Tibet

the Bradt Travel Guide

Michael Buckley

edition
3

www.bradtguides.com

Bradt Travel Guides Ltd, UK
The Globe Pequot Press Inc, USA

D0379197

N

Bradt

0 — 100km
0 — 100 miles

XINJIANG

Kashgar

Muztag
6973m ▲

KUNLUN SHAN

AKSAI CHIN
(occupied by China,
claimed by
India & Pakistan)

Mount Kailash Kora: sacred
mountain — the trek around it
is Tibet's top pilgrimage draw
page 245

Lake Namtso: among the top
five sacred lakes in Tibet
page 173

Changtang

(Northern Plateau)

TANGGU

Ali
(Shiquanhe)   Tsaka

Gakyi   Oma   Gertse

Zanda   ▲ Lungar Shan
                           7216m   Dongko

Moincer   Tsochen
▲ Kailash 6714m

Huore   *Manasarovar*   *Ngantse Lake*

Burang ▲ Gurla Mandhata   Paryang
         7728m
Simikot

**TIBET
AUTONOMOUS
REGION**

Siling Lake

Nam

Damx

*Nyaingentanglha Feng
7088m* ▲

Zhongba   ▲ Raga   **NYANCHEN TANGLHA**   **LHASA**

Saga   Sangsang   ♨ **Shigatse**   Gongkar

Yarlung Tsangpo   *Palku Tso*

Guge Kingdom ruins: surreal kingdom
of clay set in stunning desert landscape
page 239

N E P A L

▲ Shishabangma
   8012m

Lhatse   Gyantse ♨

Shegar   ♨

Tingri

*Kula Kang
7554m* ▲

BHUTA

Everest   Kangchenjunga
8848m ▲   8595m ▲

Gangtok ● Yadong

KATHMANDU ■

I N D I A

A

KEY

Capital city	■
Main town	●
Other town	○
Airport	✈
Archaeological/ historic site	⁝
Monastery	♨
Main road	═══
Other road	━━━
Railway	┅┅┅
International boundary	─ ·· ─

Shigatse, Tashilhunpo Monastery:
well-preserved temple architecture
with impressive statuary
page 206

Mount Everest base camp: the awesome
north face of the world's highest peak
will blow you away
page 229

BANGLADES

Labrang Monastery: largest monastery in east Tibet, and thronged with pilgrims
page 289

Litang/Tagong grasslands: a chance to see the fast-disappearing Tibetan nomad culture
page 267

Lhasa, Potala & Jokhang: the heart of Tibet — two World Heritage sites
page 117

Lake Basum Tso: alpine lake in pretty setting, associated with Gesar legend
page 252

Yarlung Tsangpo Grand Canyon: the world's deepest canyon — and very hard to access
page 255

Gyantse: fantastic fortress architecture, plus rare circular temple
page 193

Samye Temple Complex: historic site of Tibet's first monastery
page 181

CHINA

QINGHAI (AMDO)

Golmud

Wenquan

Yushu

Yangtse

HAN

Amdo

Nagqu

SICHUAN (KHAM)

Derge

CHENGDU

Chamdo

Mekong

Bangda

Baxoi

Litang

Kangding

Lake Basum Tso

Gyala Pelri 7294m

Barkam

Bayi

Salween

Medrogungkar

Nyingchi

Rawu

Samye

Yarlung Tsangpo

Tsedang

Deqin

Zhongdian

ARUNACHAL PRADESH

YUNNAN

Brahmaputra

Dali

KUNMING

INDIA

MYANMAR (BURMA)

CHINA

Mekong

XINING

LANZHOU

Tibet
Don't
miss...

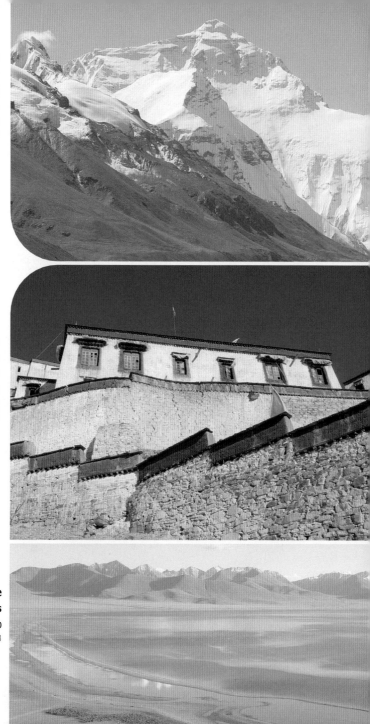

Himalayan vistas, world-class trekking
Mount Everest, north face
page 229

Tibet's fantastic fortress architecture
Gyantse Dzong
page 199

Pristine sacred lakes
Lake Namtso
page 173

above Chinese tourists changing into Tibetan dress for a photo session at Potala Square page 154

below Game changer: the train to Lhasa brings in large numbers of Chinese tourists and migrant workers page 67

top   Tibetan Buddhism and the art
        of motorcycle maintenance:
        two monks fixing a
        Zhongshen motorcycle at a
        monastery in central Tibet
        page 25

centre The old way of getting around
        — by horse page 21

right Juggling mobile phone and
        lap-dog in Lhasa page 117

above   **Rongbuk Gompa in the foreground, with the north face of Everest looming in the background**
page 228

left   **Thermal landscape with bubbling sulphurous activity, central Tibet**
page 167

below   **Ruins of the mysterious 10th-century Guge Kingdom, at Tsaparang**
page 242

AUTHOR

Michael Buckley has travelled widely in Tibet, China, central Asia and the Himalaya, visiting many Tibetan enclaves. He is author of *Eccentric Explorers*, a book about the exploits of ten fearless adventurers to the Tibetan plateau, and of a travel narrative, *Travels in the Tibetan World*. For Bradt, he has also authored *Shangri-La: A Travel Guide to the Himalayan Dream* – a concept guidebook that covers contenders for the Shangri-La crown across the Himalayan range. In the course of numerous journeys to Tibet, Buckley has hitchhiked overland from Chengdu to Lhasa, trekked around Mount Kailash and mountain-biked from Lhasa to Kathmandu.

www.himmies.com In support of this book is a special website with travellers' tales, dodgy advice, warped insights and provocative discussion related to travel in the Tibetan world. Log on to find out more.

www.WildYakFilms.com This website is companion to two short documentaries made by the author. *From Nomad to Nobody* focuses on the plight of the fast-disappearing Tibetan nomads, the stewards of Tibet's grasslands. *Meltdown in Tibet* focuses on extensive dam-building and mining in Tibet and the impact on the nations downstream.

AUTHOR'S STORY

There are things you take for granted in Tibet: magnificent snowcaps, powerful gushing rivers, hearty nomads, yaks grazing the grasslands under vast open skies. I never imagined I would have to write the following line: that landscape is undergoing drastic change. The Himalayan snowcaps are in meltdown mode, due to climate change – accelerated by a rain of black soot from massive coal-burning in both China and India. The mighty rivers of Tibet are being dammed by Chinese engineering consortiums to feed the mainland's desperate thirst for power. The grasslands of Tibet are being usurped by desert – due to climate change, and to the shortsighted Chinese policy of forcibly removing nomads from the grasslands and settling them in concrete hovels. Even yaks – the iconic creatures of Tibet – are vanishing from central Tibet.

When I first visited Tibet in the mid-1980s, none of this was apparent. This has all come to pass in a few short decades, unfolding right before my eyes. Accelerating the change was the 2006 arrival of the train to Lhasa, making possible a huge influx of Chinese settlers and tourists, and enabling exploitation of Tibet's resources on a large scale. Extensive mining in Tibet would not be possible without the train to export minerals. Nor would export of Tibet's groundwater in the form of bottled water. Nor would the construction of new mega-dams on Tibet's rivers be possible, as the train brings in materials and technology.

I believe it is the guidebook writer's duty to give the 'news' the way it is – the good, the bad and the ugly. Ugly refers to the harsh realities in today's Tibet. Tibetans live in a climate of fear: they have no say in preventing the reckless destruction of their sacred land. At the very least, a guidebook should give voice to those concerns. Despite these caveats, Tibet remains an extraordinary travel destination. If you delve into the pages of this book, you will find pockets of genuine Tibetan culture – places where the Tibetan pulse runs strong.

PUBLISHER'S FOREWORD   *Hilary Bradt*

The first Bradt travel guide was written in 1974 by George and Hilary Bradt on a river barge floating down a tributary of the Amazon. In the 1980s and '90s the focus shifted away from hiking to broader-based guides covering new destinations – usually the first to be published about these places. In the 21st century Bradt continues to publish such ground-breaking guides, as well as others to established holiday destinations, incorporating in-depth information on culture and natural history with the nuts and bolts of where to stay and what to see.

Bradt authors support responsible travel, and provide advice not only on minimum impact but also on how to give something back through local charities. In this way a true synergy is achieved between the traveller and local communities.

* * *

This has always been an important book for Bradt. Written by a recognised expert on Tibet, and used by Michael Palin during his Himalaya television series, it set the standard for sensitive coverage of this resilient country and its peace-loving culture. Visitors need this guide to help them understand and appreciate this unique place.

Third edition published January 2012   First published 2003

Bradt Travel Guides Ltd, IDC House, The Vale, Chalfont St Peter, Bucks SL9 9RZ, England
www.bradtguides.com
Published in the USA by The Globe Pequot Press Inc,
PO Box 480, Guilford, Connecticut 06437-0480

Text copyright © 2012 Michael Buckley
Maps copyright © 2012 Bradt Travel Guides Ltd
Illustrations copyright © 2012 Individual artists and photographers (see below)
Project Manager: Elspeth Beidas

ISBN: 978 1 84162 382 5
British Library Cataloguing in Publication Data
A catalogue record for this book is available from the British Library

Photographs
Text Michael Buckley (MB)
Front cover Nomad woman (MARKA/Alamy)
Back cover Monks at Ganden Monastery (MB)
Title page Mountain (MB), Snow lion mural (MB), Yak-butter candles (MB)

Illustrations Carole Vincer   **Maps** David McCutcheon

Typeset from the author's disk by Wakewing, High Wycombe
Production managed by Jellyfish Print Solutions; printed in India

CONTRIBUTORS

Bill Weir has covered a lot of ground in Tibet – experiencing it from the saddle of his trusty bicycle and on foot. He prefers to travel slowly this way in order to appreciate culture and scenic beauty. Bill revamped and expanded the Kham and Amdo section of this guidebook, covering the best routes. You can check out Bill's online Arizona guide and his latest travel stories and photos at www.arizonahandbook.com.

Bradley Rowe, contributor to the Amdo section, has been visiting Tibet since it first opened to individuals in 1984. He has spent over six years in the region, much of it on foot. His photographs appear in many publications under the name 'Stone Routes'. Apart from Amdo, his main concern is to encourage preservation of the unique ecosystems of the plateau.

Acknowledgements

INSPIRATION, INSIGHTS AND THANKS

Fellow travellers make a big difference to a project like this: on-the-road inspiration was provided by Gary McCue and Kathy Butler, Terry and James Anstey, Kat, Rene and Kris, Thijsje, Johanna, Tess, Barbara, Kozo, Pema, Jorge, Markus, Keith, Tom, John Buchanan, Rocky Dang, Shelley Guardia, Doko, Marion Lahme, John Howarth, Vassilis, Dave Turner, Tony Williams, and all the other great people I met along the way. My gratitude to Roland Hardt for mapping input, to Pat and Baiba Morrow for mountaineering research, and to Tashi Gyal and Dickyi Dolkar for help with the Tibetan language section. Chung Tsering provided Tibetan script for the language section – a laborious task. Direct text contributions were provided by Bill Weir, Bradley Rowe, Matteo Pistono, John Ackerly, Geoff Flack and Brian Harris.

YOUR INPUT

Guidebooks are like time capsules – 'snapshots' taken when the data was collected. The reader should make allowances for fluctuating rules and regulations in Tibet.

A guidebook is a two-way process: your input is invaluable for bringing the next edition up to date. If you notice details that have changed or are inaccurate, drop us a line. Marking up maps is especially useful – feel free to photocopy maps, alter them and send them along to us. I believe a guidebook must do much more than present the facts: it must make sense of them. So I welcome suggestions, comments, beefs, bones of contention, insights, travel tips and travellers' tales. Writers will be acknowledged in the next edition.

Drop a postcard or letter to Michael Buckley, c/o Bradt Travel Guides Ltd, IDC House, The Vale, Chalfont St Peter, Bucks SL9 9RZ, England; e buckeroo555@yahoo.com. Alternatively you can add a review of the book to www.bradtguides.com or Amazon.

Periodically Bradt authors post travel updates and reader feedback on the website. Check www.bradtguides.com/guidebook-updates for any news.

Contents

LIST OF MAPS

Introduction

A visit to Tibet is a strange experience, with intense emotional highs and lows. It's weird because the real Tibet no longer exists. Since their military occupation in 1950, the Chinese have systematically dismantled the Tibetan social fabric, destroyed its great monasteries, persecuted its monks and nuns, forcibly resettled its nomads in housing ghettos, and wreaked devastating damage on Tibet's pristine environment. Any description of present-day Tibet and Tibetan culture must be framed in this context of iron-fisted Chinese occupation.

'Intense' is a word that applies to many aspects of Tibet. It applies to the amazing resilience of the Tibetan people in the face of extreme adversity. Their battle has been largely a pacifist one, of suffering and enduring – a game of ultimate patience and tolerance. 'Intense' captures the feel of the landscape. The intensity of colours at this elevation is extraordinary, with glacial-blue lakes, luminous-yellow fields of mustard, deep reds and browns of barren rock landscapes, and then, up on the horizon, looms an ethereal Himalayan snowcap, backed by piercing blue skies. The colours practically glow: when you show photographs of these landscapes to people who haven't been there, they question the unreal colours – what kind of filter did you use?

Travel in the Land of Snows is a guaranteed adventure, with the wildest, roughest road routes in High Asia. Here are the highest mountains and the highest trekking in the world – and the deepest gorges. Tibetan Buddhist monasteries blend into the landscape, becoming navigation landmarks; imposing fortress ruins cling to sheer hilltops; nomads herd yaks in snow-dusted pastures; pilgrims prostrate their way across the land to reach the sacred city of Lhasa. It is this combination of extraordinary landscape, extraordinary people and high adventure that makes Tibet so special.

There is only one drawback to visiting Tibet: you can easily become addicted to the place. It makes you reluctant to leave, and as you do, you're already plotting your return – a return not necessarily to Tibet itself, but to Tibetan culture. Sadly, real Tibetan culture is more likely to be found outside Tibet, in places where refugees continue their Buddhist practices, festivals and way of life in exile – in India, Nepal and Bhutan. A chapter in this book briefly introduces these places as well.

Travel to Tibet raises important ethical questions. One of the biggest is: should you go? Should you put money in Chinese coffers, thus indirectly subsidising Chinese military bills in Tibet? Most of the tourist business is in the hands of the Chinese, and some of the travel agencies are run by the military. This raises the thorny question of lending legitimacy to Chinese government operations by visiting, but more important for the Tibetans is the moral support they get from visitors. Your mere presence in Tibet provides a 'buffer zone' in an ugly situation between Chinese and Tibetans.

Tourists love monks. This is one of the great anomalies of tourism in Tibet: the monasteries are kept open and operating because of tourist demand to see them.

Apart from Himalayan landscapes, the main tourist 'attraction' in Tibet is its monks and monasteries, its Buddhist rituals and sutra-chanting. The Chinese really have no difficulty with this – they simply cash in on it. Apart from making a buck out of Buddhism, the Chinese have absolutely no interest in Tibet's rich culture, its religion or its language. If you go, you line the pockets of Chinese travel agents, hoteliers and airline agents, but if you stay away, you isolate the Tibetans.

The position of the Tibetan exile leadership is to encourage tourism. Addressing this ethical dilemma – to go or not to go – Nobel Peace Prize laureate the Dalai Lama responded to a question posed in Vancouver, Canada, in September 2006, about repression in Tibet: 'I think you must go [to Tibet] yourself, and spend some time, not only in towns but in the countryside. Go to the countryside, and with a translator, if possible one who speaks Tibetan, if not, then one who speaks Chinese. Go there. Study on the spot. Then I think you will get a real answer.' He knows that any Western visitor to Tibet will learn of conditions there and of the aspirations of Tibetans, will not fail to be moved by the experience, and will keep the Tibetan issue alive.

The Western tourist trade in Tibet represents a small fraction of the number of visitors going to China. By far the biggest group visiting Tibet is Chinese tourists, flocking to see this exotic corner of the Motherland. According to Chinese figures, over six million tourists visit Tibet annually – most of them domestic tourists from big cities like Shanghai, Beijing or Guangzhou. And that number is expected to increase. While tourism is a mainstay of the economy in Tibet, in the overall picture of visits to China, it does not have a high profile. Basically, whether you go to Tibet or not comes down to a personal choice, to be weighed by each traveller.

If you can resolve the question of 'should you go?', the next thing to consider is 'can you go?' The Chinese are suspicious – with good reason – of the activities of independent travellers in Tibet, and have shepherded visitors into monitored, higher-paying group tours. Since major upheaval and large-scale protest across the entire Tibetan plateau in 2008, foreign visitors have only managed to gain access to Tibet on group tours. There are ways around this – particularly by visiting the eastern regions of Kham and Amdo, where such travel restrictions do not apply.

ABBREVIATIONS

ATP	Alien Travel Permit, small cardboard folder
BOC	Bank of China
CITS	China International Travel Service, the official government travel agent
EBC	Everest base camp
HHDL	His Holiness the Dalai Lama
PAP	People's Armed Police (paramilitary group)
PLA	People's Liberation Army
PRC	People's Republic of China
PSB	Public Security Bureau (police)
TAC	Tibetan Autonomous County
TAP	Tibetan Autonomous Prefecture
TAR	Tibet Autonomous Region
TTB	Tibet Tourism Bureau
WWII	World War II

Part One

GENERAL INFORMATION

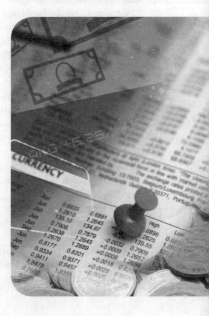

TIBET AT A GLANCE

Location The landlocked region of the Tibetan plateau is the highest in Asia, with an average elevation of 4,600m; all major rivers in Asia are sourced in Tibet

Neighbouring countries India, Pakistan, Bhutan, Burma – and China

Size/Area (km²): Ethnic Tibet: 2.3 million km²; Tibet Autonomous Region: 1.2 million km²

Climate Extreme, oscillating from freezing cold to searing heat; cool, high and dry

Status Nation under Communist occupation forces since Chinese invasion in 1950.

Population Ethnic Tibet: est. 4.5 to 6 million; Tibet Autonomous Region: 2.67 million

Capital (and population) Lhasa, population est 475,000

Other main towns Shigatse, Gyantse, Tsedang, Bayi, Ali, Chamdo

Economy Agriculture (barley, wheat, millet and buckwheat) and animal husbandry; a key industry is craft production; major mineral reserves have been identified, including uranium. It is not known how much wealth is generated from mining in Tibet, but the figures could be very high. One official Chinese source cites the discovery of over 110 kinds of minerals in Tibet, worth over US$120 billion.Mining will certainly become a significant part of economic exploitation of Tibet: most minerals are exported to mainland China.

GDP Accurate figures not known

Languages/Official language Tibetan; the official language is Chinese

Religion Maoist-manipulated Tibetan Buddhism

Currency Chinese yuan renminbi (Y)

Exchange rate £1 = Y9.92; US$1 = Y6.36; €1 = Y8.56 (October 2011)

Major airlines Air China (CA), China Southern Airlines (CZ), China Eastern Airlines (MU)

Principal airport Gongkar Airport, 60km from Lhasa

International telephone code +86 891 (Lhasa)

Time Tibet runs on Beijing time (GMT+8, PST+16)

Electrical voltage 220 volts, 50 hertz, with variety of plugs; erratic and unreliable

Weights and measures Standard metric

Flag Chinese flag – five yellow stars on red background; the Tibetan snow lion flag is outlawed

National anthem Per Gyallu (outlawed in Tibet)

National sports Meditating (temples), horse-racing (nomad summer festivals)

Public holidays Losar, Tibetan New Year – usually February; International Labour Day, 1–3 May; Chinese National Day, 1–3 October

Background Information

GEOGRAPHY

The defining element of Tibet is its extreme altitude – hovering above 4,000m. In this book, 'Tibet' refers to the entire Tibetan plateau region within the confines of the PRC. Altitude has shaped everything in Tibet – from its other-worldly landscape and majestic snowcaps to its unique flora and fauna – and its special people and culture. Yaks, for instance, are superbly adapted to their high-altitude environment – and Tibetan nomad culture is entirely dependent upon them.

The Chinese and the Tibetans refer to different-sized areas when it comes to Tibet. The Tibetans refer to the much larger area of Ethnic Tibet, encompassing the entire Tibetan plateau, and including the northeastern and eastern areas of Kham and Amdo. Ethnic Tibet or Greater Tibet covers a quarter of China's total area: Ethnic Tibet is roughly 2.3 million km², which is almost double the size of what is now called 'Tibet' (Xizang Province) by the Chinese. In 1965, the Chinese created the Tibet Autonomous Region (TAR), having previously carved off much of Kham and Amdo and assimilated them into neighbouring Chinese provinces. Even so, the TAR is huge. With an area of 1.2 million km², the TAR is roughly the size of England, France, Germany and Austria put together, measuring 2,600km from west to east, and 1,300km from north to south.

Tibet within the People's Republic of China (PRC) straddles most of the geographical feature known as the Tibetan plateau. This is often referred to as 'the Third Pole', because outside of the Arctic and Antarctic regions, the Tibetan plateau holds the world's largest store of ice, snow and permafrost.

Superlatives abound when it comes to the subject of physical Tibet: the world's highest peaks and lakes – and the world's deepest gorges – are all located here. The landlocked region of Tibet borders India, Nepal, Bhutan, Burma – and China. Major rivers sourced on the Tibetan plateau are the Mekong, Yellow, Yangtse, Salween, Irrawaddy, Yarlung Tsangpo (source of the Brahmaputra), Indus, Sutlej and Karnali. On their wild journeys off the plateau, the rivers carve deep gorges. The tail ends of these rivers feed the world's largest deltas – prime rice-growing regions such as the Mekong Delta in Vietnam, the Irrawaddy Delta in Burma, and the Ganges-Brahmaputra Delta in Bangladesh.

In the south of Tibet, bordering Nepal, lie the 8,000m-plus Himalayan giants of Everest, Lhotse, Makalu and Cho Oyu. The world's 14th-highest peak, Shishapangma, lies wholly within Tibet. The Himalaya – Tibet's natural mountain border for centuries – have the world's highest snowline, and some 37,000 glaciers. To the north of Tibet are the Kunlun Mountains, while to the west are the Pamirs and the Karakoram Range.

Most of the Tibetan plateau is over 4,000m high. It was formed millions of years ago by a collision of the Indian and Asian continental plates. A glance at a satellite

TIBET AUTONOMOUS REGION

XINJIANG

KUNLUN SHAN

AKSAI CHIN
(occupied by China,
claimed by
India & Pakistan)

Kashgar

CHINA

Golmud

Muztag
6973m

Changtang
(Northern Plateau)

Siling Lake

Namtso

Ngantse Lake

TANGGULA SHAN

QINGHAI
(AMDO)

Wenquan

Amdo

Nagqu

Brach

N

SICHUAN
(KHAM)

Chengdu

Derge

YushuO

Yangtse

Chamdo

Mekong

Barkam

Salween

Degin

YUNNAN

MYANMAR
(BURMA)

INDIA

Bangda
Baxoi
Rawu

Namche Barwa
7756m

Gyala Peri
7294m

Nyingchi

Bayi

ARUNACHAL PRADESH

Brahmaputra

Damxung

Nyainqentanglha Feng
7088m

LHASA

Medrogungkar
Gongkar Airport
Yarlung Tsangpo
Tsedang

Yamdrok Tso

Kula Kangri
7554m

NYANCHEN TANGLHA

Shigatse
Gyantse

Lhatse

Shegar

BHUTAN

Yadong

SIKKIM

Kangchenjunga
8595m

INDIA

Sangsang

Tingri

Everest
8848m

Paiku Tso

Raga

Shishapangma
8012m

KATHMANDU

NEPAL

Tsochen

Dongko
Gertse

Zhongba

Saga

Yarlung Tsangpo

Paryang

Lungar Shan
7216m

Oma

Tsaka

Gakyi

Ali
(Shiquanhe)

Moincer

Mansarowar
Gurla Mandhata
7728m

Kailash
6714m

Burang

Huore

Simikot

H I M A L A Y A

Zanda

Sutlej

Indus

INDIA

KEY

International boundary
International boundary
(disputed)
Border of TAR

0   200km
0   120 miles

map will easily delineate this zone, and will show dramatic drop-offs from the edge of the plateau to forested areas. The northern sector of Tibet is the forbidding Changtang, an immensely rocky and arid desert where nomads roam, eking out a tough living. To the northeast, in Amdo, the landscape turns to lush green, with rich grasslands irrigated by the Yellow River. In Kham, semi-monsoonal conditions and lower elevations result in copious forest cover – one of China's greatest sources of timber. The Yarlung Tsangpo River, running from the far west of Tibet to the east, is responsible for the rich pockets of farmland in central Tibet – it's considered the cradle of Tibetan civilisation, with historic Tibetan settlements along the riverbanks.

Tibet is landlocked: though many Tibetans have not seen the ocean, the pristine turquoise lakes of the plateau are vast – to the eye, the larger ones form their own inland sea. There has been little development at these lakes – Tibetans do not eat fish, and they regard a number of the lakes as sacred places. The largest lakes are Manasarovar (west Tibet), Namtso (north), Yamdrok Tso (central Tibet) and Kokonor (Amdo).

Tibet's extreme altitude makes it a special place for hardy high-alpine flora, with secrets yet to be revealed. This rare flora attracted the attention of early 20th-century British plant hunters, who discovered the Himalayan blue poppy and many species of rhododendron (there are estimated to be over 400 in Tibet). Over 2,000 species of medicinal plants have been documented by the Tibetans themselves. Herbal remedies lie at the core of Tibetan medicinal practices. For a brief introduction to Tibet's unusual wildlife, see *Appendix 1*, page 307.

CLIMATE

The climate of Tibet is cool and dry. With an average elevation of 4,500m, the weather in Tibet can best be described as extreme, oscillating from searing heat to freezing cold – sometimes in the course of a single day. It is possible to be simultaneously hot and cold, if a person's head is in the shade, but his or her legs are in the sun. Climatic conditions vary with elevation and exposure: there is little moisture in the atmosphere and intense UV rays can be problematic.

There is no best time to visit Tibet: the weather is unpredictable and, no matter which season, there are extreme conditions to deal with. Few travellers visit during the winter, however, because of treacherous road conditions, because access flights often close down for this period, and because Nepali hotel and restaurant managers head back to Kathmandu for the winter season.

SPRING March to May. Strong winds are possible and can whip up dust storms and sandstorms. However, this is one of the better trekking seasons, when conditions are not too hot.

SUMMER June to August. In this period are higher temperatures, which are conducive to staging festivals like horse-racing fairs. Most of Tibet's rainfall occurs during July and August. In southern and eastern Tibet, the Himalaya form a barrier against the rain-bearing monsoons, so Tibet does not experience heavy monsoons like Nepal, Sikkim or Bhutan. However, in Tibet rainwater build-up combined with glacial meltwater can result in rampaging rivers and flooding in the autumn.

AUTUMN September to November. As a result of the aforementioned rampaging rivers, travel in autumn is prone to delays due to mudslides, flooding and bridges that have been swept away. Otherwise, it's not a bad time to travel, and it can be sunny.

It seems incredible at the dawn of the 21st century that important new geographic discoveries are still being made. In 1998, and again in 2002, secrets of one of the world's last great uncharted rivers were finally revealed.

The river is the Yarlung Tsangpo. In the 1800s, the actual course of the river was unknown, and whether the Tsangpo (flowing from Tibet) and the Brahmaputra (flowing into India) were the same river, or two different rivers. The reason for the uncertainty lay in the river's dramatic course: for the first half of its 2,900km length, the Yarlung Tsangpo runs east through Tibet. Then it makes an abrupt hairpin turn and flows west into India – where it is called the Brahmaputra – and south again to its mouth in Bangladesh (where the river is known as the Jamuna).

This abrupt hairpin turn foxed geographers and adventurers for centuries, but equally mystifying was the river's dramatic drop: on its journey east, the Tsangpo roars into a 4,900m cleft between two mighty peaks – Namche Barwa (elevation 7,756m) and Gyala Pelri (7,294m). In a distance of around 240km, the Tsangpo plummets some 2,700m through what is now known as the Yarlung Tsangpo Grand Canyon, the world's deepest gorge. With a depth reaching over 5,300m near the Tibet–India border, this gorge is more than twice as deep as Arizona's Grand Canyon.

Geographers speculated that with such a precipitous drop, there had to be some huge waterfalls within the gorge, but because of its steep, forbidding walls, the site was considered inaccessible. In the 1880s, the British sent an Indian pundit by the name of Kinthup into the area to determine if the Tsangpo and the Brahmaputra were indeed one and the same. His task was to launch 500 small, marked logs through the gorge to determine the course of the river. After a series of epic misadventures, Kinthup completed mission impossible, launching all 500 logs (50 a day over a period of ten days), but his message back to headquarters went astray and there were no observers to witness the logs coming through at the other end.

Nobody believed Kinthup's discoveries, including his claim of sighting a waterfall 45m in height. In forays to the region in 1911 and 1913, British officer Eric Bailey confirmed Kinthup's exploration, but found only a 9m fall at the site mentioned. (Bailey later tracked Kinthup down in Darjeeling and found that a scribe had confused a thin 45m cascade from a tributary with the 9m fall on the main river, and Kinthup was illiterate: he could not read to check the account.) Bailey conclusively showed that the Tsangpo and Brahmaputra did form the same river, but he did not have the resources to fully explore the region.

Not making matters easier was the local custom of poisoning outsiders as sacrifices to evil spirits, but the British persevered. In 1924, British botanist Frank Kingdon Ward spent 11 harrowing months surveying the gorge and discovered Rainbow Falls, which, observed from a considerable distance, he estimated at nine to 12m high. His reconnaissance was described in his 1926 book, *Riddle of the Tsangpo Gorges*. Ward discovered that the Tsangpo's precipitous descent was probably not due to one or two massive cascades, but rather was the result of a near-continuous succession of violent rapids. But still the secrets remained; Ward's reconnaissance reduced the unexplored part to one raging section about 15km long.

Even satellite imagery could not probe this section, as the gorge is deep and twisted, with overhanging vegetation. In 1987, a Chinese army photographer claimed to have photographed falls in the region while flying over the Upper Gorge in a military helicopter, but no accurate measurements of the height of the falls could be made from these pictures. In fact, the unexplored section was considered impenetrable until Nepal-based explorers Ian Baker and Ken Storm made persistent attempts in the 1990s. During a 1998 expedition they found a way through – and were able to get near to the falls – by following takin (goat-antelope) tracks. Using climbing ropes, Baker and Storm rappelled down the Tsangpo walls and got up close to Ward's Rainbow Falls, which they recalculated to be 22m high, double Kingdon Ward's original estimate.

Then the team went where none had gone before: they continued their descent deeper into the canyon, and discovered a huge new waterfall, calculated at 32m high, which they christened Hidden Falls. That name probably won't appear on Chinese maps, however. Baker and Storm upstaged a Chinese scientific expedition in the same area at the same time: both teams claimed the prize discovery of the waterfall. Baker and Storm mounted an intense publicity campaign in the US to reinforce their claim, and the Chinese responded by closing the Tsangpo Gorge region to foreigners for a significant period. Among rafters and kayakers, the Yarlung Tsangpo is regarded as the Everest of white water. The river claimed the lives of two kayakers attempting first descents: Yoshitaka Takei, who vanished in 1993, and Doug Gordon, who was lost in a massive rapid while on a *National Geographic*-sponsored expedition in 1998. After Gordon's death, white-water experts wrote the Tsangpo off as un-runnable.

In early February 2002, however, a team of explorers and kayakers from seven nations began a two-month expedition through the Upper Tsangpo Gorge. Their goal was twofold: to chart some of the unvisited parts of the gorge, and to complete its first white-water descent. The 80-man ground crew included Ken Storm, who had discovered Hidden Falls in 1998, and 68 Tibetan porters lugging 1,100kg of supplies.

Expedition leader Scott Lindgren, from California, had had his eyes on the gorge for more than a decade, after pioneering descents of other Himalayan rivers. He scouted the Tsangpo several times and concluded that the flow of water was suicidally high in the spring, but that late winter might work because of the lower flow.

Seven of the world's top kayakers launched into the wild water of the Upper Tsangpo Gorge – the most fearsome they had ever seen – and went where nobody had ever been before. They survived Class V+ rapids, thundering past boiling eddies, great vertical drops, massive lateral waves and huge boulders. Alternately paddling and portaging – and seal-launching from huge boulders – the team paddled about 90% of the Upper Gorge. Then the battered group started an epic winter portage over 3,600m Sechen La, to bypass the un-runnable Rainbow Falls and Hidden Falls. The expedition members and porters threaded their way up treacherous couloirs and steep snow-slopes, which must have looked a strange spectacle with kayaks in tow. Finally they rejoined the river, but found that a flash flood had scoured the banks of the Tsangpo to near-vertical rock. At this point, Lindgren prudently decided to end the expedition. The team had covered 70 river kilometres – the first-ever descent of the Upper Tsangpo Gorge – and lived to tell the tale.

Back in the 13th century, explorer Marco Polo reported to incredulous Europeans that Chinese peasants burned a 'black rock' for heat. Today, more incredulous news: burning these black rocks is destroying the planet. Lumps of coal burned in households in China result in a tremendous output of CO_2 (not even taking industrial use of coal into account). That's China. On the other side of the Himalaya, a billion Indians are doing the same. And the emissions, known as black soot, are raining down on Himalayan peaks sited between the two heavily populated nations.

According to scientific studies, black soot deposition at some Himalayan glaciers increased 30% between 1990 and 2003. Shimmering white glaciers in theory reflect the sun's heat, while 'dirty' glaciers (caused by black soot depositions) will do the exact opposite: they will start absorbing the sun's rays, thereby accelerating glacial meltdown. Most soot in the region comes from diesel engines, coal-fired power plants and outdoor cooking stoves. Multiply the cooking stoves by several billion to get an idea of how much black soot may be floating around in the air.

This is not good news for Himalayan glaciers, which are melting rapidly due to climate-change factors. Tibet is the icebox of south Asia, with its myriad glaciers acting as major water-keeper for the entire region. With some 37,000 glaciers in Chinese-controlled Tibet alone, Lonnie Thompson, glaciologist at Ohio State University, calls the Himalayan region 'Asia's freshwater bank account'. It's an icebox where massive build-up of new snow and ice (deposits) has traditionally offset its annual run-off in rivers (withdrawals). But now the region is facing bankruptcy, because rapid withdrawals are depleting the account. Of the 680 glaciers currently monitored by Chinese scientists, 95% are shedding more ice than they are adding, particularly at the southern and eastern edges of the plateau. The glaciers are not simply retreating, they are losing mass from the surface down, says Thompson.

The first threat from glacial meltdown is GLOFs (Glacial Lake Outburst Floods). A GLOF is a large lake that is temporarily dammed by a glacier. If the 'dam' bursts, entire villages can be washed away in a deluge of mud and water. This has happened in both Tibet and Nepal. GLOFs pose serious threats in neighbouring Bhutan. Accelerated glacial meltdown in the Himalaya would lead initially to flooding from glacier-fed rivers. And much further down the road, it could lead to no water. If the glaciers vanish, the rivers would be reduced to a trickle. Monsoon rainwater alone is not enough to keep Himalayan rivers running at sufficient volume.

That's the snowline. Even more alarming is what is melting *under* the ground, in the ice below. The Tibetan plateau sits on the largest deposits of permafrost outside of the Arctic and Antarctic regions. Permafrost is found at various sub-surface depths across the entire Tibetan plateau. Due to climate-change factors, the permafrost, frozen for millions of years, is gradually beginning to thaw. In the process of thawing, permafrost could release large amounts of carbon and methane, locked in ice crystals. In permafrost regions, methane hydrate is found trapped in layers between 150 and 2,000m deep. As a greenhouse gas, methane is thought to be over 20 times more potent than carbon dioxide in its ability to trap heat in the atmosphere. It is not known what effect the release of large amounts of methane into the atmosphere would have.

WINTER December to early March. Severely cold conditions and snowfalls can shut down high passes to traffic. The Tibetans call the plateau Kangjong (Land of Snows), but the sun is quick to melt off snowfalls in the central Tibetan region. February and March are good festival months: Losar (Tibetan new year) falls in this period and during this time there are many nomads in Lhasa.

NATURAL HISTORY

Though they had no sewage systems or concept of garbage disposal, in the realm of conservation the Tibetans were light years ahead of the West (at a time when the Tibetans were still in control of their environment). The Buddhist compassion for all life – human, other animal or insect – protected Tibet's wildlife, and in a sense made Tibet one great wildlife preserve. Because Tibet was isolated from the rest of the world for so long, it sheltered rare species: even in the 1990s, species thought long extinct were discovered in Tibet (a breed of small forest pony was found in Kham, and the Tibetan red deer was found in the Shannan district). Huge herds of wild gazelles, antelope, wild asses and yaks used to graze the grasslands of central Tibet. If animals were culled, the Tibetans took only what they needed, so impact on the wildlife was minimal.

In the 1940s, American adventurer Leonard Clark reported: 'Every few minutes we would spot a bear, a hunting wolf, herds of musk deer, *kiang* (wild ass), gazelles, big horned sheep, or foxes. This must be one of the last unspoiled big game paradises.' His words were in some ways prophetic: with the coming of the Chinese in the 1950s, everything changed rapidly. Chinese soldiers machine-gunned wildlife not only for food, but for export to China – and for sport. Some of Tibet's once-plentiful wildlife now faces extinction: in the last 40 years, large mammals have gone the way of the bison in North America. Apart from supplying China with meat, there is a demand for rare animals in Chinese restaurants and for Chinese traditional medicine. This has decimated numbers of the snow leopard, for instance.

Tibetan Buddhists have a profound sense of sacred landscape. Larger lakes and mountains were sacred and were left untouched, and mining was not practised. With its harsh environment, Tibet has a delicate ecological balance – one with which the Chinese are interfering. Such interference can have disastrous consequences, leading for example to increased desertification at Qinghai Lake, or destruction of an entire ecosystem. This may well be happening with the building of a hydro-electric project at Lake Yamdrok Tso – a highly controversial project that the Chinese have rushed, with uncertain results. Other large dams are under construction in Kham and dozens more are planned. The Chinese have made a priority of exploiting Tibet's untapped oil and mineral wealth. Oil fields in Amdo produce over a million tons of crude oil a year. In 2001, Chinese scientists announced the discovery of billions of tons of oil and gas in the remote Changtang region of northern Tibet.

The Dalai Lama once said that he could understand Chinese anger with Tibetan 'separatists', but what did they have against the trees? It is estimated that over 50% of Tibet's forests have been cut down since 1959 – mostly in eastern, northeastern and southeastern Tibet. If massive clear-cutting takes place on the slopes of the Tibetan plateau, there will be nothing to stop landslides and mudslides cascading down during monsoon season into neighbouring nations like Burma and India. There could be unbridled erosion and flooding in these areas; the monsoon patterns themselves could be affected by changes in the ecological balance in Tibet. Severe flooding of the Yangtse in the late 1990s is, according to Chinese sources, directly attributable to deforestation at the edge of the Tibetan plateau. The situation

Because Tibet has the highest terrain on the planet, it's easy to break world records. China seems bent on setting human rights violations in Tibet at record levels too. Here are some highs and lows.

HIGHS

Highest mountain Everest's 8,848m summit is shared by Nepal. Many records are associated with Everest: at the north face base camp is the world's highest monastery (Rongbuk, 4,950m) and the world's highest post office (5,150m).

Deepest gorge Yarlung Tsangpo Grand Canyon, east Tibet, is around 500km in length, and thought to have a maximum depth of over 5,300m. It is sited along the course of the world's highest major river, the Yarlung Tsangpo (average elevation 4,000m).

Highest airport Bangda, 4,334m, east Tibet; also has the world's longest runway at 5,500m in length. Eclipsing this will be a new airport at Nagqu, at 4,436m in elevation.

Highest railway station Tanggula Shan Station, 5,070m, on the Qinghai–Tibet border.

HIGH AND LOW

Golmud–Lhasa railway Completed in 2005, the line is simultaneously the world's highest and its most controversial, as it has unleashed a new invasion of Chinese immigrants into Tibet.

14th Dalai Lama The world's most popular spiritual figure, and most revered religious leader among Tibetans, is officially outlawed by Chinese authorities, who denounce him as a 'splittist'.

LOWS The darker side of life in the Middle Kingdom is hard to gauge because of secrecy and a complete lack of statistics, but here's how China ranks, with an eye on the situation in Tibet.

Executions China carries out by far the world's highest number of annual executions by any nation – in fact, more than the rest of the world combined.

Human rights A report released in 2011 by Freedom House ranked Tibet among the ten Worst of the Worst for human rights violations. Tibet was identified as a territory; the nation of China was not far behind in those rankings.

Press China is among the world's worst nations for tightest control over press, media and internet, in the company of repressive neighbours like Vietnam, Burma and North Korea.

became so critical that in 1998 Chinese authorities issued a ban on logging in the upper reaches of the Yangtse and Yellow rivers.

Apart from exploitation of natural resources comes the threat of pollution. Although Chinese officials have shied away from the topic, there is evidence that remote parts of Tibet have been used for the dumping of nuclear waste. China is intent on using Tibet as a missile-launching site, targeting Indian cities. There are a number of missile bases and military airfields scattered around Tibet. Far more progressive is the Dalai Lama's vision. He calls for complete demilitarisation of the region of Tibet, to serve as a buffer between the nations of India and China. He envisages the transformation of Tibet into a sanctuary, a zone of peace – as it once used to be.

On paper, there have been attempts by Chinese officials to set up nature reserves, but in effect there is little protection or policing going on, and these are largely cosmetic. The reserve with the highest profile is Qomolangma Nature Preserve, in the Everest region, with a 34,000km² zone said to be under protection (although it is a mixed-use zone, with herders living within the boundaries). Under the guidance of renowned naturalist George Schaller, the mega Changtang Nature Reserve (around 247,000km²) was established in 1993, but poaching of Tibetan antelope proceeds at a brisk pace within its confines.

See also *Appendix 1*, page 307.

HISTORY AND POLITICS

To do justice to the subject, an account of history and politics in Tibet really requires a separate 800-page book. Even the modern era could easily provide enough content for a 500-page book. Two hefty tomes to consult are Melvyn Goldstein's *A History of Modern Tibet 1913–1951*, and Tsering Shakya's *The Dragon in the Land of Snows*, covering the period since 1947. The following is a very brief introduction, but one that should be read in combination with the section on *Tibetan Buddhism*, page 25, because in Tibet you cannot separate religion from politics.

Tibetan recorded history dates back over 2,000 years. The emergence of Tibet as a geopolitical entity dates to the 7th century AD, when warrior-king Songtsen Gampo unified the clans of Tibet. At this time, Tibet was a great military power that expanded its boundaries south into India and east into China.

King Songtsen Gampo (c AD618–649) is regarded as a great religious king – he actively spread the teachings of Buddhism in regions under his control. The king had three Tibetan queens. As Tibet's power grew, neighbouring countries sought alliances through marriage: Princess Wencheng from China was sent to marry Songtsen Gampo, and Nepal sent a royal princess as a bride.

In the 8th century, King Trisong Detsen adopted Buddhism as the official religion of Tibet, bringing Buddhism into conflict with Tibet's ancient Bon shaman religion. Tibet waged war on China, occupying the Tang dynasty capital of Xian. In the 9th century, war broke out again between the Tibetans and the Chinese, with the Tibetans emerging victorious. At the centre of Lhasa, outside the Jokhang Temple, stands a stone obelisk that affirms in Tibetan and Chinese the terms of a peace treaty concluded between King Ralpachen and Chinese emperor Wangti in the year AD823. It is written in stone: 'Tibet and China shall abide by the frontiers of which they are now in occupation. All to the east is the country of Great China; and all to the west is, without question, the country of Great Tibet.'

In 826, Ralpachen was assassinated by his elder brother Langdarma, who succeeded him and changed tack completely: he attempted to snuff out Buddhism under pressure from Bon priests. In 842, he was killed by a monk, and Tibet dissolved into chaotic factions. A hundred years later, Buddhism was introduced again in western Tibet, in the Guge Kingdom. By the 12th century, three Buddhist lineages or schools had emerged in Tibet: Nyingmapa, Kagyupa and Sakyapa. The fierce rivalry between them was not so much religious as political.

The snowcapped peaks and high deserts of the Tibetan plateau served as natural defences and increased Tibet's isolation. But in the 13th century, Tibet fell under Mongol domination. The Mongol khans ruled an empire that stretched as far as Europe and encompassed all of China. The Mongols took a great interest in Tibetan Buddhism. In 1350, Tibet resumed its independent ways, but enjoyed a special patron–priest relationship with Mongolia over the next few centuries. Invited to educate the Mongols in spiritual matters, the Tibetans in turn accepted Mongolian guarantees to stave off would-be invaders.

It was the Mongolian leader Altan Khan who bestowed the title 'Dalai Lama' (Great Ocean, or Ocean of Wisdom) on Sonam Gyatso, the 16th-century leader of the Geluk or Yellow Hat sect. This reformist school had been established in the 14th century: Sonam Gyatso is regarded as the third Dalai Lama (the title was conferred posthumously on his predecessors). The Geluk sect gradually assumed a dominant role in politics and from 1642 onwards they effectively ruled Tibet through their leader, the fifth Dalai Lama. The 'Great Fifth' (Lobsang Gyatso) managed to reunify Tibet and extended his authority to the fringes of Tibetan territory. During his reign, Tibetan culture flourished – many monasteries were erected and the Potala was rebuilt. By this time, Tibet operated under one of the most unusual forms of government in the world: a theocracy, or a Buddhocracy (a system whereby the spiritual leader is also a king figure – sometimes referred to as 'god-king' – combining religious and political responsibilities). The system lasted over 300 years, up until the Chinese invasion in 1950.

By the 17th century, Mongol power was waning, and another set of invaders stormed the Great Wall to occupy China: the Manchus. By this time, Tibet had largely demilitarised – perhaps the first nation in history ever to do so. The national priorities lay in spiritual matters. The Manchus recognised Tibet as an independent nation under the authority of the Dalai Lama, and agreed to protect the peace of the demilitarised nation. Over the next three centuries, Tibet's fortunes fluctuated, with various incursions across its borders by the forces of Nepal and China. One of the stranger chapters in Tibetan history was an invasion in 1903 by the British colonial forces, intent on opening Tibet to trade and convinced that arch-rival Russia was influencing Tibet. After blasting their way through to Lhasa, the British stayed for two months. Failing to find anyone of real authority (the Dalai Lama had fled), the British concluded a useless treaty with some head lamas and then withdrew, leaving a telegraph line and a few trade links in place.

In 1911, with China weakened by civil war, the Tibetans seized the opportunity to formally announce Tibetan independence, expelling all Chinese from Tibetan soil. Between 1913 and 1950, Tibet asserted its independent status by controlling its own affairs, signing treaties with neighbouring nations, patrolling its own borders, bearing its own flag and issuing its own currency, passports and stamps. In this regard, it was ahead of its neighbours: India and China shook off the yoke of colonial rule only after World War II.

Curiously, the main Chinese claim to Tibet goes back to an era when China itself was occupied by a foreign power – the Mongols. If Tibet really were part of China, it's odd that the Chinese waited over a thousand years before staking their claim. A better explanation would be that the Tibetans successfully defended themselves against the Chinese for more than a thousand years. Over the last two thousand years, Tibet has nurtured a culture that is very different from that of China, with a separate language and literature, separate form of religion, separate economy and central government, and distinct forms of art and architecture. Out of this rare society – based on the tenets of Tibetan Buddhism – emerged a distinct 'Tibetan-ness'. It is this Tibetan-ness that forms the basis for their claim to independence. Pre-Chinese-occupied Tibet was not a paradise. It was a medieval society that was out of synch with the rest of the world, and which paid dearly for its isolationist policy and its failure to keep abreast of the times.

POST-1950 TIBET After their victory in the long-running civil war in 1949, the forces of Mao Zedong wasted little time in announcing their next target would be the 'return of Tibet to the embrace of the Motherland'. The Chinese invaded Tibet from the east in 1950. Their justification for invasion was to liberate the Tibetans from 'feudalism'. However, it is dubious whether this came to pass: Tibetan nobility and clergy were simply replaced with harsher Chinese masters.

Under a document called the 17-Point Agreement – dictated by the Chinese in 1951 – the 14th Dalai Lama would remain at the head of the Tibetan government, but China would be in charge of military matters and other key facets. The 17-Point Agreement quickly turned into a sham: monastic lands were confiscated, tribal lands were collectivised, and it soon became apparent that the Chinese idea of schooling was very different from the Tibetan idea. Tibetans had little empathy

SAVING THE CHIRU

In March 2002, police in New Delhi intercepted two Kashmiri traders with 80 *shahtoosh* shawls. It takes the underwool of three antelope to make a single shahtoosh shawl, so that haul represented at least 240 dead Tibetan antelope. And on the international market, at US$5,000 a shawl (the average price for a fine one), the cache was worth US$400,000.

Renowned naturalist George Schaller has conducted extensive research on the chiru (Tibetan antelope) in their main habitat of Changtang in remote northern Tibet. Schaller says upwards of 20,000 chiru are poached each year for their underwool, from which shahtoosh shawls are made. This is pushing the chiru to the brink of extinction. The demand for shahtoosh shawls in the fashion centres of Western countries has boosted the trade. The wool of the chiru is the finest animal fibre in the world – finer than that of cashmere goats. This also makes it the most expensive fibre. Although the sale of shahtoosh shawls is supposedly banned around the world, they can be bought at haute couture boutiques, with clients paying up to US$20,000 for a single shawl.

The main centre for shahtoosh spinning is Kashmir, even though the trade was outlawed there in mid-2000. Kashmir is of course a renowned centre for spinning cashmere wool, also from Tibet. Poachers from Tibet trade chiru wool for tiger parts from India. The Kashmiris need the chiru wool, and the tiger parts are highly valued in Chinese traditional medicine. So here's a vicious circle involving two highly endangered species: poachers are using automatic weapons to gun down chiru so that Kashmiris can weave shahtoosh shawls to sell to high-fashion divas in the West. And Indian traders are poaching tigers, which the Kashmiris sell to the poachers in Tibet in exchange for chiru wool: the tiger parts are divided up for sale in Chinese traditional medicine potions which are mostly directed at boosting a flagging male libido.

Can Communism and Buddhism co-exist? They are both rational, non-theistic (no belief in a superior god) and altruistic philosophies. So in theory they should be able to get along with each other. The problem is communist intolerance of Buddhism, not the reverse. In the early years after the Chinese invasion, the Dalai Lama claimed that he liked some of Mao Zedong's ideas, even going as far as saying he considered himself half-Marxist, half-Buddhist. And Buddhism had long been practised in China itself. But Mao Zedong told the Dalai Lama religion is poison.

One of the main reasons the Chinese claimed they set out to 'liberate' Tibet was to free it from 'feudalism', which, it transpired, meant not only Tibetan aristocrats but also the entire monastic system. The communists lumped Tibetan Buddhism in with the old 'feudal' ways of Tibet. The monks, claimed the Chinese, did nothing: they just sat around the monasteries and exploited the people, which prevented Tibet from modernising. The question remains: what would have happened if the Chinese had not invaded in 1950? The Dalai Lama – not old enough to rule at the time – was most certainly a progressive person who intended to introduce modern ways. He was – and is – fascinated by the West and by modern inventions.

Communist countries have historically replaced Buddhist teachings with communist ideology, weakening the power of the monasteries, eliminating the privileges of monks and discrediting the monastic leadership. Persecution of Buddhists in Russia and Mongolia nearly wiped them out. So what does the Chinese communist leadership do about a region that is overwhelmingly Tibetan Buddhist in faith? Well, they set up the Chinese Religious Affairs Bureau to oversee what is happening in the monasteries, to introduce Marxism into the curriculum and to demand allegiance to Beijing. During the Cultural Revolution, statuary at main altars in some Lhasa temples was replaced with portraits of Mao Zedong. Karl Marx believed religion to be the opiate of the masses, employed by repressive regimes to divert the attention of the people from their true enemies. In a true communist society, religion does not exist – it is replaced by loyalty to the Party. A modified version of this is that religious practices that do not harm political rule can be tolerated. In Tibet, however, monks and nuns often spearhead political protest.

for the zeal of Maoism, and alongside the construction of hydro-electric stations, experimental farms and roads, armed resistance took place at various points (particularly in eastern Tibet) from 1954–59. Concerned for his safety, those close to the Dalai Lama engineered his escape on horseback to India. In 1959, he crossed the border into northeast India and into exile. Behind him, Lhasa fell into chaotic fighting. Tens of thousands of Tibetans were killed in the subsequent uprising.

In India, meanwhile, the Dalai Lama renounced the 17-Point Agreement and set up his government-in-exile.

Barely recovering from the vicious reprisals of 1959, Tibet was hurled headlong into the madness of the Cultural Revolution (1966–76), which hit Tibet harder than any other part of China.

Chinese officials would later blame destruction of monasteries on this period, when in fact many buildings were blown up or dismantled before the onset of the Cultural Revolution. With the flight of the Dalai Lama, the Chinese dissolved the remnants of the Tibetan government, and set up the Tibet Autonomous Region (1965), splitting the area of Ethnic Tibet in half. All forms of Tibetan customs and worship – public and private – were banned, including barter. Large numbers of Tibetans died in labour camps and prisons.

Since the 1960s, Chinese policy in Tibet has see-sawed – sometimes harsh and repressive, at other times loosening up. China's human rights record in Tibet, meanwhile, has been appalling, constituting one of history's worst cases of cultural genocide.

In 1987 major rioting took place in Lhasa: this was followed by intermittent demonstrations that were brutally put down by Chinese troops. Martial law was imposed in 1989 and not lifted for over a year. Since 1996, it has been forbidden to own or display any image of the Dalai Lama in Tibet: this followed in the wake of a major falling-out over the choice of the 11th Panchen Lama (see page 32). Little dialogue has taken place between the Chinese and the Tibetan government-in-exile over the issue of Tibet. China has tightened its grip on the region, ruling what is today the largest colony in the world.

The greatest uprising since 1959 took place in the spring of 2008. A protest that started in Lhasa, initiated by monks from Sera and Drepung, spread across the entire plateau, involving Tibetans from all walks of life – urban dwellers to nomads. A vicious crackdown ensued, with over a thousand Tibetans believed killed – and many more missing or imprisoned.

In mid-2011, Chinese authorities in Lhasa staged 'celebrations' to mark the 60th anniversary of the signing of the 17-Point Agreement for the 'peaceful liberation of Tibet'. Looking back on those 60 years, the Chinese see Tibet as a great success story – the socialist transformation for Tibetans from primitive feudalism to a much higher standard of living. From the Tibetan point of view, those 60 years have been a complete catastrophe, a sad story of pillage, rape, torture, dislocation and destruction – a deliberate attempt to obliterate their culture, their religion and their values.

ECONOMY AND RESOURCES

The traditional economy of Tibet is based on animal husbandry on rich pasturelands, with the raising of yaks, sheep and goats, as well as horses and mules. However, this is radically changing – and the grasslands themselves are disappearing. In exchange for

ETHNIC TIBET

The map on page 21 shows the shifting political boundaries of Tibet, old and new. The wider area encompasses 'Ethnic Tibet' – the area recognised as Tibet by the British in the Simla Treaty of 1914 (which the Chinese did not ratify). Starting in the 1920s, the area bordering China to the east was slowly encroached upon. In the 1950s, the Amdo and Kham regions were carved up and incorporated into Chinese provinces, mostly as a collection of Tibetan Autonomous Prefectures (TAPs). In 1965, the Chinese administration created the Tibet Autonomous Region (TAR), reducing the area designated as 'Tibet' to half its former size. When the Chinese refer to 'Tibet', they mean Xizang or the TAR, which embraces the former Tibetan regions of Ü, Tsang and Ngari. When Tibetans talk about 'Tibet', however, they mean the much wider Ethnic Tibet region, embracing not only central and western Tibet, but also the former regions of Amdo and Kham.

yak meat, cheese and butter, Tibetan nomads used to barter for grains from farmers. That trade has now been severely disrupted due to large-scale forcible settlement of nomads in concrete ghettos. Tibetan farmers grow barley, wheat, millet and buckwheat. In larger towns, the main traditional industry is craft production – the making of carpets, Tibetan boots, *tankas* (wall-hangings) and religious items.

Before the 1950s, industry in Lhasa was really only present in the form of a mint and an ammunition factory. Since then, light industry around Lhasa has ballooned to the point where pollution is a concern: industry includes power plants, machinery plants, printing shops, chemical factories, woollen textile plants, leather processing factories, grain processing factories, carpet factories, a concrete factory and a brewery.

A key factor in the Chinese 'development' of Tibet is finding or creating sources of energy. Hydro-electric projects are under way in parts of the plateau to tap the enormous power generated by rivers originating in Tibet. A number of these projects show little concern for the surrounding environment. The high altitude in Tibet results in intense solar radiation, which has successfully been utilised through solar panels and solar cookers. There is also great potential for harnessing geothermal energy and wind power.

Before 1950, Tibet was self-sufficient in food, with barley as the staple. In the 1960s and 1970s, the Chinese ordered wheat to be planted instead of barley, banned barter, and formed communes – a disastrous policy that led to Tibet's first-ever famines. Now Beijing claims that it has to heavily subsidise the ailing economy in Tibet, but officials fail to mention several key factors, such as how much money is drained by propping up Chinese settlers and the military in Tibet. Estimates put the number of PLA (People's Liberation Army) troops in Tibet at between 200,000 and half a million. Long convoys of military trucks are a common sight, as are military garrisons, particularly in border areas. There are at least nine military airfields in Tibet, a number of radar stations and several missile bases. Tibet has become one of China's largest missile-launching bases, capable of targeting India and other areas near the Indian Ocean.

Although officially the Tibetan economy appears to be running at a loss, a factor not mentioned is how much of Tibet's natural wealth is being taken out. Since 1959, over half of Tibet's forests have been cut down. Tibet's mineral resources were largely untouched before 1950: the Chinese have identified reserves of gold, radium, titanium, lithium, iron, lead, bauxite and other minerals, including major deposits of uranium. For religious reasons, Tibetans did not mine – disturbing the earth was considered a bad omen. Today, it is rumoured that mining accounts for over 40% of Tibet's industrial output, with scores of mining sites opening up. Large deposits of oil and gas have been discovered in Tibet's northern Changtang region. This raises the essential issue of what the Chinese are doing in Tibet in the first place. The answer is: they're doing what every colonial power has done throughout recorded history – they are exploiting the colony's resources. They are cutting down all the trees because China proper has run out of trees. And they have their eyes on Tibet's abundant fresh water resources because severe water shortages are looming in China proper.

VALLEYS OF THE DAMMED In the 21st century, as access to clean water dwindles and as population increases, nations will no longer be fighting over oil or other resources – they will be fighting over water. And the rivers of Tibet will be one of the flashpoints. Who owns a river? Does the country that controls the source of a river have the right to divert the water for its own purposes? Will neighbouring nations like India and Vietnam stand idly by as they witness 'theft' of their rivers – the damming and diversion of Tibetan rivers by Chinese engineers?

China has an acute problem with water supply. Fresh water is becoming an increasingly rare commodity in the north of China, where agriculture depends on water to sustain food production. It is estimated that up to 70% of China's rivers are contaminated – to the point where the water is not drinkable, or even usable. China's new 'emperors' are not quite sure what to do about this, but if they want to avoid mobs of starving pitchfork-wielding peasants, they have to do something – and very soon. The regions of northern China are particularly hard up for water due to intensified desertification and increased industrial pollution. A dramatic example of water crisis surfaced in late 2005, when an explosion at a chemical plant near Harbin (northeast China) released 100 tons of cancer-causing benzene compounds into the Songhua River, from which the city draws its water supply. Three million Harbin residents were in a state of panic: they were without running water for almost a week until the toxins were cleaned up. The population of China's eastern region is heavily concentrated in large cities like Harbin.

The Chinese solution to the water problem appears to be a vast project to divert river waters from the south to the north. In this scheme are three diversion sectors: eastern, central and western. The western sector eyes the Tibetan plateau as a water-diversion target. Tibet is the principal watershed of Asia and the source of its ten major rivers: about 90% of run-off from Tibetan rivers flows downstream into China, India, Bangladesh, Nepal, Pakistan, Thailand, Burma, Laos, Cambodia and Vietnam.

In Tibet, a number of Chinese engineering projects are under way to harness hydropower. Several are in operation close to Lhasa. Lying 96km northeast of Lhasa is Zhikong Hydro-electric Power Station, with a dam 1.3km long. And 120km southwest of Lhasa is Yamzhog Yumco Pump Storage Power Station, a highly controversial project that has destroyed a sacred lake. The question here is: who are these dams for? In many Tibetan areas, houses are lucky if they have power for a few light bulbs; in fact, a number of Tibetan residences rely on solar dishes or solar panels as their main source. It would appear that the energy output from the dams close to Lhasa is intended to provide power for Chinese industrial concerns – and to new Chinese housing developments springing up on the fringes of Lhasa.

Dozens of major hydro-electric projects are planned for Tibetan rivers, with an eye on exporting the electricity to Chinese cities such as Chengdu, Xining and

Lanzhou. With ultra-high voltage lines now under installation, hydro-electric power from dams in Tibet can be exported all the way to eastern China. The most disturbing project on the drawing board is a blueprint for a mega-dam in eastern Tibet on the Tsangpo River, which could theoretically generate twice as much electricity as the Three Gorges Dam. The plan is to harness the enormous hydro potential at the Great Bend of the Tsangpo. There's one glitch with this plan: downriver on the Tsangpo, millions of people in India and Bangladesh are waiting for the water resources too – relying on the Brahmaputra River.

Currently, the main Chinese engineering focus is on the Kham area (southeastern Tibet), where fast-flowing rivers are concentrated. At the edge of the Tibetan plateau in upper Yunnan, eight dams are planned for the mighty Mekong within China. Four are already in operation, three more are under construction, and an additional three are in planning stages. These dams are huge. Xiaowan Dam, towering to 292m in wall height (the height of a 90-storey building), is the largest arched dam in the world.

Opposition to China's actions is fierce from neighbouring countries, with both foreign NGOs and local environmentalists predicting environmental and social disaster. At stake is the livelihood of some 60 million people in the Mekong Basin – the majority being subsistence farmers and fishermen. The farmers are dependent on the river's rich sediment for riverside cultivation, and the people of these countries rely on the Mekong's abundant fish supply as staple food. The completion of eight dams in Yunnan could sound the death knell for the river.

MINING TIBET You may know more about the movie *Avatar* than you do about mining in Tibet, but the film offers uncanny parallels to the situation on the Roof of the World. Tibet is the largest colony in the world. Tibet is under military occupation by Chinese troops. Tibet is being ruthlessly exploited for its valuable minerals, against the wishes of the inhabitants, who deeply resent what is happening to their land. In *Avatar*, the action takes place some 150 years into the future on a distant moon called Pandora. Here, rapacious foreign CEOs and military figures seek a mineral of astronomical value called unobtanium. The only thing stopping them in this endeavour is the blue-skinned Na'vi, who refuse to allow mining on their land, which they regard as sacred. Tibetans for centuries did not permit any mining (except for gold) due to their belief that digging would scar the sacred surface of the earth. Today, many valuable minerals are being extracted in Tibet by Chinese and foreign companies. And one mineral alone would qualify for the status of 'unobtanium'. That is lithium. Lithium is used for making batteries for computers, mobile phones and many other gadgets, and lithium is a rare mineral, in very short global supply. Tibet is one of the prime sources: lithium is extracted from a handful of lakes in Tibet. In fact, you probably carry a tiny piece of Tibetan lithium around in the battery of your laptop, iPad, mobile phone or other device.

RAILWAY ON THE ROOFTOP A poster put out by China Mobile and China Construction Bank shows Lhasa as a futuristic land of high-rise buildings, telecom towers and flyover highways, with a train running through it all. There are just two Tibetan buildings depicted in the poster: Tibet Museum and the Potala Palace. This is Lhasa in the 21st century – a Chinese clone. The blueprint is to modernise, go high-rise, and bring in entrepreneurs to stimulate the market. The train in the poster has sleek aerodynamic lines like the Japanese Bullet Train or the French TGV.

And all this may yet come to pass, with the arrival of the Golmud–Lhasa railway line. It is the world's highest elevated track, eclipsing the Peruvian Central Railway of the Andes by several hundred metres. Chinese news sources wax lyrical about the engineering feat of building the railway, claiming it to be the fruit of growing national strength – and an achievement on a par with China's second manned space flight, 'which is arousing both pride and envy at home and abroad'. But for Tibetans in exile and activists abroad, the railway arouses only disgust and indignation: the project is highly controversial. The line got under way in 2001 and was completed in 2005 at a cost of over US$4.1 billion. In fact, over a four-year period, the railway racked up bills equivalent to double the entire budget spent in Tibet on education and health care since it was invaded by China in 1950. Obviously, the railway was not built for philanthropic purposes. Later, Beijing revealed that mining was a major factor in the decision to build the railway: that the income and benefits from mining would easily cover the cost of building it. Mining is not possible without the railway for shipping minerals.

The railway project took on a formidable engineering challenge, crossing bleak, frozen terrain through a region plagued with sandstorms in summer and blizzards in winter. European tunnelling engineers concluded that it was impossible to bore through the rock and ice of the Kunlun mountain range. But somehow Chinese engineers have pierced the Kunlun mountain barrier that has kept Tibet secluded for centuries – in the process creating the world's highest tunnel at 4,900m. The 1,140km line traverses the Kunlun mountain range, crossing more than 400 bridges, boring through 30km of tunnels, cresting two 5,000m passes, and running past more than 30 stations before reaching Lhasa.

American author Paul Theroux wrote in *Riding the Iron Rooster* that the reason Tibet remained un-Chinese for so long was because of the mountain barrier isolating it. 'The Kunlun Range is a guarantee that the railway will never get to Lhasa. That is probably a good thing. I thought I liked railways until I saw Tibet, and then I realised that I liked wilderness much more.'

The Kunlun 'guarantee' has been swept aside by Chinese engineering, and with that comes another threat: the railway is bound to disrupt Tibet's fragile ecosystem and impact on its rare wildlife. About 550km, or half of the line, is built over permafrost, which is unstable: any construction is bound to damage this environment. In the warmer summer months, the frozen ground can thaw during the day, which might cause railway track to buckle and sink. The Chinese claim to have made a technological breakthrough for dealing with this – by pumping cooling agents into the ground via underground pipes to ensure the earth remains frozen. The trains themselves require high-tech tinkering too, which is where foreign corporations come in. American company General Electric Transportation has a contract to supply locomotives. Two Canadian corporations, Bombardier and Power Corporation, supply special railcars, and another Canadian company, Nortel, supplies a digital wireless communications network for the railway. These companies have come under fire in the West for making possible a project that is bound to be detrimental to the survival of Tibetans, who face a massive influx of Chinese settlers arriving by train.

The railway is projected to move eight million tons of cargo annually, with at least 16 trains a day on the Golmud–Lhasa line (eight each way). The Golmud–Lhasa run takes ten to 15 hours by train, knocking at least ten hours off the best time by bus.

The Chinese claim that the TAR is the only part of China not connected by rail, and that a railway would accelerate economic and social development of Tibet. Those same two factors – viewed from a Tibetan perspective – amount to a nightmare. 'Economic development' could mean Chinese mining companies using the rail line as a way of extracting precious metals and other resources and freighting them back to China. 'Social development' could obliquely mean a new Chinese invasion – a massive influx of Chinese settlers, drawn by financial incentives and tax breaks. There are precedents here: you do not have to look any further than Golmud itself. Fifty years ago, Golmud was open steppe with nomad herders. After the railway reached town, immigrants from eastern China arrived in droves, leading to the present population of several hundred thousand and a sprawling town. A similar situation occurred, but much faster, in the remote northwest of China, in the Islamic centre of Kashgar, where the Chinese population increased by 30% in 2001 – the year after the railway to Kashgar was completed. Another major application of the railway reaching Tibet is strategic – with the line, it is easier to consolidate border defences.

There are plans to extend the railway line west from Lhasa to Shigatse (and eventually to Kathmandu), and east from Lhasa to Bayi. The long-range blueprint for Tibet calls for three more rail lines to reach Lhasa – from Lanzhou, Chengdu and Kunming.

PEOPLE

The main population groups are Tibetan and Han Chinese. The origins of the Tibetans as a race are sketchy: ethnologists place them in the Tibeto-Burman group. The earliest human habitation in Tibet can be traced back 4,700 years: it is believed that Tibetans migrated to the plateau in the late Neolithic Age. However, a recent find suggests that there was human presence in Tibet much earlier than that, as far back as the Ice Age. In 1995, researcher David Zhang Dian from Hong Kong University found remnants of a stove and 19 handprints and footprints pressed into rock on a mountain slope 85km from Lhasa. He brought back rock samples and had them dated. The tests revealed they were from the Ice Age. And in 2002, at a location 120km north of Golmud, Chinese archaeologist Xu Xinguo found artefacts dating to the microlithic period (10,000 to 30,000 years ago).

On the Tibetan plateau there are a number of ethnic Tibetan subgroups, differentiated by cultural, dress and linguistic variations. These groups include the Topa (far-west Tibet), the Khampa (east Tibet), the Golok (from the northeast), and a number of minority groups closely related to Tibetans, such as the Qiang (from upper Sichuan) and the Monba and Lhoba tribespeople (far southern Tibet, near the Bhutan border). In the Barkor in Lhasa, it's possible to see groups from very different regions who have arrived on pilgrimage to the sacred city. The groups are often identifiable by their dress. From Amdo come nomad women, with their braided hair done in 108 strands (a sacred number). The waist-length tresses must be re-done at least once a week and smeared with yak butter. In former times, Tibetan women used to wear their wealth in the form of elaborate jewellery. This still holds true to some extent – you will see Amdo women with big chunks of turquoise or amber in their hair, or worn in bulky necklaces. From Golok come nomads who wear greasy sheepskin cloaks, yak-hide boots, and often sport felt bowler hats (a legacy of British invasion) or Stetson felt hats (made in eastern China). From eastern Tibet come the quick-tempered Khampas: the men have tassels of red or black yarn braided through their hair, and a dagger sheathed at the waist – not entirely decorative. Selling goods in the Barkor are also Nepali and Kashmiri traders, and Muslims from Xinjiang.

Any statistical data on Tibet – particularly on population – is dicey; facts and figures are fudged to suit whatever propaganda department is issuing them. Basically, the Chinese do not wish it to be known that they are flooding the region with Chinese settlers. Chinese figures from 2003 put the population of the TAR at 2.67 million, broken down into 93% Tibetan, 6% Han Chinese, and 1% 'ethnic minorities' like

Monba, Lhoba and Hui. But how can this breakdown possibly be accurate? A visual check on the streets of Lhasa – or Tsedang or Bayi – shows the Han Chinese are clearly in the majority in these places, and not the tiny minority indicated. Chinese figures do not take into account the number of roving (non-resident) Chinese businesspeople in Tibet, nor Chinese military stationed there (estimated at 200,000 to 500,000 troops) – they would be registered in other provinces of China. It's possible, within the region of Ethnic Tibet, that the Chinese outnumber the Tibetans. The population of Ethnic Tibet could be 4.5 to 6 million, meaning more Tibetans live outside the TAR than in it. Within Tibet, nearly all Chinese live in urban areas, while about 80% of Tibetans live in rural areas, some continuing their nomadic ways.

LAST OF THE NOMADS Traditional occupations for Tibetans are farmer, merchant, trader or monk. But the lifestyle that really manifests the rugged spirit of Tibet is that of the hardy nomad, dependent on yaks and other animals to survive. Tibetans are among the last nomads in Asia – other pastoral nomads include the Mongols (now found mostly in Outer Mongolia) and the Turkic tribes of China's far northwest, such as the Kazaks. Tibetan nomads face a great battle to retain their way of life as the Chinese are suspicious of those on the move, and attempt to make them settle: as a result the way of the nomad is fast disappearing. Chinese policy is attempting to put an end to Tibetan nomad culture. This started with large-scale fencing of traditional nomad grazing grounds with barbed wire in Amdo and Gansu – which has led to considerable acrimony over land and water rights, and exactly who has access to the richest grassland.

Early travellers to Tibet remarked on how cheery Tibetan nomads were in the face of one of the harshest environments in Asia – a high, treeless, windswept plateau. Maybe it's their ribald sense of humour that sustains them in sub-zero temperatures and howling gales. Whatever the case, the nomads are part of the romance of Tibet, with their yaks and yak-hair tents, their elaborate costumes and jewellery, and their raucous folksongs.

The *drokpas* are pastoral nomads, moving their tents in search of pasture for their animals. Livestock – yaks, goats, sheep and horses – are central to the livelihood of the nomads, and the basis of their culture. Their movements are seasonal, linked to weather conditions and availability of pasture. Pure nomadic life is becoming rare: more often, nomadic groups move between designated areas with the change of the seasons. There are signs of 'modernisation': nomads wearing knock-off North Face jackets (not sheepskin), nomads riding motorcycles (not horses), and nomad women sporting two braids (not the traditional 108 braids). Solar panels sit on top of the yak-hair tent and power up lights at night.

True nomads are found in the grasslands of northern Tibet, and at the peripheral zones of Kham and Amdo. Hastening the demise of the nomads are occasional bitterly cold winters. The winter of 1997–98 was particularly savage, with a long snowfall and temperatures of –30°C to –40°C, which wiped out large herds of yaks and sheep. The death toll for nomads was unspecified, but it is certain that a number died.

Playing a key role in the survival of the nomads is the yak – a 'comical' creature best described as a cow with a skirt. The yak is the male animal: the female is called a *dri*, while a yak–cow hybrid is called a *dzo* (a very useful word to remember when you are playing Scrabble). Some insist that since only the females produce milk, the term 'yak butter' is incorrect. The fact is that most Westerners do not know what a

THE SILENCE OF THE GRASSLANDS

In 1979 and 1980, as part of ongoing negotiations with China, the Dalai Lama's government-in-exile sent three delegations from India to see Tibet first hand. The news was not good. The Tibetans had suffered greatly under Chinese rule. One of the things that the delegates remarked upon was the silence of the grasslands – and the emptiness of the grasslands. Where teeming herds of wild animals roamed in the 1940s, there was nothing. The animals were slaughtered by the PLA and Chinese settlers for food and for sport. The wildlife vanished from the grasslands.

These days, the grasslands themselves are in danger of disappearing. Nomadic herders and their yaks are disappearing. And the grasslands themselves are undergoing degradation: they are slowly turning into desert.

For close on 4,000 years, Tibetan nomads have grazed their yak herds on these grasslands. The nomads are the real stewards of the grasslands: they have developed sophisticated knowledge of how to maintain the pastures, knowing that they must use them again. Defying all logic, Chinese officials have targeted Tibetan nomads for forced settlement. The Chinese view nomads as backward uneducated people, and the rationale behind Chinese policy is that nomads will have access to schools and medical assistance. But there appears to be a more sinister agenda. A large factor is the ability to control the nomads in fixed settlements. Nomads are viewed as unruly and too independent – beyond government control. And another reason is that nomads are sitting on rangeland where mining ventures want to move in, or in valleys where mega-dams are planned for construction. China makes no secret of its intention to settle all the nomads within a very short timeframe. From 1995 to 2015, the objective is to transfer all of the nomads in housing settlements in remote areas, forcing them to sell or slaughter their yaks. Across the entire plateau, that involves at least two million Tibetan nomads. Tens of thousands of nomad families have been shifted to settlements that resemble concrete ghettos. Chinese policy previously 'dri' refers to, so the term 'yak' has been generalised to cover both male and female of the species for Westerners.

Wild yaks can weigh up to 1,000kg – double the size of domestic yaks. Due to their wild origins, yaks are superbly adapted to high-altitude living and cold conditions, and are sure-footed on mountain slopes. Tibetans use all parts of the yak. With a harsh climate and a lack of vegetables, meat eating is a necessity in Tibet. Yak meat is the principal meat eaten, preserved in dried or semi-dried form. The hair and hide of the yak are used for making thread, blankets, ropes, bags, clothing and boots. Yak milk, yoghurt, butter and cheese provide sustenance. Yak dung is collected and stacked – it is the main fuel source on the treeless plateau. Yaks are also used for riding (though they hate the idea), as a pack animal and in farm work (for ploughing). Yak hide is even used to make ingenious small boats.

Nomads live in thick heavy tents woven from the hair of the yak. These tents can be dismantled piece by piece, rolled up, and loaded onto yaks or horses. Upon arrival at a new site, the tent is quickly reassembled. At the centre of the tent is usually a stove, fuelled by yak dung; one corner of the tent always has a little altar. To beat the cold, Tibetan nomads cocoon themselves in long sheepskin jackets – the top and sleeves can be shuffled off when temperatures rise. Much warmer than sheep wool is fox fur, often used in hats. Cashmere goats provide particularly fine wool, highly valued in the West. After several efforts to obtain breeding stock

targeted Mongolian nomads (Inner Mongolia) and Kazak nomads (Xinjiang) for settlement. Now, with those nomad cultures virtually erased, the attention has shifted to Tibetan nomads.

Chinese authorities cite climate-change factors to account for recent degradation of the grasslands, but in fact Chinese policy is largely to blame because of a widespread fencing policy. Previously, nomads were self-sufficient, getting everything they needed from their herds, and trading any surplus for grains from farmers. Now this barter system, which has been in place for thousands of years, has been disrupted. Chinese policy targets the nomads – and also targets their livestock. Yaks go to the slaughterhouse. One estimate claims that since the ludicrous policy of 'removing livestock to restore grasslands' was put in place, over 50% of herd animals have been removed from the TAR. Travelling in central Tibet today, yaks are noticeably missing. What you see more of is cows or yak–cow hybrids: these animals are more suited to village living. Yaks like to roam.

Nomads who are forcibly settled face serious problems with food supply and quality of living. They are totally dependent on state subsidies: they have no jobs, no money, no training. In their rush to settle the nomads, Chinese officials have made absolutely no provision for retraining nomads to adjust to semi-urban life. To lure nomads to settlements, Chinese officials make pledges to open schools and clinics, but these mostly turn out to be empty promises. Nomads cannot read or write Chinese (they cannot even write in Tibetan). Without those language skills, they have very little opportunity for training to get decent jobs. And they have no skills in farming. One of the very few avenues open for nomads to make real money is to collect exotic mushrooms and herbs from the highlands in the spring. From a model of sustainability (getting everything they need from their yaks and livestock), the nomads have been reduced to beggars in their own land.

for cashmere (wrong animals, two of same sex), the British finally procured some cashmere goats and took them to the far north of Scotland, leaving them out in the freezing cold. However, it clearly wasn't cold enough – or windy enough – for the goats, who refused to grow their cashmere undercoat.

Tibetans are among the few people in Asia who thrive on dairy products – mostly yak and goat derivatives (milk, butter, yoghurt and cheese). The Mongols and the Kazaks eat similar fare. You might have trouble recognising these dairy products: yak butter floating in the tea, or tooth-breaking pieces of dried cheese, strung together like a necklace. Large amounts of tea are also consumed: three to five cups of tea are considered necessary for everyone in the morning, and some people might drink as many as 40 cups a day. Chinese brick tea was once considered so valuable it was a form of currency. Instead of milk, yak butter is used, and since sugar is hard to come by in Tibet, nomads just use salt (there are copious salt deposits found near lakes). Tea is made in a wooden churn, a long cylindrical object.

Often mixed with tea and rolled into balls is the great staple of the nomads – *tsampa*. This flour is usually made by roasting barley, but can also be made from corn, wheat, millet or oats. *Tsampa* is a tasteless flour, but highly sustaining – it is obtained through bartering, and held in cloth bags. It stores very well. Often eaten raw from the bag, *tsampa* can be consumed in cakes or soup. Another barley derivative is *chang,* a milky fermented beer that is brewed on special occasions and is frequently offered to guests. Chang can also be made from rice, wheat, corn, oats or millet. Since *chang* is home-brewed, the alcohol strength varies wildly.

LANGUAGE

Mandarin Chinese is the official language enforced in Tibet. Tibetan is spoken and written, but given a very low profile in schools and very little media exposure. The literacy rate among Tibetans is very low – thought to be less than 25%. Many have no access to proper education facilities. The Chinese practise linguistic colonialism: if a Tibetan wants to get ahead and reach the echelons of higher education, he or she must speak and write Mandarin Chinese. Very few Chinese living in Tibet speak any Tibetan or attempt to learn it.

The Tibetan language is part of the Tibeto-Burman language group, although the written form is distantly related to Sanskrit. The existence of many dialects makes it hard for Tibetans to communicate with each other. Lhasa dialect is the standard, but Lhasa court dialect is dying out. The script is more uniform throughout the Tibetan world, and although different writing styles are employed, they're more easily understood from one end of the Himalaya to the other than the spoken word. There's one catch here: the very high illiteracy rate.

The elegant Tibetan script consists of 30 consonants plus four vowels, and is easily rendered on computer in Macintosh and PC formats, though not much of this is in evidence in Lhasa, where virtually all computer access is in the much more complex Chinese characters.

Tibetan is the Latin of High Asia: it is hardly geared to the modern world. This ancient language lacks the vocabulary range for innovations like 'email', 'mobile phone' or 'barcode'. Tibetan is flexible enough, though, that English or foreign words can be imported phonetically (which is the case for a lot of geographical terms) or Tibetans can try to make up new compound words. The Tibetan word for movie is *log-nyen,* meaning 'electric picture', the word for aeroplane is *namdru* ('ship of the sky') and in Amdo the word for bicycle is *sherta* ('iron horse'). But new vocabulary requires consensus among the scattered groups of Tibetans to gain wide acceptance, and thus to be widely understood. There could be one term used within Tibet (taken from Chinese) and a completely different one used in India (deriving from English or Hindi).

Scholars of Latin have achieved more success than Tibetans in agreeing on new vocabulary. They have used the internet to achieve this standardisation and to spread the word; societies in Europe regularly publish new Latin vocabulary. Nothing resembling this occurs in the Tibetan world, where computer access is rare or non-existent. Refer to *Appendix 2*, page 312, for more about spoken Tibetan.

TIBETAN BUDDHISM

Tibetan Buddhism, practised by almost all Tibetans, is perhaps better described as 'showcase Buddhism' within the TAR, as it is rigidly controlled by the Chinese. Officially, the Chinese are atheistic, with the government and motherland as the reigning deities. The spiritual and political leader of the Tibetans is the Dalai Lama, who is vilified by the Chinese as a 'separatist' and even as 'a major hindrance to the development of Tibetan Buddhism'.

Tibetan Buddhism has all the trappings of a religion – temples, abbots, monks, monasteries, sermons, holy texts – but is actually not a religion. With no belief in a superior god or supreme being, Buddhism does not qualify: in fact, it can be equated with agnosticism. (Note, however, that the terms religion and religious are used throughout this book for the sake of convenience.) Buddhism is non-dogmatic, encouraging practitioners to question – even challenge – authority, and to rely on evidence tested with their own senses. It suggests that the practitioner, not some external force, holds the answer to his or her own happiness, with the mind being both the obstacle and the key to understanding. Buddhism can thus be more accurately called a philosophy or a form of psychology. It is primarily a belief system based around respect for all living things and the concept of compassion, providing a code of ethics to live by. Tibetans are an extremely devout people – Tibetan Buddhism forms a significant part of their lives and their identity. Material gain is not high on the list of priorities for Tibetans: spiritual fulfilment is.

At the core of Buddhism is the concern with suffering, and how to overcome that suffering and achieve a full life. The higher goal of Buddhism is to attain enlightenment, which means to be fully awake to the reality of life, to have an understanding of suffering and how it may be overcome. The Buddha is the 'enlightened one' or 'he who is fully awake'.

Buddhism is fairly easy-going: it does not require (or expect) converts, or people to spread its message. Neither does it demand sole faith in Buddhism: you can be Jewish or Christian or atheist – or communist, for that matter. Except for monks, Buddhism does not require attendance at a fixed place of worship, nor does it have stringent rules or vows to follow.

There are a number of branches of Buddhism: the three major ones are Zen (mainly identified with Japan), Mahayana (identified with Tibet) and Theravada (identified with Thailand and Cambodia). Tibetan Buddhism is unique because it is a blend of Mahayana Buddhism (originally from India) and the ancient Tibetan shamanist cult of Bon, heavily associated with magic and sorcery.

In contrast to the stripped-down tenets of Zen, Tibetan Buddhism hosts a vast pantheon of animist spirits, protectors, tantric deities shown in blissful union with their consorts, and an array of bodhisattvas and Buddhas. Other icons are real figures – founders of the various sects and past Dalai Lamas (see the *Jokhang Temple* section in *Chapter 4*, page 142, for more on Tibetan iconography).

There are few female deities in the Tibetan Buddhist pantheon; women have a low profile in the leadership of Tibetan Buddhist sects. This is a contentious area of Tibetan Buddhism, and one difficult for Western women to accept. Compared with men, women are considered to be a lower form of incarnation.

Most Tibetan Buddhists believe in reincarnation – on a higher plane, a person is reincarnated as a human, on a lower plane as an animal or an insect. But there is, in addition, belief in the concept of different realms after death. Similar to Christian beliefs in heaven and hell (which may have derived from Buddhism), there is belief in an earthly realm, a heavenly realm, a hell realm, and limbo zones like the realm of hungry ghosts. For reincarnation, rebirth in the human world is far preferable to that of hell or hungry ghosts. Only high lamas are said to be able to direct a specific rebirth in their next incarnation. See page 31 for more on reincarnation.

A related concept is karma. Tibetans believe that they may have inherited some bad karma from previous lives, a situation that must be corrected by doing good deeds in the present life. Many Buddhist practices hinge on accruing merit by doing good deeds. Merit can be accrued by making donations to temples; by assisting in the building or repair of temples, Buddha images or shrines; or by going on pilgrimages to sacred Buddhist sites. In their lifetime, many Tibetans want to undertake a pilgrimage to Lhasa and to Mount Kailash, among other holy places. Karma is cause and effect: good deeds have good effects, bad deeds have bad effects. By following the right path in this life, a person can accrue merit, with karmic carry-over to the next life. A tree drops a seed that becomes a tree – but this tree is not the same as the original one.

One of the ultimate forms of merit-making is to become a monk or a nun. In old Tibet, it was an honour for a family to be able to send a son to a monastery – this was seen as an opportunity to gain a proper education, since monasteries in old Tibet were the only schools. Tibetan culture is closely linked to Tibetan Buddhist beliefs – in former times most literature, music, dance and drama, painting, sculpture and architecture was inspired by those beliefs.

Since 1959, Tibetan Buddhism has been in a state of flux because traditions were severely disrupted by Chinese takeover, and lineage holders fled into exile. The Tibetans in exile say that real Tibetan Buddhism continues in freedom outside Tibet, but not inside Tibet. The Dalai Lama has attempted to draw the four main schools of Tibetan Buddhism together, the differences between them being more of a political nature than a religious one, but these attempts have seen little success.

The oldest school is the Nyingma sect, founded around the 7th century by Indian master Padmasambhava. The tradition is carried on through reincarnates of great teachers. The Sakya sect, founded in the 11th century, is not as prominent as the other three schools. At its head is the Sakya Trizin, who fled Tibet in 1959 and established his base in Dehra Dun, India. The Kagyu sect also emerged in the 11th century; the lineage holder is the Karmapa. The 16th Karmapa fled Tibet in 1959 and founded Rumtek Monastery in Sikkim (a former kingdom in northeast India); on his death in 1981 a search was conducted for the 17th Karmapa. Eventually a boy from east Tibet, Ogyen Trinley Dorje, was installed at the traditional seat of Tsurphu Monastery near Lhasa in 1992. Ogyen Trinley Dorje escaped into exile in 2000 and now lives in India; a rival Karmapa candidate, Thaye Dorje, also lives in India. Finally, the Geluk sect, founded in the 14th century by Tsongkhapa, is closely associated with the Dalai Lama. The lineage holder is the Ganden Tripa, who is elected every seven years in Dharamsala.

A number of new schools, sub-sects and offshoots have been founded in exile by various masters. Some very strange permutations have taken place in the West. Exiled Tibetan Kagyu lama Chogyam Trungpa (1939–87) established training centres and retreat communities where he promulgated his 'crazy wisdom' visionary approach. In 1970 he shocked his students in Scotland by marrying a young English woman and flying to North America, where he went on to establish a series of dharma centres under the banner of Shambhala International. Chogyam Trungpa was dubbed 'the cocktail lama' due to his scandalous predilection for women and wine, and his highly unconventional personality.

One thing that Tibetans in exile have attempted to do is cut down the amount of ritual involved in Tibetan Buddhist ceremonies, and to concentrate on the pure elements of Buddhism. In its 'purist form', Buddhism has gained wide appeal in the West. But how can the ancient faith of Tibetan Buddhism be in tune with the modern world? Buddhism appeals to the rational, scientific world because the Buddha did not insist that followers accept what he said: he told them to question everything, and test his words for their veracity. Attributed to the Buddha is this disclaimer: 'Like analysing gold through scorching, cutting and rubbing it, monks and scholars are to adopt my word not for the sake of respecting me, but upon analysing it well.'

That said, there remains a very unscientific facet to Tibetan Buddhism, verging on high superstition. One of the reasons that Tibet fell to the Chinese was that the clergy failed to modernise. In pre-1950 Tibet, modern advances and technology were seen as threats to spiritual life and traditional values. The clergy was highly suspicious of new gadgets and new-fangled ideas: in 1943, the Regent banned the use of motorcycles and the playing of soccer (soccer fever, which had gripped Lhasa, was seen as a powerful force that would undermine social stability).

There was – and still is – great faith among Tibetans in auspicious days and bad omens, which are interpreted by astrologers. Tibetan astrology or astronomy could hardly be called scientific: like medieval Western models, the mapping of the earth and the planets was firmly rooted in religious beliefs rather than scientific observation with telescopes. The Tibetan cosmos places Mount Meru, the abode of the gods, at the centre of the universe (it is identified as Mount Kailash on this earth). On the summit of Mount Meru is the celestial city of Sudarsana; above Meru float 25 more heavens of the gods, while under the mountain lie the hell-realms. Mount Meru is surrounded by seven rings of golden mountains and seven oceans. At the outer edge of a flat circular disk, across the outer ocean from Meru, are a few spin-off worlds, like the one we're on. This is identified as the continent of Jambudvipa, trapezoidal in shape, where inhabitants live for a century, and where the dharma flourishes. East of Meru lies the continent of Videha, which is white and half-moon shaped, with inhabitants whose faces resemble half-moons – they are said to be twice as tall as humans and live up to 500 years. Two other continents lie to the north and west – Uttarakuru, a square continent populated by square-jawed giants, and Godaniya, a circular continent populated by round-faced giants. Beyond all this are the paths of planets, with the mandalic (see *Glossary*, page 326) model enclosed by massive rings of fire.

Tibetan Buddhists have had to seriously reconsider their traditional cosmology model in the light of modern discoveries. Some Tibetans cling to the literal truth; others claim that Meru is merely symbolic. There is obviously no huge mountain at the navel of the world, there is no city on the top of that mountain, and there is no continent of lanky giants with half-moon faces to the east, either.

MONLAM AND SHOWCASE BUDDHISM To the casual tourist in Tibet, it may appear that Tibetan Buddhist culture flourishes and that freedom of religion is permitted. Monks chant in deep tones in dark assembly halls, butter-lamps are lit in monastery courtyards by shiny-eyed pilgrims, and monastic festival days such as *tanka*-unfurling festivals are dutifully observed. But while monks and pilgrims appear to go through the ritual motions – turning prayer-wheels, making offerings in temples, and prostrating – this may be all they are doing. These manifestations are largely cosmetic: the atheist Chinese tightly control what goes on through the Chinese Religious Affairs Bureau. This has led to a variety of 'showcase Buddhism' – purely ritualistic icing for tourists.

The crux of the problem for the Chinese is that monks and nuns are the ones who have spearheaded protests against Chinese presence in Tibet and demanded the right to freedom of worship, so a gathering of monks is something that the Chinese fear. Nowhere has this been more dramatically revealed than in the case of Monlam, a major festival resumed in 1986. Monlam Chenmo, the great Tibetan prayer festival, coincides with lunar New Year celebrations, and takes place around February or March. Or used to. There have been no full Monlam celebrations since 1988, after a series of explosive events.

In 1986, for the first time in over 20 years, Monlam was revived in Lhasa at the request of the Chinese. Whether this was to be a spectacle for tourists, or to show the world that religious freedoms were being resumed, is not clear. Whatever the case, photography of the 1986 Monlam pops up in all kinds of Chinese sources – in photo books, in brochures bolstering the Chinese claim that there is complete religious freedom in Tibet, and even in video format on the Beijing-produced CD-ROM *Wonders of Tibet*. But the actual festival is no longer held with all monasteries participating.

In the 1950s, with monks coming from all over Tibet, Monlam became a focus for anti-Chinese protests. On 10 March 1959, at the tail-end of Monlam, the Lhasa Uprising took place, with monks taking up guns against the Chinese, so the end of Monlam is a particularly volatile time. In 1986, over a thousand monks from the different monasteries around Lhasa gathered for rites. Huge butter sculptures were displayed outside the Jokhang Temple at the heart of Lhasa, attracting crowds of up to 10,000 people from Lhasa and the valleys beyond.

Versions vary as to exactly what happened at the third Monlam to be staged. The last day of Monlam, 5 March 1988, turned into a riot (close on the heels of the pro-independence riots of October 1987). Apparently, when a procession was in progress around Barkor Bazaar in Lhasa, some monks chanted independence slogans. Stones were thrown at them, and they were warned to keep quiet by the Chinese. When the monks repeated the slogans, a Chinese policeman advanced, drawing his pistol. A Khampa tribesman from east Tibet stepped in to defend the monks, and was shot in the head at point-blank range. Infuriated, the monks paraded the dead man's body around the Barkor. At first the Chinese did not interfere, but by the third circuit of the Barkor, they were using batons and tear gas, then guns. Eighteen Tibetans died that day: hundreds of Chinese troops stormed the Jokhang Temple and beat a number of monks to death with iron bars; other monks were thrown off the rooftop. Some 800 Tibetans were arrested.

The following year, Monlam was boycotted by the monks. On 5 March 1989, the most severe rioting erupted – as many as 100 Tibetans were killed, Chinese shops were burned, a state of martial law was declared, and all foreigners were ordered out of Lhasa. Martial law was not lifted in Lhasa for 13 months. By late 1991, the situation was back to normal, according to the Chinese. The place was once again open to tourism and it was business as usual, albeit with lots of permits, restrictions, checkpoints, and frequent chopping and changing of regulations.

In 1996, Chinese work-teams occupied all of the monasteries and nunneries in Tibet as part of an extensive 're-education' campaign that involved signing of pledges by the monks and nuns to denounce the Dalai Lama and denounce the notion that Tibet might be a separate entity from China. Pictures, writings, audio recordings and videos of the revered Dalai Lama are banned in Tibet: those in possession of such items typically receive prison sentences. Since 1996, 'patriotic re-education' has been a staple for monastic studies, with monks required to study six books with titles like *Handbook on Crushing the Separatists* and *Handbook on Ethics for the Masses*. Testing is conducted on these handbooks.

Since 1959, the annual examination to award the Geshe degree (the highest rank in the Geluk school of Tibetan Buddhism) has fallen by the wayside. The Geshe examination is traditionally in the form of a rigorous question-and-answer debate, testing the applicant's knowledge to the fullest – the equivalent of a monastic PhD. The examination in Lhasa was suspended after 1959, was revived for three years from 1986 to 1988 (along with Monlam) and was suspended again following riots in Lhasa. After a hiatus of 16 years, the Geshe examination was revived in mid-2005, when six monks in their seventies were awarded the degree by the Beijing-based Buddhist Association of China, after taking the test at the Jokhang Temple in Lhasa. This will explain why there's a dearth of high-ranking clergy in Tibet: there's very little education going on, at least not of the monastic kind. The Tibetan government-in-exile, by contrast, has continued to offer the Geshe test every year. In 2005, Chinese authorities launched a campaign to blacklist not only the exiled Dalai Lama but also key religious figures close to him – banning those *rinpoches* (high lamas) from returning to their homeland, and forbidding any contact with them.

THE DALAI LAMA He's funny, he's charismatic and he has a deep, booming voice. He's a thorn in the side of the Chinese, who vigorously protested the award of the Nobel Peace Prize to him in 1989. He cracks jokes on the Larry King show. He's been a guest editor at French *Vogue*, and has written introductions to scores of books about Tibet. He's been featured on the covers of numerous magazines, and on billboard ads by Apple Computers as one of the great thinkers of the 20th century – in the same league as Einstein and Picasso (the Dalai Lama's picture, however, did not appear on billboards in Hong Kong).

Who is he? The title is synonymous with Tibet: the Dalai Lama is Tibet's greatest campaigner. Revered as the living incarnation of the bodhisattva of compassion, Tenzin Gyatso is the spiritual leader of all the Tibetan Buddhist sects. The Dalai Lama claims he is a simple monk ('a naughty Buddhist monk') but he's much more than that: his upper arm bears vaccination scars, revealing how well travelled he is. He is a fighter for Tibetan rights, the foremost proponent of world peace, and a tireless promoter of what he calls his real religion: kindness and compassion.

The Dalai Lama is an international icon, an inspiration to millions of Buddhists, and to millions of advocates of non-violence and right living. On a global basis, he has no equal (the Pope comes to mind, but the Pope is a proselytiser, seeking converts, while the Dalai Lama isn't). He cuts across barriers of race, religion and creed. All this is even more remarkable when you consider that the Dalai Lama's first language is not English, and that no government is willing to recognise him as a political leader – they accept him as a Nobel laureate or as leader of Tibetan Buddhism. The Dalai Lama has significantly raised awareness about Tibet, and the countries of Costa Rica, Poland and Norway have voiced support for Tibet in international forums.

The Dalai Lama's life has undergone fantastic twists and turns: the stuff that legends – and Hollywood movies – are made of. The Tibetan system of finding reincarnates, based on oracles and visions, dates back to the 15th century. Since lamas in the Geluk sect were celibate, a method of selecting the leader had to be arrived at. The resulting system of choosing a reincarnate worked beautifully, with no king's sons fighting each other for the throne, and no dispute over who would reign. It was, in addition, egalitarian, since the reincarnate could come from an impoverished nomad family. The 14th Dalai Lama was born in 1935 in a cowshed in Amdo Province, of a very poor family. At the age of two, he was identified by disguised lamas as the reincarnation of the 13th Dalai Lama, and hence the spiritual leader of four million Tibetans. His family were informed they would be moving to Lhasa. The boy was installed at the age of four upon the Lion Throne in Lhasa, and embarked upon a formidable course of monastic studies – training in Tibetan Buddhist metaphysics that would continue for the next 18 years. His new home was the dark, thousand-room Potala Palace.

A month after the Chinese invaded Tibet in 1950, the Dalai Lama was rushed through an enthronement ceremony to give him his majority, and thus assume the leadership of Tibet in the face of Chinese aggression. He was just 15 at the time. At age 18, he was negotiating face-to-face with Mao Zedong and Zhou Enlai over the fate of Tibet. In 1959, at the age of 23, the Dalai Lama escaped from Lhasa – ironically disguised as a soldier – and fled into exile in India, losing his country and his people. He issued a statement condemning the Chinese. He was just a Tibetan refugee, and a humble monk – no passport, no country and no status.

The Dalai Lama still travels on a refugee's yellow identity certificate. If anyone had told him back in 1959 that he would still be in exile over 45 years later, he would not have believed it. Other Dalai Lamas had fled Tibet during political crises – to Mongolia and to India – but only for a period of a few years. Tibetans going into exile in 1959 all believed they would soon return, and have not tried to take out Indian citizenship because it would mean a loss of their Tibetan identity.

The Dalai Lama's idol is Mahatma Gandhi, from whom he learned the path of non-violence. But this path has produced no concrete results: the Dalai Lama is in a dilemma because nothing has come of his peaceful approaches in the last 45-odd years. The Chinese pre-condition for discussion about Tibet is that the Dalai Lama abandon any thought of independence. For a period, the Dalai Lama abandoned his position of asking for full independence and asked for autonomy within the PRC, a situation similar to that which existed in Tibet from 1950 to 1959. This is similar to the system guaranteed for 50 years in Hong Kong SAR (Special Administrative Region), whereby Hong Kong continues its free ways but cedes military power to the PRC. But even this did not bring the Chinese to the negotiating table, because the Chinese claim that Tibet already is autonomous and that what the Dalai Lama is really after is independence. What keeps the Dalai Lama going? 'A belief in the rights that we have,' he says. It is the Tibetan struggle in a nutshell.

After his dramatic escape in 1959, the Dalai Lama kept a low profile throughout the 1960s, engaging in personal retreats. In 1974, he took his first trip to the West. Since then he has globetrotted at an astounding rate, spreading the message about Tibet and his ideas on world peace. The Dalai Lama's most endearing quality is what he calls a 'radical informality' – his uncanny skill at cutting to the heart of the matter, and being on the same wavelength as ordinary people. He is one of Tibet's most accomplished philosophers, trained in a traditional Tibetan system, and yet he comes across as a kind of jovial uncle. In March 2011, at the age of 75, the Dalai Lama announced his 'retirement', meaning that he would focus his attention on religious matters instead of acting as nominal head of the Tibetans in exile. In August 2011, Harvard-trained legal scholar Lobsang Sangay was sworn in as Prime Minister of the Tibetan government-in-exile, taking over political duties from the Dalai Lama.

REINCARNATES Tibetan Buddhism places great faith in master teachers, or *rinpoches*, and in the concept of reincarnation. With most of these rinpoches living in exile, that means the survival of Tibetan Buddhism lies outside Tibet. There are a number of obstacles to continuing the tradition of the masters: a major obstacle is how and where to find incarnates.

In Tibetan Buddhism, only a high lama is said to be able to redirect his soul into the body of another. The young reincarnate is known as a *tulku*, or living Buddha, and is usually found in a one- to three-year-old boy (if the search takes longer, the boy could be up to six or older). Most tulkus are officially instated at four or five years old. Finding the incarnation of a high lama upon his death is a complicated matter for the Tibetans – it involves the assessing of omens and portents, consulting the state oracle, performing divinations for clues, and perhaps visiting Tibet's sacred oracle lake, Lhamo Latso. Potential candidates are screened through extensive interviews; the final confirmation of a reincarnate is made by the Dalai Lama himself.

After the Dalai Lama's flight to India in 1959, the process of finding and verifying reincarnate lamas has become even more complicated because it must be determined if the incarnate has been born inside or outside Tibet. Most are now found outside Tibet: tulkus have been found among the Tibetan exile community in India and in Switzerland. If a tulku is discovered inside Tibet, it is difficult for the Dalai Lama's emissaries to carry out the selection process. This puzzles the Tibetan community-in-exile: where are the reincarnates to be found? And if one is discovered inside Tibet, what should be done about it? Can a reincarnate be a Westerner?

Asked about his own incarnation, the Dalai Lama has said that logically if he is in exile, his reincarnate can only be found in exile. But he has wavered on the question of whether the method of finding the Dalai Lama should be altered, and whether the Dalai Lama should be chosen democratically, like the Pope. In the case of the Geluk Sect throne-holder, the process *has* been altered: the leader is elected in Dharamsala every seven years. The Dalai Lama has also taken the unusual step of saying in an interview that in future the Dalai Lama could be a woman (all 14 Dalai Lamas thus far have been men). Of course, that's only an idea, and one that would never stand a chance of getting off the ground with the Tibetan community in exile. The stories behind three controversial tulkus are briefly described here.

The Spanish lama Dharamsala, March 1987: a two-year-old boy, Osel Torres, is enthroned with much pomp and ceremony as the reincarnation of renowned teacher Lama Thubten Yeshe. Lama Yeshe was the founder of the Foundation for the Preservation of the Mahayana Tradition (FPMT), an international organisation with over 80 dharma centres worldwide. Osel ('Clear Light') was discovered through oracles and dreams by Lama Zopa Rinpoche, who took over directing the FPMT after the death of Lama Yeshe. Subjected to traditional tests, Osel passed with flying colours, and at the age of two was recognised by the Dalai Lama. The one major difference is that Osel is Western. Since globetrotting Lama Yeshe was one of the biggest transmitters of Tibetan Buddhism in the West, it was reasoned his reincarnate was Western also. Lama Osel is the son of Paco and María Torres, who were devoted followers of Lama Yeshe in Spain; the couple have five other children. Lama Osel went on to receive a formal Tibetan education at Sera Monastery in south India. Reincarnate lamas undergo severe training: without special qualities, most would collapse under the strain. The strain was greater on Osel as a Westerner – a celebrity lama scrutinised by the Western media. In Osel's case, his special monastic education did not quite do the trick: as an adult, he rebelled and reverted to being a normal citizen in Spain, saying he wanted to catch up on drinking, watching football, chasing women – and pursuing a career as a filmmaker.

The politics of the Karmapa Officially the Chinese are atheist, and have ignored the selection of reincarnate lamas as 'feudal superstition'. This attitude, however, changed because the Chinese realised that these incarnates are very powerful, so it's become more a question of politics than religion. In 1992, the Chinese recognised an incarnate in the 17th Karmapa of the Kagyu sect, enthroned at Tsurphu Monastery and assisted by the Chinese Religious Affairs Bureau. This marked the first time since 1959 that the Chinese recognised an incarnate, although it appeared in this case that they wanted to direct the choice of the incarnate. The choice of the 17th Karmapa, a boy from eastern Tibet, caused a rift among Kagyu sect followers at Rumtek Monastery in Sikkim, where the 16th Karmapa lived in exile until his death. However, it appeared from the choice of the 17th Karmapa that it was possible for an incarnate to be found within Tibet and approved by both the Dalai Lama and the Chinese. This concurrence was short-lived: in early 1995, the Chinese and the Dalai Lama had a severe falling-out over the choice of the 11th Panchen Lama (see next section). See the *Tsurphu Monastery* section in *Chapter 5* to read more about the dramatic escape of the Karmapa and the case of two contenders for the throne.

The Tibetan monk known as His Holiness the 17th Gyalwa Karmapa, Ogyen Trinley Dorje, currently lives in Dharamsala, India. He obtained refugee status in India in 2001. The most media-savvy of any title holder, he uses webcasting to reach out to his followers at dharma centres around the world (especially in the USA). He uses the tools of Facebook and Twitter; he owns a Nintendo Wii – and his favourite Western movie is *Kung Fu Panda*. One cool Karmapa – who got into a lot of hot water in 2011 when Indian police raided his monastery and found millions in cash, including a large amount of Chinese money. The Karmapa shrugged it off, saying it was donations. Among Tibet's high-profile lamas, Ogyen Trinley Dorje ranks close to the Dalai Lama, who acts as his spiritual teacher.

The case of the missing lama In January 1989, when the tenth Panchen Lama died of a heart attack at Tashilhunpo Monastery in Shigatse, the Dalai Lama's government-in-exile started collecting names of potential candidates. In 1991, a divination was performed that determined the reincarnate had been born inside Tibet. Approaches to Beijing to co-operate in a search for the incarnate were rejected, but in 1993 a message was sent to India by Chatral Rinpoche, the head abbot of Tashilhunpo Monastery, explaining that the proper rituals were being carried out. The search by a committee from the monastery (sanctioned by the Chinese) had whittled down the number of candidates. A six-year-old boy from Nagqu (northern Tibet), named Gedhun Choekyi Nyima, looked the most promising.

Several divinations were performed in Dharamsala, India, in early 1995 to determine if the boy was the right candidate, and these proved positive. On this basis, in May 1995, the Dalai Lama declared the child the official 11th Panchen Lama. At this point, all the Chinese had to do was go along with the Dalai Lama's choice – the boy was, after all, one of their own sanctioned candidates. But Chinese officials were apparently infuriated that the choice of candidates had been 'leaked' to the Dalai Lama's government-in-exile.

This time, for the first time since taking over Tibet, the Chinese stepped in – in a big way. They condemned the Dalai Lama's choice, detained Chatral Rinpoche (the abbot responsible for the search), and took the six year old in question into custody – making him the world's youngest political prisoner. Neither the boy nor his parents have been seen in public since, leading to fears for their safety.

In the meantime, Tashilhunpo Monastery split into pro-Dalai Lama and pro-Chinese factions – an estimated 50 Tibetans were detained following the fallout. In July 1995 the leading lamas at Tashilhunpo were sacked, and replaced with pro-Chinese head lamas. In November that year, 75 Tibetan Buddhist leaders were rushed to Beijing, lectured by President Jiang Zemin, told to reject the Dalai Lama's choice, and asked to prepare another list of candidates. The new candidate would be selected by drawing a ball from the Golden Urn – a lottery system from the 18th century, from an outdated Mongolian treaty.

In November 1995, another six-year-old boy from Nagqu, named Gyaltsen Norbu, was virtually hand-picked by the Chinese as the new Panchen Lama. Ten days later, a highly publicised enthronement ceremony took place. Security was tight, with hundreds of PLA troops deployed at Tashilhunpo Monastery. In January 1996, Gyaltsen Norbu was in Beijing, shown being greeted by President Jiang Zemin. The Chinese choice for Panchen Lama does not seem to spend much time in Shigatse – the reason given is safety concerns (ie: that he will be threatened by Tibetans).

The interference of atheist China in Tibetan Buddhist ritual is hard to fathom. Did it really matter to the Chinese which six-year-old boy from Nagqu was chosen? To the Tibetans it does – no Tibetan will accept a Panchen Lama who is not verified and sanctioned by the Dalai Lama. The only way the Tibetans will accept such a choice is under duress, and this is apparently the next step, as the Chinese force monks in major monasteries to swear that the Chinese choice is the only legitimate one, and to renounce the Dalai Lama. A deluge of Panchen Lama posters, pictures, books and videos spreads the word of the Chinese choice. As for the Dalai Lama's choice, black market pictures of the missing lama are sold in Lhasa, despite the risk of a jail sentence if found in possession of such a picture.

In the aftermath of these events, the abbot of Tashilhunpo Monastery, Chatral Rinpoche, was sentenced to six years in jail for 'leaking state secrets'. The head of the Tantric University at Tashilhunpo, Kachen Lobsang Choedrak, was detained; and the secretary of Tashilhunpo, Gyatrul Rinpoche, was fined and expelled for refusing to endorse the Chinese-chosen candidate. Chinese work-teams moved into Tashilhunpo Monastery to force monks to pledge their loyalty to the Communist Party – those refusing to do so were expelled or imprisoned.

Conflicting reports have been given by the Chinese concerning the whereabouts of Gedhun Choekyi Nyima, the Dalai Lama's choice. Chinese officials have variously said the boy is living in Beijing, or in a town in the north of Tibet. In 1996, in the aftermath of the Panchen Lama run-in, an intense anti-Dalai Lama campaign was launched, with the removal of all Dalai Lama pictures, including those from the Potala. Monks were told to sign pledges denouncing the Dalai Lama and approving the Chinese choice of Panchen Lama.

Despite all this, attempts by Chinese authorities to give their appointed Panchen Lama, Gyaltsen Norbu, some religious credence among the Tibetans have gone seriously astray. In 1998, when officials sought to bring the Panchen Lama to Kumbum Monastery in Qinghai, the abbot of that monastery, Arjia Rinpoche, promptly fled China to seek asylum in the US. The abbot later revealed that he did not want to be seen as a collaborator with the Chinese government.

In 2011, Chinese officials introduced new laws stipulating that Tibetan Buddhist monks must seek permission from the Chinese communist (atheist) regime for reincarnation. It is not clear how the metaphysics of that would work, but the laws are described by the Chinese Religious Affairs Bureau as an important move to 'institutionalise management of reincarnation'. Another law specifies that Buddhist monks outside of China are barred from being recognised as a reincarnation of the Dalai Lama.

MYTHOLOGY AND THE ARTS

Tibetan culture, isolated for thousands of years, developed along very different lines from that of neighbouring India or China. There are two streams to Tibetan culture: religious arts and folk arts – the sacred and the profane.

FOLK ARTS The folk arts of Tibet (the profane side) derive largely from the nomad herder culture, with hard drinking and partying at festival time, like the annual horse-racing festivals held all over the Ethnic Tibetan region. Rather like Wild West cowboy rodeos, these events are a mixture of horse races and other competitions, plus song-and-dance events. They are also a prime venue for matchmaking among the widely scattered nomad clans, so nomad women show up dressed in their finest clothing and jewellery. In exuberant foot-stomping dances, Tibetan boots become musical instruments all of their own, and with a simple horse-hair fiddle nomad musicians can create strident music. High-pitched Tibetan 'yodelling', performed by women, is especially haunting and evocative of the vast grasslands. Often performed in a welcome ceremony is the Yak Dance. Two performers don a single yak-skin costume, with one performer up front, shaking the head and horns, and the other performer at the back, wagging the tail. The feisty yak may perform back-rolls, or it may charge – with horns forward – causing members of the audience to scatter in all directions. Similar in concept is the Snow Lion Dance, again with two performers inside a single costume.

SACRED ARTS Tibetan culture is closely linked to Tibetan Buddhist beliefs – in former times most literature, music, dance and drama, painting, sculpture and architecture was inspired by those beliefs. The bulk of Tibetan literature is based on its Buddhism, as texts were printed with inked woodblocks at certain monasteries.

Two massive works of Buddhist literature are the Kanjur (Canon of Buddhist Law, 108 volumes) and the Tenjur (commentaries on the Kanjur, in 228 volumes). These are mostly translated from Sanskrit. An exception to religious literature is the epic of Gesar of Ling, the legendary king – this was a staple of Tibet's former wandering storytellers, who committed the long tale to memory. This thousand-year-old tale runs to millions of words, and is Asia's equivalent to Homer's *Odyssey*.

Unlike Theravadan Buddhist traditions, monks at Tibetan Buddhist monasteries are actively involved in the creation of artwork, using formulaic methods. Inspiration is the goal of the artwork – assisting the viewer with meditation and in attaining spiritual realisation – and thus the creation becomes far more important than the creator. As a result, most Tibetan art is anonymous. However, there are instances where great lamas and teachers also happen to be creators, like the lama-teacher-sculptor Zanabazar in Mongolia. Sculpture at monasteries is generally of bronze or copper with highlights in gold or gilt. Fine silver statuary is also found. Murals covering the entrance and interior walls of monasteries depict Buddhas and bodhisattvas, protector deities, and other themes. *Tankas* (wall-hangings, either painted scrolls or appliquéd on cloth or silk) originated as objects of meditation and were formerly used for teaching purposes by travelling lamas (no longer seen within Tibet).

Other objects to assist with meditation are mandala murals and mandala *tankas* – the mandala is a mystic circle design or cosmogram. A unique Tibetan monastic art form is the creation of sand mandalas – circular sand paintings made by monks with coloured sand over a period of several weeks. Elaborate ceremonies take place at the monastery during and after completion of the sand mandala: it is then destroyed, to indicate the impermanence of all things.

Monasteries in Tibet used to stage an annual ceremony called Cham, with masked dances and accompanying longhorn music performed by the monks. In these rituals, the monks wore masks representing demons, spirits and mythical animals. Cham dance is still occasionally seen within Tibet, but the authorities are highly suspicious of any large gathering of Tibetans, so the chances of seeing a Cham dance in Tibet are rare (in fact, the chances of witnessing one are higher in other parts of the Tibetan world).

Because of their close link with Tibetan Buddhism, many of the Tibetan arts are proscribed or no longer practised in Tibet itself. That means you have to go to the exile community for the real culture. Tibet's cerebral sacred music is showcased in albums like *Freedom Chants,* recorded in India by the exiled Gyuto Monks, who are also featured on the soundtracks for the movies *Kundun* and *Seven Years in Tibet*. These monks have mastered the Tibetan meditation technique of chanting with a deep three-note chord, which places such a strain on the vocal chords that the singer is in danger of becoming mute if he overdoes it. Oddly enough, Tibetan sacred music has found a place in New Age offerings. Firmly established with New Age musicians is a former monk, Nawang Kechog. Kechog has mastered a number of instruments including the bamboo flute, the Tibetan longhorn and the aboriginal didgeridoo: his albums include *Quiet Mind, Sounds of Peace* and *In a Distant Place* (see *Further Information,* page 332).

SAVING TIBETAN CULTURE

The ancient Tibetan culture developed along very different lines from others in High Asia. Saving this unique culture essentially comes down to the issue of religious freedom, because Tibet's cultural identity is tied in with its Buddhism, and the Chinese do not respect that religion. Ultimately, it's a question of human rights.

HUMAN RIGHTS On 10 December 1948 the United Nations adopted the Universal Declaration of Human Rights (UDHR). This document was principally crafted by Canadian law professor John Humphrey as the UN response to atrocities committed during World War II – ostensibly to ensure that horrors like the Jewish Holocaust would never happen again. In Tibet, they did happen again, within a scant ten years of that declaration. For more than 55 years, the UN has turned a blind eye to the devastation China has wreaked in Tibet, violating the majority of the 30 articles of the UDHR. In my view the UN has no moral authority left; it has become a corrupt and bloated bureaucracy. True, in 1959, 1961 and 1965, resolutions were passed at the UN demanding that China respect the UDHR in Tibet, but there was no punch behind the resolutions. They were promulgated before 1970, the year that the PRC became one of the five permanent members of the UN Security Council, with full veto power. The UN Human Rights Council today includes voting members from such bastions of liberty as China, Cuba, Syria, Saudi Arabia, Sudan and Zambia, who do nothing but thwart its human-rights mandate.

Why Are We Silent? This is the title of a 60-second cinema ad about Tibet, marking the 50th anniversary of the UDHR in 1998. The clip features six film and rock stars reading extracts from the UDHR against a background of Tibetan imagery. In early

1998, members of the Tibetan Youth Congress staged a hunger strike in Delhi. Six hunger strikers, representing the six million people of Tibet, demanded that the UN resume its debate on the question of Tibet; that it appoint a Special Rapporteur to investigate the situation of human rights in Tibet; and that it appoint a Special Envoy to promote a peaceful settlement of the question of Tibet and initiate a UN-

BLOWING IN THE WIND

Tibetan culture – ethnic stock, beliefs, customs, language, food – has little in common with Chinese culture. But possibly the best way to gauge a culture is not through its food or its customs, but through its mythology. Here, Tibetan culture truly comes into its own. On the roofs of Tibetan houses, atop nomad tents, on high passes, on sacred peaks, at holy lakes and on the upper ramparts of monasteries, you will always find prayer-flags fluttering. There are a number of varieties of prayer-flags, but the commonest are the five-coloured prayer-flags, which are printed with Buddhist mantras. Depicted in the corners of each flag are the clawed supernatural animals of the four directions: garuda (wisdom), dragon (gentle power), tiger (confidence) and snow lion (fearless joy). A fifth mythical animal, appearing usually in the middle of the prayer-flag, is the windhorse. Some of these mythical animals are found in other Asian cultures, but not the windhorse or the snow lion, which are uniquely Tibetan.

THE WINDHORSE The beautiful steed that brings good fortune, symbolised by the jewel on its back, is known as *lungta* in Tibetan. When prayer-flags snap and flutter in the breeze, the windhorse printed on them is set in motion, carrying good fortune in all directions and galloping across the sky, spreading the teachings of Buddhism. The windhorse represents uplifting energy. Prayer-flags are usually printed on cloth, using woodblocks. Some pilgrims cannot afford them, and resort to a modified inexpensive version – small squares of paper, embossed with windhorses. Pilgrims throw these in the air at sacred sites and shout 'Lha Gyalo!' ('Victory to the gods!').

THE SNOW LION When the lion made the leap over the Himalaya from India, it became the residing deity of Tibet's snowy ranges, able to bound from snowpeak to snowpeak. This friendly dog-like animal (*sengye* in Tibetan) is shown in temple frescoes with a white body and turquoise mane, or a blue body with vermilion mane and green eyes. The snow lion is a symbol of fearless joy – a mind free of doubt, clear and precise. The snow lion dance is performed at special events. Snow lions are part of the throne of Buddha, and are shown upholding the three precious jewels of Buddhism on the forbidden Tibetan flag. Snow lions appear on the crest and seal of the Dalai Lama; they also appear on Tibetan government seals of office, and on old banknotes and stamps.

There's a curious ideological battle involving snow lions, possibly because of their close association with the Dalai Lama and Tibetan nationalism. Snow lion statues stand guard at the gates of Norbulingka, the Dalai Lama's summer palace in Lhasa, but outside the front gates of the Potala stand statues of Chinese imperial lions, the same symbols of Chinese emperors found at the Forbidden City in Beijing. Chinese officials have even objected to a logo at a conference in Europe – the image in question was not the Tibetan flag, nor an image of the Dalai Lama, but simply a pair of snow lions.

supervised plebiscite to ascertain the wishes of the Tibetan people. The lengthy strike was broken up by the Indian police.

China has one of the worst human rights violation records in the world. US Department of State reports on Tibet have slammed China for 'serious human rights abuses in Tibet' and for imposing 'intensified controls on fundamental freedoms'. Evidence for reports like this is drawn from interviews with credible Tibetan refugees, who tell of forced sterilisations and abortions, as well as arbitrary arrest, torture in prisons and cases of summary execution. Despite mounting evidence, China vigorously denies any transgressions, says that torture has been completely abolished, and claims that Tibetan people have gained real democracy and equality since 1959's 'democratic reforms'. Beijing blithely churns out glossy brochures in English that quote the UDHR to back up the Chinese claim that rights are better now than they were under the Dalai Lamas. This won't explain why Tibetan monks have been given long prison sentences for translating the UDHR into the Tibetan language.

What human rights do the Tibetans want? The basic ones: the right to freedom of speech, freedom of thought, and freedom to follow Tibetan Buddhist beliefs. The right to a proper education, the right to use the Tibetan language. The rights of the child. Even the most fundamental of human rights are denied to Tibetans. These include the rights to clean water, sufficient food, a home, health care, proper education, employment, protection from violence, equality of opportunity, and a say in their future. In Tibet, Chinese violations of the UDHR are so blatant that they have led scholar Robert Thurman to say that 'Tibetans are the baby seals of the human rights movement'. The Dalai Lama puts it this way: 'The Chinese are entitled to their happiness, but not at the expense of another nation or people'. He accuses the Chinese of pursuing a deliberate policy of cultural genocide in Tibet. By the government-in-exile count, over a million Tibetans have perished – directly or indirectly – at the hands of the Chinese since the 1950s.

Population transfer Before 1950, there were no Chinese settlers in the TAR. Accurate figures on current Chinese population in Tibet are hard to come by: Chinese figures do not include the sizeable military contingent. However, it is certain that China is providing incentives to bring settlers into Tibet – higher salaries, more benefits and tax breaks. In the provinces at the edge of the TAR, Han Chinese settlers outnumber the Tibetans. The Chinese do not integrate with the Tibetans, nor bother to learn the language. Not only are they starting to outnumber the Tibetans, they are reducing them to second-class citizens in their own land. For doing the same job, Chinese workers are usually paid a higher salary than Tibetans.

In Inner Mongolia, after 1949, when the communists took control, millions of Han Chinese flooded onto the steppes, thanks to government encouragement and incentives. The Mongols are now a minority in their own land – there are 20 million Han versus four million Mongolians. Mongol nomad livelihood has been severely disrupted by Han Chinese turning pasture into irrigated farmland. All this is in breach of the Geneva Conventions. A similar scenario appears to be under way in Tibet.

Political prisoners The number of political prisoners held in prisons in Tibet ranges from over 1,000 (government-in-exile figure) to 50 (Chinese figure). The Chinese figure is skewed because Chinese officials maintain that prisoners in Tibet are common criminals, not political prisoners. If a prisoner is convicted for holding up a Tibetan flag, this is noted as 'prisoner trying to incite public disorder' so somehow it becomes a criminal offence, not a political one. Conditions in prison are poor, with beatings and torture routine. Across China, it is estimated that over 6,000 prisoners a year are executed (the exact number is not known, since figures are kept secret). For the year 2004, Amnesty International reports that 3,400 people were known to have been executed in China, a figure exponentially more than those executed in the rest of the world *combined*. By contrast, in 2004, there were 159 executed in Iran and 59 executed in the US. Some prisoners in China are executed by lethal injection, but the majority are dispatched with a bullet to the back of the head: the bill for the bullet is often sent to the family of the executed as further humiliation. There is some evidence that body parts of executed prisoners are sold on the international market. Chinese spokespeople blithely deny that any of this ever takes place.

The world's youngest political prisoner is believed to be Gedhun Choekyi Nyima, the Dalai Lama's choice for 11th Panchen Lama. His whereabouts are unknown: he has not been seen in public since May 1995. (See page 32.)

In August 1995, Ngawang Choephel disappeared in Tibet. Choephel, a Fulbright scholar, was researching traditional music in Tibet and videotaping dance and song performances. It was not for another 14 months that his mother discovered that he was still alive, and in prison. He was charged with spying for the Tibetan government-in-exile and a sentence of 18 years was handed down. After a vigorous high-profile campaign by Western supporters, and after serving six years of his sentence, Ngawang Choephel was released on medical parole in January 2002, and flown back to the US, where he applied for political asylum.

Ngawang Sangdrol is a nun who was 13 years old when she was first jailed for demonstrating for a free Tibet. After her release, she was forbidden to rejoin her nunnery. In 1992, she was arrested again for demonstrating and sentenced to three years in jail. In 1993, while in prison, Ngawang and 13 other nuns recorded Tibetan protest songs – the tape was smuggled out by a sympathiser and taken to the West. When they learned of this, the Chinese increased the nuns' sentences by a further six years. In 1996, Ngawang's sentence was increased by a further nine years. In a rare protest from the UN, in 1995 the Working Group on Arbitrary Detentions ruled the nun had been punished for exercising her rights to freedom of opinion. The group called on China to release her, in line with the principles of the UDHR – a call that was ignored by the Chinese. In 1998, as part of a campaign commemorating the 50th anniversary of the Universal Declaration, Ngawang Sangdrol was featured in a joint campaign by the Body Shop and Amnesty International, putting added pressure on the Chinese. In 2002, Ngawang was released from prison, and in 2003 she was permitted to fly to the US for medical treatment. She was granted asylum in the US shortly after, and is dedicated to working for the release of her fellow prisoners.

Religious freedom It is estimated that up to 70% of political prisoners in Tibet are monks and nuns. The reason they are imprisoned is a combination of their political attitudes and their fight for religious freedom. In the past, monks and nuns have spearheaded the Tibetan independence movement: their vows may empower them to act politically. Celibacy puts them in a better position to sacrifice their lives as opposed to those with families, and dying for Tibetan independence is a selfless act guaranteeing a human rebirth in the next life.

Since early 1996, Chinese officials have conducted a 'Strike Hard' campaign deliberately directed at monks and nuns. Chinese work-teams have been dispatched to all monasteries and nunneries in Tibet for 'patriotic re-education' (an ongoing process). Dalai Lama pictures have been banned in all temples and public places, and Tibetan monks and nuns are required to sign a five-point agreement, pledging to oppose the idea of an independent Tibet, to denounce the Dalai Lama, to recognise the Chinese-appointed Panchen Lama, to oppose those advocating independence for Tibet, and to work for the unity of 'the Motherland'. According to China's own statements, the majority of Tibet's 46,000 monks and nuns in 1,700 monasteries and nunneries have come under the programme. As a result, in the first two years of the programme, it is estimated that 14 monks and nuns died, upwards of 300 were arrested, and over 3,000 were expelled from their monasteries or nunneries. In addition, seven monasteries and nunneries were completely closed down.

In June 2002, a tent encampment established in a remote valley near Serthar in Amdo (Sichuan Province) was broken up by Chinese officials with pickaxes, and thousands of residents were ordered to leave. The encampment at one point attracted up to 8,000 monks and nuns, of whom nearly a thousand were Chinese. They were drawn by the teachings of charismatic leader Khenpo Jigme Phuntsok, who started off Larung Gar encampment with a handful of students in the 1980s. At special teaching times, the numbers at Larung Gar swelled to over 15,000 participants – hence the Chinese nervousness that led to the break-up. Khenpo Jigme Phuntsok was held incommunicado for a year in Chengdu, and died in 2004 in a military hospital.

In 2005, President Hu Jintao confided to President Bush (on an official visit to China) that China was 'continuously raising the level of human rights enjoyed by its people', but that such progress must reflect 'China's national conditions'. This gobbledegook was spoken by the same man who ruthlessly suppressed Tibetans and imposed martial law in the late 1980s (Hu Jintao was Party Secretary of the TAR from 1988–92). If anything, repression of Tibetan Buddhism appears to be intensifying. In 2005, Chinese officials launched a campaign that blacklisted not only the Dalai Lama but also key religious figures in exile close to him – who maintain links to monasteries within Tibet.

WHEN HOLLYWOOD LOCKS HORNS WITH BEIJING
Gyantse, November, 1987: a young British tourist, Kris Tait, is accosted by a Chinese soldier on a bicycle, who tries to tear off her T-shirt. She at first assumes he's trying to assault her, but when a Tibetan crowd gathers chanting 'Dalai Lama!' it occurs to her that the soldier is after the T-shirt, which appears to bear an image of the Dalai Lama printed on it. Actually the T-shirt is embossed with the face of the late Phil Silvers, a cult figure from late night BBC re-runs of the 1950s American television series, *Sergeant Bilko*. The woman manages to wrench free from the soldier, and flees to her guesthouse to change clothes. Kris Tait, an avid Bilko fan, later says there is a resemblance between Silvers and the Dalai Lama – the same quizzical eyebrows, the same thick glasses. Hollywood's dust-up with the Chinese over the Dalai Lama has just begun.

Dissolve to 1997, when the sleeves are rolled up, and the big brawls begin, as Hollywood takes on China in earnest, with full-length movies about the Dalai Lama in the works. Disney's Touchstone Pictures is faced with the most momentous decision of its corporate career – sell Mickey Mouse in China, or humour director Martin Scorsese? Which goes? Whose wrath will be greater to face – that of surly Chinese officials, or of Scorsese without his morning coffee? Scorsese is filming a movie about the early life of the Dalai Lama, one that has raised the hackles of the Chinese, who threatened to halt work on the creation of a Disneyland near Shanghai. The clash of the titans has begun.

Flashback to 1937: Frank Capra's epic, *Lost Horizon*, is released by Columbia TriStar. The film, based on the book of the same name, is the first big-budget movie to use a Tibetan setting: a Tibetan monastery high in the snowcapped mountains where the wisdom of the ages is preserved by wizened lamas. The film costs four times the amount of any Columbia TriStar film at the time, using a set considered the largest ever built in Hollywood. During World War II, Tibet remained neutral, a kind of Switzerland in High Asia (although the British Mission remained in Lhasa, without official diplomatic status). *Lost Horizon* was widely circulated among the armed forces during World War II – it bolstered the hope that there was a place during mankind's darkest days where the values of civilisation were preserved.

Sixty years later, Columbia TriStar released *Seven Years in Tibet*, quite a different version of Shangri-La – one man's vision of the last years before Tibet itself was engulfed in war and chaos.

Why the sudden Hollywood interest in Tibet after a 60-year silence on the subject? Why did the 1990s produce a rash of Tibet films? And why is Beijing upset about them? In part, Hollywood's interest in Tibet is attributable to the collapse of the USSR and the demise of the Cold War: China provides a new 'evil empire' to crusade against, in the vacuum left by the demise of Russia. China is the world's most populous nation, with expanding economic clout and a world-class nuclear arsenal. China is an up-and-coming superpower with a ruthless leadership: a change of Western attitude to China definitely occurred after the Tiananmen Massacre in 1989. Suddenly, what the Dalai Lama had been saying all along – that the Chinese were killing Tibetans – was blatantly demonstrated at Tiananmen when the Chinese opened fire on their own people. An indicator of this shift of evil empires was the plot of the 1997 James Bond film, *Tomorrow Never Dies*. No KGB here: the movie was originally slated to be about the handover of Hong Kong, but missed its timing so the script was changed to a stand-off between China and Britain, with the two teetering on the brink of war because of the ambitions of an out-of-control media megalomaniac (modelled on Rupert Murdoch!).

In part, Hollywood's interest in Tibet is related to new-found interest in Buddhism in the US, and to celebrity actors like Richard Gere, Harrison Ford and Uma Thurman supporting the Tibetan cause. Tibet has become chic following the popularity of the Dalai Lama after his 1989 Nobel Peace Prize award. The man has become Hollywood's favourite underdog – a non-violent rebel with a cause. The Dalai Lama has mingled with Cindy Crawford and Sharon Stone at Los Angeles parties. Perhaps this is not so unusual: he has been an avid fan of movies from an early age. In the late 1940s, he arranged for the building of a projection room in Lhasa to view films imported from India. In the early 1990s, he fine-tuned the script for *Kundun* (in readings with Melissa Mathison and Harrison Ford) and for *Seven Years in Tibet* (with Becky Johnston).

Another reason for Tibetmania is possibly that Tibet is the ultimate in exotic locations: there's renewed Hollywood interest in exotica following the phenomenal success of movies like *The English Patient*. More likely, however, is that Tibet is hot simply because controversy fuels box-office hits – and there's no shortage of controversy when it comes to Tibet.

In the case of *Kundun* and *Seven Years in Tibet*, the controversy started before shooting began. Both movies set out to portray an idyllic pre-1950 Tibet, with a smiling, soft-spoken Dalai Lama at the helm – a Dalai Lama sworn to non-violence. The Chinese claim that pre-1950 Tibet was hell on earth – a medieval society where Tibetans had no freedom, and slaved away as serfs for the aristocracy. Both movies show the Chinese as brutal thugs. Sony, which owns Columbia TriStar, was threatened in China over *Seven Years in Tibet*, as was Disney, but no economic sanctions were applied. Both movie directors were blocked from filming in India, which was their first choice of location. One thing's for sure: films like *Kundun*, *Seven Years in Tibet* and *Red Corner* will never be shown in China. However, there's no reason why they can't be shown in Hong Kong, where technically the laws only empower authorities to check films for violence and sex. In fact, *Seven Years in Tibet* has been screened in Hong Kong despite stern criticism from Beijing. The movie brought Ngapoi Ngawang Jigme out on the attack in Hong Kong. He complained about the movie's portrayal of himself as a turncoat who betrayed the Tibetan Army and signed the 17-point Agreement with China for its annexation of Tibet. It was poetic justice of a kind. Ngawang Jigme has rarely spoken to the press; he has lived in Beijing since 1967, where he and his clan hold high positions.

Seven Years in Tibet was also screened in Moscow, again despite Chinese Embassy objections. The Chinese vigorously protested a screening of the movie at a film festival in Japan (the film performed well in Japan, where Brad Pitt has a cult following – among teenage girls, anyway). Other Chinese objections were raised over *Kundun,* a movie that glorifies the Dalai Lama (and in one scene portrays China's great leader, Mao Zedong, as a crass, evil, chain-smoking buffoon). In May 1998, the Chinese Embassy demanded that the film *Windhorse* be removed from the Washington International Film Festival because it was meant to 'obviously smear China's policy toward Tibet'. The festival director invited Chinese Embassy officials to come to the screening of the movie and participate in an open dialogue about the film – they did not show up. The film went on to become the festival-goers' top choice.

Words are the only weapon that Tibetans have in the fight against Chinese repression of Tibetan culture and occupation of their land, and Tibetans have found words can have great impact when they are spoken on the big screen. In the US and elsewhere, Tibetans have distributed leaflets and Tibet Action Kits outside screenings of the movies. China's problem with all of this is an issue of freedom of speech. Chinese embassies around the globe have tried to muzzle Hollywood, which thus far has only succeeded in drawing more attention to the Tibetan cause.

In a world where the international community has been spectacularly silent on the topic of Tibet, the films have pricked the Western conscience, and incurred the wrath of Chinese Embassy officials. China's greatest fear is that one of these Hollywood films will become a cult hit, with television re-runs for the next 20 years – just like *Sergeant Bilko.*

2

Practical Information

Travel to Tibet Autonomous Region (TAR) is rigidly controlled. You need a Tibet Tourism Bureau (TTB) permit before you can board a plane or train to Lhasa where most trips get started. The TTB permit can only be arranged through an agent who must detail your entire itinerary for your stay in Tibet before tickets in and out can be processed. Given this rigid framework, you have to indulge in some large doses of logistics and think over your itinerary carefully.

However, outside the TAR, in the Kham and Amdo regions to the east, none of this permit hokum applies: you can travel independently and play it by ear. Hopefully, the following pages can guide you through the complex paperwork, permits, logistics and options. If you come through all that at the other end, you arrive in Lhasa – a major achievement in itself. Tibet travel regulations chop and change – so keep an ear to the ground and make allowances for modifying the following information.

WHEN TO VISIT

CLIMATE April to October is the best time. November is starting to get cold. December and January can be freezing, with heavy snow blocking high passes. Few individuals visit at this time, which means it's hard to find people to share Landcruiser rentals (see *By Landcruiser and guide*, page 77). February is Tibetan New Year and though cold it can be lively, if you can get in. April can be windy; there's a rainy season around July and August, when flooding can cut off roads and wash out bridges. Because Tibet is so large, climate conditions change from east to west and with the elevation.

TIMING, FESTIVALS AND SENSITIVE PERIODS Rules and regulations concerning travel in Tibet change as often as the weather does with El Niño, so the following sections may be out of date by the time you plan your visit. If so, make adjustments. There are several times of year when it is difficult or impossible to get into Lhasa. Winter is an obvious one – there are no flights from Kathmandu and fewer from Chengdu. The Chinese may be nervous if some military bigwig or political leader is visiting, and they might just shut the whole of Tibet down for a few weeks. Nothing is guaranteed in Tibet, and no guidebook written in stone. Allow for changing information.

The Tibetan calendar is filled with unofficial anniversaries, and security is tight at these times, with Chinese troops on alert ten days before and after the sensitive period. You may have trouble getting into Tibet or travelling around at these times. The easiest travel months are April, June and August (however, June to August is the most heavily booked period for flights into Lhasa). Among the 'hot' times are:

Losar	Tibetan New Year, around February
5 March	Commemorating major protests in 1988–89
10 March	Anniversary of 1959 Lhasa uprising, and marks the start of the Tibetan spring – protests across the entire plateau in 2008
23 May	Marks the 1951 surrender to the Chinese with the 17-point Agreement
6 July	Dalai Lama's birthday
27 September	Start of 1987 riots
1 October	1987 protest in which Tibetans were shot dead
10 December	International human rights day, which sparked a protest in 1988

Tibetans sometimes gather at countryside locations to picnic and throw *tsampa* in the air to mark special occasions – in Lhasa, this practice has been banned by Chinese authorities.

Because the Chinese are nervous about large gatherings of Tibetans, traditional festivals are low profile – indeed, for a number of years, festivals were banned outright. If you get a chance to see something more formal, like a festival in the countryside, go! If you're lucky there might be a horse-racing festival in progress at Damxung or Gyantse, or a *tanka*-unfurling ceremony at one of the monasteries within reach of Lhasa. There used to be festivals at every full moon in Tibet, but many were abolished by the Chinese authorities. The festivals that survive are based on the lunar calendar, which is complex and unpredictable (usually only announced in February, at Losar or Tibetan New Year). Ask around when you arrive in Tibet to confirm if there are likely to be any festivals in progress.

HIGHLIGHTS

A key factor in route planning is addressing this question: what do you want to see? What piques your interest? It's a good idea to pinpoint places of high interest to determine where this takes you on an actual map. Photocopy maps from this guidebook, get a colour felt pen, circle destinations of high interest – and start joining the dots.

Highlights are subjective – they really depend on your interests. Some travellers see two or three monasteries and get 'templed-out', while others seem to have an unlimited capacity for looking at monasteries. The key to visiting is to vary the sights – take in a temple or fort, go on a day hike or visit a hot spring. Sometimes you luck out and find these all in the same locale. The following is a shortlist of personal favourites, which is bound to be biased, of course. My bias is very simple: I favour things Tibetan – which may sound odd, but after you've been in Tibet a week or so, that comment will make perfect sense. Travellers come to Tibet looking for Tibet, not China. All too often what they get is a bull in a secondhand China shop. The main highlight of any visit to Tibet will be meeting the people. There are two guaranteed places you will see and meet lots of Tibetans: at festivals and at key pilgrimage sites. Tibetans have their own version of top sites, and these are sacred pilgrimage destinations like Mount Kailash – the trip of a lifetime.

TOP PILGRIMAGE SITES You will find temple tripping much more enjoyable if you mingle with Tibetan pilgrims. Important pilgrimage sites are great for seeing people from all parts of Tibet. And interacting with them. Shiny-eyed pilgrims turn out in throngs at the most sacred spots, including the Potala, Jokhang and Barkor (Lhasa); Tashilhunpo (Shigatse); Kailash (west Tibet); Kumbum and Labrang (Amdo).

TIBETAN TOWN ARCHITECTURE Distinctive Tibetan style can be found in these places: the Tibetan Quarter, Potala, Norbulingka (Lhasa); Gyantse (Kumbum, fort, plus Pala Manor); Samye; and Xiahe (Labrang). It's becoming harder to find areas of pure Tibetan architecture due to encroachment by bland Chinese concrete-and-karaoke architecture.

BEST ATMOSPHERE Certain villages and small towns have a strong Tibetan ambience, with minimised Chinese influence, which means they are great places to stay longer and absorb. These places are more likely to be backwaters. In central Tibet, they include Tidrom hot springs, Samye and Gyantse. In west Tibet, the Kailash region is excellent. This is old Tibet – Tibet lost in time – where the Tibetan pulse runs strong.

BEST FORTS The majestic administrative centres of old Tibet. Most have been destroyed but these remain: Gyantse Dzong (used in the battle against British forces in 1904) and Yumbulagang (a rebuilt fortress-temple near Tsedang). The Potala in Lhasa is a prime example of fortress architecture. These castles in the sky are testament to the supreme stonemasonry skills of Tibetans.

TOP ACTIVE TEMPLES Chanting, rituals and monastic life (even monastic debating) can be experienced at the Jokhang (the most revered temple in Tibet), Sera and Drepung (Lhasa), Ganden, Samye Monastery (the oldest in Tibet), Tashilhunpo (Shigatse – magnificent statuary), Sakya (Mongolian fortress-style temple with grand chanting hall) and Labrang (entire monastic citadel in Xiahe, Gansu). Sera Monastery in Lhasa sees regular afternoon debating.

BEST HOT SPRINGS Tidrom Nunnery, Lhasa Prefecture – beautiful valley with Tibetan village and three enclosed hot springs for bathing.

BEST DAY HIKES Back of Sera Monastery in Lhasa; hike to Hepo Ri viewpoint in Samye; hikes around Sakya; hike to top of Shining Crystal Dzong ruins in Shegar.

TOP RUINS Guge Kingdom, in Zanda, west Tibet – though mostly destroyed, excellent murals can still be seen. Set in entrancing desert terrain riddled with caves.

MOUNTAINS, TOP TREKS Kailash, sacred mountain – three- to four-day pilgrim circuit in a stunning setting. Everest, north face – a three-day trek into the base camp (you can also drive there); from here the highest trek in the world (without crampons) leads to advanced base camp at over 6,400m. Closer to Lhasa, the five-day Ganden–Samye trek is popular.

YARLUNG TSANGPO GRAND CANYON Nothing comes close to this wonder of nature: it is more than double the depth of Arizona's Grand Canyon. Opening to Chinese tourism, but difficult for foreign hikers or rafters to access. Closest approach is Nyingchi in east Tibet.

SACRED LAKES Turquoise classics include Yamdrok Tso (with backdrop of peaks in Bhutan); Manasarovar (Kailash in background); Lake Namtso, with 7,000m peaks as backdrop; and Basum Tso, east Tibet. Pilgrims undertake *koras* (walking circuits) around sacred lakes. You can ride horses part-way along some circuits, like Namtso and Manasarovar.

NOMADS AND GRASSLANDS Nomads are being rapidly settled across the Tibetan plateau, but pockets of pastoral nomadism survive. The best place to see traditional yak herding is the Kham region around Tagong and Litang, where you can make extended visits for several days, hiking or on horseback.

ADVENTURE SPORTS Multiple-day camping trips can be organised from Lhasa – for rafting, kayaking, trekking or mountain bike forays. On your own, there are super trekking and mountain bike opportunities in Kham and Amdo.

GREAT ROAD TRIPS Lhasa to Kathmandu route; Lhasa to Chengdu or Kunming; Lanzhou via Labrang to Chengdu (Amdo); Kunming via Litang to Chengdu (Kham); Chengdu via Tagong to Xining; and the Karakoram Highway. These are among the greatest road trips in High Asia. Excellent for mountain biking too.

FESTIVALS These follow the lunar calendar, and timing is unpredictable as they're often not announced. If you get a chance, go – festivals offer great people encounters. Summer (June to August) sees horse-racing fairs in Gyantse, Nagqu and Litang and other locations. Monasteries occasionally stage *tanka*-unfurling ceremonies or annual Cham dances – both majestic spectacles.

GIVE IT A MISS Avoid places where you see fake palm trees sprouting up. The worst town architecture prize goes to Tsedang, a complete Chinese town of the bathroom-tiling school of architecture, complemented by the odd fake palm. The town of Bayi in eastern Tibet is sprinkled with fake palm trees and mini-brothels. The most shocking experience in Lhasa is seeing Chinese high-rises – and fake palm trees on Yuthok Road.

TOURING STRATEGY

TWO TIBETS Since large-scale protest by Tibetans erupted across the Tibetan plateau in the spring of 2008, access to the Tibet Autonomous Region (TAR) has been severely restricted by Chinese authorities. That situation may change, so best to check on current news about Tibet travel via websites (see *Appendix 4*, page 335).

The rigid model for travel in the TAR is to present your whole itinerary upfront to an agency, which will package airfare, vehicle and tour guide for central Tibet. The easiest place to arrange all this is Chengdu (Sichuan). You can arrange fixed itineraries for central Tibet from other gateway locations such as Zhongdian and Xining, again through agencies. Once in the TAR you can lose your minders for some of the time, and more of the time if you requested 'free days' built into your itinerary.

The rigid rules applied to travel in the TAR do not apply to the vast ethnic Tibetan areas outside the TAR, in Kham and Amdo, where you are relatively free to roam (except during times of unrest).

You are thus dealing with a case of two Tibets – central Tibet (TAR) is a very expensive option that requires you to present your whole itinerary upfront so that permits can be acquired for closely monitored group touring. By contrast, to the far east, the regions of Kham and Amdo, outside the TAR, do not require permits (with a few exceptions) – and you are free to do what you please, at far lower cost – as long as your visa is valid.

Touring the 'two Tibets' requires a load of logistics. There are several important things to keep in mind when planning your itinerary in Tibet: the duration of your

Chinese visa, how tight the permit situation is, the direction of travel, and allowing time to acclimatise to altitude. This is especially true if you want to attempt trekking

VERY TIBETAN

An American Tibetologist claims that one of the key factors for determining if a person is Tibetan is whether he or she eats *tsampa* (roasted barley flour) and actually enjoys it. Here's a shortlist of other criteria that would lead to the label 'very Tibetan'. When in Tibet, if you follow these customs, you'll be just like one of the family.

SIPPING YAK-BUTTER TEA Closely allied with tsampa because the tsampa is kneaded into balls with the addition of butter tea. Tibetan nomads drink up to 50 cups a day of yak-butter tea. You should attempt at least one cup if with Tibetans, but do not drain it – as the cup will instantly be refilled.

LIGHTING YAK-BUTTER LAMPS Required etiquette in temples, though vegetable oil is mostly used these days. Some offer the more expensive yak-butter lamps as special merit-making.

TURNING THE WHEELS Follow the pilgrims at temples and you will find giant prayer-wheels in various styles. Good to keep the wheels turning.

WALKING THE *KORA* Tibetans find solidarity with foreigners walking a sacred circuit of a temple or sacred site. A great way to stretch your legs and get a workout to acclimatise.

TYING ON PRAYER-FLAGS You can buy brightly coloured cloth prayer-flags very cheaply in larger cities. Get a stack of them, and at the cairn that marks a high pass, tie some prayer-flags on – and yell *Lha Gyalo!* at the top of your lungs. That's to appease the gods and ensure safe passage. Throwing handfuls of paper windhorse squares into the air also works well.

SHARING SACRED IMAGES Tibetans can spend ages poring over pictures of Mount Kailash or the Potala. If you have prints, the family shrine always needs new additions. The ultimate addition is HHDL images – very risky to be carrying. An image for personal use tends to be overlooked by officials.

CHASING WAYWARD YAKS Some yaks may diverge from the herd. Nomads have ways of keeping them in line. The main weapon is a woven yak-hair slingshot – wielded with astonishing accuracy to target a wayward yak by firing a small stone. Takes lots of practice to get it right, though.

SIDESTEPPING THE DOG Not just any dog – it's a Tibetan mastiff, thought to be the oldest guard dog in existence. This large lion-maned dog fearlessly defends nomad tents.

MINGLING WITH NOMADS In the summer, in July and August, nomads get together on the grasslands for a giant picnic with horses. Find out where these horse-racing festivals are and rub shoulders with hardy nomads.

in Tibet, such as trekking close to Everest, or tackling the *kora* at Mount Kailash. These treks require considerable physical stamina – and complex logistical support. Another parameter is just how deep your pockets are.

These factors go hand in hand. Getting permits within the Tibet Autonomous Region (TAR) is difficult and expensive, as you must travel with vehicle and guide in a group at all times. In practice, your 'group' can be just two people – or even just yourself. Outside the TAR, such restrictions do not apply: you are an independent traveller, and can use local transport.

The best advice that can be given here is to get the longest Chinese visa you can before you enter the Middle Kingdom (China). It should be possible to get a three-month visa in Hong Kong, for instance. There are other places that dispense two- or three-month visas: check online forums. Renewing your visa within China can be tricky – Chengdu has long been notorious for a slow and difficult extension process (try nearby Leshan instead).

A prime reason for keeping the 'two Tibets' strategy in mind is that periodically Chinese officials close the door to the TAR entirely, blocking it off for a month or so because of some sensitive anniversary. That means you would only be able to visit the Kham and Amdo regions, which lie outside the TAR. These regions have much to offer, and you could spend months exploring them.

Altitude strategy: it can take a week or longer to acclimatise to altitude, so best to go slow for the first week to adjust. Be active – take lots of walks – but avoid strenuous climbs as your body adjusts. See the *Health and safety* chapter, page 99, for details. The higher you go, the more the acclimatisation time needed.

For all of these reasons, you have to think over your itinerary for the TAR very carefully, as once you have decided on a route and the timing, there may be little flexibility to alter it.

HOW LONG DO I NEED? Ten to 20 days would be good. Six weeks would be better. Two months would be ideal if you plan on going trekking. You need time to adjust to the altitude, and you should build in extra time for delays due to breakdowns, road closures, overbooked flights and so on. The Western ethic of rushing around doesn't work well here.

TRIP DESIGN/ITINERARIES

Loop or linear? That is the essential question if planning a route that is a mix of the 'two Tibets'. The following are some sample itineraries, all starting from Chengdu, that can make the best use of your time in the region. There is a lot more detail about itineraries in specific regions in chapters devoted to those regions, such as the *Exploring Central Tibet* chapter, page 167.

CHENGDU LOOPS These routes start and end in Chengdu (with a variation to start or end in Kunming). Spend a few days in Chengdu with an agent, sorting out paperwork for Tibet, which will be forwarded to a related agency in Zhongdian. Then proceed from Chengdu by road to Tagong, Litang, Xiangcheng and Zhongdian. Pick up Tibet permits and tickets in Zhongdian via the contact from your Chengdu agency. Having spent time at altitude in Kham, you should be reasonably acclimatised and can hit the ground running when you fly into Lhasa, taking full advantage of the expensive sorties there. After flying Zhongdian–Lhasa, explore central Tibet for a week to ten days or more with driver and guide – either looping to Namtso or heading for Everest base camp, or both. Trek add-in: you

2

0 ————— 200km	CHENGDU LOOPS
0 ————— 125 miles	

NOTE:
YOU COULD REVERSE THE
DIRECTION OF THE FLIGHTS
AND FLY CHENGDU-LHASA FIRST

Lhasa
Loops   Namtso   CHENGDU
                ···Tidrom   Tagong KHAM
LHASA   Namche   Litang
Shigatse   Barwa   TAR   Kangding
Gyantse   Xiangcheng
        Yamdrok Tso
Everest base camp   Deqin

KEY
····▶··· Driving route   I N D I A   ZHONGDIAN   N
····▶··· Flying route   MYANMAR   Bradt
                              (BURMA)   Kunming

could do the Ganden to Samye trek. Following the foray into central Tibet, return
to Lhasa and fly back to Chengdu (or fly to Kunming).

Note that there is no direct flight from Chengdu to Zhongdian. On the first leg
of this loop, you could fly Chengdu to Kunming and change planes for Kunming
to Zhongdian, or go by road from either Chengdu or Kunming to Zhongdian.
Paperwork for Tibet should still be done in Chengdu. Zhongdian–Lhasa flights are
low frequency: be sure to book ahead from Chengdu.

Another Chengdu loop to consider: pick up paperwork in Chengdu, fly from
Chengdu to Lhasa, and take it easy for the first few days to acclimatise. Then explore
central Tibet towards Everest base camp for the next week or longer. Fly from Lhasa to
Zhongdian. From here you can trek on your own where you please, hitting the towns
of Xiangcheng, Litang and Tagong on the road to Chengdu. Or proceed by road from
Zhongdian through Kham down to Kunming, and exit overland to Vietnam.

Another exit route to consider: leave Tibet by train from Lhasa to Xining, and
weave your way south through Amdo and Kham *en route* to Chengdu.

LINEAR ROUTES: THE ROAD TO KATHMANDU A longer, linear route design: start
in Chengdu, and arrange your group entry and itinerary for Tibet, but specify
you will fly from Zhongdian to Lhasa (not from Chengdu to Lhasa). You can then
proceed by road from Chengdu to Kham (no permits required), spend time there
and acclimatise well to altitude, get on a plane from Zhongdian to Lhasa, tour
central Tibet without having to worry about altitude adjustments, and exit by road
to Kathmandu in Nepal. This trip would take at least three weeks.

Variation for central Tibet: drive from Lhasa to Namtso and on to Shigatse.
Then go off-road to Everest base camp for a few days, with the option of trekking
in the area.

For those who love epic overland journeys, try this route: start from Kunming
and journey north the entire length of Kham and Amdo to Xining, then arrange a
train ticket to Lhasa. With a pre-arranged small group, tour central Tibet and move
on to Everest base camp and tackle the Kailash trek. Then drop down past Paiku Tso
and Zhangmu into Nepal and proceed to Kathmandu.

Bad strategy: attempting that same trip in reverse. The reason is that you are
entirely at the whims of the Chinese Embassy in Kathmandu when it comes to
approval for Tibet – and these visa folks are sure to cancel a long Chinese visa
you have previously acquired and replace it with a visa valid for the length of your
fixed group-tour itinerary in Tibet, which might only be ten days. That's why the
direction of travel is of great importance.

CHENGDU TO KATHMANDU ROUTES

KEY
----- Driving route
······ Flying route

200km
200 miles

CHINA

CHENGDU

Kangding
Tagong

KHAM

Litang
Xiangcheng

ZHONGDIAN

KUNMING

Deqin

TAR

MYANMAR
(BURMA)

Namche
Barwa

Yarlung Tsangpo

Tidrom

LHASA

Namtso

INDIA

Yamdrok Tso

Gyantse

BHUTAN

Shigatse

Sakya

SIKKIM

Paiku Tso

Tingri

Rongbuk

Everest

NEPAL

Nyalam

Zhangmu

KATHMANDU

Kailash

INDIA

N

Bradt

LHASA LOOPS

Coming from the other direction, from Tibet into Nepal, getting a Nepalese visa on arrival is a breeze. What will work, starting from Kathmandu, is a round-trip loop, flying Kathmandu to Lhasa and returning overland to Kathmandu. The agency in Kathmandu arranges the Chinese visa for the length of the tour.

TOUR COSTS AND POSSIBLE PROBLEMS Travel in Tibet is expensive. Getting there by air is expensive. Touring around in rented vehicles is expensive. Most foreigners travel the Tibet Autonomous Region in a Landcruiser with driver and guide – a combination that runs to US$130–230 a day, depending on the agency used, the itinerary and other factors. Three to five passengers can share the cost of the Landcruiser. However, five passengers means very thin passengers as that is the only way you will fit four in the back seat (with the front seat occupied by driver, guide and one passenger). A lower-cost arrangement is to travel in a larger group, say 12 people, using an arranged minibus. If you want lower-budget options, consider travel to Kham and Amdo, where group touring is not required.

Let's say you fly from Chengdu to Lhasa, spend three nights in Lhasa, drive to Namtso Lake (overnight), then drive to Shigatse (overnight), on to Sakya or Shegar (overnight), then Everest base camp (overnight), then head to the Nepal border. That's eight action-packed days and seven nights, with maybe one or two spent in the bathroom with altitude sickness. Such rapid trips are not recommended due to lack of time for acclimatisation, but for pricing purposes, this itinerary covers a lot of ground. You would be looking at about US$2,800 for the trip: split between four people that's around US$700 each, not including airfare and meals. If you have fewer than four passengers, expenses naturally go up: with two passengers, you could be looking at Tibet on a thousand dollars a week (each).

In a Landcruiser with four passengers, here's how it might break down. A tour guide at Y250 per day for eight days costs Y2,000 for the group, or Y500 a person. (For currency information see *Money and pricing*, page 73.) Permit price is around Y1,300 a person including express mail from Lhasa for permit delivery in Chengdu. Hotels in larger cities cost around Y280 for a double room; in smaller places, Y60 a bed. Total for entry fees for various monasteries along the route will be about Y650 per person. Add the entry fee at Everest base camp at Y180 a person plus Y400 fee for the Landcruiser to go there. Landcruiser for the five-day tour (not used in Lhasa) is Y1,500 a day, including cost of driver and petrol. Landcruiser return fee from the Nepal border (because the driver may come back empty) is an extra Y1,500. On top of this are the one-way Y1,590 airfare from Chengdu to Lhasa, and airport taxi pick-up for the group at Y200. Not included in the calculation are meals and drinks (probably around Y100–150 per person per day), extra charges levied at monasteries and sights for photography, and additional costs incurred for emergencies.

Negotiating for Landcruisers Because you are paying upfront for tours with vehicle, driver and guide, here are some bargaining chips. First, do not pay everything upfront. Leave a deposit (say 20–50%), with the rest to be handed over in Lhasa after you arrive there and have met your guide and driver and have looked over the vehicle. Think about what would happen if the trip gets cancelled (either by you or the agency) or if you fall sick during the trip and must leave early. What happens if your vehicle breaks down and cannot be fixed? What happens if the road is blocked by landslides? What are the provisions for a full or partial refund? It would be good to get some kind of written contract covering these items.

It's extremely important to be flexible with Landcruiser arrangements: you can't push your driver if a bridge is down, and you won't get much out of a driver if you back him into a corner. On a contract, put down a rate for extra days. If a delay is caused by the driver or vehicle breakdown, then the agency covers the cost; if the delay is due to illness of a passenger, the group covers the cost; if the delay is due to bad weather or road conditions, you can divide the cost between the agency and the group.

Some questions to be raised. What are you paying for exactly? Are your hotels included or not? What standard of hotel? Who pays for the accommodation and food for driver and guide? Who pays entry fees to the temples and other sites? Sim's Cozy Guesthouse in Chengdu offers the same tour itinerary at one price with Company A or a lower price with Company B. It's not clear what the difference is. Do Company B vehicles have bald tyres? Do their guides speak broken English? One difference will be the hotel standard: you can save money by using budget hotels in Lhasa but you will lose on clean bathrooms.

In a number of cases, it appears that agencies sub-contract. In Lhasa, I wanted to visit the office of the tour agency contracted from Chengdu, but it turned out there was no brick-and-mortar office. The contact in Lhasa worked from his apartment and put together a Landcruiser driver with a guide at the last minute for the trip. When asked for a receipt, the contact produced a letterhead bearing the logo of a company that I had never heard of.

You need to go over everything to clarify so there are no misunderstandings or shoddy arrangements. Get copies of all itineraries and paperwork. Insist on a Tibetan driver and Tibetan guide only. Insist on a Landcruiser in good shape. Some agencies may try and provide a minivan. The road to Kathmandu is in good shape, but you still need a 4x4 to go to back-country spots like Everest base camp. Even if you never use the 4x4 potential, it's good to know you have it at your disposal. Insist on no smoking in the vehicle, and insist that mobile phones be turned off inside the vehicle. The driver may attempt to use a mobile phone while driving down a huge switchback, which could prove fatal. The guide may blabber on the mobile phone to his friends in Lhasa for the entire trip unless you pull the plug.

And a very important point: tell your agency that you are running the timing, not the guide or the driver. Some guides will take charge and try to control the itinerary. There is some flexibility here. What lies on the road between towns like Lhasa and Gyantse can be truly spectacular, and worth lots of stops for photography. The guide may try and rush you through that landscape because both driver and guide have seen it all many times before. The easiest way to deal with this is to tell the driver and guide that you are all very keen photographers and expect to be stopping in many spots for photo-ops.

You may have absolutely no problem with your vehicle – just a few loose kidneys at the end of the ride. But some travellers tell horror stories about vehicles that break down (or disintegrate) in transit, drivers who refuse to follow the itinerary, belligerent guides – the nightmare goes on. A last thought on travelling: make sure you get along with the others in your group, as you'll be seeing a lot of them. If you spend 20 days on the road to Kailash, you'll want congenial company. Compatibility is a very important consideration for long road-trips like this.

LOSING YOUR SHADOW If you can afford it, arrange 'free days' to be built into your itinerary, with no destination or sights specified. This will give you more flexibility and allow you the freedom to explore on your own. On paper, the reason for these 'free days' would be to allow time for acclimatisation. For example, you could build in two or three extra 'free days' for Lhasa. These extra days need not be consecutive – they can be scattered. On the free days, you will not need a Landcruiser and driver, so that will bring the cost down. However, in theory you still need a guide shadowing you.

Here's how this might work: if you arrive fully acclimatised from, say, Kham you could step off the plane in Lhasa, lose the guide on one of your free days, rent a mountain bike, and ride all over town – on your own. Follow-up strategy: how to wear your guide out. A shocked guide, upon discovering that I rented a mountain bike in Lhasa, insisted that he had to accompany me. So I arranged for him to get a mountain bike too, and we rode out to Drepung Monastery, which is a steep climb on a bike. He was knackered by the time he got there, and I suggested that he take the rest of the day off – which he did, allowing me to carry on with my own agenda. However, I probably could not have gotten into Drepung on my own: Drepung is one of the renegade monasteries where the PSB keeps a very close eye on the monks and screens all visitors.

You might enjoy the company of your guide, in which case there is no need to follow these suggestions. Your guide may be very knowledgeable and know all the right places to go, and be great to talk with. Or your guide might be just be there on duty, looking blank and bored, following you around like a shadow.

It's very useful to have a mobile phone to contact your guide when needed in situations where you might run into trouble (he speaks on your phone for you), and also to liaise with guide and driver about when you want to depart. As a foreigner, you are expected to have a guide at all times while in Tibet, but there's nothing stipulating how long the guide is meant to be with you each day. It could be six hours, or it could be two. You decide. If you want to strike out on your own to explore, the important thing to do is to get copies (colour photocopies are best) of any permits or documents that the guide normally keeps. Those documents enable you to fob off curious officials if questioned as they provide you with a layer of legitimacy.

INTERNATIONAL GROUP-TOUR OPERATORS The majority of travellers to Tibet are on group tours. The ones that aren't often end up one way or another on impromptu tours involving Landcruisers. The Chinese would prefer that all foreigners travel this way. Why? Because tours are easy to monitor and because they get a sanitised version of Tibet. Participants are carefully insulated from the Tibetans, and chaperoned by Chinese guides with a totally warped sense of history (and no sense of culture). Group-tour operators take care of all the logistical problems – permits, transport, food and so on – but in the process you may lose out on other dimensions. Group tours to Tibet are quite costly – even the ones organised out of Kathmandu rack up the bills. How high the bills go depend on style – some operators seek out the best hotels and food in each location. They will even arrange comfortable tents for sites considered lacking in hotels of a decent standard (ie: clients will not like what they see at the outhouse). An example of this is Tidrom hot springs in central Tibet: fabulous location, but disgusting toilets at the humble guesthouses there, so high-end groups camp out in a valley close by.

On the plus side, group-tour operators seem to magically transcend all the permit obstacles, and offer a guaranteed timetable. They can mount trips and treks that individuals drool over – the vanguard of what's possible. Groups cross the border from Kailash into Nepal or India; they trek into the Karta Valley east of Everest; they engage Bactrian camels to trek into K2 base camp north of Ali; they cross the Nepalese border into Tibet with their own Western truck and driver. Some European outfits have been permitted to use their own truck and driver on the route from Kathmandu to Lhasa and onward into Qinghai and Gansu: one of these is Dragoman (*www.dragoman.com*). Expeditions liaising with Tibet Mountaineering Association (TMA) or Tibet International Sports Travel (TIST) have arranged a number of firsts – taking on trekking peaks, white-water rafting, mountain biking, hot-air ballooning and paragliding in Tibet. Commercial rafting companies have made test runs along some sections of the Yarlung Tsangpo Gorges and claim there is potential for guided trips. Because of the specialised nature of these trips, a group may be assembled from clients from different continents through outfit liaison.

For business reasons, many operators play the game of not offending Chinese sensibilities. However, some tour operators have Buddhist links and provide a tour leader who is a Western cultural expert well versed in the history and culture of Tibet. Funding generated from these high-paying tours may not benefit the Tibetans – if considering an operator, inquire whether your driver and guide will be Tibetan. If you are embarking on a trekking or mountaineering type of tour, inquire about equipment and safety conditions for porters, as the tour company is responsible for their well-being. Outfits that combine innovative trips with small groups and an ethical approach would be the most desirable.

Regardless of whether you intend to take a tour or not, check out the websites for outfits listed here to glean ideas for your own trip. The following list represents a sample of what's offered by operators, which should encourage you to research more. To find more operators, particularly those in Nepal, check other parts of this chapter and the Tibet Cultural Region Directory of the website www.kotan.org/tibet.

Australia

Intrepid Travel 11 Spring St, Fitzroy, Victoria 3065; \ 613 9473 2626; www.intrepidtravel.com. au. Small low-budget groups angled for younger travellers.

Peregrine Adventures 258 Lonsdale St, Melbourne, Victoria 3000; \ 613 9662 2700; www. peregrineadventures.com. Offers Hanoi–Lhasa–Kathmandu overland trip; allied with Exodus UK.

World Expeditions Level 5, 71 York St, Sydney 2000; ☎612 9279 0188; www.worldexpeditions. com.au

Canada
Everest Trekking 2517 York Av, Vancouver, BC V6K 1E3; ☎604 731 7650; www.everesttrekking. com. Small-group trekking & touring to Tibet, Bhutan & other parts of the plateau.

France
Terres d'Aventure 6 rue Saint Victor, 75005 Paris; ☎0153 737 773; www.terdav.com. Specialises in trekking.

Nepal
Royal Mountain Travel PO Box 8720, Lal Durbar Marg, Kathmandu; ☎+977 1 444 4378/9; f +977 1 444 4380; e info@royalmt.com.np; www.royalmt.com.np

UK
Exodus Grange Mills, 9 Weir Rd, London SW12 0LT; ☎020 8675 5550; www.exodus. co.uk. Mounts tours in central & east Tibet; runs overland trips using their own customised trucks. **Imaginative Traveller** 1 Betts Av, Martlesham Heath, Suffolk IP5 7RH; ☎0800 316 2717; www. imaginative-traveller.com. Specialises in small-group touring. **Intrepid Travel UK** PO Box 34429, London W6 0AF; ☎020 8563 8244; www.intrepidtravel.com. **Steppes East** 51 Castle St, Cirencester GL7 1QD; ☎01285 651010; www.steppeseast.co.uk

Trans Himalaya 16 Skye Cres, Crieff, Perth & Kinross PH7 3FB; ☎01764 650604; e info@trans-himalaya.com; www.trans-himalaya.com. Takes on all parts of the Tibetan plateau. **Travel Indochina** 2nd Floor, Chester Hse, George St, Oxford OX1 2AY; ☎01865 268940; e info@travelindochina.co.uk; www. travelindochina.co.uk **World Expeditions** 3 Northfields Prospect, Putney Bridge Rd, London SW18 1PE; ☎020 8870 2600; www.worldexpeditions.co.uk

USA
Adventure Center 1311 63rd St, Suite 200, Emeryville, CA 94608; ☎800 228 8747; www. adventurecenter.com. Not much listed for Tibet, but acts as an agent for Intrepid Travel UK & other outfits. **Boojum Expeditions** 14543 Kelly Canyon Rd, Bozeman, MT 59715; www.boojum.com. Offers horseback & other innovative trips to Kham region. **Geographic Expeditions** 1008 General Kennedy Av, San Francisco, CA 94129-0902; ☎415 922 0448; www.geoex.com.

High Asia Exploratory Mountain Travel 31 North Mill Rd, Princeton Junction, NJ 08550; ☎/f 609 269 5332. A goldmine for innovative ideas on trekking & mountaineering on the Tibetan plateau; this company even offers rafting & ski-touring trips in Kham. **Wilderness Travel** 1102 Ninth St, Berkeley, CA 94710; ☎800 368 2794; www.wildernesstravel. com. Focuses on trekking.

SMALL-GROUP TOURING If you organise your own small group of three or four, you can liaise with agents in Chengdu or Xining and set up customised itineraries. This should be less expensive than going with a larger foreign operator. More time-consuming (and not guaranteed to work) is to find other like-minded travellers in these places and team up for an overland run from Lhasa to Kathmandu, sharing the costs. Agencies in Chengdu or Xining may be able to place you on one of their standard fixed-departure itineraries for a route like that but because more people are involved (could be ten on a bus), you will lose flexibility and will have fewer choices. You can also liaise directly with a travel agent in Lhasa to arrange your tour: see the shortlist of travel agents in the *Lhasa* chapter, page 122. This would probably mean using Lhasa as your starting point.

NON-GROUP TOURING The only freedom you will have as an independent traveller is in the Kham and Amdo regions, outside the TAR. Here, solo travel is fine, and it is considerably cheaper than group touring in the TAR. You can try a mixed approach – join a group for touring the TAR, then revert to independent travel in Kham and Amdo. Make sure your Chinese visa covers all bases.

RED TAPE

This may sound odd, but the best place to get a long Chinese **visa** is within China – in Hong Kong. Hong Kong, since the handover, operates as a Special Administrative Region (SAR), with the Chinese Embassy simply altering its name to PRC Visa Issuing Office. The office is located in the China Resources Building in Wanchai – you can approach this office yourself, but travellers usually go through agents for convenience. In short order, in Hong Kong, you can pick up a one-month visa (can be processed next day, HK$350/US$45) or a three-month visa (HK$600/US$80). Multiple-entry visas are possible. Some travellers, especially Americans, may only be granted a one-month visa.

The Chinese Embassy insists on receiving passport photos taken with a light blue background: the travel agency can arrange this.

There are certain things with which you should be careful when applying for a visa. Do not mention Tibet or Xinjiang as destinations. Travellers have had their visa application knocked back solely for doing this, and been told they need special permission to travel to those places. Safer destinations to mention are Beijing and Shanghai. Reason for visit: tourism. Your job: do not put reporter, journalist, writer, photographer, missionary, diplomat or politician, as your visa will not be processed. These people require special permission to travel in places like Tibet – this involves a complex procedure that may not succeed. Travel agents in Hong Kong will advise you how to fill in the application.

Visas have a coding on them: the L visa (*luyo*) designates a regular tourist; the F visa (*fangwen*) is a longer 'business' visa, also issued to cultural exchange students – this visa can raise eyebrows if you stray into Tibet; the Z visa is issued to those working in China. A visa issued in Hong Kong may start running immediately (from the date of issue), which means you'll lose a week or so just getting to Tibet. Visas from other embassies usually start from the date of entry into China, and will give you a two- or three-month leeway to get there.

Embassies closer to China are the most liberal in issuing longer visas, it seems. Hong Kong is good (three-month visa or longer is possible); Hanoi is not bad (two months possible); Islamabad offers a two-month visa; the Delhi embassy may provide a two-month visa if prodded (but otherwise will only issue one month); the Bangkok embassy normally issues visas of only one month. You might try your home country to see if you can wangle a three-month visa. Explain that China is a big place and you need a long time to see it all. Visa extensions are dodgy within Tibet, but may be possible in big cities in China.

According to the Chinese, Tibet is an integral part of China. When you apply for the visa, however, do not mention you want to go to Tibet. While a Chinese visa is good for Tibet, authorities there may not extend your initial visa in Lhasa without fulfilling demands like joining a tour. Therefore get the longest visa you can – two months, three months – at the point of origin. Not all Chinese embassies abroad are created equal. Some will grant you three months, others two months maximum, and still others only one month.

Applying for a Chinese visa in Kathmandu is troublesome, because the Chinese Embassy there is in the habit of only issuing visas for the length of a tour to Tibet booked through an agent in Kathmandu. You cannot apply to the embassy as an individual: you can only approach them through a travel agent. If you already have a Chinese visa issued elsewhere and apply for a short Tibet tour in Kathmandu, the embassy in Kathmandu is likely to cancel it and reissue another visa valid for the length of the tour. If you do not want this to happen, argue the case that you want to fly on from Lhasa to Beijing after their tour and need the extra visa time.

CHINESE EMBASSIES AND CONSULATES Chinese embassies and consulates abroad are approachable for longer visas. Inquire whether the visa starts running immediately. Chinese embassies and consulates are found throughout Europe, Africa, the Middle East, Central Asia, Asia/Indian subcontinent, Australasia/ Oceania and North America.

For a complete listing of Chinese embassies and consulates, with full address data including fax and email addresses, consult the website of the Ministry of Foreign Affairs of the PRC (*www.fmprc.gov.cn/eng*). Click on the 'Missions Overseas' link for addresses for relevant embassy websites – which provide information on visa requirements and even downloadable visa application forms. A brief listing of relevant Chinese embassies follows: address and telephone data given may be the visa/consular section, which should be close to the embassy.

Western Europe

Austria Metternichgasse 4, A-1030 Vienna; 431 710 3648

Belgium Av de Tervuren 443–445, 1150 Brussels; 322 771 3309

Denmark Oregards Alle 25, 2900 Hellerup, Copenhagen; 045 3961 9889

Finland Vanha Kelkkamaki 9–11, 00570 Helsinki; 2289 0130

France 9 Av Victor Cresson, 92130 Issy-les-Moulineaux, Paris; 01 4736 0258; www.amb-chine.fr. Consulates located in Marseille & Strasbourg.

Germany Markischer Ufer 54, 10179 Berlin; 030 275 880. Consulates located in Munich & Hamburg.

Ireland 40 Ailesbury Rd, Dublin 4; 01 269 1707

Italy Via Della Camilluccia 613, Roma 00135; 06 3630 8534. Consulates located in Milan & Florence.

Netherlands Adriaan Goekooplaan 7, The Hague; 070 306 5061

Spain No 113 Arturo Soria, 28043 Madrid; 341 519 242. Consulate located in Barcelona.

Sweden Lidovagen 8, 115 25 Stockholm; 08 5793 6437. Consulate located in Gothenburg.

Switzerland Kalcheggweg 10, 3006 Berne; 031 352 7333. Consulate located in Zurich.

UK 31 Portland Pl, London W1B 1PD; 020 7631 1430; www.chinese-embassy.org.uk. Consulates located in Manchester & Edinburgh.

North America

Canada 515 St Patrick St, Ottawa, Ontario K1N 5H3; 613 789 3434; www.chinaembassycanada.org. Consulates also located in Toronto, Calgary & Vancouver.

USA 2201 Wisconsin Av NW, Room 110, Washington, DC 20007; 202 338 6688; www.china-embassy.org. Consulates located in New York, Chicago, Houston, Los Angeles & San Francisco.

Australasia

Australia 15 Coronation Dr, Yarralumla, ACT 2600; ☎ 02 6273 47890; www.chinaembassy.org. au. Consulates in Sydney, Melbourne & Perth.

New Zealand 2–6 Glenmore St, Wellington; ☎ 644 472 1382; www.chinaembassy.org.nz. Consulate located in Auckland.

Asia

Visa validity for the following embassies and consulates varies considerably. You can get two- (or even three-) month visas in Hanoi or Ulaanbaatar, but only one month (maximum) might be given in Bangkok. Islamabad may hand out two months, but New Delhi only one month. Some visas allow up to three months to get there; others may start running immediately.

Cambodia Issarak Bd at St 163, Phnom Penh; ☎ 426 271

Hong Kong SAR Ministry of Foreign Affairs of the PRC, 5th Floor, Low Block, China Resources Bldg, 26 Harbour Rd, Wanchai; ☎ 2827 1881. Classed as a 'visa-issuing office'. Travellers often use agents.

India 50D, Shantipath, Chanakyapuri, New Delhi; ☎ 011 611 6682. Consulate located in Mumbai.

Indonesia Jl Mega Kuningan No 2, Jakarta Selatan; ☎ 221 5724 3336

Japan 4–33, Moto-Azabu 3-chome, Minato-ku, Tokyo; ☎ 03 3403 3380; www.china-embassy. or.jp. Consulates located in Osaka, Fukuoka, Sapporo & Nagasaki.

Laos Wat Nak St, Sisattahanak area, Vientiane; ☎ 315 103

Malaysia 229 Jalan Ampang, 40450 Kuala Lumpur; ☎ 603 242 8495. Consulate located in Kuching (Sabah).

Mongolia CPO Box 672, Zaluuchuudyn Urgun Chuluu 5, Ulaanbaatar; ☎ 976 11 323940

Myanmar (Burma) No 1 Pyidaungsu Yeiktha Rd, Yangon; ☎ 01 221 280. There's a consulate in Mandalay.

Nepal PO Box 4234, Baluwatar, Kathmandu; ☎ 9771 413 916

Pakistan Diplomatic Enclave, Ramna 4, Islamabad; ☎ 9251 282 4786. Consulate located in Karachi.

Singapore 70–76 Dalvey Rd; ☎ 65 734 3200

Thailand 57 Ratchadapisek Rd, Dindaeng, Bangkok; ☎ 02 245 7032; www.chinaembassy. or.th. Consulates located in Chiang Mai & Songkhla.

Vietnam 46 Hoang Dieu, Hanoi; ☎ 825 3737. Consulate located in Saigon.

CUSTOMS AND SEARCHES Official Chinese sources specify that you cannot bring into China any material (CDs, DVDs, films, tapes, etc) that is 'detrimental to the political, economic, emotional or moral interests of China'. That's a very wide net. Does that include Lady Gaga and Britney Spears videos? Even if you are on a domestic flight from Chengdu to Gongkar, you may have your bags searched (body searches are rare). Customs and checkpoint searches in Tibet are of the hit-and-miss variety. Some are waved through, others get the third degree. If a suspicious item is found in a Landcruiser, all the baggage may be searched. Your baggage may be searched on entry to Tibet, while in Tibet, and on exit. Military checkpoints on the Kathmandu to Lhasa route are on the lookout for material readily purchased in Kathmandu, like Dalai Lama pictures or tapes. Some foreigners have been hauled off at a military checkpoint and questioned about books in their possession – one of these was an autobiography by the Dalai Lama. On exit, Chinese customs may be looking for 'antiques,' which means anything Tibetan that is older than 1959. One passenger had a souvenir prayer-wheel dismantled at Lhasa Airport upon exiting, to see if any messages from Tibetans were being carried in it. In case that makes you feel really paranoid, I hasten to add this was highly irregular.

ALIEN HEALTH DECLARATION You may be required to fill in a Passenger Health Declaration when flying into China or Tibet. It starts out: 'Any Alien suffering from AIDS, venereal disease, leprosy, psychiatric disorder or open pulmonary tuberculosis is not allowed to enter the territory' and goes on to solemnly ask you to declare if you are carrying any biological products, blood products, or old clothes. Your health certificate may be asked for, but probably won't be. Other

ROUTES INTO TIBET ·

The map on page 60 shows major access points into Tibet, as follows (clockwise from Chengdu):

FROM CHENGDU, SICHUAN Main air gateway to Lhasa, with daily flights, and other flights to Shigatse, Ngari, and Nyingchi. Rail route from Chengdu via Xining to Lhasa. Rough overland route to Lhasa. Frequent flights to Beijing/ Shanghai, Hong Kong/Shenzhen/Guangzhou, and Hanoi/Bangkok/Singapore.

FROM CHONGQING Direct flights to Hong Kong and Macao.

FROM ZHONGDIAN, YUNNAN Low-frequency flights to Lhasa and Kunming. The Zhongdian–Lhasa flights are staggered in winter months. Rough overland route from Zhongdian to Lhasa.

FROM KUNMING, YUNNAN Several flights a week or rough overland route to Lhasa. Bus route to Hanoi, Vietnam. Frequent flights to Bangkok, Chiang Mai, Hong Kong. Less frequent to Hanoi, Singapore, Vientiane, Phnom Penh and Rangoon.

FROM GANGTOK, SIKKIM Overland road route linking Gangktok (Sikkim) up to Gyantse and Lhasa, opened in 2006 after Beijing finally relinquished its territorial claims to Sikkim. Not much sign of foreigners using this route. The border crossing is at 4,500m Nathu La pass. This should lead to significant cross-border trade.

FROM KATHMANDU, NEPAL Direct flight or spectacular overland route to Lhasa. The flights are suspended for the winter months (November–March inclusive). Frequent flights from Kathmandu to Hong Kong, Bangkok, India and Europe.

FROM KASHGAR, XINJIANG Rough overland route via Ali to Lhasa by sleeper bus. Rail, road and frequent flights to Urumqi. Spectacular Karakoram Highway route to Islamabad in Pakistan.

FROM GOLMUD, QINGHAI Rail connection to Lhasa started in 2006, roughly paralleling the road route. The Golmud–Lhasa run is the main overland route into Tibet.

FROM XIAN, SHAANXI Infrequent direct flight from Beijing via Xian to Lhasa. Rail connection via Xining to Golmud.

Many travellers choose to enter Tibet from one point, such as Chengdu, and exit from another, such as Kathmandu, giving the opportunity to travel more widely in the region.

things you are not allowed to bring in: poisons of all kinds, opium, and foodstuffs from epidemic zones.

GETTING THERE AND AWAY

Getting into Tibet is a two-, three- or four-part operation. First you have to make it to a staging-point like Bangkok, Hong Kong, Kathmandu or Chengdu. Then you wrangle with paperwork and ticketing, run the gauntlet of Chinese officialdom into China, and strike for Lhasa. Think of this exercise as 'hitting the roof' – an oblique reference to the way you will feel when you deal with Chinese officials. It's also what will probably happen to you when you ride in a Landcruiser in Tibet.

ROUTE STRATEGIES Direction of travel becomes very important in Tibet. Getting in from Kathmandu to Lhasa is a killer (problems with permits and altitude), but exiting from Lhasa to Kathmandu is a piece of cake. Because Nepal to Tibet is an international arrival, it leads to many more visa and red-tape complications. Travellers obsessed with getting to Tibet go to great lengths: having found their route stymied in Kathmandu, some travellers have flown all the way back to Hong Kong and *back* to Chengdu, and then *back* to Lhasa! (There's also a direct Kathmandu–Chengdu flight, but it is very expensive). If you look at the map, you can see why that re-routing costs a small fortune as opposed to a direct Kathmandu–Lhasa flight. Occasionally Chengdu is blocked too – possibly because of some Chinese official visiting Tibet – and travellers have proceeded all the way up to Golmud by land, and then overland to Lhasa.

More than in most places, you need to think about your route to and from Tibet because of visa complications. There's only one consulate in Lhasa – the Nepalese (you actually don't need a Nepalese visa as you can pick it up on arrival). That's fine, but what about going overland to Kashgar, and then exiting on the Karakoram Highway into Pakistan? The nearest place for a Pakistan visa is Beijing, and that's a long, long way to go (however, there have been reports of travellers getting Pakistan visas on arrival at the border point of Sost). The overland travel situation is much easier in Kunming, which has consulates for Vietnam, Laos, Burma and Thailand. Visa acupuncture points for Asia include Kathmandu, Hong Kong, Bangkok, Hanoi, Singapore, Beijing, Islamabad and Delhi. Some visas are readily available upon arrival by land or air: these include the Nepalese visa, Thai visa, and Hong Kong entry visa.

TTB monopoly Since 2000, the Chinese-government-operated TTB (Tibet Tourism Bureau) has created a monopoly for Landcruiser travel in Tibet. The main agent dealing with the 'Tibet permit' in places like Chengdu, Kunming, Shanghai and other points is likely to be the TTB-affiliated office. So TTBS is Tibet Tourism Bureau of Shanghai (*www.tibet-tour.com*). There are also TTB offices in Hong Kong and Kathmandu. The TTB monopoly intensified after 2008 demonstrations by Tibetans across the plateau, effectively clamping down on all individual travel in the TAR.

Staging points The first stepping stone for many is to get to Hong Kong Special Administrative Region (SAR), Bangkok or Kathmandu. More information on these can be found in the sections following.

Hong Kong SAR No visa is required of most Westerners for stays of a month or longer in Hong Kong SAR. Supposedly, the economic, social and legal status quo will stay in place for 50 years from the handover to China on 1 July 1997. However,

ACCESS ROUTES INTO TIBET

this promise fell apart after just five years when dissident Harry Wu was arrested at Hong Kong Airport, held for half a day and deported. Falun Gong members have been refused entry at the airport also. There is pressure from Chinese authorities on the media and certain taboos are in place, amounting to self-censorship of sorts. Taboo topics include the Falun Gong, insulting senior Communist Party leaders, advocating independence for Taiwan or Tibet (or Hong Kong), and being off the mark about the Tiananmen massacre. The *South China Morning Post*, once among the most opinionated newspapers in Asia, laid off most of its foreign staff and replaced them with mainland stooges as reporters and editors.

All that said, there's a wide range of books available in stores, with material on Tibet freely available, but for how much longer is not known. The best bookstore is Pageone, with several branches, including Level 3 of Harbour City in Kowloon, and in the Times Square building at Causeway Bay. Hong Kong is a good place to stock up on US cash dollars, medicines or whatever else you are short of.

Chinese visas are easy to get in Hong Kong SAR, and can usually be obtained within a few days. There is a direct charter flight from Hong Kong via Chengdu to Lhasa once a week, but this is only for groups and is quite expensive. You can achieve a similar routing, but at far reduced prices, by pre-booking an air ticket from either Shenzhen or Guangzhou to Chengdu. You proceed overland from Hong Kong to Shenzhen or Guangzhou and transfer to the airport the same day. The more scenic option is the ferry to Shenzhen, which connects with an airport shuttle bus.

Hong Kong travel agents include:

Phoenix Services Agency Room 1404, 14th Floor, Austin Tower, 22–26 Austin Av, Kowloon; ☏ 852 2722 7378; f 852 2369 8884; e info@ phoenixtrvl.com. Highly recommended agent.

Star Tours & Travel 8F Wah Ying Cheong Kin Bldg, 236 Nathan Rd, Jordan, Kowloon; ☏ 852 2367 6663; f 852 2369 6173

Bangkok, Thailand No visa is normally required for most Westerners arriving in Thailand for a stay of one month. Bangkok is the major hub of southeast Asia, and an excellent place to go shopping – or visa shopping. ATM machines abound, and it's easy to turn US travellers' cheques into US cash dollars at banks, on low commission, normally around 1%. To get around town, you would be wise to keep to the Skytrain, underground Metro, or the Chao Praya express boats – everything else crawls. There are many fine bookstores in Bangkok: the two largest English-language book chains in Thailand are Asia Books and Bookazine. The Kinokuniya chain runs two mega-bookstores (the largest in the city) – one located in Siam Paragon Store (Siam skytrain) and the other in The Emporium (Phrom Phong skytrain).

Agents can arrange visas and ticketing onward from Bangkok, with direct flights to Chengdu or Kunming. One stumbling block from Bangkok is that the Chinese Embassy there will only issue a 30-day visa (compared with much longer visas handed out in Hong Kong). Khao San Road has a large cluster of travel agents – make sure the phone is plugged into the wall. A reliable agent in the Silom area is:

STA Travel Wall Street Tower, 14th Floor, Room 1406, 33 Surawong Rd; ☏ 236 0262, f 237 6005; e help@statravel.co.th; www.statravel.co.th

Hanoi, Vietnam You need a visa in advance to gain entry to Vietnam. Two-month Chinese visas are readily obtained in Hanoi within a few days. Also, getting from Hanoi overland to China is cheaper than flying. Hanoi is a very pleasant city, with lakes, cafés, bicycle rentals and streetside beer stalls (the beer is cheaper than bottled water). You can obtain cash US dollars from the Vietcombank for a small commission charge (changing from US dollar travellers' cheques). From Hanoi you can take a train to the Chinese border, then transfer for a stunning bus ride on the Chinese side to Kunming, twisting through mountainous terrain. From Kunming, you could board a plane direct to Lhasa if your paperwork is in order, or continue by rail to Chengdu and arrange a package to Lhasa from there. An alternative is to fly from Hanoi direct to Kunming. A reliable agent in Hanoi is:

New Indochina Travel 60 Tran Vu St, Truc Bach Lake; \ 844 715 0343; f 844 715 0340;   e new-indochina@fpt.vn. This agent is the STA representative for Vietnam.

Direct air routes Flights into Lhasa are usually on Boeing 737s or 757s, Airbus A340s or Airbus A320s, operated by regional carriers Air China (CA), China Southern Airlines (CZ domestic code), China Eastern Airlines (MU) and Sichuan Airlines (3U). All four carriers fly from Chengdu to Lhasa. You may still see some CAAC signs around the place, and it may pop up in the inflight magazines. CAAC stands for Civil Aviation Administration of China, which was the state monopoly until it was broken up into regional carriers, with Beijing-based Air China taking a large slice of the pie. China Southern Airlines is based in Guangzhou, while China Eastern Airlines is based in Shanghai. Hopefully, the different carriers will induce some competition, but Lhasa flights remain overpriced and are seldom discounted, even when the plane flies three-quarters empty.

Chengdu (see page 268) is the main domestic gateway to Tibet, with the best connections and options, and numerous daily flights – sometimes ten a day or more. Flights from other destinations may be less frequent, with fewer carriers. There are other flights coming into Lhasa from Chongqing, Xian, Zhongdian, Kunming and Kathmandu.

Approximate flight durations on flights to Lhasa are: from Kathmandu, one hour ten minutes; from Chengdu, one hour 45 minutes; from Xian, two hours 30 minutes. No sign of any Tibetan pilots yet – call back in another 25 years or so – but there may be some Tibetan stewardesses on the planes. They wear striped Tibetan trim on their aprons. This is progress. Inflight films may introduce you to the wonderful world of Tibet, but you would do a lot better looking out the window; the remote and savage snowy ranges between Chengdu and Lhasa are the stuff that dreams are made of.

You will not be allowed to purchase an air ticket to Lhasa from any destination unless you have the right paperwork, meaning you have to go through an agent in those places.

Gongkar Airport Pilots landing at Gongkar – which serves Lhasa – must be trained in aerial manoeuvres at 3,700m. Due to air currents, most flights in or out of Tibet are often scheduled for the morning, as the wind can pick up in the afternoon. On arrival at Gongkar your baggage may be searched, even if you are on a domestic flight. Gongkar Airport is about 75km from Lhasa and takes an hour by road on the Galashan Tunnel route. This 2,447m-long tunnel bores right through a mountain and is connected to long bridges at both ends. The Galashan Tunnel route shaved half an hour off the previous Gongkar–Lhasa route, which went via the 3,788m-long Tsangpo Bridge located just west of Galashan. A taxi from Gongkar Airport into Lhasa varies from Y130 to Y200. There is lodging and food in the town of Gongkar, an easy walk from the airport. For information on departing Tibet by air, see the *Lhasa* chapter, page 120.

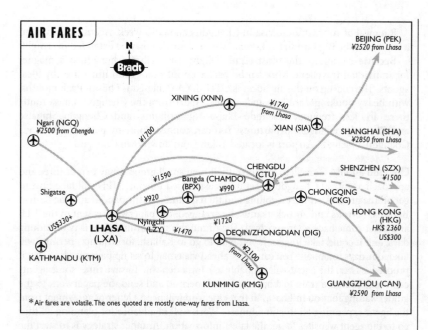

AIR FARES

N

Bradt

BEIJING (PEK)
¥2520 from Lhasa

XINING (XNN)
¥1740 from Lhasa

Ngari (NGQ)
¥2500 from Chengdu

¥1700

XIAN (SIA)

SHANGHAI (SHA)
¥2850 from Lhasa

CHENGDU (CTU)

SHENZHEN (SZX)
¥1500

¥1590
Bangda (CHAMDO) (BPX) ¥990

CHONGQING (CKG)

Shigatse

¥920

HONG KONG (HKG)
HK$ 2360
US$300

US$330+

LHASA (LXA)

Nyingchi (LZY) ¥1470

¥1720

DEQIN/ZHONGDIAN (DIG)

KATHMANDU (KTM)

¥2100 from Lhasa

KUNMING (KMG)

GUANGZHOU (CAN)
¥2590 from Lhasa

*Air fares are volatile. The ones quoted are mostly one-way fares from Lhasa.

Other plateau airports While there are a number of military airfields in Tibet, there are only a handful of civilian ones. Nyingchi Airport (elevation 2,955m, located close to Bayi, east Tibet) has a tricky landing, with planes having to approach along a winding valley. Ngari airfield, 30km from Ali (west Tibet), is up and running.

Bangda Airport, located about 100km south of Chamdo, is currently the highest airport in the world, at 4,334m. It takes an hour to fly from Lhasa to Bangda. There is another flight from Bangda to Chengdu. Confusingly, Bangda is also called Bamda, Pomda and Changdu (so there's a Changdu–Chengdu flight). Under construction in northern TAR at Nagqu is an airfield that will eclipse Bangda's record by 100m. Nagqu Airport, at 4,436m, is slated to open in 2014. Apart from these, there is an airport at Yushu, on the fringes of the TAR to the northeast. In Kham, a large airport at Zhongdian (3,275m) in Diqing Tibetan Autonomous Prefecture (upper Yunnan) started operation in 2000. The airport is officially named Diqing Shangri-La Airport: this lies in Yunnan, outside the TAR, so no permits are required to fly into this place from Lhasa. You can also fly from Zhongdian to Lhasa on a package deal similar to those offered in Kunming (from where the flight originates).

Some sample airfares (one-way): Kunming–Lhasa Y2100; Zhongdian–Lhasa Y1470; Beijing–Lhasa Y2520; Shanghai–Lhasa Y2850; Xining–Lhasa Y1750; Chengdu–Lhasa Y1590; Kathmandu–Lhasa Y2540.

Chengdu gateway Chengdu, in southwest China, is the main air gateway to Lhasa, with year-round flights and sometimes more than ten flights a day. The flight into Lhasa crosses the snowcaps of eastern Tibet, with great 757 wingtip vistas. Flight time is one hour and 45 minutes. This is the most reliable way to reach Tibet. Chengdu has frequent onward connections to destinations like Beijing, Shenzhen, Guangzhou and Hong Kong SAR; international connections from Chengdu can be made to Bangkok, Singapore and elsewhere. Chengdu has a handful of consulates, including those of Thailand, Singapore, South Korea, USA, France and Germany.

Renewal of your Chinese visa in Chengdu can take a week. Agents recommend a trip to see the Big Buddha at Leshan, where your visa may be extended overnight. Because it mounts the most regular flights into Tibet, Chengdu is a magnet for individual travellers, who can be packaged into set-group itineraries by local agents. The coding on the air ticket is CTU–LXA (Chengdu–Lhasa). Peak months, with heavy bookings, are July and August. Apart from the Chengdu–Lhasa route, there are less frequent Chengdu–Lhasa–Ngari flights, and Chengdu–Shigatse and Chengdu–Nyingchi departures. You can connect to many parts of China via Chengdu. Chengdu Airport is located 12km from downtown Chengdu.

Chengdu agents Travellers can form their own small group of say two or three and approach agents in Chengdu to set up a customised itinerary. This will take time to get off the ground, so start it rolling and then go and visit the pandas and the Leshan Buddha. Permits and air tickets must be arranged: the paperwork is sent to the TTB and must come back after approval. The minimum turnaround time is two working days, and it could take longer. If you plan to go to Kailash, for instance, permits will take four days to obtain. You can work ahead via email to set up paperwork so that it proceeds faster: the agent will probably ask for a deposit. To save time, some agents can book you on a train to Lhasa without a permit, and send the paperwork to the guide, waiting for you in Lhasa. In that case, you will need a letter of agreement from the agent explaining all this in Chinese. Work well in advance for planning all this: go to the agent websites to get the latest information. Another strategy is to start the paperwork in Chengdu, then leave by road for Zhongdian, and pick up your permit and air ticket there (forwarded by the same agent).

The best place in Chengdu to get all this together is Sim's Cozy Garden Hostel. Sim's is not 'cozy' anymore (it has ballooned to 170 rooms), and Sim and Maki who used to run the place with great efficiency have moved on to other ventures. Hopefully, what they set up endures. Sim's Cozy has a Tibet desk where you can go over itineraries and negotiate. There are also message boards where you can post messages and try to find others to join you. This is a tedious process because your timing has to match, and you need to be compatible with other travellers in the small group. For a Landcruiser, four is the maximum number of passengers. Sim's Cozy has fixed departures that you can join on set itineraries: this could be in a minivan or minibus.

Here are the main budget agents who double as running hostels:

Lazybones Hostel (40 rooms) Yangshi Jie, north of the Mao statue; ☏ 028 653 77889; e chengduhostel@hotmail.com; www. chengduhostel.com. This hostel has dorms & dbls & is well run. Décor uses parodies of Mao-era posters & other avant-garde artwork. Run by the same folks is Mix Hostel, 23 Ren Jia Wan; ☏ 832 22271; e mixhostel@hotmail.com. Both hostels can set up Tibet touring, but they probably go through bigger fish to cue it up.
Sim's Cozy Garden Hostel (170 rooms) 211 North Section 4, 1st Ring Rd; ☏ 028 819 79337; f 028 833 76882; e simscozygh@yahoo.co.jp; www.gogosc.com. Away from the centre of the city, but sits along the bus route from Chengdu

Airport. The hostel has accommodation from dorm to dbls with bath, & excellent restaurant, & loads of facilities like bicycle rental & internet. Often full, so book early.
Tibet Hotel (over 280 rooms & suites) 10 Renmin Bei Lu; ☏ 831 83388. Caters to the high-end market, with agents located on the lower floors. Rates at this deluxe hotel run Y600–1,200 a room & up.
Traffic Inn Hostel (10 rooms) Out the back of the Traffic Hotel near Jinjiang River, 6 Linjiang Middle Rd; ☏ 028 854 50470; www. trafficinnhostel.com/en. This hostel is a separate operation from the Traffic Hotel (Jiaotong Binguan). Dorms are Y20, rooms Y70 & up. Has

an office for travel bookings, including Tibet arrangements. Not as proficient as Sim's Cozy for permits, but adequate. In the Traffic Hotel next door there is a slew of agents, most likely branches of the same company, all selling the same tours – with clients commonly after 2 things: pandas & Tibet. These are actually connected: you can pass time visiting the pandas & other top sights around Chengdu while you wait for your Tibet paperwork to come through. **Windhorse Tour** C-904 Wanheyuan Apts, 1 Babao St; ✆ 862 5470; e windhorsetour@ hotmail.com. Agent for CYTS & can set up customised itineraries.

Permits to enter Tibet all pass through Tibet Hotel – the permits go through TTB Chengdu, located in Room 1418, 14th floor of Tibet Hotel, at 10 Renmin Bei Lu. You cannot get a permit directly through them – you must go through an agent. Tibet Hotel has both an airline office and a travel agent within: the latter is called Sichuan Everbright (✆ 028 831 98329).

Kunming gateway The flight from Kunming to Lhasa via Zhongdian goes several times a week. A one-way air ticket costs Y2,100. For bookings, the best plan is to stay at the Camellia Hotel (*Chahua Binguan; 96 East Dongfeng Rd;* ✆ *0871 316 3000; www.kmcamelliahotel.com; dorms Y30, dbls from Y100–300).* The Chamabar, located in the Camellia Hotel compound, is a good place to chat with travellers (and on the internet too). Kunming is connected by overland route from Hanoi in Vietnam (pick up a Chinese visa in Hanoi), and you can go overland from Luang Namtha in Laos to Kunming (pick up a Chinese visa in Vientiane – could be a multi-month visa).

Kunming agent The main agent for Tibet travel (overland or by air) is Mr Chen (*Room 3115, No 3 Building, Camellia Hotel;* ✆/f *0871 318 8114).*

Zhongdian gateway Several outfits in Zhongdian can arrange travel to Tibet, but because of less competition, these agents are pricier than those in Chengdu. You would be better off arranging a tour from Chengdu, and picking up paperwork in Zhongdian (such as air ticket and Tibet permit). Flights from Zhongdian to Lhasa are low frequency, so it is essential to book ahead in peak months. The air ticket to Lhasa is Y1,470 one-way. Going overland from Zhongdian to Lhasa is a very expensive Landcruiser trip, costing around US$3,500 for the journey. See the section on Zhongdian in the *East Tibet, Kham and Amdo* chapter, page 263, for accommodation details.

Zhongdian agents Khampa Caravan, at the centre of Zhongdian (✆ 887 68321, e *info@khampacaravan.com; www.khampacaravan.com*) offers package tours and overland tours to Lhasa for a hefty tariff. With similar services is KawaGebo International Travel, located in the square of the old town (✆ 887 73316; e *info@ yaktraveler.com; www.yaktraveler.com*). Also try the TTB-affiliated office (*Room 2206, Shangbala Hotel;* ✆ 887 822 9028; f 887 822 7892).

Xining Gateway Since the Lhasa line opened, Xining has stepped up to the plate as a viable staging point for Tibet – going by train, of course. There are flights to Lhasa, but these are irregular (Xining is a stop on the flight from Shanghai to Lhasa). See the tail end of *Chapter 8*, page 282, for more about Xining accommodation.

Xining agents There are several agents that deal with the Tibet trade. One is Tibetan Connections, located on a high floor at 5 Building, International Village

Apartment, above Lete Hostel (℡ 86 1520 256 8354; www.tibetanconnections.com). Another is Snow Lion Tours, which has several offices in Xining. One is located at Cheng Lin Mansion (*Office 121, 7 Dongdajie Rd;* ℡ 0971 816 3350; e info@ snowliontours.com; www.snowliontours.com). They also have an office in Lhasa.

Other Chinese gateways The flight from Beijing stops in Chengdu, then continues to Lhasa. Frequency may vary from once a week to daily; in any case, the Chengdu–Lhasa leg is daily. Less frequent flights go to Lhasa from Guangzhou via Chongqing (rumoured to be once or twice weekly), or to Lhasa from Shanghai via Xian and Xining (two or three times a week). There are several snags involved with these flights. The first is that they are very expensive – Beijing to Lhasa is Y2,520 and Shanghai is even more expensive. Listing of a flight on a timetable does not guarantee that the plane will actually depart. Chinese planes only fly when seat space is sufficiently filled: if not, the plane could be cancelled or delayed.

Kathmandu gateway The only international flight into Lhasa is from Kathmandu, Nepal. A group of five may be required for ticket reservations. Flights should be booked two to four weeks in advance through a travel agent. The flight costs Y2,540 one-way (US$390). To go from Kathmandu to Lhasa you need a full package price with an organised tour, including air ticket, Landcruisers, Tibet permit, accommodation, the whole shebang – probably with a minimum of eight days. It would cost at least US$800 per person for an all-inclusive week in Tibet, round trip to Kathmandu, in a group.

In Kathmandu, it seems that everyone can offer a tour to Tibet, but beware. Most of these companies operate as subcontractors and may cancel tours at the last minute due to lack of clients. They have a tendency to tell you what you want to hear: that expenses are all included (when they are not), that you can leave after the tour in Lhasa and carry on by yourself (unlikely), and that you can get a visa extension in Lhasa (highly unlikely). Make sure you know what services you are paying for, and are getting the itinerary you desire.

On these tours, there is most likely going to be a group visa – a single piece of paper covering all the people involved, and this is not stamped in your passport. That means you will be forced to stay with the group to exit China because you have no other paperwork. There's one loophole: some agents can book you on an eight-day tour from Kathmandu overland to Lhasa, and then allow you to wander off on your own in Lhasa for a few more 'rest' days.

Agents in Kathmandu do not like it if you have a Chinese visa already stamped in your passport (obtained elsewhere) as this spells trouble. The Chinese Embassy in Kathmandu is prone to cancelling a visa issued elsewhere and replacing it with a group visa valid for the length of the tour you've booked. There's a (tiny) chance you can salvage the situation by leaning on the agent and impressing upon the Chinese Embassy that the visa should remain unchanged because you will be travelling onward from Lhasa to the heart of the great motherland (Beijing) and other parts of mainland China after the Tibet portion of the trip, and China being a very large country, this will all take time. There are no guarantees this strategy will work – in fact, the chances are not good. Other embassy games: normal visa processing fee is US$58, taking seven working days. For US citizens, it's US$144 for that visa. But for a group application for travel to Tibet, you will need to get a 'fast-track' visa that takes three days to obtain, and costs US$80 for most nationalities (or US$180 for US nationals). A one-day turnaround is again more expensive.

Despite the visa handicaps in Kathmandu, there are excellent agents who can set you up with great itineraries, and do it right. You could, for instance, cue up an entire trip to Kailash, starting with a flight to Lhasa, acclimatisation and touring in central Tibet, and Landcruiser to Lhatse, meet a Nepalese crew of Sherpas in a truck there, continue to Kailash (camping out), complete the *kora*, then exit back to Nepal by road.

No Nepalese aircraft fly the Tibet route – it's all on Air China, so again the ticketing problems come up (you can't buy the ticket yourself). Kathmandu to Lhasa flights operate two or three times weekly in season (the flight is closed down for the winter months – November to March inclusive). Peak months, with heavy bookings, are July and August. The flight lasts 70 minutes, and goes straight over the Himalaya – the pilot uses Everest as a navigation landmark when turning. If you fly from Lhasa to Kathmandu, due to time-zone differences you will arrive before you left – which is neither here nor there but a handy piece of trivia to know.

Kathmandu agents You can find information about Kathmandu agents, with address, email and website listings, at www.kotan.org (go to the side panel for Tibetan Cultural Region Directory, then click on Nepal). Scores of travel agents handle trips to Tibet, particularly those around the Thamel district of Kathmandu. Some recommended agents are:

Eco Trek Thamel; 9771 442 4112; e info@ ecotrek.com.np; www.ecotrek.com.np. Covers overland tours as well as trips to Kailash.
Royal Mountain Travel Lal Durbar Marg; 9771 444 4378/9; f 9771 444 380; e info@ royalmt.com.np; www.royalmt.com.np

Tashi Delek Nepal Trek & Expeditions Thamel; 9771 441 0746; e tashidele@wlink. com.np; www.tashidelektreks.com.np

The railway Track for the Lhasa–Golmud (western China) line was completed in October 2005, with passenger services starting in 2006. The railway line closely parallels the road route, meaning that any sizeable town along the way is now a railway station. Along the line, there are 11 stations with permanent staff, 18 stations without staff, and five to ten scenic observation stops. The train can move at speeds of 100–160km/h, covering the 1,140km distance in half the time the bus takes, and in much more comfort. The railway cars have a system of oxygen enrichment, which means feeding in oxygen as higher elevations are reached; there are individual oxygen tubes for passengers who are blue in the face. A great hardship for Chinese passengers is that smoking is forbidden at altitude, because of the potentially explosive combination of oxygen-enriched air and cigarette lighters.

Despite these precautions, when you are issued a ticket, you may need to sign a slip of paper that testifies that you are aware of the risks of altitude and swear you can adapt to elevations above 3,000m. Other conditions specify that passengers with 'diabetes out of control' or 'abnormal heart beats above 100 times a minute' will not be permitted to board. Nor will 'highly dangerous pregnant women'.

The highest station along the route is Tanggula Shan, which at 5,070m is actually the highest in the world. From Golmud and Xining, the railway system across China is accessible to Beijing, Shanghai, Chengdu or Guangzhou. The 4,000km rail journey from Beijing to Lhasa can be accomplished in a mere 47 hours by express train, with only six stops along the way – effectively ending Tibet's legendary isolation.

Pricing on the Lhasa line varies, factoring in agent surcharges, the type of sleeper acquired, and the season. In high season (June to September) prices spike because of heavy bookings, meaning agents have to pay touts to acquire sleepers. Some sample prices: Xining–Lhasa Y523 hard sleeper, Y810 soft sleeper (26 hours); Chengdu–Lhasa Y845 hard sleeper, Y1100 soft sleeper (45 hours).

Much more lavish is an Orient Express style of rail travel being marketed by GW Travel in the UK and by RailPartners in North America. Their ultra-luxury cars have bathrooms, television, gourmet meals and butler service, and a price tag to match.

Road routes into Tibet There are two major road routes into Lhasa – one from Golmud and one from Kathmandu. China uses the metric system, and there are kilometre marker stones along all major routes, so you can track your progress. You can also use these marker stones to figure out turn-offs. In Tibet, there are usually road maintenance stations every 10km, just like in imperial Rome.

Golmud route The 1,130km journey from Golmud to Lhasa is an overnight epic that qualifies for the most boring bus ride in Asia. Most skip it and take the train instead. Golmud (3,200m) is a bland town of 90,000. The mostly paved road traverses high terrain, passing the world's highest inhabited place (Wenquan, at 5,100m, established by the Chinese in 1955), and shortly after crossing Tangu La (5,180m). If you've left Lhasa and reached Golmud overland, you might want to look into continuing overland from Xining via Labrang to Chengdu – a great run through Tibetan areas. For more details, check the *East Tibet, Kham and Amdo* chapter, page 286.

Kathmandu route By contrast, the Kathmandu to Lhasa route cuts through diverse altitude zones and draws you past an enthralling Himalayan landscape. However, this route is better tackled as an exit, for reasons of permits, choices and altitude. See the *Lhasa to Kathmandu* chapter for details, page 187. The first problem you will have is getting a Chinese visa. Unless you book a tour from Kathmandu, the Chinese Embassy will not issue a visa. The majority of travellers entering Tibet overland from Kathmandu do so on an eight-day tour; some negotiate a stay of a few more days in Lhasa on their own. A package includes transport by Landcruiser overland to Lhasa, hotels *en route*, and flight back from Lhasa.

Longer overland routes There are various epic routes into Lhasa that traverse the plateau and you get to see half of Tibet along the way. **Chengdu to Lhasa** overland takes about ten to 15 days without stops, and crosses some 15 high passes. Past Kangding at Xinduqiao, the route diverges, a northern branch going through Derge and Chamdo, and a southern route passing through Litang and Barkam. Both routes join up again near Bangda, and the road continues past Namche Barwa, the highest peak in eastern Tibet, at 7,756m. For a very long time, geographers speculated that there had to be a huge waterfall in the area close to Namche Barwa because the Yarlung Tsangpo dropped radically as it transformed into India's Brahmaputra River. There's no big waterfall, but the river stages a dramatic U-turn around Namche Barwa, cutting through the deepest gorge in the world.

Towns along the Chengdu to Lhasa route are mostly truck stops. Officials and truck-stop inns don't see a lot of foreigners, and problems can surface. One group in a Landcruiser, stopping at Bayi, was fined heavily for staying overnight at a non-PSB-approved hotel (PSB wanted them to stay at a very expensive approved hotel). Chengdu to Lhasa is 2,400km via Chamdo (north route) and 2,080km via Litang (south route). Some details for these routes are given in the *East Tibet, Kham and Amdo* chapter.

Coming up **from Kunming** is a stunning route that travels through the scenic towns of Dali, Lijiang and Zhongdian before joining the route to Lhasa near Barkam. Kunming to Barkam is 1,200km, and it's another 1,100km from Barkam to Lhasa. Kunming is a good staging point. If you're into long overland trips, you can reach Kunming from either the Lao Cai border (connecting to Hanoi by road) or the Ban Boten border (connecting through Laos to Thailand). Going the other way, there is a Lao consulate in Kunming and also a Vietnamese consulate, to enable land crossings into those countries. For Thailand, you can get a visa on arrival at any airport or land border crossing.

The wildest route of all into Lhasa is the 3,100km journey **from Kashgar** in the far west of Xinjiang province, southward through Yecheng and Mazar to Ali, and then on to Lhasa. The route traverses passes over 5,000m. That looks like a long stretch, but actually it can be covered in 12 days: one high-end hotel in Lhasa announced a trip using 800cc BMW motorcycles that took in Everest and Kailash along the way. The only problem was the price tag: Y44,000 for each person based on three riders. The old silk route trading town of Kashgar looks like it's a long way from anywhere, but actually it's only a few days down the Karakoram Highway from Kashgar to Islamabad in Pakistan. This is one of the greatest mountain road trips in High Asia, crossing the 4,700m Khunjerab pass. Another way of reaching Kashgar is from Bishkek (Kyrgyzstan) over the Torugart pass.

The Jules Verne challenge By stringing together some of these routes, you can develop a journey on a grand scale, clocking up over 10,000km by road. In 1992, the London-based adventure tour operator Voyages Jules Verne sponsored a car rally commemorating a historic 1907 race from Paris to Peking. The 1992 rally cars left London headed for Saigon, by way of Moscow, Tashkent, Kashgar, Yarkand, Shigatse, Lhasa, Xining, Chengdu, Nanning and Hanoi. Taking a cue from this, you can set up your own Jules Verne challenge. You can overland from Saigon up through Hanoi, continuing by road to Kunming and Chengdu, then go by road or air to Lhasa, continue by road to Kathmandu, and carry on overland all the way to Istanbul. A silk route variation would be to take the same trail to Lhasa, and head north to Golmud and Dunhuang, perhaps fly from Urumqi to Kashgar (or take a train), zip down the Karakoram Highway into Pakistan, and then travel overland to Istanbul. There's an international rail crossing from Urumqi to Almaty, connecting all the way to Moscow.

Routes restricted to high-end groups High-paying group tours walk to the Kojinath border crossing in western Tibet, trekking in for five days from Simikot (Nepal), and are then picked up by Landcruisers that take them on to Burang, and up to Kailash. A similar trek up the Indian side, crossing at Lipu Lek pass, is sanctioned for high-paying group tours. Group tours might be able to cross overland from Tibet into Nepal at Kyirong, leading into the Langtang area of Nepal, north of Kathmandu. Roads on both sides of the border have been completed – on the Nepalese side with assistance from Chinese engineers. There is little doubt that this will become a major trading route, and that tourist traffic will follow. Permits are needed on the Tibetan side to reach Dzongka and Kyirong.

Opened in 2006 after a closure of more than 40 years is Nathu La pass, 4,500m, on the Sikkim–Tibet border. This makes it possible to travel from Gyantse (Tibet) to Gangtok (Sikkim). This was the main gateway for British access to Tibet by horse in the early 20th century, coming up from Kalimpong and Darjeeling. On the Tibetan side, the road passes viewpoints looking across at Kangchenjunga, the third-highest peak in the world.

> Good heavy ammunition boots are the best for men, and stout ankle boots for women, and both may, if desired, be hobnailed. A pair of comfortable slippers are a great relief after the day's march is done, and should not be forgotten. Woollen socks and stockings are the best, and should be thick. To avoid chafing, boric powder should be dusted inside them before putting them on, and the toes and heels rubbed on the outside with soap. In the event of blisters developing, they should be pricked with a sterilised needle, Germolene applied, and a lint and cotton wool pad placed over them to protect them from further chafing while marching.

This paragraph comes from *Touring in Sikkim in Tibet*, a slim guidebook written in 1930 by David Macdonald, former British Trade Agent in Gyantse. He makes travel sound painful; in the 1930s, travellers rode or marched into Tibet with pack animals and an entourage of porters, carrying 30kg tents, a portable bath, hurricane lanterns, stove and so on. One porter was assigned to carry the tiffin basket, which contained crockery, cutlery and provisions for lunch. Times have changed – those 1930s travellers would be amazed at the strong, lightweight camping gear and clothing on the market now, with the wonders of Gore-tex and Velcro.

Even so, on a trip to Tibet, you may end up with a lot of gear. What to take? Pepper spray for the dogs? A shovel for the propaganda? A shortwave radio to get your news fix? A GPS device to find out where you are? All kinds of equipment springs to mind, but can you carry it? A good idea, before you set out, is to assemble all your gear, shoulder it, and walk a dozen blocks – or better yet, hike up the nearest mountain. Carrying luggage at altitude is much harder work than at sea level: the emphasis in your gear should be on strong, lightweight stuff that performs multiple functions. And you should remember that the gear you take is not the final weight: you may purchase souvenirs or books *en route*, not to mention food and drink, all of which will add to the burden, so you have to figure out where the weight lies, and how to reduce it without compromising on essentials like medical supplies.

High on my list, in the clothing/footwear category, would be a good pair of hiking shoes with ankle support – lightweight, strong and well broken-in. You rely on your feet a lot in Tibet. The next priority would be a strong flashlight that has a long battery life (and a supply of spare batteries). Due to erratic or non-existent electrical supply in Tibet, you constantly need a flashlight – for illuminating dark frescoes in monasteries, for finding your way around at night, for visiting the outhouse at night, etc. Clothing for dealing with extremes of heat, cold and wind is essential. Rain and dampness are not so much of a problem, as Tibet is high and extremely dry. Dust is a big problem, though. Pure cotton clothing is of dubious value in the mountains because it takes too long to dry – if you sweat, the sweat stays, and you can freeze as a result. Quick-dry synthetics are preferable, such as nylon/polyester mixes with the feel of cotton, or else cotton/polyester mixes. Silk items favoured by skiers are ideal for insulating because they're lightweight and durable. You can find silk items made in China on sale in Lhasa, along with lots of cheap outdoor clothing of reasonable quality. A thick-pile sweater and a windproof jacket (Gore-tex is good) should provide protection against biting wind and cold. For more on clothing, sunglasses and protection from the elements, read the *Health and safety* chapter (page 99), which has a rundown of essential medical supplies.

If you plan to get off the track in Tibet, you need a good sleeping bag. These are bulky, but you'll find a Chinese quilt is much more bulky – though these are supplied in most guesthouses, off the track they may not be, and you can't afford to freeze or lose sleep. If a guesthouse is already warm enough, you can use a sleeping bag to cushion the bed. A sleeping bag with a down fill is recommended because it's compact, lightweight and insulates well – get one rated to sub-zero temperatures. You can buy cheap Chinese-made sleeping bags in Lhasa for under US$50. A compact Therm-a-Rest (ultra-light air mattress) is also a good idea in case you end up sleeping on the floor of a teahouse.

In the gadget line, an altimeter may be helpful – make sure it goes to 6,000m. Some wristwatches have in-built altimeters, so the question is not what time, but how high.

The selection of camping and outdoor equipment has vastly improved in Lhasa, with a string of specialised stores along Beijing Road and Tengyeling Road. You could arrive in Lhasa in a pair of shorts and a T-shirt and be fully outfitted for camping and outdoor clothing within a few days, and at low prices compared with similar items in the West. One of the top Chinese brands is Ozark, makers of tents and other camping equipment. Discarded expedition gear may also be on sale in Lhasa.

If you are planning to go cycling or do a lot of trekking, you might want to think about importing your own freeze-dried food and other supplies. Concentrate on food that can be 'cooked' by adding hot water to the package and letting it sit for a few minutes. This way you can use the vacuum flasks of hot water supplied in most hotels. While you can buy a stove in Lhasa, it might be an unwieldy kerosene one. If you want to be sure of a light, compact stove that operates off any fuel source, bring it with you. The rot-gut Chinese liquor sold in various parts of Tibet can power a stove.

What you bring really depends on what kind of trip you're planning. If travelling in a Landcruiser, consider that luggage space in the back is minimal if sharing with three other passengers. Obviously if you want to go trekking, you will need to be fairly self-sufficient gear-wise. You may find that your backpack or main duffle bag is out of reach, buried under other baggage. Thus you need to keep a daypack with essential items such as camera and so on with you; some daypacks have an external mesh holder for a water bottle. Within easy reach also should be the food supplies if you stop for lunch: some travellers purchase a cheap vinyl bag in Lhasa to hold food supplies and things like candles, separating this from the main baggage. If staying longer in Tibet, you can use Lhasa as a base, so you could leave a duffle bag in guesthouse storage while off gallivanting around. Cargo duffles have lockable zippers on them to deter prying fingers.

While on the subject of locks and security, think about bringing your own small, sturdy padlock for hotel rooms. A number of rooms use a door-clasp secured with a padlock, but they will only supply one key. That's not convenient if you are sharing with three other people, as you would have to leave the key at front reception, and the reception person may be hard to find. A better idea is to carry your own padlock with four keys (you can have extra keys cut in the marketplace if needed).

Bring all photography supplies with you. To rephrase that: bring a lot more film or digital storage cards than you think you'll need. If you're passing through, Hong Kong and Bangkok are good places to make prints. See the section on *Photography*, page 83, for more details on filming in Tibet.

Electrical supply in Tibet is 220 volts, 50 hertz, with a variety of plugs; walls jacks mostly accept two flat-prong American plugs or two round-pin European plugs. Bring an adaptor. Supply is erratic, intermittent or unreliable, with possible blackouts. It's best to bring good battery back-up for any electronic devices, and use the power supply to recharge those batteries. A surge protector is a good idea. Some multi-plug units have a surge protector built in and so do electrical adaptors.

A couple of other notes on gear: if you don't have it, maybe your fellow travellers do. Message boards at the budget hotels in Lhasa carry ads from travellers selling sleeping bags, film, camping gear, medicines, freeze-dried food – or even left-over oxygen. Travellers can become fixated with their stuff and spend hours in needless aggravation over what to take. Get that part over quickly and shift your attention to more important matters like plotting your route, reading up on the areas you plan to visit, reading up on Tibetan culture and learning some Tibetan language (buy a phrasebook). Knowledge is the most important thing to carry with you.

And while on that subject, a note about gifts: those inflight magazines and news magazines that you might discard elsewhere would be greatly appreciated within Tibet: they make ideal gifts because it is impossible to obtain foreign magazines in Lhasa.

MAPS Research all map material before you go to Tibet, and bring it with you. Within Tibet, the only maps available are Chinese-produced. The best place to find maps of Tibet is in Kathmandu, where you can even find pirated editions of maps that are long out of print in Europe, like Stanfords's *South-Central Tibet: Lhasa to Kathmandu Route Map*.

Handy map collections can be found in several books. A highly ambitious project is *Mapping the Tibetan World* (see *Further information*, page 332), a book that collates over 280 maps, with fine detail seen nowhere else, including trekking maps. Victor Chan's *Tibet Handbook*, though somewhat unwieldy (it has been christened 'Vic the Brick'), contains a collated set of *US Department of Defense Aerial Survey Maps*. These provide selected coverage of Tibet's topography – very useful for trekkers – but they are old, and while the geographical features are fine, the size and location of towns may have changed.

For sheet maps, Hungarian cartographic company GiziMap publishes several fine maps that cover the Tibetan plateau in detail. Canadian cartographic company ITMB (*www.itmb.com*) publishes a map of Tibet with similar area coverage, as well as maps of neighbouring nations like Bhutan. German cartography of Tibet includes Berndtson & Berndtson's *Tibet*; the RV Verlag/GeoCenter map *Tibet, Nepal and Bhutan*; and Himalayan maps in the Nelles series. A series by Swiss-based Gecko Maps (*www.geckomaps.com*) features *Himalaya-Tibet* (road map), *Kailash* (trek map, plus a panoramic map), *Everest* (panoramic map), *Nepal* and *Kathmandu*. In the same series is the *Lhasa Map*, a superb theme-map focusing on Lhasa's historic buildings (meaning traditional Tibetan architecture): this map is an offshoot of the book *The Lhasa Atlas*.

Tibetans themselves never really needed maps, nor bothered to create them, except in artistic renditions. So Tibetan-created maps of Tibet are a recent phenomenon, and an attempt to fight back on the cartographic front. From the Amnye Machen Institute in Dharamsala comes the highly detailed map *Lhasa City* (issued 1995), with a separate gazetteer in English and Tibetan. The map lists 590 locations, including sites like educational institutions, prisons and PLA bases, which are of no interest to the casual tourist. That aside, the map provides an excellent overview of Lhasa, with contour lines useful for hiking sorties. Published in 1998 by Amnye Machen is *Tibet and Adjacent Areas under Chinese Communist Occupation*, with some focus on ethnic groups of the plateau. For more information on these maps, consult www.amnyemachen.org.

Surely the strangest map-guide ever produced is *On This Spot: Lhasa*, issued by ICT Washington, 2001. This unconventional map is backed up by a wealth of detail on Lhasa's rapidly changing face and its tragic human rights situation; it tells you what happens behind the scenes in the capital and includes some subversive photos. The map was released as part of an International Campaign for Tibet (ICT) initiative to educate travellers about China's occupation of Tibet, and to redress the balance in guidebooks on Tibet, which often omit information on the human rights situation. The map can be ordered through ICT's website (*www.savetibet.org*). Also available from ICT is a double-sided map titled *The Eastern Regions of Tibet*, which gives details on Kham and Amdo, with a lot of historical annotations.

Within Tibet/China The only maps available within Tibet and the PRC are the Chinese-produced ones. This is probably because of 'cartographic correctness' – Chinese maps show all of Arunachal Pradesh lying in Chinese territory, much to the chagrin of India.

On sale in Lhasa are the following maps: *China Tibet Tour Map*, a foldout map of Tibet (published by the Mapping Bureau of the TAR, 1993), *Lhasa Tourist Map* (Chengdu Cartographic Publishing House, 2004) and *Tourist Map of Tibet*, with one side featuring Tibet, and the other side devoted to Lhasa (Xian Map Press, 2010). Significantly, there are few Tibetan-language maps for sale. The best map of China is a joint-venture effort between the Cartographic Publishing House of China and Liber Kartor AB, Sweden (1995): it's a large wall map, but you could slice off the Tibet part to make it easy to carry.

Maps are very cheap in China, but the maps published in English are weak in detail, while the maps published in Chinese are more complete (a kind of reverse censorship – the Chinese need to find their way around their own colony but they don't want foreigners to access the material). For the traveller, maps with Chinese and English on them are best, so you can point to the characters for your destination when talking to Chinese drivers.

The basic problem with maps of Tibet is that the Chinese have all the data, but treat it as a military secret – it's only partially revealed in Chinese-produced maps. On Western maps, there are conflicting names for destinations depending on whether the Tibetan name, the Chinese name or the old English name is referred to, and which transliteration system is used. Everest, for example (English name), is known as 'Chomolungma' in Tibetan, and transliterated as 'Qomolangma' in Pinyin Chinese. Maps of Tibet are an ideological battleground. Tibetan-exile maps show Tibet covering the entire Tibetan plateau, while Chinese maps show the much-reduced area of the Tibet Autonomous Region, created in 1965 (Xizang Province). Street names in Lhasa may be referred to by a Tibetan name (such as Dekyi Shar Lam) or a Chinese name (Beijing Road). There are ongoing battles between cartography departments in China and neighbouring countries. Chinese maps continue to show Tibet extending into Arunachal Pradesh. Indian customs officials scrutinise books for any maps with these inflated borders, and handstamp over them this message: 'Borders neither authentic nor correct'.

$ MONEY AND PRICING

Two forms of readily exchangeable money are **travellers' cheques** and **US cash**. It's wise to carry some of both. Credit cards are of limited use in China and Tibet, and are only usable at major hotels in Lhasa (Lhasa Hotel takes them). Cash advances on a credit card are possible in Lhasa at the Bank of China (BOC). Changing travellers' cheques or US cash is not a problem within Tibet or China. The whole idea is that you spend lots of money, otherwise Tibet wouldn't be open, so you can find Bank of China branches in Lhasa, Shigatse, Tsedang, Ali and other large Chinese towns. If not, major hotels can change travellers' cheques. The two most widely recognised travellers' cheques are American Express and Thomas Cook. Although cash and travellers' cheques in different currencies are accepted by the Bank of China, in places like hotels or on the street, US dollars are more easily negotiated. If you're short on cash US dollars, you can convert US travellers' cheques into US cash at Bank of China branches for a little over 1% commission (so a US$500 cheque would net you around US$494 in US cash). There's a very small black market in US dollars, so if banks are closed, you can always change in a shop or maybe at a hotel reception desk.

Chinese currency is renminbi yuan (Y or RMB, people's money): it comes in denominations of 1, 2, 5, 10, 20, 50 and 100 yuan paper bills, and small change in the form of 100 fen to the yuan. The older 10-yuan bill shows Tibet – well, the north face of Everest – and one variety of the 50-yuan bill shows the Potala. Exchange rates hover at around Y6.5 (renminbi) to the US dollar (with travellers' cheques, a small commission is deducted by the Bank of China; rates should be uniform across the country). The rate is slightly lower for cash. Other relevant exchange rates are: Nepal, about 78 rupees for US$1 (there's a black market in US cash, with higher rates for bigger bills); and Hong Kong SAR: HK$7.78 for US$1.

Within Asia, you can use ATM machines to access your home bank account using your usual bank card with a four-digit PIN number. ATM machines are common in Hong Kong, Bangkok and Singapore, and can also be found in Kathmandu and a number of large Chinese cities (look for Bank of China ATM machines). ATM machines are not common in Tibet, but are available in Lhasa and Shigatse, where BOC branches dispense cash. You can also find them in Kham, in places like Zhongdian and Litang.

DUAL-PRICING SYSTEM Pricing in this book is quoted in either US dollars (US$10 for example) or Chinese yuan (Y20 for example) – and sometimes in Hong Kong dollars (HK$40, for instance). Because pricing fluctuates and is often negotiable, variations may occur. Pricing is not a problem for restaurants and hotels in Tibet – you get used to the expected prices fairly quickly. Prices are negotiable because of the Chinese dual-pricing system (one country, two systems). The highest expenses in Tibet are for long-distance transportation – ie: flights to and from Lhasa – and the cost of hiring Landcruisers.

PAYING THROUGH THE NOSE If you are from Europe, Australia or North America and have a beak-like nose, you are known as *da bizi* (big-nose) by the Chinese, or *waiguoren* (outland person) or *yangguizi* (foreign devil – derogatory). This is a kind of separate ethnic group – in the Chinese system, Tibetans are barbarians, and foreigners are aliens. The bigger the nose, the more you pay through it. Although in theory there is no dual-pricing system in China, in practice you can pay two, three, ten or a hundred times more for certain services. When you buy a Y100 (US$15) ticket to go and see the Potala, you are paying at least ten times the going price that a Chinese or Tibetan person pays. Negotiating prices depends on what you look like, how desperate you look, and how long you're willing to argue. You can bargain for student price for some items (such as the Potala entry ticket, and even bus tickets), but this argument may only be accepted if you're a student in China, with valid ID. Chinese who live overseas (called overseas Chinese) are often charged a rate that is above the Chinese price, but lower than the Western price. Usually, the seller deduces they are overseas Chinese (or from Hong Kong) from their clothing or cameras. Westerners of Asian ethnic background who speak good Chinese can confuse Chinese sellers as they can't rank them in the pricing system.

BUDGETING

HOTELS AND GUESTHOUSES These can be easily sized up – they fall into budget/ low-end, mid-range or group-tour (high-end) categories. Low-end guesthouses charge US$3–8 per bed in two-bed, three-bed or larger rooms. Mid-range hotels charge US$15–50 for the room (whether occupied by one person, two or three). High-end (group tour) hotels charge US$50 and up per room – the tariff can go to US$200 and up for suites in Lhasa.

RESTAURANTS The cost of food is not really a big issue in Tibet, as food, if it is available, will be available at inexpensive teahouses or restaurants, costing around US$2–5 a head for a shared meal. Restaurants in deluxe Lhasa hotels could charge US$5–15 per dish. Occasionally, Chinese-run places might try to gouge Western customers by serving up something that looks like a banquet. Be wary of places that pile on extra dishes – ones that you never ordered – or lay on extras like face towels and bowls of peanuts, as these will appear on the bill.

PERMITS AND ENTRY FEES Entry fees for monasteries and tourist attractions (forts, palaces, etc) are usually US$3–7 per person, with the asking price for major monasteries hovering around US$7 (the Potala Palace charges US$15). Posted photo and video permission fees are high: US$23 for taking still photos at Tashilhunpo Monastery and US$275 for videoing. Permission and entry fees to get to Everest base camp chalk up a significant bill. Permit fees to visit certain parts of Tibet can be high, but usually one piece of paper is issued, so all names of passport

THE BRIGHT FUTURE OF TOURISM

When not busy imprisoning monks or forcing them to renounce the Dalai Lama, Chinese authorities are preoccupied with building Tibet's bright socialist future. On the horizon are plans for more and bigger cities, improved roads, and an expansion of tourist facilities. Among Chinese tourists, Tibet is seen as an exotic corner of the Chinese realm. Miss Tibet contests have been staged in Lhasa, and fashion magazine crews from Beijing have arrived to shoot models on location (we're talking about cameras here). So you see a picture of a Beijing model posing in semi-ethnic gear outside the Potala, or posing next to pilgrims outside the Jokhang.

What's next? Well, the Chinese haven't really yet begun to tap Tibet's tourist potential. There's a lot of scope for mountaineering, trekking, horseriding tours, mountain biking, rafting, kayaking and other adventure sports. In eastern Tibet lies Yarlung Tsangpo Grand Canyon – by far the deepest in the world, and barely touched by tourism. White-water rafting has been launched on the rivers of central Tibet, while the eastern region of Kham has hosted activities like cliff-jumping (paragliding). Less well advertised are hunting trips organised to parts of Qinghai Province whereby Western hunters are allowed (for large sums of money) to shoot rare wildlife such as Argali bighorn sheep as trophies. Car rallies and motorcycle rallies across the rooftop of the world have been staged. Also on the board are plans for the creation of tourist theme locations, such as a therapeutic hot-spring centre for health care, or a fisherman's island where tourists can learn about yak-hide boats (and cruise around in them).

Practical Information BUDGETING

2

75

holders can go on it to minimise costs. Alien Travel Permits (ATPs) cost only a dollar (for the group) but a military permit can be US$10 a person. Cultural Bureau permits for Zanda and Tsaparang can run to US$50 or so. The 'permission' to buy a plane ticket into Tibet can run to US$80 a person.

TIPPING Tipping is not customary in Tibet or China. There is no tipping in hotels, restaurants or taxis. Increasingly, however, those who are savvy in the tourist trade involving Westerners are looking for tips. You may want to tip the driver and guide at the end of a Landcruiser sortie. As with all tips, the amount offered should be contingent on doing a good job – and you should indicate this early into the trip as a way to leverage higher standards. Clothing (such as a down jacket) and equipment that is no longer needed would make good gifts. In Nepal, some trek operators work on a fixed amount, collecting in advance say US$3 a day from each client for the duration of a trek, then divvying up the pot at the end of the trip between the *sirdar* (leader), the cook and the porters. That removes the tipping guesswork headache for the trekkers, and puts it back in the hands of the agency.

TRANSPORTATION Bicycle hire is about US$5 a day in Lhasa. Taxis are a few dollars to get across town. Local long-distance buses are cheap, even if you pay double as a foreigner. Hiring a Toyota Landcruiser with driver and guide runs from US$120–230 a day, depending on the agency, the itinerary and other factors. This rate includes the driver, the guide, the vehicle and the fuel, but nothing else. The formula is based largely on kilometres covered on the trip (fuel consumption), terrain (wear and tear on vehicle), rest days, and so on. The guide fee of US$25–40 a day is included with the cost of the Landcruiser.

GETTING AROUND

All roads lead to Lhasa. Sooner or later, you will end up there. Getting around the towns in Tibet presents little problem: they are mostly small enough to walk around. Larger cities like Lhasa, Shigatse and Tsedang have public buses plying the streets, and fleets of Volkswagen taxis roving around (you can also hire these by the day or half-day). Another taxi-like option is using the motorised three-wheelers and foot-powered trishaws as transport. Renting a bicycle is another excellent way of getting around, if you can find one (easy in Lhasa). In Shigatse, you can take a walking-tractor – a tractor with handlebars controlling the engine up front, and a carriage at the back – across town for a small tariff.

PERMITS AND PREFECTURES Within Tibet you are classed as an alien, and you require an Alien Travel Permit (ATP). Various annoying pieces of paper with fancy chops (Chinese signature markers) and seals dog your movements into and around Tibet – this is not like mainland China where you can virtually travel without restriction. Apart from ATPs, other permits are issued: TTB, military, Foreign Affairs, Cultural Bureau permits. Foreigners are usually never shown these documents, nor allowed to keep them – they're classed as secret. The guide will keep the permits (you could try and get a photocopy). To get an overview of the complicated situation for permits, consult the map (opposite) showing prefectures of the TAR with area codes. The TAR is divided into seven prefectures, each with its prefectural capital or seat, and each with its own telephone area code. Permits are normally only issued in the prefectural capital, although permits for any destination can be issued in Lhasa through agents. Key destinations of interest are found in the following prefectures.

Lhasa Prefecture Includes the key monasteries of Tsurphu, Drigung and Ganden, as well as Namtso Lake.

Shigatse Prefecture Gyantse and Everest base camp both fall in Shigatse Prefecture, as does Sakya.

Shannan Prefecture The prefectural capital is Tsedang. Other areas covered include Gongkar Airport, Samye, Yambulagang and Samding Monastery.

Ngari Prefecture Ali is the prefectural capital. Key sites include Mount Kailash and the Guge Kingdom.

BY LANDCRUISER AND GUIDE The Chinese insist that the only way you (as a foreigner) can get around Tibet is in a hired Landcruiser (or similar vehicle, such as a Toyota van or Mitsubishi Pajero) with a driver and guide. This works out to about US$120–230 a day which, split between four paying passengers, is less damaging. Most of the operators are connected to Chinese channels – routes may be monopolised by TTB-connected Landcruisers.

Landcruisers are the greatest expense you'll incur in Tibet. Many of them operate on the Lhasa to Zhangmu run (to the Nepalese border). You can find them for hire in Zhangmu, and possibly in Shigatse (but don't count on it). Most Landcruisers make use of Lhasa as the home base. One peculiar phenomenon you will have to deal with in Tibet is called 'hitting the roof'. This is when the Landcruiser (which has no seatbelts) hits a rut and launches those in the back seat straight into the roof. It hurts! To soften the impact, think about wearing a wool hat or something similar. The idea of padded interiors has not caught on yet.

BY TAXI Taxis are intended to be a mode for getting around larger towns like Lhasa, Shigatse or Tsedang. However, they also commute from Gongkar Airport into Lhasa, a distance of around 75km, so think about this: they're much cheaper than Landcruisers. Taxis are viable if the road is paved and in good condition: you can also hire a taxi by the half-day or full day and use it as your touring vehicle, which makes sense if three or four travellers get together to share the rental.

ON YOUR OWN You need considerable stamina, perseverance and devious ingenuity to mount your own trips in Tibet and break away from the Landcruiser syndrome. In the pre-2008 days of Tibet travel, when permits were lax, travellers hitchhiked on trucks and took local buses, or proceeded on foot. Crazy dreamers have found ingenious ways of getting around inside Tibet. Back in the early days of independent travel in Tibet, in the 1980s, two Americans transported their kayaks up to Lake Manasarovar and started paddling the Yarlung Tsangpo – they made it part of the way. A young Englishman managed to bluff his way through the Zhangmu border with a motorcycle, and he was out by the Great Wall by the time the authorities caught up with him. Others have rented (or bought) yaks or donkeys to carry their gear, and headed off on long hikes, and have indulged in camping and horse racing combination forays.

If you have money coming out your ears, of course, you can arrange to realise any dream you want through official channels. All the paperwork and aggravation might take some of the joy out of it, though. I've met several trios of motorcyclists from Europe who've been all over Tibet and Xinjiang on their imported bikes. They would not, however, divulge the cost of the entourage of vehicles accompanying them (with national guide, local guide, translators, medic, etc). A high-end hotel in Lhasa quoted a price tag of Y12,000 for each motorcyclist on a five-day sortie to Everest base camp (based on three riders, with BMW 800cc motorcycle supplied).

KAYAKING AND RAFTING Consult the website www.windhorsetibet.com (click on 'River Journeys') for details about white-water rafting and kayaking in Tibet. This outfit handles everything from first-time rafters to first descents. Wind Horse Adventure also handles multi-day camping trips with horseriding, and adventure sports like mountaineering, customised for small groups. See also www.griffonexpeditions.com.

ACCOMMODATION

Except in larger towns like Lhasa and Shigatse, be prepared for very low standards of food and lodging. It's best to bring your own supplies as back-up: bring a Therm-a-Rest (ultra-light air mattress) and a good sleeping bag to soften the beds and to stay warm, and bring packets of soup, or whatever, to compensate for the lack of restaurants.

HOTELS AND GUESTHOUSES Low-end guesthouses, teahouse inns and truck-stop places generally offer a bed and not much else. These usually work out to US$2–5 a bed, in dormitory-type accommodation with perhaps four beds to a room. If there's a dirt floor, a lumpy bed and a tap in the yard, you've hit rock bottom. Bedbugs can be a problem in low-end hotels.

A notch up are Chinese concrete-blockhouse hotels, usually with several storeys, and possibly some internal plumbing. These places charge about US$10–25 for the room, no matter if your party is single, double or triple, so you can reduce costs by sharing. The more creature comforts you get, the higher the tariff. If you get your very own bathroom, with your own plumbing, rates are even higher. Because of shoddy workmanship, it often turns out that half of these gadgets fail to function, and yet you are paying for them being in the room. Some foreigners have successfully bargained down the price of a room due to absence of electricity to power devices like the television. In this range are hotels designed for visiting Chinese, some of which may be off-limits to Westerners.

At the high end are group-tour hotels, with rooms from US$30–80 and up (if you have three people sharing a room, this may still only be US$20 a bed). These definitely have plumbing – and even hot water – and rooms with real light bulbs, and possibly even television reception. Even so, the prices for the rooms are often inflated, and discounts are frequently offered to tour operators. The hotel lobby often features a dining hall, souvenir shop, bar and so on. It may even have a foreign exchange counter and a small business section able to handle faxes and IDD calls. Even if you don't stay in a high-end hotel, you can wander in and shop or use the services there: naturally, the tariff will be higher than normal. There are hotels of this standard in Lhasa, and several in Shigatse, Gyantse, Tsedang and Zhangmu. These high-end hotels may have cheap dormitories tucked away, so it's worth enquiring.

Plumbing notes Although mid-range hotels in places like Lhasa and Shigatse provide hot showers, and solar-heated showers are popping up in places like Sakya, in more remote regions this could be a rarity. Off the track, you may be dependent on hot water from the large Chinese Thermoses at hotels, which is boiled up by solar cookers on the rooftop or with a furnace. Hotels do not automatically provide Thermoses. You may have to ask – or wheedle or cajole – to get one. By using a bucket or washbasin, you can manage basic ablutions. The hot water Thermoses can also be used for making soup or tea, and if you let it cool overnight, the water can be carried in your own bottle as drinking water. Tibetan and Chinese toilets are of the bomb-bay door design (squat and hope). They're usually filthy. In high-end hotels, there are Western sit-down models. When Shigatse Hotel started operation, fancy imported plumbing was brought in. An overweight woman on a group tour sat on one of these brand-new pieces of porcelain and the sit-down unit broke away from its mooring. The woman was not injured, but she was furious – she threatened to sue the manager over the poorly installed equipment. The hotel manager promptly confiscated the passports for the group and said that they would not be returned unless he was compensated for the full value of the imported plumbing that had been destroyed. Confronted with this, the group-tour leader decided to pay up.

✗ EATING AND DRINKING

Tibet is not noted for its culinary arts. China, however, is – ergo, find a Chinese-run restaurant if you want more variety. There's lots of variety in Lhasa – Tibetan, Chinese, Indian, Nepalese and Western cuisines are all available. On the streets you can find fresh fruit and vegetables in abundance, and fresh bread and tangy yoghurt. You can even get good fresh cheese imported from Nepal. Yak cheese is excellent, but only when made with Swiss or Norwegian technology (as it is in Bhutan, Nepal and in parts of northern India). There are some small cheese-making concerns in Lhasa that employ European technology, but more commonly what you'll find on sale are small pieces of rock-hard yak cheese, strung together like a necklace. These are almost impossible to eat, and are treated like sweets by the nomads, who suck on the pieces all day.

Tibetans are more inclined to run teahouses with low carpeted tables, which serve tea and *momos* (meat dumplings) and perhaps the odd potato. They offer lots of atmosphere, but not a whole lot of food. Lhasa is fine for food and so is Shigatse, but once out in the countryside, it's pretty much just noodles. In the wilder areas, it's

On a bicycle you have the freedom to go at your own pace and enjoy unobstructed views of Tibet's spectacular scenery. It's easy to stop and meet people, admire the views, or grab that great photo opportunity. Maps and guidebooks, supplemented by recent internet postings, will help you plan the trip of your dreams. A search on the internet will turn up interesting travelogues of cycling in Tibet.

The rewards of cycling in Tibet come with challenges of sustained high-altitude travel, changeable weather, and toughest of all – permit uncertainties. In the past, the Chinese government's attitude towards foreign cyclists has ranged from very easy-going to intolerant. The whole region may close if major anti-government protests have taken place recently or are expected to take place. Don't let this worry you: Tibet has wonderfully adventurous cycling. Just have Plan B ready in case you don't get in or through. Tibetan areas outside the TAR are well worth visiting – you'll find the same culture and scenery without the permit restrictions in northwestern Yunnan, western Sichuan, southwestern Gansu and southern Qinghai provinces.

Several routes stand out for cyclists. The classic Lhasa to Kathmandu route runs through the heart of Tibet, passing famous monastery towns and fantastic Himalayan panoramas; a side road goes all the way to Everest base camp with an amazing view of the north side of the world's highest mountain. Nearing Nepal, you can experience a jaw-dropping 4,500m descent off the plateau from Tong La pass right down into subtropical valleys.

The ride across eastern Tibet between Yunnan or Sichuan provinces and Lhasa has ups and downs like no other place on earth, as you repeatedly descend into deep valleys of the Mekong, Yangtse and other great rivers, then climb high passes. Western Tibet is the toughest of all with vast distances, few places for supplies and long stretches of unpaved road. Only the most determined cyclists have pedalled all the way from Kashgar in China's extreme west via Mount Kailash and on to Lhasa. On longer hauls like this, you might want to consider a hybrid trip: cycle for part of the distance, then put the cycle on top of a vehicle for the remainder.

The Chinese have put great effort into improving the main roads in recent years, so cycling has become easier and less dusty. Food and accommodation have also improved with more places springing up. Camping and cooking gear are more a matter of personal choice than necessities on the main routes, though it's worth carrying a tent, pad and warm sleeping bag for emergencies, or if venturing into western Tibet or other remote lands. Cyclists have loaded up with as much as 50 days of supplies and disappeared into remote uninhabited regions to commune with the mountains.

The current mood of Chinese officials will affect what sort of trip you can do. If they are lenient you may be able to come and go as you please with just a regular Chinese visa. Border areas near India are very sensitive, and you can expect to be turned back if you get close. When officials follow strict regulations, your only option may be to go on a tour, which you can arrange through approved travel agencies. A tour will involve a guide, driver and vehicle as well as the permit. This is expensive, of course, but the more cyclists in your group the lower the cost per person. It might be possible to arrange a cycling guide without the costly car, so ask around to see if this is possible. If you're in a group and have the funds, it's worth thinking about arranging a tour even if not required for the added convenience of carrying gear and a safety back-up. It's possible to have a cook come along, so you can camp and relax at the end of the day and wait to be served dinner. If tours are required and you have a low budget, consider that northern Tibet is the cheapest trip followed by Lhasa–Kathmandu, eastern Tibet, and the very long haul across western Tibet.

If you enter Tibet from Nepal, your only option may be on a tour with a group visa; any Chinese visa that you had beforehand will be cancelled. Getting the group visa changed later on to an individual visa to travel onwards through China may not be possible. If you wish to travel extensively in both China and Tibet, your best bet will be to enter China first on an individual visa, then go to Tibet and on to Nepal. And, of course, never mention 'Tibet' or 'bicycle' on your visa application.

Your own bicycle will probably be the best bet if you are comfortable with it and have the panniers and touring gear already sorted out. The other option is to buy a bicycle in Lhasa, Chengdu, Kunming, Hong Kong, or other large city in China. American mountain bikes made in Shenzhen (such as Diamondbacks) are sold around China, but these may take time to track down as they are mainly for export. You can also find Taiwanese-made mountain bikes (such as Giant brand) even in Lhasa. Panniers and accessories are available, too. Costs for bicycles and accessories tend to be lower than in more developed countries, but don't count on the same standards that you may be accustomed to at home. Long-legged cyclists may find seatposts too short and frames too small. One tall European tried to use a local mountain bike in Lhasa with a handlebar for a seatpost, but the arrangement never worked well. Avoid the cheapie Chinese-made mountain bikes, as brakes may fail and pedals break off. For shorter trips in the Lhasa area, you can rent your steed (refer to the *Lhasa* chapter for details, page 121). Many young Chinese cyclists hit the road from Sichuan Province and ride on to Lhasa (or tackle sections of this route), and they often sell their mountain bikes in Lhasa, which explains the high-quality rentals available and why bicycle accessories are on sale here. The right accessories can be the hardest things to find – such as good bicycle water bottles. Cyclists revel in wearing a wristwatch that tells not only the time but the altitude – or having a handlebar cycle computer that does the same.

Opportunistic theft is a problem in the cities and something to be aware of in the countryside. Be sure to lock the bicycle and park it in an area where it looks like it's being watched. Bus and train stations are places where you need to be extra careful. At night you can usually take the bicycle into your guesthouse or hotel.

The Chinese tend to be very helpful with taking bicycles on flights or the train. Either way, it's best to box the bicycle; bicycle shops sell boxes and enterprising Chinese were selling bicycle boxes on the sidewalk in Lhasa across from the Kirey Hotel, so ask around. Chinese airlines usually charge for overweight, but not for oversize. Trains charge a fixed fee: weight and size are not usually a factor. Your bicycle may go on a different train from you and must be checked at a separate parcel office. This is best done a day or two ahead of time.

Cyclists are a peculiar breed: talk revolves around headwinds, gradients, water quality and, in Tibet, animals. There are two animals to watch out for: yaks and dogs. Yaks are not a problem – they will bolt at the approach of a bike (mistaking it for a rival species?) but may upset the yak herder when they thunder off. Dogs, on the other hand, may come straight for you, fangs bared. The best strategy here is to pick up a stone, or at least pretend to do so. Dogs know what stones can do, as most Tibetans are crack shots. For more about dealing with dogs and cycling logistics, see *Cycling Kham and Amdo* in *Chapter 8*, page 276.

In first-class and business class on Air China flights, the Tibetan brand of bottled water labelled 5100 is served. This slick piece of marketing relies on the Chinese perception that natural products from Tibet are somehow pure and magical. The source of 5100 is a spring at Damxung to the north of Lhasa. In 2009, the 5100 company produced almost two million gallons of bottled water, which was shipped out of Tibet by train, in a business estimated to be worth over US$100 million a year. The water collected would otherwise flow through wetlands where yaks and sheep graze. It is not known how the factory's siphoning of water has impacted the ecosystem.

Close to Tingri, in western Tibet, is a water-bottling factory that claims to bottle Everest (Qomolangma) meltwater from a glacial source. As Everest's north face is an iconic symbol for Tibet, it's not clear whether the source of this bottled water is right at Everest, or whether the company is using Everest as a branding device. Certainly there is a lot of competition for using the iconic Everest north face by other water bottling companies in Tibet. Tibet's groundwater and spring water was never tapped before 2005. Only since the completion of the Golmud–Lhasa railway in 2006 has it been economically feasible to export bottled water from Tibet, shipping it by rail as far afield as Shanghai or Beijing.

An unfortunate by-product of all this bottling of water in Tibet is littering of the landscape with empty plastic bottles. If you are riding in a Landcruiser to Everest, at least make sure your driver and guide do not add to the garbage tossed out the windows.

tsampa – or roasted barley flour – all the way. *Tsampa* is boring but quite sustaining, and you can mix it with soup or noodles (some connoisseurs add powdered milk or other substances to this Tibetan goulash). Not many travellers take to *tsampa*, though more take to army-ration biscuits. Chinese packaged goods are not much more appetising. Olive-green army cans with stewed mandarins or pork or something equally disgusting are re-sold on the black market. When travelling in Tibet, you should always bring along some food as a back-up, for the times when you're stuck. You can load up in Lhasa on packaged soup and so on. Some bring in freeze-dried food from the West.

Bottled mineral water is available in Lhasa, Shigatse and larger towns in Tibet, where brands include Tibet Magic Water and Potala Palace Mineral Water. Cheaper than bottled water is Chinese beer. Since beer goes through a fermenting process, it's safe to drink, but this is not advisable at altitude until you've acclimatised (beer should not be drunk if you have the runs, either). Available Chinese brands include Huanghe (Yellow River), Lhasa Beer, Snow Beer and Pabst Blue Ribbon.

SHOPPING

Facilities inside Tibet are poor compared with those in neighbouring regions. Most of the infrastructure, buying and selling are concentrated in Lhasa, so you can glean more about shopping from the *Lhasa* chapter, page 136, and the section on *Shigatse* in *Chapter 6*, page 203. You can ship purchases (even very heavy ones) out of Lhasa without problem through China Post, the main post office. Carpet companies in Lhasa will arrange the shipping for you direct from their showroom.

ENTERTAINMENT

Unless you like karaoke bars, or parlours showing ear-splitting kung-fu videos, nightlife is mostly limited to restaurants. There are some restaurant venues where Tibetan dance is staged (see *Lhasa* chapter, page 136). For the performing arts, the best bet is to time your trip with a festival, like the Yoghurt Festival in Lhasa or the horse-racing fair in Namtso.

PHOTOGRAPHY

Tibet is highly inspirational for photography, and you will find yourself clicking through lots of pictures. So when shooting **digital**, bring as many solid-state cards (CF or SD) as you can. This is due to potential problems at altitude: you could have a problem with a back-up device that uses a hard drive. Manufacturers are reluctant to mention this, but many devices that employ hard drives are not guaranteed to work above 3,000m, because they spin on a cushion of air – and the air pressure is different at altitude, leading to possible crashes. You might have absolutely no problem – or you might end up losing all your photos stored on a hard drive. The solution to this is to use solid-state or flash-based memory. There are laptops on the market that use solid-state drives (no moving parts). Apple's iPad uses flash memory. Digital pictures can be burned to DVD as a back-up at internet cafés in Lhasa. You can make prints from digital cameras at these places too, often within a few hours. Prints would make great gifts for Tibetan friends.

Film is sold in Lhasa, but the variety is limited and the quality is dubious: it's best to bring your entire supply in yourself (there is no limit to the amount of film that can be brought in). The light in outdoor situations in Tibet is so intense that you can make wonderful use of fine-grain slide film. You will probably want a polarising filter to reduce glare. Another situation commonly encountered is exactly the opposite: a dim interior where you need high-speed film, as flash may be forbidden.

Special photography hazards in Tibet include yak butter, fine dust and frozen batteries. In freezing conditions, remove batteries and keep them in a shirt pocket, worn on your body overnight (near your body is not close enough). Fine dust is a particular hazard for digital cameras in Tibet. Some manufacturers sell 'rugged' cameras which are supposed to be sealed against dust and moisture; other manufacturers claim to have an automatic dust removal system. Avoid changing lenses outdoors to prevent dust entering the camera. Even if you keep the same lens on the camera, dust can find its way down the barrel of the lens, leaving dust spots on the sensor. As for yak butter: there is a lot of the stuff in Tibetan temples, and it may find its way onto your lens. Oily stuff on the lens is not good news. For this reason, be wary of handing over your camera to pilgrims, who may stick a yak-butter fingerprint right on the lens.

To bring in professional video or motion-picture equipment, special clearance is required, meaning you probably won't get it without a ton of paperwork and grovelling. There is no restriction, however, on bringing hand-held **camcorders** and **amateur video equipment** – plenty of Chinese visitors to Tibet bring such gadgets. The equipment is not the problem, it's how and when you use it. A policeman might overlook it if you are in a closed or sensitive region, but making a record that can later be aired in public is a very different case. Taboo subjects include the Chinese military (especially on patrol in Lhasa, or on manoeuvres and at highway checkpoints) and strategic locations like bridges or the airport. Tibetans do not appreciate camera flashes in temples, nor photography of sky burial rituals (which is particularly sensitive). Some foreigners have had their film confiscated, and even their camera equipment. At a checkpoint on the Kathmandu–Lhasa road, a bored passenger stood aside and photographed a luggage search in progress. An army officer promptly seized his camera, and it was only after considerable argument that the camera was returned, minus the offending film.

⟩ MEDIA AND COMMUNICATIONS

China's one-party state controls all forms of media, making independent reporting impossible. All local news media are closely monitored. In Tibet, foreign news media are not permitted entry unless reporters are considered pro-China and will toe the party line. The TTB produces a glossy magazine on Tibet called *Tibet Tour* (printed in Shenzhen), but this is mostly in Chinese. Slick colour brochures on human rights and other 'hot topics' are distributed to major hotels in Chengdu and Lhasa.

PRINTED MATTER Anything printed outside China may be scrutinised (and seized) by Chinese customs and at Chinese road checkpoints – like this guidebook. However, non-political books like Gary McCue's *Trekking Tibet* have been spotted for sale at the Lhasa Hotel, along with *Tintin in Tibet* (which has been translated into 27 languages, including the Tibetan language itself). 'Printed matter' extends to messages on T-shirts: these have caused Westerners some trouble, although Tintin T-shirts are acceptable, and sold in Lhasa.

Photocopying A corollary to the above is that you may have to photocopy the relevant pages of books from other travellers. That's easy to do, as there are a number of places with good-quality photocopy machines in Lhasa. Outside of Lhasa, you might try high-end hotels, as they often have a business centre for guests with photocopy, fax and internet facilities.

RADIO Tibet Radio is the official Chinese station in Lhasa, which is about all you'd want to say about it. If you bring a shortwave radio, you can pick up the BBC *World Service* (the Dalai Lama's favourite programme – he's addicted) which broadcasts in English.

Voice of America (VOA) and Radio Free Asia (RFA) are operated by the US: both broadcast in Tibetan. RFA started in late 1996 and reaches Thailand, Indochina, Indonesia and China – it espouses a free press to authoritarian governments. Apart from a Mandarin segment, there's an RFA Tibetan Service. The Chinese don't seem to like either broadcast: in mid-1998, three RFA journalists who were due to accompany Clinton on his visit to China had their visas revoked. The head of the Tibet section in Washington is Ngapo Jigme, who is one of 12 sons and daughters of Tibet's greatest turncoat, Ngapo Ngawang Jigme (Ngapo Jigme defected in 1985 and works for the Free Tibet Campaign in Washington).

Because Tibet is at such high altitude, there's excellent reception. However, around Lhasa, authorities jam signals by broadcasting on the same frequencies.

Broadcasting in Tibetan is Voice of Tibet (VOT), a station run by Tibetan journalists stationed in India and other countries (the target area is Tibet and neighbouring countries: VOT cannot be heard outside this range, but can be picked up in RealAudio on the website www.vot.org).

TELEVISION Lhasa has two television broadcasting stations: Xizang TV, which is parked near the Potala, and Lhasa TV, to the eastern fringe of town. Other stations or transmitters are located in Shigatse, Tsedang and Gyantse. A couple of channels broadcast in Tibetan, others in Chinese – these programmes run the boring socialist gamut from pig farming in central China to ear-splitting Sichuan opera performances and revolutionary ballet performed by PLA soldiers. Beijing's CCTV (China Central TV) broadcasts on four or five channels, with CCTV-9 broadcasting mostly in English or with English subtitling on the programmes.

Because of the elevation, satellite television reception is excellent on the Tibetan plateau, but dishes must be licensed and are carefully monitored. In Lhasa, the mid-range and high-end hotels may be able to pick up VTV, a kind of Indian MTV. On larger satellite dishes – notably the one at Lhasa Hotel – is CNN. Of course, the average Tibetan gets nowhere near a satellite receiver, but occasionally things work for the better. In 1996, stunned Tibetan staff at a Lhasa hotel gathered to watch a broadcast of *Larry King Live* where one of the guests was the Dalai Lama.

Hong Kong-based StarTV programming may also be available on satellite, including the Star Movie Channel (English movies), Star Sports and a Chinese movie channel, but not BBC news. In 1994, Rupert Murdoch, chairman of the News Corporation (which owns StarTV), removed the BBC news from his satellite services to China to calm tense relations with Chinese officials who complained about a BBC profile of Mao Zedong and objected to coverage of Chinese dissidents. Although Murdoch has styled himself as a foe of totalitarianism and a champion of individual liberty and free speech, in the PRC's case he decided to brush all that under the carpet because he has extensive holdings in China and ambitious plans to expand them. In 1997, the BBC came under further fire from the PRC because it aired a programme on the disappearance of the 11th Panchen Lama.

More missing news: in October 2001, AOL Time Warner signed a deal with the Chinese government to expand its Mandarin-language cable channel China Entertainment Television (CETV) into Guangdong Province, southern China. AOL Time Warner acquired CETV from a Singapore entrepreneur who said his successful formula for reaching the Chinese market was 'no sex, no violence – and no news'. CETV shows dramas, game shows and situation comedies from Taiwan and Hong Kong. The no-news part sounds quite bizarre for a company best known for CNN. Meanwhile, Time Warner Cable has agreed to distribute Beijing's CCTV-9 in the US, and that station carries Chinese news.

STAYING IN TOUCH May your mail be opened, may your phone calls be monitored, may your text messages be scanned, may your email be scrambled. This is not an ancient curse – it's a reality in today's Tibet, policed by the paranoid Chinese. The mailing system in Tibet is quite efficient – letters can get from Lhasa to Europe or North America within a few weeks. Poste Restante exists at the main post office in Lhasa, or you can have letters mailed care of specific hotels (a better option).

Sending faxes is expensive, but still cheaper than repeating complex details over the phone (when you will still be charged even if you get an answering machine at the other end). Fax is often employed by travel agents within Tibet to make bookings at hotels where the staff never answer the phone.

Once out of Lhasa or Shigatse, communication becomes more difficult. If planning to send postcards, buy all the stamps in Lhasa, because you may only find small-value stamps in other places, and they will cover the entire postcard. Bring your own posting materials if out of Lhasa. Although places are remote, if there's an army base around, there are probably communication towers and satellite dishes to serve the military. That means IDD phones, sometime even in remote corners of Tibet.

Fax and phone If you bring your own mobile phone, you can purchase a SIM card in Lhasa from a China Mobile outlet. Due to odd territorial restrictions, it is probably better to buy this SIM in Lhasa rather than elsewhere, although a SIM card purchased in Chengdu works. Be aware that in addition to heavily filtering the internet and scanning email, Beijing has issued regulations to Chinese mobile phone companies requiring them to police and filter SMS text messages. This directive followed widespread text messaging in the winter of 2003 that exposed the government's cover-up of the SARS outbreak.

You can use IDD phones to call direct from Lhasa through major hotels or at the main post office. Most China-wide and international destinations can be reached direct. Pre-paid cards are much cheaper than hotel calls – around Y4 a minute for international calls (global reach) versus Y12–15 a minute for calls placed through a hotel system. There are two kinds of card: the IC yellow phonecard, and the IP hotel phonecard. The IC yellow phonecard can be purchased with values like Y50 or Y100. You will see yellow phones on the street; they can also be found in some hotel lobbies.

Phone area codes are designated by prefecture, which is very useful for figuring out whose jurisdiction you are in for permits. The area codes are Lhasa Prefecture 0891, Shigatse 0892, Shannan 0893, Nyingchi 0894, Chamdo 0895, Nagqu 0896 and Ali Prefecture 0897. If dialling from outside the country, drop the 0 in this prefix. Let's say the local seven-digit number in Lhasa is 633 3446. If you are in Lhasa, you would dial the number as is. If you are in Shigatse trying to reach Lhasa, you would dial 0891 633 3446. If you are in Canada, trying to reach Lhasa, you would dial 011 86 891 633 3446. The 011 sequence gets you out of Canada, 86 is country code for China, 891 is area code for Lhasa (you drop the 0 prefix from 0891 for this dial-up), followed by the local number. Lhasa phone numbers are seven digits, but mobile phones are usually 11 digits (with 1390 often being the first four). That means if you are trying to reach a mobile phone in Lhasa from outside the country, you would have to dial around 20 digits.

Other areas of Tibet may have erratic five-digit numbers – or no phones at all. Some other area codes for Chinese cities are Xining 0971, Zhongdian 0887, Kunming 0871 and Chengdu 028.

THE TWILIGHT ZONE

Feeling out of synch? Having trouble figuring out what time of day it is in Lhasa? You wouldn't be the only one. All China runs on Beijing time, due to the communist craze for centralised planning, although it should strictly have five or six time zones from east to west. Even though Lhasa is thousands of kilometres to the southwest of Beijing and should be on the same time zone as Nepal (which is 2¼ hours behind Beijing time), it runs on Beijing's clock. If you fly from Lhasa to Kathmandu, that means you actually arrive before you left! So everything is out of synch in Lhasa. Sunday is the non-working day; Saturday might be a half-day. From Monday to Saturday, Chinese business hours for banks and other offices are (in summer) 09.00 to 12.30, then *xiuxi* (siesta – some offices have beds in the back rooms), and then 15.00 to 18.30. When they say 09.00, it's actually more like 07.00 in real time. Tibetans run on Tibetan time, which is like stepping back a few centuries. It's timeless: get up when the sun comes up, and go home when the sun goes down. Beijing time is Greenwich Mean Time +8 hours, or Pacific Standard Time +16 hours.

Email and internet What the fax machine was to the dissidents of the 1980s ('seek truth from fax'), the anarchic internet is to those of the new era. Surfers in Beijing can be fined if caught using the wrong websites – the crime is 'splitting the motherland'. Cybercafés are located in most of the popular tourist sites and cities of China, and in other parts of Asia (Kathmandu, Hong Kong, Bangkok, Kuala Lumpur, etc).

The rules of engagement for use of the net in China are that many sites are 'sensitive'. However, you are not told which ones. It's possible that the laws that apply to locals do not apply to foreigners. If foreigners are used to looking at their favourite newspaper and suddenly find it blocked, they might get upset. The net is your lifeline for news and information: consult *Appendix 4*, page 334, for useful sites.

Email is monitored, though with the sheer volume of web-based mail, it is hard to fathom how this could possibly work. Proof of monitoring is that some foreigners have discovered their email accounts entirely shut down – because of recent email discussion about the Falun Gong. There is good email access in Lhasa, Shigatse and Gyantse, and some email access in key towns like Golmud or Nagqu. Elsewhere in Tibet, net access may be limited or non-existent.

Your email may go through unmonitored, or it may be monitored by keywords. Words like 'Dalai Lama', 'Tibet', 'Taiwan' and 'Tiananmen Square' are bound to raise a few red flags – probably ones with yellow stars on them. If you put all those into a single sentence and add the words 'freedom', 'independence' and 'democracy', don't be surprised if your Yahoo! account suddenly starts acting funny – and vanishes from the screen. To get around restrictions, some travellers have resorted to high-tech methods that leave no trace on computers used in cyber-cafés.

CULTURAL ETIQUETTE

Tibetans are a spontaneous lot – they have no trouble breaking the ice. They'll probably examine your camera, fondle your luggage or shake you down for Dalai Lama pictures. Or give you a big grin. Tibetans have a great sense of humour, they're self-reliant, amazingly hardy, and have none of the shyness or coolness that the Chinese bring to bear on foreigners. They are usually direct, open and honest in their dealings. Tibetan women have a fairly high status, although they still do heavier work than the men. Outside of Lhasa, few Tibetans speak English: those who do are likely to have been educated in India. Put a Tibetan phrasebook to good use: any attempt at speaking the language is greatly appreciated. There are other ways to communicate: gestures like thumbs-up work well, as does singing in any language. If you're patient enough, it's only a matter of time before you are invited in for tea – or something stronger. Any kind of pictures you have are a great way of communicating. That extends to picture books on Tibet – these are engrossing to your host.

Interactions with Tibetans are not always as pleasant. Unfortunately, for a lengthy period Tibet has been open mostly to group tours, which are in the habit of handing out pens and candy to Tibetan kids: these same urchins may expect similar gifts from you, and will get antsy if nothing is forthcoming. On a more serious note, when interacting with Tibetans, you have a responsibility. When it comes to an overheard political discussion, not a lot will happen to you, a foreigner – at worst, you'll be booted out of Tibet. For the Tibetan, however, it could mean interrogation and jail. An Italian tourist interviewed a monk on video about Tibetan independence, and then took the videotape to a Chinese Embassy back in Italy to protest the treatment of Tibetans. The monk in the video was traced and received a 14-year jail sentence. Avoid putting Tibetans at risk – if a Tibetan talks to you about something politically sensitive, make sure to keep your interaction private and guard their identity. There are Tibetan informants as well as Chinese ones. Common sense will serve you well in most situations, but keep in mind just how serious Chinese authorities are towards punishing Tibetans who speak their mind, or express their support for any notion of independence.

There are several online sources related to ethical travel in Tibet. A brief one is *Tibet: The Alternative Guide*, which is viewable online or can be downloaded as a PDF from www.freetibet.org. Another PDF guide worthy of your attention is a report on understanding the environmental challenges that Tibetans face: you can download SFT's Enviroreport from www.sftuk.org/campaign/environmentcampaign/.

The following section has been adapted from a set of ethical guidelines published by the International Campaign for Tibet. You can view or download their online guide, *Interpreting Tibet: A Political Guide to Traveling in Tibet*. For further up-to-date information and advice, contact the International Campaign for Tibet (*1825 Jefferson Pl NW, Washington, DC 20036, USA; www.savetibet.org*) or ICT Europe (*Keizergracht 302, 1016EX Amsterdam, Netherlands*).

RESPECTING CUSTOMS Tibetans are extremely religious people and appreciate foreigners respecting a few simple customs; always walk clockwise around Buddhist religious sites and within monasteries or nunneries. Take hats off, do not smoke and do not touch figures or use flash photography inside monasteries or nunneries unless it has been cleared with the monks or nuns. Do not jump queues of pilgrims within monasteries nor interrupt ceremonies. Try to be an unobtrusive visitor but feel free to show interest and ask questions. It is also important not to touch the heads or point your feet towards monks or nuns, and be careful with physical contact with them. Dress appropriately when going to any religious site – remember, it is a holy place.

Sky burial Do not encroach on Tibetan burial rituals (known as sky or celestial burials). This unique system of disposing of the remains of the dead is a sacred and private affair – it is not proper for visitors to Tibet to intrude into a family's last rites. Some Tibetans believe photographs can steal their soul. At any rate, taking pictures of people can be rude and intrusive. Put yourself in their place.

SUPPORT RELIGIOUS FREEDOM Entry fees at large monasteries will go to a committee controlled by the Chinese Communist Party, and will not necessarily be used for religious purposes. Donations left on altars may benefit monks and nuns, or donations can be made directly to individual monks and nuns, or given in kind. Clothing, food, film or books are much appreciated, but don't give your dirty cast-offs. Donations to smaller, out-of-the-way monasteries will be used properly, according to traditional Tibetan custom, since they are not as tightly regulated by Chinese authorities. Items such as candles, prayer-flags, a bag of *tsampa* or some tea are always appreciated at remote monasteries. A wonderful way to spend some time with monastic people is to share your food. Walk the Barkor at sunrise with the Tibetans. It's a peaceful experience and allows you to be with the Tibetan people in a way that shows your support for their religious freedom.

BUY FROM TIBETANS If you want to support the Tibetan people, culture and economy, buy from Tibetan shops and stalls. A large influx of Chinese immigrants in Lhasa and other Tibetan cities is now taking over the economy and putting Tibetans out of work. The Dalai Lama has called this influx possibly the greatest threat to the survival of Tibetan culture. This general rule also applies to

Tibetan restaurants and tea stalls. Eat Tibetan food rather than Chinese imported foodstuffs. Inflation is also a very real problem in Tibet. You contribute to this by paying exorbitant prices to vendors, which can increase prices Tibetans must pay for goods. Don't be cheap, on the other hand. If you find a piece of finely woven cloth or a carving you like, pay a fair price for the amount of work entailed. Bargaining is a part of Tibetan life – unfortunately, being ripped off by tourists is also becoming a part of their life.

DO NOT BUY ANTIQUES Most of Tibet's artistic treasures have already been destroyed or plundered by Chinese troops. Please leave antiques in Tibet. This goes for all family heirlooms as well as religious items. Since it is difficult to tell what is antique and what is not, a good rule of thumb to follow is that if someone tries to sell you something secretly, don't buy it. Stick to public stores and stalls. Families are often forced to sell their treasured items to put food on the table. Be creative and find other ways of helping Tibetans without taking away their culture.

ECOTOURISM Help protect Tibet's wildlife – do not buy products made from wild animals, especially from endangered species (ie: skins of the snow leopard and tiger, horns of Tibetan antelope, paws of the Himalayan brown bear, or any medicinal products made from animals). If you see these items, take photographs and notify the World Wide Fund for Nature (WWF) or the International Campaign for Tibet. This holds true for cities in Tibet, as well as Nepal, China, Hong Kong or anywhere else you come across them.

Leave only footprints The Himalayan ecosystem is a fragile one. If you go trekking use kerosene, even where wood is available. Trash should be buried 30m (100ft) from a water source, paper burned, and cans and bottles packed up and taken to a hotel or large town. Do not leave this up to your guide as environmental awareness is often low, especially among the Chinese. Plan ahead and bring food that has little packaging. Bring your own water bottle that can be filled up from vacuum flasks, as the quantity of discarded plastic mineral water bottles is frightening enough. Travel light and don't demand five-course meals. Bring your own food as villages rarely have surplus. If you want to bring presents for locals along the way, think carefully. Don't bring plastic baubles or contribute to begging by handing out a lot of freebies. It is much more appropriate to share time and a cup of tea with people, or play a game of jacks with the children. Tibet is becoming littered with human waste and toilet paper, so bury excrement and burn toilet paper. Be careful where you hike as erosion and damage to fragile plants are increasingly becoming a threat to the environmental health of the plateau and mountains.

INTERACTING Try to use knowledgeable Tibetan guides. All travel companies must work through a travel operator in Lhasa. It is important to select a company that works with a Lhasa-based operator, run and staffed by Tibetans as opposed to Chinese. To quote one experienced guide, 'When you go to France, you don't want a German tour guide; when you go to Tibet you don't want a Chinese one.' Moreover, using Tibetan-staffed companies promotes Tibetan culture and employs Tibetans. Check and see if one of the Tibetan-run agencies is operating at the time of your visit to Tibet.

If you are on a tour with an official Chinese government guide, do not expect accurate answers to historical, religious or political questions. Educate yourself before you leave. Read books about the history of Tibet and its people. John Avedon's *In Exile from the Land of Snows* is a classic and the Dalai Lama's autobiography

2

Freedom in Exile is very informative (see *Further information*, page 331). Reading some Chinese propaganda before you leave may help you to recognise false statements encountered in Tibet.

Breaking away Almost everyone who visits Tibet says that the best part was their interaction with Tibetans. In small groups, wander the streets, follow the hillside paths or get outside of the town and visit a village. Revisit a monastery without the group or spend time at a tea stall in the market. Photographs of your family and neighbourhood or Tibetan communities and celebrations abroad are great conversation pieces – don't worry about the language barrier. Tibetans would much rather have you attempt their own language rather than speak Chinese. Be mindful of approaching Tibetans in front of Chinese, particularly soldiers. Depending on current Chinese restrictions, Tibetans can be openly criticised or interrogated for associations with foreigners. Always be careful around dogs; they are numerous in most parts of Tibet and are trained to protect their territory.

Being critical Don't be frightened by dire warnings that the Chinese will lock you in jail and throw away the key for your support of the Tibetans. You should, however, be careful, and never endanger the Tibetans. Let the Chinese know when you disapprove of actions such as the use of monasteries for grain storage, the malevolence shown by police in and around religious sites, and unfair hiring and school enrolment practices. You can do a lot for the Tibetans and their cause, and will most probably want to after you come to know these wonderful people.

DEALING WITH OFFICIALDOM

There are a lot of unwritten laws in Tibet. You will probably be told you cannot ride a bicycle in Lhasa (not true) and that you cannot go into the Jokhang by yourself (not true). Or that your camera or film will be confiscated if you take pictures of Chinese military at checkpoints (a good chance this could happen). There are rare

DALAI LAMA PICTURES

Since 1996 the trade in Dalai Lama pictures has been banned, and there have been several incidents of tourists being detained, interrogated and searched after they were seen giving pictures to Tibetans. Of course, the gifts most appreciated by Tibetans are photographs and postcards of the Dalai Lama and books by or about him. However, if a Chinese guide or the police see you giving them to a Tibetan, both of you could get into serious trouble. Possession of Dalai Lama images, audio tapes and video has resulted in stiff jail sentences for Tibetans.

There's nothing to stop you talking about the Dalai Lama, however – if you have seen the Dalai Lama on television or have read a newspaper story about him, tell the Tibetans about it and assure them of his good health. Tibetans like to have a Dalai Lama picture to place on their home altar if they can (under current conditions in Kham, east Tibet, images of the Dalai Lama are permitted for display). However, that's not the only picture they put there. They'd be quite happy to place a picture of the Potala Palace or the Jokhang Temple or sacred Mount Kailash there as well. Pilgrims would be very happy to receive these pictures, and they're all street legal.

occasions when rules are written down. The following Public Security Bureau (PSB) notice appeared on the walls of budget hotels in Lhasa sometime back. Curiously, there is no mention of 'Tibet' or 'Tibetans' – the latter are referred to either as 'Chinese citizens' or 'Minority Nationality'.

NOTICE: Ladies and Gentlemen: Welcome to Lhasa. So you may have safe and enjoyable travels, we would like you to be aware of the following government regulations.

1 Foreigners travelling to China must abide by Chinese law and must not endanger the national security of China, harm its public interests, disturb the public order, or engage in any other activities incompatible with tourist status.

2 If Chinese citizens are holding a rally or demonstration, it is strictly forbidden for foreigners to participate, follow along with, take pictures, or video film any of these activities. Foreigners are not permitted to interfere in Chinese internal affairs.

3 Foreigners are forbidden to distribute any propaganda material and join in any religious activity.

4 In accordance with regulations, foreign tourists must go through all registration formality and stay only at a designated hotel. Without prior permission, it is forbidden to travel in unopened areas, to operate individual business or privately take up an occupation.

5 It is forbidden to visit or photo the sky burial site according to the local government's regulations for the minority nationality's habits and customs. The tourist who breaks this regulation will be punished strictly.

BEING WATCHED Without being too paranoid about things, you should be aware that if you appear to be any kind of activist or have any connections to the Tibetan government-in-exile, your actions may be watched. You may be followed, your interaction with Tibetans noted, and your room may even be bugged. Sounds unreal? It has happened. In one case, in Beijing, a person speaking on the phone in French was asked by a Chinese wire-tapper to switch to English because he couldn't follow the conversation! In Lhasa, in 1996, a traveller wrote a political comment about Tibet in a book (for complaints) at the counter of the Bank of China. The PSB promptly tracked him down, exacted a confession, cancelled his visa and gave him an exit visa – meaning he had three days to fly out of Lhasa, back to Kathmandu. The Chinese are not good sports when it comes to criticism.

ENCOUNTERS WITH THE PSB There's no particular reason to be worried when dealing with police, army or other officials. If you are formally arrested, your embassy must usually be notified within four days. You have the right to speak to a consular officer and can demand that a call be placed to your embassy. Incidents involving foreigners in Tibet have ranged from warnings to hotel interrogations, to confinement to a hotel for four days (Dalai Lama tapes found in baggage in Shigatse after police were tipped off), to deportation. Three tourists watching demonstrations in Lhasa in 1994 had their passports confiscated. There have also been reports of Westerners being given a mild dusting-up – kicked or punched – when dealing with security officials.

China is the only country in the world to enshrine in law the concept of a 'web political criminal'. In 2000, the State Council barred nine types of content from websites, bulletin boards and chat rooms – including anything that might 'harm the state' or 'disturb social order'. Other countries have jailed bloggers for criticising the government, but no country has gone after cyber-dissidents with as much zeal as China. In April 2005, 11 years after its initial connection to the World Wide Web, China launched the US$800 million Golden Shield Project – an automatic digital system of policing the internet, in effect denying Chinese people the right to free information. The Golden Shield's objective is to monitor every thought and action of those Chinese people who use the internet. Internet 'gateways' in China mainly monitor and filter political information. Technical functions include blocking foreign websites, filtering content and key words on web pages, monitoring email and internet cafés, hijacking PCs, sending out viruses, and enabling connections between Chinese policing systems. There is a lot to keep the Golden Shield busy. China is terrified of social media networks after watching events unfold in the revolutionary 'Arab Spring' of 2011. Facebook, YouTube and Twitter are routinely blocked. In 2010 alone, it is estimated that 1.3 million websites were shut down within China.

The development of this technology has only been possible through the software, guidance and input of Western companies. Among those deeply involved are Yahoo, Microsoft, Nortel, Cisco and Sun Microsystems – and Google. Well, Google was involved, until it ran into problems with officials in Beijing. Google started out in China by omitting banned websites from its search results in China, completely blocking the BBC, for instance (the Chinese can neither watch nor read Chinese-language BBC broadcasts on the web, though the English versions may come through). Comically, in its effort to bend over backwards to please China, Google infuriated others: the Taiwanese foreign ministry discovered that the mapping software Google Earth called Taiwan 'a province of China'. When Google found out that its servers had been hacked from within China in an attempt to access information about Chinese dissidents, the company decided to pull out of Beijing and move its base to Hong Kong.

China's first web criminal, Lin Haiyin, was imprisoned for subversive actions in 2000. Since then, over a hundred cyber-dissidents have been caught in the 'web'. In September 2005, Zheng Yichun was sentenced to seven years for posting an essay to an overseas Chinese-language website, voicing the opinion that China's one-party system is 'the root of all evil'. He posted the essay to dajiyuan.com, which is popular with Chinese intellectuals overseas – and blacklisted in China, which means that nobody in China can access it anyway. In April 2005, journalist Shi Tao was imprisoned for ten years for the crime of 'revealing state secrets'. Shi Tao posted to a US website a list of topics that Chinese newspapers are forbidden to cover, including the anniversary of the 1989 Tiananmen massacre. The Paris-based organisation Reporters Without Borders claimed that Yahoo's Hong Kong unit helped Chinese authorities to link Shi Tao to a US-based website, which led to his conviction. In response, Yahoo officials said they had no choice but to abide by the 'laws, regulations and customs' of the country where it does business. Reporters Without Borders accused Yahoo of helping Chinese authorities in at least two other conviction cases. In May 2011, members of the Falun Gong in America filed a lawsuit in California against Cisco, claiming that the company helped China customise its Golden Shield Project to trace dissidents in China – in particular, Falun Gong members.

Powerful corporations like Yahoo and Microsoft are kowtowing to a sign over the gateway to the Middle Kingdom that reads: 'Abandon company ethics, all ye who enter here'. Microsoft has aided Chinese censors in removing words like 'freedom', 'democracy', 'human rights', 'Tibet', and 'Dalai Lama' from the net in China, and with software packages that prevent bloggers and others from using these and other politically sensitive words on their websites. This censorship, it appears, extends to Microsoft software such as the Chinese version of Encarta. And while Bill Gates toadies up to Chinese leaders, praising them for their 'brand new form of capitalism', there's an inherent conflict of interest with Western values – the values of democracy and freedom, privacy and integrity.

Canadian communications giant Nortel has worked for a number of years with the Chinese government to develop surveillance technology for use on Chinese citizens. This would seem to be at rather large odds with Nortel's privacy statement for the internet, which swears it will not sell, rent or share personal data with any other organisation or third party. The company's blurb on ethical business practices cites integrity as its cornerstone: 'We strive to do the right thing for individuals, organisations and society in general.' And yet Nortel is supplying a digital communications network for the Golmud–Lhasa railway line, which the Dalai Lama has denounced as a major part of China's plans for 'cultural genocide' in Tibet.

In November 2005, a group of social investment funds from Western countries called for internet firms to refrain from supporting repressive human rights practices in China and other nations. The group of 25 investment funds (based in the US, Canada, Switzerland and Australia) sent out a letter to firms ranging from Yahoo to Cisco warning of the risks involved in 'collaborating to suppress freedom of opinion and expression'. The investment fund group sending the letter included Ethical Funds of Canada, Fondation Ethos of Switzerland and Conscious Investors of Australia. They maintain that companies can – and should – retain integrity while doing business.

Are powerful companies responsible – and accountable – for ethical abuses? When it comes to cases of pollution, like accidental oil spills, definitely yes – there are laws in place, and severe penalties for offenders in many nations. In the case of internet filtering and surveillance, in early 2006 the US Congress began to address concerns that US-based internet companies are assisting the Chinese government in silencing dissidents. Under consideration is legislation for a Global Online Freedom Act to ensure global access to information on the net. But when it comes to the question of assisting genocidal regimes, it seems that governments are willing to turn a blind eye. Consider the case of New York-based IBM, conducting highly profitable business with Nazi Germany in the 1930s. There were no computers then, but there was a precursor: the IBM punch-card machine. In co-operation with Nazi authorities, IBM, working through European subsidiaries, customised punch-card machines for the sole purpose of persecuting the Jews. After World War II finished, IBM rushed to destroy evidence of its links to Nazi Germany, managed to evade any hint of responsibility for wartime reparations, and evaded any accusation of complicity in war crimes – in genocide, in fact. Investigative journalist Edwin Black details what IBM did in his remarkable book *IBM and the Holocaust*, published in 2001 (the book is supported by a website: www.ibmandtheholocaust.com).

Engaged Buddhism refers to Buddhists who are seeking ways to practically apply insights from their meditation practice and spiritual teachings to social, political, environmental and economic suffering and injustice. While the roots of Engaged Buddhism may be found in the teachings and actions of the Buddha himself, and other great teachers of the past, Engaged Buddhism can also be understood principally as a movement that began in the late 19th century as a response to Western colonialism in Asia. It is best known through its political movements, such as the struggles by the Tibetan, Burmese and Vietnamese Buddhists for self-determination, democracy and peace.

Engaged Buddhism is not simply being a Buddhist and involved in politics and social justice. Rather, Engaged Buddhists critically and creatively apply the Buddha's teachings to transform themselves and their societies. Thich Nhat Hanh of Vietnam, Ajan Maha Ghosanand of Cambodia, The Dalai Lama of Tibet, Aung San Suu Kyi of Burma, and Ajan Sulak Sivaraksa of Thailand are modern-day leaders who embody Engaged Buddhist principles and have guided organisations such as the Buddhist Peace Fellowship, the International Network of Engaged Buddhist, and the Zen Peacemakers.

When I first went to Tibet in the late 1990s, I was on a pilgrimage and did not intend to involve myself with politics in general, or practise Engaged Buddhism. The roadmap for my pilgrimage was the far-ranging travels across Tibet by a 19th-century mystic known as Tertön Sogyal. I meditated among hermits in remote sanctuaries and slept in caves where Tertön Sogyal had experienced spiritual visions. On foot, on horseback and in dilapidated buses, I crossed the same snow-covered passes that he had used to travel from eastern Tibet to Lhasa. I was searching out the living masters and yogis who uphold Tertön Sogyal's spiritual lineage and could tell me the oral history of his life and teachings.

But my pilgrimage took an unexpected turn. The more time I spent in Tibet delving into the 19th-century teachings of Tertön Sogyal, the more often I met Tibetans who wanted to tell me their stories of present-day frustration and suffering in what they see as Chinese occupation of their country. And the Tibetans spoke of their never-ending hope that one day the exiled Dalai Lama would return to Tibet. Travelling as a Buddhist pilgrim, I gained the trust of Tibetans. Political prisoners who had experienced abuse and torture in Chinese prisons showed me scars. Monks and nuns who had been kicked out of their monasteries gave me their expulsion notices from the local security bureau. I was taken to meet a Buddhist leader who had been scalded with boiling water and then jailed for five years for publicly praying to the Dalai Lama.

Tibetans not only told me their stories, but early into my pilgrimage they asked me to spirit such first-hand accounts of human rights abuses out of Tibet and into

In the Chinese system, if you are arrested, you are automatically guilty of something. Do not assume that innocence in a Western situation would mean you're in the clear in China. Chinese logic is different. Cast aside any notions of justice, put aside ideas of politeness and gentility and respect. There is no innocent here: you're either guilty and you admit it – and you'll get off lightly – or you're guilty and you deny it, in which case you'll be heavily fined, deported at your expense or otherwise punished. The arresting person would lose face if you were entirely innocent. You must leave a way out for the arresting officer – the usual method is making a written the hands of Western governments and advocacy groups. I became a courier of often graphic accounts of torture and abuse. This required evading China's vast security network of plainclothes security agents, undercover cops in monks' robes, and sophisticated cyber police. I began photographing Chinese secret prisons where Tibetan monks and nuns are incarcerated for their Buddhist beliefs. The decade-long journey in Tertön Sogyal's footsteps became a different kind of pilgrimage – one that became the dual narrative of the book *In the Shadow of the Buddha: Secret Journey, Sacred Histories, and Spiritual Discovery in Tibet.*

While I do not claim to have benefited anyone from my human rights work, I can say that I have tried to apply what the Buddha and my teachers have taught me about acting for the benefit of others. This is how I entered the path of Engaged Buddhism. I have given voice to what I have witnessed. I know in politics, ultimately, there are no winners, for every politician will die and every government will eventually fall – the real question is not if a political system will survive, but when will it fail. Because everything is impermanent, including politicians and their governments, we have a responsibility to effect change that will bring about the conditions *right now* for others to find contentment and happiness. For me this is Engaged Buddhism.

Like many others who have been profoundly affected by Tibet's unique wisdom culture, I cannot let the world forget about Tibet. China wants governments and people around the world to forget about Tibet, to turn their backs on monks, nuns, musicians and bloggers who languish in prison for their religious beliefs and their peaceful expression of political views. It is the responsibility of those who have the freedom to travel, to write and express our opinions, to talk to our governments – and to not only bear witness but act to change injustice. This is why I documented China's human rights abuses in Tibet and why I wrote *In the Shadow of the Buddha*. I do not expect everyone to take up the Tibet issue. That is not my reason for writing. Rather, it is my hope that wherever we find ourselves in the world, we never lose hope and faith and a sense of responsibility to those who are suffering in our family, in our community or in other countries.

I believe progressing on our spiritual path means doing what each of us needs to do for ourselves to bring about true and lasting contentment, beyond suffering. And accomplishing the path of social engagement means creating the conditions for others to find that same lasting satisfaction. These are the commitments I've learned from my venerable teachers, and ones that I continue to take with me.

Matteo Pistono is the author of In the Shadow of the Buddha *(for more details, see www.matteopistono.com). He is founder of Nekorpa (www.nekorpa.org), a foundation working to protect sacred pilgrimage sites around the world.*

confession. There is nothing binding about these confessions – they're not legal documents. You can promise to the hilt on a confession, and then go out and break those promises the next day.

Under no circumstances should you let someone else write that confession for you (especially in Chinese!) to be signed. Insist that you write it yourself. Irksome though confessions may sound, they are really meaningless pieces of paper. Phrases that please are 'my ancestors would be ashamed of me', or 'I will never even think of doing this again'. In the early days of Tibet travel, a British backpacker was busy writing his confession about being in a closed area when the arresting officer noticed that he'd extended his own visa – the highest level of naughtiness conceivable. Unperturbed, the traveller continued writing his confession: 'In addition to the above, I must humbly confess that I have extended my own visa, for which …'

Close encounters are usually of the PSB kind, ie: over travel permits. As long as your papers are in order, there's nothing to worry about: if you get off the track,

THE GIFT OF SIGHT   *Brian Harris*

There are estimated to be 45 million blind people worldwide: 90% of these people live in non-affluent countries. Remarkably, 80% of this blindness is either preventable or curable.

In the Tibet Autonomous Region alone, there are probably over 30,000 blind people. In the Tibetan-populated regions of neighbouring provinces, there could be a further 30,000 blind people. That makes a total of perhaps 60,000 blind Tibetans. With cataract surgery, over half of these people could see again. The main cause of cataract blindness is simply the ageing process; however, in Tibet the incidence is believed to be increased due to poor nutrition and to a greater exposure to ultraviolet light. At 4,500m there is less atmosphere to filter out its harmful effects.

The Seva Foundation in the US and its sister organisation Seva Canada are among the few NGOs working in Tibet to address the problem of reversible blindness. Seva has worked with the Tibet Development Fund, centred in Lhasa, for over seven years to help Tibetans develop eye-care services in each of the main hospitals in Tibet, by building a regional eye-care programme to reduce this immense backlog of cataract surgeries.

Although more than 40 doctors work in various eye clinics in Tibet, few have medical degrees and none are fully qualified ophthalmologists. Eye-care services in the region are very limited; the eye doctors are poorly trained, equipment is inadequate and outdated, and complication rates have been very high. Seva's Tibetan Sight Programme attempts to address these urgent needs. Seva has developed training programmes for surgical teams from each of the 12 principal hospitals in Tibet, to teach staff safe cataract surgery techniques and other eye-care skills. Seva has also supported eye camps in Tibet, providing up to 500 cataract surgeries each to supplement the limited eye-care services available. Now, the Tibetan doctors Seva has trained are conducting their own eye camps each year.

When Seva first started working in Tibet a decade ago, one of its first major goals was to find and train local medical doctors in modern cataract surgery. Among the early trainees was a team of doctors from Menzikhang, the hospital of traditional Tibetan medicine in Lhasa. Actually, Seva did not plan to work within the traditional medical model, but the Menzikhang had the space to conduct eye camps and its traditional doctors were very keen to learn modern ophthalmology. Tibetan medicine is a complex system of medical practice, inseparable from its spiritual foundation in Tibetan Buddhism. The Tibetan medical tradition has historically included a form of surgical treatment for cataract. Thus Seva was not challenging any major conceptual assumptions of Tibetan medicine. Several years later Seva also learned that Tibetan medicine includes the recognition of different eye diseases and several treatments for these conditions.

Now, after years of training and participating in many co-operative eye camps, there is an effective local cataract surgery team. But despite having excellent the legality of your travels is sometimes at the whim of the particular PSB official you are dealing with, at which point a small 'fine' may be levied, going directly into his pocket. These fines are negotiable: if he asks for US$100, wait until it drops to US$20 or US$10. Packets of foreign-brand cigarettes go down well with the Beijing Boys. Sometimes the crime is just too 'serious' and the PSB won't back off. Two Germans who were caught collecting high-altitude bug specimens were fined

surgical techniques, these doctors don't understand many of the basic tenets of Western medical ophthalmology. There are inherent dilemmas and very practical risks that arise when modern ophthalmology is incorporated into traditional medical practices without this new way of medical thinking to act as a bridge. Providing this theoretical bridge without undermining the very important traditional medical system is one of the many challenges Seva encounters in Tibet.

Another instructive example of the conundrums created by modern ophthalmology's meeting with traditional belief is when an elderly Tibetan refuses to have this free, 15-minute, sight-restoring cataract surgery because their blindness is understood to be his or her karma or spiritual destiny. It is very important to respect such deeply held religious belief.

Seva continues to work with Menzikhang because they are clearly committed to serving the poorest people in Tibet and this hospital is the most trusted by the local people. In order to develop a comprehensive blindness prevention programme, Seva is still exploring the best way to add preventative care and medical treatments for other diseases to its existing programme of cataract surgery.

Seva does seek skilled volunteers for Tibet. Ophthalmologists, optometrists and ophthalmic assistants who can make a long-term commitment are especially welcome. Non-clinical volunteers including computer and health education specialists are also sought.

The rewards? Here's what ophthalmic surgeon Dr Pratt-Johnson says of his volunteer work in Nepal, India and Bangladesh:

You soon get the feeling that you are doing so little and yet it means so incredibly much to our partners and particularly to the patients, who express their overwhelming gratitude in a mixture of gestures, tears and happy smiles. You try and wish you could do more. You return with an afterglow that warms your heart and soul. This psychologically resets the equilibrium of one's life, fulfilment and joy. We ophthalmic surgeons need to be conscious of having skills that place us in a privileged position, coming close to performing miracles – restoring sight to the blind. Share it with as many as you can. Giving through volunteering is such an adventure and a lot of fun.

For more information about Seva's work in Tibet and other parts of the world you can contact the following offices in the US and Canada:

Seva Foundation   1786 Fifth St, Berkeley, CA 94710; 510 845 7382; 510 845 7410; admin@seva.org; www.seva.org
Seva Canada   Suite 100-2000 West 12th Av, Vancouver, BC, V6J 2G2; 604 713 6622; 604 733 4292; service@seva.ca; www.seva.ca

2

over US$300 by PSB for their illicit activities. PSB officers have amusing English-language phrasebooks for dealing with foreigners in situations like this ('Please sign your interrogation' – things like that). The military – mostly teenaged recruits – do not seem particularly concerned about foreigners, except at checkpoints.

TRAVELLING POSITIVELY

For many living in the Himalaya, life is far from paradise. How is your karma-meter? Gold, silver or bronze? Giving doesn't have to mean money. It could mean lending your expertise in education, medical care, or assistance with computer operations. Here are some opportunities for working with Tibetans, both in Tibet and in exile.

rokpauk.org British-based worldwide charity Rokpa was founded in 1980, with projects in Tibet & Nepal from eye-care to education.
tibetanliberation.org/volunteer.html The San Diego Friends of Tibet website gives good ideas on voluntourism, including requests for doctors, nurses & physiotherapists, & teaching English to new arrivals from Tibet.

tibetanvillageproject.org Go on a trip & help at the same time, with projects in villages in the Kham region. Click on the Ecotourism tab.
tras.ca The Trans-Himalayan Aid Society, established in 1962, has projects in Tibet, Nepal & northern India to assist in building schools & medical centres. The NGO depends on volunteers.
volunteertibet.org Has current postings for volunteer opportunities working with Tibetan refugees in Dharamsala & other parts of India.

3

Health and Safety

in consultation with Dr Felicity Nicholson

The material in this chapter is not intended to scare you away from visiting Tibet. Rather, it is intended to make you aware of the dangers involved if you happen to get really sick, to encourage you to travel with at least one friend as a back-up in case things go wrong, and to urge you to obtain comprehensive evacuation insurance before setting off.

The following medical issues may venture into uncharted territory, especially concerning **altitude sickness**. It offers a broad outline and does not cover matters in great detail. Draw your own conclusions – and then consult other sources and experts for more thorough answers. Information on altitude sickness is hard to come by because it's not a common problem in the West. There are some books on the subject, but these tend to get out of date as knowledge evolves. For general health concerns, the Center for Disease Control and Prevention, based in Atlanta, Georgia, maintains a website (*www.cdc.gov/travel*) with the latest information on prevention guidelines and strategies. See also the shortlist of websites in *Appendix 4* under 'Health', page 335.

BEFORE YOU GO

Some important facts to know before you go: Tibetan and Chinese hygiene standards are very poor, and Chinese medical facilities within Tibet are extremely limited. Some conclusions to draw: you may have to be your own doctor in Tibet, you have to be willing to help fellow travellers in dire situations, and you have to be prepared to evacuate if the need arises.

Prior to departure, go and visit your local health unit or travel clinic (see listings overleaf) and get an armful of relevant shots. You would be wise to be up to date with **tetanus**, **polio** and **diphtheria** (all ten-yearly), **typhoid** and **hepatitis A** (Havrix Monodose or Avaxim). You would also be wise to consider **rabies** vaccine for even short trips as there is a shortage of treatment if you have not had pre-exposure vaccine before an incident. For longer trips (four weeks or longer) consider **meningitis** and **hepatitis B**. Both rabies and hepatitis B involve three doses of vaccine, which can take up to two months to give depending on the age of the traveller. Talk to your doctor and arm yourself with drugs – ciprofloxacin (for dysentery), tinidazole (for giardia or amoebic dysentery) and Diamox (to deal with altitude). Assemble a good medical kit (see page 102). Check out where your embassies lie in China and in the neighbouring region – note down the addresses and contact numbers. Bring a health certificate to China (it may be checked). Find out your blood group and record it on that document. If you haven't had time to get all or any of your vaccinations/medicines before you leave home then the **Ciwek Clinic** in Kathmandu is an excellent place to go. It is run by Western doctors and is located across the street from the British Embassy and the British Council (☏ *442 4111*).

TRAVEL CLINICS AND HEALTH INFORMATION A full list of current travel clinic websites worldwide is available from the International Society of Travel Medicine on www.istm.org. For other journey preparation information, consult www.tripprep. com. Information about various medications may be found on www.emedicine. com. For information on malaria prevention, see www.preventingmalaria.info.

UK

Berkeley Travel Clinic 32 Berkeley St, London W1J 8EL (near Green Park tube station); ℡ 020 7629 6233
Cambridge Travel Clinic 48a Mill Rd, Cambridge CB1 2AS; ℡ 01223 367362; e enquiries@cambridgetravelclinic.co.uk; www. cambridgetravelclinic.co.uk; ⊕ 12.00–19.00 Tue–Fri, 10.00–16.00 Sat
Edinburgh Travel Clinic Regional Infectious Diseases Unit, Ward 41 OPD, Western General Hospital, Crewe Rd South, Edinburgh EH4 2UX; ℡ 0131 537 2822; travel helpline ℡ 0906 589 0380; www.link.med.ed.ac.uk/ridu; ⊕ Mon–Fri 09.00–12.00. Provides inoculations

& antimalarial prophylaxis & advises on travel-related health risks.
Fleet Street Travel Clinic 29 Fleet St, London EC4Y 1AA; ℡ 020 7353 5678; www. fleetstreetclinic.com. Vaccinations, travel products & latest advice.
Hospital for Tropical Diseases Travel Clinic Mortimer Market Bldg, Capper St (off Tottenham Ct Rd), London WC1 6AU; ℡ 020 7388 9600; www.thehtd.org. Offers consultations & advice but only for the complicated traveller. Check the website for opening times & how to get an appointment. Runs a health line (℡ 0906 133 7733) for country-specific information & health

TRAVEL-RELATED DVT

Deep vein thrombosis (DVT) is a concern where long-haul immobility is involved, as in long airplane flights, lengthy bus rides, Landcruiser jaunts that last for days, and riding Chinese railways for several days to get closer to Tibet (or indeed into Tibet). Prolonged immobility may cause blood clots to form in the legs. Although most clots are reabsorbed without the passenger ever becoming aware of the problem, some clots may break off and travel through the blood vessels to the lungs, causing life-threatening complications.

People at the highest risk and who should seek medical advice before they go are:

- People with heart disease
- People with cancer
- People with clotting disorders
- People who have had recent surgery, especially on the legs
- Women on the pill or other oestrogen therapy
- Pregnant women

The main symptoms of travel-related DVT are swelling or pain of the foot, ankle or calf, usually on just one side. A blood clot moving to the lungs can cause chest pain and difficulty in breathing. To prevent DVT on aeroplanes or trains, the solution is simple: stay mobile. Walk up and down the aisles, do exercises to contract leg muscles, and drink lots of fluids (but not alcohol). For long-haul bus or Landcruiser trips, you will just have to find a way to do similar things – creative yoga on the bus, or getting out of a Landcruiser periodically to stretch. For more information about travel-related DVT, go to the website www.travelhealth.co.uk and run a search for the topic.

hazards. Also stocks nets, water purification equipment & personal protection measures.

Interhealth Worldwide Partnership Hse, 157 Waterloo Rd, London SE1 8US; ☎020 7902 9000; www.interhealth.org.uk. Competitively priced, one-stop travel health service. All profits go to their affiliated company, InterHealth, which provides health care for overseas workers on Christian projects.

MASTA (Medical Advisory Service for Travellers Abroad) London School of Hygiene & Tropical Medicine, Keppel St, London WC1 7HT; ☎0906 550 1402; www.masta.org. Individually tailored health briefs available for a fee, with up-to-date information on how to stay healthy, inoculations & what to bring. There are currently 30 MASTA pre-travel clinics in Britain. Call ☎0870 241 6843 or check online for the nearest. Clinics also sell malaria prophylaxis memory cards, treatment kits, bed nets & net treatment kits.

NHS travel website www.fitfortravel.scot. nhs.uk. Provides country-by-country advice on immunisation & malaria, plus details of recent developments, & a list of relevant health organisations.

Nomad Travel Store/Clinic 3–4 Wellington Terr, Turnpike Lane, London N8 0PX; ☎020 8889 7014; travel-health line (office hours only) ☎0906 863 3414; e sales@nomadtravel.co.uk; www.nomadtravel.co.uk. Also at 40 Bernard St, London WC1N 1LJ; ☎020 7833 4114; 52 Grosvenor Gdns, London SW1W 0AG; ☎020 7823 5823; & 43 Queen's Rd, Bristol BS8 1QH; ☎0117 922 6567. For health advice, equipment such as mosquito nets & other anti-bug devices, & an excellent range of adventure travel gear.

Trailfinders Travel Clinic 194 Kensington High St, London W8 7RG; ☎020 7938 3999; www. trailfinders.com/clinic.htm

Travelpharm www.travelpharm.com. The Travelpharm website offers up-to-date guidance on travel-related health & has a range of medications available through their online mini-pharmacy.

Irish Republic

Tropical Medical Bureau Grafton St Medical Centre, Grafton Bldgs, 34 Grafton St, Dublin 2; ☎1 671 9200; www.tmb.ie. A useful website specific to tropical destinations. Also check website for other bureaux locations throughout Ireland.

USA

Centers for Disease Control 1600 Clifton Rd, Atlanta, GA 30333; ☎800 311 3435; travellers' health hotline ☎888 232 3299; www.cdc.gov/travel. The central source of travel information in the USA. The invaluable *Health Information for International Travel*, published annually, is available from the Division of Quarantine at this address.

Connaught Laboratories PO Box 187, Swiftwater, PA 18370; ☎800 822 2463. They will send a free list of specialist tropical medicine physicians in your state.

IAMAT (International Association for Medical Assistance to Travelers) 1623 Military Rd, 279, Niagara Falls, NY 14304-1745; ☎716 754 4883; e info@iamat.org; www.iamat. org. A non-profit organisation that provides lists of English-speaking doctors abroad.

International Medicine Center 920 Frostwood Dr, Suite 670, Houston, TX 77024; ☎713 550 2000; www.traveldoc.com

Canada

IAMAT Suite 1, 1287 St Clair Av W, Toronto, Ontario M6 1B8; ☎416 652 0137; www.iamat.org

TMVC Suite 314, 1030 W Georgia St, Vancouver BC V6 2Y3; ☎1 888 288 8682; www.tmvc.com

Australia, New Zealand and Singapore

TMVC ☎1300 65 88 44; www.tmvc.com.au. 31 clinics in Australia, New Zealand & Singapore, including: *Auckland* Canterbury Arcade, 170 Queen St, Auckland; ☎9 373 3531; *Brisbane* 6th Floor, 247 Adelaide St, Brisbane, QLD 4000; ☎7 3221 9066; *Melbourne* 393 Little Bourke St,

2nd Floor, Melbourne, VIC 3000; ☎3 9602 5788; *Sydney* Dymocks Bldg, 7th Floor, 428 George St, Sydney, NSW 2000; ☎2 9221 7133

IAMAT PO Box 5049, Christchurch 5, New Zealand; www.iamat.org

South Africa and Namibia

SAA-Netcare Travel Clinics P Bag X34, Benmore 2010; www.travelclinic.co.za. Clinics throughout South Africa.

TMVC 113 D, Malan Dr, Roosevelt Pk, Johannesburg; ☎ 011 888 7488; www.tmvc.com. au. Consult website for details of other clinics in South Africa & Namibia.

Switzerland

IAMAT 57 Chemin des Voirets, 1212 Grand Lancy, Geneva; www.iamat.org

EVACUATION INSURANCE You are strongly advised to carry comprehensive air evacuation insurance for a trip to Tibet. Hopefully, you won't have to use it. Your best strategy if you fall really sick in Tibet is to get right out of Tibet – and China – as fast as you can, and make a beeline for somewhere with better hospitals, like Singapore. Use regular scheduled flights to get out of Tibet if possible. If the plane looks full, insist that a regular passenger gets bumped off the flight for the emergency patient.

Evacuation by chartered flight can cost a fortune. Check your travel insurance to ensure that it covers emergency evacuation costs and, more specifically, if it will cover evacuation by crews like SOS/AEA, which has clinics in Beijing with expat doctors and imported medicines. Better yet, take out direct insurance with SOS/ AEA (check their website www.internationalsos.com for addresses and contact numbers, and see the section on evacuation that follows, on page 112).

HIMALAYAN MEDICAL KIT Failing adequate health care in Tibet, you really need to be your own doctor. There are Chinese pharmacies in Lhasa, but medication may bear Chinese instructions and may not be familiar to Western eyes. Kathmandu and Hong Kong are quite well stocked with Western drugs and will issue medication without prescription. You can easily find drugs like Diamox in Kathmandu (check expiry dates). While you can't be a travelling drugstore, you'll need a larger than usual medical kit in Tibet. If travelling with a friend or a small group, divide up a medical kit to share the weight. Camping and outdoor stores in the West sell pre-packaged medical kits that you can customise to your needs (you can even find 'Himalaya kits'). Items like antiseptic cream and Band-Aids (plasters) are hard to find in Lhasa. Take along a Swiss Army knife with scissors and tweezers. You'll need your own water bottle and purifying tablets (or filter).

A medical kit may contain a ready-made package – sealed and labelled – with sterile needles and syringes. It is highly recommended you carry these in case blood samples or injections are required. Make sure that you obtain a certificate signed by a doctor stating that they are for your own personal use for medical situations. Take along any prescription drugs you need, as well as back-ups of things you are dependent upon – such as glasses. Your chances of finding contact lens solution in Shigatse are zero: dust can be a major problem for contact lenses in Tibet (take along regular glasses as a back-up). Glasses or no glasses, dust can cause eye irritation – you might want to pack soothing eyedrops.

Read the following sections for ideas on arming yourself for the rigours of Tibet – you will need medications like cough lozenges, codeine-based medicines and decongestants (for colds); moisturisers, lip balm, sunglasses, sunscreen and other balms will help combat the effects of sun, wind and altitude. Recommended drugs for Tibet include: Diamox to help acclimatise, Ciprofloxacin for diarrhoea associated with blood or mucus and/or a fever, tinidazole for giardia and amoebic dysentery and a phial of chlorine dioxide tablets for purifying water.

Travellers may buy a medical kit but overlook the importance of the medical knowledge required to go with it. A pocket-sized booklet would be worth bringing along – there are several on the market. Notable are two booklets by the same author, Dr Stephen Bezruchka, both published by The Mountaineers Books in 2005: *The Pocket Doctor: A Passport to Healthy Travel,* and the more specialised *Altitude Illness: Prevention and Treatment.* Also check out Medex travel at high altitude online for an excellent guide. If you're leaving Tibet and returning directly home, you should consider selling or donating your precious cache of medicines and other supplies to incoming travellers. Drugs like Diamox have an expiry period and will be of little use to you in the West anyway.

THE BUDDY SYSTEM When you go diving, you use the buddy system. You watch out for your friend underwater, which is an alien environment and a potentially dangerous one. You could draw close parallels in Tibet: high altitude is an alien environment. If someone gets altitude sickness, he or she becomes confused and disorientated, and cannot make the right decisions. Someone else has to take those decisions. Back yourself up in Tibet with at least one buddy. And be prepared to watch out for others in a Landcruiser group if someone falls sick.

COMMON HEALTH AND SAFETY PROBLEMS IN TIBET

RUNNING ON EMPTY To keep your system ticking properly, you need good nutrition and high fluid intake. And that's hard to achieve outside Lhasa. So carry vitamin pills, freeze-dried soups and extra food supplies (such as dried fruit) to supplement the meagre local offerings. You should think in terms of what can be 'cooked' with the hot water supplied in vacuum flasks in hotels and truck stops: check the cooking times on soup packets (ideally, only a few minutes in hot water). Packets of soup are the best item here – soup is easily prepared and gives the illusion of a hot meal. *Tsampa*, the Tibetan food staple, is sustaining but tasteless – it can be mixed in with soup to make it more palatable. You can get run down without proper nutrition intake: this makes you more susceptible to coming down with other ailments.

FLUID INTAKE Two essentials concerning water: making sure the water is safe to drink; and drinking enough of it. Even though Tibet is high and the water looks crystal clear, it could be contaminated by herders and livestock on higher ground. It's best to always filter water or boil it. Staying hydrated is essential in Tibet to combat dryness and the effects of altitude. Even if you have to overload your system, keep drinking your quota of water – about four litres a day. If you get a case of the runs, you'll lose a lot of body fluids, so you need to keep drinking water to stay hydrated. You can buy bottled water in Lhasa and larger towns in Tibet – make sure the seal is intact. The water supplied in Chinese Thermoses in hotels is usually reliable since it has been boiled at high temperature. You have to wait for this to cool down, or else drink it in tea. You should take along your own water purifying devices – chlorine dioxide tablets can be purchased cheaply in the West. Chlorine-treated water tastes unpleasant but you can buy another tablet that removes that taste. Or take Gatorade flavouring crystals with you to neutralise the taste. These and other electrolyte powders (such as Electrolade) are sodium and potassium, which will help restore body fluid balance (one of the main ingredients in sweat is sodium).

HYGIENE HAZARDS Washing and cleaning activities are a low priority with Tibetans: explanations range from lack of hot water to layering themselves with

3

dirt to protect the skin from sun. Both Tibetan and Chinese hygiene standards fall far short of western Europe. You have to be careful about the handling of food and water – do not accept the cold face-towels offered in restaurants. Stick to well-cooked hot food in restaurants (noodles are fine). Boil it, peel it – or forget it. Some travellers prefer to use their own eating utensils, such as an aluminium mug and spoon (soup can be served in the mug).

Although hot showers are readily available in Lhasa, Shigatse and Gyantse, in the rest of Tibet you may not be so lucky. Solar hot showers are on the rise, there are the occasional hot springs to soak in, but that's about it: the rivers and lakes are pretty cold. Out of Lhasa, you have to rely on the Thermos of hot water supplied to your room (or ask for it). The Thermos is a source of hot water for tea, or for making soup – and can also be used for bathing. A metal basin is often supplied in the room (sometimes with a special wooden stand to hold it), so you can pour water in and wash yourself in stages (hair one day, and so on). Another technique is to soak a thin towel (preferably your own) and apply it Japanese-style, as in a sushi restaurant. Thin, spongy Western sport towels are ideal for this as you can wring them out to dry quickly.

DIARRHOEA Because of low hygiene standards, it is eminently possible that you will get a case of the runs. Usually, this is not a problem – just stick to a simple diet with liquid back-up: water, clear soups and unsweetened juices. Do not drink beer or milk, and avoid spicy or fatty foods as they can aggravate your condition. The problem should pass within a day or two. In Kathmandu you can buy packets of rehydration salts – a mixture of glucose and salt. If these are unavailable, you can make your own by adding two or three teaspoons of salt and a similar amount of sugar to a litre bottle of purified water. Packets with electrolyte rehydration powders (sodium/potassium crystals) are efficacious. If problems persist, it may be a case of bacterial diarrhoea – refer to the section on *Intestinal bugs* (page 106).

THE ELEMENTS Sunburn, windburn, chapped lips, lobster-face and red-eye are definite hazards in Tibet due to the (at times) ferocious effects of the sun, wind and cold. Once you get cracked lips or chapped hands, you'll find these take a long time to heal and can be very bothersome. Moisturisers are the answer: bring along hand- and face-cream moisturisers (though these can also be purchased in Lhasa). You need a good sunblock cream and Chapstick. A hat of some kind – preferably covering the ears and neck – is essential, as are high-quality sunglasses or glacier glasses that block UV rays (ideal are dark polarising lenses). The use of certain drugs such as the antibiotic Tetracycline can render a person more sun-sensitised, and result in bad sunburn. One of the greatest hazards in Tibet is dust. It can get into your eyes, so contact lenses are not a great idea – dust can be very irritating if it gets under them. A silk scarf or bandanna, wrapped around your nose, throat and mouth (bandito style) will generally filter the dust out of your breathing apparatus in extreme conditions, and the same scarf can be used round your neck to keep you warm in a sudden change of temperature.

ACUTE EXPOSURE It can get *very* cold overnight in Tibet – and if you happen to be in the back of a truck, you may get frozen solid. Silk articles, favoured by Western skiers, are especially useful for countering the cold – they're light and pack easily (balaclavas, long johns, T-shirts, scarves, gloves). Wool and polypropylene clothing also insulates well. A woollen *tuke* or similar headgear will go a long way towards countering the cold. A dangerous condition, caused by rapid heat loss, is hypothermia: this is brought about by physical exhaustion when cold and wet.

Symptoms include uncontrolled shivering. Shelter is the most important thing here: strip off wet clothing and replace with dry. In severe cases, the person should be stripped and placed in a sleeping bag with another person to share body heat. Do not rub affected limbs.

Frostbite is the most extreme result of rapid body-heat loss. It affects the tips of the extremities first – toes, fingers and nose. In these areas the blood freezes, preventing circulation as ice crystals expand in the cells. Again it is essential to find shelter, and immerse the affected part in lukewarm water if available. Surface frostbite can be thawed with another person's body heat – do not rub the affected part. Snow blindness results when bright sun reflected off snow (or ice or water surfaces) burns the cornea of the eye. The eyes feel like there is grit in them, appear bloodshot, and eyelids may puff up and swell shut. The condition is alarming but temporary – rest and soothe the eyes with cold compresses or eye drops, and the problem should clear up in a few days. Wearing glacier glasses with total UV block is the way to prevent this condition.

COUGHS, COLDS AND SORE THROATS Respiratory ailments are quite common in Tibet, and can turn very nasty when combined with the effects of extreme dryness and altitude. Take care. These are not your normal colds – they can be persistent and debilitating. Virulent (mutating) strains of flu, originating in China, can be knockouts. The best way to avoid this syndrome is to make sure you don't undergo drastic changes of body temperature. Make sure that you have clothing that you can layer on or off, to cope with the extremes of heat and cold – sometimes occurring on the same day in Tibet. This also applies to sleeping arrangements – there's not much heating in hotels in Tibet. Bring your own medicines for coughs, colds and sore throats. Some stronger drugs (codeine compounds) can be multi-purpose – for headaches, pains, coughs or colds.

TUBERCULOSIS The 'white plague' is threatening to make the comeback of the 21st century. Vaccines, antibiotics and improved hygiene nearly erased TB from industrialised nations; however, the disease now appears to be resistant to most of the drugs previously used to treat it. Tuberculosis thrives in crowded and dirty living conditions where both ventilation and the people are poor. Tuberculosis certainly is a problem in Tibet, Nepal and India: the airborne bacteria are transmitted through coughing, sneezing or spitting by people in an infectious stage of TB. Conditions can be very smoky in Tibetan teahouses – with a fire burning away in the middle, and no ventilation. Catching TB is a matter of repeated exposure to the bacteria over a period of time.

AVIAN FLU Sporadic lethal outbreaks of avian influenza A (H5N1) have been reported in China and other Asian countries since 2003. These outbreaks have occurred among wild birds and bats; among domestic chickens, ducks, quail and pigs; and more alarmingly, among humans. The H5N1 virus has devastated poultry stocks across Asia, killing or prompting the slaughter of millions of chickens and ducks since 2003. Outbreaks are not expected to diminish: it is likely that avian flu has become endemic in the region. If the avian flu virus strengthens its ability to transmit through human-to-human contact (and there have been cases where this has happened), an influenza pandemic could result – as humans have little or no pre-existing immunity, and drugs or vaccines to counter avian flu are in experimental stages. Avian flu is spread through saliva, nasal secretions and faeces from infected birds. Most cases of avian flu infection in humans have resulted from contact with infected birds or contaminated surfaces. There have now been reports from the World Health Organisation that avian flu can also be caught through eating undercooked infected poultry or possibly eggs. Ensure that all food is well cooked and if in doubt don't eat it. This is less likely to happen in Tibet as poultry is not a staple on the plateau (though there was a minor outbreak of bird flu among chickens at a farm close to Lhasa in mid-2005). However, Tibet does have lots of wild birds – and wild birds are known to play a role in spreading the virus. In June 2005, Chinese news sources reported that over a thousand birds died of the H5N1 virus at Quanji Town in Qinghai Province, to the northeast side of the plateau. Among the dead birds were bar-headed geese, great black-headed gulls, ruddy shelducks and great cormorants.

Mainland China is a high risk for mutant strains of avian flu developing. With an estimated 14 billion domestic poultry – 70% kept in backyards – China is a ticking time bomb. Any outbreak of the H5N1 virus among humans within China could severely disrupt tourism, or even shut it down for a period. It's essential to keep an eye on news and internet sources to stay up to date on where outbreaks may have occurred and on other information. Since the Chinese government is slow (or inaccurate) on reporting these, stick with foreign web sources. Here are some sites to consult: www.cdc.gov/travel; www.pandemicflu.gov; www.internationalsos.com (go to News section and click on 'Pandemic Preparedness').

At present, the most promising drug capable of reducing the severity of bird flu is Tamiflu (the commercial brand is Oseltamivir, made by Swiss company Roche). The prime ingredient of this drug is shikimic acid, derived from the spice-fruit known as star anise. Star anise is useless on its own – it has to be extracted and mixed with several other ingredients to be effective.

SARS Severe Acute Respiratory Syndrome (SARS) was first detected in Hong Kong in November 2002. The illness spread to more than two dozen countries worldwide with devastating results, before being brought under control. Symptoms include high fever, headache and body aches. Mild respiratory problems are present at the outset, later developing into a dry cough and pneumonia. To prevent the spread of SARS in Asia, devices appeared at major airports with the capability of scanning incoming passengers for high forehead temperature. In 2003, Tibet was closed to travellers for most of the high season because of SARS outbreaks in China. This closure was designed as a barrier to prevent the possible spread of SARS from China through Tibet into Nepal. There are a lot of unknowns about SARS, with a race under way to find an effective vaccine. Keep an eye out for recent developments.

INTESTINAL BUGS AND WORMS If diarrhoea is persistent, with blood or mucus in the stool, this indicates a more serious illness such as amoebic or bacillary dysentery. In this case, you need a stool test to identify the culprit – merely guessing and indulging in 'drug cocktails' may be detrimental. Facilities to identify bugs like this are not available in Lhasa; the nearest place is a Western-run clinic in Kathmandu (Ciwek clinic, see page 99). From Chengdu, the closest reliable medical testing facilities are found in Bangkok, Singapore and Hong Kong. For bacillary dysentery (recognised by blood or mucus in the stools, which may be accompanied by a fever), the best treatment is to take Ciprofloxacin (500mg tablet repeated ten to 12 hours later) or Norfloxacin. More of a problem is giardia, caused by a microscopic parasite that can elude some water filters (iodine kills it). Giardia-like symptoms include stomach cramps, sulphurous burps or gas, and persistent diarrhoea: it's like something is bubbling away down there. You can treat it with tinidazole (another drug is metronidazole, also known as Flagyl, though this is not as good and has more side effects).

Various types of intestinal worms are also prevalent in Nepal – the larvae are often present in unwashed vegetables or undercooked meat. Intestinal worms are awful to contemplate, but not of great concern since drugs like mebendazole are highly effective in killing them. Stool tests can detect the culprits.

HEPATITIS Hepatitis is a viral infection of the liver, primarily spread through contaminated food and water (hepatitis A) or dirty needles (hepatitis B). Since both types are prevalent in Nepal and Tibet and prevention is better than cure, obtain vaccinations prior to travel. At the very least have one shot of either Havrix Monodose or Avaxim (for hepatitis A). This will last for a year when a booster dose can be given to extend coverage for at least 25 years. Protection for hepatitis B (Engerix B) consists of three shots over a minimum of 21 days (for those aged 16 or over). You can now do both at once (again three shots over 21 days) by using Twinrix. For those under 16, the minimum time for hepatitis B or the junior Twinrix is over two months so allow plenty of time before travel. You would also be wise to have typhoid vaccine.

ALTITUDE SICKNESS When Sherpas say climbing is in their blood, they may mean it literally. Sherpas have a physiology adapted to the high-altitude environment – their blood has a higher red-cell count and their lung capacity is larger. Ability to adapt to altitude is thought to be in your genes. That may mean you either have the high-altitude genes or you don't. If you do, you can adapt quickly; if you don't, it will take longer – or so the theory goes. At higher altitudes, air pressure is lower and the air is thinner. Although it contains the same percentage of oxygen as it does at sea level, there's less oxygen delivered in each lungful of air. So you have to breathe harder, and your body has to convert to more red blood cells to carry the oxygen through the system.

Altitude sickness is something of a mystery. It does not appear to depend on being in shape: athletes have come down with it, and it may occur in subjects who have not experienced it before. Altitude sickness can occur at elevations above 2,000m, and about 50% of people will experience some symptoms at 3,500m. The higher you go the more pronounced the symptoms could become. So adjustment is required at each 400m of elevation gain after that.

Terrain above 5,000m (common enough in Tibet) is a harsh, alien environment – above 6,000m is a zone where humans were never meant to go. Like diving at depth, going to high altitudes requires special adjustments. To adapt, you have to be in tune with your body. You need to travel with someone who can monitor your condition – and back you up (get you out) if something should go wrong. Consider this: if you were to be transported in a hot-air balloon and dropped on the summit of Everest, without oxygen you would collapse within ten minutes, and die within an hour. However, a handful of climbers have summited Everest without oxygen: by attaining a degree of acclimatisation, they have been able to achieve this. A similar analogy could be drawn with flying in from Chengdu, which is barely above sea level, to Lhasa, at 3,650m. That's a 3,500m gain in an hour or so. You need to rest and recover. Coming by land from Kathmandu, you rise from 1,300m up over a 5,200m pass at Tong La – a gain of 4,000m over a few days (to soften the blow, it would be worth staying a few days at Nyalam, which is 3,750m).

The study of altitude sickness is still evolving. Recent studies suggest that altitude sickness may be due to leaky membranes – which are more permeable as you go up in elevation. It was unknown if a person could survive above 7,500m without oxygen until 1978, when Messner and Habeler summited Everest. Actually, a hundred years earlier, in 1875, French balloonist Tissandier reached 8,000m after a three-hour ascent and lost consciousness: the balloon descended and Tissandier survived but his two companions died. Messner was told he would come back from Everest a raving madman, or, at the very least, a brain-damaged automaton if he attempted the peak without oxygen. Messner got his timing right, got to the top, and went on to bag all the 8,000m peaks without oxygen. Climbers like Messner, however, will admit to impaired functions at higher elevations – and to strange encounters. Messner recalls talking to his ice axe, talking to his feet, talking to an imaginary companion and having hallucinations.

Altitude strategy It is essential to take it easy for the first three or four days after arriving at altitude; most acclimatisation takes place within the first ten days (it can take two or three months to fully acclimatise). When reaching altitude, most travellers experience discomfort – headaches, fatigue, nausea, vomiting, lack of appetite, swelling or tingling of the hands or feet, difficulty sleeping. This condition is usually mild and short-lived. Headaches can be treated with paracetamol or ibuprofen: if a headache persists, or intensifies – or if the person wakes up with a headache – this is a sign of real altitude sickness. The critical question is how to distinguish between mild altitude sickness and more serious cases. You don't acclimatise by sitting around doing nothing – get some simple exercise like walking,

HIGH-ALTITUDE DRUGS

This text comes with a few caveats. Mainly, that there are a lot of unknowns when it comes to altitude sickness. What works for one person may not work for another. The only guaranteed cure for altitude sickness is immediate descent to lower elevations and administration of oxygen to the patient. Drugs can reduce symptoms of altitude sickness, but may also mask symptoms: the taking of these drugs should never be used to avoid descent or to enable further ascent.

HERBAL DRUGS Dr Stephen Bezruchka, in his book *Altitude Illness: Prevention and Treatment* (Mountaineers Books, 2005), says:

> The herb, Ginkgo biloba, 80mg to 120mg twice a day, beginning five days before ascent and continued a day at altitude, appears to prevent AMS. It interferes with platelet activity in the blood, so its safety for those taking other drugs that have such effects is unknown. It also improves blood circulation to the hands in the cold. Its role at altitude remains to be clarified, but it has few side effects and should be considered.

Chinese visitors to Tibet use a variety of traditional herbal medicines to counter the effect of altitude, but what is in these remedies is often not specified. The fruits of the Chinese wolfberry are thought to be efficacious for altitude problems, but the plant that shows up most frequently in herbal remedies is the Tibetan Radix rhodiolae plant, which grows on the plateau at elevations of 3,500 to 5,000m. Also known as 'plateau ginseng', this plant, according to Chinese sources, is efficacious for relieving high blood pressure, high blood fat, diabetes, senility and 'internet addiction'. In any case, it appears to improve blood flow, which is good at altitude. Rhodiola concoctions are sold in Lhasa in capsules, as a liquid in glass phials and in various teas. Cans of rhodiola and drink lots of water. Do not drink alcohol, as it contributes to dehydration. Smoking, of course, will be a major problem at altitude.

Never underestimate altitude – it can be a killer. Go slow, be careful, experiment before you go higher. The climber's maxim is 'walk high, sleep low' – climbers may trek higher during the day, but retire to lower levels to sleep. The maximum rate of ascent when trekking should be about 400m a day. If you're acclimatised to Lhasa (3,650m) you really need to undergo a second acclimatisation phase to handle a visit to Lake Namtso (at 4,650m). On a brighter note, once you've acclimatised to a particular altitude, the altered blood chemistry should stay with you for about ten days. So if you acclimatise to the 5,000m level and then go down to 3,500m, you should be able to go back up to 5,000m again without ill effects, provided you do so within ten days.

ACUTE MOUNTAIN SICKNESS Acute mountain sickness (AMS) is a general term for a whole raft of altitude-related maladies. Symptoms of AMS include gastrointestinal turmoil (loss of appetite, nausea, vomiting), extreme fatigue or weakness, dizziness or light-headedness, and difficulty breathing or sleeping.

A case of severe AMS may result in high-altitude pulmonary oedema (HAPE), when a small amount of fluid that appears in the lungs at altitude is not absorbed normally. Instead, it accumulates, obstructing the flow of oxygen and drowning the victim in his or her own fluids. Symptoms include rapid respiratory rate and rapid

drink (on sale in Lhasa) list rhodiola, honey, water and citric acid as ingredients. Another drink available around Lhasa is a kind of high-altitude tea. Similar to *maté de coca* (the Andean remedy, from coca leaves), this tea is said to relieve headaches, insomnia, nausea and dizziness brought about by altitude. The tea is called *Gaoyuanan* and is made in Tibet. You can buy a box of sachets in Lhasa at several of the hotels or at Dunya Restaurant (which serves it as 'altitude relax tea').

DIAMOX Diamox (acetazolamide) is a diuretic that can help alleviate the symptoms of altitude sickness. It does not prevent you getting altitude sickness, nor does it solve the problem, but it may ease your passage when, say, arriving in Lhasa by air, or when going up and over and down a pass within the same day. It may also improve the quality of sleep at altitude. Since it's a diuretic, it leads to increased urination and to dehydration, so you need to keep drinking more if you use it. Other side effects include a tingling sensation in the lips and fingertips, and the medication may give a strange taste to carbonated drinks. There is now good evidence that if it suits you it is worth taking as it reduces the chance of getting altitude sickness. Do a trial at sea level for two days at least two weeks before travel. Take a 250mg tablet in the morning and again at 16.00. If there are side effects then try halving the tablet. If you still get side effects then it is probably best to avoid using it as a prophylactic medicine. People who are allergic to sulphur drugs should not try this. If it suits you then start taking the tablets two to three days before reaching 3,500m and continue to maximum altitude and for two to three days after if you are continuing to be at altitude. If a person comes down with Acute Mountain Sickness (AMS), then the first thing to do is to descend at least 500m. If treatment with Diamox is considered necessary, then the dosage can be increased to 250mg every six hours.

pulse, cough, crackles or wheezing in one or both lungs, frothy or bloodstained sputum, and severe shortness of breath. Another serious complication is high-altitude cerebral oedema (HACE), where the fluid problem is in the brain. A person with HACE is disoriented, has an unsteady gait and trouble using the hands, is irritable, suffers from drowsiness and nightmares, and may suffer hallucinations. Memory, judgement and perception are impaired.

To counter HAPE and HACE, mountaineering expeditions sometimes tote a Gamow bag, which weighs about 8kg. It is a body-enclosing bag that can be hand-pumped to replicate atmospheric pressure at much lower levels. Recent studies suggest that a one-hour treatment corresponds to a descent of 1,500m: this leads to short-term improvements, but nothing lasting. Some group tour operators carry a tank of oxygen to deal with cases – but that tank may only hold 30 minutes of oxygen (Landcruiser drivers sometimes carry oxygen). Drugs like Diamox are also used to counter the effects of altitude (see box, page 108). The best solution, however, in all cases, is simply to transport the patient to a lower elevation as fast as possible (if this means moving in the middle of the night, do so). Unfortunately, on the Tibetan plateau, descent to lower elevation is not always feasible. In serious cases, the focus is often evacuation by road to Kathmandu, or by air to either Kathmandu or Chengdu.

ACCIDENTS AND RECKLESS DRIVING By far the biggest potential threat for travellers in Tibet is possible injury caused by vehicle collisions or road accidents. It's unknown how many foreigners have perished in Tibet due to driving accidents, but there have certainly been cases of trucks and Landcruisers being totalled, and foreigners killed. There are no safety devices along precipitous mountain roads in Tibet and few warning signs. Your fate rests with your driver's road skills.

Drivers range from excellent to downright dangerous. Assess the state of your driver and his judgement calls – if he's going too fast or taking unnecessary risks, tell him. Some macho drivers seem to make a sport out of overtaking everything in sight – on blind corners or perilous cliff edges. If the driver makes a dangerous move, signal for him to pull over and stop, and explain that there is no rush to reach the destination (you don't mind arriving half an hour later), and therefore there is no need to overtake all the time. Get the driver used to the idea of going slower so you can take in the scenery and make photo stops. A tired driver is definitely a hazard: if the driver looks sleepy, keep him awake – or rearrange the itinerary so you stay in the nearest hotel, where he can rest up. Danger increases exponentially with driving at night. Visibility is much reduced, and drivers may choose not to turn on their headlights, preferring to navigate in total darkness, which is deadly.

You are bound to experience some pretty close calls in Tibet. One Landcruiser hit a flock of sheep – resulting in a smashed front windshield. The passengers were all right, but the incensed shepherd had to be compensated, and the group continued, albeit a bit frozen with the windshield missing. In another situation, our driver played 'chicken' with a military convoy, doing daredevil overtakes on mountain roads with sheer drop-offs. After overtaking all the trucks, the driver called for a pit stop – at which time all the army trucks overtook us again.

You most likely don't want to even think about this, but you have to consider what would happen if there was an accident. The biggest problem could be loss of blood. It's not known to what degree hospitals in China or Tibet screen their blood – tainted blood carries all kinds of viruses, including hepatitis and HIV. Then there's the question of whether your blood type will even be stocked. Blood Type O is rare. The Chinese neither have nor store Rh-negative blood for transfusions: you'd have to be evacuated to the nearest Rh-negative country.

DOGS Tibetans are fond of dogs: these hounds perform guard duties in many villages around Tibet. Dogs are believed to be reincarnates of renegade monks who didn't quite make the grade, and hence are accepted at monasteries. Some are in good shape; others are mangy and flea-bitten. Sometimes dogs operate in packs around monasteries, in which case they can be benign (lazing around, or curled up in corners) or they can be extremely dangerous. Travellers have been attacked and dragged to the ground in some places, and then rescued by monks. This can lead to lacerations requiring stitches – not a pleasant thought.

If a bite from a dog punctures the skin, it can lead to a far greater problem: rabies. If you are bitten, scratched or licked over an open wound by a dog or *any* warm-blooded mammal, clean the wound thoroughly with soap and water, working the soap into the wound for at least 15 minutes. The incubation period for rabies is variable, depending on where the victim is bitten. If the victim is not given the appropriate treatment then the result is fatal. Dogs are known to carry rabies in Tibet and rabies is endemic in most parts of Nepal, where rabid street dogs are a cause for concern. Following any potential exposure get to medical help as soon as you can and ensure that you receive the correct treatment. If you have not had three pre-exposure rabies vaccines before travel then you need two products: a preformed antibody called rabies immunoglobulin (RIG) and five doses of vaccine. RIG is often hard to come by so ensure that they offer you both products but if not then evacuate to Singapore or Hong Kong. You can obtain pre-exposure vaccinations before you go. Three injections are ideally given over a minimum of 21 days and if you have had these then you will no longer need RIG, just two further doses of vaccine given three days apart. You can get post-exposure rabies vaccine at the People's Hospital in Lhasa, and also at clinics in Kathmandu. (There is only a small chance of getting RIG in either of these places, so having the pre-exposure rabies vaccine becomes worthwhile).

The best strategy here is not to get bitten in the first place. Treat all dogs, or indeed any warm-blooded mammal, with extreme caution: carry a stick, or an umbrella, or pick up a stone if a dog approaches. If a dog attacks, try and clobber it on the sensitive snout area.

CHINESE MEDICAL FACILITIES

Chinese hospitals are of a very low standard in China generally, and completely primitive in Tibet, when compared to Western medical facilities. It could be said that should you fall ill, rather than stay in a hospital you would do a lot better by taking a good hotel room. I have personally seen, in Tibetan clinics, rusting antiquated equipment, and filthy wards and operating theatres. There's a shortage of sterile equipment and supplies; the most basic facilities for diagnosis and treatment are generally absent; doctors and nurses are poorly trained. Surgical gloves may be washed and re-used – and the same with syringes. A disturbing trend in some hospitals in Tibet is to subject the patient to a cardiogram, an X-ray and a glucose drip – regardless of what illness is presented – and then charge for these services. Other hospitals are prone to giving the patient lots of antibiotics.

In Lhasa, the best facilities are at the Military Hospital, but this place is not usually accessible to tourists. The People's Hospital has an emergency centre, but no mechanism for dealing with seriously injured people. An Italian NGO has been supplying equipment and training at the People's Hospital. Costs for foreigners staying at the People's Hospital in Lhasa can be very high, and payment may be

3

expected in Chinese cash (travellers' cheques will probably not be accepted, and nor will credit cards).

The nearest places in China for good medical attention are Chengdu (a hospital can run to US$120 a day for foreigners), Hong Kong (even more expensive) and major cities like Beijing and Shanghai. Elsewhere in Asia, any place that has a lot of foreign embassies is good for clinics and hospitals with Western standards, often staffed by Western doctors. The best are found in Singapore, Nepal (the Ciwek clinic – see page 99) and Bangkok. See also *Medical services* in Lhasa, page 138. This is why having good medical insurance is so important.

MEDEVAC CREWS

International SOS is a Singapore-based medevac organisation which comes under the umbrella of parent company Asia Emergency Assistance (AEA). International SOS will evacuate to Hong Kong or Singapore if possible; there are branch offices in Beijing, Shanghai, Guangzhou and other locations in the PRC. Check their website (*www.internationalsos.com*) for contact numbers. Their head office is at International SOS (*331 North Bridge Rd, #17-00 Odeon Towers, Singapore;* 65 6338 *2311; alarm centre* 65 6338 7800; f 65 6338 7611; e *corpcomm@internationalsos. com*). The Hong Kong office is International SOS (*16 World Trade Centre, 280 Gloucester Rd, Causeway Bay;* 852 2528 9998; alarm 852 2528 9900; alarm f 852 2528 9933). Another emergency medical assistance firm is MEDEX, whose packages are more economical for long-term travellers. See their website (*www. medexassist.com*) for details: there are regional offices located in Beijing, Hong Kong, Singapore, Thailand, the Philippines and Japan. AEA has been able to fly a Lear jet from Hong Kong into Lhasa for an evacuation, but the procedure is extremely complicated and costly.

RISKY SITUATIONS AND EVACUATION

The best advice that can be offered in risky medical situations in Tibet is this: when in doubt, evacuate. Get on a scheduled flight to Kathmandu or Chengdu (an alternative is to take a Landcruiser down to Nepal, but this could take three days or more). If the patient can be brought to Gongkar Airport without too much trauma, then you can organise the evacuation yourself. When sufficiently pressured, airline authorities will bump passengers off a regular flight to Chengdu or Kathmandu to create space for an emergency case, so the idea is to get to Gongkar Airport as fast as possible.

Although helicopter evacuation is employed for injured trekkers in Nepal, it is simply not an option in Tibet. Although the Chinese military have Sikorsky and Boeing CH-47 high-altitude choppers, these are strictly for military applications and under no circumstances will be diverted for civilian use. The elevation limit for conventional helicopters is around 6,000m (although a French helicopter pilot landed on the summit of Everest in May 2005). If the condition of the patient is not too critical, and there is leeway of a few days to transport, another option is use of a Landcruiser as an ambulance – getting the patient down to Kathmandu as fast as possible.

If it's a case of altitude sickness, it's essential to get oxygen for the patient as fast as possible. Lhasa Hotel has oxygen 'pillows' (pillows with nasal tubes attached); you can also buy oxygen in a sort of aerosol can (or larger tank) in Lhasa itself at a commercial outlet just west of the Potala.

The above evacuation advice is offered because (a) medical facilities in Tibet are very basic and (b) there is no system of helicopter rescue in Tibet. Travellers have died in the past after not being evacuated, and so these risks should be taken very seriously.

SAFETY AND SECURITY

As with any Third World travel situation, you need to keep your wits about you in Tibet. Theft of luggage is uncommon on the plateau, but it does happen. Ditto with rented bicycles – lock yours in a secure, highly visible location. Luggage has even gone missing from some budget hotel storage rooms in Lhasa; to reduce the risk of this happening, identify your baggage with your passport number prominently displayed on an attached label. Keep an eye on your bags when on the move. Pilfering of personal items is known to be a risk when trekking in some areas, particularly the Everest region.

Because of the heavy Chinese military presence in Tibet, armed robbery or similar crimes are extremely rare, though in old Tibet banditry certainly existed in more remote areas. A greater threat to life and limb is on Landcruiser sorties and through resulting confrontations that may develop on these trips. Apart from the major health hazard it presents, high altitude is known to befuddle the brain, making you irritable and unable to focus when making decisions or when judgement is required. And there are important decisions that need to be made: for example, to size up quickly those on whom your life depends. That means that, if a Landcruiser or taxi driver refuses to slow down and keeps overtaking recklessly, you may have to bail out.

Confrontations between Landcruiser drivers, guides and passengers over changes of itinerary or other problems can turn ugly. Incidents have involved both Tibetan and Chinese driving crews. In the Everest region, when a Landcruiser driver and his guide (both Tibetan) refused to drive beyond Rongbuk Gompa for the extra dozen kilometres to Everest base camp, a passenger swore at the guide. The guide picked up a rock and hurled it at the passenger. The rock missed, but the passenger was in a state of shock that he would even attempt such a thing. Disagreements between passengers themselves can also turn nasty. Other arguments may erupt over permits and permission with Chinese authorities, who are not noted for their politeness. In all of these situations, mediation skills are called for: stay cool, be patient, be polite yet insistent, and keep your temper to yourself.

WOMEN TRAVELLERS

Although Tibetan Buddhism promotes a code of respect, there have been cases of harassment of Western women by Tibetan men, especially on crowded buses and when hitching rides in trucks. Tibetan women dress modestly, with little flesh exposed, and that may be the key here: a Western woman wearing shorts and a revealing top may send out the wrong message, and is bound to attract the wrong kind of attention. For these reasons, travelling solo in Tibet is not advisable for a woman. However, a woman who speaks enough Tibetan – and who dresses modestly – should not have a problem. Chinese men and Chinese military appear to have little interest in sexual advances to Western women, perhaps due to the phenomenon of numerous Chinese prostitutes plying their trade at karaoke bars in the larger towns of Tibet.

DISABLED TRAVELLERS

Until the 1990s, there was only one elevator in the whole of Tibet, at what was then known as the Holiday Inn in Lhasa. Tibetans used to sneak into the hotel to experience this wonder of the Western world. That will give some idea of the problems facing disabled travellers: Tibet can be a very rough ride. If hotels lack elevators, think about monasteries – none of them have anything remotely resembling an elevator. And monasteries and fortresses are often built on hilltops, with steep access.

Still, if a blind climber can overcome the obstacles and make it to the top of Everest, then nothing is impossible. Erik Weihenmeyer made it to the summit in 2001 from the Nepalese side. In 2004, he came to Tibet to visit his friends Sabriye Tenberken and Paul Kronenberg, the co-founders of Braille Without Borders (*www.braillewithoutborders.org*) – a project in Lhasa to help blind Tibetans. Erik inspired blind teenagers at this school to climb on Rongbuk Glacier at the north side of Everest. A documentary called *Blindsight* was released in 2006, describing these encounters. The best advice for disabled travellers is to ensure that you are going with a travel agent knowledgeable about potential problems and hazards, and who can provide the logistical support and help needed. Navyo Nepal (*www.navyonepal.com*) is a Kathmandu-based operator with experience in organising tours for disabled travellers in Nepal and Tibet.

TRAVELLING WITH CHILDREN

Tibet presents challenges for travel with young children, as the dryness and altitude can make them irritable. Then again, as so few foreigners come to Tibet with children, this is of great fascination to local Tibetans, who fawn over the kids. Be aware that medical facilities are sub-standard in Tibet, so you will need to second-guess on the medical front and arrive well-prepared for any contingencies. It's hard to say what would make Tibet entertaining for kids. Monasteries, probably not. But kids love yaks – they are new creatures to marvel at. Going to see the yak dance at a place like Shangri-La Bar in Lhasa will be a definite hit.

To set up connections with Tibetan culture, buy some picture books for kids. Available in Delhi or Kathmandu is a ten-page book titled *I am a Yak,* which introduces nomad culture. Others in this series published in India include *How the Yak got his Long Hair, A Snowlion's Lesson,* and *The Three Silver Coins.* In the West, Tibetan folklore and Buddhist animal tales are available in books for young readers. And the classic story about the yeti is found in Herge's comicbook, *Tintin in Tibet.*

GAY TRAVELLERS

There are no particular taboos or caveats for gay and lesbian travellers visiting Tibetan regions. Buddhism is an easy-going religion, and highly tolerant. In a country (China) where men (or women) often stroll hand-in-hand as a show of friendship, gay travellers should not raise any eyebrows. Some tour agents market gay and lesbian tours to Tibet, or have done so in the past. These include Out Adventures (*www.out-adventures.com*) and Hanns Ebensten Travel (*www.hetravel.com*).

Medicine buddha

Part Two

THE GUIDE

LHASA ORIENTATION

G F E D C B A

1
2
3
4

Yerpa

Ganden,
Nyingchi

Bumpa Ri

see page 127

Himalaya
• TMA

Xianzu

Jiangsu

see page 129

Ramoche
Temple

Jokhang

Swimming pool •

Norling

Northa
Khangsang

Namtso
Galyiling

Tashi Mandala

Potala

Jarmalingka
Island

see page 151

Karaoke bars

Grand Hotel Tibet

CITS •

Tibet
Nepalese consulate

Lhasa

Tibet
Museum

International
Grand

Norbulingka

see page 160

N Bradt

0   500m
0   500yds

Kyi Chu (Lhasa River)

→ Railway station

• Foreign Trade Building

Golmud

Gongkar airport,
Shigatse, Gyantse,
Tsedang

4

Lhasa

Telephone code 0891

SECRETS OF THE CITY

The name Lhasa is thought to derive from the Tibetan words *lha* (sacred) and *sa* (earth). In the late 19th and early 20th centuries, Lhasa was the most reclusive city on the face of the planet – a sacred place that was as difficult a goal as Mecca to reach. Even the greatest Western explorers of the era – Nikolai Prejavalsky, Sven Hedin – failed to make it.

Now this shroud of secrecy has been ripped away, to reveal ... a humdrum Chinese town. Lhasa is one large Chinatown now, with rows and rows of faceless Chinese apartment blocks and government buildings. 'It's just another Chinese city with a few Tibetans thrown in for colour,' says a Tibetan-born American visitor. The most disturbing aspect of Lhasa is not only the overwhelming Chinese presence: it is the Tibetan absence. The Tibetans are a minority in their own capital. The population of Lhasa is estimated at 475,000. A hefty number are migrant workers from provinces like Sichuan, working in markets, restaurants and as taxi drivers. And a sizeable contingent of Lhasa's population is an occupation force – Chinese military, paramilitary, police and bureaucrats.

If you are disappointed with Lhasa, or feel cheated of the mystique you had expected, you won't be the first. The eccentric English traveller Thomas Manning tried to forge a route through to Peking, and by chance reached Lhasa in 1812, disguised as a Chinese physician. He found the Potala extraordinary, and the rest of the place a dump. Here's his description of Old Lhasa, one of the first 'snapshots' of the Potala ever recorded by a Westerner:

> The road here, as it winds past the palace, is royally broad; it is level and free from stones, and combined with the view of the lofty towering palace, which forms a majestic mountain of a building, has a magnificent effect. The roads about the palace swarmed with monks; its nooks and angles with beggars lounging and basking in the sun ... As a whole [the Potala] seemed perfect enough; but I could not comprehend its plan in detail ... If the palace exceeded my expectations, the town as far fell short of them. There is nothing striking, nothing pleasing in its appearance. The habitations are begrimed with smut and dirt; the avenues are full of dogs ...

Manning not only managed to get to Lhasa, he also gained an unprecedented audience with the seven-year-old Dalai Lama (IX), which he recorded as a moving experience. Almost a century later, in 1904, the invading English under Francis Younghusband found their triumphal march into Lhasa impeded by piles of refuse, stagnant pools of water, open sewers, and various rabid animals foraging for putrid scraps of food. They did, however, note that the ... eaming gold roofs of the Jokhang and other temples restored the balance in favour of the majestic.

Lhasa was never a big city. There was no census taken in the Lhasa of 1949 or earlier, but the population was estimated at 30,000. There were an additional 7,000 monks at Sera Monastery and 9,000 monks at Drepung. This brought the figure to around 45,000, and probably double that number would be in Lhasa during festivals. Lhasa's design was based not so much on practical as sacred aspects. In the 7th century, King Songtsen Gampo moved his capital from the Yarlung Valley to the site of Lhasa. Later, as the residence of the Dalai Lamas, Lhasa became the religious centre of Tibet, and the seat of government. Lhasa was (and is) dominated by the Potala Palace, the winter residence of the Dalai Lama, with his summer palace, the Norbulingka, below. Within the front, walled section of the Potala was the entire Tibetan government administration, where the nobles lived. These buildings have now largely disappeared. Across town, separated by meadows, was the Jokhang Temple with a market and artisan section. A third edifice was the Palace of the Regent – the man who ruled in times when the Dalai Lama was not of age.

Old Lhasa disappeared with the Chinese invasion of Tibet in 1950 and with the flight of the Dalai Lama to India in 1959. Transformation was swift: few of those Tibetans who fled in 1959 would have recognised Lhasa in 1964, when pro-Chinese writer Israel Epstein said:

> Lhasa is becoming a beautiful modern city. Not long ago, the Potala, the temples and
> a few mansions stood amid hovels and cesspools of medieval squalor. Now there are
> miles of well lit, asphalted streets and underground drains … Electricity is supplied to
> 90 per cent of all homes for illumination and often for cooking (ex-serfs and slaves get
> it free). A working people's Cultural Palace and a hall seating twelve hundred is used
> for meetings, plays and films; there are also two other film theatres. A State Emporium
> built this year, the biggest of many new shops and stores, sells everything from needles
> and thread to sewing machines, bicycles and transistor radios …

Picture this process accelerated over the next 40-odd years, and you get an idea of what's occurred in Lhasa. A Tibetan resident commented that Lhasa had changed more since the 1990s than it had over the previous few hundred years. The urban area of Lhasa has rapidly expanded, with many new Chinese-built apartment buildings and offices. By Chinese figures, the number of vehicles in Lhasa has risen dramatically, but few parking facilities have been built to keep pace with this. Meanwhile, more than 40 auto retailers have set up shop in Lhasa, notching up brisk sales of private cars and SUVs. In northern Lhasa, an industrial fringe has cropped up, with a concrete factory and a brewery. And the coming of the railway to Lhasa is bound to accelerate Chinese construction and development – and pollution. Condominium developments have sprouted around Lhasa in readiness for a real estate boom generated by the arrival of the railway.

While technological change is a positive thing, the fact is that in Lhasa these changes have not been in the interest of the Tibetans – they're for the Chinese. The Tibetans 'still preferred independence to electricity, and freedom to sewers', as French explorer and writer Michel Peissel put it. The Chinese settlers demand electricity and street lighting, Chinese soldiers need roads, and Chinese officials need cultural palaces, and girlie bars and karaoke salons with their glitter and neon. Rows of barbershops near the Potala do a brisk business late at night. Why? Because they are fronts for prostitution – one of Lhasa's dirty secrets. Holy city or whorehouse? For Tibetan pilgrims, Lhasa remains the Holy City, but to even the casual visitor, the Chinese layering of scores of bars and karaoke salons is glaring. And that's not to mention the heavy Chinese military and paramilitary presence, with army bases ringing the city, and a network of prisons. The end result is that Lhasa has become increasingly sinicised. You see it in small details, like the statuary around the city – pairs of Chinese lions outside the entrance to the Potala, a Chinese dragon sculpture in the fountain in Potala Square, a concrete statue of Chinese mountaineers atop Everest, Chinese flags flying at strategic points, and glowing Chinese neon signs at night.

Since the arrival of the railway in 2006, followed by mass tourism Chinese style, Lhasa has turned into a kind of theme park – what you might call 'Tibet Disney'. Parts of the capital have Tibetan trimmings and appear Tibetan, but in fact are not. There are quasi-Tibetan-style buildings. Chinese department store staff may dress Tibetan style.

An official report talks of plans to build a miniature version of the Potala Palace in Lhasa to satisfy tourist demand.

Patrolling this 'theme park' is a large security force, one that is heavily armed. PLA troops in camouflage fatigues occupy bunkers on the main streets of Lhasa. Small groups of PLA with machine guns patrol the back alleys. Other teams, dressed in black with SWAT shoulder patches, keep an eye on pilgrims near the Jokhang. Sitting on rooftops under Coca-Cola umbrellas are soldiers with high-powered guns, scanning the Barkor below with binoculars.

LHASA GOES HIGH-RISE

When you picture Lhasa, you may not conjure up a metropolis of high-rises and soaring telecom towers, but this is the way Lhasa is going: upward. Previously, the only building that approached a skyscraper was the Potala, which gets most of its height from the hill it sits on. It is still the tallest place in town, but only because of the hill. Back in 1990, the tallest structure in the Lhasa Valley was a wing of the Holiday Inn, reaching a height of seven floors, with a lift – the only one in Tibet at the time and an object of great curiosity among Tibetans. But now there are lots of lifts in Lhasa, and they ride much higher. The Tibet Foreign Trade and Economic Co-operation Building, to the west side of Lhasa near the Kyi Chu River, takes the skyscraper prize with 17 floors, shimmering with a green-tinted glass façade. Other tall glass façades belong to the China Telecom building (ten floors) and the Tibet International Grand Hotel (11 floors). On the Sera Road is a 13-storey block – the ominous City Police HQ. These soaring steel and glass towers do not exactly blend in with existing Tibetan architecture: glass was rarely employed in pre-1950 Tibet (it had to be brought in overland from India) and Tibetan traditional buildings were rarely built higher than four floors. There is still lots of scope for new architectural monstrosities in Lhasa as Chinese architects continue to experiment with slapping mock-Tibetan façades onto Chinese structures, or mixing the two styles – resulting in spectacular clashes.

Very few new buildings in Lhasa have been constructed with Tibetan architectural flair: one instance is the Tibet Museum. Another is Lhasa Railway Station, which does not go high-rise, but extends horizontally. The Chinese architects claim this structure is based on traditional Tibetan elements, with an inward-sloping façade. It does, at least, have an element of fortress architecture, with little glass showing on the exterior.

To make Lhasa more attractive to coastal entrepreneurs (who, according to the Chinese, 'go to Tibet to offer their expertise to help develop the local economy') some anomalies have popped up. Chinese office blocks are going up around the town; for the first time in its long history, Lhasa is seeing traffic jams, caused by the importation of taxis. Chinese taxi drivers can earn up to five times as much in Lhasa as they can in other cities; other incentives for Chinese immigrants include preferential tax and loan policies. Keeping track of investments is the Tibet Stocks Business Centre, which has a satellite feed listing prices on China's stock exchanges in Shenzhen and Shanghai. Keeping Chinese residents comfortable requires improved communications, so Lhasa is hooked up to China's main mobile phone networks. Satellite reception is provided in Lhasa by Xizang TV and by LBTV. There is, however, a blackout on foreign media and connections: there are no foreign news agencies in Lhasa, there is virtually no foreign television reception, foreign radio signals are jammed, and only a handful of carefully screened foreign NGOs are allowed to operate within Tibet.

GETTING THERE AND AWAY

Getting to Lhasa is practically synonymous with getting to Tibet, since Lhasa is the main transport hub: all flights and overland travel are routed through the capital. Consult the route descriptions in the *Practical information* chapter, page 59, for details on the intricacies of long-distance travel to Tibet (Lhasa) by road, rail or air.

Lhasa **railway station** [165 C4] lies 4km to the southwest of town, on the south bank of the Kyi Chu. For reasons of tight security, taxis are not permitted to draw up next to the station entrance: you must walk a fair distance from the taxi pick-up point. A taxi into town is around Y40. The station is a strange piece of architecture – a mock-Tibetan structure with inward-sloped façade. Two major bridges close to Lhasa were constructed to link with the railway. There's a white triple-arched railway bridge with a 929m span several kilometres to the west of Lhasa. And close to the Foreign Trade Building downtown is a motor vehicle bridge spanning the Kyi Chu to provide access to downtown Lhasa from the railway station. For locals, the long-distance **bus station** [116 B3] in Lhasa is located to the southwest side of town, near the Tibet Museum.

Lhasa is the hub for **plane arrivals and departures** to Tibet. Ticketing to and from Chengdu, Zhongdian, Ngari, Kunming, Beijing or Kathmandu should be booked several weeks ahead, especially around peak holiday periods like National Day. There is an airline booking office downtown (\ 633 3446), located just north of Tibet Post Hotel. The airline ticket office runs its own buses to the **airport** for Y35 per passenger. Taxis charge around Y130 for the run to the airport.

GETTING AROUND

Lhasa is a small town. It's easy to navigate by prominent landmarks like the Potala or the TV tower atop Chakpori Hill. Key roundabouts can be readily identified by statuary – Golden Yak statues, Mountaineers-on-Everest statue. You could call them the 'Golden Yak roundabout' or the 'Mountaineers-on-Everest roundabout'. The 13-storey City Police HQ, a glass-and-steel block with two small towers at the top, is a key landmark at the northern side of town.

BY TAXI Foot-powered bicycle-taxis rove the streets – they seat two passengers. Regular Volkswagen cabs (imported from east China) cruise the streets and are easy to flag down. They don't have meters – you usually pay a flat rate of Y10 for any distance, but if your destination is a long way out, it may be Y15. You can also hire taxis by the hour, or by the half-day or full day for touring, which makes sense if you have three or four people.

BY BICYCLE Cycling is an excellent way of getting around Lhasa – since the town is mostly flat, you can go a long way, even on a gearless Chinese roadster. Flat is easy, but if you tackle any inclines, you need to be well acclimatised, as the altitude can be a knockout.

There are at least three places renting mountain bikes in the vicinity of the Yak Hotel [129 B1]. The best one is hidden down a back alley. Take the alley next to Dunya Restaurant, keep walking and you will find the place, which is called HDF Youth Hostel. This hostel caters to young Chinese cyclists who have come in from as far away as Sichuan. They often end up selling their bikes. You can rent good-quality mountain bikes here, including Taiwanese imports with front suspension, for about Y60 a day. On Beijing Road, close to Kyichu Hotel, is Spinn Café [129 B1] which has decent bike rentals. Their website (*www.cafespinn.com/en/*) is informative. A few blocks away, attached to the Kirey Hotel [129 D1], is a small shopfront that offers bike touring, but on the expensive side. These outfits may arrange bike tours around Lhasa, including combination jeep-bike touring around Lhasa Valley and beyond, with guide. They also sell bike accessories like water bottles, helmets, bicycle gloves and so on. If you want to mount your own day trip, head east on the road to Ganden: there is far less traffic in this direction. See the section *Outskirts of Lhasa*, page 162, for ideas on where to bicycle around Lhasa.

BY LANDCRUISER Most travellers will get around in Landcruisers. Four-wheel-drive vehicles are the best way to go anywhere in Tibet. The 4x4 vehicles sighted include the Mitsubishi Pajero and the Beijing Jeep Cherokee, but Toyota Landcruisers are the most common rental vehicles available in Lhasa. They are preferred by drivers in Tibet because Mitsubishis or Nissan 4x4s are considered unreliable and difficult to fix on the road. Some Landcruisers are mighty long in the tooth – they've probably broken world mileage records, but the odometer has long ago stopped functioning so you'll never know. A good choice, if you can afford it (you have to pay more) is the Toyota Landcruiser 4500, which has double-capacity fuel tanks, giving it a range of perhaps 700km without refuelling. It comes with an array of fog lights and other extras, and rides higher off the ground. However, the Landcruiser 4500 normally only seats four passengers (meaning three passengers plus guide), while the older long-

ADVENTURE SPORTS

Lhasa has nowhere near the number of adventure tour outfits that operate out of Kathmandu, but things are starting to pick up: some adventure tour operators from Nepal have shifted their focus and their expertise to Tibet. Most adventure tour operators (such as those for mountain biking) make arrangements with clients long before they get to Tibet. However, if you have built 'free days' into your itinerary for Lhasa, it is possible to arrange small-group adventure touring on the spot. Two options that spring to mind are bicycling around Lhasa, or combination jeep-biking. And in a group of four or more, you can join exhilarating rafting trips out of Lhasa, either as day trips or multiple-day camping sorties (see the box in *Exploring Central Tibet* chapter, page 169).

in-the-tooth Landcruiser seats five passengers (four passengers plus guide). This is because of front-seat configuration, which is bucket seat for the Landcruiser 4500 (driver and one passenger in front). In the older Landcruiser you can squeeze a driver and two passengers in the front seat (although this is not entirely comfortable because of the gear sticks). If you can afford it, go with three paying passengers and guide (this is what group tours regularly do). If you all have a lot of gear, the baggage weight alone will limit the vehicle to three passengers. If you have say seven people, you could hire two Landcruisers, sharing one guide.

Landcruisers cost about Y900–1,550 (US$130–230) and upwards a day, depending on the route, the distance, the itinerary and so on. Pricing may be based on kilometres covered: calculate on about Y4 per kilometre in a Landcruiser. If you go into Everest, there's a lot of wear and tear on the vehicle, which operators don't like, so the price will rise for that itinerary. If you're making a one-way run to the Nepal border, the agency expects a return subsidy to cover cost of fuel (even though the driver will probably pick up new passengers).

Landcruiser checklist It is worth checking the vehicle a few days before heading out of Lhasa. Get the driver to take you for a short spin to Drepung or Sera. Are the tyres bald? Do the seats have any springs left in them? Are the ashtrays full of cigarettes? What about mirrors – does your vehicle have any? These are basic things that can – and should – be remedied before you set off on a cross-Tibet saga. If you are going to pay through the nose for vehicle hire, make sure the vehicle is in decent shape, or demand another one. Same with the guide: if he mumbles incoherently in broken English, ask to have him or her changed. A guide has to speak adequate English – that is part of the job description.

BY BUS AND MINIBUS Although a local minibus system exists, most travellers don't bother with it unless heading out to, say, Drepung Monastery or Sera Monastery (buses for both can be picked up along Beijing Road, at the intersection west of Kyichu Hotel). Enquire at your hotel about which bus to take for a longer journey. You can mostly walk or bicycle around town.

The following information will not be of much use to those on pre-arranged tours. But the day may return when restrictions are lifted: think of this as information about how the locals get around. At around 06.30 minibuses patrol the streets near the Yak Hotel [129 B1] looking for local passengers for Shigatse, Samye or Nagqu. Sometimes they're parked in the alley towards the Ramoche Temple. There are crack-of-dawn pilgrim bus departures from the west side of Barkor Square, heading for Ganden (and less frequently to Tsurphu or Drigung). For Gongkar Airport, there are airline bus departures several times daily from the airline ticket office, located just north of Tibet Post Hotel. Minibuses also congregate in the vicinity just south of the Norbulingka. Around the corner from this is Lhasa's main bus and minibus station, with a large board listing places all over the map. But they probably won't sell you a ticket. Destinations they may sell tickets for include Tsedang, Shigatse and Damxung. In the past, foreigners have gotten around refusal to sell tickets by ambushing the bus on its way out of town (the fare goes in the driver's pocket). One foreigner managed to hop on a bus to Chengdu – a trip of about two weeks.

PRE-ARRANGED TOUR AGENCIES

There are a number of agencies in Lhasa, which handle travel with small or large groups that have made all arrangements before entering Tibet or China. A number of Lhasa travel agents have offices in the hotels. It is difficult to recommend a travel agent in Lhasa because the trade is heavily controlled by the TTB and Chinese official management. Here are some that are recommended:

Shangri-La Tours [127 C2] Ohdan Hotel; 656 3009; f 634 4009; e info@shangrilatours.com; www.shangrilatours.com. Small operation, but smaller in Tibet is actually better – this agency is very attentive to detail & goes the extra distance. The agency is Tibetan-managed, with Tibetan guides.

Shigatse Travels [129 B1] Yak Hotel compound; 100 Beijing Donglu; 633 0489; f 633 0482; e info@shigatsetravels.com; www.shigatsetravels.com. With lots of experience in Tibet, this agency has links to a sister agency in Nepal.

Spinn Café [129 B1] 135 Beijing Donglu; 595 23997; www.cafespinn.com. Arranges some budget adventure touring, & gives sound advice on website.

Wind Horse Adventure North Minzu Lu; 683 3009; f 683 6793; e wha@public.ls.xz.cn; www.tibetwindhorse.com. Specialises in high-end, customised tours & innovative trekking, bicycling, mountaineering, camping & rafting trips.

The agencies operating out of the ground floor of Lhasa Hotel are higher priced and CITS-linked; across the street is the head office of China International Travel Service (CITS), with TTC (Tibet Tourist Corporation), Tibet Adventure Travel and Tibet/China Travel Service all coming under the CITS wing. Handling sports aficionados is TIST (Tibet International Sports Travel), operating from the grounds of the Himalaya Hotel. Close by is the TMA (Tibet Mountaineering Association), which deals with mountaineers. Golden Bridge Travel Service is run by the PLA, and Asian Dragon Travel is run by the dreaded PAP. The catch is that agencies linked to the military or CITS can arrange permits more easily than others.

PERMITS AND PAPERWORK

Start early on the origami mastery in Lhasa: to expedite permits and paperwork, and for saving time at hotel check-in, obtain photocopies of your initial passport page plus Chinese visa page, showing entry stamp – all collated onto a single sheet of paper (possibly back to back). You can hand this photocopy over to a hotel desk, for instance, where they will spend ages copying down all the details by hand. Also procure copies of any paperwork that your guide is holding, such as Tibet Tourism Bureau (TTB) permit, Alien Travel Permits (ATPs) and so on, on the pretext that if the guide loses these items or cannot find them, you would have back-up copies.

What permits does your guide hold? Well, definitely a TTB permit, plus ATP for towns *en route*. Most Landcruisers with foreign passengers carry a TTB sticker on the front window that says 'China Tibet Tour'. For more remote locations in far west or far east Tibet, extra permits are required – military permit (for restricted areas and getting past military checkpoints), Foreign Affairs Permit, and Cultural Bureau Permit (for visiting sites of special architectural or cultural interest such as the Guge Kingdom). These can take time to obtain in Lhasa.

NEPALESE CONSULATE The only consulate in Lhasa is the Royal Nepal Consulate-General [165 D3] (683 0609 or 681 5744; f 683 6890). The visa-issuing section is located near the road at the north side of the Norbulingka (10.00–12.00 Mon–Fri). You can pick up a 30-day or 60-day Nepalese visa within a day for US$30 or Y240. Double-entry or multiple-entry visas can also be obtained (price will

4

double or triple), and there may be a half-price visa valid for 15 days. It's not really necessary to obtain a Nepalese visa as you can get the same visa for the same price on arrival in Nepal by air or by road. However, some like the cachet of the exotic visa issued in Lhasa.

⌂ WHERE TO STAY

The following hotels and guesthouses are arranged by location and pricing. Location means a lot in Lhasa – the closer you are to the Barkor area, the better, because that's where all the Tibetan action is and where you can stroll around at will. There are other factors to consider. How is the plumbing? What time does the front door close at night? Is there secure storage if you leave bags behind for a week or more? Apart from location and price, there's one very important factor to consider: who runs the place? More kudos to you if you stick with Tibetan management.

As for Chinese management: well, they may not want you in their hotel at all. Apartheid is a standard Chinese practice, segregating Chinese tourists from foreign tourists. A number of hotels are restricted to Chinese only, and PSB would rather keep foreigners isolated in a select number of hotels where they can keep an eye on them. To the southeast side of the Barkor, the Khada Hotel appears to be for Tibetan truck drivers. Out near the Mountaineers-on-Everest roundabout, the

TIBET CHIC: CHINESE TOURISTS

It's late afternoon on the rooftop of the Jokhang, and a Chinese woman with her hair braided Tibetan style (with small chunks of turquoise in it) is on her mobile phone, chatting with relatives in Shanghai. The monks are doing a roaring trade selling drinks and lucky charms to a cluster of Chinese tourists, all happily snapping pictures of each other. Among them are some 'military tourists' – in uniform, off duty and carrying cameras with big lenses.

These are well-heeled Chinese tourists; a trip to Tibet is not cheap. Some wear their wealth: one tourist I met came armed not only with a video camera but with two digital still cameras – he downloaded the images to his laptop and then sent them off to friends from a cybercafé in Lhasa. Tibet is a 'cool' place to go among the wealthy. In 1997, statistics say 260,000 Chinese visitors came to Tibet; by 2001, that number had doubled, and by 2005, the number had quadrupled, with over a million Chinese tourists visiting Tibet that year – though it is unclear whether 'military tourists' are included in this count. By 2010, the figure had reached over six million Chinese tourists annually, which is more than the entire population of Tibetans living in ethnic Tibet.

The Chinese tourist phenomenon in Tibet means that you will inevitably mix with sometimes unwieldy numbers of them at key sites, like the Jokhang. Interactions are interesting here – not a single Chinese tourist I came across would venture an opinion on the Dalai Lama or Buddhism in Tibet. Of course, to broach such topics with Chinese settlers, hard-nosed administrators or the military living in Tibet is impossible, but you'd think that a Chinese tourist might be willing to talk.

An obligatory stop for Chinese visitors is Potala Square, where they dress up in Tibetan cloaks and fox-fur hats to have their photos taken with the Potala in the background. Dress-up charades in fact abound in Lhasa: Chinese women posing as Tibetan women (wearing Tibetan-style long dresses) have been sighted working

Plateau Hotel seems to cater exclusively to a Chinese clientele. The same appears to be true of Gold Grain Hotel, which is a bland 50-room block on Yuthok Road, with prices in the mid-range. Close by this is Ying Binguan, which is exclusively reserved for visiting Chinese officials. Catering to well-heeled Chinese clientele is the modern Tibet Royal Hotel, with a big disco-karaoke complex, on the southern section of the Lingkor. Out on 'Karaoke Row' (west of the Golden Yak roundabout) are some glitzy Chinese places with names like Hotel Dream Paris. And scattered around Lhasa are hotels that deal mostly with Chinese group tours, like the Century Grand Hotel or the Snow Mountain Grand Hotel. The hotels specialising in Chinese clientele are not detailed in the following selection, because they are boring, away from the centre, and the staff mostly do not speak anything other than Chinese.

Addresses are confusing in Lhasa because street names keep changing. Three different names may be in use: Tibetan, Chinese and Western. For instance, Dekyi Shar Lam, Beijing Donglu and Beijing East Road are one and the same road. Beijing Zhonglu and Beijing Middle Road are the same. And Tengyeling Road is the same as Danjelin Road. Some names derive from a feature found along the road, or connected to it. For instance, Norbulingka Road leads to Norbulingka Summer Palace. Yuthok Road is named after an ancient covered stone bridge, which is actually still there – it has been transformed into a long gift shop (located about a block west of Barkor Square).

in department stores, selling tickets at key attractions, and as receptionists in some hotels.

Despite communist leadership vilification of the Dalai Lama, trendy Chinese can shop for Tibetan jewellery at boutiques in Shanghai, or buy an astonishing variety of Tibetan products (made by state-run companies) like ginseng-berry juice or Tibetan barley wine (Shangelila label). And though China is officially atheist, Buddhism is resurfacing, with some high-profile figures openly practising the religion. You will find, at some pilgrimage sites around Tibet, Chinese participating in rituals like tying on prayer-flags, burning juniper and chanting 'Om Mani Padme Hum' (see the entry 'mantra' in the glossary).

That's exactly what Chinese chanteuse Dadawa did on a track of her 1995 album, *Sister Drum*. Dadawa achieved the remarkable feat of infuriating both Tibetans and Chinese simultaneously with this album. Dadawa (Moon) is her adopted Tibetan name: her real name is Zhu Zheqin. On the album she croons songs like 'Sky Burial' and 'The Sixth Dalai Lama's Love Song'. In the cover art, she appears dressed in monastic robes, but her hair is not shaven (it is hidden under a monastic hood) and she is wearing jewellery, which neither monks nor nuns do in Tibet. In London, Tibetans gathered outside the office of her record label to protest exploitation of Tibetan culture. But in Tibet itself, reticence turned to jubilation when Tibetans discovered that in the background track of her top hit was the voice of a woman praising the Dalai Lama in Tibetan! Dadawa had to recall her album and have it re-edited, and her videos are still banned in Tibet. In 2002, a Tibetan monk attending a Dadawa concert in Beijing expected to hear a twisted version of his culture. However, he said he was pleasantly surprised to hear Dadawa accompanied by Tibetan musicians, who were allowed liberties not extended to their brethren in Tibet itself. Dadawa's albums are partly responsible for the phenomenon of Tibet Chic, which draws legions of Chinese tourists to visit Tibet.

Pricing notes: many hotels in Lhasa charge the same for single, twin (two beds) or double rooms (either one large bed, or two beds). Others offer discounted rates for singles, but the interpretation of 'single' seems to vary. Some hotels charge more for single rooms because 'single' means one large bed, and there may be a balcony or additional features in this room. Some hotels include all service charges in the price; others include breakfast as well – and even, in high-end hotels, free oxygen! In mid-range and high-end hotels, a service charge of 10% may well be added to bills. These hotels claim to accept a wide range of credit cards: American Express, Visa, Diners, MasterCard, Dragon, JCB, Great Wall and Peony. The high season for travel to Tibet is April to October: prices may fluctuate seasonally, dipping lower in the shoulder (between high and low seasons) and low seasons. Travellers have bargained lower rates than those posted on the reception boards, especially for stays of a week or longer. Rates can plummet in winter months, along with temperatures (and no heating).

LOW-END TO MID-RANGE HOTELS A number of hotels in Lhasa offer accommodation from dormitory up to deluxe double rooms. Though few backpackers manage to get into Lhasa these days, there are many young Chinese backpackers on the loose – and lots of low-end hotels that cater to them. The tariff in this group is Y20–50 for a dorm bed, Y80–200 for a double room and Y200–400 for a double with bath. The hotels listed in the Barkor and Sera Road areas are mostly Tibetan-managed or Nepalese-managed, which is why they are placed upfront here. Those in the Lingkor area are likely to be Chinese-run.

A British traveller who stayed at a mid-range hotel (included with an arrival tour by mistake) says that his Y500 room at the Shangbala Hotel was equivalent to a Y50 room at the Yak Hotel (but with no bathroom included at the Yak for this price). For a double with bath, much better value is to stay at the Yak or Snowland for around Y260, or at the Flora Hotel for Y180. Very popular with travellers are the Tibetan-run Yak, Kirey, Snowland and Banakshol hotels, which operate on a similar formula – they offer a range of accommodation, and have on-site shop, email and internet access, restaurant and travel agents. These hotels have hot showers, laundry facilities and will store baggage while you're off on a trip. Some hotels offer a few services for free, like free laundry (at the Banakshol) or free internet. In the low-end to mid-range price category, Nepalese-managed hotels are a good choice because they favour Tibetan staff and Tibetan-style décor: these include the Mandala, Dhood Gu, Gorkha and Kyichu hotels.

Barkor area

🏠 **Snowland** [129 B2] Off Barkor Sq; ☎ 632 3687. This Tibetan-managed courtyard-style hotel is popular with backpackers & those on group tours. Good central location, but toilets are sloppy (if staying in dorms or a room without bath). Hot shower stalls are grubby. Has email centre, bike rentals & FIT travel centre (official monopoly, high prices). *Y25 dorm (4-bed to 8-bed); Y30 common trpl (per bed); Y180 dbl. In the newer wing Y250 dbl with bath, plus some deluxe rooms.*

🏠 **Yak** [129 B1] (130 rooms) 100 Beijing Donglu; ☎ 632 3496; f 633 6906; e lhasayak_

hotel@hotmail.com. A large, efficient operation with central courtyard. The quiet main section is removed from the road. Excellent rooftop teahouse with expansive views. Cleaner than Snowland. Rooms range from dorm to deluxe, & include buffet b/fast at the Dunya Restaurant next door. *The ground-floor dorms around Y40 a bed. Rooms with common bath Y100, or Y150 for a trpl (no bath). Higher-end rooms Y260 dbl with shower; Y380 standard; Y550–650 deluxe; Y1,500–1,888 suite.*

🏠 **Kirey** [129 D1] (100+ rooms) 105 Beijing Donglu; ☎ 632 3987. Though lacking in

BARKOR AREA

KEY
━ ━ Barkor pilgrim walking route
─ ─ Lingkor pilgrim walking route

0 ───── 200m
0 ───── 200yds

People's Hospital
Tibet Emergency Centre, 1120

N
Bradt

Khaide Nangma Club
New Century
Tianhe
Department stores
Gold Grain
Department stores
Yuthok Bridge
YUTHOK ROAD
BEIJING ST

see Potala Area map, page 151

Tibet Royal Hotel & Top View Disco
JIANGSU ROAD

Bank of China
NIANGRE ROAD
Markets
Airline office & buses
Tibet Post

City Police HQ (13 storeys)
DZUK-TRUN ROAD
Bank of China
Jinbo
Ramoche Temple
Tent makers
Ohdan
Bicycle Hostel
Yak
Kyichu
Spин Café
Institute of Tibetan Medicine
Snowland
Tromsikhang Market
Kirey
DUOSENGE RD
Barkor Square
Peace

see page 129

Sera
China Telecom
Bank of China
Gang Gyen
Banakshol
Pata
Barkor Bazaar (pilgrim route)
Ani Sangkhung Nunnery
Xiongbala
The Jokhang
Mosque
Khada

Plateau
Holy Swan
Mountaineers on Everest statue
Bank of China
E LINGKOR ROAD

Lhasa Municipal People's Hospital & Emergency Centre
(DEKYI SHAR ROAD)
Tibet PSB (travel permits)
Karaoke bars
Tibetan mini-mart
E LINGKOR ROAD
St Regis
(TSANG GYUN SHAR ROAD)
Lhasa carpet factory (government run)

Furniture makers
Sunlight

TV Tower
Lhasa Broadcasting & Television Centre
Eastern Bus Station (private companies)
Tibet University

Stadium
TMA,
Himalaya Hotel

imaginative design, this hotel is well managed & packed with good features, like its internet café & free baggage storage. Shangri-La Restaurant at the courtyard centre stages dinner-dance soirées. *Rooms Y30 dorm (in 3- to 9-bed rooms); Y70 dbl; Y150 dbl with bath.*

🏠 **Cool Yak Hotel** (around 30 rooms & some suites) Tengyeling Rd near Snowland Hotel; ✆ 685 6777; e coolyak@gmail.com. *Y360 standard rooms, Y580 deluxe.*

🏠 **Barkhhor Namchen House** Off the Barkhor; ✆ 679 0125; www.tibetnamchen.com. Well managed Tibetan-style place. *Y60–70 dorms.*

🏠 **Dong Cuo Youth Hostel** [129 E1] On Beijing Rd, same vicinity as the Kirey; ✆ 627 3388; f 633 0683. Favoured by Chinese backpackers. *Dorms Y30–40 a bed; Y70 trpl room (no bath); Y130 sgl with bath; Y180 dbl with bath.*

🏠 **Banakshol** [129 F1] (around 100 rooms) Beijing Donglu; ✆ 632 3829. Has bike rental; FIT travel centre (the same rip-off one as in Snowland). Rooms range from budget upward – the better ones are those on the upper floors, where there's more sunlight. Walls are thin – a definite minus. Tibetan management is very friendly. *Y25 dorm (in 30 rooms of 4–5 beds); Y30 sgl (10 rooms); Y60 dbl (45 rooms); Y150 with bath (20 rooms with deluxe Tibetan-style décor).*

Potala area
🏠 **Airway Hotel** [151 F2] Just east of the Potala; ✆ 683 4444. Hotel is bland, apart from this draw: *rooms start at Y180 & rise to*

Sera Road area
🏠 **Gakyiling** [116 E2] (48 rooms) Off Sera Rd on side street; ✆ 632 6685. Favoured by NGO groups. *Y230–280 dbl; Y370 suite.*

🏠 **Tashi Mandala** [116 D2] Near Gakyiling. Arrayed around a Tibetan-style courtyard, this hotel is also a favourite of NGO groups. Price negotiable, depending on length of stay.

Lingkor area
🏠 **Gorkha Hotel** [129 C4] (around 40 rooms) 45 Jiangsu Lu, South Lingkor Rd; ✆ 627 1991; f 627 1993; e tibetgorkhahotel@yahoo.com. This splendid hotel lies on an alley off the main road. It is built around several enclosed gardens, with the back castle-like structure originally being

🏠 **Flora** [129 F4] Off east Barkor on Hobaling Rd, near the mosque; ✆ 632 4491; f 632 4901; e florahtl@hotmail.com. This hotel is well run, with a small courtyard garden café & internet section. *Main building has 20 rooms for Y180 dbl, or Y270 trpl, including bath – excellent value.*

🏠 **Kailash** [129 A1] 143 Beijing Donglu; ✆ 632 2220. Group-tour hotel with some Tibetan-style standard rooms & some attempt at Tibetan décor, with Tibetan staff, although it's Chinese-run. *Prices similar to Kyichu Hotel, rooms for Y160 sgl or Y380 dbl.*

🏠 **Ohdan** [127 C2] (25 rooms) Near Ramoche Temple; ✆ 634 4999; f 636 3992; e ohdan_guesthouse@yahoo.com. Large 4-storey building with restaurant-bar on the ground floor, & a 5th-floor rooftop café with great views. The ground-floor Tibetan-style restaurant stages special movie nights, *momo*-making classes & other events. *Rooms with bath & TV for Y160, & 2 sgls for Y180 a piece.*

🏠 **Mandala** [129 B3] (35 rooms) South side of Jokhang Temple, 31 South Barkor St; ✆ 633 8940; f 632 4787. Centrally located group-tour hotel & has Tibetan staff & Nepalese management. On the ground floor is a great dining area & bar; you can access the rooftop for terrific views over Lhasa, with the Jokhang in the foreground. *Y190 sgl; Y270 standard dbl; or Y370 trpl.*

Y280–320 for Potala views in west-facing rooms on upper floors.

🏠 **Norling Hotel** [116 E2] Sera Rd; ✆ 636 1888; f 634 2198. *Rooms Y480–580.*

🏠 **Northa Khangsang** [116 E1] (30 rooms) Sera Rd; ✆ 634 1734; f 634 1735. The hotel is oddly constructed around a cavernous Tibetan-style foyer with teahouse; the room interiors are Western-style. *Rooms Y360–480 & up.*

the old Nepalese (Gorkha) consulate. The hotel is Nepalese-managed & has a restaurant facing an interior courtyard garden – a pleasant place to hang out & have a drink, even if you are not staying at the hotel. Tibetan tent teahouse on the roof. 25 rooms are standard dbls. *Y50 dorm*

THE TIBETAN QUARTER

Lhasa WHERE TO STAY

4

129

(6-bed); Y220 common room; Y250 trpl (no bath); Y390 standard (with bath); Y570–700 for a suite.

🏠 **Pata** [129 F2] (18 dbl rooms) East Lingkor. Tibetan-style hotel with 3 floors; great balconies with potted plants. Some NGOs lodge here. Tibetan-run. Rooms Y120 each.

🏠 **Peace** [129 B4] (38 rooms) 10 Jiangsu Rd, South Lingkor; 📞 632 4253; 📠 634 8612. A concrete block with Tibetan trimmings, & Chinese-run. In an isolated spot – not much

atmosphere. Y288 sgl; Y380 standard; Y260 trpl; Y680 suite.

🏠 **Tibet Royal Hotel** [127 A4] (24 rooms, 6 suites) South Lingkor; 📞 675 7849. Sports a mock-Tibetan façade, but is Chinese to the core. Has a large entertainment-disco-karaoke complex at the back called Top View Disco, with an advanced light & sound system, & a rabbit-warren of karaoke rooms leading off it. Favoured by the military brass. Y268 rooms; Y388 suite.

MID-RANGE HOTELS

Tariff is Y400–975 (US$60–150) for a double in these hotels, rated three-star by Chinese tourism authorities. You can easily tell classier hotels by lifts in the lobby, oxygen piped into rooms (or supplied through a machine), and saunas. Although they may have some token Tibetan interior design, the following mid-range hotels are Chinese-run (except for the Dhood Gu and Kyichu, which are Nepalese-run). Most offer rooms with hot water, colour television, IDD phone, air conditioning and other comforts. Lobby facilities include business centre, fitness centre, travel agent, gift shops and so on. A peculiar item on the tariffs is the 'o'clock room': this is a room that is rented by the hour for Y100–200, probably for short-time flings. Even the high-end Tibet Hotel has them.

🏠 **Kyichu** [129 A1] (aka Kechu or Kecho) (around 50 rooms) 149 Beijing Donglu; 📞 633 1541; 📠 6335728; 📧 kyichu@public.ls.xz.cn; www. kyichuhotel.com. This Nepali-managed hotel hosts small 5-storey wings enclosing a garden. Very clean, highly recommended. Excellent restaurant & giftshop. Y380 sgl; Y480 dbl; Y560 trpl; Y680 suite.

🏠 **Shangbala** [129 B2] (70+ rooms) 1 Tengeling Rd; 📞 632 3888; 📠 632 3577. Chinese blockhouse with some Tibetan trimmings, used by tour groups. Strange atmosphere. Pricey. Y400–800 sgl or dbl.

🏠 **Dhood Gu** [129 C1] (67 rooms) Near Tromsikhang market; 📞/📠 632 2555; 📧 dhoodgu@ yahoo.cn. 5-storey Tibetan-style hotel. The rooftop has fine views of the Potala. Most rooms Y420 dbl; Y520 Potala view; some cheaper.

🏠 **Xiongbala** [129 C4] (83 rooms) 28 Jiangsu Lu, South Lingkor; 📞 633 8888; 📠 633 1777. Comfortable place with adequate rooms: some upper-floor rooms have Potala views. Mixed reviews from foreign guests due to spotty service & haphazard management style. Y400–550 standard; Y1,900–2,500 suite.

🏠 **New Century** [151 G2] (80 rooms) Beijing Middle Rd; 📞 833 4895. Has 2 lifts. Y500 standard; Y1,000 suite.

🏠 **Grand Hotel Tibet** [151 A1] (540 rooms) 195 Beijing Zhonglu, west of the Potala; 📞 682

6096; 📠 683 2195. Patronised by visiting delegations. Dining Hall Number One has a capacity for 1,000 guests at a conference. The 'Oxygen Bar' turns out to be part of the hotel clinic, with a few armchairs where you can siphon from an oxygen bag for a fee. Rooms arrayed in 4 wings. Y160 economy dbl (about 100 rooms); Y280 standard (185 rooms); Y460 deluxe (180 rooms); Y2,000 suite.

🏠 **Xianzu Hotel** [116 E4] Xianzu Island to the southeast side of Lhasa; 📞 871 5888; 📠 671 5333. The hotel incorporates a lot of Tibetan design in the buildings. It has a pleasant outdoor café set in large grounds; close by is an outdoor swimming pool. You could cycle over & partake of these features without staying there. The place is a magnet for Tibetan picnickers who come to pavilions in the grounds. Y330 common room; Y580 sgl; Y680 standard.

🏠 **Himalaya Hotel** [116 F3] (130+ rooms) 6 Lingkor Donglu; 📞 632 2293; 📠 633 2675; 📧 himalayahotel@tist.net. Rooms with bath, arrayed in several wings, the main one being a high-rise building. Sports-related groups often lodge out this way because TIST (Tibet International Sports Travel) & the TMA (Tibet Mountaineering Association) have offices in the vicinity. There are possible traditional dance performances taking place at night here. Y580 sgl; Y750 standard; Y900 & up for suites.

BOUTIQUE HOTELS Mostly sited in Lhasa's **old quarter**, the following places are boutique hotels imbued with history. Old Tibetan courtyard housing has been lovingly restored to turn structures into mini-hotels with Tibetan décor – and loads of character. Some are former residences of nobles or important dignitaries in old Lhasa. All are small – and expensive, hitting the high-end range. Even if you don't lodge here, while wandering the Barkor back alleys, you might want to take a peek to see what the traditional architecture looked like. You might be able to access the rooftop restaurant in some cases.

⌂ **House of Shambhala** [129 D1] (9 rooms) 7 Jiri Erxiang; ☎ 632 6533; www.shabhalaserai. com. Stylish boutique hotel down a quiet back alley. Has a great rooftop terrace. The hotel is the pet project of Lawrence Brahm, a former New York lawyer who lives in Beijing & who is obsessed with finding Shambhala. Nearby, also run by the owner, is Shambhala Spa. An offshoot of the hotel, called Shambhala Palace, also in the old quarter, offers 17 rooms (Y765–1,200). *Y675–1,050.*

⌂ **Lingtsang** (9 rooms) South of Barkor Sq; ☎ 689 9991; e lingtsanghotel@163.com; www. lingtsangboutiquehotel.com. A boutique hotel in what was once the residence of a tutor of the

Dalai Lama. On the roof is a restaurant with views of the Jokhang. *Y600 standard; Y1,660 deluxe.*

⌂ **Yabshi Phunkhang** (21 rooms) Beijing Donglu; ☎ 632 8885; www.yabshiphunkhang. com. This heritage building underwent a 4-year restoration. The hotel is constructed in a complex that long ago was built for the parents of the 11th Dalai Lama. Large rooms. *Y1,000–1,800.*

⌂ **Trichang Labrang** 11 Luguwu Xiang; ☎ 630 9555; www.trichanglabrang.com. Former residence of Trijiang Rinpoche, previous tutor to the 14th Dalai Lama. Great courtyard garden, but rooms are a bit lacking for the price. *Y280–500 sgl/dbl; Y880 deluxe.*

HIGH-END HOTELS Lhasa's top hotels charge Y1,000 a room and up, and are all Chinese run. These are rated four-star by Chinese tourism authorities; the St Regis Lhasa Resort claims five-star status. Up and coming are more high-end hotels operated by luxury chains InterContinental Group (with 1,200 rooms in first phase) and Shangri-La Hotel Group (with 350 rooms).

⌂ **Brahmaputra Grand Hotel** [165 G4] A long way east on Jiangsu Lu; ☎ 630 9999; www.tibethotel.cn. Listed here more as a place to visit, because of its bizarre private museum, with *objets d'art* collected by supermarket tycoon Zhang Xiaohong. The 2nd-floor museum houses ethnographic displays, displays of Tibetan armour & opera masks, & displays of turquoise & amber jewellery. The Tibetan statuary is top-notch, but the black-&-white photos displayed are simply reproductions of historic photos taken by early foreign visitors to Lhasa. The museum seems to have more gutsy displays than the government-run Tibet Museum at the other end of town. Besides which, the Brahmaputra Grand Musuem is free. Oh yes, & it is a hotel – a vast, sprawling hotel. *From Y1100 sgl; Y2200 dbl; Y4,800–9,800 suites.*

⌂ **Tibet International Grand Hotel** [116 B3] (80+ rooms) South Minzu Rd; ☎ 683

2888; f 683 2919; e tigh@tighotel.ls.xz.cn. 11-storey high-rise block: the all-glass exterior reflects the structure's original intent of being an office tower for China Telecom (which owns the present hotel). TIGH is angled for businesspeople, & has little in the way of atmosphere. There are Chinese & Western restaurants on the 3rd floor, & panoramic views from the top floor. Near the fitness centre in the basement area is a small indoor pool, but it is not heated. *Y800 standard or sgl; Y1,200–1,800 suites.*

⌂ **Jiangsu Ecological Garden Hotel** [116 E4] (Jiangsu Shentai Yuan Hotel) Xianzu Island to the southeast side of Lhasa; ☎/f 632 8666. Set in parkland, but the buildings are dreary, & b/fast is Chinese only. *Y1,088 standard; Y1,288 sgl; Y1,900–2,900 suite.*

⌂ **Tibet Hotel** [116 B2] (200+ rooms) 64 Beijing Middle Rd; ☎ 683 4966; f 683 6787. A mock-Tibetan abomination of a building that is favoured by Asian group tours & Chinese clientele. Unfriendly & surly staff: has a VIP wing where staff are trained not to snap at guests. The giftshop is worth checking out. *Y880 sgl or standard; Y980 trpl; Y2,800 suite.*

⌂ **Lhasa Hotel** [116 B2] (468 rooms & suites) 1 Minzu Lu; ☎ 683 2221; f 683 5796; e sales@lhasahotel.com.cn; www.lhasahotel.com.cn. Has a swimming pool – but nobody seems to use it, because it's poorly maintained (or simply because there may be no water in it). Even if it is a luxury hotel, Lhasa Hotel has its problems. Built in 1985, it is falling apart in places, with water-damaged walls. Lhasa Hotel still has a sign up saying 'Former Holiday Inn Lhasa', but does not explain the background (see box, *The Former Holiday Inn*, below). The hotel boasts 3 tower wings, each with a lift (the 1st to arrive in Tibet). The hotel has the full gamut of services, including telecom & business centre, currency exchange counter & several giftshops. There's a fitness centre with sauna & jacuzzi. Restaurants include the Tibetan-style Himalaya (styled like a Tibetan teahouse), Chinese-style Kailash & the Western-style Hard Yak Café. The banquet hall can seat 600. Lhasa Hotel appears to be one of

THE FORMER HOLIDAY INN

In late 1997 it was announced that the Holiday Inn management group would not renew its contract for running the branch in Lhasa – the only luxury hotel in Tibet at the time. No reason was given, and the international giant continues to run its numerous other branches around China. Victory was claimed by various campaign groups in the West, particularly the Free Tibet Campaign in England, which launched a boycott of Holiday Inn operations and those of its British parent company, Bass PLC (brewers of Bass beer), in 1993. In 1997, Students for a Free Tibet and 50 other Tibet support groups joined the campaign.

In its heyday, the Holiday Inn Lhasa was run in partnership with the Chinese government and was the largest foreign currency earner in Lhasa – catering to well-heeled group tours. The original hotel was completed by the Chinese in 1986: the Holiday Inn corporation modernised the building and renamed it. A trusted brand name like Holiday Inn brought a certain amount of prestige, a veneer of respectability, and a seal of approval for Chinese operations in Tibet. There were even Miss Tibet contests conducted in 1992 to attract tourism during the slack winter months. You had to wonder how long it would take McDonald's, Pizza Hut and the rest of the multi-national gang to get there in the wake of Holiday Inn.

After the Holiday Inn management left, the building reverted to its original name, Lhasa Hotel, but the sign out front and the hotel brochures still bear the legend: 'The Former Holiday Inn Lhasa'. A hilarious account of life at the former Holiday Inn is given in Alec Le Sueur's book, *Running a Hotel on the Roof of the World*. Although Tibetans work at the hotel, there is no Tibetan presence in the management – profits only benefit the Chinese. Top-ranking Chinese military like to stay there, and it appears that the staff are in cahoots with security forces.

Foreign protesters have now moved on to targeting other Western luxury hotel groups operating in Lhasa, such as InterContinental. Another enterprise sparking protests is the beer company Pabst. Pabst Blue Ribbon operates a Sino–American joint venture: in 2001, their Chinese partner strung up a large banner in Lhasa congratulating the Chinese on the 50th anniversary of the takeover of Tibet. There is one other beer joint venture in Lhasa: Carlsberg has shares in Lhasa Beer company.

the rare hotels in Lhasa permitted to have CNN broadcasts (via Beijing) relayed to the TVs in the guestrooms. For the price of a drink you can drop in & watch CNN & other programmes on satellite TV by going to tiny Chang's Bar, on the ground floor. *Y1,050 standard; Y1,600 Tibetan-style; Y2,100–3,000 suites; Y8,888 presidential suite (US$1,300+ a night).*

🏠 **Four Points by Sheraton** (103 rooms & suites) On a side road off Jiangsu Lu; ✆ 634 8888; www.fourpoints.com/lhasa. Part of US-based Starwood Hotels Group, this place opened in 2006 & is rated 4-star. *Y1,480–1,580 standard rooms; Y2,580 superior rooms; Y3,400 suites.*

🏠 **St Regis Lhasa Resort** [129 F4] (122 rooms, 28 villas & 12 suites) 22 Jiangsu Rd;

✆ 680 8888; f 630-8888; e reservation.lhasa@ stregis.com; www.stregis.com/lhasaresort. Also run by the Starwood Hotels Group, this sprawling hotel occupies a large corner on the south side of Lhasa & started operation in 2010. Constructed with Tibetan features in both architecture & décor. Currently the only 5-star hotel in Lhasa: a rating no doubt acquired because of its functioning swimming pool – a gold-tiled pool that is part of Iridium luxury spa, along with 6 treatment suites, yoga studio & meditation garden. On the ultimate Lhasa pampering list, the St Regis offers butler service, plasma TV sets, & in-room Wi-Fi. *Y3,000 standard rooms; prices go into orbit from there.*

✗ WHERE TO EAT

Lhasa is well supplied with food: you can even buy fresh bananas (from Central America), peaches and mangoes from street vendors. You can throw together your own food in Lhasa: there are places where you can find fresh-baked flatbreads, delicious yak curd (yoghurt) and bananas – start putting these things together and you'll have a great breakfast. It's fun to wander the streets around the Barkor to get your daily yoghurt.

A number of restaurants listed here double as suppliers of food for trekkers and those on Landcruiser trips. In the self-catering line, department stores around Lhasa stock a good range of fruit juices, dried fruit, almonds, nuts and Dove chocolate. Mini-marts do well, too: Norling mini-mart, a Tibetan-run place on East Lingkor Road near the Flora Hotel, stocks supplies like trekkers' muesli from Nepal, mango Frooti drink, peanut butter from India, sunblock and so on.

Watch out for dirty restaurant kitchens – diarrhoea and food poisoning are the threats here. Many travellers in Lhasa have stomach problems or coughs, colds and flu. Stomach problems are probably traceable to water that's not properly boiled, or to uncooked vegetables. Near Tashi I are several Muslim noodle houses with hearty fare at low prices: these bear green banners with the Muslim crescent moon on them. Opposite Sheng Shia Hotel, west of the Potala, is a string of hot-pot places where food is cooked at the table. Watch out for heavy Chinese food or greasy food. Peking duck, for instance, is very rich – and hard on your system.

If you are feeling really acclimatised, you can wash down dinner with some wine (alcohol will go to your head very quickly at altitude). Avoid the cheap Chinese champagne on the shelves – this is only good for bathing in. The bottle to purchase is Dynasty white wine, which is made in Tianjin as part of a French joint-venture enterprise. Another good brand is Great Wall red.

✗ **Makye Ame** [129 D3] Back of the Barkor. This 2nd-floor restaurant has a laid-back atmosphere & big bay windows overlooking the Barkor, where you can watch the Tibetan pilgrim world turn & turn. The restaurant is Tibetan-run & serves an eclectic menu from *thukpa* (noodle

soup) to pizza. You can also visit for drinks alone – go up to the tented rooftop section for even better views of the Barkor. Makye Ame also rents books if you leave a deposit. The restaurant has branches in Beijing & Kunming. Behind Makye Ame is a lot of history. Makye Ame is thought to be the name of a beautiful woman that the 6th Dalai Lama pursued while in disguise. The original tavern on this site was said to be the trysting place – & was thus allowed the honour of having its exterior painted in royal yellow.

✗ Dunya [129 C1] Next door to Yak Hotel; ☏ 633 3374. Dunya has cornered the market in safe eating: the place is run by Europeans & is very clean & spacious, with wooden tables, candles at night & a great ambience. It features a mixed menu, including Tibetan, Italian & Indonesian. On the menu is 'yak sizzler', which is yak steak, French fries & vegetables served in a hot skillet – so hot that it sizzles.

✗ Potala Traditional Snack Bar Opposite the Yak Hotel [129 B1]; ☏ 633 6664. Offers a mixed Tibetan, Nepali & Western menu & can get busy at night. The upstairs section showcases a scale model of the façade of the Potala Palace, set into the wall. Next door is Ganglamedo (see *Bars*, page 136), which offers similar fare.

✗ New Mandala Restaurant [129 B2] To the west side of Barkor Sq, located on an upper floor with views. This place has Tibetan décor & is mostly set up for group tours. Chase after cheeses: you can maybe get a tasty nutty-flavoured yak-cheese brought in via Nepal. This cheese is hard to find in Lhasa, for some reason.

✗ Naga [129 B1] Tengyeling Rd; ☏ 655 0758. Cave-like décor on ground floor, with low seating. Good atmosphere – serves meals & snacks, with Nepali, Tibetan & Western fare. Try the upper floor, too.

✗ Snowland [129 B2] Snowland Hotel. A few notches up in décor & price is Snowland Restaurant, in Snowland Hotel but a separate operation, with Nepali cooks. This place is very comfortable, with a larger section at the back for group tours. On the menu is a selection of Western, Chinese, Tibetan & Nepali food. The Tibetan dishes are curious: yak tongue salad, yak noodle soup, yak fried chilli. The b/fast menu may sound more

familiar, serving muesli with fruit & curd (tangy yoghurt), banana milk porridge or scrambled eggs & coffee. Ask about their tasty yak cheese, which is made locally & can be purchased by weight. Snowland restaurant also sells supplies for those off on excursions: you can buy excellent brown bread, canned goods, Swiss chocolate & other delicacies imported from Nepal.

✗ Norling Restaurant [129 A1] Kyichu Hotel. Overlooking a courtyard garden, this upscale restaurant serves great Indian, Nepalese & Western fare with wonderful atmosphere, though it's a tad pricey. You can dine at outdoor tables in the courtyard garden – a pleasant retreat from the trenches & pillboxes on Beijing St outside.

✗ Kailash [129 F1] Banakshol Hotel. This Nepali-run restaurant serves great vegetarian food, rents out books (inc guidebooks) & sells trekking food supplies.

✗ Tashi 1, Tashi 2 Family-run & with fair prices, but food is bland. Tashi 1 is upstairs on the corner of Tengyeling Rd & Beijing Rd. Tashi 2 is inside the Kirey Hotel [129 D1]. On the menu are yak burgers, spaghetti, French fries, vegetable dishes & apple *momos*.

✗ Yeti Café [129 F1] 206 Beijing Xilu (Beijing West Rd), close to Lhasa Hotel. Has a big menu of Sichuan, Western & Tibetan food. The café features Tibetan-style teahouse décor, with carpeted seats. It can handle groups. In this area are trendy cafés, catering largely to a Chinese clientele.

✗ Lhasa Hotel [116 B2] Has several overpriced restaurants, including the Hard Yak Café (serving yak burgers) & an ice-cream café (with good gelato). The Himalaya restaurant at Lhasa Hotel serves a range of food from Indian to German, plus Tibetan dishes like yak tartare, or minced yak with Tibetan spices. Traditional Tibetan music groups sometimes perform at the restaurant.

TEAHOUSES AND ROOFTOP CAFÉS There are pleasant teahouses in Lhasa where you can soak up the views as well as the drinks. One of these is **Lukhang teahouse** [151 F1] in the northeast corner of Lukhang Park – it offers a great view of the back of the Potala and is a peaceful place. The teahouse serves 'eight treasures tea' and there are often fresh flowers on the tables from the adjacent nursery. Another viewpoint on the Potala is from the front, at a **Chinese pavilion** with restaurant and teahouse [151 F3], overlooking a lake to the Potala's south side. There's a Tibetan-style teahouse inside the **Red Palace** [151 E1] of the Potala itself.

The Dalai Lama's image has been banned in Tibet since a major fallout over the choice of Panchen Lama in 1996. Even more incriminating are tapes or books by him or about him, or movies about him. Even the Potala Palace is bereft of his portrait – the last big portrait was taken down around 1997. The image you might see in monasteries (possibly) is of a younger Dalai Lama with Mao Zedong in Beijing in the 1950s, as this seems to be politically correct. Otherwise, the Dalai Lama is commonly denounced as a 'revolutionary splittist' or 'a wolf in monk's garb'.

But the irrepressible Dalai Lama is easy to find on the internet. You can bring him up at any time – he's on so many sites, they can't be blocked. He pops up on the cover of all his books, for starters. In a cybercafé in Lhasa, I was hunting for information on the Karmapa (who is not yet blacklisted by the Chinese), when a magazine cover popped up. It was an issue of *Time Asia*, with a cover story on political repression in Tibet. And featured on the cover were two monks in burgundy robes – the Karmapa and the Dalai Lama. *Time Asia* itself is firewalled in China, but somehow this cover arrived by a different route, past the firewall. Amazed Tibetans crowded round the screen to witness this, probably the first time they'd seen a photograph of the two high lamas together. But the cybercafé operator, fearful of having his licence revoked – or fearful of starting a riot – asked me to switch sites.

On the rooftop of the **Jokhang** [129 C2] is a tented teahouse, run by the monks, although only in the summer months, and mainly for tourists. Offering a great view across Barkor Square is the fourth-floor rooftop patio at the **New Mandala Restaurant** [129 B2]. Most ignore the menu and just settle for a beer or a fruit juice – and the view, of course. Around the back of the Barkor, **Makye Ame Restaurant's** [129 D3] rooftop on the third floor has great views over the parade of pilgrims. From various hotel rooftops, you can also get good views of Lhasa, and see paper kites launched from other rooftops. These include the rooftop of the **Mandala Hotel** [129 B3], the fifth-floor teahouse at **Yak Hotel** [129 B1], the fifth-floor rooftop café at **Ohdan Hotel** [127 C2] and the rooftop of the **Dhood Gu Hotel** [129 C1].

The ultimate for views may be the **TV tower restaurant** [127 F2], way up the top of the TV tower in eastern Lhasa. This is a revolving restaurant where the Chinese have actually got the direction right for a change – it revolves clockwise. Revolving is hit and miss, as is the food. But you'd go for the views (assuming the place is open and accessible).

ENTERTAINMENT AND NIGHTLIFE

Lhasa's handful of hotels and restaurants are nightlife and entertainment venues by default: they are gathering points for information exchange. Source and sauce: other travellers provide the latest information, and you digest it over a steaming bowl of noodles. **Snowland** [129 B2], **Tashi 1**, **Dunya** [129 C1] and **Kailash** [129 F1] restaurants function as traveller cafés. This is how travellers mostly pass their nights. Chinese nightlife consists of crooning, carousing and chasing Sichuan women around in karaoke bars or places like **Top View Disco** [127 A4] (some Westerners venture in here, too). Tibetan nightlife consists of crowding into tiny video salons where sound distortion and flasks of *chang* are the big things.

Lhasa ENTERTAINMENT AND NIGHTLIFE

4

DINNER-DANCE SHOWS AND NANGMA CLUBS The **Shangri-La Restaurant** [129 D1], located inside the Kirey Hotel, stages dinner-dance shows. The cost is Y50 including buffet dinner, or you can probably arrange to pay Y20 for the show and just order a drink. Dinner starts at 19.00; the show takes place from 19.30 to 20.30. The performance is a mix of traditional dance and music, with the highlight being the exuberant yak dance, performed by two Tibetans hidden inside a yak skin. It is traditionally performed as a welcome dance. The 'yak' rolls on the floor, flicks its tail around, and charges into the audience.

Scattered around Lhasa are more than 30 Nangma nightclubs, which get under way from 23.00 onwards and host a range of live singers and dancers, and a dance floor upfront. These places are the closest you'll get to Tibetan nightlife, and are great fun. Tibetan singers are garlanded with *katas* during performances – some end up with so many scarves they have trouble moving around. One of the better-known Nangma clubs is **Khaide** [127 A2], located on Beijing Road near Tibet Post Hotel.

BARS Popular with foreigners is the upstairs bar at **Dunya Restaurant** [129 C1], next to the Yak Hotel. You can't miss the Heineken sign out the front (the bar was set up by a Dutchman). Opposite the Yak Hotel is **Ganglamedo** [129 B1], a trendy Chinese-run restaurant and bar: the food is bland, but the place is fine for drinks, and stays open late. Next door is **Potala Traditional Snack Bar** – a good place to quaff Lhasa Beer or Snow Beer. There are a number of small bars catering to upscale Chinese visitors: some have imaginative décor.

SHOPPING

If you can't find it in Lhasa, you probably won't find it anywhere in Tibet, except possibly in Shigatse. Whether outfitting for a trip or shopping for Tibetan artefacts, Lhasa has the biggest selection, though it has nothing on Kathmandu.

CAMPING AND OUTDOOR GEAR Camping and outdoor supplies in Lhasa are very good: you could arrive in Lhasa with nothing and be fully kitted out within a few days. There are numerous outdoor equipment shops around Lhasa, particularly along Beijing Road and Tengyeling Road. These vary from small shops to cavernous stores, selling a range of top Chinese brands like Ozark. A few of the larger stores are located to the west of Lhasa, such as **Wilderness Outside Camp Store** near the Golden Yak roundabout.

Chinese-made equipment is cheap compared with what it would cost in the West. Sleeping bags can be purchased for under US$50. North Face jackets and vests go for low prices: these could be copies, or could be factory off-runs. Other brands on sale include Mountain Hardwear and Columbia. Some places stock high-quality imported gear, including stoves and useful gadgets. Others sell gear recycled from mountaineering expeditions – and may rent this equipment, too. Department stores sell formless but functional clothing, and there's PLA surplus gear for sale on the streets. If you are looking for a good sleeping bag, you should check the noticeboards at places like the Snowland, Kirey and Yak hotels, as fellow travellers will advertise there.

FRESH/PACKAGED FOOD If you're going on a long trip – for instance, to Kailash – stock up on as much food as you can in Lhasa (the only other place to get supplies is Shigatse). For fresh food, go to **Tromsikhang** [129 C1], the Tibetan market to the north of the Jokhang. This has the biggest selection (for items like potatoes, dried fruit and so on). Department stores downtown are a source of packaged goods, such as teabags, chocolate and biscuits. **Lhasa Department Store** [151 F3] has a good stock in its mini-mart. For muesli, peanut butter and other items imported from Nepal try **Snowland Restaurant** [129 B2] or **Kailash Restaurant** [129 F1] (Banakshol Hotel). There is a Tibetan-run **mini-mart** on East Lingkor Road [129 F3] with a good stock of Nepalese-imported items.

TIBETAN ARTEFACTS The main array of souvenir shops lines **Barkor Bazaar** [129 D3], but watch out for Chinese clones. Some souvenirs are obviously not Tibetan at all: a few brass Buddha statues are from Thailand; others come from Kathmandu. Much the same stock is sold at giftshops in major hotels at more inflated prices, at souvenir kiosks at the Potala entrance, and at the Norbulingka. Watch out for fake turquoise and other stones if buying jewellery. The dilemma faced by purchasers who do not know what they are looking at is best exemplified by the trade in *dzi* stones. These are agate talismans with 'eyes' that involve human crafting in the process. If a *dzi* stone is an ancient heirloom, passed down for generations, it could be worth millions of yuan. If it is a brand-new import from Taiwan, it might be worth Y10. Even experts flounder when it comes to telling the difference between valuable *dzi* stones and worthless ones.

You might want to get to the source of items crafted in Lhasa, as the **factories** are a sight themselves. There are several Tibetan **tent-making workshops** in the city – the easiest to find is in an alley near the Yak Hotel [129 B1]. Among other items, this place sells fine cotton door-hangings with Tibetan lucky symbols hand-embroidered on them. At the eastern side of the Barkor (located down alleys north of the mosque; follow signs) is **Dropenling** (*www.tibetcraft.com*), run by a non-profit UNDP-backed artisan enterprise and designed to bolster Tibetan handicrafts in the face of rampant Nepalese and Chinese imports. On sale are *tankas*, weavings, silverware, woodcarvings, saddle carpets and other handcrafted items. You can watch craftsmen at work, which makes it well worth a visit.

There are several **carpet factories** in town, including one to the southeast side of Lhasa and another out near Drepung. **Potala Carpet Factory** [165 B3], 300m past the turn-off for Drepung, welcomes visitors – you can see women weaving and singing here as they work on complex patterns. There is an exhibition and retail room on the premises. Check out the various designs: a Tibetan dragon has four claws, the Chinese imperial dragon has five.

BOOKS AND MAPS You might dredge up the odd map, poster or Tibetan music cassette from the **Xinhua Bookstore** at the west end of Yuthok Road [151 F3]; otherwise, pickings are slim. There's also a Xinhua Bookstore branch out near Lhasa Hotel. Prices for maps and books can be absurdly low if produced by the Chinese government. Maps in Chinese characters are easy to find; maps in English are more difficult and not nearly as detailed. *Lhasa Tourist Map*, produced by Chengdu Cartographic Publishing House, is a sheet map dated 2004 and selling for Y16. This large, double-sided map carries an impressive wealth of detail and a selection of mini-guide material. However, it is missing some newer details like the bridge leading over the Kyichu River close to the railway station. For those details you would have to hunt down the more recent *Tourist Map of Tibet,* published in 2010 by Xian Map Press: one side of this sheet map features Lhasa, and the other side shows the TAR.

The souvenir shops at **Lhasa Hotel** [116 B2] and **Tibet Hotel** [116 B2] are good for books, though more expensive. **Guxuna bookstore** [129 B1] on Tengyeling Road has an array of books, but mainly in Chinese. **Souvenir kiosks** at key sights around town also sell books and postcards. Rule of thumb: when you see something you really want, bargain and buy it – you might not see it again. Other Chinese bookstores are scattered around; there's one at the east side of Barkor Bazaar.

OTHER PRACTICALITIES

BANKING The main branch of the Bank of China [151 D2] is located just northeast of the Golden Yak roundabout. It provides full services, including credit card advances (although commissions can be high) and ATM machines. The BOC is open 09.00–18.30 Monday to Friday (in winter, 09.30–18.30); from 10.00–17.00 Saturdays; and possibly open Sundays. There are sub-branches in a few other locations – notably one near the Banakshol Hotel, which has an ATM machine. Major hotels like Lhasa Hotel [116 B2] have their own exchange counter, but the rate is not as good. ATMs for the BOC in Lhasa dispense a maximum Y2,000 per card per day, while those for the Agricultural Bank offer a maximum of Y1,000 per day.

MEDICAL You're best off moving to a comfortable hotel in the event of a medical problem. High-end hotels usually supply oxygen pillows and may have a doctor on call. Hospitals in Lhasa cost a fortune for foreigners to stay in, and the medical attention is dubious anyway. Lhasa's finest is the Military Hospital at the north end of town, but that's not for foreigners. The People's Hospital is basic, although one unit is supported by an Italian NGO project for equipment and training and there's an X-ray unit there. The Emergency Centre [129 G1] (✆ 120 or 632 2200) at this hospital has a small ambulance. This is the best option for foreigners in trouble.

BLIND MASSAGE THERAPY Massage therapists in a programme set up by Braille without Borders run a small, efficient massage operation, located on the second floor of a building opposite the Kailash Hotel [129 B1]. A relaxing one-hour acupressure massage costs Y80; appointments can be booked by phone

---

HAVING A BLAST

Need a blast of oxygen? A high-altitude cocktail? Lhasa Hotel was reputed to have rooms where oxygen was piped in, but this system no longer seems to function because guests kept going out and leaving the oxygen on. If guests have trouble with the altitude, they are usually given an oxygen pillow to make sleeping smoother. There is nothing more scary than sleeping at altitude and waking up in the middle of the night completely out of breath, heart pounding, gulping for air, with a throat like the Sahara. This is where the oxygen pillow comes to the fore – it is a pillow of oxygen with nasal tubes attached. The pillows are also taken along on Landcruiser or minibus trips from Lhasa Hotel in case a guest is feeling under the weather. Landcruiser drivers may also keep a tank of oxygen in the vehicle, rather like a fire extinguisher unit. Oxygen does not solve the acclimatisation problem, but it does provide temporary respite.

Several outfits in Lhasa sell oxygen devices, manufactured as far afield as Xiamen. These range from small scuba-like tanks to aerosol spray-cans for those who need a blast of fresh air. You can rent the scuba tanks for a dollar or so a day (with a large deposit). The capacity is 30 minutes of oxygen. At top-end hotels guests can use a card system to hook up to a larger oxygen-dispensing device.

(632 0870). The brochures claim massage will ease altitude problems and jet lag and relieve headaches – by increasing blood circulation, of course. And brochures suggest you might need to recover from 'travel-related back and neck pain' – probably an oblique reference to the rigours of Landcruiser travel. The massage therapists are all blind. If you want to learn more about the remarkable training of blind people in Lhasa, you can visit Braille without Borders, found down a back alley just west of Peace Hotel [129 B4] (enquire about exact visiting hours, as the facility is only open for tours several times a week). The training facility was set up by Sabriye Tenberken, a blind German woman who worked out the first-ever system for rendering the Tibetan language into Braille. For more about this, consult their website (*www.braillewithoutborders.org*).

COMMUNICATIONS AND MEDIA The Potala **post office** [151 F2], the main branch for telecommunications, lies near the Potala on Beijing Road. The sending of regular mail and parcels takes place here; bring along your own packing materials as few are supplied (for larger items, you might have to open your package for customs inspection). Some hotels deliver mail to the post office.

Part of the China Post complex on this block is a large store devoted to Chinese magazines – everything from car magazines to fashion periodicals – to keep the settlers happy. The news is all from China, and thus all screened. In English, there are only stray copies of *China Daily* floating around, and even those are hard to come by. There is a media blackout in Tibet: you cannot find any foreign magazines at all. So you have to resort to internet news sites, a number of which are blocked. And despite the great advances the Chinese say they have made in Tibet, not a single Tibetan newspaper is on sale in the shops of Lhasa. There is a pathetic rag the size of a newsletter called *Tibet Daily*, but that is rehashed propaganda, and is only sold by roving vendors.

Fax and phone There's a long-distance calling office next door to the main post office [151 F2] (calls are most likely routed through Beijing); the same office will allow you to send faxes. Faxes can also be sent from some hotel business centres, but that will be more expensive. International phone calls can be placed through hotels, even at the budget hotels. To keep costs reasonable, use pre-paid calling cards, which can be bought for fixed amounts like Y50 or Y100. These come in two main varieties. A pre-paid IC card can be activated by dialling a number sequence, either on a hotel phone or at one of the tiny telecom shops found around Lhasa. A pre-paid IP card (China Telecom is best) can be used with a yellow phone, with booths found on the street, and sometimes also in hotel lobbies. The country code (China) is 86; the Lhasa area code is 0891 (for calls within China) or 891 (for incoming international calls). Another possibility is net phoning via services like Skype.

Mobile phones If staying longer in Tibet and China, set yourself up with a SIM card for a mobile phone from China Mobile (office near China Post). Their SIM card can be installed on the spot: you can switch to English-language menu, and you can top up the talk time with pre-paid cards of Y50–500. The network includes SMS text messaging, which can be sent in English, Chinese characters, even Tibetan script. Mobile phone and SMS coverage reaches across China, but does not extend to Hong Kong SAR. The reason for this is simple: the press in Hong Kong is much freer than in China proper, and text messaging is a method of relaying news. You should be aware that Chinese mobile phone companies may police and filter text messages – do not write anything risqué on SMS. Mobile phone and SMS reception

4

across Tibet can be erratic as it depends on whether there is a telecom tower within range. But these reception towers can pop up in remote places – such as Rongbuk *gompa*, near Everest base camp.

Email and internet Net access is available through a growing number of cybercafés, and through hotels and guesthouses. Connection speeds vary – connection is sometimes good, sometimes slow and sometimes non-existent (come back later). Internet use is cheap – mostly under Y5 an hour. A number of the low-end to mid-range hotels in Lhasa have small internet cafés. The ones at the Kyichu [129 A1], Yak [129 B1] and Snowland [129 B2] hotels are good. Upper-end hotels have internet access through business centres, but this could prove more

KHAMPA MONA LISA

Mona Lisa's enigmatic smile undergoes a twist in Lhasa. You may see her painted with Khampa-style dress and turquoise jewellery studded in her hair. This is definitely not traditional. The painting is part of an effort to break away from traditional Tibetan art forms, which in the past focused exclusively on religion. Khampa Mona Lisa is definitely a very different take on iconography. Several paintings of her have been spotted – some created by Tibetan artists, some by Chinese artists.

Located at the northeast corner of the Barkor is a three-floor gallery displaying modern works by members of Gedun Choephel Artists' Guild. The guild is Lhasa's only centre of modern Tibetan art, although the painting of modern themes has generated a cottage industry among Han Chinese artists resident in Lhasa, vying for the tourist market. These artists paint the Van Gogh-style wares and other high-kitsch art seen hanging on café and hotel-lobby walls in Lhasa, and on sale to Western and Chinese tourists in small shops.

For centuries, Tibetan artists painted only formulaic *tanka* art for monasteries: Gedun Choephel Artists' Guild was started up in 2003 with the aim of expressing Tibetan themes in modern styles, ranging from realism to surrealism. There are more than 20 artists in the group. Gade, an artist in his thirties, attempts to bridge the old world of Tibet with the modern globalised world: he paints Buddha images that include references to Hollywood movies, sentences in English and Russian, even short SMS messages.

The group takes its name from Gedun Choephel, a Tibetan intellectual and accomplished artist from Amdo who headed south to India in the 1930s to visit important pilgrimage sites. The chain-smoking Choephel had formidable powers of concentration – he could debate with the best of them, even when totally inebriated. Apparently, Choephel could cause monastic debating opponents to freeze into shocked silence. His unorthodox views upset many people in high places, including the British colonial rulers of India, the aristocrats and the ruling clergy in Tibet. After 13 years in India and Sri Lanka, Choephel decided to return to Lhasa in the mid-1940s to write the definitive history of independent Tibet. He was promptly thrown into a dank dungeon in Lhasa on trumped-up charges. In 1949, when communist invasion of Tibet seemed imminent, a general amnesty for prisoners was declared in Lhasa. Choephel emerged from jail in emaciated condition, dressed in rags, a shadow of his former self. Tibet's foremost intellectual died in 1951 at the age of 46, but his legend lives on, inspiring many young Tibetans.

expensive. Cybercafés are sprinkled around town: these are closely monitored by 'internet police'. For email, it's difficult to see how such a large volume of messages could be scrutinised, but monitoring is done by flagging keywords like 'Tibet', 'independence' or 'democracy'. Chinese authorities are extremely sensitive about what you can access on the net (see *Appendix 4* for websites, page 334). Taboo sites are those concerned with human rights, Tibetan exile groups, Taiwan; the list goes on. That means sites could be blocked or firewalled, but it's surprising what you can still pick up in Lhasa. If you do get through to sensitive sites, it could mean trouble for the cybercafé owner. However, there is no official list of what is forbidden and what is allowed. In theory, though, there is filtering software in place at cybercafés that will block certain sites: if sensitive material is not filtered, the café could be closed down. It is dubious whether foreigners are subject to these regulations – the logic being that foreigners are accustomed to viewing such sites.

Satellite television High-end hotels may have satellite television reception: some can pick up VTV (India) or StarTV (Hong Kong). Access to these stations is strictly controlled: even if the hotel has a satellite dish, this does not guarantee it has permission to receive certain channels (for which a decoder is needed). Lhasa Hotel seems to have the best contacts for permission, with CNN broadcasts from Beijing available in guest rooms: there's a place within the hotel (Chang's Bar) where non-guests can watch the tube. The larger the dish, the greater the reception: satellite receivers require special permission to operate within China, and the foreign programmes are not intended for local eyes. Xizang TV (XZTV) and Lhasa TV (Lhasa Broadcasting and Television Centre) are the local stations. Tibetans mostly watch XZTV. CCTV-9 from Beijing broadcasts news daily in English (all programmes on this station are broadcast either in English or else Chinese with English subtitles, as this is Beijing's pan-Asian voice). CCTV channels 1 to 12 are broadcast from Beijing; there are about 30 more regional channels that are picked up in Lhasa.

PHOTOGRAPHY Internet cafés found within hotels can burn DVDs and CDs, and offer printing services on photo-quality paper. Prints of Tibetan friends will make fine gifts. Print film is sold in Lhasa, but quality may be suspect. High-speed film and black-and-white film are very difficult to find.

WHAT TO SEE

ORIENTING YOURSELF To get a better idea of the layout of Lhasa, there are a number of places that offer expansive views. The Jokhang rooftop has stunning views, and the rooftops of hotels like the Mandala, Yak and Ohdan offer views over the Barkor and beyond.

Traditionally, Tibetan pilgrims approaching the holy city embarked on four sacred circuits: the inner circuit of the Jokhang Temple (called the Nangkor), the 20-minute outer circuit of the same temple (around the Barkor), a 25-minute circuit of the Potala Palace (called the Tsekor), and a 90-minute circuit around Lhasa itself (called the Lingkor). The first three are eminently possible, but the Lingkor is no longer easy to follow – it has been disrupted by modern Chinese buildings. The description of sights that follows is based on clockwise circuits of the Nangkor, Barkor, Tsekor and Lingkor – that is, starting at the Jokhang Temple, and spiralling outwards around Lhasa.

There is one very good reason why you should follow these ancient walking routes: the pilgrims, with their fervent devotional practices, are in fact the main 'sight' of Lhasa, if it can be phrased that way – and their interaction with sacred sites is what makes these places so special. Many visiting Lhasa are disappointed by what they see – a large Chinese city, essentially. The Potala is a museum, and it's easy to feel that tightly controlled temples are more interested in ensuring that you have paid the exorbitant entrance fee than helping you understand the faith that is at the heart of Tibetan society. To get a glimpse of a more spiritual Tibet, try the Jokhang early in the morning and queue with the pilgrims (be prepared for the crush when the doors open!) or pace the Barkor *kora* at dusk (several times). If you have more time, be sure to hike to the sacred sites and *koras* at the outskirts of Lhasa – at Bumpa Ri, and at Pabonka (above Sera), for instance. The pilgrim pulse fares better on the edges of Lhasa at the former great monastic citadels of Sera and Drepung.

You have to read between the lines in Lhasa when it comes to the sacred and the secret. There's been so much upheaval in the Holy City that half the time you don't know if what you're looking at is sacred or not – whether the statuary at the Jokhang is real or not, whether the West Gate is original or reconstructed. From the real to the unreal, from the sublime to the ridiculous: one minute you're admiring the stunning structure of the Potala – and the next minute, you're examining a fake palm tree, wondering how on earth that ended up on the streets of Lhasa.

ENTRY PROTOCOL AND FEES Despite what agencies and guides tell you, it is possible to access key sites in Lhasa by yourself – but have lots of paperwork handy, such as passport (for Potala and Jokhang) and copy of TTB permit. The charge to enter the Potala is Y100 a person, and it's Y85 to go into the Jokhang. The Norbulingka charges Y60. Sera has a Y50 entry fee, and so does Drepung. Sera and Drepung may be difficult to get into because they each have a large police station building situated near the entrance, snooping on all visitors. Entry fees at other sites around Lhasa generally range from Y20 to Y60. It all starts to add up. Hefty extra fees are levied for taking still pictures inside top attractions (a charge of Y30–150 is common). The charge for taking video is astronomical (around Y850–1,800 per video camera).

BARKOR AREA There are two areas left in Lhasa where the Tibetan pulse can still be felt: at the Potala (a faint museum pulse) and Barkor Bazaar (throbbing pilgrim pulse). Other than that you're looking at Chinatown. It seems absurd to put it this way, but you really have to visit the 'Tibetan Quarter' – the quarter around the Jokhang Temple and the Barkor – to catch any Tibetans in action. Sadly, this quarter only comprises a small fraction of Lhasa's land area.

The Jokhang [129 C2] The Jokhang or Tsug Lakhang (central cathedral) is Tibet's most sacred temple – the heart of Tibet – with streams of pilgrims coursing through. The temple was built in the 7th century by King Songtsen Gampo when he moved his capital to Lhasa. Apart from his three Tibetan wives, the powerful Songtsen Gampo had two wives offered by neighbouring nations – Nepalese queen Tritsun and Chinese queen Wencheng. The Jokhang was originally designed by Nepalese craftsmen to house a Buddha image brought by the Nepalese queen. Upon Songtsen Gampo's death, Queen Wencheng switched the statue she had brought (the Jowo Sakyamuni) from the Ramoche Temple to the Jokhang, apparently to hide it from Chinese troops. That's why one part of the Jokhang (Chapel 13) is called the Chapel where the Jowo was Hidden. In time, the Jowo Sakyamuni statue became the chief object of veneration. The Jokhang was enlarged and embellished by subsequent rulers and Dalai Lamas. Although the building is as old as Lhasa, much of the statuary is quite new. During the Cultural Revolution, the temple was used as a military barracks and a slaughterhouse; later it was used as a hotel for

Chinese officials. Much of the statuary was lost, destroyed or damaged, so it has been replaced with newer copies of the originals.

In 2000, the Jokhang was inscribed on the UNESCO World Heritage List as an addition to the Potala Palace, which is good news because it may bolster protection of the buildings in the immediate vicinity.

Outside the Jokhang Fronting the Jokhang are flagstones where Tibetans gather to prostrate before the temple. A bit further back are two small walled enclosures with obelisks inside. One enclosure shelters two stone obelisks with an edict in Chinese about curing smallpox – the edict, from 1794, is largely illegible because Tibetans gouged pieces out of it, supposing that the stone itself had curative properties. The second enclosure, with a tall thin obelisk, bears a bilingual inscription about a peace treaty between Tibetan king Ralpachen and Chinese emperor Wangti, concluded in AD823, delineating the borders between the nations of China and Tibet. The brick enclosures around the obelisks were put up when Barkor Square was created in 1985.

Access In the morning, you can enter the Jokhang directly through the front doors; otherwise, entry and exit may be via a side-door courtyard. An entry fee of Y85 is charged: for that you get a tacky ticket with a 3D image of the Jokhang embedded. It may not mean much to you, but hang on to that ticket – it makes a super gift for Tibetans in remote regions. It's best to visit the Jokhang in the mornings, from 09.00 to noon. Parts of the Jokhang may be closed on Sundays. Entering the inner sanctum of the ground-floor chapels may be difficult for Tibetan pilgrims. As a tourist, you are privileged to be allowed in. Photography is allowed in certain parts of the Jokhang – if in doubt, ask first. Second-floor chapels may be closed off and only accessible to monks residing at the Jokhang. You should respect this limitation. It should be all right to access the rooftop, however, and you might be able to visit the rooftop at times when the ground-floor chapels are closed.

The rooftop You can take a staircase near the ticket booth at the front straight up to the golden rooftop of the Jokhang, with excellent views over Lhasa rooftops and the Potala in the distance. In the summer months there is a tented teahouse up on the Jokhang rooftop, run by the monks. Visiting the rooftop seems to be a privilege reserved for tourists – both Western and Chinese – as you don't see Tibetan pilgrims up here. The monks at the teahouse do a roaring trade with Chinese tour groups, selling Jokhang talismans and postcards, as well as T-shirts, books, souvenirs and drinks. Chinese tourists excitedly chatter on their mobile phones to callers across China (they even talk on mobile phones when visiting the shrines in the Jokhang – including the Jowo shrine). Although it can, at times, turn into a Chinese photo-taking zoo, the rooftop is a bright, peaceful spot – a refreshing place after the dark, smoky chapels of the Jokhang interior. There are beautiful ornaments hanging from the eaves of the gilded sloping roofs, some in the shape of dragons, others in the shape of mythical birds.

Ground-floor icons Walking through the dark corridors and chapels of the Jokhang, you enter another world. Dim light is provided by a galaxy of butter lamps; the air is thick with the odour of yak butter and incense; echoing through the halls is the sound of murmuring from throngs of Tibetan pilgrims. If your timing is right, the inner sanctum may reverberate with the sound of deep, hypnotic chanting of monks at prayer. About a hundred monks live at the Jokhang, residing on the upper levels.

THE JOKHANG

Nangkor

Staircase to upper floor (no access)

6 Tsongkhapa Chapel

7 Amitabha Chapel

8 Jowo Sakyamuni (main image)

9 Jampa Gonpo Chapel

10 Chenrezig Chapel

Statues of guardian kings (between chapels)

Glass case with Avalokitesvara image

5 Jampa Truze Chapel

Inner Sanctum

Maitreya statue (large)

Small Avalokitesvara image

Nangkor

4 Avalo-kitesvara Chapel

Padmasambhava statue

3 Eight Medicine Buddhas

Milarepa statue

Maitreya statue (large)

Maitreya statue (small)

11 Re-constructed chapel (rows of Buddhas)

12 Jampa Chezhi (small standing Jampa image)

13 Chapel where the Jowo was hidden

Nangkor

14 The Seven Mighty Buddhas

2 Amitabha Chapel

1 Tsongkhapa & his Eight Disciples

Side chapel

Side chapel

16 Chapel of the Dharma Kings

15 Nine Aspects of Amitayus

NOTE:
Some ground-floor chapels in the Jokhang have been destroyed and reconstructed, and statuary has been defaced, replaced, restored and shifted around, so this plan may not match exactly: use it only as a rough guide. Chapels may close and reopen, depending on reconstruction.

Open courtyard with butter lamps (former assembly area for monks)

N • Bradt

Steps leading to rooftop

Main doors (🕘 09.00–11.00 except Sundays)

Ticket booth (🕘 09.00–19.00 daily)

Open courtyard

Prostrators assemble on flagstones here

Entrance

THE JOKHANG

Some of the chapels in the Jokhang have been destroyed and reconstructed, and statuary has been defaced, replaced, restored and shifted around, so the plan opposite may not match exactly with what is on the ground. Chapels may close and reopen, depending on reconstruction. With this jumble of old and new, it is also debatable which statuary is original and which is copied.

The world you enter seems quite complex and confusing, with no point of reference, no rhyme or reason. However, that may be a matter of familiarising yourself with the icons of Tibetan Buddhism which, admittedly, are bewildering in their scope and number. If you want to explore Tibetan temple iconography, the Jokhang has the lot – a virtual Who's Who of the Tibetan Buddhist pantheon. Using the plan of the Jokhang in this section, you can identify which images are Avalokitesvara, Sakyamuni, King Songtsen Gampo and so on. The same icons pop up in many other temples in Tibet, and are referred to in other parts of this book. Only some of the ground-floor chapels are described here: the emphasis is on the icons.

Unlike most temples, the Jokhang is not identified with a particular sect. Leaders and teachers from the different sects are shown in statuary and murals. **Tsongkhapa** (Chapel 1) is the founder of the Geluk (Yellow Hat) sect. There's a finer image of him in Chapel 6, wearing a monk's robes and a pointed yellow cap; he lived from 1357 to 1419. Between Chapel 3 and Chapel 4 is an image of the great poet-saint **Milarepa** (1040–1123), with his hand cocked to one ear so that he can better hear the music of the spheres and the voice of teachings. The sage appears with skin of a greenish hue – a case of nettle anaemia (he dined solely on nettle soup for a number of years). Milarepa was a founding member of the Kagyu sect. Another historical figure seen in chapels and in larger statues at the inner sanctum is **Padmasambhava**, the 8th-century tantric Indian master who is credited with establishing Buddhism in Tibet. He is the founder of the Nyingma sect, and is shown with a stern expression and a curled moustache, wearing a folded red hat.

In the Tibetan pantheon are many Buddhas and bodhisattvas. A bodhisattva is a being on the way to becoming a Buddha, but one who has decided to delay the pursuit of nirvana and devote himself or herself to the welfare of others. The Dalai Lama is thought to be an emanation of **Avalokitesvara**, the bodhisattva of compassion (*Chenrezig* in Tibetan). Often shown in a standing statue, Avalokitesvara has 11 heads (one of which is wrathful) and multiple arms, and may be encircled by a thousand hands. The many heads are said to have burst from the original head as a result of contemplating the suffering of living beings.

The figure of Avalokitesvara is found in several parts of the ground floor – in Chapel 4, outside Chapel 5 in a glass case, in Chapel 10, and right at the centre of the inner sanctum. The image in Chapel 4 has a long story behind it: some parts of the statue are original, some are copies. The image was commissioned by Songtsen Gampo in the 7th century. During the Cultural Revolution, this image and others were tossed into the streets. Tibetans managed to salvage a wrathful and a peaceful aspect of the faces of Avalokitesvara, and the images were smuggled out via Nepal to India. The faces were eventually made into a new image of Avalokitesvara at the Tsug Lakhang in Dharamsala.

Tara (*Drolma* in Tibetan) is said to be the spiritual consort of Avalokitesvara, and possesses more than 20 forms. **White Tara** is identified with Queen Wencheng and the fertile aspect of compassion, while **Green Tara** is identified with Queen Tritsun and the motherly aspect of compassion. Green Tara is the patron female saint of Tibet; she sits with her right leg extended slightly, resting on a lotus blossom. Tara sits cross-legged upon a lotus flower. She is easily recognised by the eyes depicted in the palms of her hands: she is believed to have sprung from a tear of compassion falling from the eye of Avalokitesvara. While there is little statuary of Tara in the ground-floor chapels, her image appears in a number of murals. A Tara fresco is shown on a wall recessed at the back of Chapel 16.

Tibetans believe that the historical Buddha (Sakyamuni) is the Buddha of the present era, but only one of the many Buddhas to appear in the past, present and future. The Buddha is 'he who is fully awake' – an enlightened being. **Amitabha**, appearing in Chapel 2, is the Buddha of Infinite Light (*Opame* in Tibetan) – usually depicted in a red colour, with hands clasping an alms bowl. The Panchen Lama is thought to be an incarnation of Amitabha. A row of eight **Medicine Buddhas** is shown in Chapel 3 – these are the Buddhas of healing, and caring for the sick. **Jampa** is the Buddha of the Future, also known as Champa or the Maitreya Buddha. This Buddha is not usually shown cross-legged, but seated conventionally on a throne. The Jampa statue shown in Chapel 5 is a copy of one brought to Tibet from Nepal by Queen Tritsun. In Chapel 9 is an image of Jampa (brought in from Drepung to replace a destroyed image); this statue was once paraded around the Barkor at Monlam. In the inner sanctum are two Jampa images.

The centrepiece of the Jokhang is a 1.5m-high gilded statue of **Jowo Sakyamuni**, the Buddha of the Present, born in 543BC in Nepal. The image was brought to Tibet by Queen Wencheng. It depicts the Sakyamuni Buddha at the age of 12: features such as long earlobes and a cranial bump are special marks of the Buddha. The highly revered statue bears an elaborate headdress and is encrusted with jewels; pilgrims crowd in to make offerings, and to walk around the statue.

Revered as deities are the early religious kings of Tibet, who converted to Buddhism. Easily identified in the ground-floor chapels is **King Songtsen Gampo** (c AD608–650), the first of the great religious kings, considered to be a manifestation of Avalokitesvara. He wears a high orange or gold turban; his Chinese wife, **Queen Wencheng**, is on the viewer's right; his Nepalese wife, **Queen Tritsun**, on the viewer's left. This is the arrangement for a group to the left of the Jowo Sakyamuni image. The three great religious kings of Tibet are found in the Chapel of the Dharma Kings (Chapel 16) – the central figure being Songtsen Gampo; to the viewer's right, **Trisong Detsen** (the second religious king, who ruled from AD755 to 797); and to the viewer's left, **Tri Ralpachen** (who ruled from AD815 to 838).

Entering or exiting the inner Jokhang sanctuary, you pass two **side chapels**. The one to the left (on the north side) contains a statue of Palden Lhamo, the main protective deity of the Jokhang, as well as of fierce guardian deities. To the right, on the south side, are three Naga deity statues, also with a protective role.

Barkor Bazaar

Barkor Bazaar [129 D3] Barkor Bazaar is a lively combination of marketplace, pilgrim circuit and ethnic melting pot. The 20-minute hexagonal circuit, running clockwise around the Jokhang and other structures, is always busy, especially at dawn and dusk. Join the pilgrims for a few circuits – it's good for exercise and for people-watching.

The Barkor has been remodelled to suit Chinese whims: it was completely repaved in 2003 with flatter stones (hence easier to drive over), and a series of Tiananmen-style lamp posts were put up around the circuit, matching those at Potala Square.

At the front of the Jokhang, just inside the temple, you can see some of the original stones. The flagstones are worn smooth, polished from many years of pilgrims performing prostrations. Two-metre-high conical incense burners billow clouds of smoke, and the smell of juniper fills the air. Vendors – mostly Chinese making a buck off Buddhism – sell *kata* scarves (see *Glossary* appendix, page 326), prayer-flags and prayer-wheels to the pilgrims. Arriving on pilgrimage from far-flung regions, such as the Kham or Golok areas, pilgrims mutter mantras as they circumambulate. You might see nomad women from eastern Tibet, their long tresses smeared in yak butter; or an old woman leading her favourite sheep around the circuit; or a proud Khampa from eastern Tibet with tassels of red yarn braided through his hair, and a dagger on his belt (not entirely decorative); or a hardy prostrator with rubber apron and padded gloves flinging himself forward on the ground, completing the circuit on his stomach.

The Barkor is a magnet for beggars seeking alms, and for pilgrims seeking funds for their return home (and to support themselves in Lhasa in the meantime). More sophisticated are sutra chanters: for a small sum, they will recite from sacred texts. And finally, there is the bazaar itself – shops and businesses line the entire circuit. Competing with these are open-air stalls laden with souvenirs and household goods; and there are roving vendors with bags of Tibetan music cassettes or other items. Since 1987, Barkor Bazaar has assumed another role – as the focus of protesters who encircle the Barkor when demonstrating against the Chinese occupation of Tibet. This explains the presence of police and security personnel in the area, ready to intercept any demonstrators.

Barkor Square [129 B2] Officially, Barkor Square was completed in 1985 to mark the 20th year of the creation of the TAR. Unofficially, it was built to provide full military access to the troublesome Tibetan quarter and the maze of alleyways in the Barkor beyond. In the process, the Jokhang – previously hidden from view – has been exposed by a large plaza. There used to be a small square in front of the Jokhang – used as a marketplace – but nothing on the scale of the present plaza. This architectural approach might suit a grand European cathedral, but it is a travesty when applied to an intimate corner like the Jokhang.

Barkor Square is lined with shops and eateries, but it is also an elaborate parking lot for army trucks should trouble arise. A lot of older housing was ripped up and then replaced with mock-Tibetan shops, but these do not quite look the same. For one thing, the outer walls of these newer buildings are vertical, not bevelled as in old Lhasa. Old Lhasan housing is conservative in style, with an 'extraordinary biblical severity ... preserving for us living architectural forms of ancient civilisations', as one writer noted. Typical housing consisted of flat-roofed two- or three-storey structures made of stone or sun-baked brick. Some buildings in the Barkor area date back to the 17th century and have withstood the test of time. Like the great masons of ancient Egypt or the Inca Empire, Tibetans used no nails or cement: they fitted large blocks of stone closely together and relied on gravity, which meant inward-sloping walls were constructed.

In the PRC, squares like this are used for mass shows of solidarity with the Party, but occasionally (as at Tiananmen Square in 1989) they can be used for mass demonstrations against the Party. In Barkor Square, if 20 or so Tibetans congregate, the police will break the gathering up, nervous of a repeat of the rioting that has taken place in the past.

Barkor back alleys The Barkor area was proposed as a UN World Heritage Site, but ironically it did not qualify because of too much destruction. However, in 2000, the Jokhang Temple was inscribed on the World Heritage List, so hopefully that will slow down Chinese dismantling of the area. The Chinese are systematically tearing down as much of the old quarter as possible on the grounds that the buildings are unstable: these same buildings are then replaced with newer ones of a similar design. The area around the Barkor used to be prime real estate, with residences of high-ranking nobles or lamas. Some of the better-preserved residences are at the southeast side of the Barkor: here you can find Labrang Nyingba, the former residence of aristocratic families.

Despite destruction and reconstruction, the Barkor area is a real delight for strays and alley cats, with small markets and temples tucked away, and Tibetans playing billiards. You can explore on foot or bicycle. Around here, you step into a time warp, catching glimpses of what life must have been like centuries, or even a millennium, ago. Ramoche Temple, to the northern side of the Barkor, is thought to date back to the 7th century – it is older than the Jokhang. The Ramoche is Lhasa's second-largest temple and is best viewed during prayer sessions (early morning or late afternoon) for real atmosphere. An entry fee (usually around Y20 or Y30) is charged; you might be allowed to access the rooftop, with good views of the area. The wide alley that leads to the Ramoche Temple is lined with curious shops, some merchants selling gold teeth, others gilded temple-top ornaments.

Waiting for you to discover them are a host of small temples and shrines tucked into the back alleys. Easy to find are two temples directly at the back of the Jokhang (east side), off the Barkor circuit. The larger of these is Meru Nyingba, founded in the 17th century as the Lhasa residence of the State Oracle. On the edge of the Barkor area, on the southeast side, is Ani Sangkhung, one of the three nunneries in Lhasa. Upward of 80 nuns live at Ani Sangkhung, while a number of nuns from this place are serving time in Drapchi Prison for demonstrating. The nunnery is difficult to find – keep asking for Ani Gompa. Also in this vicinity are several small mosques, combining Muslim and Tibetan architectural features.

BEGGAR WITH A MOBILE PHONE

Lhasa has an air of mystery and intrigue still – but not quite the way you'd think. The big mysteries today are what all those Chinese buildings are, with the guards out front holding AK-47s or with pistols on their belts. The Chinese military have their own living quarters, exclusive markets, teahouses, restaurants, bars, discos and clubs tucked away, but you can walk into some of them. A lot of buildings are off-limits or Chinese-only or sensitive, and photography is frowned upon. Army bases are self-contained units with high walls – they usually have their own shops and facilities within, including their own video-cinema.

To assist the paranoid Chinese in their endeavours to snoop on Tibetans is a nefarious network of informants – human listening posts – and video surveillance cameras. The video cameras are mounted around the Potala and Barkor areas, and at major intersections of the city. The cameras were initially sold by Western countries to China for use in monitoring traffic flow. Since Lhasa doesn't have a traffic flow problem, obviously they are being put to other uses here. The Chinese network of Tibetan informants includes plainclothes police, monks in robes, and beggars. One Tibetan described these people as 'Tibetans who do Chinese work'. In the Barkor area, a man in rags was seen begging one moment, and the next using a mobile phone to inform police of what was going on. The Chinese are convinced that demonstrations by the Tibetans could flare up at any moment. And then there is the threat of bombs. There have been sporadic reports of bomb blasts around Lhasa since the mid-1990s. The nature of the bombing is mysterious, and Chinese authorities have largely remained silent on the subject. The bombs do not appear designed to cause loss of life – rather, to drive home a message of protest.

In June 1995, police defused an explosive device at the Qinghai–Tibet Highway monument, an obelisk to the west of the city, opposite the bus station. The

Institute of Tibetan Medicine [129 A2] Tibetan medicine is an amalgam of herbal cures, astrology and Tibetan Buddhism. No surgery is used – for this, the patient would have to go to other practitioners. Diagnosis in Tibetan medicine is done mainly by reading the pulse (urine samples are also checked). By reading the pulse, a traditional physician determines which humour-flow (bile, wind or phlegm) has been blocked, or is excessive, and which herbal remedies to prescribe to set the system in harmony. Apart from the three main 'humours' there are over 20,000 'channels' operating through the body. Though this may sound like medieval alchemy, in fact there is strong evidence to suggest the herbal cures, developed over a millennium, have considerable effect.

Since the medical college on Chakpori Hill was razed in 1959, the institute is the only traditional medicine facility left in Lhasa. In its present form – a bland concrete building located just west off Barkor Square – the institute opened in 1977. It has in-patient, out-patient and pharmaceutical production sections, as well as an astro/medical teaching institute.

Put together a small group and you can arrange a short tour of the Institute (☉ *09.00–12.30 Mon–Sat*), which will include a visit to a second-floor museum, and the top-floor medical *tanka* room. Here hundreds of rare medical *tankas* are stored – teaching devices showing which plants should be collected, anatomical charts with energy channels, and so on. You will be shown copies of the originals. In the same section are three statues of famous medical practitioners. In the middle is a white-bearded figure (Yutok Yonten Gonpo, 9th-century founder of Tibetan

monument commemorates the completion of roads linking the TAR to the provinces of Qinghai and Sichuan. Authorities were nervous because the explosive device was discovered a few months before the 30th anniversary of the founding of the TAR, scheduled for September 1995. With 500 government officials and their families from all over China expected for the celebration, security was considerably tightened, and half-a-dozen checkpoints established on the Gongkar–Lhasa road. Two European tourists who took photographs of the obelisk a week later were detained and questioned for two hours, and had their film confiscated. In another 1995 incident, a tourist sent a fax from the Holiday Inn speculating about a bomb explosion: Chinese police intercepted the fax, arrested the tourist, detained him for 48 hours, and then deported him.

In May 1996, Chinese authorities admitted to three bomb blasts in Lhasa, blaming them on separatists. In December 1996, a bomb damaged the gatehouse of the Metropolitan District Government Offices. The blast was confirmed on Tibet Radio, which described the incident as 'yet another counter-revolutionary bombing staged by the Dalai clique in Lhasa City' and calling it 'an appalling act of terrorism'. A substantial reward was posted for information leading to the capture of the person or persons responsible.

There are closed-circuit surveillance cameras mounted inside the Potala to eavesdrop on the caretaker monks there. Even though the Potala is Lhasa's major tourist attraction, and one of its most sacred sites, its last resident – the 14th Dalai Lama – is vilified by the Chinese. His picture is banned, along with that of the young 11th Panchen Lama (the one chosen by the Dalai Lama). So the whole trade in Dalai Lama and Panchen Lama pictures – once freely pursued in the Barkor – has simply gone underground.

medical science), flanked on the left by the regent of the Fifth Dalai Lama (Desi Sanggye Gyatso, 17th-century founder of Chakpori medical college) and on the right by the most renowned physician of the 20th century (Khyenrab Norbu, physician to the 13th Dalai Lama).

POTALA AREA
The Lingkor The Lingkor is the outer pilgrim circuit of Lhasa, taking about 90 minutes to complete on foot (or half that time by bicycle). Hardy pilgrims with prayer-wheels and pet dogs (or pet sheep) follow the route, perhaps breaking the journey for a spot of food shopping *en route*. Once they realise that you are joining them for the *kora*, you will get lots of reassuring grins and thumbs-up gestures. There is no finer way to get into the spirit of Lhasa – what's left of Lhasa, that is.

Tibetans still follow the full Lingkor circuit, though it has lost much of its sacred appeal on the eastern and southern sides, where small bars and karaoke salons have mushroomed. These places may be fronts for prostitution. Nudes or noodles? Probably a bit of both, washed down with beer. Prostitutes are flown in from Sichuan Province. Other fronts: barbershops west of the Potala, and certain restaurants with partitioned sections. How big is the trade? Very big. At Jarmalingka Island Bridge, the news doesn't get any better. An old wooden bridge here used to lead to an undeveloped area where Tibetans would congregate under the trees for picnics. The bridge was torn down and replaced by a wider concrete one – to develop Jarmalingka. The island's greenery disappeared, and the area sprouted into a Chinese entertainment zone, with row-housing, nightclubs, hairdressers, brothels, karaoke bars, fairground, restaurants and hotels. The area is today known by various names – Kumalingka, Taiyang (Sun Island) and Zhonghe International City.

The Lingkor as a sacred circuit really gets under way at a cairn of stones with some prayer-flags, just west of Jarmalingka Bridge. This marks the turn-off for a walking track that leads to the Blue Buddha. If you bicycle the route, there are steps near the Blue Buddha which require you to carry the bike. Otherwise, it's easy riding, with smooth, flat sections.

Blue Buddha [151 C3] The way up past the south base of Chakpori Hill is a staircase lined with prayer-flags. Further on is an entire cliff face depicting religious figures, which have been carved in bas-relief and painted in bright colours. Some carvings date back over a thousand years, with countless additions over the centuries. The largest carving is the Blue Buddha, shown seated in a meditation pose. In this area, pilgrims pay their respects, and off to the side, carvers chip text into *mani* stones. If you follow the pilgrims, heading north, you'll reach another Petrochina station at Dekyi Nub Road. Just before reaching that junction, set back off the road lies Kundeling Gompa, a small active monastery that is little visited. On Dekyi Nub Road is a section with some well-worn rocks. These are special rubbing stones that pilgrims apply their knees or backs to. From here, pilgrims continue to the Golden Yak statues.

Golden Yak statues [151 C2] Two Golden Yak statues, which now sit in a park overlooking a major roundabout, were unveiled in May 1991 to celebrate the 40th anniversary of the 'peaceful liberation' of Tibet by Chinese troops. Tibetans have christened the incongruous statues 'Tenzin and Raidi', a reference to the two Tibetan deputy secretaries of the Communist Party in Tibet who are trotted out when the Chinese need to present a Tibetan face to the media. In the background at this site sits the modern office building housing Xizang TV (XZ TV), the main radio and

KEY
- – – – Lingkor pilgrim walking route
- ····· Tsekor pilgrim walking route

POTALA AREA

see Barkor area map, page 127

Lingkor to Mountaineers G on Everest Statue

People's Hospital

Bank of China $

NIANGRE ROAD

DZUK TRUN RD

Lukhang X teahouse

Lukhang Temple

Lukhang Park

Three Chortens

Airline office & buses

Tibet Post

Airway

Chinapost Main PO/ Telecom

DZUK SHAR RD (BEIJING ST)

New Century

Markets

Tianhe

Gold Grain

YUTHOK RD

Dept stores

Department stores

Lhasa Department Store Hotel

Lhasa Dept Store

Xinhua Bookstore

KANGANGDUO NANLU

Chinese Pavilion/ Teahouse X

Markets

JIANGSU LU

Tibet Royal Hotel & Top View Disco

Lingkor, west side G

bars

Red Palace

N Tower entry/exit

Potala Palace

Central staircase

Admin office

White Palace

West Gate (reconstructed)

DEKYI-NUB RD

Flagpole

Potala Square

Concrete monolith, marking 50 years of colonial repression

Gardens

Bridge to D Jamalingka Island

Alley around outer enclosing wall of Potala

Gate

P

Bank of China $

XZTV

Horse on Globe statue

Golden Yak statues

Chorten on rocks

Nunnery

Third Pole Camping

Palha Lupuk Cave-temple

Chakpori Hill TV tower 3756m

Steps

Chorten

PetroChina

Rubbing stones

Sheng Shia

PetroChina

Kundeling Gompa

Tibet Tourism Bureau (TTB)

DEJI LU

Blue Buddha & rock paintings

PAP HQ

Century Grand

TSANG GYUN NUB ROAD

DEKYI NUB ROAD

Nightclubs & karaoke bars

Hotpot restaurants

China Telecom building

Karaoke bars

Grand Hotel Tibet

NORBULINGKA ROAD

Norbulingka

Kyi Chu (Lhasa River)

N

Bradt

0 ——— 200m
0 ——— 200yds

4

TV broadcasting unit in Lhasa. The operation is solar-powered. The Golden Yak statues are something of a navigation landmark, referred to in this section as the Golden Yak roundabout.

Three Chortens [151 E1] From the Golden Yak roundabout, the Lingkor route heads northward, turning through a park where the route is lined with vendors – a chance to indulge in some food shopping. Proceeding onward, you arrive at a busy junction with three *chortens* (shrines). All change at Three Chortens: you can diverge and complete the Tsekor (circuit of Potala Palace), or you can access entry to Lukhang Park, or you can carry on with the whole Lingkor route. Or combinations of these routes. From the three *chortens*, Lingkor pilgrims march north on a narrow walkway that is sectioned off from Lukhang Park by a wire fence. They stop to feed geese and fish in Lukhang Lake and give money to beggars, thereby gaining more merit. A bridge festooned with prayer-flags is located near the main road: this spot offers fine views of the back of the Potala Palace. At the end of the bridge, there is a gateway that leads into Lukhang Park. The Lingkor route continues eastward but loses its lustre – and its purpose – among bland Chinese buildings.

The Tsekor The Tsekor is a *kora* (complete loop) of the outer enclosing walls of the Potala Palace. The following description proceeds clockwise from the West Gate, though you might want to start at Lukhang Park if coming off the Lingkor circuit.

West Gate [151 D2] As part of the 1995 'celebrations' of the 30th anniversary of the founding of the TAR, Lhasa's West Gate and two accompanying *chortens* were resurrected. Passing through the *chorten*-like West Gate was once the only way into the sacred city, and reaching it was the dream of many explorers. It was the gate that British troops marched through in 1904; the gate that Heinrich Harrer and Peter Aufschnaiter reached in rags in 1946, after two years of wandering. Now you see it, now you don't: the original West Gate was completely destroyed in the Cultural Revolution, and then completely rebuilt for the 1995 ceremonies. Tibetan pilgrims pose next to the 1995 version of the West Gate for photographs, but Tibetans say that the structure was not properly consecrated by monks, and in any case there are no hidden treasures within the *chorten*-like structure that required consecration. Nevertheless, there is some fine artwork lining the interior of the West Gate, especially a mandalic mural on the inside ceiling.

From the West Gate, pilgrims proceed north along a narrow walkway lined on one side with an endless row of prayer-wheels, and on the other side with an endless row of stalls – and vendors shouting their wares. This walkway follows the outer Potala Palace walls to the three *chortens* area. From here, you can carry on to complete the Tsekor circuit, or you can take a stroll through Lukhang Park and rejoin the Tsekor.

Lukhang Park [151 F1] The park at the back of the Potala was a site where the Tibetan aristocracy used to picnic or drink tea. It has since lost its noble atmosphere – it's down at the proletariat level now, renamed Jiefang (Victory) Park. However, you can still take tea here, and contemplate the excellent views of the Potala. There are three entrances to the park – one at the northwest side, one at the northeast and one at the south side. At the entrances, you pay a token fee (extra for a bicycle). Lukhang Park attracts picnickers, strollers and people relaxing, and it's great for cycling around. At the northeast corner is a teahouse with outdoor tables and umbrellas overlooking a small artificial lake, with the towers of the Potala looming above. A plant nursery is attached to the teahouse: potted plants and flowers make *right*   A small dam under construction in Kham, east Tibet; Chinese engineering projects are steadily encroaching on Tibet's beautiful landscapes page 17

below   Big bend of the Yangtse, *en route* to Deqin page 265

bottom   Deep green valley and village, eastern Tibet page 251

top   Nomad woman milking a yak,
Lake Namtso page 173

centre   Unloading a yak-hair tent — from
a yak, of course page 23

left   Rock-hard pieces of yak cheese,
strung together in clusters that
resemble necklaces page 79

top — Dancers parading before a horse-racing event in Gyantse page 196

above left — Rare display of Cham dancing at a monastery in central Tibet; behind the masks are monks page 167

above right — Nomad women dressed in their finest, at a horse-race festival in Nagqu page 285

below — Archery contestants at a horse-race festival in central Tibet; the riders fire at a target while galloping page 167

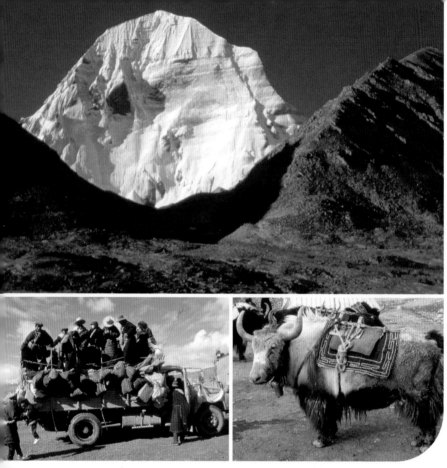

top   North face of Mount Kailash, the most revered peak in Asia, and close to the source of four major rivers page 244

above left   Pilgrims getting off a truck at the start of the Kailash circuit page 245

above right   Pack yak unloaded at Darchen, west Tibet page 22

below   Prime trekking territory — views of a valley with village on the route to Everest base camp page 223

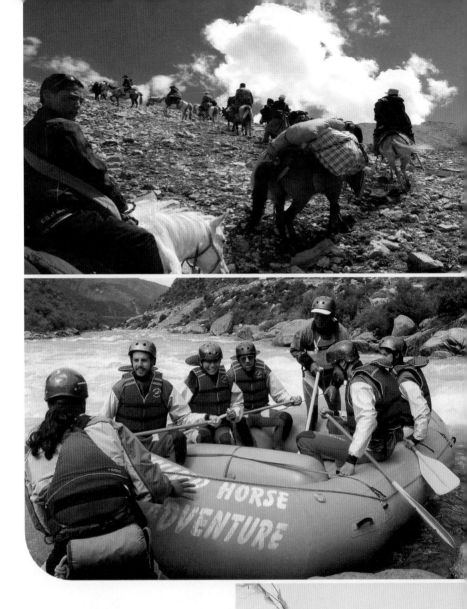

top   **Horse trekking in Kham to visit a nomad encampment** page 257

centre   **Pushing off in a raft on the Drigung River, close to Lhasa** page 169

right   **Riders have to deal with the elements — here, fresh snow on a high pass** page 80 *top left* Khampa from east Tibet holding a *gau* (portable shrine), an amulet worn around the neck that contains the image of an important spiritual figure page 20

top right Nomad woman at horse-racing fair, Nagqu page 20

above left Lhasan woman with chunks of turquoise braided in her hair; in old Tibet, the wealth and status of aristocratic women was denoted by the quality and amount of jewellery worn page 20

above right Khampa with fox-fur cap and large amber beads page 20 this a very pleasant place. You can park yourself over a cup of *ba bao cha* (eight treasures tea) – this is provided in a cup with a lid, and contains a big lump of rock sugar with dried berries and herbs, to which steaming hot water is added.

Lukhang Temple [151 E1] On an island in the middle of the lake is Lukhang Temple, a tiny three-storey chapel constructed in the form of a mandala. The building of the temple is attributed to the Sixth Dalai Lama, and it was used as a quiet retreat for arcane meditation practices by successive Dalai Lamas.

Lukhang Temple is one of those corners that provide an illusion of old Lhasa: it is sequestered in greenery, with only the back of the Potala visible, so you can get

THE MYSTERIOUS SIXTH

The Sixth Dalai Lama was Tsangyang Gyatso, whose name means 'Ocean of Melodious Songs'. He is thought to have lived from 1683 to 1706. He took over as Dalai Lama under very unusual circumstances. The Fifth Dalai Lama had died during the construction of the Potala but his death was concealed by the Regent for some 15 years to ensure completion of the work (the Fifth Dalai Lama was replaced by a double and was said to be engaged in long meditation retreats). The Sixth Dalai Lama took over as an adolescent, not an infant like his predecessors. He did not take any celibacy vows and was never fully ordained as a lama. He showed little interest in either his political or religious duty. His passions lay elsewhere. He was a prolific rake – no woman in Lhasa was said to be safe from his indulgences:

> I dwell apart in the Potala
> A God on earth am I
> But in the town the chief of rogues
> And boisterous revelry

Lukhang Temple has been variously described as the Sixth Dalai Lama's personal retreat, and as his favourite trysting place. He was said to sneak out of a back gate of the Potala to meet his lovers. Apart from his love of wine and women, he was renowned as a melodious singer of love songs, and writer of romantic lyrics:

> Drops of rain wash away
> The love songs written in
> Black and white
> But love, though unwritten,
> Remains long after, in the heart

Despite his behaviour, the Sixth was revered by the people, who came to the conclusion that the living Buddha had two bodies – one which stayed in the Potala and meditated, and the other that got rotten drunk and chased Lhasa women. The Sixth disappeared under mysterious circumstances at the age of 23. One account claims that he had a son by a special lover, and that high lamas – fearing the office of the Dalai Lama would become hereditary – drove the Sixth into exile and imprisoned his lover and their son. Another account claims he was murdered at Litang.

a feeling for what Tibet once was. There are a few monks currently in residence at Lukhang Temple. You can visit, but not all parts of the building are accessible. There are murals on each of the three storeys: the most interesting are those on the third floor, believed to date to the 18th century. You will need a flashlight to see these gems – they are protected by a wire shield, which doesn't make the viewing any easier. The murals show subjects that are rare to find in Tibetan temples today. Among them are depictions of Indian ascetics in yogic poses, and others striking blissful tantric poses. One wall shows the stages of human life, with detailed anatomical pictures acting as a kind of Tibetan medicine primer (in which system an imbalance of humours leads to sickness and dysfunction). Attached to this is a set of murals based on *The Tibetan Book of the Dead*.

Potala Square [151 E3] Potala Square was created in 1995 in time to mark 'celebrations' for the 30th anniversary of the TAR. A large area of ramshackle Tibetan housing was razed to create the paving; the inhabitants were moved to concrete housing north of the Potala. The concept of a large square or plaza is alien to Tibetan town planning: this is a Chinese idea. The Tibetans would have no use for such a square because it allows the bitter winter wind to roar through. Potala Square has a lot in common with Beijing's Tiananmen Square, including the same chandelier-lamp fixtures with propaganda speakers attached. Tiananmen Square was Mao Zedong's creation, designed for military parades and mass solidarity parades, and meanwhile used for weekend amusement like photography or kite flying.

This is exactly what Potala Square is used for: the military use it as one big parking lot; concerts for the military have been staged here; shows of force and parades by the PLA have taken place; and trade fairs with vendors promoting Chinese products have been conducted here. Potala Square is the premier Chinese photo-opportunity site. There is a slew of photo-shops just to the west of the square, catering to Chinese tourism. A flagpole at the front of the square is a favourite place for Chinese tourists to have their photos taken. All Chinese dignitaries and military honchos arriving in Lhasa stop near the flagpole to have photographs or video taken with the Potala in the background.

In 2002, a 37m-high concrete monolith was constructed near the fountain to commemorate the 50th anniversary of the liberation of Tibet. This monstrosity, said be an abstract rendition of Everest, is flanked by two concrete bunkers, intended as exhibition halls. The monument is reported to have cost US$1.7 million to build, prompting exiled Tibetans to call it a million-dollar insult. Directly in front of the monolith is a hidden musical fountain – for special events, waterworks spring up, synchronised with music from loudspeakers.

On a more positive note, in time for the 40th anniversary of the founding of the TAR in 2005, some shoddy Chinese shops were pulled down to the west side of Potala Square, and in their place a green belt with gardens was added. This green belt is a favoured spot for Tibetans to take photos.

Palhalupuk Cave-temple [151 D3] As an extension of the Tsekor circuit, pilgrims diverge to visit Palhalupuk, an extraordinary cave-temple set into the lower section of Chakpori Hill. You can reach it by a path leading from the West Gate; entry is Y20. The brown and ochre-coloured Palhalupuk temple, with a dozen monks in residence, offers a superb viewpoint of the Potala, giving it a foreground of rocks and trees. Close by are two small caves – the larger one is lined with several rows of brightly painted bas-relief images, believed to date back as far as the 7th century (which qualifies them as the oldest in Lhasa). The central image here is Sakyamuni, while at the back is a small statue of Palden Lhamo, the protectress of Lhasa. The intimate scale of the temple and cave make Palhalupuk very special – it offers perspectives that you will find nowhere else in Lhasa. There's a second (minor) cave with an image of Avalokitesvara in the vicinity; above Palhalupuk to the right is a small active nunnery. Another hike to consider is up Chakpori Hill. This hill was once crowned by the fortress-like medical college of Lhasa – the institute, founded in the 15th century, was razed by shelling in the 1959 uprising. The hill is now crowned with a TV tower, which you may be able to climb partway for views of the Potala.

Potala Palace [151 E2] The Potala was inscribed on the UNESCO World Heritage List in 1994. The citation says: 'The Potala, winter palace of the Dalai Lama since the 7th century AD, symbolises Tibetan Buddhism and its central role in the traditional administration of Tibet.' Chinese authorities conducted a five-year multi-million-dollar restoration of the Potala, completing work in 1995. Why restore a palace that is the former abode of Public Enemy Number One? Because it's a major tourist attraction, of course – and one that generates millions of dollars in income annually. Unlike the Jokhang or the monasteries around Lhasa, the Potala is run by Chinese tourist authorities: the practice of Buddhism is essentially banned in the palace.

Once humming with spiritual activity, the Potala is now a lifeless museum, a haunted castle. A lot of the Chinese restoration was directed at the enclosing walls, which were damaged by Chinese shelling during the 1959 uprising. Adding considerably to the bill is the 'wiring' of the Potala. Electrical hook-ups have been enhanced and video surveillance cameras have been installed throughout. The cameras are to monitor the 60-odd caretakers at the Potala, who pad around in purple trenchcoats. On a more practical note, fire extinguishers and other devices have been installed (following a disastrous fire that broke out in 1984 due to a short circuit).

Below the Potala, within the enclosing walls, used to lie the Tibetan administrative quarter of Shol. Some buildings in this zone have been destroyed. One building has been turned into a hotel; the others are used as art galleries, souvenir shops, or occupied as residences. Before 1950, Shol quartered the offices of the Tibetan government, Tibetan Army officials, guard offices and a prison. Other sections of the Potala were used to house Namgyal Monastery, as well as a community of monks and a school for monk officials.

History and architecture The Potala is a 13-storey castle – rising over 117m high – built of rammed earth, wood and stone. Crowning a mass of solid rock, the maze-like structure contains over 1,000 rooms, and is thought to house 10,000 shrines and 200,000 statues. The architecture at first appears to be regular, but is not – storeys are not continuous, and access to halls may be hidden behind pillars or shrines. The walls – varying in thickness between 2–5m – were strengthened against earthquakes by pouring in molten copper. No steel frame was used, and no nails were used in the woodwork. The Potala is a layered structure: successive Dalai Lamas worked on the project. Although original construction dates back to the 7th century, the White Palace was not completed until 1653, and the Red Palace not until 1694: at this time, the wheel had not been introduced to Tibet, so stones were lugged in on donkey-back, or on the backs of humans. Simple equipment was used to fashion this skyscraper – an achievement on a par with the building of the pyramids.

The skyscraper itself created a transport problem. The Potala had no plumbing, electricity or heating, so there was a constant stream of porters with water for tea, yak butter for the prayer lamps, and firewood for the fireplaces. The Dalai Lama was

portered in and out of the palace in a palanquin; high lamas were piggybacked up
to the entrance of the Potala by porters.

Access Opening hours for the Potala seem to chop and change, and vary with the
season. You can follow the logic of the hours described here, but there could well
be modifications. The Potala is supposed to be open to tourists from 09.00–17.00
daily, including holidays. The best time to visit is mornings; the last tickets are sold
around 15.00. In high season (July–August), there are long queues to get in. Tickets
were previously limited to 1,600 visitors a day, but that figure was boosted to 2,300
after the July 2006 opening of the railway. After the daily maximum is reached, even
Tibetan pilgrims (who pay Y2) are turned away. To discourage visitors, the palace
is contemplating a steep increase in ticket admission prices. This would also be in
the interests of preserving the architecture itself, which is at risk from heavy use
by tourists. To avoid disappointments and queues, in peak season you should buy
tickets ahead – buy them after 14.00 on the day prior to your visit. Important note:
to purchase tickets, you need to show proper ID such as a passport. Entry costs
Y100 for big-noses; in the 'slack season' (1 November–31 March) the ticket price
may be reduced. Photography of interiors at the Potala is not permitted, though you
can shoot in exterior courtyards.

Due to heavy demand, with conga-lines of tourists snaking through the
Potala, a tactic of limiting your time in the palace has been adopted. Your guide
will try and rush you through in 90 minutes, start to finish. For some folks,
that's fine. Others like to go slower. The one-hour stipulation, like many other
rules in Tibet, is unwritten. Therefore, ask your guide to show you where it says
you only get one hour to visit, and just ignore the pressure. The tide of humanity
surging through may speed you along on certain stretches, particularly if you
get caught in throngs of pilgrims. Fisticuffs have broken out at entrances to
certain highly revered rooms as pilgrims and Chinese tourists jockey for the
best vantage points.

The Potala is open to Tibetan pilgrims, who pay a token entry fee. It appears
that the pilgrims are allowed entry on Monday, Wednesday and Friday mornings,
but this could change. When there are lots of pilgrims, key shrines may become
very crowded, with long queues. Here's a paradox: things are much more lively
with Tibetan pilgrims around (you can observe what they are doing – muttering
mantras, flinging *katas*, and spooning yak butter into lamps at shrines) but at the
same time, it's more crowded and uncomfortable. The solution here is to visit the
Potala several times: first to see the architecture and statuary, the second time to go
and mingle with the Tibetan pilgrims.

Entry to the Potala is via the central staircase, which is taxing to negotiate at
altitude – take it slowly here. Group tours may have permission to access easier
ways of reaching the top of the Potala. Only a fraction of the Potala's thousand-
odd rooms are accessible to the touring public: the contents of many are rumoured
to have been destroyed or carted off. The rooms seem to open and close without
rhyme or reason, so the following description may hit the mark – or it may not.
You should be able to follow the overall logic. The way things are currently set up,
you enter the palace by the central staircase. From there you mount staircases to
the open rooftop area of the Potala, and then spiral downward to the bowels of the
building, where you exit by the north tower. This is actually a car ramp. Heading
down from the north tower at the back of the Potala, you get a view of north Lhasa
that is not revealed from the rooftop: a sea of apartment blocks stretching towards
Sera – the heavy Chinese concrete hand at work.

Inside the Potala The Potala is divided into the White Palace and the Red Palace. The White Palace was secular in nature (used for offices, a printing house and so on), while the Red Palace fulfilled a religious function (comprising the tombs of the Dalai Lamas, scores of chapels and shrines, and libraries of sacred texts). Most of the White Palace is inaccessible; you can see a fair number of rooms in the Red Palace.

The 14th Dalai Lama's quarters Huffing and puffing up staircases, you arrive at an open rooftop area of the Potala. Green-maned snow lions are the gargoyles here – pilgrims touch the mouths of the lions and ring attached bells. To the west side of the open area are the former living quarters of the 13th and 14th Dalai Lamas, attached to the White Palace. The only section accessible here takes you into the former reception hall, dominated by a large throne. On the wall nearby hangs a portrait painting of the 13th Dalai Lama, but a portrait of the 14th that used to hang alongside it has been removed. So ludicrous is the Chinese removal of 14th Dalai Lama images that in a lavishly illustrated Beijing hardcover about the Potala, he is only seen in one picture – shaking hands with Mao Zedong in 1954.

In the same reception hall, near the entrance, is a large mural of the legendary land of Shambhala. Beyond the hall lie the private quarters of the 14th Dalai Lama. You may or may not be allowed to see these, depending on the mood of caretakers. Try tagging along behind an official tour. At the 14th Dalai Lama's tearoom and meditation room, pilgrims leave *katas* and other offerings; beyond is His Holiness's bedroom, vacant since 1959.

The Red Palace Entering the Red Palace from the rooftop area, you spiral downward through four levels, eventually exiting at the North Tower. The upper levels of the Red Palace enclose an open skylight space, with chapels arrayed in a gallery-like rectangle around it. Interspersed through the many chapels and shrines of the Red Palace are the eight gold-plated stupas, each containing the salt-dried body of a past Dalai Lama – from the Fifth to the 13th, with the exception of the Sixth, who disappeared. Four of the reliquary stupas are on the upper level, and four are on the ground level.

Upper level The upper level provides access to chapels with the stupas of the Seventh, Eighth, Ninth and 13th Dalai Lamas. You may have difficulty getting permission to see the stupa of the 13th Dalai Lama, which is 14m high, made of gold, and fronted by a three-dimensional mandala said to contain 200,000 pearls. The tomb ranges over several storeys and is well lit. One wall bears fine murals of the 13th Dalai Lama surrounded by his ministers and tutors, as well as scenes from his life. Another highlight of the upper level is the former throne room of the Seventh Dalai Lama, which contains a beautiful silver image of 11-faced Avalokitesvara, the bodhisattva of compassion – this statue was commissioned by the 13th Dalai Lama.

Revered by Tibetan pilgrims as the most sacred part of the entire Potala is the **Avalokitesvara Chapel** (Phakpa Lakhang), on the northwest side of the upper level. The tiny chapel gets very crowded when there are lots of pilgrims. It is reached by a small triple staircase. The centre of pilgrim attention is a tiny gilded standing statue of Avalokitesvara, thought to have come from Nepal. Legend has it that the image was found miraculously embedded in a Nepalese sandalwood tree when its trunk split open. Flanking it are two other images derived from the same source, one of Avalokitesvara again, the other of Tara. To the right of this chapel is the massive funerary *chorten* of the Seventh Dalai Lama, rising to a height of 9m, and studded with precious stones. Next to that is the tomb of the Ninth Dalai Lama.

Lhasa **WHAT TO SEE**

4

Mid-levels Downstairs, there is a Tibetan-style tearoom with a souvenir shop. On the same level is the Cultural Relics Museum, which charges Y10 entry and features a display of armour and instruments. There are two levels of galleries at the mid-levels, but rooms on the lower level are most likely to be closed (these contain murals depicting the construction of the Potala and major Tibetan monasteries). The highlight of the mid-levels is the **Kalachakra Chapel** (Dukhor Lakhang), which contains a stunning three-dimensional mandala of the palace of the Kalachakra deity. Made of copper and gold, it measures over 6m in diameter. To one side of the mandala is a life-sized statue of the multi-headed, multi-armed Kalachakra deity in union with his consort. On shelves nearby are the seven religious kings of Tibet and the 25 kings of the mythical realm of Shambhala.

Very popular with Tibetan pilgrims on this level is the oldest chamber in the Potala, the Chapel of the Dharma Kings, thought to have been the meditation chamber of King Songtsen Gampo. This cave-within-the-castle is approached by a ramp; the niches lining the cavern are filled with statuary of past kings, royal family members and ministers. The most highly regarded statue is that of Songtsen Gampo himself. You can expect a pilgrim traffic-jam in this area and foreign group tours are likely to be ushered past the line-ups.

Ground level After negotiating several steep, dark flights of stairs, you come into a large assembly hall with columns – the Great Western Assembly Hall. This is the largest room in the Potala Palace, with dozens of pillars wrapped in raw silk. It contains the throne of the Seventh Dalai Lama; the walls are coated in murals and appliqué *tankas*.

There are four chapels open on this level. The first you come to is Lamrin Lakhang, dedicated to the ancient lineage masters of the Geluk school, particularly Tsongkhapa. The next chapel, Rigdzin Lakhang, is dedicated to the great Nyingma lineage holder, Padmasambhava, showing eight manifestations of the master; in the same line-up of statues here are seven other great Indian masters.

The next chapel, Dzamling Gyenchik, contains the astounding tomb of the Fifth Dalai Lama, which reaches a height of over 14m, and is said to contain 3,700kg of gold. It is studded with jewels and precious stones. In this line-up of tombs are eight more dedicated to Sakyamuni Buddha, commemorating the eight major events in his life. In the same chapel are the more modest stupas of the Tenth and 12th Dalai Lamas, who both perished as minors, failing to attain their majority. The Dalai Lamas from the Sixth through to the 12th all died young and under mysterious circumstances – possibly poisoned.

The last chapel on the ground level is Tungrab Lakhang, featuring a central double throne with two statues – a gold one of Sakyamuni and a silver one of the Fifth Dalai Lama. This chapel contains the tomb of the 11th Dalai Lama; three statues of the Buddha (past, present and future); and statues of the eight Medicine Buddhas.

You can exit Tungrab Lakhang by a dark hidden corridor at the back of the statues – this leads out of the rear of the Potala at the North Tower.

NORBULINGKA AREA

The Norbulingka [116 B3] In contrast to the lofty, monumental Potala, the Norbulingka is a small-scale, down-to-earth summer palace. In former times, an elaborate procession would wind out of the Potala, escorting the Dalai Lama to the Norbulingka, his home for up to six months of the year. In better days, the walled summer palace exuded an idyllic atmosphere, with picnic pavilions and well-tended gardens, peacocks roaming the grounds, and Brahminy ducks flocking to the lakes.

Norbulingka in fact means 'Jewelled Garden'. Visiting in the 1930s, members of a British delegation were astonished to find roses and petunias flourishing at 3,650m, as well as hollyhocks, marigolds, chrysanthemums, and rows of potted herbs or rare plants. In addition, there were apple, peach and apricot trees – though the fruits did not ripen in Lhasa – and stands of poplar trees and bamboo.

The Norbulingka was shelled during the 1959 uprising, and a number of buildings were destroyed. Following a long period of dereliction, in 2003 the gardens and grounds of the Norbulingka underwent extensive restoration, bringing back the greenery, the floral beds and the miniature lakes. The Norbulingka is mainly identified with the 13th and 14th Dalai Lamas, who commissioned most of the structures you see here. In 2001, the Norbulingka was added as an extension of the Potala for inscription on the UN World Heritage List, along with the Jokhang Temple. The citation quoted preservation of the last vestiges of traditional Tibetan architecture: what is meant here is saving the last traditional structures in the face of rampant Chinese development and reconstruction in Lhasa.

Access The Norbulingka is open 09.30–12.30 and 15.30–18.30 (summer hours) Monday to Saturday. Tickets cost Y60. To get to the Norbulingka, you can walk, bicycle, take a taxi, or take a number 2 bus from the Barkor Square vicinity. Although there are several gateways at the Norbulingka, the only one open for entry–exit is the East Gate, where a ticket booth is located. If on a bicycle, you may be permitted to cycle around the grounds of the Norbulingka, which are quite spread out. When Tibetan opera is held here during the Yoghurt (Shoton) Festival, around August or September, the grounds are crowded with picnickers. Flanking the massive east gates of the Norbulingka are two snow lion statues, draped in *katas*. Tibetans like to get their photograph taken next to the mythical snow lion (the one to the left side shelters a lion cub). The snow lion is the symbol of Tibet – it is reputed to be able to jump from one snowcapped peak to another. Only a few buildings inside the Norbulingka are open. Others are locked up, used as storage, or as residences or offices by those involved with the upkeep of the Norbulingka. More recent building additions are souvenir kiosks selling drinks, souvenir books and Tibetan artefacts.

Residence of the 14th Dalai Lama The main attraction at the Norbulingka is Takten Migyur Potrang, the summer residence of the 14th Dalai Lama. It's a pilgrimage site for Tibetans, who leave *katas* and other offerings in the various rooms here. The building was constructed from 1954–56, and was the place where the Dalai Lama meditated before he escaped to India. Access is only to rooms on the upper floor.

In the assembly hall, murals portray a detailed history of Tibet, from its mythical beginnings to its early kings to the discovery of the 14th Dalai Lama. Several other rooms can be seen here: the Dalai Lama's study chambers, with a beautiful *tanka* of Atisha; and his bedroom, with an Art Deco bed and a 1956 Phillips radio (a gift from India). A side door leads to a bathroom with state-of-the-art (for Tibet at the time) plumbing. You may be allowed to visit a small library and a meditation room.

In the reception hall is a carved golden throne which was used to carry the Dalai Lama when he went outside the Norbulingka for special occasions. One entire wall of the reception hall is covered with fine murals, painted in 1956 by artist Amdo Jampa. The murals show – with photo-like realism – the 14th Dalai Lama at the centre, flanked by his mother at the right, ministers and relatives at the left, secretary below him, his four tutors above him, various tribes of Tibet at lower right, and foreign dignitaries at lower left. Under all this is a row of mythical figures. Among the foreign

THE NORBULINGKA

Ticket booth

Main entrance at East Gate

Souvenir kiosk

Souvenir kiosk

Shabten Lakhang

Souvenir kiosk

Tibetan Opera performance area during Yoghurt Festival

Souvenir kiosk

North Gate (no exit)

Takten Migyur Potrang, summer residence of the 14th Dalai Lama

Fountain

Artificial lake with pavilions

Kelsang Potrang, summer residence of the 8th Dalai Lama

Former stables

Gardens

Drunzig Potrang, Retreat of the 13th Dalai Lama

Library & Former stables

Water tower

Chensek Potrang, summer residence of the 13th Dalai Lama

Display of old vehicles

Woods

Mini zoo

0 50m
0 50yds

N

Bradt

160

dignitaries you can make out Hugh Richardson (hat and tie) who originally worked for the British and stayed on to represent the new Indian government. Also visible is an Indian dignitary, a Russian wearing medals, and a Mongolian ambassador. Unfortunately, most of the mural – especially the section showing the Dalai Lama – is likely to be roped off, and light reflections make it difficult to view. An overhead surveillance camera ensures that pilgrims get no closer. This is one of the rare images of the Dalai Lama still left in Lhasa and thus the object of great veneration by pilgrims passing through, an activity the Chinese do not wish to encourage.

The opposite wall bears a large portrait of the Great Fifth Dalai Lama, surrounded by smaller portraits of the First through to the 13th Dalai Lamas. As you exit the doorway, there's a round Shambhala fresco with a Kalachakra mandala. Harder to access are other sections of the building, including the dining room, and various meeting and reception rooms.

Retreats, vintage cars and a mini zoo Moving along through the grounds of the Norbulingka, of milder interest is **Kelsang Potrang**, the summer residence of the Eighth Dalai Lama, completed in the 18th century. This section may be closed; if it's open, you can view some fine *tankas* depicting White Tara. On the eastern wall in this area is a viewing pavilion that looks over the opera grounds. The Dalai Lamas would sit here to take in performances, which are still held during the Yoghurt Festival (in August or September). The festival derives its name from traditional offerings of yoghurt to monks at this time. To the west of this, in a separate compound (approached from the west wall), is **Drunzig Potrang**, constructed as the library and retreat of the 13th Dalai Lama. It has the atmosphere of a place of worship, with an assembly hall redolent of butter-lamps. It contains a newer wooden statue of Avalokitesvara, and thousands of sacred texts. Nearby is an area with outdoor pavilions, probably used for picnics or drinking tea. Following substantial renovations, the ponds here have been revived, which has brought wild birds back – you might even spot some bar-headed geese.

There are several locations where horses were formerly stabled, though these are hard to pinpoint today. The back of each stable was decorated with bright frescoes of equestrian subjects, ranging from horse anatomy to legends of flying horses, and nearby was the Dalai Lama's garage.

The Dalai Lama's cars, however, have been shifted over to a display of vehicles at Chensek Potrang. A fair walk away, in the northwest corner of the grounds, **Chensek Potrang** is the summer residence of the 13th Dalai Lama. It was built in 1922, and is preserved much as it was in 1933, when the 13th Dalai Lama died. Only the assembly hall may be accessible.

Inside the Chensek Potrang Chapel is a fascinating display of vehicles, ranging from palanquins (covered litters for one person, moved on foot by bearers) to landaus (elaborate horse-drawn carriages with side lamps). There is even a bicycle and a tricycle (gifts from the British to the 13th and 14th Dalai Lamas). This is all the more fascinating when you consider that the wheel was not much used in pre-1950 Tibet, and the use of vehicles like motorcycles was banned by the monastic powers.

In the courtyard here you might be able to make out the rusted remains of several cars that originally belonged to the 13th Dalai Lama and were inherited by the 14th Dalai Lama. The cars were gifts from British political officers, carried in pieces by yaks over the Himalaya from India and reassembled by an Indian chauffeur and mechanic. Two were 1920s Baby Austins (one with the number plate Tibet 1); the third was a 1931 orange Dodge. They were used for special occasions, and were the only cars in Tibet at the time, apart from an American Jeep. Their range was limited by a lack of roads and a lack of fuel, which had to be carried in from India. By the 1940s, they had fallen into disrepair, but the young 14th Dalai Lama managed to get them running again. He took a Baby Austin out for a spin at the Norbulingka – and promptly crashed into a tree. One of these cars was later adapted to power a generator for the 14th Dalai Lama's private cinema. Somewhere in the inner gardens of the Norbulingka there used to be a film theatre, constructed in 1949 for the Dalai Lama by Heinrich Harrer (there was another cine-projection room at the British Mission, run by radio operator Reginald Fox).

In the same vicinity, south of Chensek Potrang, is a derelict mini **zoo**, with some cages lying empty. In residence is a motley collection of bears, spotted deer, rhesus monkeys, foxes, lynxes, Argali bighorn sheep, bar-headed geese and bearded vultures, none of whom look especially thrilled about living on bare concrete. Looking very out of place are some imported lions.

Tibet Museum [116 B3] Located in the same vicinity as Norbulingka Summer Palace is the largest structure built in Tibetan style in the last few decades, which is ... a museum. Completed in 2000, the multi-million-dollar Tibet Museum encloses a vast exhibition space, spread over three floors. It is long on ethnography and short (or warped) on history; short on religion, and very short on the Dalai Lamas. There is only one photograph of the 14th Dalai Lama on display – taken when he was a child – but in the caption for this picture, he is not identified as the 14th in the lineage. He is identified as the reincarnation of the 13th. The museum is liberally sprinkled with Chinese propaganda: the history section features such items as an original copy of the 17-point Agreement signed in 1951, marking Tibet's takeover by the Chinese; and the Golden Urn, used by the Chinese to determine their choice of the 11th Panchen Lama in 1995.

Despite this slant, with its large collection of manuscripts, *tankas*, masks and costumes, the museum marks the passage of a great civilisation, with original, striking art and architecture. The ground floor focuses on prehistory and manuscripts and *tankas*; the middle floor is largely devoted to nomad culture; and the top floor concentrates on Tibet's flora and fauna. One small salon features rare *tankas*. Among these is a beautiful 15th-century masterpiece portraying White Tara in silk appliqué. In the same salon is a patchwork embroidery *tanka* of the deity Hevajra, with figures added in silk, satin and brocade: a slight 3D relief effect results from the use of cotton batting as stuffing.

The museum has a huge ground-floor giftshop, selling everything from books to *dzi* stones. Given out with tickets are audio-tour devices programmed with different languages – available in English, Chinese, Japanese and, yes, even in Tibetan. Entry tickets are Y30, or Y20 for students. The museum is open daily, 09.00–13.00 and 14.00–18.00. The museum has extraordinary security procedures at the entrance. It is like going through security at an airport, with large scanning devices and frisking of tourists. And as at airports, water bottles and cigarette lighters are confiscated. They cannot be taken inside the museum.

OUTSKIRTS OF LHASA

BIKING AND HIKING One of the saving graces of Lhasa is its clean air – far cleaner than in Kathmandu or other Asian cities. Compared with Chinese cities, traffic in Lhasa is light, and the place is ringed by mountains. The outskirts of Lhasa present great hiking and bicycling opportunities. You can combine those by hiring a mountain bike and setting off, later exploring on foot. Offering novel perspectives on Lhasa

Valley are ridge-top viewpoints – at Bumpa Ri to the southeast side, above Sera to the north side and at Gephel Ri to the northwest side. The easiest one to tackle is Bumpa Ri. To get to the base of Bumpa Ri, you can bicycle out over Lhasa Bridge, which spans the Kyi Chu River. The bridge was built in 1965 – it is 530m long, and is guarded by sentries at both ends. Find a place to keep your bike and climb up towards prayer-flags planted on top of Bumpa Ri. If you want something less strenuous, you can take on smaller hills in this area, also planted with prayer-flags. For a return trip by bicycle, consider cycling west along the south bank of the Kyichu River – there's a dirt road here that leads to a long bridge spanning the river close to the railway station.

At the back of Sera Monastery are fine hiking trails linking shrines. You can take a bus or minivan service to either Sera or Drepung monastery, bicycle out, share a taxi, hitch a ride, or walk. If you have a mountain bike, day trips or overnight trips can be mounted – due east and northeast of Lhasa are the best directions to go, as there is less traffic.

Sera [165 F1] The three great Geluk monastic citadels close to Lhasa – Sera, Drepung and Ganden – developed a considerable rivalry in old Lhasa. They were all established in the early 15th century – Ganden in 1409, Drepung in 1416 and Sera in 1419. Sera's population hovered around 7,000 monks, eclipsed by the 9,000 at Drepung, while Ganden's quota was probably 5,000 monks.

Sera, 4km to the north of Lhasa, was at one time famous for its fighting monks, who spent years perfecting the martial arts. They were hired out as bodyguards to the wealthy, and even took on the Tibetan Army in 1947 during protests following the imprisonment of Reting Rinpoche. Once a year, the fighting monks of Sera used to race starkers along the Kyi Chu riverbank for several kilometres to toughen up. Sera means 'merciful hail' – the origin of the name is thought to derive from the fact that Sera was in constant competition with Drepung ('rice heap monastery') and that the 'hail' of Sera destroyed the 'rice' of Drepung. Today, only a few hundred monks remain at Sera, a shadow of its former self. You can wander around and view the interiors of the two main colleges – Sera Me and Sera Je – as well as the main assembly hall.

Monastic debating One of the biggest draws at Sera is Tibetan-style debating, which takes place in the afternoon, starting around 14.00 or 15.00. Weather permitting, the venue is an open courtyard to the north side, where monks gather on cushions under the shade of trees. They debate religious and philosophical questions in the peculiar Tibetan style of slapping the palm of the hand to make a point. All highly photogenic. Monastic debating is the method used for passing exams to obtain monastic degrees, though this system has lapsed under communist control.

Entry to Sera costs Y50. Near the entrance to Sera is a monastery restaurant that serves noodles, vegetables and bread at low prices. There's a pleasant outdoor section at the back, shaded by birch trees, where pilgrims gather.

Hiking behind Sera A bigger draw than the temple interiors is the hiking out this way. Behind Sera to the northeast, on a mountainside, is the hermitage of Tsongkhapa – a simple shrine. In the vicinity are striking rock carvings, painted on boulders. A walking circuit around Sera takes about an hour to complete. If you are well acclimatised, there are more ambitious, longer, steeper hikes behind Sera that offer superb views. Dotted around the hill backing Sera are a number of caves, hermitages and sacred sites that are among the oldest in Lhasa. A circuit of sorts leads past Sera to Pabonka, a small temple with two dozen monks; from there you can carry on to Tashi

Choling Hermitage, and climb a ridge to Chupsang Nunnery, which has 80 nuns in residence. This makes for a worthwhile but fairly strenuous day.

Sera to Drepung Instead of going back through downtown Lhasa to get from Sera to Drepung, you can take a more interesting short cut by traversing a marshy area southwest of Sera. Some of the time there's a dirt road to follow, other times not. It's possible to bicycle most of the route, which leads past a rock quarry. Unless you have a mountain bike with gears, it's better not to attempt the steep route up from the base of the hill leading to Drepung. Leave the bike with a shop owner (with a token payment) and hitch a ride with whatever comes along (most likely a walking-tractor or number 3 bus).

Drepung [165 B2] If Sera used to be famous for its fighting monks, Drepung was famed for its scholars. Spectacularly sited – enclosed on three sides by boulder-strewn peaks – Drepung is an entire monastic town that once housed a community of some 9,000 monks, qualifying it as the largest in the world. There are perhaps 500 monks living here today, although their numbers are uncertain following a major re-education campaign in the late 1990s, where monks were forced to denounce the Dalai Lama. Drepung has been singled out as a priority for re-education because of its larger contingent of monks and because of its previous involvement in Lhasa demonstrations.

Drepung is 8km west of downtown Lhasa. You can bicycle out this way, or take a number 3 bus, which runs past the Potala and goes all the way up to the gates of Drepung. The monastery charges a Y55 entry fee. On the way in or out of Drepung, you might want to visit the Potala Carpet Factory [165 B3], which is about 300m west of the turn-off to Drepung. You can see women weaving and singing at the factory.

Like other large-scale monasteries, Drepung is divided into colleges with attached residences, rather like a campus where different disciplines are pursued. There are four major colleges – Ngakpa, Loseling, Gomang and Deyang. In previous times, all the monks at Drepung would gather on special occasions at the vast main assembly hall. Now the hall is little used. The hall is three storeys high: you can climb onto the flat rooftop for great views over Lhasa Valley (Drepung lies a few hundred metres above Lhasa). If you like climbing, there's a very strenuous hike behind Drepung to the top of Gephel Ri. The climb up and back would take a full day and you need to be very well acclimatised, as the top of Gephel Ri is 5,200m in altitude.

Nechung [165 C2] On the lower slopes of the hill leading up to Drepung is Nechung Monastery, a small temple that fulfilled an important function in old Lhasa. It was the seat of the state oracle, who was consulted by the Lhasa government when making important decisions. The monks who lived at Nechung were trained in the secret rituals that accompanied the trances of the oracle. When in a trance, the oracle was said to be possessed by the spirit Dorje Drakden – the oracle shook, trembled, barked, rolled his eyes and stuck out his tongue. Monk-attendants quickly strapped on the oracle's impossibly heavy headpiece and he would dance around. Questions were asked, cryptic answers were given. The state oracle's last cryptic answers in Tibet concerned whether the Dalai Lama should leave or not – the answer was interpreted as yes. The state oracle himself escaped to India with the exodus of exiles in 1959: he died in 1985, but his successor was found, and the tradition has been kept alive in Dharamsala, India.

In keeping with its unusual function, Nechung Monastery has some strange, striking and imaginative murals lining the walls of the inner courtyard and main

LHASA VALLEY

N

Bradt

0 ———— 2km
0 ———— 1 mile

Gephel Ri ▲

Drepung

Nechung

Potala Carpet
Factory

Cement factory

Railway
station

Foreign Trade
Building

Golmud

Tsedang,
Gongkar Airport,
Gyantse, Shigatse

▲ 4272m

CITS

Tibet

Norbulingka

Lhasa
Nepalese consulate

Tibet Museum

Kyi Chu (Lhasa River)

Pabonka

Military
hospital

Chupsang
Nunnery

Sera

Sera Tse

Tashi Choling

Sky burial site

Northa
Khangsang

Lhasa beer
brewery

Drapchi

Swimming pool

Gakyling

Ramoche

Jokhang

Potala

Jamalingka
Island

TMA

Himalaya

Brahmaputra
Grand

Bumpa Ri ▲

Yerpa

Ganden,
Nyingchi

To the north of Lhasa is a kind of 'dead end', with Drapchi Prison, Lhasa Military Hospital and – to the northeast – a large flat-topped boulder, on top of which sky burials take place. Upon death, the body is thought to return to one of the elements – earth, air, fire, water or wood. Earth burial is rare in Tibet: the ground is hard to break up, and could be frozen in winter. Cremation (return to fire) is also rare because wood is a scarce commodity. A high lama might be cremated, and the ashes placed in a silver *chorten* in his monastery. Two other forms reserved for high lamas are wood burial (the body is placed in a hollow tree trunk) and embalming (the body is preserved in a seated pose by an ancient Tibetan embalming technique). Water burial – whereby the body is eaten by fish – is reserved for small children and paupers.

In Tibet, the most common form of dispatching the dead is not under the ground, but the opposite – releasing the body to the air. This is sky burial. The body is taken to a site on a rock on a mountainside and hacked into pieces with machetes. The bones are pounded together with *tsampa*, and when the work is complete, a signal is given to waiting flocks of vultures – which know the timing well – to feast on the rock. This way, the body is thought to be taken closer to the heavens. Sky burial takes place all over Tibet, but is more common in Lhasa because of the larger resident population.

In the mid-1980s, travellers were allowed to sit near the rock where sky burial takes place. As long as they were respectful of the customs and did not take photos, they were tolerated by the Tibetans. However, a number of ugly incidents involving photography upset the Tibetans. In particular, one Westerner climbed up behind the rock, intending to sneak photographs of the site with a long lens. In the process, he scared off the vultures who sit on the ridge above the sky burial site, so they did not come down at the completion of rites – a very bad omen. Since the early 1990s, the site has been off-limits to tourists. However, you may be able to see the sky burial ceremony at Drigung Monastery, to the northeast of Lhasa, and at other sites around the Tibetan plateau, such as Litang.

Tibetans are not the only people to dispatch the dead this way. The Parsees in India follow a similar custom. However, the ancient Parsee religious custom may soon disappear because the vultures that eat the bodies are headed for extinction in India. Populations of both the long-billed and white-backed vulture have crashed since 1996 due to a virus of some kind.

chapel – paintings of flayed humans held from the rafters by serpents, figures with dangling eyeballs, disembodied heads and legs, wrathful deities with garlands of skulls, and other ghoulish artwork. It also features an array of mythical animals, such as murals of snakes and dragons coiled around support beams in the main hall. There's a statue of Dorje Drakden in the main assembly hall, as well as a photograph showing the Nechung Oracle in a trance. Adjoining chapels were once used by the various Dalai Lamas when they visited or conducted retreats here. Some 20 monks currently reside at Nechung.

5

Exploring Central Tibet

Lhasa is not Tibet – it is too heavily Chinese-influenced for that. If you want to see a more genuine Tibet, you have to get out into the countryside, where 80% of Tibetans live. This chapter covers areas within easy reach of Lhasa by Landcruiser. You might also consider combination routes involving Gyantse and Shigatse when on a round trip out of Lhasa. See the *Lhasa to Kathmandu* chapter, page 187 for details on Gyantse, Shigatse and sites further west.

While destinations when touring by Landcruiser are commonly monasteries, what's along the way is often more interesting. If you see an opportunity to stop or get off the track, take it. On one trip, we spotted some horseriders in costume. We pulled over and got the driver to ask where they were going. It turned out there was a horse-racing and archery event not far away. We spent several hours watching the races and drinking *chang*. Our Tibetan driver didn't mind – he was enjoying himself, too.

If you string together a lot of temples on a Landcruiser trip, you run the risk of becoming 'templed out'. That is, after visiting the first two or three temples, they all start to look the same. The key to a well-designed trip is variety – visit a temple, a fortress, then take in some countryside, and make impromptu stops along the route. Samye is a good combination of natural sights (eg: crossing of the Yarlung Tsangpo River) and temples. A visit to Lake Namtso places more emphasis on natural beauty.

Some of the sites mentioned here (Tsurphu, Damxung, Samye, Tsedang) can be reached by Landcruiser with driver and guide over a period of two to seven days, depending on how much ground you want to cover, splitting the tariff between four or five passengers. If you are not overnighting, permits should not present problems – you can visit on a day trip. However, be wary of Tsedang and Samye, which have active PSB officers who will check on you – even in the daytime. It's worth keeping in mind that PSB does not work on Sundays.

NORTH OF LHASA

Popular destinations north of Lhasa are Tsurphu Monastery and Lake Namtso, and the monasteries of Ganden, Drigung, Tidrom and Yerpa. There are several possibilities for touring this northern sector by Landcruiser: you could head straight for Lake Namtso on a two-day sortie; or you could easily spend five days going to Namtso and cutting across overland to Lhundrup, Reting and the monasteries of Drigung, Tidrom and Ganden. Some travellers just target the valley with Drigung, Tidrom, Ganden and Yerpa in two or three days. Locals reach these places by taking pilgrim buses, leaving downtown Lhasa early morning from Barkor Square.

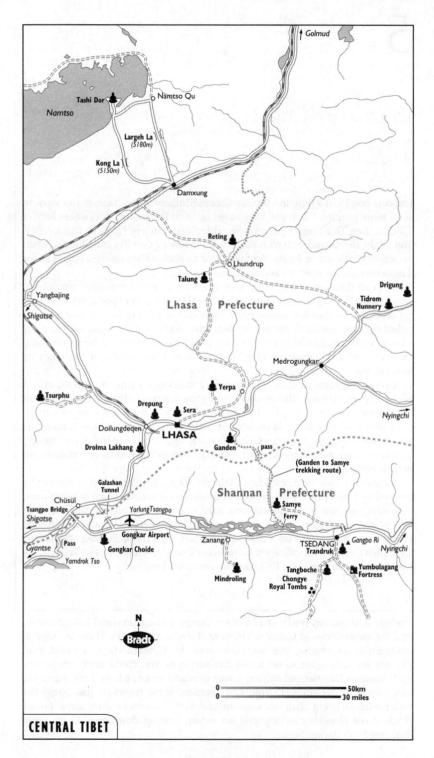

↑ Golmud

Namtso

Tashi Dor

Namtso Qu

Largeh La
(5180m)

Kong La
(5150m)

Damxung

Reting

Yangbajing

Shigatse

Lhundrup

Talung

Lhasa   Prefecture

Drigung

Tidrom
Nunnery

Medrogungkar

Tsurphu

Yerpa

Drepung

Sera

Doilungdeqen

LHASA

Nyingchi

Drolma Lakhang

Ganden

pass

(Ganden to Samye
trekking route)

Galashan
Tunnel

Chüsül

Shannan   Prefecture

Tsangpo Bridge

Samye
Ferry

Shigatse

YarlungTsangpo

Gongkar Airport

Zanang

TSEDANG

Gangpo Ri

Gyantse

Pass

Gongkar Choide

Trandruk

Nyingchi

Yamdrok Tso

Mindroling

Tangboche
Chongye
Royal Tombs

Yumbulagang
Fortress

N

Bradt

| 0 | | 50km |
| 0 | | 30 miles |

You can also indulge in trekking (which can be rough in Tibet) at various points. With Landcruiser pick-ups, hardy trekkers have embarked on longer forays: you could, for instance, trek from Samye to Ganden, drive from there to Tsurphu, hike on to Yanbajing Gompa, drive on to Tashi Dor, and then trek back to Damxung.

SAMPLE ITINERARIES When working out itineraries, you should keep road conditions in mind: what looks like a short distance on the map might be over atrocious roads, which means it will take a long time to cover the ground. The run from Lhasa up to Damxung is along a sealed road and thus a very fast ride; however, the side road to Tsurphu is abysmal and will chew up a lot of Landcruiser time. The sector from Ganden to Damxung cuts through a high rough dirt road and will consume at least eight hours, probably longer.

RAFTING IN CENTRAL TIBET

Tibet has excellent potential for rafting, with numerous rivers to run. Taking on a handful of rivers with commercial tours is Raft Tibet, with a small office in downtown Lhasa near the Shangbala Hotel on Tengyeling Road. This comes under the wing of high-end touring company Wind Horse Adventure. The rafting operation was originally set up by Chris Jones from Tasmania and Sharyn Smith from Canada. Wind Horse operates one-day trips close to Lhasa as well as customised multiple-day rafting trips in central Tibet, and kayak descents further afield. All equipment for rafting (and kayaking) is supplied, and the company uses professional Nepalese or Tibetan rafters. A minimum of four rafters is required for a trip. You must be acclimatised to altitude to handle a rafting trip – meaning that you have spent four or five days at altitude already.

The outfit's most popular sortie is a half-day on the Tolung Chu. Recommended for getting the real feel of rafting in Tibet is a one- or two-day sortie on the Drigung River. On the one-day version, rafters start from Lhasa early morning and are driven several hours to a put-in point. They are provided with wetsuits and thermal clothing, and after brief safety instructions, are dispatched into class III and IV rapids on the Drigung River, experiencing the raw power of the river as no onlooker can. The day trip covers about 25km downriver on the Drigung. Clients are returned to Lhasa the same afternoon, somewhat shaken up. A two-day version of this trip would take in more white water, with overnight camping in a valley near Tidrom Nunnery. Consult the website www.windhorsetibet.com and click on River Journeys for more details.

Chris Jones and a Nepalese rafter named Ram made a first kayak descent of the Drigung River in 2003: the knowledge gained from that expedition is what led to the first commercial white-water rafting trips on the river. Chris says there is much to explore on the rivers of Tibet, with stunning rapids up to class V+ in a number of regions. He can organise custom rafting and kayak descents. He has led expeditions for first kayak descents of Rong Chu (Everest region), Yigung Tsangpo (north of Lhasa), Parlung Tsangpo (east Tibet) and the Sutlej (far west Tibet). In remote regions like this, Chris says, villagers often gather at the banks to cheer on the strange riders in their plastic boats. Others may run away, unsure what kind of demon spirits these might be on the water.

Three-day itinerary: Lhasa to Namtso/Tashi Dor
Day 1 Lhasa–Tsurphu–Damxung (overnight Damxung)

Day 2 Damxung over Largeh La to Tashi Dor (overnight Tashi Dor)

Day 3 Hike or horse trek at Namtso for a half-day, and drive back to Lhasa

Three-day itinerary: Lhasa to Ganden, Drigung, Tidrom and Yerpa
Day 1 Visit Ganden for half a day and drive to Drigung (overnight at Drigung)

Day 2 Drive to Tidrom hot springs (overnight at Tidrom)

Day 3 More time in Tidrom, drive to Yerpa (extended hiking time needed), drive back to Lhasa

ESCAPE FROM TIBET

Times have changed dramatically since Heinrich Harrer's account of his amazing escape in *Seven Years in Tibet*, tracing his flight from a British internment camp in India to the safe haven of neutral Tibet in the early 1940s. Since 1959, the escape route has been in the opposite direction, away from Chinese oppression.

That's exactly what the Karmapa miraculously carried out at the dawn of the new millennium. The youth – then 15 years old – was growing increasingly restless about his monastic education. He had been denied access to his spiritual mentors: the Chinese had reneged on promises to allow these lamas to visit Tibet, and refused to allow the Karmapa to visit India. Worse still, he was clearly being groomed as a patriotic alternative to the Dalai Lama. It was simply a matter of time before he would be called upon to denounce the Dalai Lama publicly.

The stakes for the 17th Karmapa to attempt an escape from the Chinese were very high: any mistake would be costly for the highest-profile religious figure living in Tibet. Meticulous planning was essential. In late December 1999, the Karmapa informed his Chinese minders that he was going into solitary retreat in his private quarters for a week, and would not entertain any visitors. Nothing unusual about that, or greatly suspect. But parked outside the monastery was a Mitsubishi SUV, requisitioned by a senior Tsurphu monk for a fund-raising trip. And distracting the attention of everyone inside – including Chinese overseers – was a newly acquired television set.

Late on the night of 28 December, with monks and minders engrossed in the new television, the Karmapa changed into civilian dress, slipped out a back window at Tsurphu, jumped into the waiting SUV and stole off into the night. At Tsurphu, meanwhile, his teacher and cook kept up the charade of attending to him while 'on retreat'.

The Karmapa's real retreat was from Tibet: he and his four trusted companions proceeded on a circuitous route across Tibet in the SUV, travelling day and night. They dodged military checkpoints along the way: fortunately, during winter there was little military presence, with several posts unmanned. Approaching a dangerous checkpoint by night, the Karmapa and two others got out of the SUV and skirted the area on foot, scraping their hands and legs on thorn scrub in the darkness. To their immense relief, the SUV driver eventually showed up: he had driven past the checkpoint in darkness.

Five-day itinerary: Lhasa to Drigung, Tidrom and Namtso
Days 1 and 2 Same as above (Lhasa–Ganden–Drigung–Tidrom)

Day 3 Depart early from Tidrom and drive to Reting and Damxung (a long day over rough dirt roads; overnight in either Lhundrup or Damxung)

Day 4 Drive to Lake Namtso (overnight at Tashi Dor)

Day 5 Hike or horse trek at Namtso half a day and drive back to Lhasa (or continue on the Kathmandu route)

TSURPHU MONASTERY Lying 70km northwest of Lhasa, Tsurphu is the traditional seat of the Karmapa, head of the Karma Kagyu sect. At the beginning of 2000, the Chinese-sanctioned 17th Karmapa made a dramatic escape from Tsurphu,

And then the SUV simply drove across the unmanned Nepalese border right into the kingdom of Mustang. Here, they abandoned the SUV and switched to travel on foot and by horseback. Hiring fine horses from the Mustang region, they rode hard from Lo Monthang for a few days to reach Kagbeni, and then forged on to a helicopter rendezvous site at Manang, on the Annapurna circuit. From Nepal, they telephoned Tsurphu to find out what was happening: when a stranger answered, they hung up (the fates of the teacher and the cook at Tsurphu are unknown). Flying into the Pokhara vicinity, the Karmapa and his entourage took a taxi to the Indian border, bribing their way past Nepalese border guards.

From here, train and taxis took them through northwest India to Dharamsala. The Karmapa arrived, exhausted, on the morning of 5 January 2000. An hour later, he was greeted in an audience with the Dalai Lama. It was a moment of astonishment and delight – the meeting of two bodhisattvas, and the end of an amazing journey.

The Karmapa's escape echoed the flight of the Dalai Lama from Tibet 40 years earlier. The Dalai Lama is the one person in the world that the Chinese did not want the Karmapa to meet. The Chinese insisted the Karmapa left the motherland on a shopping trip – to get his hands on a black hat, certain musical instruments, and other ceremonial items belonging to his predecessor, the 16th Karmapa, who was based at Rumtek Monastery in Sikkim. You can almost imagine the headlines in China: Soul Boy Steps out of Motherland on Black Hat Shopping Expedition.

The black hat they talk about is sacred. The rightful owner must keep one hand on the hat while wearing it, as it is reputed to have the ability to fly away by itself. That's because, according to legend, the black hat is woven from the hair of countless *dakinis* – celestial female deities, or 'sky walkers'. First mentions of the flying crown date to the 12th century; the present hat dates from a few centuries later and was smuggled out of Tibet to Rumtek. Controversy rages as to whose head the crown will grace, since there is a rival Karmapa candidate in India, but both young Karmapa appointees seem impervious to the conflict. There's a lot more than a hat at stake here: worldwide Kagyu sect assets are estimated to be worth over US$1.2 billion. Who is the real Karmapa? Will he ever take up residence at Rumtek? Will he wear the sacred black hat? Will it fly off his head? Whatever the case, Ogyen Trinley Dorje is not out on a religious-relic shopping spree: he has been granted refugee status by the Indian government.

crossing into India just as his predecessor, the 16th Karmapa, had done 40 years earlier. Though the escape was a major embarrassment for the Karmapa's Chinese overseers, the 17th Karmapa has somehow avoided being blacklisted: photographs of him are displayed at the monastery. However, the *gompa* (monastery) does not attract the same volume of pilgrims as it used to – previously, many travelled here to receive the young Karmapa's blessing. There is an air of dereliction at the monastery today; following a witch-hunt for collaborators in the escape, the monastery was turned upside down and many older monks were replaced with novices. Several hundred monks currently live at the monastery.

The monastery was founded in the 12th century by the first Karmapa, Dusum Kyenpa. As the seat of the Karmapa, Tsurphu was the headquarters for instruction of monks from far-flung monasteries of the order, some as distant as Kham. In the 1950s, Tsurphu was home to a thousand monks. In 1959, the 16th Karmapa left for exile in Sikkim, where he founded Rumtek Monastery. Tsurphu Monastery was razed during the Cultural Revolution, but a few parts have been rebuilt, including the impressive assembly hall. The monastery flies its own flag, a blue and yellow ensign. In May 1997, sacred Cham dances were performed at Tsurphu as part of festivities for Saka Dawa (Buddha's birthday) under the watchful eyes of Chinese officials – this dance had been banned for decades. The most curious part of the monastery is a back protector chapel where (dead) animals appear to be the offering: previously whole stuffed yaks, a kangaroo and stuffed birds were suspended from the rafters, but on my last visit these had all been removed, and only stuffed tiger heads remained.

Getting there Tsurphu lies 70km northwest of Lhasa, at the end of a dirt trail off the main road (the turn-off is at the KM3853 marker stone). It takes about two hours to reach the monastery from Lhasa: there is an inclined rough road to get to Tsurphu, which sits at 4,420m. Should the need arise, there's a small monastery guesthouse and shops near the gates. Travellers are likely to reach Tsurphu by **Landcruiser**. Locals hop aboard a daily pilgrim bus that departs early in the morning from the west side of Barkor Square, Lhasa, and returns the same day in the afternoon. One other option here: you could **trek** out of Tsurphu by embarking on a four-day foray northwards, to Yanbajing *gompa*, which lies close to the highway, 15km southwest of Yangbajing town.

The case of the two Karmapas There are currently two contenders for the title of 17th Karmapa, both living in India. And how exactly were two Karmapa candidates chosen? The selection ripped the Tibetan exile community apart. The lineage of the leaders of the Karma Kagyu sect of Tibetan Buddhism goes back to the 12th century. The 16th Karmapa was born in Tibet in 1924. After fleeing Tibet in 1959, he founded Rumtek Monastery in Sikkim as his principal seat in exile. He died in the US in 1981, but followers could find no letter or sign from him on how to locate the next incarnate. Four regents of the Kagyu sect in Sikkim were appointed to conduct the search for the 17th Karmapa: Situ Rinpoche, Gyaltsap Rinpoche, Jamgon Kongtrul Rinpoche and Shamar Rinpoche. In 1990, Situ Rinpoche said he found a letter left by the 16th Karmapa, giving clues about his reincarnate. The letter was not shown to the other regents until 1992: its authenticity was disputed. Nevertheless, in April 1992, with Chinese approval, a search party of lamas left Tsurphu Monastery to find the new incarnation.

A few weeks later, Jamgon Kongtrul Rinpoche was killed in a car accident – he had previously been designated as the person to find and check the incarnate. A boy from a nomad family in eastern Tibet – appearing to match details given in the letter – was brought to Tsurphu in July 1992. The boy was officially recognised by the Chinese – the first time they recognised a Living Buddha since 1959. On evidence from the search party, the Dalai Lama then recognised the boy also. In September 1992, eight-year-old Ogyen Trinley Dorje was enthroned in an elaborate ceremony at Tsurphu by Situ Rinpoche and Gyaltsap Rinpoche, with Chinese media and government widely represented.

Meanwhile, in Sikkim, violence flared at Rumtek Monastery as rival camps of monks brawled over the Karmapa issue. Indian troops were brought in to hold the peace. The 16th Karmapa's monks were evicted, and Situ Rinpoche's monks forcibly occupied the grounds in late 1993. In 1994, Shamar Rinpoche announced in Delhi that the true Karmapa had been found – a boy from Lhasa by the name of Thaye Dorje. The boy was able to procure travel papers to leave Lhasa by way of Chengdu and Hong Kong to India, where he now lives.

NAMTSO CIRCUIT Namtso is Tibet's largest saltwater lake, and at 4,700m, also one of the highest. You would be unwise to visit Namtso shortly after arriving in Lhasa, as the altitude can be very hard on your system. However, if you have been around Lhasa for a while and are contemplating taking trips at higher elevations, Namtso is a good testing ground: spending a few days here will help you acclimatise to the 4,500m zone. You might want to consider step-by-step acclimatisation strategy: Lhasa lies at 3,650m, Tidrom is 4,300m, Namtso is 4,700m and Everest base camp is around 5,000m. Some arrange Landcruiser trips for two days up to Namtso; others hire a Landcruiser for five days or more to take in the much wider zone of Reting, Tidrom and Drigung monasteries. And others head up for Namtso, and then onward to Everest and Kathmandu.

Along the Lhasa to Namtso direct (paved) route, you pass by **Yangbajing** (elevation 4,155m), where a small settlement has developed around geothermal power units supplying Lhasa. Yangbajing hot springs, which are 4km off the main highway, are nothing to get excited about – the water is channelled into a large concrete swimming pool with a few deckchairs lying around. It's all a bit derelict and scummy – and expensive to boot. Next stop (about two hours from Yangbajing) is **Damxung** (elevation 4,200m), a deadly boring Chinese-built town 170km from Lhasa. Think of this town as an elaborate truck stop – or a glorified railway station – on the Golmud run. There are a number of hotels and guesthouses. Located at a crossroads on the west side of town is **Tienfu Hotel**, a green-tiled building, with beds for Y60 each. Along the main road of Damxung is **Pema Hotel**, charging Y150 for common room, Y180 for a triple and Y270 for a standard room: this is probably the best choice of a rum lot. Close by is **Jinzhu Hotel**, with rooms a bit higher in price. There are a number of roadside restaurants in Damxung where truck drivers congregate – you can negotiate rides with them to Lake Namtso.

A further 40km from Damxung brings you to **Lake Namtso**, reached by two routes – in a Landcruiser you can enter one way (motoring over Largeh La, 5,180m) and leave by another route (over Kong La, 5,150m). At a tollgate near Damxung, a Y80 entry charge is levied to enter Namtso Lake Nature Reserve. Driving on the paved road over Largeh La, it takes an hour to reach Lake Namtso: the road runs through a grassland valley, with the odd nomad encampment visible, and herds of yaks, sheep and goats roaming around. For the nomads, life is dependent on yaks: they live in yak-hair tents and use yak-dung as their main fuel source. Some travellers trek into Lake Namtso – a tough hike taking 12 hours (one-way)

Overnighting at Tashi Dor is recommended because bus tours from Lhasa can overwhelm the area during the day: if you stay overnight, it's more tranquil when you take in sunset and sunrise. There are several possibilities for basic lodging at Namtso. The area close to Tashi Dor is crowded with tent guesthouses and metal or thin wooden shacks, each charging about Y50 a bed. Some group tours bring their own tents and camp out. Further back from the lake is a more permanent structure where guests can stay. There are some teahouse-type restaurants operating out of tents, selling soup or noodles. Bring extra food, a flashlight and a good sleeping bag if you can – nights are freezing. There is private generator lighting and electrical supply for a few hours at night.

Namtso is a sacred lake: there are cave-temples, shrines, hermitages and a nunnery for contemplation at **Tashi Dor**. That is, assuming you can get away from the annoying vendors of cheap jewellery and other shoddy wares, and those intent on talking you into posing with various animals for photos (for which you pay, of course). Two large rock towers near the nunnery are considered to be sentinels for the region. It's worth spending a day or more exploring the area, hiking in the hills around Tashi Dor, and poking around the cave-temples. Hermits from the Kagyu and Nyingma sects occasionally occupy the caves in the area. The beautiful turquoise hues of the lake are a source of inspiration, and the vistas will redefine your sense of space. In the distance, to the south, the 7,088m snowcap of Mount Nyanchen Tanglha looms up, along with the range of the same name. A walking circuit of Namtso is a tall order indeed. The lake is roughly 70km long and 30km wide, with a surface area of 1,940km²: it takes nomad pilgrims up to 20 days to circle it. A short walk to the east of Tashi Dor is a site that operates as a bird sanctuary – between April and November there are good chances of sighting migratory flocks, including, if you're lucky, the black-necked crane.

One method of covering more ground in a shorter time is to hire some horses at Tashi Dor. If you hire them, make sure you also hire a mounted Tibetan horseman to come with you. There are a number of reasons for this strategy – mainly that the horses may refuse to go anywhere unless the horseman is present. If you hire the horses for five hours, you should be able to get a fair distance along the lake to the west side, and with the help of the horseman, you can visit nomads in their tents in this area. Some wealthier nomad families have jeeps, trucks and motorcycles, but their business is still the same as it ever was – milking yaks, making yak cheese, churning yak-butter tea.

CLASSIC GOMPAS, MOUNTAIN SETTINGS Northeast of Lhasa are a number of ruined or semi-active monasteries, amid spectacular settings. Getting to these places takes you right off the track into small villages. Roads are rough, and the going can be slow.

Ganden Located 40km east of Lhasa, Ganden is a Geluk lamasery founded in the 15th century. Additions in later centuries increased its capacity to support upward of 5,000 monks. Ganden was dynamited to rubble during the Cultural Revolution. Remarkably, a number of its main halls have been rebuilt from scratch. In early 1996, following a ban on Dalai Lama pictures, the 400 monks at Ganden were involved in a riot. PLA troops arrived and fired on the monks – two were believed killed and a number were injured. It is thought a hundred more monks were arrested; an equal number probably fled into the hills. Life has since returned to Ganden. There is a large population of monks (currently estimated at around 400), and reconstruction has continued at a brisk pace. A permanent PSB building up on the hill above the monastery guesthouse keeps a wary eye on everything.

Locals reach Ganden by riding an early morning pilgrim bus from Barkor Square in Lhasa. Ganden Monastery has a Y25 entry fee, and posts a Y20 still camera fee, plus a whopping Y1,500 video camera fee (Y750 for 'inland tourists', meaning Chinese). You can stay at the basic but pleasant **monastery guesthouse**, near the front gates. The tariff is Y15 a bed in six-bed dorms. Trekkers, Landcruiser arrivals, pilgrims and visiting monks or nuns all lodge here. Further on is a monastery-run shop, selling the usual dismal selection of packaged noodles, sweets and candles.

The main assembly hall of Ganden is located near a vast square: it is a white structure with gold-capped roofs. If your timing is right, you can hear monks chanting. There are many gilded images of Tsongkhapa in the main chapel. Pilgrims come to be tapped on the head with Tsongkhapa's hat or else the 13th Dalai Lama's shoes. Adjacent to the main assembly hall is a maroon and ochre building which houses a Sakyamuni Buddha statue. A section of this chapel is devoted to the hand-printing of scriptures from woodblocks. In one corner is the *gonkhang* (protector chapel), which is only open to men and which showcases wrathful deities such as 32-armed Yamantaka and six-armed Mahakala, on a horse with a crown of skulls. You can access the rooftop of this building for views.

Ganden is set in a natural, hilly amphitheatre. You can hike around the monastery on a one-hour *kora* route, with stunning views over the surrounding valleys. Start from the monastery guesthouse and go up the hill to a white building with a red flag and a satellite dish (this is the PSB building); from there head for hilltop prayer-flags and follow other prayer-flag markers along the route, and other pilgrims. At the far end of the clockwise *kora* is a rock that is said to be able to talk.

Ganden-to-Samye trek For those with stamina and a good food supply, there's an arduous four- to five-day trek from Ganden to Samye, over several 5,000m passes. Groups arrange a guide, cook, yaks and yak handlers to carry gear – all are self-sufficient with food and camping equipment. Even for just two trekkers, the entourage for a tour might encompass seven or so yaks loaded up with food and cooking gear, and tents. Yaks are apparently not permitted to walk right into Samye, so you would have to carry gear for the last stretch, or use a walking-tractor. The trek to Samye starts on the hill above Ganden guesthouse.

Tidrom Nunnery Further to the northeast, about 110km from Lhasa, lies Tidrom Nunnery, which is set in a beautiful valley with numerous hermitages and caves in the surrounding hills. Miraculously, there's hardly a Chinese building in sight, although the nunnery has a huge satellite dish mounted on its traditional rooftop. The nunnery, though small, is home to over a hundred nuns. Pilgrims and visitors come to Tidrom for the **sulphur hot springs**, also frequented by the nuns. The hot springs are said to have magic healing powers – or at the very least, to be good for the treatment of arthritis, gastritis and other ailments. It's a detox for the soul, anyway, to be in such a purely Tibetan atmosphere.

A charming aspect of Tidrom is that it is a walking zone: no vehicles can enter the village. Landcruisers and other vehicles stop at a parking lot at the edge of Tidrom, a short walk from the hot springs. The nunnery offers a few rooms, and a castle-like structure nearby offers beds for Y20 apiece in large rooms, with clean toilets outside. There is also **accommodation** in tents. Rooms at the guesthouse directly overlooking the hot springs are overpriced and dingy, with rank pit-toilets: beds go for Y40 each. Offerings of food in Tidrom are meagre, so best to bring some back-up supplies. The nunnery runs a small restaurant serving potato curry soup or *thukpa*, and there are a few teahouses.

At the hot springs, Tibetans bathe either in swimsuit or birthday suit. Piping-hot water at this altitude (4,320m) can be a shock to the system, and can make foreign visitors feel dizzy. Best to take this in small doses until you get accustomed: take a dip for ten minutes, get out, rest, and go back in again. Those with high blood pressure or a heart condition (or if pregnant) should not partake. That said, these have to be the finest hot springs in central Tibet: the springs are located right near a river, where the water bubbles under a great rock and disappears. There are three hot spring pools with attractive stone-laid enclosures surrounded by wooden fencing (no concrete!). One pool is for men, another for women, and the third pool is mixed: it is extra-hot and lies across a small footbridge. You can get a hot stone treatment, of sorts – there are hot stones below your feet if you step into a pool. Locals rub against smooth hot submerged stone as a kind of massage. No yak-yoghurt scrubs or *tsampa* rubs on the menu, but then again, you're not subjected to flaky New Age music, either. All very low key.

If you stay overnight, you can indulge in a moonlit soak with candles, and – if skies are clear – a magnificent canopy of stars overhead.

Hiking above Tidrom is rewarding, in terms of views and photography. You can hike up to several small *gompas*; there are also nomad tents in the vicinity.

Drigung Monastery Close to Tidrom is Drigung, a monastery impossibly grafted onto a sheer cliff face. Drigung (elevation 4,150m) was originally the base of the Drigung sub-order of the Kagyu sect, dating from the 12th century. At one time it housed over 500 monks. Going up switchbacks in a Landcruiser, you may pass a donkey bearing a body under a blanket: Drigung is reputed to have the best sky burial (*danchag*) ceremony of all. It is said that bodies dispatched here will not fall down into the 'three bad regions'.

The monastery is intriguing due to its location: it offers stupendous views over the entire valley – you can clamber up to the gold-capped roofs for better vistas. You can visit Drigung and move on, or you can stay the night at the **monastery guesthouse**, which has two 12-bed dorms. Although the dorms are basic, the atmosphere is special, as you are staying inside the monastic grounds. Monks supply hot water in Thermoses, and there's a small shop selling packaged noodles, candles and drinks. Some group tours camp out in the valley below.

Previously, a large sign was posted near the monastery entrance saying that visitors are not permitted to witness **sky burials** at Drigung. Obviously, photographers sneaking shots with long lenses have upset the monks to the point where they have banished visitors from the sky burial site altogether. Whether this situation will change remains to be seen – ask your guide or driver. In case the monastery policy on visitors does change, here is some information on sky burial (see also page 166). The sky burial site is located about 600m from the *gompa* – a trail to get there starts just below the monastery and then turns uphill. You gain about 200m of elevation on this hike and it takes about 15 minutes to reach the site from the monastery. The site is a large fenced-off area surrounded by prayer-flags. It's high on a ridge, with a large rock at centre-stage. The ceremony takes place on the rock, with monks present to bless the departed. Sky burial does not take place every day: sometimes there is no body. Other times, there could be four bodies. The timing is also a bit random, but about an hour after sunrise is the probable time. Vultures assemble on the upper slopes waiting for their cue to descend to the rock. This spectacle is not for the faint of heart – it's a grisly ritual where bodies are chopped into pieces and fed to the vultures.

Yerpa, Talung and Reting Three other monastic sites worth looking at lie north of Lhasa: Yerpa, Talung and Reting. **Yerpa**, 45km northeast of Lhasa (well off the main road), used to be a complex of monasteries, with more than 80 meditation caves tucked away in the hills. The area suffered extensive damage during the Cultural Revolution: restoration is ongoing, but in 1998 a major setback occurred when Chinese officials destroyed several temples and caves. There are, however, half-a-dozen restored temples to reach. Getting to Yerpa is not easy; a Landcruiser takes about half an hour from the turn-off to reach the foothills of Yerpa. The driver parks in a village, and then you embark on a strenuous hike. A steep trail ascends to about 4,400m, so you must be acclimatised.

Further north is a rough back route leading to Lake Namtso (see map, page 168). In this direction, the once-great **Talung Gompa** lies in ruins, a victim of the Cultural Revolution. Several temples have been restored and over a hundred monks have taken up residence. The monastery overlooks a village.

If you continue along this route past Lhundrup, you'll reach **Reting**, about 150km from Lhasa. Reting, at an elevation of 4,150m, is the seat of the Reting Rinpoche: this lineage started in the 18th century when the Seventh Dalai Lama appointed his tutor as abbot of Reting. Several of the Reting Rinpoches served as regents during the minorities of the Dalai Lamas. The Fifth Reting Rinpoche ruled from 1933 to 1947 during the minority of the 14th Dalai Lama, and was actually responsible for his discovery. Involved in political intrigue and sexual scandal, the Fifth Reting Rinpoche died in prison in 1947.

There is considerable controversy over the authenticity of the current Reting Rinpoche, a boy essentially chosen by Chinese officials. Born around 1998, the boy lives near the river at Reting in a small monastic compound which has an unusual architectural feature: a police station has been built backing right onto the entrance, effectively blocking it. This means all comings and goings to the compound are closely monitored by Chinese authorities. Any arrangement for a brief audience with the Reting Rinpoche has to go through the police, who will be present to ensure that no unusual messages (or ideas) are passed on. The police will most likely specify a silent audience – no talking and no photographs. Pilgrims can present the Rinpoche with a *kata*, which he will place back over the offerer's head.

Little is left of the splendour of Reting Gompa – it was all destroyed in the 1960s. Sited on a hill, a small assembly hall has been rebuilt, with a few dozen monks in residence. You can visit for a Y30 entry fee. The area is remarkable for its grove of juniper trees, which appear to be twisted and gnarled as an arboreal response to the problems of high altitude and high winds. You can stay in a small **guesthouse** at Reting Gompa with teahouse attached, with beds for Y35. That would be the best option as it appears authorities do not welcome travellers in the nearby village of Lhundrup, which has a few poky shops and a gas-refuelling station where Landcruisers can fill up (remind your driver as this is the only one in this region). Backing Lhundrup is the startling and seemingly unreal vision of a perfectly conical mountain. Driving times: Tidrom to Reting is about five hours on rough roads, and Reting to Damxung takes about three hours on rough roads.

YARLUNG VALLEY

Southeast of Lhasa lies the cradle of Tibetan culture – the Yarlung Valley. The Adam and Eve of Tibet – from a myth involving a monkey and a demoness – were supposed to have dwelt in Tsedang. The Yarlung dynasty kings had their base in the Yarlung Valley – in the 7th and 8th centuries, they unified the Tibetans and strengthened their identity as a nation. The burial mounds of all the Yarlung dynasty kings are at Chongye. However, these are rather dull to look at: the main attractions southeast of Lhasa are the Samye Temple Complex and Yumbulagang Fortress. By Landcruiser, you can visit half-a-dozen sites mentioned here in two or three days. If you're planning to do any hiking, allow more time. You can trek from Samye to Ganden by an arduous route over high passes. You need to be completely self-sufficient for a trip like this. Some group tours tackle the trek with guides, and yaks, donkeys or horses to carry gear.

LHASA TO SAMYE

Drolma Lakhang The exquisite Tara Temple (Drolma Lakhang) is one of the best preserved in central Tibet. This temple lies along the main road, 25km out of Lhasa. It is associated with the Bengali sage Atisha who arrived in Tibet to teach in the 11th century. He died in this area in 1054. The temple is dedicated to the goddess Tara, with whom Atisha had a strong connection. The temple was apparently spared damage in the 1960s because of a request from the government of Bengal, where Atisha is a highly revered figure. The temple is small and active, with 25 monks. The most striking feature is a *sutra* chanting chapel where 21 life-sized bronze statues of Tara enclose the space. The main image is a Sakyamuni statue; to the left is a small statue of Atisha. On the upper floor is a library, plus some meditation rooms.

Gongkar The name Gongkar is today associated with Tibet's only commercial airport, but in the days before the first planes arrived in the 1960s, it was known to Tibetans as the location of Gongkar Dzong and Gongkar Choide. The *dzong* (castle) was mostly destroyed, but Gongkar Choide remains. The monastery is located 10km west of the airport (turn off at the KM84 marker and go 1km off the road). It was ransacked during the Cultural Revolution: the main hall was used as a barley silo, and murals were defaced with Mao Zedong slogans. Despite the destruction, the surviving mural work at **Gongkar Choide** makes it worth the visit.

THE CASE OF THE STOLEN BUDDHA

Among the statues at Drolma Lakhang is one that has been on a sort of world tour. This is a 1,200-year-old statue of the Buddha that was stolen from Drolma Lakhang in April 1993 by two men with a minivan. It was immediately sold to smugglers in Chengdu for an estimated US$300,000 according to a report in the *People's Daily*. Then it disappeared without trace, until Lhasa customs discovered that it had been shipped to the US, where a buyer was prepared to pay US$8 million for it, according to the news source. The FBI seized the Buddha statue on arrival, but demanded photographic evidence that it had come from Drolma Lakhang before they would return it. The Tibetans did not have such evidence. Finally, after two years of wrangling, Lhasa customs found a picture taken by a foreign tourist, and the FBI returned the statue to Drolma Lakhang in late 1997.

Interpol estimates that the black market in stolen art and antiquities worldwide results in upward of US$10 billion changing hands annually, making it the world's biggest illegal trade after arms and drugs. The motivation is vast profits with a short turnover time. Original Tibetan art is, of course, highly sought after, and there is little doubt that Chinese smugglers have been involved in the traffic, dismantling Tibet's heritage piece by piece.

Gongkar Airport (elevation 3,700m) lies further east, just off the main road to Tsedang. It was constructed in the late 1970s, with elaborate terminal facilities and a second runway added in 1994. Not far from the airport gates is a crossroads with a cluster of small Chinese hotels and restaurants, and a mini-mart. Several **guesthouses** in this area charge Y30–50 a room; the best is a second-floor guesthouse, running along the top of a string of restaurants. There's also a ramshackle Tibetan guesthouse in the vicinity. Within the airport compound is the **Airport Hotel** (↝ *618 2447*), with 115 rooms ranging from Y140–380. The airport has a post office and a bank with foreign exchange facilities (near the gates).

By Landcruiser or taxi, it takes about an hour to drive the 70km from Lhasa to Gongkar, on the route over two bridges connecting to Galashan Tunnel. Gongkar falls in Shannan Prefecture but it is open without permit. That means you can use Gongkar Airport zone as a base to reach out into the Yarlung Valley. You've heard of airports with duty-free zones – this one is a PSB-free zone. Do not confuse Gongkar Airport with Gongkar County (the village 10km east of the airport) or Gongkar Choide (the monastery 10km west of the airport).

Mindroling Gompa Mindroling is the largest Nyingma sect monastery in central Tibet (a second large Nyingma lamasery is Dorje Drak, on the north bank of the Yarlung Tsangpo). Founded in the 17th century, Mindroling was razed by the Mongols in the 18th century, then rebuilt, and again razed during the Cultural Revolution (and rebuilt). Mindroling's imposing façade is constructed in monastic citadel style; the *gompa* impresses with its surprising size and austerity, and skilful construction in stone. The most important chapel lies at the back: it houses a huge Sakyamuni image. To get to Mindroling, turn off the main road near Zanang (aka Zhanang or Dranang) – the monastery is a further 8km away, on a dirt trail.

SAMYE Samye, an attractive walled temple complex, sits at 3,650m on the north bank of the Yarlung Tsangpo. Samye is fascinating because you get a feel for old Tibet as the buildings are all Tibetan (with rare exceptions). Samye is also unusual because it is fully enclosed by a wall with gates at the compass points. Within the walls, most things are run by the monastery. There's a cluster of small guesthouses, restaurants and shops just outside the east gate, along with China Post. There is some build-up, too, outside the west gate, but nothing at the south gate and very little at the north gate.

Getting there If you are in a **Landcruiser**, you have several options. The easiest way to get to Samye is to drive the entire way from Tsedang by crossing the Tsangpo at a bridge just east of Tsedang (see map, page 168) and doubling back on the other side of the river. This means you can be flexible with the itinerary because the driver remains with you. If taking this route, you might want to visit Tsedang (Yumbulagang) first, so you can overnight in Samye.

The second option is to drive to the ferry crossing on the south bank of the Yarlung Tsangpo, opposite Samye: this means leaving your Landcruiser and driver behind till you return by the same ferry. Some local transport that connects with the ferry: a regular **bus** to the Samye ferry crossing (Y35 a head, takes about four hours); hiring a taxi from Lhasa (about three hours, costs around Y180 for the whole taxi); or taking a **taxi** from Tsedang (taking about 40 minutes, Y80 for the taxi). Transport drops you on the south bank of the Yarlung Tsangpo River at a

TOP DOG

If you are in the Gongkar Airport vicinity, or passing by on the way to Samye, make a stop at a Tibetan mastiff breeding facility in the area. The guide or driver should know the location. This breeding facility houses around 300 dogs, mostly Tibetan mastiffs, but there are no Tibetans in sight: the entire operation is run by Chinese entrepreneurs. There's a charge of about Y80 levied on visitors if you want to walk around and take pictures.

Why such a big facility? Here's the short explanation: in March 2011, a red-haired Tibetan mastiff sold for the jaw-dropping sum of US$1.5 million to a coal baron in northern China. The pure-bred male was, he said, 'an investment' – to be loaned out for stud duties (with a price-tag probably exceeding US$20,000 per session). Red is a lucky colour: the dog has been christened 'Big Splash'. Prior to that sale, the record price for a Tibetan mastiff was set in 2009, when a wealthy woman bought one for US$586,000 –and sent a convoy of 30 Mercedes-Benz cars to the airport in Xian to pick up her new dog. Those extraordinary sales figures make the Tibetan mastiff the most expensive dog in the world.

The dogs at Gongkar are much more affordable – with price tags starting in the region of US$3,000 to US$12,000. The Tibetan mastiff has become the ultimate status symbol for super-wealthy Chinese. The lion is considered lucky by Chinese, and the Tibetan mastiff has a lion-like mane. Xinhua News Agency reports that among the must-haves for the ultra-rich in north China are these three: a beautiful young wife, a Lamborghini and a Tibetan mastiff – the bigger and more ferocious, the better. That puts the Tibetan mastiff into the similar status class as the chihuahuas of socialites in Hollywood. But the Tibetan mastiff is not the sort of dog you carry with one arm. It is about the size of a St Bernard, and just as slobbery. It grows to over 80kg and is known for fiercely defending its master.

Thought to be the oldest guard dog in existence, the Tibetan mastiff has a bloodline going back thousands of years. It evolved as a guard dog for nomads, usually tied up close to the yak-hair tent as a security measure. The dog alerts nomads to intruders, and has been known to take on livestock predators such as wolves and snow leopards. Tibetans nomads, however, are not involved in any way with the current craze in China for mastiffs. All the breeding operations are Chinese run. And in China, it takes very wealthy patrons to ensure the mastiff is itself guarded. In Beijing, if a dog exceeds a certain height, it can be confiscated and killed on the spot by vigilant authorities. A Tibetan mastiff would exceed those height limits.

small compound (KM155 marker stone) with a truck stop inn and a few small shops. A Landcruiser driver waits with the car for a day or two while the guide takes you along on an hour-long ferry ride across the Yarlung Tsangpo. On the other side, a truck picks you up for the 20-minute run into Samye. The 'ferry' is a barge designed for the transport of goods back and forth from Samye. There have been a number of nasty arguments between foreigners and locals over the cost of the barge and the truck. Passage should cost Y10 a person if shared with Tibetan passengers, and a similar amount for a truck on the other side. The ferry will cost more if you and your group are the sole passengers (the whole boat costs Y90 a crossing). Bargaining doesn't work well here as this is a monopoly situation and the operators know it. To avoid ill feelings, leave the matter in the hands of the guide (if you have one), and focus instead on the entrancing Yarlung Tsangpo vistas. Because the barge has to navigate around sandbars, the trip across the Yarlung Tsangpo can take up to an hour. The route changes seasonally with the water levels.

Where to stay and eat The best place to stay is **Samye Monastery Guesthouse**, which lies just outside the walls at the east gate. Rooms with bath go for Y100–200. The hotel is comfortable, but the restaurant is basic, with dull variations on noodles and dumplings.

There are several small guesthouses just outside the walls at the east gate, including **Mount Hepori Hotel**, and a few places to eat, including **Friendship Snowland Restaurant**.

Nightlife Because of very little ambient light around Samye, there is a fantastic star-show at night – assuming clear skies. Find a rooftop somewhere, lie down, and gaze at the canopy of stars.

What to see and do
Samye Temple Complex Samye is thought to be Tibet's first monastery and its first university. It has been deconstructed and reconstructed a number of times. The monastery is thought to have been founded in the 8th century by King Trisong Detsen, in consultation with Indian sage Padmasambhava. The temple was destroyed during civil war in the 11th century, by fire in the 11th and 17th centuries, by earthquake in the 18th century, and by Mao Zedong's fanatical hordes in the 20th century. Today, only a fraction of its original 108 buildings survive or have been reconstructed. Adaptations for visitors within the walls include the monastery guesthouse with restaurant and monastery shop. Most Samye villagers live outside the walls.

Samye's layout is based on Buddhist cosmology: it is a mandalic 3D replica of the Tibetan Buddhist universe. The temple complex has been constructed according to the principles of geomancy, a concept derived from India. At the centre of the Tibetan Buddhist universe lies a mythical palace on top of Mount Meru, which at Samye is symbolised by the main temple (Utse). Surrounding this is a great 'ocean', with four great island-continents, and eight subcontinents. If the colour-coded *chortens* look a bit out of place in this scheme of things; it's because they were razed during the Cultural Revolution, and were only reconstructed in the early 1990s, in new brick, with synthetic paints, and without much finesse. Renovation and reconstruction of other parts within the walls is ongoing.

The complex is bounded by an oval wall (the original wall was a zigzag design), pierced by four gates and topped by 1,008 small *chortens* that represent Chakravala, a ring of mountains that surrounds the universe. The wall itself has been hastily restored, using a large amount of concrete – the favourite material of the Chinese.

There are currently about a hundred monks attached to the main temple. The monastery was built long before the rise of the different sects in Tibet. In the late 8th century, Trisong Detsen presided over a debate at Samye between Indian Buddhists and Chinese Zen Buddhists concerning which type of Buddhism should prevail in Tibet. The Indians won. Since that time, the monastery has come under the influence of various sects, such as the Nyingma, Sakya and Geluk traditions. Even today, influences are eclectic. Entry to Samye Monastery is Y40, with Y150 extra charged for interior photos, and Y1500 for video.

Samye Utse The three-storey temple faces to the east. The upper storeys were removed during the Cultural Revolution, but the gleaming roof was restored in 1989. To the left of the main entrance is a 5m-high stone obelisk; erected by King Songtsen Gampo, it proclaims the Indian school of Buddhism to be the state religion. Inside the main assembly hall of the Utse are statues of the early kings, and images of Padmasambhava and Atisha. The inner sanctum contains a beautiful Sakyamuni image. To the right side of the assembly hall is a Gonkhang or tantric protector chapel with odds and ends like a stuffed snake and an old musket. To the left of the assembly hall is the Avalokitesvara Chapel, with a fine bas-relief portrait of the bodhisattva.

Upstairs, you can access several chapels and might even be allowed to view the former quarters of the Dalai Lama.

On the second floor is an open gallery with a long string of murals, some depicting the history of Tibet; there is also a damaged mural of the fabled land of Shambhala here.

North of the Utse temple lies the Chapel of the Moon, and to the south, the Chapel of the Sun. Four *chortens* are positioned respectively to the northeast (green), southeast (white), southwest (red) and northwest (black).

Ling Chapels While Mount Meru is connected with the realms of the gods, humanoids are supposed to live on the four island-continents (*ling*) across a vast ocean, flanked by satellite islands or subcontinents (*ling-tren*). These are all symbolised by one- or two-storey chapels at Samye, some lined with murals, and graced with pleasant courtyards with gardens and potted plants. Others lie in a decayed state, awaiting restoration.

Jamphel Ling, at the east side, is dedicated to Manjughosa. In the 1980s it was a commune office. At the southern end, Aryalpo Ling, dedicated to Hayagriva, was where Indian scholars lived during the great debate of the 8th century. It has undergone some restoration of its murals; on the upper storey are strange murals depicting creatures riding scorpions, dragons and bears. The chapel immediately west of this is worth a visit: it has been renovated with a full set of murals.

Jampa Ling, the chapel near the west gate, is dedicated to Maitreya (*Champa* or *Jampa* in Tibetan) and is where the Chinese monks resided during the 8th century. At the entrance hall is a mural showing Samye as it once was. Jangchub Semkye Ling, at the north, was dedicated to Prajnaparamita. Inside is a 3D scale model of Samye. This building is undergoing restoration – it was previously used for wood storage.

Just east of Jangchub Semkye Ling is a north-facing red-walled building – Pehar Kordzoling, a protector chapel. Samye's Sanskrit texts were once stored here in the care of the protector deity Pehar. Pehar's mandate was to watch over the monastery's treasures: among these was a leather mask that was believed to come alive, with the rolling of bulging eyes. After several centuries at Samye, Pehar was removed to Nechung Monastery in Lhasa, and became the protective deity of the state oracle. There was also an oracle at Samye: Pehar's job at Samye was taken over by Tsemar, the red protector, who sat in judgement of the souls of men once a year: evil-doers

Ganden (trek)

Tsangpo ferry ← ↑ → Chimphu Valley caves

North Gate
(Main entrance)

(wall)

(wall)

Jangchub
Semkye Ling

Pehar
Kordzoling

Moon
Chapel

Black Stupa

Green Stupa

Jamphel Ling

Mt Hepo Ri,
Tsedang by road →

Shops
● ●

West Gate

Jampa Ling

Utse

Entry

Truck
parking

East Gate

✕
Friendship
Snowland

Shop

to small hotels,
restaurants,
China Post →

Red Stupa

Site of
Sun Chapel
(destroyed)

White Stupa

Aryalpo
Ling

(wall)

Monks' quarters
& study area

(wall)

South Gate

N

Brad†

0 |━━━━━|100m
0 |━━━━━|100yds

ORIENTATION

Although the plan given here is aligned to the north (and the modern main
entrance is at the north), in Tibetan Cosmology it was more likely aligned
to the west, with the main entrance at the east gate. Solution: turn your
book sideways so that west appears at the top of the map.

were chopped to shreds. Pehar Kordzoling is adorned with unusual mural work
featuring skulls; though under renovation, the chapel appears to be a site where
special rituals are carried out.

Following Chinese occupation, villagers were encouraged to treat the walled
sanctuary of Samye as just another part of the village, so pigs, cows, braying donkeys
and sheep were herded through the muddy wasteland. Along with a large band of
dogs that hung out on the flagstones near the Utse, this gave Samye a somewhat
earthy and surreal air – you would round a corner looking for a sacred temple, and
instead stray across a pig wallowing in the mud. Although the dogs still lounge

around, the other animals have been pushed back outside the walls again (although herders occasionally bring their flocks through).

Hiking at Samye To the east of Samye you can hike to a ridge called **Mount Hepori**, which offers a terrific bird's-eye view of the town. To get there, walk out of the east gate, go to the end of the village, and then veer right to find the trails that lead up the foothills to the ridge-top temple. The hike takes about 30–40 minutes. If there are pilgrims around, you can follow them: they make offerings at the ridge-top temple shrine, festooned with prayer-flags. From this vantage point, you can see the elliptical shape of Samye's walled enclosure and something of its cosmic plan. The walls used to be circular (apparently before 1959), but were rebuilt as elliptical. About 500m south of the south gate you can see a grey, three-storey building enclosed by a high wall: this used to be one of the three queens' residences, but there's no access to the place (the other two residences were apparently destroyed).

To the far northeast of Samye is **Chimphu**, which is riddled with hermitage caves (there are said to be 108 of them). Monks and nuns come for retreat here: if visiting, take some *tsampa* and candles as donations. It takes about 40 minutes on a walking-tractor to reach the general area, then a three-hour hike (round trip), so you'd have to allow five or six hours for the visit. If arriving by walking-tractor, make sure the driver waits to take you back to Samye.

There is a five-day trek between Samye and Ganden monasteries. See the *Ganden* section above, page 175, for details.

TSEDANG (*Tsetang, Zedang, Nedong; 3,600m; capital of Shannan Prefecture; telephone code 0893*) Tsedang is a Chinese town – or to put it more bluntly, a Chinese eyesore. This is the shape of things to come, as more Chinese settlers move in. With a population over 50,000, the town functions as a Chinese hub in central Tibet. In contrast to traditional Tibetan architecture, which blends into the mountain and desert environment, Chinese structures here look totally jarring, with bland concrete blocks finished in bathroom tiling and blue-tinted glass. And the addition of fake palm trees along some boulevards doesn't help. Behind the concrete curtain, there was an ancient Tibetan town at Tsedang, but it has been marginalised – remnants of an old Tibetan quarter exist to the east of the market area with an active *gompa* and a nunnery. Due to a military presence, there is a surfeit of karaoke bars and bars stocked with young women.

Tsedang is mostly used as a stepping stone to destinations like Yumbulagang Fortress. There are a few **hikes** on the eastern side of Tsedang that are of middling interest. A four-hour hike takes you up a mountain trail to **Gangpo Ri monkey cave**. This cave is revered as the mythical site where a monkey (an emanation of Avalokitesvara) consorted with a demoness (an emanation of Tara) to give birth to six children, later leaders of the Tibetan clans. The monkey then instructed them how to cultivate grains in the fertile valley, so Tibet's first cultivated field is supposed to be in the Tsedang area. This tale of the origin of the Tibetan race, involving descent from a monkey, has an oddly Darwinian touch.

Getting there Tsedang is 196km from Lhasa and 97km from Gongkar Airport. Locals use buses running to Tsedang from Lhasa. A **taxi** from Lhasa is possible: the road is smooth, paved and flat, so you can get there in under three hours.

Getting around The choice is between regular Volkswagen taxis, motorised three-wheel contraptions (seating two) or bicycle trishaws (also seating two).

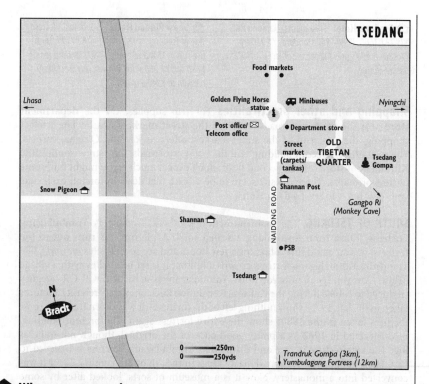

Food markets

Lhasa

Golden Flying Horse
statue

Minibuses

Nyingchi

Post office/ ⊠
Telecom office

Department store

Street
market
(carpets/
tankas)

OLD
TIBETAN
QUARTER

Tsedang
Gompa

Snow Pigeon

NAIDONG ROAD

Shannan Post

Gangpo Ri
(Monkey Cave)

Shannan

PSB

Tsedang

N

Bradt

| 0 | 250m |
| 0 | 250yds |

Trandruk Gompa (3km),
Yumbulagang Fortress (12km)

Where to stay and eat A strange cat-and-mouse game goes on with hotels, guesthouses and restaurants in Tsedang, which seems to be a PSB-Mafia-dominated monopoly. Travellers who have tried to stay in non-Chinese-operated guesthouses or restaurants have been visited by Tsedang PSB officers and told to move along. A number of Chinese hotels refuse to accept foreigners, including the Golden Crane Hotel. That means, essentially, that you are stuck with overpriced officially approved hotels. Even restaurant owners, intimidated by the PSB, may inform Westerners they cannot eat in the restaurant. PSB officers have been seen trailing travellers around the town. Travellers should make efforts to break this stranglehold when it comes to restaurants (try buying drinks only at a Tibetan teahouse to annoy the Beijing Boys), but there doesn't seem to be a way round for hotels, as the PSB can easily close down Tibetan-run guesthouses.

Taking all this into account, the best thing you can do about Tsedang is give the place a miss as an overnight stop. You can aim instead to stay in Samye or Gongkar.

The rough centre of Tsedang is a dusty traffic roundabout with a golden flying horse statue in the middle. Most activity takes place on Naidong Road, the street running south of the roundabout. Arrayed on or close to Naidong Road are the following hotels.

Shannan Post Hotel (60 rooms) 10 Naidong Rd; ↘ 782 1888; f 782 0688. Rooms are in several wings. *Y238 minimum common room; Y328–488 standard room; Y666 suite (although posted rates for Chinese guests are much lower).*

Shannan Hotel (53 rooms) 13 Naidong Rd; ↘ 782 6168; f 782 1855. *Y280 economy, Y380 standard; Y680 suite; Y880 deluxe suite; Y80 for 'o'clock room' (a short-time room for Chinese military & consorts).*

☖ **Tsedang Hotel** (190 rooms) Naidong Rd; ✆f 782 1668. *Y680–880 standard; Y1,220 trpl; Y1,380–8,200 suites (all prices subject to a 10% service charge).*

☖ **Snow Pigeon Hotel** (50 rooms) Western side of Tsedang; ✆ 782 8888; f 782 7777. High-rise run by China Telecom. *Y680 standard room; Y880 sgl; Y1,280 suite (but you can most likely bargain to Y340 a room).*

Shopping and other practicalities For trip supplies, try the **department store** near the main crossroads, and also the **street markets** nearby. For artefact shopping, the west end of the street markets offers *tankas* and Qinghai carpets. The **post office/telecom** building is at the main crossroads. One street south is the **Xinhua bookstore** (on the second floor; don't expect much – you might find some posters or maps). There doesn't seem to be a bank that deals in foreign exchange: your best bet is to try Tsedang Hotel.

SOUTH OF TSEDANG The main attraction south of Tsedang is **Yumbulagang Fortress,** 13km from town along a sealed road. A pilgrim bus runs out to the fortress, or you could hire a taxi for a few hours and see several sites *en route*, like Trandruk. Yumbulagang fortress crowns a hilltop; it is set in a valley with a village below. Now you see it, now you don't. Yumbulagang is in the RRDCR-CR category (reduced to rubble during the Cultural Revolution and completely rebuilt). Pictures taken in the late 1970s show nothing left of the fortress – it was shorn from the rock. Pictures taken in the 1980s show the entire fortress again. The present building, reconstructed in 1982, is a pretty good copy of the original, though not quite as big. The architecture is rare and distinctive: Yumbulagang Fortress is believed to have been built by the Yarlung dynasty kings in the 7th or 8th century. Later it was converted into a monastery. Now it is a museum of sorts, looked after by some Geluk monks. Waiting at the base of hill leading to Yambulagang are horsemen seeking lazy tourists for the ride up to the fortress. There may even be the odd camel awaiting your arrival. Hiking or riding up to the hilltop fortress, you can clamber up through several storeys to the two-tiered chapel at the top. From this eyrie, there are fine views of the patchwork of fields in the village below.

On the way out to Yumbulagang, or on the return trip, you can visit **Trandruk Gompa (Falcon-Dragon Temple)**, originally built by King Songtsen Gampo in the 7th century. The monastery is 7km from Tsedang, reached by a good road. The monastery is a warren of chapels: in an upstairs chapel right at the back is the monastery's treasure. Locked in a dusty glass case is a precious *tanka* depicting Avalokitesvara, whose ghost-like image is reputed to be composed of 30,000 pearls sewn into a red tapestry.

A different fork from Tsedang leads 17km south to **Tangboche Monastery,** which, though in a sorry state, is worth checking out for the murals covering the walls of the assembly hall. These murals were commissioned in 1915 by the 13th Dalai Lama (whose image naturally appears among the murals). A further 13km southwards brings you to Chongye, where the tombs of all the Yarlung dynasty kings are located. **Chongye Royal Tombs** consist of massive earth mounds, which all look pretty much the same except for their size. This has led to much confusion over who is actually entombed within. The largest tomb is believed to be that of the 7th-century warrior-king, Songtsen Gampo. On top of this tomb is a small chapel, reached by a flight of stairs – it features a statue of Songtsen Gampo, flanked by two of his wives and two important ministers.

6

Lhasa to Kathmandu

THE GREATEST ROAD ROUTE IN HIGH ASIA

The Lhasa to Kathmandu route ranks, in my mind, as the finest in High Asia – because of the ethereal views. You are motoring across the roof of the world, powering over five passes – festooned with prayer-flags – all above 4,500m. If you take the Gyantse route, winding up to Khamba La pass, you come to stunning views of the Turquoise Lake (Yamdrok Tso) with snowcaps on the Bhutanese border. Three great monasteries – at Gyantse, Shigatse and Sakya – lie along the road route. If you have arranged it with the driver and guide, you can drive all the way to Everest base camp – a magical spot that will (almost literally) blow you away. Even without the base-camp trip, on a clear day you can see some 8,000m peaks right from the roadway, including Cho Oyu (8,153m), near Tingri. And then there's a fantastic drop right off the Tibetan plateau – from high-altitude desert, switchbacking down to tropical Nepalese jungle. There is nothing in High Asia that can compare to this roadshow. Lhasa to Kathmandu is an excellent adventure. Nobody said the trip would be easy, though.

LOGISTICS AND TIMING You can take a one-way trip, Lhasa to Kathmandu and cross into Nepal, or you can take a round trip from Lhasa, going all the way to say, Nyalam, and then heading back to Lhasa. Because the road is paved and in good condition, you can make it from Nyalam to Lhasa in a long day of driving. Most destinations in this chapter fall under the jurisdiction of Shigatse Prefecture. For that reason, your guide may have to stop at Shigatse PSB to arrange permit stamping and paperwork.

A lot of navigation information is carried in the Lhasa to Kathmandu map (pages 188–9). You can work out turn-offs and where you are by a system of kilometre marker stones by the roadside. This is the best way, for example, to find Milarepa's Cave (which is not visible from the road). The entire route from Lhasa to Kathmandu is 938km if you go via Gyantse, but 865km if you take the direct Lhasa–Shigatse route. If you take side trips to Shegar and Sakya (highly recommended) you add 56km to the journey, since Sakya lies 21km off the main route. There's a major detour of 70km off the main route to reach Everest base camp (refer to the *Star Treks* chapter, page 223).

Without stops or obstacles, fast drivers can make the run from Lhasa to Zhangmu in two days, overnighting at Tingri. With stops, the trip would require a minimum of four days. It's recommended you allow six to seven days, depending on side trips. If you include Everest base camp, build in time for possible delays. Approximate driving times along the route:

Lhasa to Shigatse	6–10 hours (depending on route taken)
Shigatse to Lhatse	3½ hours
Lhatse to Shegar	3 hours

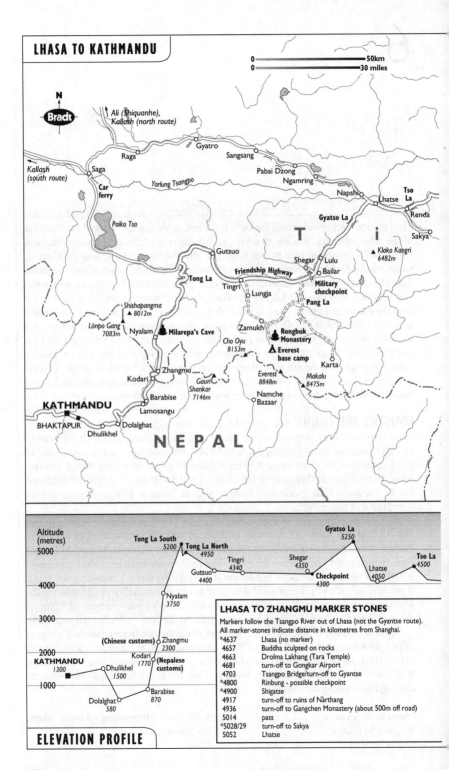

LHASA TO KATHMANDU

0 ▭▭▭▭▭ 50km
0 ▭▭▭▭▭ 30 miles

N

Bradt

Ali (Shiquanhe),
Kallash (north route)

Gyatro
Raga   Sangsang
Kallash   Saga   Pabai Dzong
(south route)   Ngamring
      Car   Yarlung Tsangpo   Napshi   Tso
      ferry   Lhatse La
                                                                Renda
      Paiko Tso   Gyatso La
                                                            Sakya
                           Gutsuo
                                      Shegar Lulu   Klako Kangri
                                                      6482m
                    Tong La   Friendship Highway Bailar
                           Tingri Lungja   Military
                                             checkpoint
      Shishapangma   Pang La
      ▲ 8012m
Lönpo Gang   Nyalam ▲ Milarepa's Cave Zamukh ▲ Rongbuk
7083m   Cho Oyu   Monastery
                   Zhangmu   8153m   ▲ Everest
      Kodari   Gauri   base camp
                           Shankar   Everest ▲   Karta
             Barabise   7146m   8848m   Makalu
                                             ▲ 8475m
KATHMANDU Lamosangu   Namche
                                    Bazaar
BHAKTAPUR   Dolalghat
      Dhulikhel   **N E P A L**

T   i

Altitude (metres)		Gyatso La 5250	

Altitude (metres)

5000 — Tong La South 5200 / Tong La North 4950

Tingri 4340   Shegar 4350   Gyatso La 5250   Tso La 4500

Gutsuo 4400   Lhatse 4050

4000 —   **Checkpoint** 4300

Nyalam 3750

3000 —

(Chinese customs) Zhangmu 2300

2000 —
KATHMANDU 1300   Kodari 1770 (Nepalese customs)
      Dhulikhel 1500

1000 —   Barabise 870

      Dolalghat 580

ELEVATION PROFILE

LHASA TO ZHANGMU MARKER STONES

Markers follow the Tsangpo River out of Lhasa (not the Gyantse route).
All marker-stones indicate distance in kilometres from Shanghai.

*4637	Lhasa (no marker)
4657	Buddha sculpted on rocks
4663	Drolma Lakhang (Tara Temple)
4681	turn-off to Gongkar Airport
4703	Tsangpo Bridge/turn-off to Gyantse
*4800	Rinbung - possible checkpoint
*4900	Shigatse
4917	turn-off to ruins of Nàrthang
4936	turn-off to Gangchen Monastery (about 500m off road)
5014	pass
*5028/29	turn-off to Sakya
5052	Lhatse

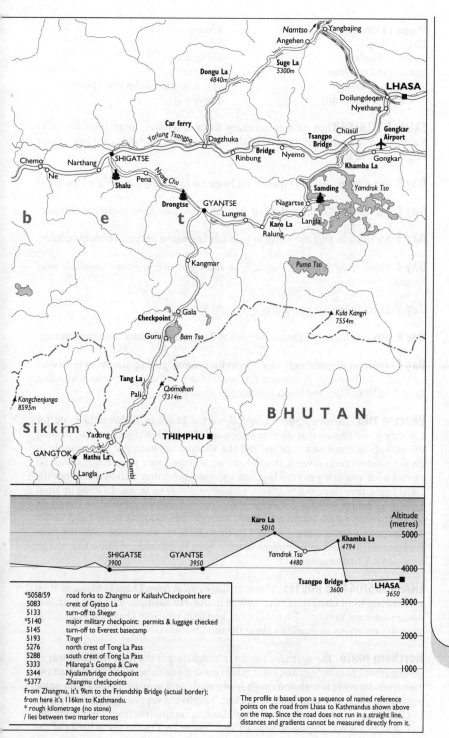

Namtso   Yangbajing
Angehen
Suge La
5300m
Dongu La
4840m   LHASA
                                    Doilungdeqen
                                    Nyethang
Car ferry   Chüsül   Gongkar
Yarlung Tsangpo   Dagzhuka   Tsangpo   Airport
                    Bridge   Bridge
Chemo   Narthang   Rinbung   Nyemo   Gongkar
Ne   Khamba La
SHIGATSE
Shalu   Pena   Nyang Chu   Samding   Yamdrok Tso
Drongtse   GYANTSE   Nagartse
b   e   t   Lungma   Langla
                    Karo La   Langla
                    Ralung

                Kangmar   Puma Tso

                    Gala   Kula Kangri
Checkpoint   7554m
    Guru   Bam Tso

Tang La   Chomolhari
Kangchenjunga   Pali   7314m
8595m
Sikkim   B H U T A N

    Yadong   THIMPHU
GANGTOK   Nathu La
    Langla   Chumbi

	Karo La 5010				Altitude (metres)
					5000
SHIGATSE 3900	GYANTSE 3950		Yamdrok Tso 4480	Khamba La 4794	
					4000
			Tsangpo Bridge 3600	LHASA 3650	
					3000
					2000
					1000

*5058/59	road forks to Zhangmu or Kailash/Checkpoint here
5083	crest of Gyatso La
5133	turn-off to Shegar
*5140	major military checkpoint: permits & luggage checked
5145	turn-off to Everest basecamp
5193	Tingri
5276	north crest of Tong La Pass
5288	south crest of Tong La Pass
5333	Milarepa's Gompa & Cave
5344	Nyalam/bridge checkpoint
*5377	Zhangmu checkpoints

From Zhangmu, it's 9km to the Friendship Bridge (actual border);
from here it's 116km to Kathmandu.
* rough kilometrage (no stone)
/ lies between two marker stones

The profile is based upon a sequence of named reference
points on the road from Lhasa to Kathmandu shown above
on the map. Since the road does not run in a straight line,
distances and gradients cannot be measured directly from it.

Shegar to EBC	4 hours
EBC to Tingri	5 hours
Tingri to Nyalam	4½ hours
Nyalam to Zhangmu	2½ hours
Zhangmu to Kodari	11½ hours (includes checkposts)
Kodari to Kathmandu	4 hours.

SAMPLE ITINERARY A sample itinerary for a seven-day foray from Lhasa to Kathmandu (via southern route through Gyantse with a stop at Everest base camp) might look like this:

Day 1 Drive from Lhasa to Gyantse via Nagartse (Samding), overnight Gyantse

Day 2 See more of Gyantse, short drive to Shigatse, hike *kora*, overnight Shigatse

Day 3 Morning in Shigatse, drive to Sakya, hike around Sakya, overnight in Sakya

Day 4 Drive from Sakya to Shegar, hike at Shegar; overnight at crossroads near Shegar

Day 5 Drive to Everest base camp, overnight there

Day 6 More time at EBC, then drive back to Tingri and Nyalam, overnight Nyalam

Day 7 Drive to Friendship Bridge. Cross into Nepal, pick up transport to Kodari and on to Kathmandu. If crossing the border later in the day, overnight at either Kodari or Dhulikhel, and reach Kathmandu on day eight.

Reverse trip The description here follows the Lhasa to Kathmandu route for the very good reason that it's more approachable in that direction due to both the altitude acclimatisation factor and the visa/permit situation. It is possible to do the road route in reverse, if you have an arranged tour from Kathmandu. Be careful what you bring in your baggage – suspect literature, such as that about the Dalai Lama, may cause big problems. Guidebooks may be targeted. Going up from 1,300m in Kathmandu to a 5,200m pass, you may be in no mood or condition for sightseeing, as you may have trouble with altitude sickness. Some Landcruiser drivers carry a small tank of oxygen in the vehicle for this reason. Starting from Kathmandu, it would be far preferable to fly from Kathmandu to Lhasa first and go by road back to Kathmandu.

LHASA TO SHIGATSE ROUTES There are three routes from Lhasa to Shigatse. If on a round trip from Lhasa, you can combine routes. For example, for a long loop, you could motor via Yamdrok Tso to Gyantse, and then return to Lhasa via Yangbajing, stopping at various monasteries along the way.

Northern route The northern route via Yangbajing is the least-travelled way of getting from Lhasa to Shigatse, but it makes sense if you've been off to Lake Namtso. This splendid route is high and rough (not paved), and sometimes used if for some reason the main westward route is blocked. Yangbajing supplies geothermal power to Lhasa; there is a hot-spring pool here. Heading southwards from Yangbajing you motor across two high passes, Suge La and Dongu La. On the north banks of the

Yarlung Tsangpo you can detour along a rough road to Menri Gompa, a small Bon monastery. You cross the Yarlung Tsangpo by car ferry to Dagzhuka, and join the main western route to Shigatse. Approximate driving time (no stops) on this route is Lhasa to Yangbajing, two hours; Yangbajing to Suge La, 2½ hours; Suge La to Dagzhuka ferry crossing, 2½ hours; Dagzhuza to Shigatse, two hours.

Western route This road follows a canyon running along the Yarlung Tsangpo – it is used by Chinese military and supply trucks to get from Lhasa to Shigatse in the fastest time. It thus sees the heaviest traffic, with convoys of military trucks heading through. The road runs beneath steep canyon walls, and rock falls may block the road entirely. Slabs of roadway have also been known to disappear into the Yarlung Tsangpo, because engineering skills haven't quite been perfected. The bridge spanning the Yarlung Tsangpo near Rinbung is one-way, meaning that there can be traffic line-ups when the flow is against you. Driving time on this Lhasa to Shigatse route is about five to six hours if there are no delays or problems.

Southern route This route via Gyantse to Shigatse is much more dramatic, taking in the beautiful lake of Yamdrok Tso. It is longer, more winding and rougher, so it is not used by supply trucks. This means minimal traffic and far superior views. On the southern route, exiting Lhasa, you cross the Tsangpo Bridge and wind up to Khamba La, with stunning views. Down the other side of Khamba La you reach Nagartse, a village with a small restaurant, plus a guesthouse. If you can, arrange a side trip to Samding Monastery. From Nagartse, the road climbs over Karo La and heads for Gyantse. Approximate driving time on this route is Lhasa to Khamba La, 1½ hours; Khamba La to Karo La, three hours; Karo La to Gyantse, 2½ hours; Gyantse to Shigatse, two hours.

SOUTHERN ROUTE TO GYANTSE

Drolma Lakhang Exiting Lhasa on either the western route or the southern route (as above), you can visit this well-preserved temple, about 25km from Lhasa. See *Exploring Central Tibet* chapter, page 178, for details.

Yamdrok Tso From Khamba La, where prayer-flags are buffeted by the winds, you get a magnificent view of Yamdrok Tso (the Turquoise Lake), with the large snowcap on the horizon being Kula Kangri (7,554m) on the Bhutanese border. From this vantage point you can see why the Tibetans consider Yamdrok Tso to be a sacred lake. It is Tibet's largest freshwater lake. Your contemplation of the views at the pass may be interrupted by a circus of aggressive vendors – who sell photo-ops with yaks, Tibetan mastiffs or sheep.

Winding down from Khamba La towards the shore of Yamdrok Tso, you can see a hydropower plant, with four Austrian-made turbines. This plant is part of a hare-brained Chinese scheme that drains the lake water to produce electricity for Lhasa during peak demand. The plant is designed as a pumped storage plant with a 90MW capacity. The project has been a total disaster since its inception in 1985. In 1986, due to vigorous objections from Tibetans headed by the Tenth Panchen Lama, work was halted, but was resumed after the Panchen Lama's death in 1989. Overriding international campaigns, the Chinese went ahead with construction, with disastrous results. In 1993, in the village of Dramalung, close to the project, all freshwater wells completely dried up, forcing villagers to rely on the lake for their water supply. In 1996, reports filtered through of the complete collapse of a tunnel leading from the lake to the turbines. The plant started generating power in the late 1990s.

Western environmentalists are concerned that the water level at Yamdrok Tso could drop significantly – or, in a worst-case scenario, that the lake might completely drain away. Authorities in Lhasa insist this is not the case: they say they will pump water back from the Yarlung Tsangpo to replenish the lake water. But even if this were true, it means snow-fed lake water would be replaced with muddy river flow, with uncertain ecological results. One result is certain: the sacred lake is bound to lose its natural deep turquoise colour. Pumping water back up into Yamdrok Tso requires a separate power source: a new dam, under construction on the Nyang River, 30km east of Gyantse, is said to be that source. The building of this dam has spawned an entire town of corrugated roofing, housing Chinese construction workers and engineers.

Nagartse and Samding Monastery Nagartse is the only sizeable village near Yamdrok Tso: Landcruiser drivers headed for Gyantse may break up the long day with a rest stop here. Nagartse has a few restaurants (Lhasa Restaurant, Holy Lake Restaurant) and several guesthouses. Technically a permit is required to stay overnight: Nagartse and Yamdrok Tso are under the jurisdiction of Shannan Prefecture.

Yamdrok Tso is shaped like the pincers of a crab: in the grip of them lies the monastery of Samding, about 8km from Nagartse. You can reach it by Landcruiser from Nagartse, or hike in. Nagartse PSB does not seem to like travellers visiting this one, so be discreet when visiting. The monastery is on a hilltop, reached by a set of switchbacks; a few dozen monks are in residence. There are expansive views across the valley from Samding.

Samding Monastery has an odd history. The monastery was probably founded in the 13th century and was associated with the Bodong sect, initiated by Bodong Chokle Namgyel (1306–86). The sect never gained much prominence, although a number of temples within radius of Samding followed its precepts.

At one time, Samding appears to have had both monks and nuns in residence, and was run by an abbess, one of the only female incarnations in Tibet. The lineage goes back to the 18th century. In 1717, legend has it, the abbess (venerated as Dorje Phagmo or the 'Thunderbolt Sow', believed to be a reincarnation of Tara) transformed herself and her cohorts into pigs to save them from a Dzungar (Mongol) attack. For centuries, the lineage continued uneventfully, until the year 1937. That year the acting Regent of Tibet announced that the Sixth Dorje Phagmo had been recognised in a young girl, even though the Fifth was still at large. He argued that the transference of souls actually took place in this case before death. The Fifth Dorje Phagmo died the following year, but the Tibetans would not accept the Sixth as the true incarnation and three other candidates were put forward. The matter was hotly disputed by the nominated girl's father, and a costly legal battle drained the funds of Samding and tore its monks and nuns apart with internal strife.

The Sixth Dorje Phagmo (the girl selected in 1937), it appears, hardly took up residence at Samding, since the legal wrangle carried over into the 1950s. In 1959, she fled to India, but the same year decided to return to Tibet by way of China. She then sided with the Chinese and made it clear she did not wish to be a Living Buddha anymore. She married and had three children, and held a high government position in Lhasa when last heard of.

If a community of nuns and monks with an abbess at their head sounds like good material for a novel, there is one that draws inspiration from Samding. In his suspense novel *The Rose of Tibet*, author Lionel Davidson combines Yamdrok Tso and Samding to create a place called Yamdring Monastery.

Ralung Gompa Between Yamdrok Tso and Gyantse is a turn-off that leads 5km along a rough dirt road to the tiny *gompa* of Ralung. This monastery used to be much bigger, but its Kumbum and main halls were destroyed. What remains is a single structure, housing a handful of monks, who commute on motorcycles. The place is located in a quiet valley and is little visited.

GYANTSE *(Gyangtse, Gyangze, Jiangzi; 3,950m)*

Gyantse was established as the personal fiefdom of King Pelden Sangpo, in the 14th century. His successor, Rabten Kunsang Phapa (1389–1442), extended the fiefdom's range, and constructed Palkor Choide Lamasery and the mighty Kumbum, both of which are still standing today.

In later centuries, Gyantse developed as an important centre of the wool trade in Tibet, and a bustling caravan stop on the trade route from Lhasa to India. That route – leading to Sikkim and Bhutan – was closed by the Chinese after they took over in 1950. Gyantse has since fallen into obscurity, its role usurped by Lhasa under the Chinese. This situation, however, has left Gyantse intact as a Tibetan architectural entity, which is something quite rare amid all the Chinese destruction and reconstruction. Gyantse has a largely Tibetan population – perhaps around 20,000. There is a huge fort at one end of town, a walled-in monastery grounds at the other end, and a ramshackle marketplace with older buildings and alleyways between fort and monastery.

In the late 1940s, Italian photographer Francesco Mele passed through Gyantse. Here's his description of the market:

> Its market is rich, due to the wool trade and the Indian and Chinese imported objects sold there. The shops are near to the main street, and many of them are simply tents. Here women wearing silver and turquoise jewellery sell clothing and household articles… There are even some Nepalese and Bhutanese salesmen, and a few Muslims who have taken the few weeks' journey from Ladak in order to sell their products in Gyantse. Muslims are often employed as butchers of yak and goat here, since the Buddhist religion forbids Tibetans to kill animals. Fresh and dried beef and mutton hang in every part of the market, giving it an oddly surrealist appearance.

Gyantse market appears to have died: there isn't a whole lot happening around the old quarter anymore. Instead, various smaller street markets are scattered around the town. Nevertheless, Gyantse is a great place to visit, and will give some idea of what an intact Tibetan town must have looked like.

Buildings in Gyantse date back as far as the 14th century. One of these is the massive *dzong* (fort), occupying a strategic hilltop at the southern end of town. The *dzong* guarded the road to Lhasa, and the invading British expedition of 1903 found it a formidable obstacle. The British eventually stormed the *dzong*, the Tibetan defenders capitulated, and there was no further resistance on the road to Lhasa.

Although the last of the British forces withdrew in 1908, several vestiges of British presence remained in Gyantse, in the form of a British Trade Agent, a British wool-agent station, a British post office (with a telegraph line running to India), and later a British-run school for upper-crust Tibetan children. By the 1940s, a great deal of Gyantse's sheep-wool production was slated for export to British India. There was little interest in yak wool, which was too harsh in quality, although in the pre-synthetic era, the beards worn by Santa Clauses in US department stores were made from yak-tail hair. Gyantse became a funnel for the export of wool due to its location, and wool was brought here from outlying areas of Tibet.

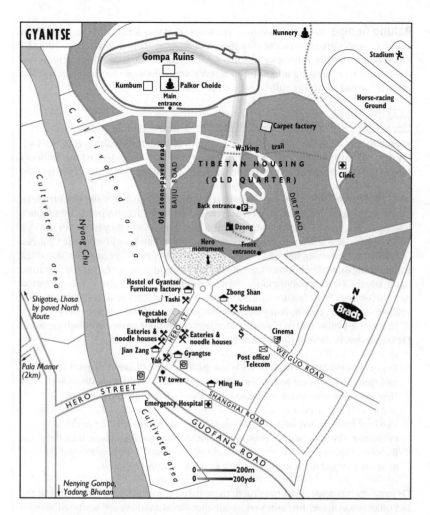

GYANTSE

Nunnery

Stadium

Gompa Ruins

Kumbum Palkor Choide
Main
entrance

Horse-racing
Ground

Carpet factory

Cultivated road

Walking   trail

TIBETAN HOUSING

(OLD QUARTER)

Clinic

Baiju Road

Old stone-paved road

Nyang Chu

Cultivated area

Back entrance

Dirt Road

Dzong

Hero
monument

Front
entrance

Shigatse, Lhasa
by paved North
Route

Hostel of Gyantse/
Furniture factory
Tashi

Zbong Shan

Sichuan

Vegetable
market

Bradt

Pala Manor
(2km)

Eateries &
noodle houses

Eateries &
noodle houses

Cinema

Jian Zang

Gyangtse

Post office/
Telecom

Yak

TV tower

Ming Hu

Hero Street

Weiguo Road

HERO STREET

Emergency Hospital

SHANGHAI ROAD

Cultivated area

GUOFANG ROAD

0   200m
0   200yds

Nenying Gompa,
Yadong, Bhutan

The 1950s saw a period of severe dislocation in Gyantse. In 1954, the town was nearly destroyed by flooding; in 1959 the local industries were virtually dismantled with the exodus of artisans from Tibet and the removal of others to work camps. After putting down the 1959 revolt, the Chinese imprisoned 400 monks and laymen at the monastery of Gyantse. During the Cultural Revolution, the monastery itself was ransacked and dismantled – items of value were either destroyed or shipped back to China. Gyantse Kumbum, however, was spared. Since 1980, the Chinese have attempted to stimulate the handicraft production for which Gyantse was so famous. But if there has been any stimulation, there is little evidence of it in Gyantse's present-day marketplace.

In the late 1990s, Chinese authorities embarked on a propaganda blitz in Gyantse, naming it 'Heroic City' in praise of valiant Tibetan resistance to British troops in 1904. In Chinese terms, the logic runs thus: 'Tibetan patriotic soldiers safeguarded state sovereignty and territorial integrity – defending the Tibet-China Motherland.' These propaganda efforts were most likely tied in with a round of Brit-bashing after the 1997 handover of Hong Kong. First there was the 1997 release of *Red River Valley*, a Shanghai-made epic movie about the British in Tibet, with on-location filming at Gyantse. This was followed by renaming the main street of Gyantse 'Hero Street', and the erection of a huge obelisk as a monument to heroic Tibetan fighters. The monument makes a convenient navigation landmark, right near the town's central roundabout.

GETTING THERE Motoring over several stunning passes on the back route from Lhasa is the best way to get to Gyantse. This trip should take about six hours – longer if you stop *en route*. If arriving by **Landcruiser** and overnighting, park the vehicle within your hotel grounds. Locals use buses that run from Lhasa via Shigatse to get to Gyantse. It's a 90km trip.

GETTING AROUND Gyantse cleaves into several distinct zones. To the northern end of town is the old quarter, with Tibetan housing. To the southern end of town, south of the central roundabout, are newer Chinese concrete blocks and Chinese facilities like the bank, post office, cinema and so on. At all compass points around the town are cultivated fields. There are stupendous views of Gyantse from the uppermost ramparts of the fort.

If you're with a **Landcruiser** driver and your time is short, have him drive you to sites like Pala Manor, the main monastery, the *dzong* (reached by motor road at the back), and Ani Gompa. Pala Manor can be visited by Landcruiser as a stop on the way to Shigatse, or incoming from Shigatse. Gyantse's key destinations would be easy to get to by **bicycle**, if you can lay your hands on one. Gyangtse Hotel has a few bikes, but only for their guests, and they are expensive at Y5 an hour, or Y50 a day. An alternative is hiring a **bicycle trishaw** driver in town. If you have more time, Gyantse is a pleasant place to stroll around – you can reach key destinations **on foot**, though it's a long way out to Pala Manor.

WHERE TO STAY Some hotels in Gyantse appear to favour Chinese guests, such as Zong Shan Hotel. For exact locations of the following hotels, see the Gyantse map, opposite.

Hostel of Gyantse Town Furniture Factory Central roundabout. Comfortable, with rooms including TV. There are no showers in the rooms, but hot water is provided in the public shower at certain hours if there are enough guests. Foreigners may not be permitted to stay here. *Y35 dorm beds.*

Gyantse Dhugu Hotel (30 rooms) 817 3165. Adequate standard hotel. *Y160 dbl; Y180 sgl.*

Jian Zang Hotel Hero St, southwest of roundabout; 817 3720; f 817 3910; e jianzanghotel@yahoo.com.cn. Best pick of a rum bunch in Gyantse. *Y380 standard rooms.*

Gyangtse Hotel (138 rooms) Shanghai Rd, towards the river; 817 2222; f 817 2366. The most expensive hotel in town (the plumbing actually does work). This is the place for high-end group tours, with a large dining hall & a souvenir shop. The hotel rents bikes for Y5/hr or Y50/day, but only to guests. Has a business centre, & to one side of the compound is Pala Manor Recreation Centre, offering haircuts & massage. *Y460 standard; Y575 trpl; Y770–Y1,200 suite. Tibetan-style rooms more expensive.*

WHERE TO EAT Scattered around town are small eateries, some with only two or three tables. For real Tibetan atmosphere try **Tashi Restaurant**, near the central roundabout (on the second floor), a Tibetan-style teahouse serving palatable food. There's a string of small restaurants along Hero Street – Muslim, Tibetan and Chinese styles on offer. The second-floor **Yak Restaurant** is found here, opposite

Jian Zang Hotel. Along the same strip (set back off the road) is a small fruit and vegetable market where you can buy peaches and bananas. In the mornings, you may find tiny bakeries serving hot baked goods. Stores in Gyantse are not as well stocked as they are in Shigatse.

OTHER PRACTICALITIES Facilities in Gyantse are limited, but include a half-hearted attempt at a department store (shelves bare) and a half-hearted attempt at a bank (staffed by Chinese who appear to have perfected the art of camouflaging themselves as non-bank workers). Further down the street is the **post office**, with long-distance telecom capabilities if you goad the staff. Chances of making long-distance connections are better at the **cybercafés** found at the southwest side of town (see map, page 194). For medical problems, your best bet is likely to be the **Emergency Hospital** on Shanghai Road, past Gyangtse Hotel. Avoid the clinic at the northeast side of town, as it's unsanitary. Gyantse at night is subject to the occasional tuneless wailing from karaoke bars or the sound of kung-fu epics emanating from video salons or Tibetan teahouses; there's also a movie theatre with an antiquated sound system.

WHAT TO SEE
Horse-racing festival The time when Gyantse really comes to life is during the horse-racing festival, held in the first week of the eighth lunar month (usually sometime in late July or early August). The horse-racing ground is to the northeast side of town. Festivities last for about five days. The jockeys are young boys: the winners (both boy and horse) are festooned with white ceremonial scarves. Large parades, with dancers and singers, and monks in full regalia, accompany the opening and closing ceremonies.

Old quarter Gyantse is a great town to walk around. The Tibetan part of town, toward the gates of Gyantse Gompa, is a fascinating medieval jumble of alleyways, with cows roaming through. Gyantse market used to be located along the stone-paved road close to the main monastery. There's no plumbing in the old quarter, and water comes from street taps – and little electrical supply. However, solar cookers have been introduced by the Chinese: these concave-shaped reflectors are found on the flat roofs in the old quarter – they can bring a kettle of water to the boil in a few minutes.

There is a walking trail through from the monastery towards the horse-racing ground, which cuts through a cleft in a high ridge (see map, page 194). Along the way is **Gyantse Carpet Factory**, where all work is done by hand – carding the wool, spinning, dyeing and weaving. This small operation is a shadow of what Gyantse once was. There's also a clothing factory in Gyantse. A worthy destination to the northeast side of town is **Ani Gompa**, a nunnery with 30 nuns in residence. A tiny chapel here contains a large wooden prayer-wheel and some life-sized frescoes, including one that shows the Tenth Panchen Lama (a mural near this used to show the current Dalai Lama, but, under orders, the head was repainted in the likeness of the Fifth Dalai Lama). Behind the nunnery is a cliff face with hermit caves; there's a sky burial site in the vicinity.

The monastery Pictures taken by Leslie Weir on a visit in 1930 show a complex of 16 monasteries within the high walls at the north end of Gyantse (Weir was a British Trade Agent at Gyantse). The monastic town has been razed with the exception of a few of the larger buildings. The monastery goes under different names: Palkor

Geoffrey Flack

After invading in 1903, the British negotiated the right to set up telegraph and post offices in Tibet. This gave the Tibetans access to the international postal system. There were a handful of British post offices, the earliest starting around 1906. The British were not permitted to establish a post office in Lhasa, but three British post offices linked the main trading corridor from Tibet to India: at Gyantse, Phari and Yadong. The mail then went on to Kalimpong, in India.

The postal system for external mail in Tibet was primarily used by Nepalese and Indian traders. Delivery was accomplished by runners: the monasteries, for instance, had their own runners. Ponies were also used, and in the 1930s a Dodge truck operated on part of the route to India. The runners, like most Tibetans, were illiterate and could only identify traders' mail by handmarked symbols on the envelopes. The mail could be delivered in a fairly short time: officials in Lhasa used to subscribe to newspapers in Calcutta, which might arrive a week or so later. Considering the altitude of the passes along the route, the runners did a remarkable job.

In 1910 the 13th Dalai Lama, who had fled to India, asked the British company of Waterlow to design a Tibetan stamp. Waterlow produced some proofs with a snow lion on them, the symbol of the Dalai Lama. These were rejected by the Tibetans, but they kept the proofs, and the Waterlow design was copied for the first Tibetan stamp issue of 1912. Tibetan stamps were a very haphazard affair. The 1912 issue, done in five different *trangka* values, was printed off woodblocks of 12 stamps. Stamp colour largely depended on what inks were available in the marketplace. Tibetan cancels never bore dates, and the random print-runs were never announced – the 1914 issue of stamps was not discovered by the West until 1942.

If you were living in Lhasa in the 1930s and you wanted to get a letter to England, life got complicated. There was no British post office in Lhasa, and Tibet was not a member of the International Postal Union. So you needed two sets of stamps on an envelope – Tibetan and Indian. In Lhasa, they'd cancel the Tibetan postage and forward the item to the Tibetan post office in Gyantse. Somehow the letter would make it across town to Gyantse's British post office, and then go on to Yadong and India, where it entered the international postal system.

Incoming mail was virtually impossible to orchestrate unless sent care of a trader in Gyantse or Phari, who would affix the Tibetan postage and forward the letter. In the process, the actual stamps would be dwarfed by a selection of wax seals, handstamps, chops and registration marks. Red wax seals could only be used by Incarnate Lamas. Few of the Dalai Lama's letters went beyond Sikkim. They were carried by private runners, and enclosed ceremonial silk scarves and perhaps a small bag of gold dust. They could only leave the Potala on auspicious dates.

By the early 1950s, stamp collectors were rushing to buy Tibetan postage. The majority of fake Tibetan stamps and covers started to appear at this time, though the hobby goes back to 1920. Buyers who are offered earlier Tibetan stamps in Kathmandu will probably be shown forgeries nine times out of ten. Covers are now forged so well that only a handful of world experts can tell the difference.

Geoffrey Flack (www.tibetanpost.com) is a recognised expert on Tibetan stamps, resident in Canada.

Lhasa to Kathmandu   GYANTSE

6

Choide is the older name, but the Chinese refer to it as Palchoi Temple or Baiju Temple, and the road leading up to it as Baiju Road.

The monastery is only accessible by the south gate, where an entry fee of Y45 is charged (additional fees are collected by the monks for photography within the main temple and the Kumbum). The Kumbum appears to be open only in the mornings – in any case, this is the best time to visit. Chapels can be dark, so bring a flashlight.

The Kumbum The main sight of Gyantse is the immense *chorten* or Kumbum in the grounds of the walled monastery at the north end. It was built in the 14th century by Rapten Kunsang Phapa. Kumbum means 'having 100,000 images', and Gyantse Kumbum may well live up to that description. The *chorten* is a deluxe model and quite innovative in its architecture – there is nothing like it elsewhere in Tibet. It has 70 small interlocking chapels that you visit as you spiral your way to the golden plume at the top. Each chapel contains fine statuary, and murals painted in the 15th century by Newari artists.

In aerial perspective, the *chorten* is shaped like a mandala, the embodiment of the Lamaist universe. Pilgrims circumambulate this giant wedding-cake structure: the inner spiralling circuit of the *chorten* is a meditational aid, with the top canopied section representing the highest plane of wisdom. How far you can ascend depends on how adept you are at convincing the caretaker monks to allow you to proceed. The best strategy is to try to follow pilgrims, since entrances to upper regions are hidden behind statues and in dark alcoves (some may be locked). Right near the top you come out below the large all-seeing eyes of Buddha, painted on the upper walls. The chapels here are larger and contain intricate tantric murals and mandalas. Although it may appear you cannot go higher, in fact there are ladders leading above the all-seeing eyes through a trapdoor to an open wooden turret, under the top umbrella-like structure. From here there are panoramic views of Gyantse.

Palkor Choide Lamasery This monastery is believed to have been constructed in 1418–25 by Rapten Kunsang Phapa. Though in the past it served the Sakya and Geluk orders, it is presently looked after by Gelukpa monks. The monastery has miraculously survived with some original statuary intact. More interesting than the ground floor assembly hall are the chapels on the second floor. On the third or uppermost floor is a shrine to Sakyamuni Buddha, with huge tantric wheel murals of Sakya deities.

Hero monument Facing the central roundabout is a huge three-sided obelisk, with text or characters on each side in Chinese, Tibetan and English. The English side reads: 'Gyangtse Mount Dzong Monument to Heroes'. The monument is set in a large park and was constructed in the late 1990s. The Chinese-style monolith is made of concrete and finished in marble: it sits on a dais similar to one at the Temple of Heaven in Beijing, with Chinese imperial lions – not Tibetan snow lions – standing guard.

Around the base of the obelisk are bas-reliefs which are falling apart, but fascinating. The front section shows the battle of 1904 with Tibetans throwing down rocks, British troops (easily identified by pith helmets and guns) and what appear to be characters with Chinese dress and swords (not historically correct, as there were no Chinese soldiers or advisers at Gyantse in 1904). A side panel shows the British with heavy machinery, and the back panel shows PLA troops waving Chinese flags and people holding portraits of Mao Zedong.

The fort This brooding 500-year-old colossus crowns a hilltop at the southern end of Gyantse. The fort's foundations are of 14th-century vintage, while the thick walls were probably constructed later.

There are two ways to reach the *dzong*: by car or on foot. Landcruisers can drive up the back of the *dzong* by a switchback road to a parking lot. On foot, access to the *dzong* is by a set of steps at the southeast side, proceeding through the *dzong*'s huge doors to the ticket office. If on foot, consider exiting the *dzong* by walking down the switchback motor road at the back. This will land you up in the old town, close to the monastery (see map, page 194). The *dzong* is in theory open 08.00–20.00 in summer and 10.00–18.00 in winter and spring; the entry fee is Y30.

View from the top You can climb right to the top battlements, which offer a superb view of Gyantse town and make a great photo perch. Within the *dzong*, there's actually little to see. Various buildings and battlements were blown to smithereens by Nepalese invaders, then British invaders, and again by the favourite cohorts of Mao Zedong (the Red Guards), leaving a lot of rubble lying around. Even so, it is one of the best-preserved forts in Tibet. A restored section includes a chapel with some dark murals and newish Buddhist statuary.

Toiling on upwards, you come to a viewable room labelled 'Dungeon', which contains a tableau with life-sized figures, one a Tibetan aristocrat (as judge) and four others involved in flogging a prisoner. This is meant to show the harsher side of the feudal serf system in old Tibet. Other descriptions of these nasty feudal times include binding a prisoner in cowhide and throwing him in the river, and scooping out eyeballs or intestines. The Chinese may have overlooked the fact that similar penalties (if not worse) were meted out in imperial China during this era.

A set of Chinese-built concrete steps leads straight up from here to the top of the fort. Mounting these steps can be strenuous – a bit like Stairmaster at altitude. The top turret is about 4m² in size and offers breathtaking views (in all senses of the word – you are actually over 200m higher than the town). This eyrie makes an excellent vantage point for orientation and photography.

Pala Manor Over a bridge, on the west side of Nyang River, is a junction with several turn-offs. To the west you can drive or walk 3km to Pala Manor, which is an old noble's house in the middle of a small village. The manor belongs to the 'feudal' days when an aristocrat ruled the village and surrounding lands. The walled three-storey manor – mostly constructed of wood – features the former tearoom and stables.

Pala fled Tibet in 1959 and lived out his days in exile. A tableau upstairs shows Pala and his cronies (one the abbot of Palkor Choide Monastery) indulging in the game of mah-jong, drinking tea and taking the occasional shot of whisky. This is meant to show decadence but in today's China, half the population is addicted to mah-jong. You are shepherded around and shown three or four rooms on the uppermost floor. One of these reveals Pala's personal larder – stocks of Kraft cheese, Britannia biscuits and Diamond Jubilee confectionery. Next is a lounge room of sorts, with an ancient gramophone and snow-leopard or monkey-fur covers on the cushions. A meditation room features stained glass imported from India.

Downstairs is a room that looks like a shop, with glass cases showing imported wines and goods from France, the US, the UK, Australia and India. There's a wardrobe crammed with boots, ceremonial wear and fur hats, while another case shows roller skates, football boots and a football (very progressive for Tibet – football, introduced by the British, was banned by the monastic authorities in the 1940s). On the wall is a picture of Pala in the late 1940s and another picture taken in 1956 in India – also in the line-up is the young Dalai Lama, Ling Rinpoche (his tutor) and Ngawang Jigme (who was later to betray the Tibetans).

The extensively restored manor is a showpiece on how the people of Gyantse were exploited by Tibetan nobles – that's before all the major buildings of Gyantse were blown up by the Chinese. To drive this point home, you are escorted across the street from Pala Manor to some dark hovels where servants used to live. The captions all tell the same story: life is far better under Chinese rule. One caption describes a carpet maker who used to live in a 10m^2 hovel with dirt floors at Pala Manor, but after Chinese liberation was able to shift to a 400m^2, two-storey home with three cows, a horse, 23 sheep and a colour television.

SIDE TRIPS FROM GYANTSE A turn-off on the west side of Gyantse leads directly south to **Nenying Gompa**, about 20km from Gyantse. This is an active monastery set in a small village. The monastery was nearly destroyed by the invading British in 1903, and later rebuilt, only to be destroyed again during the Cultural Revolution (and then rebuilt). The road here leads southward all the way to Yadong, at the border of Sikkim. There's a military checkpoint at Gala. After that, there are views of Mount Chomolhari from the road. Further south, with the opening of the Tibet–Sikkim border to trade in 2006, there is a border crossing but only for the Chinese it seems.

HEADING NORTHWEST FROM GYANTSE It's a fast, flat run from Gyantse to Shigatse – the ground can be covered in a matter of several hours. There are two monastery stops you can make. The first is at **Drongtse Monastery**, a small place famed for its slate bas-relief carvings. Drongtse is about 9km from the junction in Gyantse. A second possibility is **Shalu Gompa**, which is reached by a turn-off 18km short of Shigatse. The *gompa* is 4km off the main route (you can also visit Shalu on a day trip from Shigatse – see page 208).

SHIGATSE *(Zhigatse, Xigaze, Rigaze; 3,900m; capital of Shigatse Prefecture)*

Shigatse, the second-largest town in Tibet, has a population of around 60,000. The massive monastery of Tashilhunpo dates from the mid-15th century. Shigatse was the power base of the King of Tsang in the 16th century: he was defeated in battle in 1642 by the Mongol leader, Gushri Khan. In 1652, the Fifth Dalai Lama bestowed the title of Panchen Lama on the abbot of Tashilhunpo Monastery. From that time on, the authority of the Panchen Lama outweighed that of the Lhasa-appointed district governor, who occupied the defeated king's castle (the present-day ruined *dzong*) in town.

Apart from Tashilhunpo Monastery and a small Tibetan quarter, Shigatse is heavily Chinese in character, by which is meant an ugly concrete sprawl. There's a weird wind blowing through Shigatse. It's the wind from Beijing, the dusty wind of the Gobi. Look at a Chinese map of Shigatse and you can get some idea of what has transpired. A Chinese map I picked up barely mentions any Tibetan features. Apart from the usual 'No 1 Bus Team' and 'No 2 Guesthouse' is this curious entry, 'Building for Overseas Tibetans'. Could this be the fabled shop where Tibetans from Nepal come to buy their souvenirs?

Some glaring omissions on the map are the large army bases that ring the town. Shigatse is something of a glorified army base, with huge barracks punctuating the landscape. The arrival of the PLA en masse was not auspicious. In 1960, the PLA surrounded Tashilhunpo Monastery (which had hitherto escaped reforms) and seized all 4,000 monks within. Some were later executed, some committed

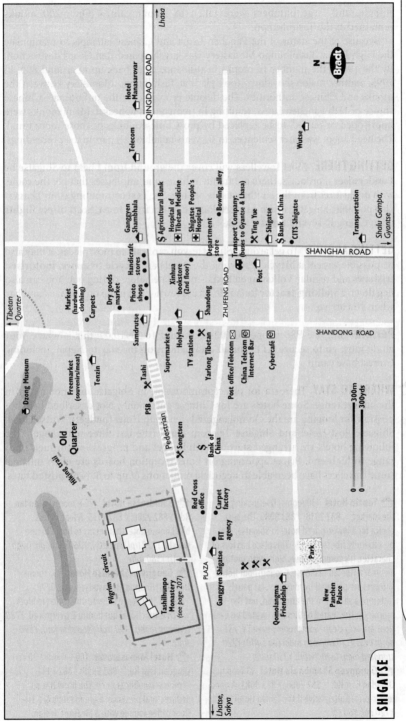

SHIGATSE

Lhasa → *Lhasa*

QINGDAO ROAD

↑ Hotel Manasarovar

↑ Telecom

Ganggyen Shambhala

↑ Wutse

$ Agricultural Bank
✚ Hospital of Tibetan Medicine
✚ Shigatse People's Hospital

Department store

● Bowling alley

Transport Company (buses to Gyantse & Lhasa)

✕ Ying Yue

↑ Shigatse

$ Bank of China

● CITS Shigatse

↑ Transportation

Shalu Gompa, Gyantse

SHANGHAI ROAD

↑ Tibetan Quarter

Market (hardware/ clothing)

Carpets ●

Dry goods market

Photo shops

Handicraft stores ●

● Xinhua bookstore (2nd floor)

● Shandong

Post ⊠

ZHUFENG ROAD

Samdrutse ↑

↑ Tenzin

● Freemarket (souvenirs/meat)

● Dzong Museum

↑ Tibetan Quarter

Old Quarter

● Supermarket

● Holyland

✕ TV station

✕ Yarlong Tibetan

SHANDONG ROAD

PSB ●

✕ Tashi

Pedestrian

✕ Songtsen

Post office/Telecom ⊠
China Telecom Internet Bar @
Cybercafé @

$ Bank of China

Hiking trail

Pilgrim circuit

● Red Cross office

● Carpet factory

● FIT agency

✕ ✕ ✕

Tashilhunpo Monastery (see page 207)

Ganggyen Shigatse

PLAZA

↑ Qomolangma Friendship

New Panchen Palace

Park

↑ *Lhatse, Sakya*

N ● Bradt

0 ———— 300m
0 ———— 300yds

suicide, and large numbers were taken to labour camps. Only 200 monks remained at the Tashilhunpo.

Because of the status of the Panchen Lama and Chinese attempts to manipulate the High Lama, Tashilhunpo Monastery was largely spared Red Guard destruction. By the 1980s, the number of monks in residence crept back up to around 800. In 1995, another major showdown took place at Tashilhunpo Monastery between the monks and Chinese authorities. The dispute erupted over the unfortunate Chinese choice of 11th Panchen Lama, resulting in tremendous upheaval. Many monks were imprisoned or ousted, to be replaced by pro-Chinese monks or those more timid. The head abbot was later sentenced to six years in jail for his part in the proceedings.

GETTING THERE Most travellers will cover the ground from Lhasa to Shigatse by **Landcruiser**. For locals, there are frequent buses and minibuses that ply the route, with departures from the southeast side of Shigatse. **Taxi** commuting from Lhasa is also possible. Shigatse Peace Airport, located 45km from town, hosts direct **flights** from Chengdu several times a week.

GETTING AROUND To get around Shigatse, you can **walk** to most places. It may also be possible to rent a **bicycle**. Prowling the streets are **bicycle trishaws**, **motorised trishaws** and regular **Volkswagen taxis** – negotiate before setting out. You can also flag down a **walking-tractor** for a ride across town – just jump on the back and pay when you arrive.

Permits Shigatse PSB is open 09.00–13.00 and 16.00–19.00: this is where your guide must go to secure ATPs for all destinations on the way to Nepal, including Everest base camp.

WHERE TO STAY There's a lot of accommodation in Shigatse, but not much in the budget range. Some hotels are for Chinese guests only. Not described here but possible for lodging are the Qomolangma Friendship Hotel (budget), Wutse Hotel, Shigatse Post Hotel and Shigatse Telecom Hotel (the last three mid-range). The following hotels are arranged starting with budget and progressing through mid-range to high-end. Prices appearing on hotel reception boards are often inflated: some travellers have been able to negotiate reductions of up to 50% off posted rates.

Tenzin Hotel (30 rooms) Overlooking the market; ☎ 882 2018; f 883 8080. The best choice for a lower-priced hotel in Shigatse, run by a friendly Tibetan family. This place has lots of character. It's several storeys high, with rooftop views & a Tibetan teahouse. Ground-floor hot showers are powered by rooftop solar panels (attempt a shower in the afternoon, not the morning). The shared bathrooms located on each floor are very clean. Some rooms have TV. *Y35 dorm bed; Y120 common room (no bath); Y220 standard room (with bath); Y250 suite.*

Ganggyen Shambhala Hotel (33 rooms) Qingdao East Rd; ☎ 882 7666; f 883 3681. A good lower-priced alternative if the Tenzin Hotel is full. *Y120 dbl; Y60 sgl.*

Samdrutse Hotel (90+ rooms) Qingdao Rd; ☎ 882 2280; f 882 1135. A featureless blockhouse hotel that seems to host Chinese guests. *Y120 trpl (no bath); Y260 sgl or dbl (with bath); Y580 suite.*

Ganggyen Shigatse Hotel (60 rooms) Near Tashilhunpo Monastery; ☎ 882 0777; f 883 0171. A large Chinese-run concrete block, which is functional but boring & overpriced. *Y280 common room; Y190 trpl; Y468 standard; Y890 suite.*

Hotel Manasarovar (80+ rooms) 20 Qingdao East Rd; ☎ 883 9999; f 882 8111; e mnsrvr@public.ls.xz.cn. The hotel has an architectural presence: a grand lobby & a 1st-floor coffee lounge with a pleasant design.

There are several restaurants within the hotel. Comfortable mid-range hotel. *Y280 common room; Y320 trpl; Y480 deluxe (with bath); Y1,380 Tibetan suite.*

⌂ **Holyland Hotel** (90 rooms) 5 Shandong Rd; ☎ 882 2922; f 882 1990. Fancier hotel with lifts. *Y500–800 standard; Y900 & up for a suite.*

⌂ **Shandong Hotel** (110 rooms) 5 Shandong Rd; ☎ 882 6138; f 882 6124. Ugly white-tiled building with green windows. Towering 9 storeys, this hotel laid claim to being the tallest in town – but has since been eclipsed by the cheeky Agricultural Bank, a block north. The hotel boasts in-house movies; some rooms have oxygen machines. A number of restaurants lurk within the hotel. The lobby bookstore selection is good. *Y358–400 standard room; Y888–1,580 suite.*

⌂ **Shigatse Hotel** (125 rooms) Shanghai Middle Rd, southeast side of town; ☎ 882 2525; f 882 1900. Group tour or expedition hotel. Supposed to be the top-rated hotel in town, but has a derelict atmosphere. Facilities include an exchange counter, small business centre, gift shop, bar & several restaurants. *Y550 dbl; Y600 trpl; Y1,880 & up for deluxe suites.*

✗ **WHERE TO EAT** One positive thing the Chinese brought to Shigatse is stir-fried food. If you are a vegetarian, or simply fancy a vegetable top-up, a good tactic is to shop for fresh vegetables at a small market and take these to the restaurant, where, for a fee, they will cook it all up.

Two excellent restaurants are located along the market street leading to Tashilhunpo Monastery. **Songtsen Tibetan Restaurant** (☎ 883 2469), offers Nepali sets, yak sizzlers, yak *momos*, tandoori and lassis. With a similar range of Nepali, Tibetan and Indian fare is **Tashi Restaurant**, upstairs near the PSB office. Because of their popularity with group tours, it can take a long time to get served in these restaurants if you hit peak hour in the evening. The same is true of **Third Eye Restaurant**, located next door to the Ganggyen Shigatse Hotel.

SHOPPING AND SUPPLIES Shigatse is one of the best places in Tibet to replenish your stocks or add to them. It is second only to Lhasa. For trip supplies, check out the department stores first, as these carry canned and packaged goods. Shopping for Tibetan artefacts is best in the Tenzin Hotel area – at the freemarket, and further east for carpets and handcrafted items. There are also several handicraft shops in town, and a gift shop at Shigatse Hotel. Chocolate and biscuits can be purchased at several well-stocked supermarkets on Shandong Road, in the vicinity of the Holyland Hotel. Shigatse is so big it even has its own bowling alley (the only other place like this in Tibet is in Lhasa).

OTHER PRACTICALITIES Shigatse Hotel and Shandong Hotel have giftshops with a good supply of maps and books, and may even stock film and batteries. The Xinhua bookstore up the street is fairly useless, though you might stray across a map or poster here.

Banking The Bank of China is near Shigatse Hotel – this is the main branch where you can change travellers' cheques. Smaller branch offices of the BOC downtown may only deal in cash. Some ATMs around town dispense cash to foreign cards: a few are open 24 hours.

Medical There are two hospitals in town, and you would do well to steer clear of both of them.

Email and internet China Telecom Internet Bar is a large cybercafé run by China Post – it is located next door to the main post office and is supposed to be open 24 hours. Further south along the same street is a cybercafé. Several smaller places are found opposite the Xinhua bookstore and vicinity. High-end hotels have internet access in the business centre.

WHAT TO SEE

Pilgrim circuit Just as interesting as Tashilhunpo Monastery (see page 206) is the cross-section of pilgrims who come from far and wide to pay homage. Pilgrims follow a circuit that starts at the gates and circles clockwise around the monastery. Off to the northwest side of the circuit is a sky burial site. Instead of completely looping around Tashilhunpo, most pilgrims continue on a path eastward that finishes at the market in Shigatse's old quarter. There are lots of prayer-flags and *mani* stones that mark the route – just follow the pilgrims, and keep an eye out for

MIDNIGHT RAID

It was close to midnight and Jane (not her real name) was cocooned in her sleeping bag. A loud banging on the door shattered her dreams. Her midnight visitors were six men from the Shigatse Constabulary – they burst in, shouting: 'We know who you are!' and 'Where is your Swiss friend?'

Jane could not determine what she had done to incur their wrath, but she was quite shaken by the experience. The men demanded her passport and papers – which she handed over – and interrogated her for several hours. Meanwhile, soundly snoring away on the other side of town, in a deluxe hotel, were the real targets of the raid: Andy (from the US) and Marie (from Switzerland). After staying in a string of spartan hotels, they'd decided to splurge and clean up.

Shigatse police had been looking in the wrong place. They should have been looking for an American male, not a female. Andy's crime was that he had slipped through and made it to Kailash. This was shortly after 11 September 2001, and everything in west Tibet had closed down due to massive military movements in the west by Chinese troops racing to seal off the Afghan corridor and crack down on the Muslim population in Xinjiang. Andy and Marie, determined to see the mountain of their dreams, hitched rides, hid under blankets in the back of trucks and made it through to Ali after an epic trip on dusty back roads, dodging police and walking around checkpoints at night.

In Ali, they were arrested, fined, and told if they wanted to go to Kailash, it was possible, but only on a high-paying Landcruiser tour. The tour would be one-way Ali to Kailash, and then on to the Nepal border, where they would have to leave Tibet. The problem was, Andy and Marie both had air tickets from Lhasa to Chengdu, and luggage in Lhasa, with precious film in it. However, seeing no way out of the situation, they paid up for the exorbitant Landcruiser deal, got to Kailash and walked the *kora* of their dreams.

But a funny thing happened on the way to the Nepal border: at 04.00, Andy and Marie slipped out of the hotel in Nyalam, and started hitching towards Lhasa. They got as far as Shigatse that day, and took an expensive hotel room. The furious Landcruiser chaperones phoned Shigatse Police, but somewhere along the line the genders got mixed up, and Shigatse Police thought they were looking for an American female in a low-end guesthouse. Andy and Marie made it back to Lhasa, where they were briefly interrogated and then promptly put on a flight to Chengdu.

dogs. The entire circuit takes about an hour and a half. This hike is good orientation for surveying Shigatse from an aerial-type perspective. A good touring plan would be to spend the morning at Tashilhunpo Monastery, visit the carpet factory and new Panchen Palace in this vicinity, and then hike the *kora* to the *dzong* at the east side of Shigatse in the afternoon.

Old quarter, freemarket and *dzong*

The Tibetan quarter, near the *dzong*, is quite lively, with a skein of alleys to wander around. There's an extensive freemarket selling all kinds of souvenirs, such as Tibetan boots, stirrups, hats, bolts of cloth and dried legs of lamb. The target audience is Tibetans (legs of lamb) and tourists (souvenirs). Nearby are several Tibetan teahouses and *chang*-drinking hangouts.

Photographs from the 1930s show Shigatse Dzong looking like a mini-Potala, with the same classic lines. The fort continued to function as the offices of the *dzongpon* (district governor) until 1950. It was dynamited to rubble during the Cultural Revolution, and remained in ruins for many years. And then, miraculously, from 2005-07, the structure was completely rebuilt in concrete, but otherwise faithful to the original. There are plans to open the *dzong* as a museum of Tibetan culture. All in the interests of generating revenue from tourism, it seems. You can climb up (or drive up) and clamber around the area for good views overlooking the old quarter rooftops.

Carpet factory

A short walk from the front gate of Tashilhunpo Monastery is Ganggyen Carpet Factory, which first started operations in 1987 as a project initiated by the Tenth Panchen Lama. To get the project off the ground, he invited the same Tibetan businessman who started up the highly successful Tibetan carpet-weaving venture in Kathmandu to get involved. The factory is part-owned by Tashilhunpo Monastery, and a slice of the profits is donated each year to the monastery. Ganggyen Carpet Factory employs several hundred Tibetans, most of them women. If work is in progress, you can drop in and walk around, and see hand-looming at work. Women weavers often sing as they work – most of the weaving is done from memory, which is quite a feat considering the intricate designs. In addition to carpets, the factory sells wool jackets, sweaters, belts, scarves, bags and blankets. Tibetan horsemen use carpeting as a saddle base: these horse carpets are made here. For carpet purchases, shipping can be arranged right at the factory.

New Panchen Palace

South of Tashilhunpo Monastery is a compound with a high wall where the Panchen Lama supposedly stays when in Shigatse. On the rare occasions that he actually is Shigatse, the palace will therefore be closed to the public. The compound hosts Tibetan-style palatial buildings enclosing a garden courtyard. The original palace at this location dates to the 19th century. In 1955, the Tenth Panchen Lama reconstructed and expanded the palace. The main three-storey structure is larger than the Dalai Lama's summer palace in Lhasa. As you enter the main building, there are magnificent contemporary murals depicting scenes of the King of Shambhala riding forth to do battle with the forces of evil. The kingdom of Shambhala is depicted in a circular mandalic shape, surrounded by snowcapped peaks. Continuing on into the Panchen Palace, rooms are bare of furniture, but you will see chandeliers and stained glass imported from India. You may be shown a room on the second floor with some personal effects of the Tenth Panchen Lama – his writing desk and so on. The most startling exhibit is his stuffed dog, which looks like a large Alsatian. The dog apparently survived its owner by ten years, which raises the question: if the Panchen Lama was reincarnated, did the dog recognise its former owner as the 11th Panchen Lama, or reject him as a fake? (Speaking, in this case, of the enforced Chinese choice of 11th Panchen Lama.)

Tashilhunpo Monastery

The Tashilhunpo is the seat of the Panchen Lama, a topic that raises blood pressures on all sides. The monastery is highly sensitive because of the controversy surrounding the 11th Panchen Lama. Pictures of the Chinese-appointed 11th Panchen Lama abound as icons at the monastery, but that's about all you'll see of him – he is sequestered in Beijing, supposedly for reasons of education. There are monk-stooges hanging about: take care what you do or say here. Tashilhunpo is immense, a monastic city with temples, assembly halls, living quarters and administrative offices. At its height, it housed up to 5,000 monks. Today, the figure is probably closer to 700.

Tashilhunpo Plaza

Near the gates of the monastery is a plaza where you can find caricatures of yourself. There are life-sized statues of foreigners – one with a camcorder, another on a mountain bike, and a backpacker with a diary of some sort. Pilgrims and locals pose with these statues for pictures, or else attempt to get onto the mountain bike handlebars, or fondle the woman with the camcorder. These frozen foreigners are very popular.

Access

The grounds of Tashilhunpo Monastery are only fully accessible in the morning. In theory, the monastery is open 09.00–12.00 and 15.30–18.00. However, in practice, fewer chapels seem to be open in the afternoon. Although there are a number of gates (including one at the northeast wall), only one is sanctioned for entry and exit – you pay a foreigner's entry fee of Y55. Certain halls charge Y150 for photographs or Y1,800 for video. Pilgrims follow an internal temple circuit which is described here, and also an external circuit around the monastery walls.

Main structures

As you look northward from the front gates of Tashilhunpo Monastery (see plan opposite), you will see several buildings that stand out as taller than the rest. You can roughly identify these off the plan. At the back right wall is an enormous *tanka*-unfurling the height of a nine-storey building. This is where massive *tankas* of Buddha are unfurled during summer festivities. To the left of the grounds, the largest building is the Maitreya Chapel: it is here that pilgrims begin their tour of the monastery.

The **Maitreya Chapel** houses a 26m-high statue of Maitreya, the Buddha of the Future (*Champa* in Tibetan), seated on a lotus throne with the right hand in a symbolic teaching pose (which looks like an 'OK' gesture, in which forefinger and thumb are pressed together in a circle). The statue is gold plated: the structure is made of tons of copper and brass, moulded on a wooden frame. Tibetans believe that Champa will return to preside over the world when all human beings have earned deliverance from suffering. Pilgrims crowd in to make offerings and murmur mantras as they make an inner circuit around the statue itself. The fortress-style building that houses the Maitreya was built from 1914–18 by the Ninth Panchen Lama.

The newest building at the Tashilhunpo is the **Tomb of the Tenth Panchen Lama**. It was completed in 1993 and is similar in design to that of the Ninth Panchen Lama. The Chinese government is reported to have donated 500kg of gold for use in constructing the Tenth Panchen Lama's tomb, which may explain the Chinese-style roof. A gilded, jewel-encrusted stupa encloses the embalmed body of the Tenth Panchen Lama, who died in 1989. A life-sized statue of the Panchen Lama is shown at the front of the tomb. Surrounding the stupa are intricate murals. Above the

TASHILHUNPO MONASTERY

Tanka-unfurling festival wall

Tomb of the 9th Panchen Lama

Second-floor walkway from 10th to 4th tombs

Tomb of the 4th Panchen Lama

Tunnel

Kelsang Courtyard

Tomb of the 10th Panchen Lama

Tsongkhapa Chapel

Assembly Hall

Kitchen

Maitreya Chapel

Tantric College

Museum

Philosophy College

N

Bradt

Traditional medicine clinic

200m

Main entrance

ROAD

Town centre

tomb are other sections. You can reach the top floor by a staircase to the left (west side) of the building. Up a few flights of stairs, you reach a room with a gigantic 3D Kalachakra mandalic sculpture and impressive mandala murals on the walls.

Finding the following corridor is a bit tricky: your best bet is to follow the pilgrims. On the second floor, at the southwest side of the building, is the entry to a dim corridor-walkway lined with small, dark chapels heading east. This corridor is lined with Buddhas large and small, Tibetan scriptures, *tankas*, and with side chapels displaying statues of Tsongkhapa and the Kalachakra deity. The corridor leads from the Tomb of the Tenth to the Tomb of the Fourth Panchen Lama. This tall, russet gold-roofed building houses a large silver stupa, enclosing the embalmed body of Losang Chokyi Gyeltsen, the Fourth Panchen Lama.

Moving along, through a tunnel, you come to the gold-roofed Tomb of the Ninth Panchen Lama. It was completed in 1988 and was consecrated by the Tenth Panchen Lama only a week before his own death. During the Cultural Revolution, the bodies of the Fifth through to the Ninth Panchen Lamas were hidden and their identities were confused, so eventually all the remains were placed in a single tomb.

This tomb is attached to an elaborate complex that is the oldest part of Tashilhunpo Monastery, **Kelsang Courtyard**. The courtyard is enclosed by multi-storey galleries. Strolling around the different galleries gives you an idea of what the place looked like in centuries past. On the east side of the complex is a printing studio where scriptures are made from woodblocks. To the west side at the mid-levels is a large assembly hall where monks congregate for sutra chanting. Leading off this is a medieval kitchen with mammoth copper cauldrons, giant implements, and fires burning away on a scale that would have had *Macbeth*'s witches cackling. This is where food for all the monks is prepared. Debating between monks may take place in Kelsang Courtyard.

Heading back southward, you come to the **Tantric College**, where, if your timing is right, prayer ceremonies may be in progress in the assembly hall. In the courtyard of the **Philosophy College**, monks gather in the mornings to debate the finer points of Buddhist philosophy, vigorously emphasising points with their unique, over-arm slapping technique.

Right near the gates is a small monk-run **clinic** that offers Tibetan traditional medicine services. There are over 20 monk-doctors doing diagnosis and dispensing herbal medicines to Tibetan patients.

The Panchen Lama, Tibet's second-highest incarnate, traditionally has a seat at Tashilhunpo Monastery in Shigatse. The Panchen Lama (literally 'Precious Scholar') was also known as the Tashi Lama. There is considerable confusion over the number of Panchen Lamas in the lineage. This is because, in the 16th century, the Fifth Dalai Lama declared Losang Chokyi Gyeltsen (then the abbot of Tashilhunpo Monastery) to be the fourth reincarnate in a line that retroactively dated to the 14th century. He also declared him to be a manifestation of the Buddha Amitabha. From this time on, the elder of either the Panchen Lama or the Dalai Lama served as tutor for the other.

Tibetans have never recognised the Panchen Lama's authority to rule over Tibet: his jurisdiction was always restricted to the Shigatse area. However, the Chinese have seen fit to promote rivalry between the Panchen Lamas and the Dalai Lamas.

The Tenth Panchen Lama was born in 1938 in the Koko Nor region (Amdo). He fell into communist hands and was certified in Xining in 1949; his qualifications as an incarnate were accepted under duress by Lhasa. He was then brought to Shigatse in 1952 by the PLA as the Chinese were determined to belittle the Dalai Lama's authority. After the Dalai Lama fled Tibet in 1959, the Tenth Panchen Lama developed, by early accounts, into a mouthpiece for the Chinese. However, after the PLA raided Tashilhunpo Monastery in 1960 and disbanded the monks, the Panchen Lama changed tack and started to openly support the Dalai Lama. In 1961, when asked to move to the Potala to replace the Dalai Lama, the Panchen Lama flatly refused to do so, and dropped out of public view. In May 1962, he delivered a blistering 70,000-character report on conditions in Tibet to Mao Zedong, and demanded that mass arrests be halted and religious freedom restored. This document was kept secret for three decades until an anonymous source turned it over to Tibet Information Network (TIN) in London. TIN had it translated and issued in book form in London in 1998 under the title *A Poisoned Arrow*, which is what Mao Zedong called the report.

Side trip to Shalu Gompa To the south of Shigatse (18km away, then an extra 4km off the road) is Shalu Gompa. Shalu is most associated with 14th-century scholar Buton, a prolific translator and writer of sacred texts. During the Cultural Revolution, these precious texts were destroyed. The upper part of the monastery was also destroyed – donations from Chinese patrons account for the present-day green-glazed tiling on the Mongolian-style roof. Parts of the monastery lie derelict, with faded murals, due to lack of funds to renovate. The murals are faded and sooty, making artwork difficult to discern.

There are about 60 monks living here. Shalu's claim to fame is that it is thought to be the place where *lung-gom* runners trained. In the absence of motorised vehicles, the delivery system in ancient Tibet used relays of runners. The monasteries had their own runners – called *lung-gom* or trance-runners. The monks bounding along in a trance were reputed to build up their leg muscles by running on a pile of grain – while meditation masters provided rigorous mental training. During important religious festivals, the monk with the greatest physical and mental abilities would be selected to run to Lhasa – without food, rest or drink. That's a distance of over 200km. If really true, imagine the impact this esoteric training could have on endurance sports at the Olympics. There's no sign of any murals showing the *lung-gom* runners at Shalu, however.

In 1964, the Panchen Lama was asked to denounce the Dalai Lama at the height of the Monlam prayer festival in Lhasa. A crowd of 40,000 gathered outside the Jokhang, and the Panchen Lama delivered a stunning speech of solidarity with the Dalai Lama, and in favour of Tibetan independence. He was promptly placed under house arrest, denounced as a reactionary and brought to trial. After being beaten to induce confessions, the Panchen Lama disappeared, along with his parents and entourage.

The Panchen Lama was taken to Beijing and sentenced to ten years in prison in 1967, much of it spent in solitary confinement. From time to time he was taken out for 'struggle sessions' in a Beijing sports stadium, where he was humiliated in front of thousands of people. In 1978 he was set free again, supposedly a fully reformed man. He lived in Beijing, where he held an important government post. He was married to a Chinese woman and had a daughter: while he was alive, his wife pretended to be his personal secretary to preserve the Panchen Lama's spiritual standing among Tibetans, since none of the Panchen Lama lineage holders had married.

Eventually the Tenth Panchen Lama returned to Lhasa and Shigatse for extended visits, during which he again became increasingly critical of Chinese policy in Tibet. In 1989 he was found dead of a heart attack in Shigatse, at the age of 50. Although he was seriously overweight and a prime candidate for a heart attack, many Tibetans believe he was poisoned. When he died, the Chinese infuriated his wife by trying to bar her from memorial ceremonies at Tashilhunpo Monastery. She obstinately continued to live in Panchen Lama's Palace in Beihai Park, Beijing, in a building that is destined for the Chinese-sanctioned incarnate, the 11th Panchen. The 11th Panchen Lama is one of the most hotly disputed reincarnates in the history of Tibet. To read more about him, refer to the *Tibetan Buddhism* section in *Chapter 1*, page 32.

Technically, you need a permit to visit Shalu Gompa (obtainable from Shigatse PSB). In practice, if you just take a day trip to Shalu Gompa, the chances are nobody will check for permits.

SHIGATSE TO TINGRI

About 15km west of Shigatse you pass the ruins of **Narthang Monastery**, formerly one of Tibet's three great woodblock printing lamaseries. The other two were at Kumbum (Amdo) and Derge (Kham). Now only Derge Monastery survives as a large-scale printing works for sacred texts. The high crumbling walls of Narthang are visible behind a roadside village: a few monks have returned to the lamasery and several minor buildings have been restored. Further westward, you cross Tso La; shortly after this, at a place between KM5028 and KM5029 marker stones is a turn-off to Sakya, a highly recommended detour of 21km.

Then you can motor on to **Lhatse** (aka Lhaze or Lhartse), elevation 4,050m. Lhatse could be renamed 'Karaoke-ville'. Everything in Lhatse is strung out along the highway – karaoke bars, eateries, a few truck-stop hotels, a theatre and a gas station.

A haven for the road-weary in Lhatse is the **Tibetan Farmers Hotel** (✆ *832 2336*) at the eastern fringe of town, with clean, cosy rooms for Y35–130 in a Tibetan courtyard-style structure with potted plants. The hotel restaurant has good food

At Tashilhunpo and many other monasteries in Tibet you will see what appears to be familiar iconography. Inlaid with turquoise are large emblems called *svas-tikas*. *Svas-tika* is the Sanskrit; the Tibetan word is *yungtrung*. There are two Tibetan designs used – one pointing clockwise (Tibetan Buddhist), the other with a counterclockwise orientation (ancient Bon religion).

No, this has not been taken from the Nazis. Very much the other way around. The Nazis stole this ancient Tibetan symbol for peace and longevity. Then they put it on a white background and tilted it at an angle – and it turned into a symbol of war and destruction. The ancient Buddhist symbol of peace and prosperity (linking of opposites) has been forever tainted by the Third Reich's iconography.

Before the 1930s, the *svas-tika* was used in the West for peaceful applications. It was used as a publishing logo by the Theosophists, and also as a logo in books by Rudyard Kipling. On the Everest expedition of 1924 to Tibet, it was used at the four corners of commemorative stamps for Everest postcards. Probably the most spectacular misunderstanding for the *svas-tika* was in December 1943 when a plane flying the Hump (over the eastern Himalaya from India to China) ran out of fuel. Five American airmen parachuted from the plane into the night – and landed in the vicinity of Tsedang. Seeing what he thought were swastika shapes painted on some houses, the pilot went ballistic: he thought he had somehow stumbled into German-controlled territory. The ancient Indian *svas-tika* symbols are actually painted on Tibetan houses to bring good luck.

and atmosphere too. The overpriced **Shanghai Hotel** offers a lot more creature comforts but less atmosphere – and a hefty tariff at Y380 a room (you can bargain). Other options for hotels range from **Lazi Highway Hotel** (west end of town) to **Lhatse Hotel** in the middle of town (✆ *832 2208*), which has rooms for Y80–200, but offers dorm rooms as well. Finding a restaurant in lovely Lhatse is never a problem – there are over 40 of them lining the main drag, catering to truck drivers that come through. For more upscale fare, try **Lhatse Kitchen** inside the Shanghai Hotel. There are some hot springs located 11km from Lhatse; they're a bit derelict, with springs channelled into concrete pools, and an entry fee of Y25. At the western edge of Lhatse is a Tibetan *gompa*.

The road forks just west of Lhatse, with a branch heading northwest to Kailash, and southwest to Kathmandu. There may be a checkpoint near the junction. After crossing Gyatso La – at 5,250m the highest pass on this route – you reach the Shegar area (see page 214).

SAKYA (*Sagya, Sag'ya; 4,000m*) Sakya ('Grey Earth') was once the base of the Sakyapa sect that rose to power in the 13th century. The founder of the Sakyapa was Drokmi, who set up a monastery in Sakya in the 11th century. The Sakyapa were strong on magic and sorcery, and permitted their abbots to marry and to drink liquor. This led to hereditary rank (the post alternates between two families), and to a rather unsavoury reputation for worldliness among the monks. Although rank is hereditary, it is believed that seven incarnations of the Buddha of Wisdom (Manjushri) have appeared in the lineage of the Sakyapa.

The rise of the Sakyapa was largely due to 'the Mongol connection'. In the mid-13th century, Mongol warlord Godan Khan invited the leader of the Sakya sect, Sakya

Pandita, to educate his people spiritually. Sakya Pandita accepted the task and under Mongol overlordship, the Sakya school gained great political influence. The Mongol link continued with the succession of Phagpa (nephew of Sakya Pandita) and Kublai Khan. The power of the Sakyapa declined in the late 14th century as the fortunes of the Geluk tradition rose, but Sakya retained its links with Mongolia over the centuries.

In 1959, at the age of 14, Sakya Dagtri Rinpoche was enthroned at Sakya Gompa, becoming the 41st Patriarch (his title is also the Sakya Trizin, or throne-holder). Almost immediately after the event, he and his entourage of teachers and personal staff fled to India. It took Chinese soldiers several months to get to Sakya after the 1959 uprising in Lhasa. The Chinese told the 500 monks at Sakya Gompa that they had supported the Khampa rebels, so the monastery was seized, grain stocks confiscated, and monks and nuns were submitted to *thamzing* ('struggle-sessions' – self-criticism and public-criticism sessions where those accused are humiliated and beaten up in front of a crowd of locals).

After getting used to such strange phenomena as trains, cars, buses and aeroplanes, the Sakya Trizin set up a base in exile at Dehra Dun, in Uttar Pradesh, with a Sakya centre and college established in the 1960s. Today there are Sakya centres all over the world, and the throne-holder has toured extensively, teaching in Europe, America and Asia.

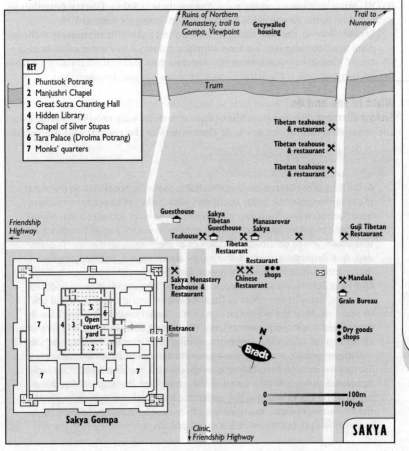

KEY
1 Phuntsok Potrang
2 Manjushri Chapel
3 Great Sutra Chanting Hall
4 Hidden Library
5 Chapel of Silver Stupas
6 Tara Palace (Drolma Potrang)
7 Monks' quarters

Ruins of Northern Monastery, trail to Gompa, Viewpoint

Greywalled housing

Trail to Nunnery

Trum

Tibetan teahouse & restaurant
Tibetan teahouse & restaurant
Tibetan teahouse & restaurant

Friendship Highway

Guesthouse

Sakya Tibetan Guesthouse

Teahouse

Tibetan Restaurant

Manasarovar Sakya

Guji Tibetan Restaurant

Restaurant

Sakya Monastery Teahouse & Restaurant

Chinese Restaurant

shops

Mandala

Grain Bureau

Dry goods shops

Open courtyard

Entrance

N

Sakya Gompa

Clinic, Friendship Highway

0 ———— 100m
0 ———— 100yds

SAKYA

Meanwhile, back in Sakya, the bathroom-tiling school of architecture is honing in on the south bank. A huge boulevard with street lighting was constructed at the east side, leading right into the village. Video bars screening noisy Chinese kung-fu movies are sprouting up. When the dust settles, this transformation will mean a largely Chinese urban style on the south bank except for the monastery and a cluster of nearby buildings, but the north bank is still Tibetan in character.

Sakya is reached by a side road: it is 21km from the main Lhasa–Kathmandu highway. Locals use pilgrim buses to reach Sakya.

Where to stay and eat Top of the line for lodging is **Manasarovar Sakya Hotel** (✆ *824 2222*). A standard double goes for Y280, triple Y380 and Y688 suite. Dorm accommodation may be available for much lower pricing. This place is brought to you by the same folks who run the Yak Hotel in Lhasa and Hotel Manasarovar in Shigatse. The hotel is outstanding (for Sakya, anyway) because it has showers in the rooms – solar-generated hot water should be available in the afternoon and evening. The hotel runs its own restaurant with palatable food. Around the corner to the south is the **Grain Bureau Hotel**, with spotty triples for Y35 a bed and limited plumbing devices. At the lower end of the scale, Sakya has some Tibetan truck-stop hotels with – I almost choke on the word – 'beds'. For these, it's a case of BYOB (bring your own sleeping bag). Among these is **Sakya Tibetan Guesthouse**, located close to the *gompa*, with dorm-type beds going for around Y20.

There are hole-in-the-wall eating houses around Sakya: the **monastery teahouse** is a good place to hang out, but food supply is minimal. For more substantial fare, try some Chinese-style restaurants that are close by – pick out what you want from the kitchen and have it stir-fried. Some tiny shops can also be unearthed.

What to see and do

Sakya Gompa The immense Mongolian-style outer walls of Sakya Gompa dwarf any other structure in the town. At the corners of the *gompa* walls are corner-

SAKYA'S HIDDEN LIBRARY

At the back of the Great Sutra Chanting Hall at Sayka Gompa is a library that runs the entire length of the north–south wall, with shelves of sacred texts reaching from floor to ceiling. The library is hidden from view and access to it may not be possible – to get in, you need to find someone to unlock a small wooden door that allows you to go around the back of all the statues on display. It's pretty dark so a flashlight is needed. The musty atmosphere is positively medieval, evoking the fabled lost library of Alexandria. The library shelving here is about 60m long, 10m high and 1m deep, and filled with thousands of dusty Buddhist scriptures, many hand-copied by Tibetan calligraphers and illuminated in gold or silver ink. Near the northwest corner is a huge manuscript illuminated in gold called the Prajnaparamita Sutra. This is an 8,000-line basic scripture of all schools of Mahayana Buddhism, setting forth the Bodhisattva path to enlightenment in conversations between the Buddha and three of his disciples. The book is so large it requires its own special rack: the pages are 1.75m wide. Apparently Sakya's library survived the ravages of the Cultural Revolution because the books were hidden underground. Above the portico leading to the monastery's central courtyard is another room housing rare Sanskrit palm-leaf manuscripts, but this section is out of bounds.

turrets and watchtowers. The monastery is thought to date to the 13th century, at which time the Sakyapa were powerful enough to employ not only large numbers of Tibetan workers and artisans, but also artisans from India, Nepal and central China to decorate the monastery.

Access is only by the east gate, where an entry fee is charged. You cross a courtyard to gain entry to the inner temple, which surrounds another open courtyard. From this courtyard, try to find a staircase that leads to the upper deck of the monastery, overlooking the central courtyard. You can also walk along the outer parapets for good town views.

Getting into the monastery chapels often requires finding the right monk with the right key. You can tour the main structures here in a clockwise circuit, keyed to the map on page 211.

At the **Phuntsok Potrang** (palace), only an upstairs chapel may be accessible, containing fine murals and statues. Phuntsok Potrang is the former residence of one of the principal lamas of Sakya. The post of leadership in the Sakya sect alternates between two families, one formerly occupying Phuntsok Potrang, the other occupying Drolma Potrang opposite. The next in line for Phuntsok Palace lives in exile in Seattle, USA. **Manjushri Chapel** is a large chamber once used for important rituals. It contains a number of bookcases, and glass cases enshrining several thousand bronze statues. The statues of Manjushri and Sakyamuni Buddha here were rescued from the rubble of Sakya's northern monasteries.

The **Great Sutra Chanting Hall** is lofty and spacious – the roof is supported by four rows of pillars, with ten pillars in each row. At the base of the massive tree-trunk pillars are lotus-patterned stone pedestals; between the pillars are low carpeted benches with seating for some 400 monks. If you're lucky, Sakya monks may be conducting a sutra-chanting session, in which case you'll experience the acoustics of the hall. The main visual focus of the hall is the row of massive gilded Buddha statuary at the west wall. These statues are surrounded by thousands of artefacts, seals, ceremonial props, ritual vessels and books amassed from all over Tibet. A small doorway leads to a large hidden library behind the statues.

Continuing the clockwise circuit, you come to the **Chapel of the Silver Stupas**, which contains 11 silver stupas enclosing the remains of the past throne-holders of the Sakya lineage. Six more stupas (enclosing the remains of important past abbots of Sakya) are found in a small chapel just to the north. In the **Tara Palace** are five stupas of important throne-holders from this family branch. The Tara Palace or **Drolma Potrang** is the former residence of the current Sakya throne-holder, now living in Dehra Dun, India. Only the upstairs chapel is open, displaying superb murals; the altar has images depicting the longevity triad of Amitayus, Vijaya and White Tara.

Hiking at Sakya North On the north side of the river there used to be a monastic complex of 108 chapels. Most were destroyed during the 1960s, but some were converted into houses. Today, the north side is mostly composed of grim, grey-walled Tibetan housing, with brushwood and yak dung lining the ramparts of dwellings, and livestock living in the courtyards. You can hike on the northwest slope up to a small restored *gompa* and viewpoint (you need to find a monk to open the doors here). A precipitous path leads from the monastery along the northeast ridge to **Rinchen Gang Labrang**, an active nunnery rebuilt in 1988, and currently home to about 30 nuns. You can also do the reverse route – go directly from Sakya town up to the nunnery and find the back route to the monastery. Sakya is right off the main road, so it lies in a completely rural area, and there are other directions you can walk into the countryside. Or the countryside may come to you, as herders and traders propel yaks, donkeys or sheep right through Sakya town.

SHEGAR (*Shekar, Shelkar, Xegar, Xin Tingri, New Tingri; 4,350m*) Shegar, set back 7km off the main road, is a small Tibetan settlement with an active monastery at the northern end, at the base of a peak. Right up the rock peak are the imposing ruins of **Shining Crystal Dzong**. The castle was formerly the residence of the governor of Shegar. In 1924, a member of the British Everest expedition marvelled at the fantastic castle, perched on the 5,000m mountaintop, appearing to be fused to the rock. Today barely a single piece stands upright; it was destroyed during the Cultural Revolution.

At around the same time, the extensive **monastery** of Shegar was also destroyed. It once housed 300 Geluk monks, but today there are only a few reconstructed buildings, with a handful of monks in residence. It's worth visiting the monastery building at the base of the mountain, and then hiking up through the ruins towards the peak (watch out for the nettles). There is a path to the summit, but it's difficult to find; take along a local kid as a guide. The path starts about halfway up, to the left of the ruined fort, and winds around the back of the mountain to the prayer-flags at the very top, where, on a clear day, you are rewarded with views of Everest. The old quarter of Shegar is the village clustered closer to the *gompa*. The Chinese section is further southwest, in the vicinity of the post office.

Where to stay and eat The **Shelkar Hotel** is a Chinese concrete compound with a lack of plumbing, overpriced rooms and surly staff. Most travellers skip Shegar itself and stay at the hotels near the main highway and the higher-priced **Qomolungma Hotel** (see below). For food in Shegar, there's a Chinese restaurant opposite Shelkar Hotel, and there are several shops with small, low-quality selections of consumer goods.

SHEGAR TO TINGRI (*Major military checkpoint 7km west of Shegar junction*) At the turn-off to Shegar is a busy junction with a handful of hotels and restaurants. Travellers usually opt to stay here and visit Shegar on a day trip. The junction is also the launching point for the ride to Everest base camp (EBC).

There are over a dozen **truck-stop inns** at the junction: the cosiest is Shigar Snowland Hotel (aka Kangjong), with a Tibetan teahouse serving food. Rooms are Y50 each, with no showers. Other truck stops include Mount Everest Home Inn and Chengdu Jiudian Hotel – both for around Y40 a room.

Set back from the crossroads are two higher-priced hotels. **Everest Service Centre Hotel** (✆ 826 2833) has about 15 rooms, some with bathroom included – though the plumbing is highly erratic, if not completely shot. There are doubles and triples for Y50 a bed. This is the Fawlty Towers of Everest – the building was originally slated to be an interpretation centre for Qomolongma National Nature Preserve, with displays about wildlife and environment in a mini-museum. This will explain the derelict museum and art gallery on the ground floor, and the grand dome over the reception area. This place is where EBC tickets are issued – the guide or driver picks them up here.

About 600m from the Shegar turn-off is the **Qomolungma Hotel** (aka Dingri Zhufeng Hotel; ✆ 826 2775), which is a large Chinese-run operation with restaurant, bar and giftshop. Get your Everest T-shirts and souvenir Everest fossils here. Group tours stay here before heading off to EBC. The hotel's 60-odd rooms are expensive, but there are some cheaper dormitory-type rooms. The majority of the rooms are standard doubles at Y360. There are also three-bed rooms for Y460, and a suite for

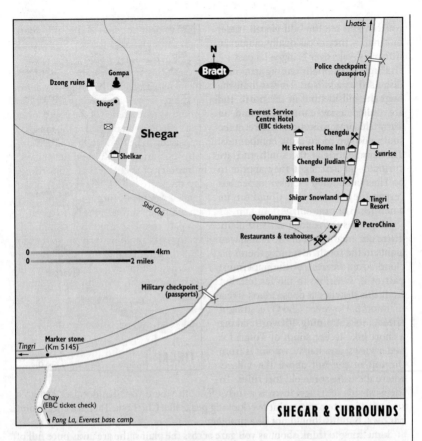

Y865. There are 12 rooms that act as dorms, of sorts: Y240 for a six-bed room with
no toilet or shower (so Y40 a bed), and Y320 for a four-bed room with toilet but no
shower (so Y80 a bed). You can use an outside shower for these rooms. And finally,
there is a Y50 'hour' room, with shower. It's not clear who uses a room like this, the
Chinese military or filthy Everest returnees.

Travellers tend to settle for the food offered in the hotels and guesthouses,
though this is pricey for what you get. There are some restaurants at the Shegar
junction: one called **Zhuang Yuan Sichuan Restaurant** offers a ten-page English
menu, but again it's pricey.

Coming from the direction of Lhasa, before you reach Shegar, there is a **police
checkpoint**. Beyond Shegar crossroads, there is a **military checkpoint** 7km west
of the junction (at roughly the KM5140 marker stone). This is the most important
checkpoint on the Lhasa to Kathmandu route – your documents will be checked,
and your luggage may be searched. Have your passport and papers ready. From
here, it's 5km west to the Everest turn-off at the KM5145 marker stone. See the *Star
Treks* chapter, page 225, for more details on this major side trip.

TINGRI *(Tinggri, Dingri, Dengre, Old Tingri, Lao Tingri, Tingri West; 4,340m)*

Tingri is a Tibetan village arrayed over a hillside. It was once a Tibetan–Nepali trading
centre for grain, goods, wool and livestock. This trade largely died out after 1959 but

you can still see the odd Nepali trader in Tingri – they occasionally saunter in with a few yaks over Nangpa La pass.

Tingri is essentially one big army base disguised as a village. Tibetan housing hugs the hillside, but at the north end are walled army compounds and an army telecommunications centre; at the south end are more army compounds. The compounds at the south end are curious – at first sight they appear to be Tibetan buildings. Closer inspection reveals they are Chinese. Could this be a new form of camouflage?

Tingri lies at the edge of a vast plain. There are great views of the Himalayan giants to the south, assuming there's no cloud cover. Everest, or the uppermost part of it, is visible to the far left, but from this distance it doesn't look like a mammoth. However, Cho Oyu, straight ahead, looks stunning. It's worth taking a short hike to the south of Tingri for better views; another viewpoint is from the top of the hill above the village, where there are some old fort ruins. To

the west side of Tingri town is a turn-off south where your Landcruiser can go a short distance to a viewpoint overlooking peaks like Cho Oyu. There's a checkpoint bar here, but this should not be a problem.

Something to think about as you gaze across the plains: the area was once full of gazelles, blue sheep, antelope and wild asses, who were remarked upon by Everest expedition members in the 1920s and 1930s. This fabulous wildlife sanctuary has completely disappeared – it was decimated by Chinese PLA troops with machine guns, hunting animals for food or for sport. Now all you can see are the odd herds of domesticated sheep, goats or yaks.

WHERE TO STAY AND EAT Facilities in Tingri are strung out along the highway. There are half-a-dozen **Tibetan inns**, including Amdo Guesthouse, Dingri Sunshine Hotel, Lao Dengre Hotel, Everest Guesthouse and Rong Sha Hotel. The best of the bunch (Amdo Guesthouse and Lao Dengre Hotel) have cosy Tibetan teahouses with carpeted seating low on the floor. Others like the Himalaya Hotel are more for truck drivers who are not picky about plumbing. You can order *momos* (meat dumplings) and potatoes at the guesthouses. The spartan rooms are around Y25–30 a bed, but can rise to Y80 at the Himalaya Hotel. Both Amdo Guesthouse and Dingri Sunshine Hotel claim to offer hot showers at certain hours for Y10 if you're a guest, or Y15 if you're an outsider. Out of town, about a kilometre to the west, is **Tingri Snowland Hotel**, with good views of Himalayan peaks from the courtyard. Rooms are Y70.

A kilometre east of Tingri along the main road (KM3193 marker stone) is **Everest Snowleopard Hotel**, a huge compound used by group tours. Everest base camp permits can be obtained here. The hotel contains over 50 rooms, priced at Y260 a double, but try bargaining – you might be able to cut that price in half, so

Y120 for a four-bed room would be more reasonable. The hotel is clean and has a large central courtyard with secure parking for vehicles. There are generator lights for a few hours a night, and televisions in the rooms. There is a small teahouse to one side, and even an 'Everest View' room (on the second floor, in the centre).

Apart from hotel eateries, there are several restaurants along the road – notably the **Sichuan Restaurant**, offering stir-fried dishes. Next to the Himalaya Hotel is the Nepali-run **Third Eye Restaurant**. A few mini-marts and small shops complete the 'strip' here. Further into Tingri village, there's very little, although you can stray across some tiny shops with a Tibetan teahouse at the back.

TINGRI TO KATHMANDU

From Tingri westward, in clear weather, you get spectacular views of Himalayan peaks, especially from passes. Tong La is a double pass, with its north crest at 4,950m and its south crest at 5,200m. You may be able to glimpse the 8,000m hulk of Shishapangma from this vicinity. After this, it's downhill all the way to Nyalam, and on to Nepal. There are two more checkpoints *en route*: the first is on the west side of the bridge spanning the Matsang River at Nyalam (strategically placed: you must go across the bridge); the second checkpoint is just above Zhangmu.

MILAREPA'S CAVE Nearing Nyalam, close to the KM5333 marker stone, is Milarepa's *gompa* and cave. The *gompa* is hidden from view at the roadside, but your guide should know where it is. If not, find some local kids to show you the way. You need to find a caretaker with keys to the cave and *gompa*, which might require some funds. Milarepa, the 11th-century sage who enlightened his students through music and poetry, never founded any monasteries. He lived a mostly itinerant existence in remote areas, living in caves and dining on nettle soup. The mystic is easily recognised in pictures and statuary due to his greenish skin and having his right hand cocked to his ear. Milarepa's cave is set inside a tiny *gompa*, which was destroyed during the Cultural Revolution but rebuilt in the early 1980s with the help of the Nepalese. In the cave you can see handprints made by Milarepa, illustrating the time when he employed his mystical powers to prevent a huge overhanging rock from falling while a disciple moved a smaller rock in place as a support pillar. Although the cave first belonged to the Kagyu sect, it was taken over by the Geluk order centuries ago.

NYALAM (*3,750m; checkpoint on west side of bridge spanning Matsang River*) Nyalam is a truck stop on the Lhasa to Kathmandu route, with a fair range of hotels and small restaurants. The centre of town is a large parking lot for trucks and other vehicles; there's another truck-parking area on the southeast side of town, next to a large karaoke complex. Because the town is easily supplied from Zhangmu, there is a much greater range of food and goods available here. Along the main road, commerce is mostly operated by Chinese or Nepali merchants, although some shops are run by Tibetans. Take a side street to the west to find the old Tibetan quarter, with traditional-style stone buildings and yaks lounging in doorways. There is a small *gompa* at the northern end of this street.

Further afield, Nyalam is the base for trekking to Shishapangma base camp (see the *Star Treks* chapter, page 234). Even if you have no intention of trekking to the base camp, the initial part of this route – accessed from the northwest end of Nyalam – is well worth a day-hike, or an overnight hike if you take a tent and sleeping bag.

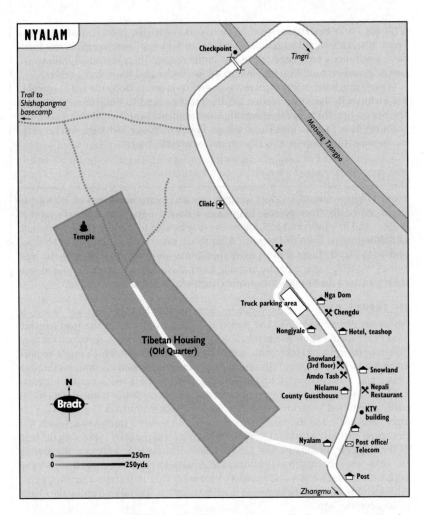

NYALAM

Checkpoint

Tingri

Trail to Shishapangma basecamp

Matsang Tsangpo

Clinic

Temple

Tibetan Housing
(Old Quarter)

Truck parking area

Nga Dom

Chengdu

Nongjyale

Hotel, teashop

Snowland
(3rd floor)

Amdo Tash

Snowland

Nielamu
County Guesthouse

Nepali
Restaurant

KTV
building

N

Bradt

Nyalam

Post office/
Telecom

0 ————— 250m
0 ————— 250yds

Post

Zhangmu

If you're coming from Lhasa, a highly unusual treat in Nyalam is ... trees. Stacks of wood are piled up, later to be used as fuel. Nyalam is low enough for poplar trees to grow, and other wood is brought in from forested slopes lower down.

Where to stay and eat Nyalam is well supplied with hotels, small restaurants and shops, but nothing fancy. The Tibetan-style **Snowland Hotel** is one of the best choices here, but is often full as expeditions use it. Rooms are Y60 a double. The hotel has a rooftop deck. Among the other hotels and guesthouses are **Nyalam Hotel** (Y20 a room), **Nga Dom** (Y30 a room), **Nielamu County Guesthouse** (Y60 a room – recommended) and the bland-looking **Post Hotel**. A string of restaurants lines the main road near the truck parking area. The **Nepali Restaurant** is good, serving large silver platters with *dhal* and lots of side dishes. Also try **Snowland Restaurant**, located on the third floor of the building opposite Snowland Hotel. For real atmosphere, nearby **Amdo Tash Restaurant** is the best – you can choose between Tibetan low couches or Western-style seating. On the breakfast menu: apple muesli and chocolate pancakes.

NYALAM TO ZHANGMU From Nyalam, there's an amazing drop off the plateau, down through lush jungle terrain with gushing waterfalls and singing birds all the way to Zhangmu. It's a 'gorge-ous' ride – this is one altitude shift you'll remember for some time to come. Because of cascading water (sometimes springing straight over the cliff sides near the road) the route here is prone to rock falls and landslides, especially in the monsoon season. Because it is at a much lower elevation, Zhangmu is liable to much heavier monsoon rains than, say, Nyalam.

The Chinese name for the entire route between Lhasa and Kathmandu is the 'Friendship Highway'. The Chinese name a lot of border features into neighbouring countries like this: Friendship Gate (Youyi Guan, the border crossing into Vietnam) and Friendship Bridge (Youyi Qiao, the border crossing into Nepal). It's not clear whether the Chinese constructed the Friendship Highway as a military route into Nepal, but the Chinese designed and built the road on the Nepalese side all the way into Kathmandu. The two countries remain on very good terms – for the moment.

ZHANGMU (*Dram, Khasa; 2,300m; checkpoint at top of hill above Zhangmu*) There's little to see in the border town of Zhangmu (pronounced Jang-moo) unless you like watching Nepalis, Tibetans and Chinese unload and reload goods and haggle over currency exchange rates. Hair stylists, karaoke bars and loose women abound. Zhangmu is no longer Tibet – it's more like a Nepalese trading town, with Nepalese

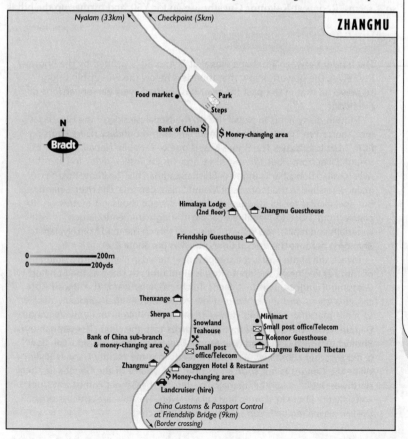

products everywhere, Nepalese moneychangers, Nepalese merchants and scores of Nepalese porters. The town is arrayed along some steep switchbacks that snake down to the Chinese customs and immigration post. Half the town appears to be a construction zone, so things may well have changed from the description here.

Out of synch Nepal is 2¼ hours behind Tibet, which operates on Beijing time. Thus when it's 12.00 (noon) in Zhangmu (Chinese immigration post), it's 09.45 in Kodari (Nepalese immigration). Bear this in mind when considering banking hours and immigration post hours of opening. Sunday can be a non-working day in Zhangmu, although the main bank is still open.

Where to stay and eat At the mid-levels of Zhangmu are some **budget guesthouses**. Ask to see a room before putting any money down; rooms can be more basic than you might imagine. Lower down is the main group tour hotel, the cavernous **Zhangmu Hotel** (✆ *874 2221*), which is in cahoots with CITS. If entering or exiting, you can use the ground-floor bar at the Zhangmu Hotel to take a breather, or to clean up. Although the rooms at Zhangmu Hotel are expensive (Y400 for a double), you can talk your way into cheaper dorm rooms downstairs at Y50 a bed. **Ganggyen Hotel**, opposite, has similarly priced dorm beds, and cheaper doubles at Y150. The further north you are in Zhangmu, the cheaper the hotels, or so it seems. Rooms at **Kokonor Guesthouse** go for Y50, and further up the hill is

---

THE RIVER FROM TIBET

The border between Tibet and Nepal at Zhangmu is defined by the Bhote Kosi River, the powerful flow that thunders below the Friendship Bridge – so powerful that in the past the river has washed away earlier versions of the bridge.

Though many rivers in Nepal rise on the Nepalese side of the Himalayas (not sourced in Tibet), there are important trans-boundary rivers coursing from Tibet into Nepal. The Bhote Kosi is one of these. In Nepali, Bhote Kosi means 'River from Tibet' (*Bhot* = Tibet, and *Kosi* or *Koshi* = river). In Tibet the river is called Rongshar Tsangpo or Shishapangma Chu. The Bhote Kosi has its main watershed in the foothills of Mount Shishapangma. The river is narrow, but spectacular for its staggering drop of several thousand metres on its course from Tibet to Nepal, cascading through tremendous gorges with waterfalls and rapids. You will experience all this on the road from Nyalam to Zhangmu because the road at times parallels the Bhote Kosi.

In fact, the Bhote Kosi is the steepest river rafted in Nepal. With a gradient of 15m per kilometre, the Bhote Kosi is eight times as steep as the Sun Kosi (Matsang Tsangpo), which it feeds further downstream. The Bhote Kosi carves a steep and direct drop at the Nepal border that gradually eases to more placid streams and calmer pools with a 46km run at Lamosunga Dam in Nepal. The Sun Kosi then joins forces with the Arun (Tibetan name: Bhumchu), which is sourced near Mount Everest on the north side. The flow is fed by other tributaries – and then feeds into the mighty Ganges River. While the Ganges is not sourced in Tibet (the source of the Ganges lies in northwest India), a number of major feeders for the Ganges come from Tibet – mainly the Bhote Kosi, Arun and Karnali rivers. The intricate river system of the Himalayan region is complex and interconnected.

the **Friendship Guesthouse**. Intriguing for its name is Zhangmu Returned Tibetan Hotel, also in this area.

In the food line, you can rifle through the shops in lower Zhangmu, bearing good stocks of Indian and Nepalese goods such as mango fruit drinks and biscuits from Kathmandu. The town has several mini-marts with a good range of chocolate and other delicacies for the deprived. **Snowland Teahouse** is just north of Ganggyen Restaurant (at the eponymous hotel). Group tours eat in the dining hall at Zhangmu Hotel.

Other practicalities

Banking If exiting Tibet, you can change residual Chinese yuan back into US dollars (with original bank receipts). A much better deal is to change Chinese yuan into Nepalese rupees. Change either at the Bank of China (BOC, two branches) or with moneychangers close by. It's preferable to do these transactions inside a shop rather than on the street: always carefully count the money offered before presenting your part of the deal. The BOC is in theory open from 09.00–12.00 and 15.00–18.00, running on Tibetan time. In Zhangmu you can pay for goods in either Chinese yuan or Nepalese rupees, but once out of Zhangmu, Chinese yuan are useless anywhere in Nepal (you can, however, trade them with travellers at guesthouses in Kathmandu).

ZHANGMU TO KODARI From Zhangmu town, it's 9km straight downhill to Chinese customs and immigration, parked right next to the Friendship Bridge. If you are leaving Tibet, your driver and guide will bid you farewell here. On exit, Chinese customs may search baggage looking for 'antiques', which means anything older than 1959. Immigration checks are simple – you are stamped out.

Those entering Tibet at Zhangmu are usually in an arranged group headed for Lhasa. There are several hurdles here. The first is clearing immigration and being stamped in. The second is the baggage check: customs may be thorough and they will be looking for pro-Tibetan material that is available in Kathmandu. Then you set about changing money, and proceed northward.

The Friendship Bridge is the real border crossing, with the Bhote Kosi River delineating the border. Halfway across the bridge is a dividing line – one half of the bridge belongs to Nepal, the other half to China. At exactly this point, it seems, you should switch sides of the road – from right-hand drive (China) to left-hand drive (Nepal). Nepal immigration is in Kodari, 2km from the Friendship Bridge. Your passport is checked here – if you have no visa, you will be stamped in. You just provide US$25 (cash only) for a 15-day visa, US$40 for a 30-day visa or US$100 for a three-month visa. A passport photo is required. Nepal customs is a bit further down the line near Tatopani.

KATHMANDU The Nepalese capital is only five hours away by jeep. A ride of 114km along a paved road from Kodari brings you into the bazaars of Asan Tole, in old Kathmandu – in former times the trading crossroads of the empires of India, China and Tibet. You'll find more apple pie, ice cream, shampoo and English newspapers in a 200m stretch of a street in the Thamel area of Kathmandu than you will in all of Tibet. The trick is not to go berserk when faced with such myriad choices. The sudden change of diet can wreak havoc on your system: switching to apple pie and ice cream after months of living off biscuits in Tibet can be traumatic. Still, clean white sheets, Swedish massage and doses of BBC won't hurt. They may even be therapeutic.

Kathmandu has great resources for things Tibetan: there are Tibetan monasteries scattered around the valley, and there are Tibetan-run hotels, shops and travel agents

6

in Kathmandu's Thamel district. If you are incoming from Tibet, Kathmandu has all the forbidden and seditious material on Tibet that Chinese officials so diligently search baggage for. Kathmandu has one of the highest concentrations of English bookstores of any place in the Indian subcontinent. Lots of secondhand books are available as well. The result is that you can find just about any book on Tibet ever printed. You can find Free Tibet T-shirts, flags, and many handcrafted Tibetan items that are superior in quality to those found in Tibet – carpets, for instance. All this is something of an anomaly (or a money-spinner?) because the Nepalese government is heavy-handed in preventing or squashing pro-Tibet demonstrations – or even simple gatherings of Tibetans in Kathmandu. There is an increasing presence of Chinese military advisers in Nepal, and Chinese embassy staff in Kathmandu have been observed directing operations by Nepalese police beating and arresting Tibetan demonstrators.

It's wise to keep an eye on internet media for current information on areas of Nepal that might be trouble hotspots. Keep in mind that Nepalese news sources are heavily censored: they tend to paint a rosy picture of the place, glossing over potential trouble.

Where to stay There are many hotels in Kathmandu to choose from. A reliable one with good security, peaceful ambience and central location is **Kathmandu Guesthouse**, in Thamel (977 1 470 0632; e *info@ktmgh.com; www.ktmgh.com*). Here you can get dorm rooms, or you can splurge on rooms with garden views for US$40 a night. In the same compound are adventure **tour operators** who can fix you up with everything from mountain-bike tours to white-water rafting.

7

Star Treks

HIGH-ALTITUDE FORAYS TO EVEREST, KAILASH AND BEYOND

This section describes some treks in western Tibet that individuals have successfully tackled, but which are highly challenging, both in terms of physical effort and dodging demands for permits. The rewards? We're talking about a backdrop of the highest peaks on earth here – moonscapes, star treks and stellar vistas! Trekking in Tibet is expeditionary in nature, even if you are part of an organised group. Yaks and porters will ferry supplies. This is one of the few places in the world where trekking is assisted by behemoths, in the form of sturdy yaks. If you plan to trek on your own, you should be looking at the regions of Kham and Amdo in far-eastern Tibet, as you can get past permit restrictions there (see *Chapter 8*).

The more remote the location, the longer the list of permits you will need. Getting permits for Kailash or Guge in far-west Tibet could take a week of wrangling in Lhasa – and the process is still not over, as other permits need to be acquired *en route*. In other words, start early on the paperwork.

Trekking should entail minimal impact on the local people, and respect for the environment. You can start with your travel agency, by insisting that your driver and crew do not throw garbage out the window of a Landcruiser – and that any tips given will be contingent on their respect for the environment.

When trekking in an arranged group, ask in advance about conditions for porters. It is the responsibility of the operator to ensure adequate equipment and safety for porters, so by all means press the operator on these concerns. Are the porters properly clothed and equipped for the rigours of mountain travel? In Nepal, there have been a number of accidents – and deaths – involving porters, due to lack of adequate footwear, clothing and gear, poor medical care, and neglect and mistreatment by trek leaders. A porter should not be setting out with a 50kg load to tackle a high snowbound pass in tattered running shoes, but this has happened. Such neglect can result in frostbite. The International Porter Protection Group (IPPG) is lobbying trekking companies to ensure that porters have adequate equipment and that they are provided with the same standard of medical care as trekkers and leaders would themselves enjoy. This means that in the event of illness, a porter is not simply paid off and sent back down a mountain alone – which has resulted in deaths from altitude sickness in Nepal in the past. In Tibet, altitude sickness should not be an issue for porters as Tibetans are well acclimatised. However, some Nepalese trekking outfits bring in their own porters from Nepal who could be from lowland areas, rather than Sherpa porters, who are from highland areas. In Tibet, porters are more commonly used on large expeditions. Organised trekking trips in Tibet are more likely to be yak-supported, or with combinations of porters and yak caravans.

Two excellent guidebooks cover trekking routes in Tibet in detail. Kotan Publishing's *Mapping the Tibetan World* provides details on trekking not only in

Tibet but also across the Himalayan range. Gary McCue's *Trekking Tibet* would make a great companion volume to this book if you are keen on trekking. McCue covers treks in the Kham and Amdo regions in his book as well.

A handful of classic Tibet treks – enough to keep you busy for quite some time – are described in the following section. The approaches and trailheads are all reachable by Landcruiser.

Some trekkers get greedy: you can bag several of the following base camps in a single Landcruiser trip. The route might run from Lhasa to Everest base camp, then on to Kailash, complete the *kora* there, and exit to Nepal via Nyalam. This can all be accomplished in 14 days.

TREKKING IN THE EVEREST REGION

There are three main targets in the Everest area: Rongbuk (Everest north base camp), Karta (Everest east base camp) and Cho Oyu base camp. You can reach Rongbuk by Landcruiser. Two staging points to bear in mind are Shegar to the east and Tingri to the west. Refer to the Lhasa to Kathmandu route map in *Chapter 6*, pages 188–9, for locations.

Everest is not in the same class as Kailash when it comes to being a sacred peak. For one thing, the monastery at Everest was only established early in the 20th century (the shrines at Kailash go back to the 13th century). More importantly, Kailash has always been off-limits for climbers, and there are no throngs of Tibetan pilgrims headed for Everest because you can't circumambulate the mountain. Nevertheless, Everest is known to the Tibetans as Chomolangma, which transliterates as Queen (*jhomo*) on an Ox (*glangma*), otherwise more prosaically rendered as 'Mother Goddess of the World'. Tibetans believe that the goddess Miyo Langsangma resides atop Mount Everest: her mount is an ox, although other images show her astride a tiger. She is one of the five Tsering sisters; according to legend, each of these five goddesses inhabits a high peak in the Himalayan region. The goddess is not one to tangle with lightly. Witness what happened to the first expeditions. In 1921, Tibet opened expedition attempts on Everest to British climbers. The monks at Rongbuk were none too keen on the idea of climbers wending their way up a sacred peak: they predicted dire things would come to pass – which, in the case of Mallory and Irvine, they did. The monastery practice of blessing climbers rather than cursing them appears to have started in the late 1920s or 1930s when Nepali Sherpas were employed by the British as porters and cooks. Because Sherpas are Tibetan Buddhist, monasteries started dispensing blessings for safe passage on the mountain. Sherpas climbing from both sides visit monasteries before going to base camp, where they light butter lamps in supplication of various deities. At base camp itself, Sherpas make offerings of *tsampa* and *chang* to the goddess Chomolangma in the belief that the wrathful goddess will turn a blind eye and allow them passage. *Tsampa* is thrown skyward; ice axes and other gear also get a ritual blessing before climbers go higher.

DRIVING TO RONGBUK Everest base camp is remarkable in that it's a drive-in approach. The rough road to the base camp at the north side of Everest was engineered in 1960 for Chinese mountaineering attempts on the summit.

If you start from Shegar crossroads in the morning, you should be able to reach Rongbuk Monastery by mid-afternoon, all going well. The distance is around 100km, and driving time is around three to four hours for the whole stretch. Tickets to enter Qomolangma National Nature Preserve are issued at the Everest Service Centre near the Shegar crossroads. You will need a Y180 entry ticket for each person, plus a Y400 vehicle entry ticket (this bill should already have been included with your touring itinerary). Your passport is checked at a military checkpoint west of Shegar, and the EBC tickets are checked at Chay (there is no check on the way out, only on the way in). Take your time along this part: the views are stupendous. At **Pang La**, there are views of the entire Himalayan range. You can stop in Tashidzom for noodles at **Benba Guesthouse**, which has a cosy teahouse out the back. From here, a half-hour drive brings you to the village of **Pasum**. Should you require it, Pasum has accommodation in hotels (Snowman Hotel, Y40 a room) and in teahouse tents (around Y15 a bed). Or you can just carry on to Rongbuk and sleep there.

TREKKING TO RONGBUK There are two routes into Rongbuk on foot – from the Shegar end, or from the Tingri end. Trekkers tend to favour the walk in from the Tingri end because there's no checkpoint to contend with and it's easier to hire pack animals in Tingri. However, if your equipment is not that good, or your intention is to get a ride in and trek back, then you should stick to the Shegar route, which has more in the way of lodging and teahouse support. You can combine the routes by taking one route in and the other route out (and consider a side trip to Cho Oyu base camp on the Tingri route). You might want to think about hiring a mule (or yak) and handler to carry supplies and food. Animals are scarce when harvesting is in progress; if you're only going one way with a pack animal, the handler may want compensation for the return journey.

From Tingri The walk into Rongbuk takes about four days. If you are on foot, it seems you dodge permit fees, since you do not go past any checkpoint on this route. The first day's target is not particularly strenuous: the village of **Lungjhang** (4,500m), with beds available. The next day *is* strenuous – it's best to work your way towards the base of **Lanma La** and camp out near a herder's camp. The next day, you can trek over Lanma La (5,150m) and make it to the village of **Zhommug**, where basic lodging awaits. Zhommug is not far from the jeep road that winds in from Shegar: you should be able to reach Rongbuk by the end of the fourth day of trekking.

From Shegar You essentially walk along the jeep track to Rongbuk. The trek takes three to four days; there are enough lodges along the way to qualify this as Tibet's first 'teahouse trekking' route. Starting out from the Tibetan truck stop at the KM5133 marker stone, you can walk to the Everest turn-off at the KM5145 marker stone. There is a checkpoint at **Chay** for EBC tickets. You can hire a mule at Chay for the trip as far as **Tashidzom** (Peruche, 4,075m), where there are some Tibetan-run lodges and a few shops. On the next leg of the journey, between Tashidzom and Chosang, you can stay in **Pasum** (4,100m), which has teahouse-lodges with cheap beds. The last place with beds is Chosang, but trekkers have found the folk here particularly light-fingered and cold-hearted, so you may want to skip this place. From here it is a steady climb to Rongbuk.

Trek alert Tibetan villagers in the Everest region are notoriously prone to thievery. You have to consider that there are not a lot of shops out this way: taking things from visitors is somehow considered fair game. Even hosts at village inns will brazenly take small items, and when confronted, think it is no big deal. Keep an eye on gear that you can't do without – watch those water bottles. Always negotiate carefully and establish prices before consuming any food or drink at teahouses in the area, as there have been problems. Another alarming problem is that innkeepers in the Everest region have been known to beat up their wives. So what do you do –

Nepal border

Hot springs

TINGRI

Phung Chu

Lungjhang

0 ——— 10km
0 ——— 6 miles

Ra Chu

Zhommug

Lanma La
5150m

Chophug

Chosang

Kyetrak

Cho Oyu base camp
4970m

Rongbuk Monastery
4950m

Puse La
5300m

Rongshar

Chobo Rabtsang
6666m

Everest North Face
base camp
5150m

Nangpa La
5710m

Cho Oyu
8153m

Gyachung Kang
7952m

Camp 1

Rongbuk Glacier

East Rongbuk Glacier

Camp 2

N   E   P   A   L

Base camp

Camp 3

Kala Pattar

Lho La

Everest
8848m

Gokyo

Gorak Shep

Khumbu Glacier

Namche Bazaar

Lhotse
8501m

KEY
===== 4x4 dirt road
····· Walking trail

Lhatse

SHEGAR
(EBC tickets)

Shel Chu

Military checkpoint

Chay
(ticket check)

Pang La
5150m

Tashidzom (Peruche)

Pasum

Dzakar Chu

Doya La
5180m

Phung Chu (Arun)

N

Bradt

Karta Changri

Karta
3750m

Karta Chu

Karta Yulba

Kartaphu

Karta Valley

Langma La
5330m

Everest East Face
base camp
5050m

Kangshung Glacier

Shao La
4970m

Kama Chu

Pethangtse
6710m

Kama Valley

ignore this late at night, or try to step in? It's a tough call. Donkey and yak handlers can be hard to get along with and argumentative. This has little to do with language, and more to do with temperament.

RONGBUK (*Dza Rongphu; 4,950m*) Rongbuk Gompa, the highest monastery in the world, was established sometime in the early part of the 20th century, under the Nyingmapa sect. Its history is sketchy. Rongbuk Valley was known as the 'sanctuary of the birds'. There was a strict ban on killing any animal in the area. Domestic animals could be eaten as long as they were slaughtered outside the valley. The British Everest reconnaissance party, arriving at Rongbuk in 1921, found the animals of the valley extraordinarily tame: wild blue sheep would come down to the monastery. There were hundreds of lamas and pilgrims engaged in meditation in a cluster of brightly coloured buildings. The British did not meet the Head Lama on their first expedition as he was off doing a year's 'time' in a cave. It was common for hermits to go on meditation retreats in caves in the valley, subsisting on water and barley passed to them once a day.

The monastery was razed in the 1960s. At the instigation of Red Guards, Tibetans were encouraged to disassemble the buildings for raw materials, such as precious wood beams. The monastery's stupa was split in two and ransacked of its treasures. The abbot of Rongbuk fled over the Himalaya and established a new monastery at Junbesi in Nepal.

In the late 1980s and early 1990s, rebuilding took place at Rongbuk and its monastery has been resurrected, along with the stupa that figures prominently in tourist photography of the scene. Rongbuk Gompa is unusual because it has a mixed community of monks and nuns – about 20 or so live here. Surrounding the monastery is a village, and there are cave retreats scattered around the hilltops.

There are great day hikes around Rongbuk: you can clamber around and get fantastic views of the north face of Everest. The Big E will blow you away – literally, if a wind comes howling down the valley. Everest does not always co-operate – it might be obscured by low cloud. But if the sun is out and it's clear, Everest will take your breath away, too. At the north face of Everest, you are looking at the highest mountain face on earth.

Where to stay Rongbuk is very popular with both Western and Chinese travellers, the latter group loaded with expensive cameras and barking into their mobile phones (there is a telecom tower right at Rongbuk that enables mobile reception). Due to this popularity, rooms can be in short supply. You can stay at a simple 15-room **guesthouse** run by Rongbuk Monastery for Y40 a bed (three or four beds in a room). The common toilet is the pits. Hot water in Thermoses can be obtained, but don't expect luxuries here – nights can be very cold, and electricity is in short supply. A teahouse attached to Rongbuk Monastery guesthouse serves noodles. The nunnery uphill has a few rooms for guests.

Across the way is the ritzier 'Pink Palace', aka **Drufung Binguan** (✆858 4535), with 12 rooms going for a hefty Y300 each. Chinese architects are not noted for their good taste, or for trying to fit designs into the environment – this one hits a new high under the heading 'abominable'. Doors may be missing, leading to cold temperatures. The plumbing works periodically – sometimes down to one squat loo for the entire hotel. The hotel has a large second-floor dining hall with partial Everest views.

Beyond Rongbuk, a few kilometres further toward Everest base camp, are **tent camps**, where up to five tourists at a time can lodge. The maximum number of five tourists has been set so that a single tent does not corner the business. Thus larger groups are divided into different tents. The tents routinely charge Y40 a bed and offer simple meals cooked on a central stove. Watch your stuff – there are no doors that lock. Might be better to leave gear locked in the Landcruiser. A few problems with the tent camps: there's no privacy (your tent host shares the space with you), the central stove can make the interior quite smoky, and you can freeze your butt off at night. A good sleeping bag comes in handy here.

North Face base camp
From Rongbuk (or from your tent camp) you can walk or take a bus for the final stretch out to the North Face base camp, at an elevation of 5,150m. The base camp is 8km from Rongbuk. This might better be termed 'Everest Tourist base camp', as the real base camp for mountaineers lies further on. The tourist base camp is a motley collection of tent teahouses and other temporary structures. You can stay in a teahouse for under a dollar a night. Tibetan vendors pursue visitors and try to sell them fossils and cheap jewellery. The area is a glacial moraine – a bleak and desolate place – but awe-inspiring because it is so close to the Big E. It is also home to the highest post office in the world, a kiosk run by China Post, where for an extra fee, you can drop a postcard or two that will be franked with an Everest postmark.

At the edge of the tented area is a sign that says you are not allowed to proceed further, on risk of paying a fine of US$200. That is, unless you sign up for a four-day trek at US$100 a person. By strange coincidence, there is a tour agent at base camp who can arrange this very trek for hard cash, but you must have your own trekking and sleeping gear. The four-day trek would take you out to the real mountaineering base camp and back.

Beyond base camp lies a trek described by Gary McCue (*Trekking Tibet*) as 'the Highest Trek in the World … an incredible journey to Camp III (6,340m) and to the base of the North Col via the East Rongphu Glacier'. McCue says that the ascent is possible without climbing gear, though it would be advisable to have items like crampons when traversing the glacier. You need excellent back-up and considerable logistics to undertake such a strenuous – and potentially hazardous – journey.

THE BIG E
At higher elevations, Everest is scoured by 100km/h winds: the constant threat of avalanche, being crushed by an ice serac (a pinnacle of ice on the surface of a glacier), falling down a crevasse, or succumbing to altitude make it a deadly peak to climb.

In 1921, the Tibetan government opened the Himalaya to the British. The first nine expedition attempts on Everest were made from the Tibetan side in the 1920s and 1930s, because Nepal was inaccessible to Europeans at the time. None of these teams succeeded. Early expedition climbers wore woollens, thick tweeds, Norfolk jackets and studded leather boots. The only hardware was ice axes and primitive crampons, but oxygen tanks were also lugged along. On the third expedition attempt, in 1924, George Mallory and Andrew Irvine were making good time for the summit when they were enveloped in cloud and never seen again (but see page 231). Whether they succeeded in gaining the summit remains one of mountaineering's great mysteries. Another mystery concerns Eric Shipton, who, connected with these British attempts, photographed footprints left by the Yeti (known as *migyu* in Tibetan). Given to practical jokes, it seems likely that Shipton faked the footprints. Failing to summit Everest, Shipton and his climbing cronies set about bagging a host of first ascents on lesser peaks around Everest.

Since the 19th century, Tibet has attracted more than its fair share of visionaries and eccentric travellers; with Everest, spectacularly so. In 1934, British ex-army officer Maurice Wilson announced that he was going to crash-land a Tiger Moth on the slopes of the mountain and climb from there to plant the Union Jack on the summit. Incredibly, Wilson got financial backing, learned how to fly and flew all the way to India, where officials promptly seized his plane. Spurred on by his megalomaniacal brand of divine faith, Wilson found his way through Tibet disguised as a deaf and dumb monk. At Rongbuk, he got on famously with the head lama. Wilson apparently believed that earlier British expeditions had cut an ice stairway straight up the mountain – he thought he would simply climb this staircase and pray his way to the top. He had little equipment, no warm clothing and no mountaineering experience. Another British expedition of 1935 (under Eric Shipton) found his frozen body at around 6,700m.

In 1947, Canadian climber Earl Denman sneaked into Rongbuk to assault the mountain: he got above Camp 3, but turned back. This was the last attempt from the Tibetan side for some time, as the Tibetans banned the issue of travel permits to Tibet. In 1950, after the Chinese invasion, no foreign climbers were allowed in. Western attention had already shifted to Nepal, which had become accessible after 1949. In May 1953, New Zealander Edmund Hillary and Sherpa Tenzing Norgay 'knocked the bastard off' (as Hillary put it), summiting from Nepal as part of a British expedition.

Meanwhile, from the Tibetan side, the Chinese would not allow climbers to attempt the route until they had succeeded in putting Chinese mountaineers on top first. In 1959, the Chinese and the Russians undertook a joint reconnaissance. With the rift between China and Russia in 1960, China carried on the work alone, and then stepped into the Everest spotlight in a big way. In March 1960, the Chinese claimed that all of Everest, as well as an 8km stretch south to Namche Bazaar, belonged to China. At the time, China was busy testing the limits of Indian and Nepalese patience in border disputes. The Everest claim did not sit well with the Nepalese prime minister, who made a counter-claim that all of Everest belonged to Nepal, including parts of Rongbuk Glacier. The same month, a 214-man Chinese expedition arrived at Rongbuk base camp for a summit attempt. A Chinese and Tibetan climbing team reached the summit, but there were no photographs as the summit attempt took place at night. In 1975 (by which time the border between Tibet and Nepal had been firmly delineated as running across the summit) the Chinese mounted another huge expedition. One Chinese and eight Tibetans gained the summit and left a tripod there as definite proof of their ascent. The potential for Tibetan climbers on the slopes of Everest, as opposed to Sherpa climbers, has been little realised, largely because of Tibetans fearing the wrath of the peak's resident goddess. But Tibetan climbers are superbly adapted to altitude and certainly up to the challenge if taboos can be overcome. Of the eight Tibetan climbers who summited in 1975 from the Tibetan side, one was a woman, simply identified as Phantog. Phantog (also known as Pan Duo) was not only the first woman to summit from the north side of Everest, she narrowly missed being the first woman ever to summit Everest (Junko Tabei, a Japanese woman, summited from Nepal ten days earlier). To put this in perspective: the first Sherpa woman would not reach the summit of Everest until 1993 – almost 20 years later.

In 1980, the Chinese, satisfied that their claim had been accepted, opened the north side again to foreigners. In August 1980, in contrast to the huge Chinese teams, came a team of two – Italian climber Reinhold Messner and his girlfriend. In one of mountaineering's most extraordinary feats, he made it to the top of Everest, solo and without oxygen, on a variation of the route pioneered by Mallory and Irvine. Two years earlier, climbing from the South Col, Messner and fellow-climber Habeler had been the first to climb the mountain without oxygen. Until they attempted this feat, it was unknown if a climber would survive reaching the top without oxygen, as past 7,000m is known as the Death Zone (no further acclimatisation is possible). At Everest's peak, a climber without oxygen could suffer debilitating physical and mental problems. Messner did not go in entirely blind – he was a passenger on an unpressurised plane flying at high altitudes, and tested himself without oxygen for short periods. Other climbers have since reached the top of Everest without oxygen, including a female climber, Lydia Bradey from New Zealand, who summited in 1988.

In 1986 Messner claimed another record – the ascent of all 14 peaks over 8,000m, including ascents of Everest and Shishapangma in Tibet. To date, only a handful of climbers have repeated the feat. Messner also narrowly missed being the first in the race to bag the highest peak on all seven continents. This record fell to Canadian climber Patrick Morrow, who added Carstensz Pyramid (in West Irian/Papua New Guinea) to the equation. More than a hundred climbers have since bagged the Seven Summits. New Zealander Rob Hall raised the bar by conquering the Seven Summits in seven months. Others have gone on to bag the Seven Summits plus the two poles.

Where will it end? Well, there's still the snowboarding record up for grabs: climb the Seven Summits and snowboard down. In 2001, Marco Siffredi snowboarded from the summit of Everest to Advance Base Camp, while a year earlier, Davo Karnicar made the first true ski descent from the summit via the South Col. Marco Siffredi made another snowboard attempt on the Hornbein Couloir in 2002 – and was never seen again. Another Everest descent record: in September 1988, French climber Jean Marc Boivin paraglided from the summit, landing at Camp 2 (Nepalese side) in 11 minutes. The first septuagenarian summit was achieved in May 2003 by 70-year-old Japanese climber, Miura. But the most incredible feat of all is by the man who did – quite literally – go in blind: Erik Weihenmayer, a blind climber from the US, reached the summit in May 2001. Weihenmayer went on to bag the Seven Summits.

Almost 90% of Everest climbers fail to reach the summit. Nevertheless, at the last count, over 2,400 ascents of Everest have been successfully made (including repeat summiteers), the majority from the Nepalese side (the year 2004 alone saw 330 summit ascents). Meanwhile, over 190 deaths have been recorded in climbing attempts on Everest and, grisly but true, most of the bodies still lie where they fell. Roughly a third of the deaths recorded are of Sherpas. Many of the Sherpas act as porters, but others have developed reputations as fine climbers – Apa Sherpa has summited Everest 14 times, and Ang Rita Sherpa has summited the peak ten times without oxygen. In May 2005, Nepalese couple Pem Dorjee and Moni Mulepati were the first to marry on the summit.

Politics at the top: Everest is the only place in Tibet where the Tibetan flag can be flown without interference. Sherpa climbers tackling Everest from the Nepalese side are prone to leaving small Tibetan flags fluttering from the summit; they also leave an image of the Dalai Lama in the snow at the summit. When he summited in 1996, Jamling Norgay (son of Tenzing Norgay, who summited in 1953) left an ice axe with the flags of Tibet, Nepal, India, the USA and the UN flying from it – which appears much larger than life in an IMAX movie about Everest.

In May 1999, a remarkable discovery was made by climber Conrad Anker at around 8,100m on the upper slopes of Everest. He found George. After going missing for close on 75 years, George Mallory turned up on the internet, of all places: a photograph of his bleached torso was posted by expedition members to their website (*www.mountainzone.com*). This did not sit well with descendants of the Mallory family (including Mallory's grandson, George, who summited Everest in 1995), and nor did other media exposure of the body, including a cover-photo for *Outside Magazine*. Those selling the pictures claimed that the photographs were proof that Mallory had been found. Edmund Hillary said it was disgusting to expose the body in such a fashion; that the dead should be given some respect.

For Edmund Hillary, there were some tense moments: in Mallory's pockets were notes that showed he was toting more oxygen canisters than previously thought, which means he and Irvine might have been able to make the summit. But no camera was found on Mallory's body. So who got to the top first? Edmund Hillary let slip in his autobiography that he could lay claim to being first, a few steps ahead of Tenzing Norgay. Meanwhile, it was discovered that Tenzing Norgay was not Nepalese at all, but of Tibetan blood, so one of the premier summiteers, fittingly, is Tibetan. He grew up in the village of Moyun, in the Karta Valley, in the shadow of Everest. Seeking a better life, his parents left Tibet and walked over to the Nepalese side: Norgay grew up in Sherpa country. He later eloped with a Sherpa woman named Dawa: looking for work, they trekked to Darjeeling, the base of all the early Everest expeditions. Tenzing Norgay kept his real origins obscure, and finally took out Indian citizenship under the patronage of Prime Minister Nehru. Tenzing Norgay never lied about his origins, but he didn't quite tell the truth, either: it was not until after his death in 1986 that the full story emerged. Here's an intriguing link: Norgay and Mallory may have actually met. Mallory's 1921 expedition passed

MOUNTAIN BURIAL

One of Everest's less salubrious records is being the highest rubbish dump in the world. Some expeditions have been undertaken solely to clear out the hundreds of oxygen bottles and canisters strewn at the highest camp, about 900m below the summit. Something that cannot be as easily removed, however, are the bodies of dead climbers. Because of the weight, carrying back dead alpinists from this zone – at these high altitudes – is exceedingly difficult. Instead, if possible, bodies of climbers are simply pushed into crevasses, a method of dispatch known as 'mountain burial'.

That's indeed if there's still a body left. Macabre sightings at high elevations include partial cadavers. These act as grim landmarks, and reminders of how thin the line is between life and death up here. The area above 7,000m is called the Death Zone because the body cannot acclimatise here. Climbers have to move quickly in this zone before their strength is sapped by dehydration, cold and high altitude.

It is said there is no morality above 8,000m. If climbers stop to help another climber at this elevation, they will most likely have to abandon their own summit attempt. In a 1996 summit attempt, two Japanese climbers on the Tibetan side were heading for the top when they came across three Ladakhi climbers from an Indian expedition. The Ladakhis had summited but had been forced to spend the night out – though horribly frostbitten they were still alive, and moaning unintelligibly. Not wanting to jeopardise their ascent, the Japanese climbers simply sidestepped the Ladakhis – not offering food, water or oxygen – and carried on to the summit. On the way down from the summit they again passed two of the Ladakhis, who were left to die where they had fallen. Interviewed soon after their descent, one Japanese climber explained that the Ladakhis looked 'dangerous'; the other Japanese climber said: 'We were too tired to help. Above 8,000m is not a place where people can afford morality.'

through Moyun, the village where young Tenzing Norgay lived, and spent the day there. Tenzing Norgay was seven years old at the time.

And here's another conundrum: is climbing in the genes? Edmund Hillary's son Peter summited Everest, Mallory's grandson George did too, and both the son of Tenzing Norgay (Jamling) and his grandson (Tashi Tenzing) have summited, making that a three-generation affair.

On 14 May 2005, one man made it to the top of Everest without the hard slog. French test pilot Didier Delsalle made aviation history when he touched down on the summit in his turbo-engine AS350-B3 helicopter for a few minutes. This broke the record for the highest helicopter landing – a record that actually cannot be bettered. By doing this, Didier Delsalle improved the possibility of rescues in future. In fact, he mounted a helicopter rescue of two Japanese climbers on the way out.

KARTA (*Everest East Face base camp; 5,050m*) After driving by 4x4 jeep from either Shegar or Tingri (see map) a rough road lands you in Karta. From there, this arduous ten-day loop takes you through the Kama and Karta valleys with views of Everest's Kangshung Face. Of the three faces of Everest, this is the one rated the most daunting to climb, and the one rarely viewed by Westerners. The 1921 British expedition, exploring the Karta Valley on its reconnaissance of Everest, decided the approach was out of the question. It was not until 1981 that an American team tried to summit the Kangshung Face. They failed, but another expedition with some of the same members succeeded in 1983.

Of the treks described so far, the Karta loop is the most taxing, requiring considerable logistical support. Several outfits can arrange trips, starting from Kathmandu, stopping to trek at Karta and moving on to Lhasa. If you are very determined and well supplied with food and camping gear, you should be able to put together your own trek.

Caveat Porters and yak handlers in the Karta area have a notorious reputation for being unreliable and reluctant companions. On group tours, histrionic scenes have included porters getting drunk on *chang* at breakfast and not getting under way with the yaks until noon, thus throwing out the daily trekking targets. Furious arguments can erupt over what loads are to be carried on the yaks, porters can be rough in handling duffle bags, and yak handlers may stop and demand extra money before continuing. So it goes on. They are also known to be fond of pilfering loose items.

Kangshung trek To save time and conserve energy, it would be advisable to get a ride to the trailhead village of Karta. The approach by road is initially the same as for Rongbuk, with a turn-off at Peruche. From Peruche to Karta is about six bone-jarring hours by Landcruiser, with repeated river fords. You could trek in – the scenic 90km from Peruche to Karta would take three or four days (a donkey and guide can be hired in Peruche to assist).

Everest East Face base camp can be reached by several routes: a ten-day loop takes in several of these. There are two high passes *en route*: trekkers pick the lower one (Shao La, 4,970m) to go over first as this allows more chance to acclimatise. At the base of Shao La are two glacial lakes, where good campsites are found. If the weather is clear, there are good views of Everest, Makalu and Lhotse from the top of Shao La. Shao La leads into the beautiful Kama Valley which is surprisingly coated with meadows full of rhododendrons and, further on, forests of pine and fir. Westward along the Kama Valley there are many streams to cross, and meadows with wildflowers. From this vantage point, there may be views of Chomo Lonzo.

The trek continues to Everest East Face base camp, at a site called Pethang Ringmo by British climber George Mallory. If the weather is co-operative, there are unparalleled views of the Kangshung Face and Kangshung Glacier.

The return trek is made via Langma La, at 5,330m, with steep rocky sections giving way to more gentle pastures. At the Kama River is the medieval village of Lundrubling, with solid houses of stone and timber. With a few hours' trekking to the east, you return to Karta Yulba, which is close to the jeep road at Karta.

CHO OYU BASE CAMP Lesser known than Everest – but no less spectacular – is Cho Oyu, an 8,153m behemoth. You can see the peak quite clearly from Tingri. The walk out (or drive) to its base camp crosses the plains of Tingri in the same direction as the Rongbuk trail. Cho Oyu base camp is nestled at 4,970m. You can take a day hike from here towards Puse La for good views. Near Cho Oyu base camp is Kyetrak, with the ruins of a salt depot on the old trading route from Nepal, crossing Nangpa La. The glaciated route is still used by the odd Nepalese trader, and as an escape route by Tibetan refugees, which might explain Chinese military manoeuvres in the area.

SHISHAPANGMA BASE-CAMP TREK

Shishapangma is the only 8,000m peak totally within Tibet (the others – Everest, Lhotse, Cho Oyu and Makalu – lie on the Tibet–Nepal border). For a long time it was not a question of climbing Shishapangma, but getting to see it. It was not until 1951 that Peter Aufschnaiter (the Austrian who escaped with Heinrich Harrer to Tibet, see page 152) was able to get within 10km of Shishapangma to photograph it. This was only the second photograph taken of the mountain, the first being an aerial one taken in 1950. Shishapangma was the last of the 8,000m giants to fall to climbers.

The first ascent of Shishapangma (Xixabangma) was achieved in 1964. In March of that year, an army of over 200 Chinese support personnel and climbers gathered at the north base camp. Climbers swore to plant the five-starred red flag on the summit 'for the honour of the party and the socialist construction of the Motherland' (as described in the magazine *China's Sports*). The climbers not only put the red flag on the summit, they also deposited a bust of Chairman Mao. The summit was reached by four Tibetan and six Chinese climbers, one of whom, Wang Fuchou, had climbed Everest four years earlier. In 1980, a German climbing team summited the peak; in 1982, British climbers Doug Scott and Alex MacIntyre reached the top via the southwest face. French climber Didier Givois and two companions not only summited Shishapangma, they telemark-skied back down it.

Ironically, since the Lhasa–Kathmandu route opened to tourism in the 1980s, Shishapangma has become the most accessible of the 8,000m peaks. There are two approaches to Shishapangma. You can drive to Shishapangma north base camp by heading north out of Nyalam, and taking a fork to the west that leads to Lake Paiku Tso. Heading along this road is another fork to the south, leading to the village of Serlung. Here you can hire yaks and handlers if you want to trek in, or just motor on for the last 15km from Serlung to the north base camp at 4,900m.

Shishapangma south base camp, at 4,980m, can be reached by an in-and-out trail from Nyalam, taking about four or five days for the round trip. You head out northwest of Nyalam, following a river through alpine valleys. Because Shishapangma is a conglomerate peak (with several possible summits), it's difficult to determine where the real summit lies.

There are two main targets in west Tibet, both taking about a week to reach from Lhasa. The main focus of interest – for both pilgrim and trekker – is Mount Kailash. A second spectacular site is the ruins of the Guge Kingdom near Zanda. You can visit both if you have lots of time and money, and luck on the road.

Another variable here is that you may not want to return to Lhasa, or even start from Lhasa. Kailash can also be approached, or left, from the road going down to Kathmandu. There is a short cut around the south side of (Lake) Paiku Tso, which skirts close to Shishapangma north base camp. Group tent-trekking tours from Kathmandu either drive up through Nyalam or use another five-day walk-in route from Simikot (far western Nepal) to Burang. Indian pilgrims arrive as part of a lottery system: they come over the Lipu Lek pass to Burang, then on to Kailash. Some Western group tours have been allowed to follow this same route, trekking in through the Garhwal Himalaya and over Lipu Lek pass.

ROUTES FROM LHASA Travel to Kailash is like one of those epic Marco Polo diary entries: 'Five or six days' hard journey to the west, you come to a great snow-covered mountain which is considered very holy by the Tibetans, who leave articles of clothing as proof of their pilgrimage to it'. The pilgrimage to Kailash has long been considered the most difficult in Asia, due to the sheer distance, harsh weather conditions, the high altitude and lack of any supply points. No matter which way you go, the trip is arduous and you need good planning. Timing is everything at Kailash. It's snowed-in for much of the year, but June and July are generally good months to go. August is not good – monsoon rains can wash away roads and bridges leading in. September is possible. Treks at Kailash start and finish at Darchen, an encampment on the south side of the peak. There are half-a-dozen routes to Kailash, all of them arduous and time-consuming. Consult the Tibet Autonomous Region map, page 4, for an overview of routing.

HIRING VEHICLES A Landcruiser driver would be most reluctant to travel alone on any of the Kailash routes. If he gets stuck in mud or trapped while fording a river, there's no way out. If he breaks down, he's stranded in the middle of nowhere, with no chance to get help. You have some options: arrange to hire two Landcruisers, or consider hiring a Landcruiser and a truck. The cost for a single Landcruiser in high season including driver, guide and permits is around Y18,000 for a simple 12- to 15-day tour, though you can bargain as low as Y14,000 with some agencies. For a 16- to 20-day tour, the cost of a Landcruiser might rise to Y25,000. With three Landcruisers, say with 11 people, you can bargain substantial discounts. The Landcruiser–truck combination works this way. A Landcruiser can seat three (preferable) or four paying passengers plus guide and driver. A Chinese Dongfeng truck seats two paying passengers in the front cabin, plus driver. The truck acts as a tow vehicle if the going gets rough – it can haul the Landcruiser to the next town for repairs. In the back of the truck are all the supplies for the trip: food, fuel, camping gear and so on. You can rotate passengers through the two vehicles. Take as much food and water with you as you can manage from Lhasa: potatoes, vegetables, dried fruit, roasted walnuts, anything that will last the distance. Some folk take along lots of liquid supplies, too. Another good transport configuration is one truck and two Landcruisers, if you can find enough people for the journey. This makes more efficient use of the truck by sharing it between two Landcruisers. The full circuit of Lhasa via the north route to Kailash and back to Lhasa on the south route is just over 3,000km, a major road trip.

Tibetan pilgrims get to Kailash sitting in the open back of a Dongfeng truck, getting thrown around like a sack of potatoes and showered in dust.

PERMITS AND CHECKPOINTS Visiting the region of west Tibet may require a modest stack of permits – TTB, Foreign Affairs Bureau, military and PSB ATP. The paperwork starts in Lhasa, continues in Ali or Darchen, and may require more work in places like Zanda. For visits to Guge and Kailash, permits seem to work better on the north route via Ali rather than the south route via Paryang. Of course, on group tours, the agent takes care of permits, so most groups go in via the south route. On the south route, there are checkpoints at Saga, Paryang and Barga (close to Kailash); further checkpoints are located near Moincer and before Zanda; but there are no checkpoints on the north route, except possibly close to Ali.

SOUTH ROUTE The south route to Kailash from Lhasa, via Lhatse and Paryang, is more direct (a total of 1,200km), so it is the first choice of tour agencies in Lhasa as well as organised group tours from either Lhasa or Kathmandu. There are some high passes on the south route: Paryang and Huore both sit at 4,500m, and between them is a pass of 5,180m. Most travellers take the south route up to Darchen, but if heading back for Kathmandu, consider taking the short cut via Paiku Tso.

Although the south route has been substantially upgraded, with new bridges and improved surfacing, it is still a long, bleak journey with minimum altitudes of 4,500m and few settlements with only basic facilities. With the exception of Saga, which has a newish hotel, all accommodation along the south route to Kailash is in basic guesthouses with concrete or dirt floors, bedding of dubious cleanliness, electricity (solar or generator) limited to a single dim bulb and filthy squat toilets, often in a corner of the compound, open to the elements. They cost around Y60 per night (Y120 at Darchen), but bargain if there are not many visitors. Food is expensive and may be limited to dull variations on noodles – it pays to visit the Lhasa vegetable market and fill a sack with produce that lasts well in the dry atmosphere and can be given to the restaurants to cook. Make sure you have plenty of warm clothes, even in summer: a sleeping bag is highly advisable if not strictly essential. Hot water in vacuum flasks is readily available so take drinks, soups and so on, as well as snacks. Try to have a water container that can be filled up from the vacuum flasks as the quantity of discarded mineral water bottles is quite large enough.

Leaving the highway at Lhatse, the road continues 115km to **Sangsang**: it is better to stay here if you cannot reach Saga as the 4,800m altitude at Raga (113km on) and the biting cold wind should only be experienced if there is no choice. **Saga**, 181km from Sangsang, is the usual first day stop for those leaving from Lhatse, and assuming the highway is in good order and you have a good vehicle it should even be possible to complete the 450km from Shigatse in a very long day. Saga is a larger town with a checkpost (located just before town) and a strong military presence. The ferry over the Tsangpo for the road to Tingri lies just to the west, but the main road heads north over a small pass and follows a feeder stream down to the Dargye River. This is an excellent **camping site** with clear steams flowing from a snow mountain to the east. Crossing various tributaries of the Yarlung Tsangpo, the road passes some ruined watchtowers before old Dzongba where there is a reasonable truck stop 157km from Saga. From here until Paryang there are no reliable camping spots, but there are dramatic sand dunes and some stunning views of the Himalaya. You may also see herds of wild ass (*kyang*) or gazelle (*gowa*) in the region and even the occasional black-necked crane (*trung trung*). Unfortunately the elegant Tibetan antelope (*chiru*) is no longer found in this region due to severe hunting for its *shahtoosh* wool. The scattered nomad houses use well water either in their compounds or in shared locked huts. Only in the wet season do thin streams flow from the hills into the brackish pools that dot the plain leading south to the Tsangpo.

Paryang, 232km from Saga, is the usual stop after Saga, and has several truck stops and restaurants. There are good camping spots about 20km further on; in some seasons sand midges can be a problem. The final checkpost with adjacent teashops is just before the approach to the Marium La pass, which at 5,180m is the highest point on the road, some 126km after Paryang. From here it is a simple but 90km-long descent to Lake Manasarovar, past another lake and a large flagpole shrine that marks the first view of Kailash. If you fork left here you come to an excellent campground beside a river leading into Manasarovar, although this has become popular in recent years, particularly during the spring Saga Dawa full moon period when many Indian groups camp at this site. It is an ideal place to spend a rest day and perhaps hike a few hours to visit the attractive Seralung Gompa. Alternatively, you may decide to move on to Chiu Gompa on the northwest corner of the lake, or on to Darchen at Kailash, both around 50km away. The ugly town of Hor is poorly appointed and there is little reason to stop here or at Barga, where the roads to Burang and Ali divide. However, both have checkposts where permits may be examined.

NEPAL ROUTES Group tours are able to trek across a pass from western Nepal into Burang, where Landcruisers take them on to Kailash.

If exiting Kailash and heading for Kathmandu, there is a short cut – you can cut from Saga (4,500m) around the south side of beautiful (lake) Paiku Tso to the Tong La pass, and on to Nyalam on the Kathmandu route (see the *Lhasa to Kathmandu route* map on pages 188–9 for details). This is recommended only as an **exit route**, because of the altitudes involved, and because there is nowhere to rest and acclimatise. The cheaper Nepalese travel agents favour this route as an incoming way to reach Kailash because it avoids the expense of a flight to Lhasa and the cost of touring in central Tibet. Larger Indian groups often take the Paiku Tso bypass route in long convoys of Landcruisers. However, a sudden rise to 5,200m followed by a long rough journey over 4,500m means that several passengers die each year, and are cremated at a hill near Kailash.

North route The longest way to Kailash is from Lhasa via Lhatse and Gertse to Ali, then south to Darchen. *En route*, you could make a side trip to Zanda and Tsaparang. Lhasa to Kailash by this route is around 1,900km (the Ali to Darchen stretch is 330km). A return to Lhasa can be made on the south route via Huore and Zongba to Saga. From here you either continue onward to Lhasa, or cross the Yarlung Tsangpo by ferry at Saga, detour around the south side of Paiku Tso and head for Zhangmu on the Kathmandu route. Roads are in reasonable shape on the north route because this is the truck-supply route to Ali and its army garrisons. Some parts need no roads at all – the trucks forge their own route across grassland.

There are some horrible, polluted, soul-destroying truck-stop towns *en route*. No-name hotels have rough and tumble facilities, if any at all – hot water supply comes in vacuum flasks. Some towns like Tsochen and Gertse have a few small restaurants hidden away. This is the main Lhasa–Ali–Kashgar truck and military supply route, so truck stops cater to the driving crews. Among the truck stops are Sangsang (4,520m), Raga (4,800m), Tsochen (4,650m), Dongco (4,400m), Gertse (4,400m), Tsaka (Yanhu) and Gakyi (4,450m). There are some high passes of 5,000m and 5,200m north of Tsochen. Distances on this route: the main road leaves the southern route 6km after Raga and heads north past some hot springs to Tsochen, 275km away. A further drive of 260km brings you to Gertse, where herds of sheep laden with backpacks of salt are a common sight in the autumn. From there it is a further 385km to Gakyi on the upper Indus, and a final 110km from Gakyi into Ali. The wild terrain in-between truck stops makes the journey more than worthwhile: you might see wild asses, antelope and even black-necked cranes. There are a few hot springs along the way, too.

Kashgar route Connecting Ali through Yecheng to Kashgar is the wildest route of all. In the past, when Tibet was more accessible to backpackers, some travellers stocked up on food supplies and managed to hitch from Kashgar to Ali, paying the driver. A trip like that would require sitting in the cab: due to a sudden rise in altitude, this route can be fiercely cold, even in summer. For travellers, the stumbling block is **Yecheng**, 250km south of Kashgar, where passage depends on the mood of the PSB men. Sometimes they let travellers through with a friendly wave and no hassles; other times they may intercept travellers and send them back to where they came from. You can rent a vehicle in Yecheng to cover the stretch from there to Ali for around Y3,200 – split among several passengers, that's not too damaging. There are occasional sleeper buses taking 48 hours to cover the Yecheng–Ali route for Y800 a seat. The route traverses one of the highest, bleakest roads in the world, with no supply points along it. Apart from the stunning views, there's little of interest along this route except near Rutok, where some ancient **rock carvings** are found on a cliff near the road. Kashgar is in a remote corner of the PRC, but the Karakoram Highway to Islamabad provides a convenient exit or entry (open May to November, with a valid Pakistan visa).

ALI AND THE GUGE KINGDOM

If you're headed into Kailash by the south route, you may never get to Ali, which would be no loss at all. Well worth a foray north of Kailash, however, are the sites of Toling and Tsaparang (the ancient Guge Kingdom; pronounced *Goo-gay*), and Tirtapuri. The following section describes the approach to the Guge Kingdom from Ali. If you are coming up the road from Kailash, make adjustments and skip sections to suit. If approaching from the south, permits have to be secured in Darchen.

ALI (*Shiquanhe; 4,220m; capital of Ngari Prefecture; telephone code 0897*) Ali is a Chinese concrete monstrosity of a town, with some of the ugliest post-Mao proletarian-monolithic socialist-realist architecture in Tibet. It's composed of concrete cubicles and wooden kiosks, with garbage all over the place. Still, at least there's a lion statue in the middle, not a Mao statue. The town is Chinese to its rotten core – no Tibetan towns existed out this way except for the old capital of Gartok (a nomad tent encampment that has disappeared without trace). Although it is commonly called Ali, the town is also referred to by the name of the river it is located along, the Indus, which the Chinese refer to as Shiquanhe and the Tibetans call Sengghe Tsangpo ('River issuing from the Lion's Mouth'; hence Sengghe Drong or 'Lion Village' is the Tibetan name for Ali).

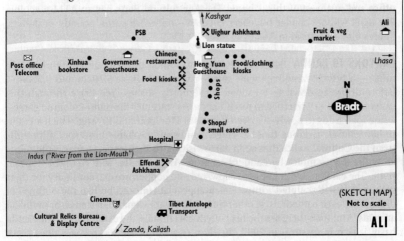

Ali is easily the biggest town in western Tibet, with the largest military garrison of the region. Army platoons jog around the streets in formation at six in the morning, and again around sunset. After sunset the top brass head for the karaoke bars and help themselves to the women. Otherwise, there's not a whole lot to see in Ali, apart from a place called the **Cultural Relics Bureau**, which has a display centre. The main reason for visiting Ali is shopping – for food and for permits.

Getting there There's an airfield called Ngari Gunsa, 30km from Ali, with **flights** from Lhasa several times a week. Air China flights from Chengdu land in Lhasa for refuelling and then continue to Ngari Gunsa, elevation 4,274m. The Lhasa to Ngari leg takes around 1½ hours.

A glance at the map will show Ali is strategically sited at the junction of the north route from Lhasa, the south route from Kashgar, and onward routes to Zanda and Kailash. Locals may arrive by sleeper bus, covering the distance from Lhasa to Ali in two days.

Where to stay and eat There are over a dozen hotels in town, of which half are tourist class, meaning rooms with attached bath. Among these are the **Guge Dynasty Hotel** and **Xiangxiong Hotel** (both expensive, with rooms over Y500 a night); in the mid-range price category are **Shenhu Binguan**, **Heng Yuan Guesthouse**, and **Ali Hotel**, all around Y120–140 for a double. Near the bus station are some cheaper hotels where beds go for Y30–40 but you may not be permitted to stay there. For food, the best bets are **Uighur restaurants** dishing up central Asian food like kebabs and nan. Just north of the lion roundabout is **Uighur Ashkhana**, a popular place, while close to the Indus river is **Effendi Ashkhana**, serving more extravagant dishes. To the southwest side of the lion statue is a Chinese restaurant with quite palatable Sichuan food. Otherwise, there are several supermarkets around town (one is located next to Heng Yuan Guesthouse). There are also eateries on the road to the south. Food kiosks in this vicinity may have little nuggets hidden away, including chocolate bars, pineapple in jars, crackers and candles.

Other practicalities You can stock up on **supplies** like shampoo here. The kiosks around town are the best bet; there's not much in the 'department stores'. Facilities to the western side of town include a small **Xinhua bookstore**, a **post/telecom office** and just west of this, a **bank**. The Agricultural Bank has an ATM machine. The bank will not change travellers' cheques – only cash euros, pounds, or dollars. There's also a **hospital** in Ali.

CANYONS TO ZANDA From Ali, the road to Zanda traverses an entire mountain range – a breathtaking trip, with snowy passes as high as 5,200m and 5,500m – before dropping down to a canyon with ghostly shapes. You drive through this canyon along a dry riverbed to reach Zanda. As you enter the multi-coloured gorges, a side road leads to newly discovered caves at **Dungkar** and **Piyang**, which are said to have murals rivalling those at Guge. You would probably need special permits from the Cultural Relics Bureau in Ali to visit. With such a spectacular route, allow an entire day to motor by Landcruiser from Ali to Zanda, with frequent stops *en route*. The canyons, with hues of yellow, red and copper, are extraordinary for their phantasmagoric sculpted forms, which appear at times to be like the outlines of dream castles or cathedrals, at other times like gigantic guardian statues or mythical animals. And then there are the near-mythical animals: the extinct ones. The Zanda basin is rich in fossils – in 2007, the skull of a woolly rhinoceros was unearthed, thought to be over three million years old. This woolly rhino is believed to have used its shovel-like horn to clear away snow and find vegetation. Research suggests that Tibet may have acted as an evolutionary cradle for mega-herbivores, allowing for adaptation to extreme cold – essential for the survival of Ice Age giants such as the woolly mammoth and the woolly rhino.

ZANDA (*Tsanda, Tsada, Zada, Thöling, Toling; 3,660m*) Zanda is the Chinese name for the ancient Tibetan town of Toling, once the capital of Ngari (west Tibet). Remnants of this capital are scattered around town and the surrounding hills; there are dozens of *chorten*-like structures towards the Sutlej River.

Zanda has a spectacular setting, but it is little more than a glorified army garrison – facilities are for the military, not for the stray tourist. There's a big army base at the southern end of town, and an old Tibetan quarter at the northwest end. In-between is a main drag with several **guesthouses**, one of which belongs to the military. The one near Toling Gompa is preferable – there are balcony rooms upstairs, and there's a tap in the courtyard with running water. Several small Chinese restaurants line the main strip (try **Sichuan Shifang**), and there are some tent-shops (selling supplies out of tents). There's also a **post office** (with telephone), and the **Agricultural Bank** has ATM access though it's not certain this will work. Zanda even has **internet** access.

Permits If you want to visit Toling Gompa in Zanda or the ruins of the Guge Kingdom in Tsaparang, you may need permits from the Cultural Relics Bureau, located near the bank. Tsaparang requires separate permits from Lhasa, Ali and Zanda – put them all together and you are allowed to visit.

Toling Gompa The main sight in town is the largely abandoned Toling Gompa. Toling dates back to the 11th century when a structure was built by Yeshe O, the king of Guge. Assisted by scholar Rinchen Zangpo, he led a revival of Buddhism in western Tibet. Buddhism was snuffed out in a few short years in central Tibet by King Langdarma (who ruled AD838–842), a staunch supporter of the Bon faith. Upon the assassination of Langdarma, Tibet was broken up into lay and monastic pockets of influence. The Guge Kingdom became an enclave that was vital for the survival of Buddhism. King Yeshe O and Rinchen Zangpo promoted cultural exchanges with Indian Buddhists. Although over a hundred monasteries were built

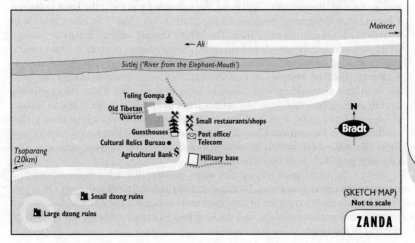

StarTreks ALI AND THE GUGE KINGDOM

7

in the western region (which at that time encompassed Ladakh), Toling became the most important centre of Buddhist study, and its reputation grew with the arrival of 11th-century scholar Atisha from India. Eventually the kingdom was sacked in the 17th century. In the mid-1960s, Red Guards trashed Toling Gompa.

The main draw at Toling today is the fine **murals** in the few chapels remaining. In addition to destruction by Red Guards, murals in the White Temple have suffered water damage. Similar to those at Tsaparang, the murals are in early Newari and Kashmiri styles, both rarely seen in Tibet. You need a powerful flashlight to view them. The entry fee for Toling Gompa is Y80.

Out of town On ridge-tops to the southwest of Zanda are two *dzongs* (citadels) made of clay. This is the most peculiar hiking you'll ever do: scrambling over sand and dealing with crevasses of clay. Access to the larger *dzong* (the one to the west) is via a steep trail, and then through a sloping tunnel carved out of clay. Above the tunnel are former cave dwellings and dangerous crevasses. From here you continue climbing, and reach a vantage point with a magnificent view of the Sutlej Valley.

TSAPARANG Located 26km west of Zanda (a one-hour drive) are the extensive ruins of Tsaparang, the once-powerful capital of the 10th-century Guge Kingdom. The main building material is not stone, but clay, with walls, buildings, secret tunnels and escape exits all fashioned from this material. Thousands of people lived here in cave dwellings in this kingdom of clay, which appears to have been operational in the 10th and 11th centuries. Little is known of the history of the **Guge Kingdom**, but some of the exceptional murals at Tsaparang portray realistic scenes with courtiers and visiting dignitaries, and give some idea of how people lived.

To access temples at Tsaparang, you need the caretaker to open the doors, and you need to pay an entry fee of Y110. The Tibetan caretaker lives in a small house near the main gate: if he's not at home, he's probably in the tiny village visible not far away from the ruins. The caretaker may want to see your paperwork, and may insist that no photographs be taken inside the temple structures. Interior photography of the site is a very sensitive point; official permits for photography are complex to obtain (from Beijing), and expensive if you do manage to get them.

Tsaparang is built tier on tier up a clay ridge. The best-preserved parts are the lower ramparts; at the very top are excellent views of the area from the *dzong*. As you go through the gate into Tsaparang, the first thing you see is the **Rust-coloured Chapel**, thus designated because its function is not clear – it bears murals of Tsongkhapa, Sakyamuni and Atisha. The **White Temple** suffered extensive damage to its statuary, but its murals remain intact. Some murals portray Avalokitesvara, the 11-headed, thousand-armed bodhisattva of compassion. The mural style is Kashmiri. The **Red Temple** was destroyed and left open to water damage, but even so, its murals are striking, with beautiful large Tara frescoes. There are engrossing murals here, apparently depicting scenes from daily life at Guge – in one section envoys are arriving by donkey at the court; another part shows a high lama giving teachings. The **Yamantaka Chapel** is dedicated to its resident tantric deity Dorje Jigje: the walls bear murals of deities locked in tantric *yabyum* embraces (see *Glossary*, page 327) with their consorts.

From here, wend your way up clay steps, passing through a fantastic winding tunnel to the uppermost ruins. There's an entire **ruined citadel** at the top. Once past the tunnel, there is a complex of chambers and passageways: the citadel had its own water supply in times of siege, and the king had an escape route tunnel that led off the rear of the ridge.

Steps up to
Tsaparang Dzong &
Demchok Mandala Chapel

Yamantaka Chapel

Red Temple

White Temple

Caretaker's residence

Front gate

Rust-coloured Chapel

(SKETCH MAP)
Not to scale

Bradt →N

TSAPARANG
Lower Ramparts

At the top, the most impressive structure is **Tsaparang Dzong** – the king's simple summer palace – with expansive views over the valley. There are several temple complexes at the top: the most important is the tiny **Demchok Mandala Chapel.** This chapel is usually locked – if you manage to get in, you can view the remains of a large 3D mandala, which was smashed in the Cultural Revolution. The chapel is a *gonkhang* or protector temple, and the site of initiation rites. It is thought that in times of crisis, the king and ministers would come to this chapel to ask for protection or direction. The chapel is dedicated to the protector deity Demchok, who is depicted in murals with his consort Dorje Phagmo. Fascinating tantric murals cover the walls: a flashlight is needed to view them. Depicted are rows of dancing *dakinis*, the female deities who personify the wisdom of enlightenment; below these are gory scenes of disembodiment from hell realms.

TIRTAPURI While Kailash is the main sacred site of western Tibet, there are a number of others on the pilgrim's wish list. After Lake Manasarovar, the most revered site is Tirtapuri, a yellow-streaked rocky landscape with hot springs. After encircling Kailash and Manasarovar, Tibetan pilgrims come to Tirtapuri for a relaxing circuit – the *kora* is only an hour, and there are grassy meadows for picnicking as well as hot water for soothing tired limbs. Tirtapuri lies 10km southwest of Moincer (which has a basic guesthouse), approachable by Landcruiser or truck. There is a short circuit in the Tirtapuri region – you can follow the pilgrims as they walk past elaborate *mani* walls, and sacred caves set in red and white clay cliffs, and pay their respects at a small monastery to a shrine of Guru Rinpoche. Though the entire Tirtapuri circuit takes just an hour, you could allow several hours to stop and drink in the atmosphere and the landscape. At the site, pilgrims bathe – or dip their feet – in several sulphurous **hot spring pools**, which can accommodate three or four people. The hot springs are reputed to have healing powers, and Tibetans search the waters for pellets of lime, for medicinal purposes. Just being able to feel hot water is therapeutic enough for Western visitors. There are plans for a bathhouse, supplied by the milky-white steaming pools, along with a small guesthouse at the *gompa*.

KHYUNGLUNG Beyond Tirtapuri, the side road bends west down the Sutlej, past the important Bonpo *gompa* of Gurugem. After passing through a small gorge, it reaches the village of Khyunglung, about 30km from Moincer. A further 3km

7

onward, reached by a footbridge, is a remarkable **cave complex** associated with the ancient kingdom of Shangshung. A short visit of three to four hours would allow you to poke around in several of the caves and climb up to the silver castle, although much longer would be needed to visit the whole site.

Khyunglung has been described as a cave city, but it has few of the features associated with a permanent settlement. The caves are all of similar size and simple construction, with a raised shrine for fires at the rear without a chimney. Instead of broken pottery and other artefacts found in abandoned caves elsewhere, there are bones, feathers and furs, some quite recent. It would appear that rather than a city, this place acted more as a gathering place for Bonpo shamans on auspicious days, with their retinue perhaps camping near the modern village. Whatever its origins, it is a unique and mysterious site. Since the recent building of a road to Khyunglung (which lies less than 100km from Darchen), it is possible to visit Khyunglung, Gurugem and Tirtapuri on a day trip from Kailash, but remember to get permits in Darchen if you do not already have them.

THE KAILASH REGION

Kailash is the centre of the universe – or at least the Tibetan Buddhist universe. In the Tibetan world view, at the cosmic axis of the universe lies Mount Meru, the abode of the gods. Mount Kailash is thought to be an earthly manifestation of the mythical Meru. Things are not as simple as this, however, as the Tibetan world view incorporates existence in multiple dimensions. The Tibetan name for Kailash is Kang Rinpoche ('Precious Jewel of Snows'); the dome-shaped peak is symmetrical like an uncut diamond, with a permanent cap of ice and snow. At 6,714m, the mountain is modest by Himalayan standards, but nevertheless impressive to view. The peak is sacred to Tibetan Buddhist and Bon adherents, and to the Hindus and Jains of India.

In the late 19th century and early 20th, Kailash assumed mythical dimensions among Western geographers and explorers. For a long time there was reputed to be a high mountain that was the source of the great rivers of India. But Tibet was inaccessible, so geographers were unsure if this was myth or fact. Finding the source of India's great rivers was a prime geographer's puzzle, on a par with finding the source of the Nile. The British employed Indian pundits, who, disguised as pilgrims, measured distances with prayer-beads, and tossed marked logs into rivers to find out where they would pop up further down the line in India.

Eventually, it was discovered that the headwaters of four of Asia's mightiest rivers lay within 100km of Kailash – the Indus, the Yarlung Tsangpo (which later emerges in India as the Brahmaputra), the Karnali (a major tributary of the Ganges) and the Sutlej. Remarkably, the mouths of the same rivers end up as far as 3,000km apart. The Tibetans know the rivers by more prosaic names, identified with the four cardinal directions and four legendary animals. Thus the Indus becomes the 'River issuing from the Lion's Mouth' (Sengghe Tsangpo or Sengghe Khambab, at the north), the Yarlung Tsangpo becomes the 'River from the Horse-Mouth' (Tamchok Khambab, to the east), the Karnali becomes the 'River from the Peacock-Mouth' (Mabchu Khambab, to the south), and the Sutlej is the 'River from the Elephant-Mouth' (Langchan Khambab, situated in the west).

DARCHEN Also known as Tarchen or Dharchen (4,620m), Darchen can best be described as a cross between a Tibetan tent encampment and a Chinese truck-stop depot. A few tents and adobe hutches dispense noodles and tea, and there are some shops by the river on the eastern side of Darchen. There's not a lot of choice when it

Map labels: Zanda, Ali; Moincer; Tirtapuri Gompa; Tirtapuri Hotsprings; Principal source of the Indus; Drira Puk Gompa; Drolma La; Choku Gompa; Kailash 6714m; Zutrul Puk Gompa; Darchen; see page 247; Sutlej; Barga; Chiu Gompa; Langpona Gompa; Huore; Samsang; N Bradt; 0 — 40km; 0 — 25 miles; Tseti Tso; Manasarovar; Seralung Gompa; Raksas Tal; Gosul Gompa; Gurla La 7728m; Trugo Gompa; Source of the Tsangpo; Gurla Mandhata 7728m; INDIA; Lipu Lek Pass; Burang; NEPAL; Karnali; Kojinath; Himla; KAILASH REGION

comes to **places to stay** – rooms are little more than a bed for Y60 in four-bed rooms, with communal toilets. Among these are Pilgrim Hotel, Lhasa Holyland Hotel, and Sun and Moon Guesthouse. Competition for rooms is heavy at peak pilgrimage months, with hotels like Gangdishi guesthouse being fully booked by Indian pilgrims. Prices tend to be high for what you get (which is little more than a rock-hard bed), so you may have to bargain. Also useful to know is that you can leave your gear here when trekking, in a locked storeroom. There's similar-priced lodging at another compound run by the PSB. It's a good idea to hang around Darchen for a day or two to acclimatise, perhaps taking a day hike up to Serlung Gompa.

There is a small **clinic** in Darchen with oxygen supply, where altitude sickness can be treated. Group tours are also known to use the military hospital in Burang, and may also race clients (patients) over the pass into Nepal to Himla, where helicopter evacuation can possibly be arranged.

KAILASH *KORA* The circuit around the sacred mountain is known as the Kailash *kora*. Tibetans complete the circuit in one long day, starting before dawn and finishing after nightfall. Unless you are super-humanoid, don't attempt this at altitude. The minimum time for most Westerners to complete the circuit would be two days. Most allow three to four days. If you have a tent and want to dawdle, taking in the landscape at a leisurely pace, plan on five days or more. An annoying Y50 fee is levied for the Kailash *kora*. What price for accumulating merit? There are rumours of a fast track for doing this: there is ominous talk of the Chinese building a motor road around Kailash, presumably with a toll gate

In group-tour arrangements, porters or yaks (or both) are deployed to carry camping gear and guest duffle bags. The cost is Y60 a day for porter or yak. The group tours sleep in tents close to monastery guesthouses. Previously, individuals could stay in the monastery guesthouses on the *kora*, but that option seems to have closed down. Don't expect much in the way of food on the circuit, although there may be some teahouse tents along the way. Sometimes the *gompa* guesthouses sell noodles. A clean water supply is essential, so take water bottles and filtering devices (water can also be boiled).

Fellow hikers at Kailash are mainly Indian and Tibetan pilgrims. The Tibetans come from as far away as Kham, usually arriving by 'pilgrim truck'. Tibetan pilgrims comprise many different nomad groups with a fascinating array of costumes, particularly the women. Women coat their faces in *tocha* – a cosmetic made of concentrated buttermilk or roots – to protect the skin from dryness and UV rays. Indian pilgrims come as part of a lottery system run by the Delhi government, in

POWERING UP AT KAILASH

In Darchen, you can stock up on last-minute supplies, and get your pilgrim supplies, too. At tents and shops at the northeast side of Darchen, pilgrims purchase prayer-flags (to drape at the passes), small squares of paper with windhorses embossed on them (to fling around at the main pass), and for good measure, prayer-beads (to mumble mantras with, to get over the high passes). The windhorse (*lungta*) is a beautiful steed who brings good fortune (symbolised by the jewel on its back) wherever it goes. It is also painted on prayer-flags – the wind sets the horse in motion, carrying good fortune in all directions.

In their lifetime, all Tibetans aspire to make the sacred pilgrimage to Kailash – some travel enormous distances in the backs of open trucks to get there. Pilgrimage is considered healthy and holy – the most popular time to attempt Kailash is after the annual harvest. When it comes to the Kailash *kora*, there's a kind of merit point system involved: the more you suffer, the greater the merit earned. Some pilgrims attempt not one circuit, but three (often on consecutive days in one season) or 13 circuits, or 108 circuits (spread over a number of years), which assures entry into nirvana. Prostrators, who proceed with inchworm-like motions, flinging themselves to the ground, take 15 to 25 days to complete the Kailash circuit, and must prostrate through anything in their path, be it snow, mud, slush, or whatever. If you see a prostrator going in an anticlockwise direction, it must be a Bon adherent. For Bon believers, Kailash is the spiritual centre of the Shangshung ancient empire of western Tibet.

Punctuating the Kailash circuit are sacred markers in stone – carved *chortens*, carved *mani*-stones and cairns with prayer-flags. Offerings made by pilgrims at these sites might include pins (said to sharpen mental faculties), discarded clothing (as proof the pilgrim has been there) or *tsampa* (thrown in the air as protection against evil).

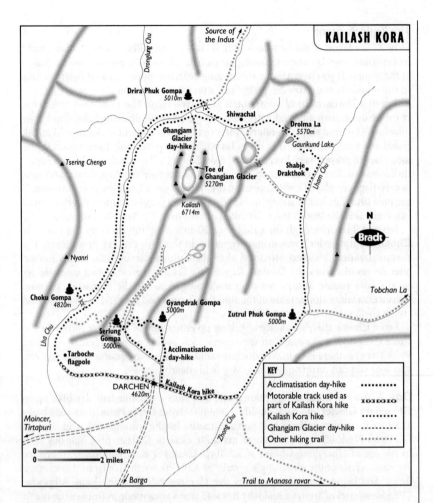

Source of
the Indus

Drongjung Chu

Drira Phuk Gompa
5010m

Shiwachal

Drolma La
5570m

Gaurikund Lake

Ghangjam
Glacier
day-hike

Toe of
Ghangjam Glacier
5270m

Shabje
Drakthok

Lhom Chu

Tsering Chenga

Kailash
6714m

Bradt

N

Nyanri

Tobchan La

Choku Gompa
4820m

Gyangdrak Gompa
5000m

Zutrul Phuk Gompa
5000m

Lha Chu

Serlung
Gompa
5000m

Acclimatisation
day-hike

Tarboche
flagpole

DARCHEN
4620m

Kailash Kora hike

KEY

Acclimatisation day-hike ··········
Motorable track used as
part of Kailash Kora hike ıoıoıoıo
Kailash Kora hike ··········
Ghangjam Glacier day-hike ---------
Other hiking trail ··········

Moincer,
Tirtapuri

Zhong Chu

0 ———— 4km
0 ———— 2 miles

Barga

Trail to Manasarovar

operation since the early 1980s. Each year, up to 10,000 Hindus from all parts of India apply. Finalists are chosen, and after fitness tests, this number is whittled down to about a thousand. Hindu pilgrims are allowed ten days in Tibet. Travelling in groups of around 35, the lucky lottery winners walk across Lipu Lek pass where they are met by Chinese guides and the sacred circuit of their dreams gets under way. However, these lottery pilgrims are dwarfed in number by those wealthier Indian pilgrims entering on their own via Nepal and travelling in Landcruiser convoys.

Acclimatisation hike Strongly recommended is a day trip up to Gyangdrak and Serlung *gompas*, due north of Darchen. These *gompas* are situated at 5,000m: you can complete a triangular loop in about six or seven hours, returning to Darchen by nightfall. One snag: the uppermost part of the trek requires a permit. However, you can avoid the permit situation by stopping short of Gyangdrak Gompa. This hike serves several functions: you can adapt to the altitude somewhat (by hiking high but sleeping low) and you can find out how to pace yourself at altitude. If intending to trek around Kailash with your own backpack, you might want to take the full load with you on the day hike to find out just how heavy it is.

The Kailash circuit

Day 1 The target of the first day's walk is usually Drira Phuk Gompa, about eight to ten hours from Darchen, including stops. That's because there is accommodation at the *gompa*. If you have your own camping gear, that opens up a lot more options in the schedule, since you can pretty well stop where you want.

Leaving Darchen, head west: you'll know you're on the right trail when you come across a cairn adorned with prayer-flags, and with discarded clothing left by pilgrims – tattered shirts, sweaters, worn-out runners and old socks, as well as yak heads and goat horns. Further on is **Tarboche**, a large flagpole from which flutter long lines of prayer-flags. Every year, at Saka Dawa (full moon day in May or June), thousands of Tibetans gather to celebrate. The flagpole is taken down, and new prayer-flags are placed on it, replacing the tattered ones from the previous year. If the pole tilts after it is raised again, it is considered a very bad omen. Pilgrim trucks can reach this site by dirt track, so this is often where Tibetans start the *kora*.

Beyond Tarboche, high on a ridge – a 20-minute climb up from the trail – is **Choku Gompa**, which was originally set up in the 13th century as a shrine. The current building was reconstructed after the Cultural Revolution, and is looked after by monks from the Drukpa Kagyu sect (as are the other two monasteries on the *kora* route). Shiny-eyed pilgrims crowd in to see the monastery's famed treasures: a white stone statue of the Buddha Opame and a sacred silver-embossed conch shell, said to have been Milarepa's.

From Choku, there's a choice of hiking up either side of Lha Chu ('River of the Gods'), through a canyon with impressive rock peaks, such as Nyanri. At Drira Phuk Gompa, there is a simple concrete building with a few rooms where you can stay – or you can camp out in the grassy fields nearby.

Day 2 You can build in an optional rest day, with a possible half-day hike up to **Ghangjam Glacier** and back. Building in a rest day at **Drira Phuk** gives your body a chance to recover, and will help you acclimatise for the arduous walk over Drolma La. Drira Phuk offers the chance to get quite close to Kailash, on a half-day hike to the toe of Ghangjam Glacier at 5,270m. Assuming clear conditions, there are awesome views of the glistening icy walls of Kailash's north face from this vantage point. You begin to understand why the Tibetans call the peak Kang Rinpoche ('Precious Jewel of Snows'), and why it is said that a wish made in front of the north face will definitely come true – one day.

Day 3 Heading out of Drira Phuk, you begin the tough ascent to Drolma La. This is the longest haul on the circuit – it takes about ten to 12 hours to walk to Zutrul Phuk. Out of Drira Phuk is a bizarre sight: a field littered with discarded clothing. The place is **Shiwachal**, named after a cremation ground in Bodhgaya, India (Shiva-tsal). In this symbolic field of death, pilgrims must leave behind a personal item – clothing, a lock of hair, or even a few drops of blood – as proof of being there. A rock pillar in the middle of Siwachal is covered with scraps of cloth and bracelets.

Toiling upward, you reach **Drolma La**, which is the focus of the entire *kora*. Drolma La means 'Pass of Tara'; a large boulder depicting Tara is festooned with prayer-flags. Tibetans attach their own prayer-flag, and leave coins, locks of hair or other mementoes of their passage; they fling windhorse squares into the air and shout '*Tso tso tso! Lha Gyalo!*' ('Victory to the gods!'). Down the other side of the pass is a beautiful greenish tarn called **Gaurikund Lake**. Hindus are supposed to take a dip here, but ice skating might be more appropriate. You continue down, down, down – on a descent that is taxing on the knees – to meadows where

Tibetans picnic. Eventually, you reach Zutrul Phuk Gompa, which has a basic concrete guesthouse attached.

Day 4 Around the Kailash *kora* are relics left by the great cave-dwelling ascetic Milarepa, who engaged in a competition with sorcerer Naro Bon Chun. At **Zutrul Puk Gompa**, the reconstructed monastery encloses a cave that Milarepa fashioned with his bare hands – there's a statue of him within. The caretaker monk will show you around, although you may need a flashlight. The final showdown between Milarepa and Naro Bon Chun is said to have taken place on the peak of Kailash: in the ensuing duel, Naro Bon Chun fell, and in so doing, is said to have carved a long vertical cleft in the mountain's south face.

And so, totally knackered, you head back to Darchen to complete the Kailash circuit. Fortunately it's a level or downhill walk to Darchen, and it doesn't take that long to dribble back into town.

CHIU GOMPA South of Darchen is a scene that frequently appears in photographs of Kailash: a monastery crowning a hill in the foreground and Kailash poking up in the background. The monastery is Chiu Gompa, the most impressive of the *gompas* encircling Lake Manasarovar. It's an easy drive from Darchen.

The ancient monastery is thought to have been the last resting place of the sage Padmasambhava, where he and his consort achieved 'rainbow body'. You can work your way up to the top chapel, with views of the entire area. The **guesthouses** close to Chiu Gompa are cheaper than those of Darchen, and have much better views. They have the added advantage of a bathhouse where sulphurous **hot springs** are channelled, offering the great luxury of washing your hair in hot water. If you are moving on to Manasarovar, this is the place to stay the night rather than Darchen.

MANASAROVAR Tibetans undertake several *koras* in the Kailash region: the first of Kailash itself, the second of Lake Manasarovar, and then a visit to Tirtapuri (some pilgrims tackle Lake Manasarovar first). Lake Manasarovar draws Hindu pilgrims who come for ritual bathing in the icy waters: full submersion in the waters is claimed to ensure enlightenment (Tibetan Buddhists, by contrast, settle for a sip and a splash over the head). Indian pilgrims pick up pebbles from the lakeside and fill containers with holy water when returning home.

A complete circuit of **Lake Manasarovar** is around 90km: the route is perfectly flat and lies at 4,560m in altitude. A walking circuit of the lake takes about four to five days. An option is horse-trekking: you hire horses to ride around the lake, with packhorses carrying gear. If you do this, be sure to take a Tibetan wrangler along.

Eight monasteries encircling the shores of the lake were once so sited to represent the Dharma wheel with its eightfold path. They were destroyed during the Cultural Revolution, but some have been partially restored and remain active. Even if you don't attempt a circuit of Manasarovar, it's well worth driving past Chiu Gompa as far as Gurla La for a glimpse of magnificent **Gurla Mandhata**. If you can, try to continue as far as Burang.

If you are contemplating the Manasarovar circuit bring sunscreen and insect repellent. You can start and end the circuit at Chiu Gompa, where there are places to stay. An alternative starting point is the town of Huore (where horses can be hired), ending at Chiu Gompa again (not a complete circuit, but close) – this will cut down the walking time. Foreigners rarely undertake the Manasarovar circuit (usually they are spent after the Kailash trek) but the lake offers pristine hiking, with birdlife visible at certain parts, and a slew of monasteries or ruins along the way. The route usually proceeds from Chiu Gompa past Langpona and Seralung *gompas* to Trugo and Gosul *gompas*, passing by the small lake of Tseti Tso, and continuing north back to Chiu Gompa.

Raksas Tal While Manasarovar is identified with the positive forces of light (the sun), the lake next door, Raksas Tal, is aligned with the forces of darkness (the moon). For this reason, Raksas Tal is shunned by pilgrims – its waters are rumoured to be poisonous (actually, they're not), as opposed to the healing waters of Manasarovar.

THE ROAD TO BURANG Right down south, close to the Nepal–India border, is the old trading town of Burang, also known as Purang or Taklakot. Burang lies at 3,900m in elevation. The distance from Darchen to Burang is around 110km, a three-hour drive. Indian pilgrims enter via Lipu Lek pass and Burang to get to Darchen; Western trekkers are permitted to take a five-day hike from Simikot (in Nepal) to Burang (or over the Lipu Lek pass), and take a Landcruiser to Kailash. Burang makes a great drive from Darchen, passing between Lake Manasarovar and Lake Raksas Tal, and driving right by Mount Gurla Mandhata.

Gurla Mandhata, though 7,728m high, appears to be quite low from this perspective, and the summit appears so close you almost imagine you could get out and start walking up it. Which is exactly what a couple of American climbers once did (unofficially), telling their startled driver to come and fetch them in a few weeks, after they'd bagged the peak! Gurla La, a pass of 4,600m, offers spectacular vistas, as does Ara La (4,200m). Southward are the pretty villages of Garu and Topa, with handsome, handcrafted houses.

BURANG Burang is an old caravan stop on the banks of the Karnali River. Today it functions as a military outpost, with lots of men in green running around. It is aligned along a north–south road: at the north side is a military checkpost (your documents will be scrutinised); towards the south side are some small **restaurants** and shops, an **expensive guesthouse**, the **post office**, **bank** and **PSB office**. Staying in Burang is a problem as the sanctioned guesthouse is an overpriced dump. It's difficult to find an alternative. While restaurants are mediocre, you may be able to buy fresh vegetables at a street market and take them to a restaurant to be stir-fried. Stocks of canned fruit and other items are quite good.

There's good **hiking** and a few things to see in Burang – you can combine several options by taking a western fork out of town. Head towards a bridge that spans the Karnali at the northern end of Burang. There's a small bazaar selling clothing, and some food (a small eatery here) with a few snooker tables. Continue west on a trail that leads up a steep hillside. Set into the cliff face is a remarkable cave-temple, **Gokung Gompa**. The caretaker monk will show you around for a token fee. The monastery ranges over three storeys, set within caves. Cave-dwellings are used as houses in this area. If you carry on over the top of a crest, you'll come to the **Nepalese Bazaar**, where Nepalese goods are sold in exchange for Tibetan wool, which is rolled into huge balls. Concrete shopfronts offer Nepalese and Indian goods, portered in from the Nepalese town of Darchula.

To the northwest of Burang, on a hilltop, you can make out the ruins of Shembaling Gompa. Once the largest monastery in the region, it housed several hundred monks, but was completely destroyed in the Cultural Revolution. Today the biggest active monastery in the region is at the pretty village of **Kojinath** (Korja or Kojarnath), situated 15km southeast of Burang, on the Karnali River right near the Nepalese border.

8

East Tibet, Kham and Amdo

This chapter cleaves into two distinct zones – east Tibet (lying within the Tibet Autonomous Region, TAR), and the parts of Kham and Amdo that are located outside the TAR. These two zones are as different as chalk and cheese when it comes to permits and freedom of movement. In east Tibet, within the TAR, you are hamstrung by permits at every turn, and restricted to Landcruiser travel and expensive hotels. Outside the TAR, however, in Kham and Amdo, you can travel by public transport and make your own hotel choices – which will be a lot cheaper. You can combine the two Tibets in a single trip if you orchestrate the logistics.

The distinction between east Tibet and the Kham region is a murky one. In old Tibet, large swathes of eastern Tibet and Kham were the same entity. The division is an artificial one that was concocted by Chinese officialdom – no doubt to divide and conquer the troublesome Khampas. 'Kham' has thus become an abstract concept – one that is referred to by Tibetans but not mentioned on Chinese maps. The former region of Kham now straddles four Chinese provinces, comprising over 47 Tibetan Autonomous prefectures and counties (there is some confusion over the exact number of prefectures and counties with Tibetan populations). Of the estimated 47 prefectures and counties quoted, roughly half lie within the TAR in east Tibet, and half lie outside the TAR – with six counties in Qinghai, three counties in Yunnan, and 16 counties in Sichuan.

EAST TIBET, WITHIN THE TAR

Few travellers venture into east Tibet because of its lack of key attractions, because transport is difficult, and because it is hard to get permits (parts of east Tibet remain closed, probably due to military presence). As a foreigner, you are restricted by the Public Security Bureau (PSB) to higher-end hotels in most towns, which means you end up paying over Y200 for a double room. But if you want to get right off the track, east Tibet is the place to go.

Loop or linear? That is the route decision to make in advance if using Lhasa as a launching pad. You could make a large loop from Lhasa through east Tibet to Bayi, within the TAR, and come back to Lhasa. Or you can go from Lhasa all the way through east Tibet via Bayi to Derge or Deqin. Once you reach Derge or Deqin, you are in Kham, where you can drop the Landcruiser and carry on by yourself. The permit brouhaha stops here.

There are few major monasteries along these routes through east Tibet, but excellent scenic spots abound. And the most scenic of all is tough to access: the Yarlung Tsangpo Grand Canyon – the deepest in the world. This is without a doubt a world-class wonder, but the problem is how to get to see it. There are permit hurdles to overcome.

Lhasa to Derge or Deqin takes about 12 days, allowing time for sightseeing, though you could do the trip in eight days. The tariff is likely to be over US$2,500 to cover the cost of vehicle, driver and guide. And the price could rise to US$3,500 for the package.

Lhasa to Chengdu is 2,400km via Chamdo (north route), and 2,080km via Litang (south route). On the first part of the route, you could undertake a tour to Samye and Yumbulagang, and then kick off from Tsedang (see the *Exploring Central Tibet* chapter, page 184). Here you enter Nyingchi Prefecture. Highlights of this region include the sacred lake of Basum Tso; the sacred peak of Mount Bonri; Mount Namche Barwa; and visits to Monpa, Lhoba and Tengpa villages. However, with the exception of Basum Tso, permits for these places are hard to come by.

GETTING TO BAYI Landcruisers headed from Lhasa to either Derge or Deqin save considerable driving time by travelling along the north route to Bayi, which is mostly paved. The southern route from Lhasa to Bayi is much rougher and thus takes a lot longer, but winds through spectacular scenery. Some travellers combine both routes as a way of exploring east Tibet: they complete a one-week round-trip loop from Lhasa. The following paragraphs briefly describe that loop, so extract the parts you need to suit your journey. Be aware that the permit situation in east Tibet is difficult: some places require four permits (see *Lhamo Latso*, below).

About 280km east from Lhasa and 48km east of Kongpo Gyamda is a turn-off northward, leading another 47km on a paved road to **Basum Tso** (Basong Tso, Draksum Tso; 3,470m). The lake can be reached in five or six hours' drive from Lhasa. This ethereal lake is associated with the legend of King Gesar of Ling, Tibet's epic poem. You can visit enchanting **Tsosum Gompa**, on a tiny island reached by a pontoon walkway (Y50 entry fee). This small *gompa* was rebuilt by Dudjom Rinpoche, the highest-ranking Nyingmapa lama from the Kongpo area. Dudjom Rinpoche died in exile in 1987. Several nuns look after Tsosum Gompa.

There is a two-day pilgrim circuit around the lake, but modern pilgrims don't bother – they just take a speedboat for an hour to reach the sacred spots up one end of the lake. There is a landing spot up the far end where you disembark and walk inland to a waterfall site where pilgrims rub themselves against revered stones and squeeze into impossible cave crevices. Join a group on a boat and you can get there for maybe Y40 a person (hiring an entire small boat will cost around Y400 an hour). You can stay in bungalows at **Basum Tso Holiday Resort Hotel**, complete with a large dining hall. There are 30 double rooms for around Y140 each.

On the southern leg of this route, south of Bayi lies the region of Kongpo, with a distinct ethnic group identified by their traditional dress. You will see Kongpo people coming to visit the nunnery of **Lamaling**, which lies 26km south of Bayi and a further 4km off the road (an easy day trip from Bayi). Lamaling is a tower-like structure with an internal octagonal wooden frame. It is set in grounds with lush gardens and fir trees, and operates its own restaurant. Overseeing Lamaling is Dechen Yudron, who is the eldest daughter of Dudjom Rinpoche, the supreme head of the Nyingma sect who passed away in 1987. Dudjom Rinpoche married twice, and had nine children, some of whom still live in Tibet while others live in exile.

Along the south route to Lhasa from Bayi lies another great draw for pilgrims: the sacred lake of **Lhamo Latso**. This place hits the jackpot in the permit sweepstakes: you need four permits (TTB, Foreign Affairs, military, and ATP from PSB). That normally takes three days of wrangling in Lhasa. Assuming your paperwork is in order, after a rough haul from Bayi via Miling and Namshan, you reach Gyatsa. There are decent hotels in all these places. From Gyatsa, a turn-off to the north heads for about two hours' drive on a rough road to reach Chongkogye Gompa (4,500m), where rude lodging can be had. The *gompa* was largely destroyed in 1959. From Chongkogye, another drive of 40 minutes – and payment of Y50 per foreigner entry fee – brings you close to a viewpoint for Lhamo Latso. You need to be very well acclimatised to march up the final hill to the viewpoint, as it rests at prayer-flags at 5,250m. From the viewpoint you can see Lhamo Latso, the oracle lake, at some distance. The lake sits at 5,080m. In former times, high lamas would venture out to Lhamo Latso to induce visions used in divinations. In the early 1930s, visions conjured up here helped direct Reting Rinpoche's search for the 14th Dalai Lama.

In the spring, this area is busy, with tent teahouses acting as lodging for those who've come in search of Chinese caterpillar fungus and high-altitude herbs. The spring is peak time for pilgrims to engage in a *kora* of Lhamo Latso, which could be accomplished on a long day trip, entering from this point. It's also possible to camp out and undertake treks of several days in this beautiful region. Further west of

THE MAGICAL BLUE POPPY

The fabled blue poppy of Tibet was first brought to the attention of the West by British officer and spy Eric Bailey, who spotted some when riding a pony near the Tsangpo in east Tibet in 1913. He pointed out the location to plant hunter Frank Kingdon-Ward, who collected the seeds at the same location in 1924. And sparked near pandemonium when the Royal Horticultural Society displayed the flower in 1926.

Poppy expert Bill Terry says: 'Among plants, none display such a palette of primary colours as the Asiatic poppies. There is no red redder than the red of punicea, no yellow more buttery than integrifolia. The white of superba is whiter than white. The imperial purples of lancifolia and delavayi are unmatched. No blue can compare with the blue of a perfect grandis or betonicifolia.'

There are dozens of poppies of different colour that grow in the Himalayan range, but the most striking is the tall *Meconopsis grandis*, a flower with incredibly blue petals flowering a metre in height at around 4,000m in alpine scree or woodland. The flower is very hardy: it has been observed with the hairs on its stem encased in ice. But the flower is not magical. It has no known medicinal properties.

Because Tibet has long been off the map, unscrupulous marketers have traded on general ignorance in things Tibet-related. Lancôme makes a perfume that says it captures the essence of the Himalayan blue poppy – which is actually not possible, because the blue poppy has zero fragrance. Yves Saint-Laurent created a line of cosmetic cleansing products based on 'health-giving Himalayan Blue Poppy water'. This, he claims, leaves the skin 'relaxed, purified and delightfully replenished'. And a healing spa in Alaska, where blue poppies grow well, advertised a Himalayan Blue Poppy Treatment, where the blue poppy is touted as having health-giving properties.

What will work as a health tonic (a tonic for the senses, at least) is to see for yourself the tall blue poppy growing, in the highlands of Tibet. In the vicinity of Lhamo Latso, if your timing is right, you will see clusters of tiny blue poppies – a different variety. To see the tall Himalayan variety, you need to go on an arduous quest – maybe into the Tsangpo Gorges like Frank Kingdon-Ward. Or go to Bhutan where the blue poppy flowers in the early monsoon. *Meconopsis grandis* is the national flower of Bhutan.

Gyatsa and Lhamo Latso, the road continues to Tsedang and Samye (see *Exploring Central Tibet* chapter, page 167).

BAYI (*2,950m; capital of Nyingchi Prefecture; telephone code 0894*) In Chinese, Bayi means '8–1', referring to the founding of the People's Liberation Army on 1 August 1927. There's a heavy PLA presence around Bayi – the place is riddled with army garrisons. Tibetans joke that 8–1 stands for eight Chinese for every one Tibetan, which is about the ratio you'll see on the streets of Bayi. The population is around 60,000. Bayi is a totally Chinese town, built in the 1950s and much expanded since – there was originally nothing in the way of Tibetan structures here. So what you see around town are white-tiled structures, China Telecom advertisements, fake palm trees and army garrisons. And mini-brothels. There is a strong relationship between the last two. It is more than a coincidence that Bayi, the second biggest town in eastern Tibet (after Chamdo), with the biggest army garrisons, also hosts the largest array of brothels in eastern Tibet. Mini-brothels line whole boulevards in Bayi, with prostitutes openly plying their trade.

For aliens visiting Bayi, accommodation is restricted to a handful of high-end hotels, an arrangement monitored by PSB. Other (cheaper) Chinese hotels are not permitted to deal with foreigners. The sanctioned bastions for foreigners include **Azalea Hotel** (\ *582 3222; with rooms for Y600*), **Nyingchi Hotel** (*around 75 rooms;* \ *582 1300; Y390 standard room, Y490 deluxe*), and the **Post Hotel**, off Hongkong Road (*around 55 rooms;* \ *588 9666; Y150–220 possible for a room, Y390 standard, Y430 trpl*).

There is limited **internet** access in Bayi, and an **ATM** machine at the Agricultural Bank that accepts foreign cards.

Bayi is often confused with the much smaller town of **Nyingchi**, 18km to the southeast. Nyingchi, also known by the names Nyingtri or Linzhi, is an old Tibetan settlement that has been eclipsed by Bayi (which is probably a good thing). But with the opening of a civilian airport near Nyingchi, and with speedboat sightseeing departures along the Yarlung Tsangpo close to Nyingchi, the pace might be picking up. There are direct **flights** from Chengdu to Nyingchi once a week. Landing at Nyingchi is apparently quite challenging as the plane must fly along a winding valley. At 2,950m in elevation, the airstrip is quite low (for Tibet).

There is some dickering over whether the capital of Nyingchi Prefecture is Nyingchi or Bayi. Think of these as twin monstrosities: the commercial power and military might are concentrated in Bayi, but Nyingchi still carries some clout and is the name that may materialise on permits. In any case, Bayi is easily the largest town in Nyingchi Prefecture, so that qualifies it as the capital by default.

BAYI TO BAXOI ENIGMAS Along the Bayi–Baxoi stretch lies some fascinating terrain which is extremely difficult to access. This is due to several factors, such as lack of both infrastructure and decent roads. But it also has to do with Chinese military presence, as the region is highly sensitive as it lies close to the Indian border. In the past there have been clashes between Chinese and Indian troops in the region over the borders of Arunachal Pradesh (occupied by India but claimed by China).

About 10km south of Nyingchi town is sacred **Mount Bonri**, which, as the name suggests, is an important pilgrimage spot for Bonpos (followers of the ancient Tibetan Bon faith). Bonpos circle the mountain anticlockwise, taking two days, but if you are attempting this, you should allow three.

In 1924, two British expeditions crossed paths in Lhasa. One was the ill-fated Everest expedition, heading west with the objective of summiting the mighty peak. The second expedition was heading in the opposite direction, east to the Yarlung Tsangpo Gorge, as it was then known. The expedition was led by botanist Frank Kingdon-Ward, with the eccentric Lord Cawdor in tow to provide financial backing. The object was to collect new plant species, and to hunt for a colossal waterfall, rumoured to be 30m tall.

Kingdon-Ward's expedition found waterfalls, but not a colossal one. He collected a staggering amount of flora – some 250 species, including the fabled blue poppy. And he overlooked a terrific discovery right under his nose. He was exploring in a canyon more than double the depth of Arizona's Grand Canyon, deeper than the Rio Colca in the Peruvian Andes, deeper than the Kali Gandaki in Nepal. The definitive discovery that the Yarlung Tsangpo Grand Canyon is the deepest in the world was not announced until the mid-1990s. The colossal 30m waterfall that Kingdon-Ward was hunting was not definitively identified until 1998.

Only now is the canyon starting to be launched as a world-class attraction – surely the eighth wonder of the natural world. The problem, as in Kingdon-Ward's day, is remote and inaccessible terrain. The canyon contains many rare species of flora and fauna, but trails through its wooded slopes are few and overgrown. The weather can be wet (very wet), foggy and unpredictable – the canyon hosts its own unique microclimates. And for foreigners, there's another great obstacle: Chinese officialdom. The main access point is close to Nyingchi, which lies close to a heavy military traffic zone.

Hopefully, this situation will change and this remarkable canyon will be easier to access for foreign hikers and even foreign rafters. Chinese tourists are able to reach the area. They start out on a day's drive from Nyingchi Airport, followed by an arduous two-day hike to Zhacu village. Close to this spot, there's a vantage point with stunning views over a bend in the river, where the mighty Yarlung Tsangpo wraps around the base of Mount Namche Barwa.

A recent addition at this site is the Namche Barwa Visitor Centre, designed by avant-garde Beijing architect Zhang Ke. The centre houses an exhibition on the history of the canyon, a contemplation space and hiker facilities (including a medical clinic for those struggling with altitude). Down by the river is another facility, a small boat terminal where trips can be taken in direction of Namche Barwa.

You would think that a major attraction like the Yarlung Tsangpo Grand Canyon should be preserved in pristine shape, with revenue derived from tourism. Sadly, that is not the case. Chinese officials have chosen a path of exploitation of resources, in a way that will be highly destructive. The Yarlung Tsangpo is slated to be extensively dammed in the coming years. It is not only the world's highest river with the world's deepest gorge; it has far and away the world's greatest hydro potential, at the Great Bend of the Tsangpo. A proposal made by Chinese engineering consortiums calls for construction of Motuo Dam at the Great Bend, with a staggering output of 38,000MW. That would be more than double the output of the Three Gorges Dam – currently the world's largest.

East Tibet, Kham and Amdo   EAST TIBET, WITHIN THE TAR   8

Nyingchi is the gateway to the Yarlung Tsangpo gorges. Treks into the gorge area are possible but this would have to be arranged well in advance – you won't be able to organise anything from Bayi or Nyingchi because of a complicated permit situation. There are even speedboat cruises from Nyingchi along the Yarlung Tsangpo River – but at the time of writing, only Chinese tourists were allowed on these high-powered vessels.

An unusual feature of Nyingchi Prefecture is that the altitude can dip quite low, with lush forest and monsoonal weather, and that means that Namche Barwa may be obscured by cloud. At 7,756m, **Namche Barwa** is the highest peak in eastern Tibet. The Yarlung Tsangpo stages a dramatic U-turn around Namche Barwa, cutting through the world's deepest gorges (for more on the Tsangpo gorges, see the *Geography* section in the *Background information* chapter, page 6).

Highly scenic parts of the Bayi–Baxoi stretch that are accessible lie at **Pomi** (stunning valleys in the vicinity, plus Dodung Monastery) and **Rawu** (beautiful pine-forest area with lakes and sandy inland beaches). Both are worthy stops for picnicking, photography and hiking. Both have basic accommodation available, but the towns of Pomi and Rawu are eyesores, with the military and loggers given the run of the place.

BAXOI VIA CHAMDO TO DERGE From the area close to Baxoi, the road splits – northeast to Derge or southeast to Deqin. The longer route is via Chamdo to Derge.

Chamdo (*Qamdo; 3,240m*) Chamdo is the major town in east Tibet and the capital of Chamdo Prefecture. It also runs under the name Changdu. It's an administrative town of 80,000 people, with a fair sprinkling of high-rises and the usual Chinese concrete-and-karaoke mayhem layered on top of dilapidated Tibetan structures. Foreigners who make it through the permit hoops are expected to stay at **Chamdo Hotel**, which is right next door to the PSB office. Overlooking Chamdo is the Geluk monastery of Jampaling, with close on a thousand monks in residence. The *gompa* dates to the 15th century. About 100km south of Chamdo is Bangda (aka Qamdo Bangda, Bamda, Pomda, Changdu) Airport, a military airport which functions as a civil airport as well. Commercial **flights** from Lhasa to Bangda were tested out in 1999 on Boeing 757s, and there are chartered flights from Chengdu to Bangda. Bangda Airport, at elevation 4,334m, is the highest commercial airport in the world. It's about 2½ hours by road from Bangda to the city of Chamdo.

About 280km east of Chamdo, reached by a long mountainous drive, is **Derge Monastery**, the star attraction on the long-haul Lhasa to Chengdu northern route. Once you get to Derge, permit problems vanish. The dividing line for the TAR is the Yangtse River, and Derge lies 26km north of the Yangtse bridges. There are even privately run guesthouses to choose from in Derge. See the *Derge* entry in the *Routes through Kham* section, page 274, for details.

BAXOI TO DEQIN The road runs from Baxoi via Markham (turn-off to Litang and Chengdu possible) and dips down to the Mekong River past the TAR border, climbs high above the river, then swings into Deqin, set in a high valley in Yunnan's northwestern corner. Once out of the TAR, the Landcruiser ride may end – unless you have negotiated further driving. Permit hokum ceases in Deqin, so you can do what you like once in Yunnan. Onward from Deqin, you can proceed by regular bus or hired vehicle to Zhongdian, and then either loop via Daocheng and Litang to Chengdu, or make a run via Lijiang and Dali to Kunming. See following sections for details on these destinations.

These regions offer thrilling experiences of Tibetan culture, grand Himalayan Mountains and expansive high-altitude grasslands of the Tibetan Plateau. This is the Tibet that spells adventure, as in trekking, visiting nomads, horseback treks, bicycle expeditions – all the things that would be prohibitively expensive in the permit-ridden TAR. A journey here could take from a few weeks to many months; you'll probably want to visit again. Kham includes much of the eastern third of the Tibetan Plateau; Amdo the plateau's northeastern corner. Each region has its distinct dialects, customs and architecture. You'll not only find fewer restrictions on your travels here compared with official Tibet (TAR), but also that the Tibetans tend to be more relaxed and friendly. In fact, according to Chinese statistics, there are more Tibetans in the Chinese provinces adjoining the TAR than there are within the TAR itself.

Religious life and the artistic splendour of the great temples of these regions compare well with those in Lhasa and central Tibet. In fact, there is more religious 'freedom' in regions of Kham. In parts of Yunnan and Sichuan, photos of the Dalai Lama are openly displayed in monasteries, and revered rinpoches in both Kham and Amdo attract a number of followers when giving teachings. Trekking and cycling opportunities abound. Summer (May–September) is the best time to come, when wildflowers flourish and hillsides turn green with lush grass. Tibetans will be out camping on the grasslands with their herds of yaks, sheep and horses. The last stronghold of the beleaguered nomad culture rests in Kham. Summer is festival time: you might catch one with Tibetan-style singing, dancing, competitions and the grand finale – the horse race. Spring and autumn can be good travelling as well, though snowstorms can upset your plans and the grasslands won't have their flowers and greenery. Winter can be brutally cold with the prospect of stalled transport. Even in summer, the air is cool on account of the 2,000–4,000m elevations. Rain showers often pass through during the summer months, yet soon yield to the intense light of the sun. For maximum enjoyment, allow time to meet people along the way and soak in the wonderful views. Also, by gaining elevation slowly in the early stages, you'll greatly reduce the chance of acute mountain sickness. Banks and ATMs quickly thin out in the high country, so carry a load of Chinese cash to get you through.

The following route ideas are just a few of the many possibilities. We begin with the vast expanses of Kham – Tibetan lands to the east of the TAR and now in northwestern Yunnan, western Sichuan and southeastern Qinghai provinces. Farther north, Amdo spreads across most of Qinghai Province to the northeast of the TAR and includes a bit of northern Sichuan and southwestern Gansu provinces. Qinghai Province has a rather unsavoury reputation as the gulag of China, due to its prison camps in the middle of nowhere. Dissidents and political prisoners are dispatched here. Due to their desert locations, it's hard to escape these camps, which is the whole idea.

Key destinations in Kham and Amdo include huge monasteries, the objective of pilgrims who travel great distances to see them: Zhongdian, Litang, Tagong, Derge, Dzogchen, Sershul, Yushu (Jyekundo), Kumbum, Tongren and Labrang. Trekkers will find remote monasteries, picturesque villages and great snow mountains. Cyclists will be challenged by spectacular high passes in the back country: see the box, *Cycling Kham and Amdo*, page 276. There is much to explore in Kham and Amdo.

The descriptions here are route-based for the simple reason that Kham and Amdo cover vast areas. You can easily incorporate the routes with your TAR travels. In the grand scheme of your trip, these routes also fit well with travels in other parts of China and in southeast Asia. Travellers tend to start in the south and work their way north, so descriptions here start in Yunnan Province and wend their way north to Qinghai Province. Routes are equally good in either direction, though northbound may be more attractive in early spring and southbound a good idea in late autumn. Information about the large gateway cities of Kunming, Chengdu and Xining is included with the routes.

ROUTES THROUGH KHAM
Gateway: Kunming You'll likely pass through Yunnan's capital on your way to or from southern Kham. Set beside Lake Dian at 1,890m, Kunming has a very pleasant climate nearly year-round. You can enjoy the fine **temples**, **parks** and **museums** while getting ready for onward travels. The city offers excellent air, rail and road connections within the province, many other cities in China, and nearby countries. You can **fly** to Lhasa, though this requires the usual permits and 'tour', which can be arranged by a local agent. Kunming is very close to border crossings with Laos and Vietnam, easily reached by **bus** on expressways. Your only option for the Vietnam connection at present is by bus. A new rail link is in the works to Vietnam and will replace the historic French-built line. You can pick up a visa for Vietnam in Kunming; or from the other direction China visas can be obtained in Hanoi. Most nationalities can get their Lao visa at the border, or you can visit the consulate in Kunming. If you're coming from Laos, Chinese visas are available in Vientiane (longer Chinese visas may be possible to obtain here).

Where to stay and eat The **Camellia Hotel** (Chahua Binguan) (*96 Donfeng Donglu;* \ *871 316 3000; www.camelliahotelkunming.cn*) has hosted travellers for decades with dorm and mid-range accommodation; travel agents have offices here. **Kunming Cloudland Youth Hostel** (*23 Zhuantang Lu;* \ *410 3777*) is very popular for its pleasant atmosphere and just about any service a traveller could desire.

CARVING UP TIBET

Vast tracts of what were formerly the Tibetan territories of Kham (east of Lhasa) and Amdo (northeast of Lhasa) were carved up by the Chinese into four neighbouring provinces of the TAR. Tibetans referred to this area as 'Four Rivers, Six Ranges', later used as the name of a Khampa guerrilla resistance movement. The Chinese christened the new slabs of territory 'Tibetan Autonomous Prefectures' (TAPs). The process started under the Chinese Kuomintang regime before 1949, and continued under the communist government from 1950 into the 1980s. Some of the TAPs are enormous: Ganzi TAP in Sichuan, for instance, covers about one-third of Sichuan's land area. On the fringes of the plateau are smaller areas called Tibetan Autonomous Counties (TACs), where Tibetans and other nationalities live in mixed communities. Some TAPs are also occupied by Tibetan-related minority groups, such as the Qiang people of northern Sichuan. The ethnic Tibetan area can be roughly correlated with the Tibetan Plateau. On the plateau, the Tibetan nomad culture is still present; where the plateau drops off, the descent is made to Chinese towns. However, there has been lots of Chinese infiltration since the 1950s.

To find out more about these regions, the International Campaign for Tibet (*www.savetibet.org*) has a range of publications, including a printed map, *The Eastern Regions of Tibet*. An excellent website for finding out more about travel in Kham is *www.khamaid.org/travel/*.

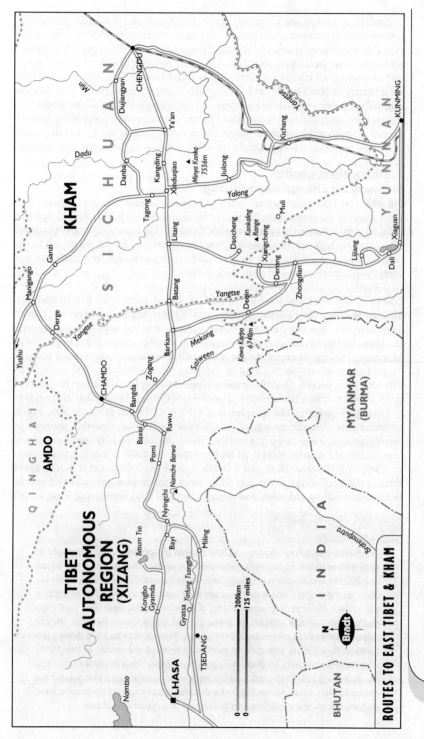

ROUTES TO EAST TIBET & KHAM

0   200km
0   125 miles

N

TIBET AUTONOMOUS REGION (XIZANG)

QINGHAI

AMDO

KHAM

SICHUAN

YUNNAN

MYANMAR (BURMA)

INDIA

BHUTAN

LHASA
TSEDANG
Namtso
Kongbo Gyamda
Gyatsa
Basum Tso
Bayi
Miling
Yarlung Tsangpo
Nyingchi
Namche Barwa
Pomi
Rawu
Baxoi
Bangda
CHAMDO
Zogang
Barkam
Deqin
Kawa Karpo 6740m
Zhongdian
Yangtse
Batang
Derge
Yangtse
Yushu
Manigango
Ganzi
Litang
Daocheng
Xiangcheng
Derong
Konkaling Range 6740m
Muli
Yalong
Lijiang
Dali
Xiaguan
Xichang
Jiulong
Minyo Konka 7556m
Kangding
Xinduqiao
Tagong
Danba
Dadu
Ya'an
Dujiangyan
CHENGDU
Min
Yangtse
KUNMING
Mekong
Salween
Brahmaputra

And if it is mushrooms you desire, there are entire streets in Kunming lined with **restaurants** specialising in mushroom cuisine. There are thought to be 850 species of edible mushroom found in Yunnan. Deep in the hills, Tibetans (often former nomads) make their livelihood from collecting varieties like chanterelles, morels and matsutake, which are exported to Japan and Europe. The Tibetans also look for a variety of black truffle, and for the highly prized *yartsa gunbu* – or Chinese caterpillar fungus – valued for its supposed anti-ageing and aphrodisiac properties. Hotpots are the traditional Yunnan way to savour mushrooms – steeped in a broth flavoured with local ham, for instance. Other dishes include stir-fries with porcini and green pepper, and fungus salad with wild herbs and black vinegar. Bon appetite!

Southern Kham wonders
Kunming via Zhongdian to Tagong
Old Dali Old Dali makes an enjoyable stop between Kunming and Lijiang. City walls encircle the restored buildings of the centre. It's very touristy, yet makes a good base for side trips to villages around nearby Erhai Lake. A fantastic mountain hike contours high on the slopes of Cang Shan above; a chairlift hoists you to the heights, where you follow a wide well-made trail southward to a cable car that brings you back to earth and a bus back to Dali.

Lijiang (*2,600m*) Lijiang was used by explorer Joseph Rock as his base in northern Yunnan Province to begin his journeys into Tibetan lands – and you can launch from here, too. The city has much to see, especially in the large and atmospheric old town, and good transport connections. The shining 5,596m Jade Dragon Snow Mountain (Yulong Xueshan) to the north will likely entice you onward towards Tibet. Lijiang is well worth a visit to meet the Naxi, a minority descended from Tibetan Qiang people. Most likely you will prefer to stay in old Lijiang (Naxi part of town, closed to motor traffic) rather than the new Chinese Lijiang that surrounds it.

Lijiang's wonderful **old quarter** is a UNESCO World Heritage Site, but is unfortunately overrun by legions of Chinese tourists who ramble through in unruly groups, ransacking the shops. There are lots of Naxi-style courtyard inns in the old quarter to suit all budgets, and the food is a brilliant selection of European, Chinese, Naxi and Tibetan – quite an eye-opener if you've spent time in the back country. You can while away time in pleasant cafés and bistros in Lijiang's bustling old town, and sample the local Naxi homemade wine, which

NAXI OLD-TIMERS

The Naxi are an intriguing group. Their ancient pictograph script is thought to derive from shamans. Naxi shamans used to conduct rituals similar to Tibetan oracles (the last shamans in Lijiang have long departed). The Naxi not only lay claim to the world's oldest dance score, they lay claim to the oldest orchestra, the oldest musical instruments and the oldest musicians. Naxi orchestra performers average around 80 years old in Lijiang. That's because they're the only ones who remembered the music when it was banned during the Cultural Revolution. The elderly musicians revived the music in the 1990s and are now passing on their skills to a new generation of performers. You can listen to a Naxi orchestra performance every evening at a venue near the centre of old Lijiang. Above the orchestra are photographs of those who have departed from the orchestra and passed on to the heavens above.

CHENGDU

Tagong

Kangding

TIBET
(TAR)

Lhasa

Barkam

Litang   Xinduqiao

Minya Konka
7556m▲

Ganzi Tibetan
Autonomous
Prefecture

SICHUAN

Xiangcheng

Daocheng

Yalong

Jiulong

Deqin

🛕 Gongaling

Yading ○

Kawa
Karpo
6740m

Muli Tibetan
Autonomous County

Zhongdian

Lugu
Lake

○ Muli

Xichang

Diqing Tibetan
Autonomous
Prefecture

Tiger Leaping
● Gorge

Ninglang

N

Bradt

MYANMAR

Lijiang

Yongsheng

Yangtse

Solween

Mekong

Dali

YUNNAN

Xiaguan

KUNMING

0 ▭▭▭▭▭ 160km
0 ▭▭▭▭▭ 100 miles

↓Bus to Vietnam border

tastes similar to port. The old quarter is actually the safest place to be: in 1996, an earthquake levelled the modern part of Lijiang, but left the old wood and stone Naxi buildings mostly intact, which speaks volumes about modern Chinese construction techniques.

The old village of **Baisha** just north of town is a fine day trip, as are several Tibetan monasteries. Farther north, an Italian-built cable car runs almost 3km up the flank of **Jade Dragon Snow Mountain**, reaching 4,500m at the top of the lift. The rapid ascent can easily cause altitude sickness: Chinese tourists not only rent parkas, they purchase oxygen canisters. Be warned that you'll have to pay very high entry and cable car fees on the mountain.

Lugu Lake The lake (2,688m), northeast of Lijiang, is the centre of the fascinating Mosuo ethnic group. Mosuo women do not marry: they instead take lovers for the length of time that suits them. Children belong to the household of the woman. Getting to Lugu Lake is an all-day affair of seven to eight hours that crosses the deep gorge of the Yangtse, then climbs high into hills. Alternatively you could overnight at Ninglang, which is itself of interest as a market town with minority groups; it's three to four hours from Lijiang. Small towns and villages around Lugu Lake offer hostels and hotels.

Upward to Zhongdian On the way, you have the option of branching northwest off the main highway to the **First Bend of the Yangtse** at Shigu, where the great river makes a nearly 180° bend to change not only its course, but the course of Chinese history. Back on the main highway, you'll cross the Yangtse and reach the main turn-off for **Tiger Leaping Gorge**, one of the top sights of Yunnan. A road goes all the way through the gorge, but a trail high above provides the best way to experience the scenic splendour. The trail is doable in one long day – or you can

SHANGRI-LA SHENANIGANS

Nobody with their marbles intact would mistake Zhongdian for Shangri-La: it's a bland Chinese city full of concrete and karaoke, which doesn't fit the bill. But Zhongdian is being marketed as the gateway to Shangri-La, in rivalry with other candidates like Yading and Lijiang. This time, all of Diqing Tibetan Autonomous Prefecture is being pushed as a composite (large monastery in one part, classic pyramidal mountain in another) which helps explain the 2002 official name change from Zhongdian County to Shangri-La County. And this will also explain Diqing Shangri-La Airport, the official name of Zhongdian's airport, on the outskirts of town, with flights to Chengdu, Kunming and Lhasa. The Kunming–Zhongdian–Lhasa flights are likely to be staggered in winter (December–May), but the Kunming–Zhongdian flights should be more regular. Many businesses in Zhongdian blithely use the Shangri-La logo without rhyme or reason: Shangri-La Bus Station, Xianggerila Mini-mart, and so on. It's just another day in Shangri-La.

According to Yunnan spin doctors, Zhongdian is the only possible site for Shangri-La. According to the Sichuan spin doctors, however, the real Shangri-La is located in Yading. Shangri-La County (formerly Zhongdian County) is one of three counties that make up Diqing Tibetan Autonomous Prefecture (the other two counties are Weixi Lisu and Deqin). Diqing TAP covers a grand 23,870km² and is sparsely populated, with around 400,000 people, of whom perhaps 30% are Khampa, or ethnic Tibetan. The percentage rises in Deqin County (population 60,000, of whom perhaps 75% belong to Tibetan or Tibetan-related minority groups).

Due to all the regional dogfights in these parts over which place is the real Shangri-La, Chinese authorities came up with a novel solution. In 2002, they announced the creation of a huge zone to be developed for tourism in western Yunnan and Sichuan, to be called the 'China Shangri-La Ecological Tourist Zone', with development investment projected to run to billions of dollars. This drew howls of protest from exiled Tibetans, who say this is yet another marketing ploy to exploit the Tibetans, and that there can be nothing remotely resembling the utopia of Shangri-La if it falls under Chinese domination. In any case, the Shangri-La Ecological Tourist Zone idea has since vanished into thin air – just like Shangri-La.

For more hoopla about Shangri-La, you can delve into Bradt's guidebook, *Shangri-La: A Travel Guide to the Himalayan Dream*.

take your time and overnight at village guesthouses. Several trails also drop from the road to raging rapids, hemmed in by one of the deepest gorges in the world.

You have a choice of two routes onward to Zhongdian: the main highway takes a direct route north, or you can go through Tiger Leaping Gorge and continue on a winding mountain road past icy 5,396m Haba Mountain, the travertine terraces at Baishuitai, and up into Tibetan country.

Gateway: Zhongdian Set at a lofty 3,275m, Zhongdian has been christened 'Shangri-La' by the Chinese. The old Tibetan name is Gyalthang. It's the largest town in Diqing Tibetan Autonomous Prefecture and the one with the most facilities.

At the centre of Zhongdian is an entirely new old town – a convincing reconstruction of Zhongdian's old Tibetan quarter, done after Zhongdian was awarded the Shangri-La name by Beijing. With the name of Shangri-La comes tourist expectations, so the old town was built to match those expectations, making it rather like a carbon copy of Lijiang's old town. To add authentic touches, even the new roofs have been carpeted in moss. Every night there is ethnic dancing at the main square of the old town to complete the picture of happy, smiling minorities. The main sight of Zhongdian is **Sungtseling Monastery**, a citadel founded in the 17th century by the Fifth Dalai Lama. Sungtseling has a spectacular setting and is worth half a day of roaming around. It's an easy 5km bus ride north of town.

Tour operators Agencies around town can organise onward travel by air or Landcruiser to Lhasa. The plane originates in Kunming, stops in Zhongdian and continues to Lhasa. However, planes can be overbooked because there are only flights several times a week from Zhongdian, as opposed to the numerous daily flights from Chengdu to Lhasa. Best to book your Zhongdian–Lhasa flight well in advance, via an agent in Chengdu. The air ticket to Lhasa is Y1,470 one-way.

An overland trip by Landcruiser from Zhongdian to Lhasa is ultra-expensive, costing in the region of US$4,000 for 12 days. The reasons for this exorbitant pricing are hard to fathom, but there seems to be little way around it by bargaining with agencies. There are two agencies close to the old town that deal with foreign individual travellers.

Khampa Caravan, at the centre of Zhongdian (887 828 8648; f 887 828 8870; e *info@khampacaravan.com; www.khampacaravan.com*), offers package tours and overland tours to Lhasa for a hefty tariff. With similar services is **KawaGebo International Travel**, located in the square of the old town (m 139 8877 3316; e *info@yaktraveler.com; www.yaktraveler.com*). Agencies seem to go through the TTB Yunnan office.

Zhongdian basics There's an **ATM** machine at the entrance to the Old Town. You can get **internet** access around the corner at **Noah's Restaurant** – which is a great place to eat. There are lots of small restaurants of good standard around the old town. You can even get a good Western breakfast: near the old town square; try **Compass Café**, which serves fresh-baked goods, along with muesli and scrumptious Western food. Zhongdian has **nightlife** attached to restaurants. At the south side of the old town near the big white *chorten* is an upstairs club and dance-bar where Tibetans hold open-mike nights for singers. In the same vicinity are some Tibetan restaurants that sell yak burgers and yak-steak sizzlers.

There's no shortage of low, mid-range and high-end accommodation in Zhongdian. In and around the old town are small cosy boutique hotels and backpacker lodges. You may want to pull out the sleeping bag here: there's little in the way of heating in the rooms even for mid-range accommodation. Hotels simply provide extra blankets or quilts. For budget accommodation, **Kevin's Trekker's Inn**, just outside the old town entrance, is highly recommended, with dorms from Y30 to rooms at Y120. Closer to the square in the old town is **Dragoncloud Guesthouse** (*www.dragoncloud.cn*) with dorms for Y30 and rooms for Y80–160, arranged in a courtyard that replicates old Chinese-style. Boutique hotels with Tibetan architectural features can be found. A fine one is **Kersang's Relay Station** at the south end of the old town: the place is homey, with lots of wood used in the construction, and there are great views from the rooftop deck. Rooms cost Y200 and up.

You can also stay in Tibetan bed and breakfasts that are converted manors; several are located along the road leading to Sungtseling Monastery. Right near the gates of monastery is the mid-range **Songtsam Hotel**, a finely designed place with lots of atmosphere. Another higher-end hotel with character, located on the outskirts of Zhongdian, is **Banyan Tree Ringha** (*www.banyantree.com/en/ringha/ overview*) with beautiful Tibetan touches in the décor, and fireplaces in the rooms – and a huge price-tag to boot.

Far less successful in emulating Tibetan style is a monstrosity in the centre of Zhongdian called the **Holy Palace Hotel**, which claims to take its name – and its architectural inspiration – from the Potala Palace. Except that the Potala does not have a karaoke-nightclub warren on the rooftop. The tariff is steep: Y700 and up for a double room. The luxury **Paradise Hotel** on the main street of Zhongdian

THE TEA-HORSE ROAD

If you are attempting the long overland haul from Lhasa via Deqin to Lijiang (or the reverse route), you are actually following stages of the ancient Tea-Horse Road.

In the 7th century Tang Dynasty, Tibetan traders discovered tea on the eastern borders of Tibet, in Yunnan. Tea quickly became a Tibetan staple. In exchange for tea, they traded horses. The Chinese cavalry needed war horses, and the Tibetans had developed a special bloodline of horses – a stocky breed, renowned for endurance and stamina at high altitude.

And so the Tea-Horse Road developed – Chinese tea going west, Tibetan horses going east. The route stretched several thousand kilometres, traversing numerous high passes and taking three months or more to complete. There were over 60 relay stations along the maze of routes. Litang and Lijiang were among these relay stations – market towns trading in musk, furs, herbal medicines, salt, cloth, tea and horses.

Although the Chinese sold them the worst-grade tea-leaves, the Tibetan could never get enough of the stuff. At times, caravans of up to 500 yaks would converge in a town at the frontier of Tibet, waiting for tea to be loaded. This low-grade tea became such an addiction for the Tibetans that tea bricks – stamped with Chinese characters for the weight – were used as actual currency in the Land of Snows. You can find these huge tea bricks on display (and for sale) in shops in Zhongdian and Lijiang.

The lucrative ancient trade in horses has long gone. The Chinese military are no longer interested in horses. But the Tibetan addiction to tea remains – and so does the nomad passion for horses. In the back-country, a fast horse is a status symbol, providing transport over rugged terrain. And Tibetan nomads love horse-racing festivals.

features a giant skylight – a Plexiglas dome enclosing the entire hotel grounds; rooms start at Y880 for a double, and extend to Y8,800 for a presidential suite. This place is rated five-star – not because it has tennis courts, but because it has a full-on hyperbaric chamber where those suffering from the effects of altitude can go to take a breather (before going back to chain-smoking in the lobby).

Side trip to Deqin and Minyong Glacier For most travellers this will be an out-and-back trip, but if you're one of the lucky people to have arranged it, this is also a route to Lhasa, entering the TAR near Yanjing. From Zhongdian, the highway heads northwest over a minor pass, then plunges into the deep gorge of the Yangtse. Near the river you'll come to a crossroads; turn left across the bridge for Deqin and follow the river to Benzilan, a town with hotels. From here the going gets tough with a long climb up and over a triple pass (4,000–4,300m) to Deqin. Nearing Deqin, you'll see a long row of *chortens* at a viewpoint where you can enjoy a splendid panorama (weather permitting) of Mount Kawa Karpo, an icy peak of 6,740m on the Yunnan–Tibet border and its female counterpart, 6,054m Miacimu to the south. Mount Kawa Karpo is also known as Mount Kawagebo or Mount Meili Xueshan.

The frontier town of **Deqin** is the capital of the county of the same name and sits at 3,290m in a side valley high above the Mekong. The spectacular five- to seven-hour bus ride from Zhongdian covers close on 200km. In Deqin, a guesthouse with character is **Dexin Tibetan Hotel** (📞 *0887 841 2031*), with dorms and rooms. More creature comforts can be had at the Meili and other hotels.

For scenery, head 10km beyond Deqin to **Feilaisi viewpoint**, where the rising sun lights up a string of 6,000m peaks like candles. At centre stage is Mount Kawa Karpo (aka Mount Kawagebo in Tibetan or Meili Xueshan in Chinese), which at 6,740m is Yunnan's highest peak. At Feilaisi's white *chortens*, Chinese photographers indulge in strange Tibet chic rituals – chanting *Om Mani Padme Hum*, throwing rice in the air, and tying on prayer-flags. The peak of Kawa Karpo is sacred to the Tibetans and has temples and a challenging *kora*. You may wish to club together with other travellers and rent a taxi out to Feilaisi at dawn and then motor on across the Mekong to the Minyong Glacier.

Impressive vistas continue beyond Feilaisi as you follow a road cut in cliffs. At a junction, the road to the TAR continues ahead, while the route to **Minyong Glacier** switchbacks down to a bridge across the Mekong, fast flowing in its narrow inner gorge and far removed from its setting in southeast Asia. With an early start you could visit Minyong Glacier on a day trip. Or stay at one of the guesthouses in the little town of Minyong near the trailhead and explore more of the area. The trail climbs through forest to the glacier and a temple, then keeps climbing on a boardwalk directly over the edge of the ice for better and better views of the glacier tumbling down Mount Kawa Karpo. See Gary McCue's *Trekking Tibet* (see page 331) for other hiking possibilities in the area, including the inner and outer *koras* of Mount Kawa Karpo.

Deqin and Minyong are the end of the road – the farthest point in Yunnan you can access without crossing into the TAR. That means you have to double back unless you have arranged permits to cross into the TAR, or unless you are particularly sneaky. If you're heading north to Litang, there's no need to go all the way back to Zhongdian; instead, get transport to Derong (turn left just beyond the Yangtse River bridge) and on to Xiangcheng at the Zhongdian–Litang highway.

North to Litang From Zhongdian, you have a choice of taking the direct highway or a longer and more varied and populated route that drops down to the Yangtse

River and winds up a tributary to Derong (which has hotels) and climbs up valleys with prosperous Tibetan villages; on the way you may wish to stop at the 'Wild West' town of Xiangbala to see the colourful **Redaqupiling Temple**. Both routes have passes and good mountain scenery before meeting **Xiangcheng**, which has hotels and an impressive hilltop monastery. The monastery is large and active, with monks on motorcycles commuting from here into town. There are sweeping views from the hilltop where the monastery is located. The area around Xiangcheng is dotted with prosperous villages and two- or three-storey farmhouses. It's worth stopping in Xiangcheng to explore.

From Xiangcheng, the highway twists over a 4,870m pass and drops to the tiny settlement of Sangdui and the turn-off for Yading Nature Reserve. You could visit Bangpu Monastery, about 1km north of Sangdui. The highway to Litang climbs onto a vast treeless plateau and a few more passes before the descent to Litang.

Side trip to Yading Nature Reserve On the way, you'll pass through Daocheng (Dabpa), a small, bland town 28km in from Sangdui with a handful of guesthouses. It's the main transport centre for bus connections. There's a big Tibetan monastery 10km northeast of Daocheng called **Yangteng Gompa** (Xiongdeng Si in Chinese), which houses tens of thousands of Buddhist scriptures as well as many Buddha figures; it's located at the top of a winding switchback route, about 30 minutes by car from Daocheng.

Yading Nature Reserve embraces a realm of crystal-clear gurgling streams, and luxuriant forests of larch, pine, cypress, fir and oak, and majestic snowcaps with cascading glaciers and odd-coloured glacial lakes. To the Tibetans, this region is sacred ground: it is thought to be among the two dozen legendary hidden valleys scattered through the Himalaya, as described in Buddhist scriptures. Each hidden valley is said to have been consecrated by a great Tibetan guru. Clues are contained in Tibetan guidebooks on how to find them, but these places can be very dangerous and difficult to reach. There are three important mountains here: Chenresig (Avalokitesvara; 6,032m), Jambeyang (Manjusri; 5,958m) and Chanadorje (Vajrapani; 5,958m); these have never been climbed and are sacred to Tibetan Buddhists for representing the compassion, wisdom and energy essential to reach enlightenment and the end of suffering. Tibetans believe that it would be sacrilege to climb them, and dream of making a *kora* or pilgrimage around one or all of the mountains. Fifteen *koras* are said to be equal to the accumulated virtues of 100 million murmurings of the sacred mantra *Om Mani Padme Hum*, so some very strenuous hiking could save considerable wear and tear on the voicebox.

Human habitation is minimal: there are no permanent residents inside the reserve apart from roving Tibetan shepherds. The nature reserve, first designated in the late 1990s, is pristine and pollution-free; the superb mountain vistas are a tonic for the senses. Shielded by the mountain range, the region has its own microclimate, with an ever-changing show of clouds dispersing over the snowpeaks, and a great interplay of lighting conditions revealing new colours.

If all that doesn't take your breath away, the altitude will: it's over 4,000m up here. Chinese tourists come armed with oxygen pillows, oxygen canisters and traditional herbal remedies to counter the debilitating effects of high-alpine air. Touted by Sichuan spin doctors as the 'Last Shangri-La', the region attracts lots of well-heeled Chinese tourists, but remains largely unknown to Westerners.

Tourists can either hike into the area or opt, as most do, for a horseback ride. Tourists are led by Khampa wranglers, and seated on woven Tibetan carpeted saddles. The first photo-op stop is near tiny **Tsengu Gompa**, the only temple in the area. Within a few hours by horse, you reach a view-spot known as **Luorong Pasture**, 14km from the trailhead, where overnight camping is provided in tents. From this spot, it's possible to hike up towards a 4,700m pass to see pristine tarns, including one magical lake where, it is said, the future can be divined. If you have more time and camping gear, attempt a *kora*: the small *kora* encircles Chenresig and takes about three days. The big *kora* circumambulates all three sacred peaks in about six days.

Sichuan's Konkaling range has never been easy to get to, or trek around. Yading Nature Reserve is only accessible about six months of the year. You can rule out the winter – when the area is snowed in – and write off the monsoon period, when heavy rains reduce the trails to mud. The best times to tackle the route are April–June and September–November. The access route to Yading snakes in over high passes from the town of Daocheng. It's about 90km from Daocheng to Yading village at the trailhead.

The only accommodation in the Yading area is in **tented camps**. The nearest hotel is in the town of Riwa (the nearest large village to Yading). On the way into or out of Yading, make a point of stopping at **Konkaling Monastery**, located west of Riwa. This Gelukpa monastery is the largest in southern Sichuan, housing over 500 monks. In the morning, they're all seated in the lofty main prayer hall, which reverberates with the sound of chanting.

Litang (*Lithang; 4,010m*) Litang is a town with a dusty high street lined with bland Chinese shops and small businesses. It is best used as a launching pad to visit the nearby grasslands and see nomad herders. Club together with other travellers and rent a minivan for the day for Y500 or so.

Litang's claim to fame is the annual **horse-racing festival**, which is supposed to take place on nearby grasslands in the first week of August. It was started up by Chinese officials to boost tourism, with fixed dates from 1–7 August. On 1 August 2007, a nomad called Rungye Adak snatched the microphone at centre stage and delivered a short speech about nomad grazing problems, about freedom of religion, and about the return of the Dalai Lama. He was promptly arrested and sentenced to eight years in jail. There has not been a horse-racing festival held near Litang since then, though it may come back. In the meantime, look for other horse-racing festivals in the vicinity around this time.

Around the town, **Litang Gompa** is worth the visit. Litang was a hotbed of resistance to Chinese rule, and the monastery was bombed and strafed by Chinese planes in 1956. It has since been rebuilt and is fairly active. On the outskirts of town at a hilly spot is a **sky burial site**. Some hotels drive guests over to witness the ceremony (assuming there is a body that day), charging Y100 for each tourist. This macabre form of profit-making needs to be discouraged out of respect for the Tibetans. You can hike to the spot yourself, or can arrange to have your driver get there in the morning before going out on a day trip to the grasslands. Do not attempt to take photographs at the sky burial site.

Practicalities The **ATMs** at the Agricultural Bank will dispense cash. There are several places to stay not far from the bus station. The **Potala Inn** is adequate, with hot showers available; cost is Y180 for a double. Along the main street are some decent **eateries** serving stir-fried food. You can buy fresh food in the small market at the centre of town.

Litang to Tagong You're on Highway G318, the southern and most-used overland route between Chengdu and Lhasa. Numerous high passes and steep drops into valley bottoms make this a very challenging highway no matter which direction you head from Litang. Some 18km east out of Litang you have the option of a short cut north via Xinlong to Ganzi in the northwest corner of Sichuan. The main highway east twists up into high country, culminating in a 4,487m pass before a wild descent into a forested valley and the city of Yajiang on the Yalong River, a major tributary of the Yangtse. A climb over a 4,475m pass brings you to a highway junction in a wide valley just before Xinduqiao, a trading town. The northern branch of the Sichuan–Tibet Highway branches off here; turn onto it for Tagong, just a short 33km jaunt north up the valley, which narrows to a little gorge before opening onto the Tagong Grasslands.

Tagong The gorgeous setting at 3,750m and a handful of Westerner-friendly guesthouses and restaurants have made Tagong a traveller's centre, though it's still small-scale. The **temple** is well worth a visit with three main chapels full of Tibetan artwork, a *chorten* field behind, and a *kora* lined with prayer-wheels. Across a stone-paved courtyard from the temple you'll find the most popular traveller hangouts: **Sally's Kham Restaurant** serves Western, Tibetan and Chinese food; nothing fancy, but good. Sally and some of her helpers speak English and can tell you about the area. Sally also runs **Snowland Guesthouse**, which is above and beside the restaurant; simple rooms cost about Y30 for one person, Y50 for two in two-bed rooms; larger rooms are available too; the bathroom has a hot shower, two squat toilets and a wash-basin sink. **Khampa Café and Arts Centre**, on the third floor of a nearby building, has a very good café with Western and Tibetan food; you have a choice of brightly painted Tibetan-style indoor seating or sitting on an outdoor patio overlooking the temple. A small gallery sells Tibetan arts and crafts; an American woman, Angela, oversees the operation and runs a website (*www.definitelynomadic.com*). Sally and Angela can advise on arranging horse and **walking treks**. The Tagong area has many good walks among the high grassy hills to temples, a stupa, and viewpoints.

Onward from Tagong From Tagong, there are route choices. You can carry on eastward to reach the major gateway city of Chengdu, or you can continue north from Tagong, on a spectacular overland route to Yushu. In case you are starting from Chengdu, the following paragraphs give the connecting route from Chengdu to Tagong.

Gateway: Chengdu Chengdu sits at just 500m, giving it a warm climate where even bananas can grow, despite the proximity to the Tibetan Plateau just to the west. Surprisingly relaxed for such a big city, Chengdu is a pleasant place to hang out before or after a journey through Tibetan lands. You can enjoy fine temples, museums, parks, varied cuisines and nightlife. Probably the most popular sight is the **Giant Panda Breeding Research Base** just northeast of the city, where you can watch pandas feeding and frolicking in late morning before they begin their epic naps: the easiest way to visit is with a tour arranged by one of the hostels.

This huge city and capital of Sichuan Province has long been the easiest place to arrange transport and tours to Lhasa and the TAR; try agents at **Sim's Cozy Garden Hostel** and **Traffic Inn Hostel** if you're looking to do this. Cyclists can arrange rentals and tours in the TAR and elsewhere with Chengdu-based **Bike China Adventures** (*www.bikechina.com*). The city has the best transport connections in the region with an extensive network of air and rail connections to Lhasa and many Chinese cities; international **flights** connect with Europe and many Asian cities. **Bus** routes fan out to the far corners of Sichuan and to Chongqing. See *Practical Information*, page 63, for more details on Chengdu.

Where to stay Hostels provide great-value accommodation, cafés, Tibet tours and many traveller services.

Mix Hostel 23 Ren Jia Wan, Xing Hui Xi Lu; 028 8322 2271; www.mixhostel.com. North of the centre, it is well run & cheaper than other hostels in town. *From Y30 dorm; Y70 sgl; Y80 dbls (bath down the hall).*

THE JIULONG ROUTE: XICHANG TO TAGONG

Few Westerners know this alternative route into Tibetan lands that leads through deep river gorges, pretty Tibetan villages and alpine meadows. Side roads branch off to viewpoints and trekking routes of the western side of a range crowned by 7,556m Gongga Shan (Minyak Gangkar to Tibetans). You could also exit by this route, travelling from Tagong via Jiulong to Xichang, and then hopping on a train from Xichang to either Chengdu or Kunming.

XICHANG Xichang is a large, sprawling city about 375km north of Kunming on the main rail line and highway to Chengdu; there's an airport here, too. It's best known for the Xichang Satellite Launch Centre (XSLC) about 64km to the northwest and used for launching geostationary communications and weather satellites. More accessible, the Buddhist and Taoist temple complex of Lu Shan spreads up the forested slope above the west shore of the large lake, Qionghai Hu, 7km south of town. A good museum near the start of the trail illustrates the history of the local Yi minority. On the way to Lu Shan you'll pass a park with sculpture and an architecturally interesting theatre complex. Hotels are widely scattered around town.

XICHANG TO JIULONG An expressway gets you most of the 75km north to Mianning, where the scenery begins. The route to Jiulong climbs past village fields, meadows and dense forest to a pass, then drops precipitously down the Yalong River. The route follows the river upstream through some narrow gorges, then turns up the Jiulong River to Jiulong, nestled in a valley at 2,960m. Nearing town, you'll see more and more signs of Tibetan culture – architecture, prayer flags and traditional dress.

JIULONG The town has a main street, Tuanjie Dajie, with most of the hotels, restaurants and services; at the end you come to the town square and a big hotel, the Longhai Dajiudian, starting at Y160 for a room. Wuxuhai, an alpine lake 25km to the northwest and 800m higher on a paved road, has idyllic scenery amidst craggy mountains; lodging, food and horseback rides may be available.

JIULONG TO TAGONG Now you're in Tibetan country as the road leaves the last villages and follows wide valleys through conifer forests and meadows past summer camps of herders to a lofty pass, then down a narrow valley to the first village, Kunkashi at the KM99 marker stone; here you can detour east to trailheads for Gongga Shan. The main road follows valleys past very attractive Tibetan villages and joins Highway G318 just 8km east of Xinduqiao. You'll pass some hostels and hotels on the way into town, though Tagong is a more appealing place to stay, about 37km to the north.

⌂ **Sim's Cozy Garden Hostel** 211 North Section 4, First Ring Rd; ☏028 8335 5322; www. gogosc.com. Farther north & offers more services. *Y35–45 dorms; Y70–240 rooms, some with private bath.*

⌂ **Traffic Hotel** 6 Lin Jiang Zhong Lu, just west of Xinnan Lu; ☏028 8545 1017; www. traffichotelchengdu.cn. Venerable hotel in the centre of town, offers great value. *Y50 sgl rooms with bath down the hall; dorm beds & en-suite rooms available as well.*

⌂ **Traffic Inn Hostel** 6 Lin Jiang Zhong Lu; ☏028 8545 0470; www.trafficinnhostel.com/ en. Just behind the Traffic Hotel & a separate business. *Y35–40 dorms; Y90–180 rooms.*

Chengdu to Tagong routes The quick and easy way goes **via Kangding**, eight hours by bus thanks to good highways and the 4km Erlanshan Pass Tunnel. Flights to a new airport nearby may be available. Kangding has Tibetan temples and traveller's guesthouses and restaurants, though it's mainly a Chinese city. Another two hours by bus will get you to Tagong.

For more of an adventure, consider one of the three routes **via Danba**, a small city hemmed in by the valley of the Dadu River. It's a good base to visit nearby Tibetan villages. The middle route goes **via Wolong**, once famed for its giant panda sanctuary. The 2008 Sichuan earthquake changed all that and left massive devastation behind (even the pandas departed). The road through Wolong has reopened but will probably remain under construction forever. You'll see how dramatically the mountains have been transformed by huge landslides and how people's lives have changed. From Chengdu's Chadianzi bus station, you'll most likely take a bus to Dujiangyan in less than an hour, then look for onward transport to Wolong, probably a minibus. You may have to overnight at a basic hotel in Wolong, then enquire about transport over 4,523m Balangshan pass and down to Rilong, a possible base to explore the three valleys of Four Girls Mountain (Mount Siguniangshan); accommodation is easy to find. The road is good on this side of the pass and continues down the valley to Danba. A southern variation avoids Wolong by going **via Ya'an** and a pass over the Xiling Snowy Mountain, then descends to the Danba road west of Rilong; you would probably need your own transport for this. A northern alternative loops via Wenchuan, Miyaluo, Barkam and Jinchuan. Parts of this road were badly damaged in the 2008 earthquake.

In **Danba**, the **Dengba Hostel** just north of the Rilong–Danba highway junction is great value for dorm beds or rooms. Another hostel is across the street and you'll find hotels here and around the downtown area, about 2km north. **Suopo Village** is famed for its stone towers, picturesque houses and views. It's close enough you could walk it: from the Rilong–Danba highway junction, head south 3km and turn left on a dirt track just past a blue and white building, follow the dirt track 1.8km across a suspension bridge and downriver to the main part of the village; eventually this will be upgraded to a motorable road. It's worth hiring a guide to take you inside some of the old buildings and one of the towers. **Jiaju Tibetan Village** has a stunning setting in a bowl high above the valley, about 7km north of Danba. **Zhonglu Village** has towers and homestays about 11km northeast on the road to Rilong.

From Danba, a road heads southwest up a craggy gorge that could have come out of a Chinese painting. The road leaves the gorge for a climb to a 3,907m pass, then runs across a plateau past Garthar Choide Monastery to Bamei, where you may need to change transport for the 27km to Tagong.

Northern Kham splendours

Tagong via Ganzi to Yushu This journey through northwestern Sichuan takes in some of the very best Tibetan landscapes and culture, including many large monasteries and temples. If time limits you to just one excursion in Kham and Amdo, this is the one to do. Derge, famed for its printing monastery, is a worthwhile side trip: it's also a gateway to the TAR on the northern Sichuan–Tibet highway. Yushu, just across the border in Qinghai, was hit by a massive earthquake in 2010 that killed more than a thousand people and destroyed most of the town and surrounding monasteries. It is undergoing reconstruction, and continues to be a major transit centre of the region.

The ride from Tagong goes through beautiful grasslands to a minor pass at 10km. Trees appear along the road as you drop into the valley on the other side. Look for dark grey barren ridges of Bamei Stone Forest on your right at about 22km. In another 5km, a group of Sichuan restaurants mark a turn-off on the right for Danba, a worthwhile side trip (see opposite) via high grasslands and a forested gorge. Continue straight 300m into **Bamei** and you'll see a large *chorten* and many small ones on the right. **Golden Sun Hotel**, on the left across from the *chorten*, is run by a friendly Tibetan woman who speaks a bit of English and is a good cook. Twin rooms with bath are Y200, smaller twins without bath are Y100, and plain triples without bath are Y30 per bed. Check out the small collection of regional photograph books at the counter in the restaurant. You could probably get a discount on the more expensive rooms if business is slow. The basic **Lucky Hotel** is a bit further on the left and has a restaurant. A few more hotels and restaurants are farther along in the centre of Bamei.

Hillsides on the 79km drive to Dawu have a mix of grasslands and conifer forests – very lush and green in summer with lots of wildflowers. At 37km you enter the Long Deng Grass Land and continue climbing to a pass at 46km, then corkscrew steeply down into a narrow forested valley with very attractive village houses of log and stone construction. You'll pass lots of *chortens*, too. **Dawu** (Daofu) is a large town on the Jianshui River at 2,980m; the golden-roofed Nyitso Monastery is visible on the hillside to the right just past the centre of town. None of the hotels has a sign in English, but it's easy to spot the large Tibetan-styled **Ling Que Shi Hotel** on the right just before the centre; rooms with bath may go as low as Y100 after bargaining; cheaper rooms without private bath are available as well. Chinese restaurants, including a vegetarian one, are nearby.

The gently rolling highway heads 72km northwest up the Xianshui He Valley, a major tributary of the Yalong River. You'll see pretty village houses and note how the architecture changes as you travel through the Tibetan lands of Kham. The vast spread of Drango Monastery and its Tibetan village come into sight well before the town of Luhuo itself. A large silver sculpture in a traffic circle marks the entry to **Luhuo**, set at 3,200m. The big **Golden Yak Hotel** across from the traffic circle may be the only place that accepts foreigners; a slightly run-down and noisy room with bath might go for Y100 after a discount. Lots of Chinese and Tibetan restaurants are nearby and across the street. From Luhuo it's possible to take another road north over a pass, then east to Barkam (aka Barkham, Maerkang or Markang) and beyond with several options for north Sichuan or Chengdu. You could even loop back to Bamei via Danba. **Drango** ('Head of the Rock') **Monastery** perches high on the hillside north of Luhuo and has a huge, well-decorated assembly hall. A series of *tankas*, said to have been done by a renowned artist, are easy to miss – step back from the altar and look up to see them. Monks are friendly, but watch out for aggressive dogs.

Ganzi (*Garzê, Kardze, Kandze; 3,394m*) The grassland and mountain scenery on this 97km stretch is spectacular. Once past Luhuo, you continue up a valley of grasslands and bits of forest to Zhuwo at 52km, the last village before the highway begins a 19km climb to a pass with a splendid panorama of the glacier-clad

Inhabitants of the Tibetan Autonomous Prefectures in Sichuan and Yunnan have a lot more freedom than in Tibet; people appear much more prosperous, with Tibetan entrepreneurs often living in castellated structures (complete with satellite dish on the roof) and driving SUVs. And you will see large Dalai Lama pictures in monasteries in Kham, something that would not be tolerated by Chinese authorities in the TAR.

Historically, the Kham region was beyond the reach of the central Lhasa government and was dominated by heads of powerful clans prior to Chinese invasion. The tall brawny Khampas have a reputation as the fierce warriors of Tibet: in the 1950s, Khampa guerrillas engaged in stubborn resistance to Chinese incursions, and protected the Dalai Lama on his 1959 flight into exile. Though considerably subdued under Chinese rule, the Khampas are nonetheless not intimidated by the Chinese, and are aggressive traders who can be encountered as far off as Nepal and India.

Chola Mountains, crowned by 6,168m Chola Mountain. Tents of yak herders lie scattered across the grasslands near the pass. The descent through intensely green valleys leads to the Yalong River and Ganzi, set beside a small swift-flowing river dividing Ganzi into east and west halves. The highway follows the main street, Chuanzang Lu.

Hidden away near the centre, the old and atmospheric **Ganzi Den Gompa** has two halls with fine paintings and sculptures: devoted worshippers prostrate and make *koras*. Look for a gateway with little white *chortens* over a small lane on the north side of Chuanzang Lu between Dongda Jie and Qinghe Lu; or, from the Himalaya Hotel, go up Dongda Jie a bit and turn left up a narrow footpath. **Garzê Monastery** sits prominently on a steep hillside on the north side of Ganzi above the tightly packed Tibetan quarter. You can reach it by walking up the street on the west side of the small river, then curve left a bit on tiny lanes to a staircase that leads to the assembly hall. You'll probably need to ask directions, though getting lost amongst the twisting walkways can be fun. Or grab a taxi most of the way. Monks debate in the afternoons in a tree-shaded courtyard to the left of the stairs below the assembly hall. Inside, there's a pantheon of Buddhist deity statues, a central Sakyamuni Buddha and lots of very small statues of Sakyamuni Buddha and Tsongkapa. Walls have large paintings, mainly of fierce protectors. Look up near the centre of the hall to see a row of large *tankas*. The highest seat is reserved for the Dalai Lama or Panchen Lama, and is piled with *katas*.

Ganzi basics The **Himalaya Hotel** at 13 Dongda Jie was run-down and musty on last check. However, next door is a newer and far **nicer hotel**, also with a Tibetan-style front, but no English sign: there's a choice of twins with bath outside, singles with bath, and twins with bath. These hotels are to the north (right when coming into town), a short way up Dongda Jie. A hotpot **restaurant** lies a bit farther up Dongda Jie on the right. An **internet** café is on the left on Qinghe Lu, just north of Chuanzang Lu. Farther up Qinghe Lu is a mid-range hotel on the left and a fair-sized supermarket just beyond; an **ATM** is on the right side roughly across from the hotel. Lots of small and large restaurants are on this street as well. West on Chuanzang Lu across the small river, you'll see a large covered market to the left, a good place to stock up on fruit. Beyond the market area is the major cross-street

Dajin Jie; turn left for the popular **Golden Yak Hotel** and another hotel across the street. Minibuses park on this street and there are Tibetan restaurants.

Ganzi vicinity Head out into the countryside to see other **monasteries**. Dongtong (Dongtok) Monastery and the new Dingkhor Chorten are about a 20-minute south walk across the Yalong River, then take the right fork. Pongo Monastery is across the Yalong River, then about one hour on the left fork. Beri Monastery is 15km west of town on the north side of the Yalong River. Dargye (Dagei Si) Monastery, nearby hot springs, and **Dargye Monastery Deshi Hotspring Guest House** are farther west near Rongbatsa, about 30km from Ganzi (check http://khamaid.org/travel/dargye.htm for info and a map). Hadhi Nunnery, a two-hour walk from here, is home to about 56 nuns. If you're headed south toward Litang, there's a shortcut via Xinlong: the turn-off is 10km east of Ganzi.

Derge via Yaqing (Yarchen) and Baiyu Instead of taking the main highway to Derge via Manigango, take this back road across superb scenery and past many monasteries. Nearly all transport heads to Yaqing, a very popular religious centre near the halfway point; here you can get onward transport to Baiyu. From Ganzi, the route follows the main highway across the Yalong River towards Manigango, then turns south up past villages, then summer camps to a 4,800m pass at 37km with fine scenery all the way. A few mud bogs on the steep 14km descent to the Ah Shi Chu may slow your vehicle. A little shop on the right before the river bridge is a popular stop for instant noodles and maybe other food. A gentle climb through a granite boulder-strewn landscape leads to a broad pass at about 23km. You might like to try a developed hot spring with private bathing pools 21km beyond the pass: look for a walled compound on the left. You'll then pass a couple of villages with *gompas*, set in a grassy valley with a few forests. At 114km from Ganzi you arrive at the signed junction for Yaqing, 7km to the south: there's a checkpost at the turn-off and police may register you.

Yaqing Yaqing is a religious centre that attracts huge numbers of monks, nuns and laypeople. There are at least two guesthouses/restaurants here; ask people for directions. Expect to pay an overpriced Y50 per bed and don't count on a toilet. Shops are scattered around and are fairly well stocked. Yaqing has two large temples, great piles of mani stones, prayer-wheels and *kora* routes. It's an amazing place to see.

Continuing 120km farther west via a 4,613m pass (25km from the Yaqing junction) and Ronggai checkpost (106km from the junction), you will reach **Baiyu** (Pelyul). Pelyul Monastery, towering above the town, dates from 1665. It was built by the king of Derge. Set in a valley at 3,261m, Baiyu is a large town with accommodation and restaurants. For much of the 115km north to Derge, you'll follow the Yangtse River; two bridges cross to the TAR 26km before Derge. Even without permits, you could probably get away with going to the other side to inspect abandoned stone watchtowers. The mountains on the Sichuan side harbour many remote monasteries and trekking possibilities that you may wish to seek out. Gary McCue's *Trekking Tibet* has an entire chapter on this region.

Derge via Manigango and Tro La The 92km stretch to Manigango follows the wide valleys of the Yalong River and tributaries, with the minor 4,045m Mukri La about halfway. Many *gompas* line the way and you can make detours to others, such as Beri and Dargye, but you'll have to ask for directions as these are not signed in English on the highway. Icy peaks of the Chola Mountains rise to the south. Manigango, at elevation 3,886m, is a scruffy little crossroads town. It has a large hotel that offers twins with toilet and shower down the hall at Y80, but you might get them for less; try your luck for a hot shower in the evening as the water may be cold in morning. The hotel has a restaurant, but you will probably get better service at one of the small restaurants across the street. If you arrive early, consider stocking up on food in Manigango, then heading another 12km on the highway towards Derge to camp at the very pretty alpine lake Yihun Lhatso (4,025m) at the foot of the towering Chola Mountains and their glaciers. You can admire the scenery and go hiking; horserides may be available.

You get a view of the lake from the highway on the 42km climb to Tro La (Chola Pass), probably the most dramatic motorable pass in Sichuan. A sign at the top gives the elevation as 5,050m, but most maps place this closer to 4,900m. Pavement gives way to bumpy dirt on switchbacks up steep slopes on both sides of the pass: the views keep getting better and better as you near the top. Conifers and meadows fill the valleys on the other side all the way down to Derge. A sign on the left, 30km beyond the pass, marks the turn for Mondrak Monastery in a very pretty and remote setting less than a kilometre off the highway. Small villages line the valley farther down and you'll reach **Keluodong** (Khorlomdo) with a hilltop *gompa* and simple restaurants 86km from Manigango. Below here the Zhil Chu Valley narrows into a gorge that runs for 9.5km, then opens up at a large *chorten* and a group of rock paintings that you may want to visit. At 114km from Manigango, you pull into the large town of Derge. Two bridges lead across the river to the main part of town, which is predominantly Chinese. But if you head up the side valley you'll reach the far more atmospheric Tibetan quarters and the Bakong Scripture Printing Lamasery, which attracts Tibetan pilgrims and the few Western tourists that venture this way.

Derge (*Dêgê*) Tucked in a deep valley at 3,220m, this former kingdom holds **Bakong Scripture Printing Lamasery**, the largest woodblock printing temple left in the Tibetan world (two others were destroyed, in Narthang and Shol). There are two kinds of ink used here – black for religious texts and red for medical ones. Some 300 laymen under the direction of the abbot assemble texts by hand for shipment to temples in Qinghai, Gansu and Sichuan provinces, as well as to the TAR itself. The lamasery possesses several hundred thousand woodblock plates and a library with rare Sanskrit editions. It's very atmospheric, with two large and well-decorated halls downstairs and the printing operation upstairs. Be sure to climb up the ladder to the roof for fine panoramas and a tiny hall. This is a good vantage point from which to snap photographs of the two-man teams who rapidly turn out hand-printed pages.

From the centre of town, walk five minutes up Bagong Jie; admission is Y50. From the lamasery, continue up the valley on the road past a row of *chortens* and prayer-wheels to see recently restored **Derge Gonchen**, a large monastery with a splendid assembly hall. You might enjoy a stroll along the narrow lanes of the Tibetan houses and a small temple on the hillsides nearby. Several hotels line the highway. The cheaper hotels (from about Y50) may lack showers and English signs, but there's a bathhouse near the river. The pretentious three-star **Que'ershan Binguan** is across the first bridge, then right along the river.

Beyond Derge The highway continues on to Chamdo in the TAR, where you have the choice of continuing west to Lhasa on the northern route via Nagqu or turning south and catching the southern route via Bayi. If you're thinking of trying to slip through without permits, be aware that the PSB in Chamdo has been extremely vigilant about nabbing permit-less foreigners even during times when the PSB in other parts of the TAR have been relaxed. Whether or not the TAR is in your plans, the short trip to the Yangtse River is a pretty one. The highway continues down the Zhil Chu Valley, meeting the Yangtse in 24km and following the great river 1km to a turn-off for the bridges. You could probably get away with slipping across to the TAR side for a close look at two abandoned stone towers; smaller towers poke out of the hillsides on both sides of this long strategic spot. A rougher road continues south 89km on the Sichuan side to Baiyu, passing tracks and trails to a great many remote monasteries. You could also loop back to Ganzi via Baiyu; see *Derge via Yaqing and Baiyu*, page 273.

Dzogchen Gompa Many of the temples in this vast monastery complex glitter with gold. The setting at 3,960m in a meadow, hidden from the main road, is superb – it's worth a side trip from Manigango even if you're not headed all the way to Shiqu. From Manigango, you'll travel the road northwest towards Shiqu and Yushu across grasslands, past a lake then up a long climb to 4,571m Muri La. There are expansive views of grasslands and mountains all the way up. In contrast, the descent is steep and enters a valley. A *mani* wall and *chortens* stand just beyond the turn-off on the left, 50km from Manigango, though the monastery complex is almost completely out of sight, hidden by a glacial moraine beyond the little market town of Zhuqing (Ganda).

There's a **hotel** signed in English on the right 1km from the turn-off and this is probably the best place to stay unless you are undertaking studies at the monastery. The hotel is more of a homestay, with the family living downstairs and four-bed rooms decorated in Tibetan style upstairs (just Y15 per bed). The hotel sign advertises a restaurant/café, but serves only simple Tibetan fare. The town stretches about 1km beyond the hotel with many shops and a few restaurants; try the little Chinese restaurant in a police building on the right. A little farther on the left across a bridge is a bathhouse and a restaurant, both signed in English.

Allow a full day to explore Dzogchen Gompa. If you have an interest in Tibetan Buddhism, you are likely to find people studying here who speak English (also see *www.dzogchenmonastery.cn/index.html*). The monastery comes into view just a short walk beyond Zhuqing and past several *chortens*. Wooded hills and glacier-clad peaks above the monastery also invite exploration. The first group of buildings includes a large assembly hall with fine wall paintings, *tankas*, and a row of giant statues, mostly of the Buddha. A new assembly hall sits next to it. A nearby temple has a highly ornate golden roof. Shira Sing Buddhist University, the large red building topped with gold, is about 20 minutes farther up the valley. Zangdok Palri Institute has a beautiful new temple with a golden roof about halfway up the valley. The English-speaking Patrul Rinpoche is in charge and has a following of European disciples (he also has a centre in Belgium). Far up the valley you'll reach another golden-roofed building, the Temple of Great Perfection and Dzogchen Pema Tung Great Perfection Retreat Centre, or 'Pema Tung' for short. An ornate Buddha statue is inside. Nearby buildings provide housing for guests and retreatants; you might be able to stay here. If you cross the river before Pema Tung, a trail leads up a glacial moraine for views of an upper valley, rapids and mountains. You can mount day hikes here – or a trek of several days over a high pass to Keluodong (Khorlomdo). Wildflowers grow in great profusion during summer.

Dzogchen to Shiqu This 173km drive curves through immense grasslands and a few minor passes. Many Tibetans set up herder camps in summer. At 6.5km from the Dzogchen turn-off, there's a rudimentary hot-springs pool on the right and a restaurant on the left. The shallow pool isn't much, and there's no privacy, but you can get a pleasant soak (no charge). Monks come here at night to bathe under the cover of darkness, so it's a strictly male scene then. At 11.3km, you reach a bridge and junction; a road goes right 10km to Shechen (Zhechen) Monastery, said to be welcoming to Westerners. In another 36km on the main highway, you'll see Juo Gompa on the left and a little restaurant on the right. There's a 4,570m

CYCLING KHAM AND AMDO   *Bill Weir*

All of the Kham and Amdo routes in this chapter make fantastic bicycle rides. Cyclists enjoy meeting people along the way, unobstructed views, fresh air and the freedom of the open road. You don't need to be athletic or undergo training to ride the routes, rather just be in good shape and pace yourself. Taking it easy at the beginning of the ride helps greatly in acclimatisation.

A reliable bicycle and the ability to maintain it will be essential as you cannot count on finding a bicycle shop if something goes wrong. Take a folding spare tyre, a couple of tubes, spare cables, brake pads, chain lube and basic tools. A tent, warm sleeping bag and pad should be carried for the odd long section between accommodations, if you get caught out late or in an unexpected storm. Chinese and Tibetan cuisines are widely available, so there's no need to carry a stove. A down jacket worn under a waterproof shell will keep you from freezing on long descents in rain or snow; mittens will be appreciated on the descents as well.

Most of the time you can find a hotel or guesthouse, and Tibetan families will often invite you inside their house or tent if you ask. Highways and some side roads have paving, but be prepared for sections of dirt and the inevitable construction areas. If dogs come after you, the best thing to do is to stop and pick up some stones, then wait for the dog owners to come out and restrain them. If nobody's home, then flag down a passing vehicle. Tibetans are major-league throwers when it comes to pelting dogs with stones, and you'll be able to make your escape. The worst thing to do is to try to outrun the dogs – the dogs will love the chase, but might nip at you.

KUNMING TO TAGONG A ride the length of Yunnan Province crosses an astonishing variety of landscapes with many minority cultures. You could start from northern Laos or Vietnam as well as the provincial capital Kunming. You'll likely come through the atmospheric old towns of Dali and Lijiang on your way to Tiger Leaping Gorge. Instead of taking the main highway to Zhongdian from here, try the smaller road through Tiger Leaping Gorge and past Baishuitai (travertine terraces) for the best scenery and light traffic. The terrain just keeps getting grander on the side trip to Deqin and Minyong Glacier. More river gorges, high valleys and half-a-dozen passes will get you north to Litang. Yajiang is the next town east, but too far for one day on account of the passes to be climbed; you'll probably need to camp or seek shelter somewhere, though villages are very sparse. Just one big pass, doable in a day, and a short climb up a valley brings you to Tagong.

XICHANG TO TAGONG VIA JIULONG Like the ride from southern Yunnan, this route provides gradual acclimatisation as you climb into Tibetan lands. The scenery begins just outside Mianning on a climb past fields and forest to a pass, then a steep descent to the Yalong River, where you turn up this great river and its tributaries to Jiulong. Wuxuhai makes an idyllic day trip from here. Continuing north, you're looking at a long day for the 48km climb past forest and meadows pass 65km from the Dzogchen turn-off, then a descent into a broad grassy valley. Xiazha (Tsatcha), about 23km along the valley, has several restaurants and a bunch of shops, then it's 11km to a gentle pass of 4,365m. The descent takes you into the broad valley of the Yalong River, though the river isn't visible until farther up the

to a high pass, then a drop through an alpine gorge and lush picturesque valleys with Tibetan villages. Continue upriver to Tagong.

TAGONG TO XIEWU Bamei, Dawu and Luhuo make convenient overnight stops on the way to Ganzi with a few passes to tackle and superb scenery. Ganzi to Manigango is just a day on the main highway, or you take the adventurous back road via Baiyu and Derge. The 114km between Derge and Manigango over 5,050m Tro La will be your highest and toughest in the region, best done over two days. Dzogchen Gompa is the highlight on the three-day ride from Manigango to Shiqu. Sershul Monastery, an easy ride beyond Shiqu, is another great monastic complex worth a visit. A pass marks the border with Qinghai Province and a great descent into Xiewu.

XIEWU TO XINING This long haul across grasslands and a bit of semi-desert has no major monasteries or snow mountains unless you leave the main road. Tibetans are as friendly as elsewhere and foreign visitors still a novelty. The highway is nearly all paved and tends to have a smoother surface than roads in northwestern Sichuan; traffic is mostly light.

XINING TO LHASA Highway G109 will take you all the way. Most of this long ride runs across Qinghai Province, and you don't need any permits for this part. If permits are required for the TAR, costs will be relatively low because the TAR part of the ride is so short. The spectacular high-altitude Namtso lake is a recommended side trip. Only on the last day into Lhasa do you leave the high grasslands for a fun ride down a gorge and valley.

XINING TO CHENGDU You can put together a route connecting Amdo's great monasteries and a great variety of valley, plateau and mountain country. For example, you could head to Tongren's monasteries and temples, perhaps stopping in Xunhua for a side trip east down the Yellow River Gorge and up to the alpine lake in Mengda Nature Reserve. Next, cross into Gansu Province to experience Labrang Monastery, then continue south into Sichuan Province via Heitso, Luchu, Langmusi and Zoige to see monasteries and temples along the way. Down at Chuanzhusi, you have choices of turning north to Jiuzhaigou National Park, east to Huanglong National Park or south to Songpan; from any of these you could continue through deep valleys to Chengdu.

Have a look at travelogues on the internet for route ideas; cyclists have mapped out other challenging trips that you may wish to try. I have cycling travelogues online of all the main routes: a Bangkok–Chengdu ride via Litang at www.arizonahandbook.com/Thai_China.htm, and lots more from Kham and Amdo regions on www.crazyguyonabike.com (enter 'Bill Weir' in the top search bar to locate entries).

8

valley. In another 40km, Junyung Monastery appears on the left, and then you'll see a dam on the Yalong River several kilometres farther. The highway leaves the main valley for the final stretch to Shiqu, passing Bunyming Monastery on the right along the way.

Shiqu (*Sêrxu*) This town set on open grasslands at 4,305m will seem like a big city after days of travelling through villages and tent camps. **Accommodation** tends to be very poor value, but you'll find lots of **restaurants**, both Chinese and Tibetan, and many well-stocked shops. One hotel set back on the right just before the first crossroads has rooms from Y80, but no showers. Continuing another block on the highway, the big Shangdeenyma Hotel has poorly maintained twins with attached bath for Y220, but don't count on hot water; ask for a discount. For **internet**, continue west on the highway past the Shangdeenyma Hotel to the next intersection, then turn left 1.5 blocks: two internet cafés face each other on opposite sides of the street.

Sershul Monastery A drive of just 31km along the highway and over a minor 4,570m pass takes you to this large complex spread up a hillside at 4,255m. In contrast to all the golden roofs and fancy halls at Dzogchen, here everything is more earthy and plain, though very atmospheric. Lots of dogs are around, so be on guard for the rare aggressive one. The best way to see Sershul is to walk the *kora* route that encircles it. Start at the long row of prayer-wheels lining the front, then follow pilgrims clockwise and hike up high on the hillside with fine views of the monastery and the expansive valley beyond. You can make side trips into the halls along the way. For a place to stay, try the simple **guesthouse** (Y25 a bed) upstairs in the last large building on the left before the highway crosses a river to the monastery. Conveniently, there's a Tibetan restaurant at one end of the guesthouse and a Chinese one at the other. A **public bathhouse** (Y10) is downstairs. The only trick with the guesthouse is finding the woman with the keys who runs it. Other restaurants are nearby, along with shops where you can get groceries, fruit, or outfit yourself in Tibetan clothing. Farther along the highway on the right, you could try the **monastery guesthouse**.

From Sershul, you'll see the kilometre posts count down to zero on the gradual 45km climb to 4,700m Anba La. On the way, look for new settlements at 13km and 33km for people made homeless in the Yushu earthquake. The pass marks the boundary between Sichuan and Qinghai provinces. From the top, the highway switchbacks down a steep slope to a valley, then cruises into the junction town of **Xiewu** (Xiwu; 3,905m) in another 22km. Here you'll reach Highway G214, one of China's most remarkable highways. It runs from near Laos in the far south of Yunnan Province through the entire length of Yunnan, continues through the TAR, then goes north through most of Qinghai Province.

From Xiewu, Yushu is 47km south, while Xining is 764km north. Drogon Gompa has a spectacular setting on a steep hillside above Xiewu. It's worth a visit to see a few of the halls and valley views; the uppermost hall is a protector chapel (women not allowed inside). There's a *kora* route around the *gompa*, also connecting with a row of *chortens* and an enclosed large prayer-wheel just above town. Morning is the best time for finding halls open and for photography. Xiewu has at least two **guesthouses**, but they're not signed, so you might have to ask. Chinese and Tibetan **restaurants** are easy to find. There's a **public bathhouse**: head south from the junction toward Yushu and it's on your left. This may be your last chance for a bath for a long time if you are headed north towards Xining. The 47km drive south to Yushu is very pretty and crosses the Yangtse River about halfway.

Yushu (*Gyegu, Jyekundo; 3,769m*) Yushu was almost totally destroyed by a severe earthquake in 2010 that killed several thousand people. Reconstruction is progressing, so check with other travellers about reopening of monasteries and hotels. Also ask about the July horse-racing festival. The town continues to be a major transport centre, with **buses** headed north to Xining and southwest (via Xiewu) into Sichuan; an airport may have **flights**. The road south from town provides a gateway into the TAR and Riwoche Monastery, then comes to the Chamdo–Nagqu highway, the northern route to Lhasa.

WILD AMDO ROUTE

Yushu to Xining This 811km drive crosses a vast expanse of high grasslands and a bit of desert, providing an opportunity to see and meet friendly Tibetans – many out in summer at camps with their yaks, horses and sheep. The highway is nearly all paved, and tiny towns provide places to stay. Unlike the drive through northwestern Sichuan, you won't see any great monasteries or glacier-clad peaks, though adventurous travellers can detour off the highway to see these. You are likely to see wildlife such as graceful Tibetan gazelles, wolves, birds of many kinds, marmots and thousands of pikas. Eagles, hawks and owls hang out, and you might even see a seagull, far from home

From Yushu, the highway returns back across the Yangtse on the 47km to Xiewu, then begins a 17km climb to Yan Pass (Yingkuoshan) at 4,458m. Summer camps dot the grasslands around the pass, down the other side and out onto a vast valley beyond. At 102km from Xiewu you'll arrive in the spread-out **Qingshuihe**, which has two adjoining **guesthouses** at the far end (north) of town on the right, both with rooms upstairs. The second one is recommended because the Tibetan family welcomes foreigners: beds in four-bed rooms are Y30. You can find good food at Chinese, Hui Chinese and Tibetan **restaurants**. Although it's a large town, don't expect any exotica such as flush toilets, showers or internet. Farther north you cross gentle 4,824m Bapengke (Bayanhar) pass 64km from Qingshuihe. Beyond, you'll roll over minor passes, where the countryside turns arid – with sparse grass and sand dunes, though many valleys have lakes. Shallow lakes of the Yellow River headwaters come into view 180km from Qingshuihe. Then you'll reach the turn-off for **Madoi** (Maduo; 4,205m), one of the larger towns in these parts with several hotels (one with Wi-Fi).

Another 80km onward, and over a 4,485m pass, and you reach Huashixia. A turn on the right leads past 6,282m **Amnye Machen**, a snowcapped peak sacred to Tibetans. Another turn-off for the area is 12km north of town. You can join Tibetan pilgrims on a week-long *kora* of Amnye Machen if you're self-sufficient, or you can arrange a trek through an agency. This is one of the top sacred sites of Amdo. Unfortunately, the peak isn't visible from the main highway. Huashixia has one **hotel**, on the right just past a police station at the far end of town: beds in four-bed rooms cost from Y30 and a single is Y60. Lots of restaurants and shops are nearby.

As you near Wenquan, 78km farther north, you'll see hot springs at the edge of town, but sadly the site is trashed and lacks bathing pools. A Tibetan **sacred spot** of hillside prayer-flags and *chortens* is just beyond Wenquan and worth a look. On the 109km to Heka, you'll roll over 4,499m Deng Pass at 16km and tunnel through Heka Mountain at 94.5km, then descend to **Heka**, surrounded by bright yellow-green fields of rapeseed at a balmy 3,290m. Try the **hotel** on the right just past a hospital near the beginning of town. Rooms start at Y50 for a single and have the luxuries of an indoor toilet and a solar shower down the hall; many restaurants are nearby. The highway rolls over ridges, some of which are sand dunes covered by vegetation on the 75km to **Gonghe**, way down in a valley at 2,855m. There's a **hotel**

8

ROUTES THROUGH AMDO

on the right, across from and a bit before the bus station, where a twin room with attached shower goes for a bargain Y60. Several other hotels are in town as well, along with many Hui-run restaurants.

From here you have two choices to continue on to Xining. Buses will take the main highway direct to Daotanghe (3,355m) in 42km, but if you arrange your own transport, you can take a very scenic tourist road up the valley (go straight through Gonghe without making any turns), then into grassland hills – culminating at 3,740m Luo He Ya Kou Shan pass and the first view of Qinghai Lake. A swift descent with good views of the lake twists down to Highway G109 on the west edge of a tourist town, known as '151' after an army camp once located here. You can find restaurants and hotels, but prices will likely be high and bargaining worthwhile. Boat tours go out on the lake from the shore.

Qinghai Lake (*Kokonor, or Blue Lake*) The lake that gives Qinghai Province its name is a huge saline lake with excellent pastureland in the surrounding hills. The rail link goes north of the lake but the road continues for over 100km on the south side through fields of yellow rapeseed and wheat. Many of the farmers are recent Muslim immigrants, and there are some tensions with the Tibetan herdsmen, whose winter pasture they have taken over.

On the western side of the lake is a birders' hotspot (season is March to early June) called **Niao Dao** (Bird Island – but actually it is a peninsula). Lying about 50km from the cheap guesthouses at Heimahe, Niao Dao bird sanctuary is inhabited by cormorants and, in spring, by bar-headed geese, gulls, terns and even an occasional black-necked crane. You can also reach Niao Dao by bus direct from Xining Bus Station – a journey that takes about five hours.

Back on the main route: turn right on busy Highway G109 for the 50km to Daotanghe and another 101km to Xining: a left turn would take you on the long haul to Golmud and Lhasa. At 8km past Daotanghe you have a choice of continuing on the expressway or turning left on a paved loop road to Riyueting – a pass famed as the route taken long ago by Princess Wenchang on her journey to Tibet and now marked by a pair of small pavilions and lots of prayer-flags. It's very popular with Chinese tourists to take in the grassland scenery and snap photographs. The small city of **Huangyuan**, 49km beyond Daotanghe, is worth a stop to see **Zanpulinka Palace**, a four-story temple-like building on the left as you enter town. The six-floor **Huangyuan Xinshui Hotel** has good rooms nearby on the right just beyond the river bridge.

Xining The capital and largest city of Qinghai Province has a population of 2.1 million and spreads out at the junction of three valleys at 2,275m. It's a pleasant city with many parks and Westerner-friendly hostels and restaurants. You may want to stay a few days to see the sights, whether you need to acclimatise before heading onto the Tibetan Plateau, or just want to take in city life after a spell in the back country. Most of the city is on the south slope of a valley, so you'll likely be heading uphill when going south, downhill when going north. A river flowing from the south bisects the centre and has parks along it; most places to stay and eat are east of this river. The cool dry air will come as a welcome change if you are travelling from lower elevations to the east. The Bank of China has ATMs at many locations around the city.

Where to stay Try to reserve ahead in summer, especially at the hostels. **Lete Youth Hostel** (*5 Bldg, International Village Apartment, 16th Floor;* 0971 8202080, *8202090; www.xnlete.com*), has wonderful views atop a high-rise just south of the centre. Prices range from Y25 per bed in a dorm to Y120 for a double room. The hostel features English-speaking staff, regional maps for sale, internet computers, free Wi-Fi, Western breakfasts and a coffee bar. Tibetan Connections above the hostel is recommended for arranging trips and permits for Tibet and tours of Qinghai Province. **Sunshine Pagoda International Youth Hostel** on Wenhua Jie (✆ *0971 821 5571; www.tdyg-inn.com/english.htm*) is centrally located. If you would like a hotel room, try one of the many near the centre, such as **Gongshang Hotel**, on the right up a little lane south of Datong Jie (✆ *0971 823 2881*) with rooms from Y120. There's a big neon sign (in Chinese) over Datong Jie pointing the way to the hotel. Many of the cheaper hotels, from about Y100, congregate in the Dongguan Mosque area, with the best values on side streets. Try **Hepin Binguan** on the southwest corner of Gonghe Lu and Zhongnanguan Jie, one short block south of Dongguan Dajie.

✗ ***Where to eat*** The **Casa Mia** restaurant (*10–4 West Wusi, Chengxi District;* ✆ *0971 631 1272*) serves great Italian cuisine for lunch and dinner and has an English menu. It's about three blocks west of the museum; upstairs is non-smoking. **Greenhouse** (*22, 222 Xiadu Dajie;* ✆ *0971 820 2710*) has good made-to-order sandwiches and pizzas (both highly recommended), pastries, muesli, smoothies and coffee. There's free Wi-Fi and it's popular with Westerners, but the restaurant lacks a non-smoking area. Look for it on the north side of the street between Huayuan Nanji and Nan Xiaojie on the east side of the centre. A little farther east and south, **Amdo Cafe** (*19 Ledu Lu;* ✆ *0971 821 3127; www.amdocraft.com;* ⏰ *09.00–20.00 Mon–Sat*) has good pastries, coffees and teas along with Tibetan crafts and postcards in a non-smoking setting. It is located on the east side of the street, halfway between Xiadu Daji and Kunlun Zhonglu, one block east of Nan Xiaojie. For views atop a revolving restaurant, you might try the 28th floor **Rotary Western Restaurant** at 55 Xi Dajie.

What to see The **Qinghai Provincial Museum** at 58 Xiguan Daji and West Wusi Lu is worth a visit for exhibits on Qinghai's history, Tibetan arts and the July bicycle race around Qinghai Lake. **Jinta Si**, the small Tibetan temple on the south side of the centre at 19 Hongjuesi Jie (just east of Nan Dajie), has three large standing Buddhas and many smaller statues. **Beishan Si**, a Taoist temple complex just north of town on the lower slopes of Beishan (best to take a taxi), has a huge two-storey hall near the entrance, many small halls and a flower garden to the left, and several more halls high up on the steep hillside, reached by steep steps or a winding trail. **Ding Xiang Yuan** is a large Chinese Buddhist temple complex below Nan Shan: the entrance is just east of the Kunlun Bridge Traffic Circle. Visit the **landscaped park** atop Nan Shan for greenery and views. If you're into classical Greek and Roman sculpture, a park high atop Beishan north of town is full of them (take a taxi). A large Chinese Muslim (Hui) community lives just east of the centre near the large Dongguan Mosque; colourful lights play on the mosque exterior after dark.

Kumbum Monastery This large monastic complex is located 26km southwest of Xining. To get there, look for a bus or taxi on the west side of the road just south of the Kunlun Bridge Traffic Circle. Admission is a steep Y80.

Kumbum (Taersi in Chinese) is the most famous monastery in Amdo and one of the six great Geluk monasteries of the Tibetan plateau. In its prime, Kumbum once housed 3,000 monks, but under Chinese rule it was closed down for a period. Since it reopened in 1979 the monastery has housed about 400 monks, with half the buildings functioning in museum mode. The former abbot, Ajia Rinpoche, fled in 1998 to seek asylum in the US: he was the highest-ranking monk in the Chinese Communist Party.

Situated in the largely Muslim county of Huangzhong, the temples here were protected during the Cultural Revolution and contain some of the greatest artworks of Amdo. However, Kumbum is a major Chinese destination, and the monks are tightly controlled, which affects the atmosphere. There is a guesthouse here with rooms ranging from Y80, with cheaper hotels on the market streets, though you can base yourself in Xining and visit for the day by public bus or minibus taxi.

Kumbum is the birthplace of Tsongkhapa, founder of the Gelukpa sect in the early 15th century. Inside a spectacular green-tiled building is a silver pagoda containing the earthly belongings of Tsongkhapa. The monastery is thought to have been built (in the 16th century) around a legendary pipal tree, said to bear a Buddha-like image on every leaf. The tree is accredited with magical powers. The temple is famed, too, for its elaborate yak-butter sculptures – in the shape of animals, landscapes and religious figures – which can reach 15m in length. Festivals at Kumbum attract large numbers of Tibetan pilgrims. Because Kumbum is easily accessed (being so close to Xining) it unfortunately also attracts large numbers of Chinese tourists, who stand next to cardboard cut-outs to have pictures taken. The monastery has a disturbingly commercialised air about it. The best times to visit are at festival times: tour agents in the Xining hotels can tell you of any up and coming festivals.

Taktser The birthplace of the present Dalai Lama, Taktser is about 27km eastwards from Kumbum, and about 7km from the small attractive monastery of Shadzong. Tsongkhapa spent some years at the mountain-top *gompa* of Shadzong, and the 13th Dalai Lama also visited and meditated there. Today, this small forested zone is popular with picnickers at weekends. Taktser itself is situated on a ridge above the valley; the Dalai Lama's humble house was reconstructed in 1986. The easiest way to visit these sites is to hire transport for a day in Xining or try your luck hitching at the turn-off. Tour agent **Tibetan Connections** (see page 65) occasionally puts together a group tour for Taktser and other off-the-beaten track sights near Xining. A little-used side road leads through the hills from Taktser to Kumbum.

NORTHERN ROUTE TO LHASA

Xining–Golmud–Lhasa Once notorious for having one of the world's most miserable bus rides, this route has become a breeze now that the rails go all the way. The road journey is much slower and will appeal to those who enjoy expansive views across desert landscapes and lofty grasslands. Highway G109 runs all the way and is nearly all paved, though parts will be under construction. Most of this journey lies within Qinghai Province, so you won't need permits until the last section across the TAR, and this part of the TAR tends to be relatively relaxed, so independent travel *might* be possible. Check with other travellers and online forums for the latest word. Cyclists looking for an adventure will enjoy this route: there's less up and down than a ride across eastern Tibet or the run from Lhasa to Nepal.

Xining to Golmud This 780km section of highway skirts the south shore of Qinghai Lake, then the southern edge of the Qaidam Basin – a vast area of salt marsh, saline lakes and desert *playas*. For notes on visiting Qinghai Lake and Bird Island, see page 282. The train skirts the north shore of Qinghai Lake, then across Qaidam Basin.

Golmud Commonly pronounced and spelled Geermu, this city of about 200,000 lies at an elevation of 2,800m. It has a leafy centre with parks. Seemingly in the middle of nowhere, Golmud exists to serve oil, gas and other mineral-extraction industries in the Qaidam Basin. The PSB has prohibited small hotels from accepting foreigners, so your options may be limited to the expensive **Golmud Hotel** (*43 Kunlun Zhonglu;* \ *0979 842 4250; rooms start at around Y400*). Or try the better-value **Tian Long Hotel** (*1 Bayi West Rd; corner with Zhongshan Rd, across from Ertong/Children's Park;* \ *0979 846 1612; rooms from Y100*). Golmud has a variety of Chinese **restaurants** including many Muslim noodle restaurants, which are very popular throughout Qinghai. Supermarkets provide your last chance to stock up on exotic fruit and other goodies for hundreds of kilometres in any direction.

Golmud to Lhasa You're looking at 1,260km by road, 1,142km by rail, on routes that roughly parallel each other. Because nearly all passengers now go by train, roadside businesses have suffered from fewer customers, and some settlements have faded away. You can count on finding something at least every 100km, with the accommodations tending to be very basic and cheap while restaurants are good and cheap. Larger communities have internet cafés, but you're unlikely to find bathhouses or hotels with showers until the towns of Amdo, Nagqu and Damshung in the TAR. There's a checkpost 33km south of Golmud staffed by a few bored soldiers who probably won't be interested in you.

The route enters a valley and begins a long gentle climb with constantly changing panoramas of arid mountains. Farther along, the valley widens with striking views of sand dunes and the glacier-clad Kunlun Mountains The climb peaks at the 4,767m Kunlun Shankou pass, 160km south of Golmud. From here until the final descent into Lhasa Valley you'll be rolling across high grasslands above 4,000m. Just before Tuotuohe, 422km south of Golmud, you cross the broad Yangtse River at a site famed among the Chinese as the First Bridge over the Yangtse. At 615km south of Golmud you'll top out at the highest pass on the route, 5,231m Tanggu La on the Qinghai–TAR border – with great panoramas of mountains, glaciers and valleys. A Tibetan tent restaurant at the pass may serve noodle soup and *tsampa*. There's no checkpost. Another 90km and a minor pass brings you to **Amdo**, a rough-and-tumble-looking town, but people are friendly. **Hotels** tend to be basic with the usual pit toilet out back. There's said to be one hotel with a shower, or you can use the public shower (Y8) just east on the left from the central junction. An **internet café** is located just north on the right from the central junction. Amdo has lots of Chinese and Tibetan **restaurants**. You'll find many Tibetan posters and other souvenirs for sale. A pleasant stroll leads west from the central junction, then left past Tibetan houses up the grassy hillside to prayer-flag-festooned towers and a good view of the Amdo area.

Back on the highway, another 138km gets you over a 4,880m pass and down to **Nagqu**, the first city since Golmud. Drop by **Shabten Monastery** to meet the friendly monks and see colourful artwork. Nagqu has a **horse-racing festival** every August, but instead of being held on grasslands close to the city, the venue has shifted to a concrete stadium where the audience is a long distance from the racers and performers. **Nakqu Hotel** and others in the centre have expensive rooms. Or try the basic **Keyan Hotel** (no English sign) on the right side of the highway most of the way through town and across from a giant army building. Basic single rooms cost Y40, 'deluxe' rooms with sink and toilet go for Y80, but you'll have to visit a public bathhouse for a shower. Nagqu has **restaurants**, **supermarkets** and **internet cafés**. The highway continues through grasslands past views of snow peaks 166km to Damshung. Although the town has plenty of Chinese and Tibetan hotels, restaurants, supermarket and internet, it's best known as the turn-off for Namtso, one of Tibet's largest and most beautiful lakes. For more on Namtso, refer to *Exploring Central Tibet* chapter, page 173.

The 75km from Damshung to Yangbajing (Yangpachen) provides more views of the icy Tanggula Range, crowned by 7,162m Mount Nyanchen Tanglha. The Tibetan village of Yangbajing is 2km off the highway to the right and has basic hotels and good restaurants. Clouds of steam rising in the distance mark geothermal activity where there's a hot springs resort, but it costs a hefty Y100 for a dip or Y300 for the hotel. From Yangbajing, the highway follows a roaring river down to the Lhasa Valley. You'll see trees for the first time in many days. Getting through the Chinese outskirts of **Lhasa** takes a long time. When you sight the lofty Potala Palace, you've finally arrived.

EXPLORING CENTRAL AMDO
Xining via Aba to Chengdu This route could be very tough going, with a complete lack of buses (try trucks instead). It goes through the heartlands of the Golok nomads, who are known for their stubbornness and, previously, fierce banditry. Many Golok nomads are now being settled in concrete housing developments under official Chinese policy to remove the nomads from the grasslands.

Xining to Guide and Golok Close to Kumbum, the main road heads south over the mountains and down to the Yellow River at Guide, 75km from Xining. This is a more attractive route than the road that heads off the Yushu highway before the Sun Moon pass. Guide is a poor, largely Muslim county town, and there is little reason to stop here, apart perhaps for the hot springs fed into bathhouses some 15km southwest of town. There are several monasteries in the nearby side valleys, but all are poorly appointed and there are very few monks.

The main road south is the main route to Golok. It bypasses the small counties of Guinan and Tongte. Roads west from the main road lead to bridges over the Yellow River from either of these two towns to link up with the Xining–Yushu route. Guinan and Tongte are hardly ever visited, but worth a day or two if you have the time. All monasteries are outside town; the most important is Serlag, but the muddy track that leads to it may be impassable.

After Tongte, the road leads down again to the Yellow River at Radja Gompa, 220km from Guide, which is an enclave of Golok and has long been important in Amdo's history. Truck stops and basic restaurants are available on the south side of the bridge and the monastery is at the foot of the holy mountain Khyunggon, which takes half a day to circumambulate.

Golok Two hours (70km) further south on the grasslands is the prefectural capital of Golok (aka Dawu or Machen), 210km from Huashixia on the Yushu road. This is an entirely new town with a single very long high street, although all facilities are concentrated near the crossroads. The **county guesthouse**, which you may be forced to stay in, is a little more expensive than the others, but offers occasional hot showers.

From here, it is possible to arrange for guided tours of the seven-day **Amnye Machen circuit**, though this can be very expensive. Roads west lead to Xueshan, the traditional starting point of the seven-day circuit. In trekking terms, this is a fairly easy walk, with two gradual passes of 4,500–4,900m, and is best done in May–October, when pilgrims abound and nomads will have their flocks in the area. Although the trek can be completed in seven days at normal walking pace (around five hours a day), complications could arise with the weather, making it longer. Camping gear is essential. Winter is extremely cold in Golok, with temperatures often below -30°C, but summer rainfall is relatively light and bearable.

From here, a road leads southwest 80km towards the small county town of **Gabde**. The side valleys down to the Yellow River from Gabde shelter several important monasteries of the Geluk, Nyingma and Jonang sects. A small monastery 12km along the main road to Darlag holds frequent festivals attended by thousands of Golok. **Darlag** (aka Dari or Jumi) can be reached in under two hours (50km) from Gabde or directly from Huashixia (195km) on the main Xining to Yushu road. It is beside the Yellow River and the most important nearby monastery is 15km west of town – a large Nyingma monastery called Traling (Chalangsi in Chinese).

From Darlag, the road goes 105km southeast to **Mendrang** (Manzhang in Chinese) village on an upper tributary of the Yangtse. A rough road leads from Mendrang for a distance of 65km to the Nyingma monastery of Tartang, one of the largest in Golok (a number of festivals are held here each year, particularly a winter festival). Sixty kilometres south of Mendrang is Beima county, one of the most attractive areas of Golok, lying between the rolling grasslands of the Yellow River and the forested gorges of southern Amdo. It is similar in landscape to Serthar, Zamthang and Aba counties in Sichuan and, like these, it possesses many monasteries. There are numerous large monasteries in these four counties.

Before reaching town is a nine-storey tower and a road west that leads to one of the wildest valleys in Tibet. But it is just south of town that the most remarkable *gompas* are found, in unique style with many *mani*-stone walls. This is a back road to Aba and although there is no bus, it is well worth hiring a vehicle to go this way, taking two days if possible and stopping at the *gompas en route*.

From Mendrang the road heads east past the Golok's other holy mountain, **Nyangpo Yurtse** (5,369m), set in a remarkably pristine environment of craggy peaks and lakes, an area not used for grazing. The road continues to the tiny county town of Jigzhi (260km from Darlag), a truly remote nomad town. There is a very infrequent bus service on a rough sandy road which crosses the Yellow River twice to reach the county town of Machu in Gansu, from where roads lead to Lamosi (Langmusi) and Gahe near Luchu on the main Linxia–Zoige road. If you travel this roundabout route from Xining to Machu, be sure to allow extra days for bus problems or sightseeing.

This route then joins the Labrang–Songpan route as far as Zoige. Then it heads east back to the elbow of the Yellow River and south 135km to the grasslands county town of Hongyuan (which can also be reached from Songpan in 180km). Hongyuan is a small, modern county town set in a broad grassy valley. The large monastery of Mewa lies in a side valley nearby, and houses over a thousand monks.

Fifty kilometres south is a turn-off to the county town of **Aba**, one of the richest regions in Amdo. Traders from this region, including monks working for the many large monasteries, can be found all over Tibet. Aba and Zamtang contain huge monasteries: within walking distance of Aba are vast *gompas* from the Geluk, Bonpo and Jonang sects, as well as smaller Sakya and Nyingma centres. Zamtang has two valleys, the easternmost of which also has a huge Jonang presence and several small Nyingma *gompas*. Starting from 2008, there has been considerable trouble at **Kirti Gompa** in Aba, with the monastery locked down a number of times by the PLA and Chinese police. Several monks have committed suicide by immolating themselves as a form of protest. Kirti *gompa* houses over a thousand monks – or used to (many have been arrested). Access to the area may be blocked by military checkpoints.

Leaving the grasslands over a pass, the road enters Gyarong, a series of forested gorges where small kingdoms of the Qiang survived until early last century. The dialect and costumes here are distinct from other areas of Amdo. At Sonmalu the main road heads southeast through the county of Lixian to Wenchuan and thence Chengdu (328km from Sonmalu). Around 60km west of Sonmalu lies the prefectural capital of Barkam, a large administrative centre of little interest to travellers (Barkam is 200km from Hongyuan). Villages nearby, however, both on the valley floor and on small plateaus set on steep slopes, are worth a visit. At a junction 25km west of town, a road goes south to Danba, with onward connections to Tagong, Litang and Kangding. Further west from the junction, the road joins the Do Chu River, which can be followed west toward the remote counties of Serthar and Zamtang.

AMDO MOUNTAIN TWISTER

Xining via Labrang to Chengdu Highways twist across rugged mountains, linking prominent temples amidst spectacular scenery on the route from Xining to Chengdu. You can also approach this region from Lanzhou, the capital of Gansu Province and home to an excellent provincial museum. Tongren has several monasteries and temples worth a visit, if you are heading southeast from Xining or southwest from Lanzhou. From Xining, it's a quick trip east down the Huang Shui Valley to Ping'an, then south over the Laji Shan. You may wish to go via Xunhua and make a side trip east through Jishi Gorge of the Yellow River (Huang He) and up a side valley to Tian Chi ('Heaven Lake') in an alpine setting at Mengda Nature Reserve before continuing on to Tongren.

If you start from Lanzhou, you can stop at Yongjing, 80km to the southwest, for the boat ride to **Bingling Si** ('1,000 Buddha Caves'). Like other grottos on the Silk Routes, you can see many Buddhist scenes sculpted and painted in alcoves hewn from cliffs. The remote setting in a tributary of the Yellow River protected them during the Cultural Revolution. A Y5 taxi ride from Yongjing will take you to the boat ticket office at the reservoir, just above the dam. Covered speedboats are the most popular option and take just an hour to reach the site and cost about Y110 a person. Slow boats also do the trip, but would take most of a day. At Bingling Si, you pay the Y50 entry fee, then walk a paved loop past the grottos and a 27m-high Maitreya Buddha. You must stay with your guide and group and return on the same boat. From Yongjing, get transport to Xunhua – via the Jishi Gorge if you can – then continue to Tongren.

Tongren *(Repkong)* Tongren is a town famed for its traditional fresco painters. Maze-like lanes lead through 700-year-old Rongwo Gongchen Monastery here. You'll also find hotels and restaurants in town. Try the **Huangnan Hotel** (*18 Zhongshan Lu;* \ *872 2293*) or **Post Hotel** (*122 Zhongshan Lu;* \ *872 4555*). Both have dorms and rooms. **Wutun Xiazhuang Monastery,** famed for the high-quality paintings of resident artists, has upper and lower sections 6km north of town. Large paintings on the walls show the Buddha and his supporting cast: these have been recently painted with great skill by local artists. The oldest chapel houses a great statue of Maitreya (Future Buddha).

The main attractions of the area are the two small **art schools** Yangoo and Mangoo (known as *Wutun* to the Chinese) which have provided mural and *tanka* painters for all of Amdo's monasteries. You'll likely see artists at work and have the opportunity to purchase a painting.

Several other monasteries are found in the hills and 25km south of town is a hot spring where you can bathe. Shortly before the hot spring, a side valley west leads past an important Bonpo *gompa* toward the holy mountain of Amnye Shachung (Jakhyung).

Head west across the Longwu He to see the colourfully decorated **Gomar Great Chorten**. Brightly painted bas-reliefs depict bodhisattvas, guardians and decorative designs. After walking the *kora* and spinning the prayer-wheels, you can climb up to the higher levels, finally reaching a shrine room filled with Buddhist statues, paintings, books and a photo of the Dalai Lama. You could walk the 6km back to Tongren on a small road.

The 100km journey southeast to Xiahe has a lot of variety. It starts with 14km north along the Longwu He Valley, passing many Buddhist *chortens*, temples, villages and fields, then turns up a canyon reminiscent of the American southwest. Mud-walled Buddhist villages blend perfectly into the arid landscape. Guashizeshi village has a large *gompa*. A couple of passes later, you arrive in Ganjia Grasslands in Gansu Province, and a third pass takes brings you to Xiahe, a town next to the impressively large and active Labrang Monastery. Xiahe and Labrang lie along the Daxia He (Sang-chu) Valley at 2,920m. Hotels, restaurants and other travellers' needs are in the Chinese section east of Labrang and the Tibetan quarter is to the west. The town cleaves into distinct populations: Tibetan, Hui Muslim and Chinese. Strangely enough, Tibetan devotional items like prayer-wheels and *katas* are mostly sold by Hui Muslims (who are Chinese except for their religion).

Labrang Monastery Labrang Monastery was founded in 1709 and rapidly grew to become one of the six great Gelukpa monasteries. The main assembly hall was rebuilt after being destroyed by fire in 1985, but most of the other halls survived the Cultural Revolution relatively intact, and contain beautiful works of art. You will most likely see elaborate yak-butter sculptures. The monks' quarters have been rebuilt in recent years and some are spacious and comfortable. A 3km *kora* lined with prayer-wheels surrounds the complex and is well worth the walk. The temples and colleges of Labrang can only be visited on a morning or afternoon official tour. Labrang acts as a major teaching centre and monks come from not only the 108 satellite *gompas* scattered throughout nearby counties, but also from central Tibet and Mongolia. Thus the number of monks is somewhat fluid, although there are likely to be around 2,000 here. There is also a small nunnery and Nyingma temple on the far side of the complex. You can be sure that with such a large contingent of monks, the Chinese keep a close eye on proceedings. Surveillance was stepped up upon the arrival of the Chinese-appointed Panchen Lama to take up residence in 2011 – in an attempt to legitimise his religious role.

At a cool 2,900m, **Xiahe** makes an excellent base for hiking. Foreigners tend to stay longer than intended at Labrang, not only because of the monastery and Western food, but also because of the opportunity to see the surrounding hills and grasslands. Bikes can be hired to reach the Sangke grasslands region, where picnics are available in Tibetan-style tents, and where horses can be hired. The nearby hills offer good opportunities for day walks, and you may be offered butter tea and yoghurt if you reach the nomad camps higher up, but beware of dogs! The most vicious dogs are chained up, but some of the others do present a serious danger if you enter their territory unbidden. Carry a walking stick, some stones or a *gokor* (a lump of lead on a string) if you plan to visit these areas. The dogs around the monastery are generally very docile, but still should not be approached.

Langmusi On the north side of Hezuo (Heitso), just an hour southeast of Xiahe, you'll see the unusual **Milarepa Buddhist Palace**, a temple tower with eight storeys. Each floor has a gallery of statues from the Tibetan Buddhist pantheon, along with large paintings and *tankas*, many of which tell the story of Milarepa, a great yogi who overcame enormous difficulties to attain enlightenment. Three hours south of Hezuo brings you to the turn-off for **Langmusi**, a Chinese–Tibetan town that straddles the White Dragon River on the Gansu–Sichuan border. A walk north across the river leads up to Sertri Gompa. A sky burial site is higher up, and visitors may be allowed to watch from a respectful distance. On the Sichuan side, you can walk south to Kerti Gompa, then continue up a gorge past a few sacred caves for some good hiking. Many travellers enjoy riding a horse across the countryside with Langmusi Tibetan Horse Trekking. Guided walking trips are also available.

From the Langmusi turn-off, the highway heads southeast over a small pass, then across swampy grasslands to Zoige, a town at 3,470m with a fine monastery. Hotels and restaurants are near the centre. Continuing southeast, you'll experience vast grasslands, then drop steeply into a valley to the junction town of Chuanzhusi. This place relies almost entirely on the tourist trade and has lots of hotels and restaurants, but many businesses will try to overcharge, so be prepared for a little negotiating.

You have three options for continuing to Chengdu: north to Jiuzhaigou, east to Huanglong, or south to Songpan. Small taxis, minibuses or jeeps can be hired for journeys to the national parks of Huanglong or Jiuzhaigou. Expect a hefty tariff for the 105km journey to Jiuzhaigou. You could try sharing a taxi with others, or try joining an existing group in a minibus.

Jiuzhaigou Famed for its alpine landscapes, Jiuzhaigou lies to the north over a 3,200m pass. It is billed as China's 'first five-star resort'. What that means is that this scenic area can cause serious damage to your wallet: be prepared for very high entry fee and bus fees to see the park. The park entry fee alone is Y80 to Y220, depending on the season. *En route* to Jiuzhaigou is a large Bonpo monastery called Gamal Gonchen, with over 400 monks and a nearby nunnery. Once over the pass out of the Min Valley, there are numerous guesthouses near the park entrance but, along with park fees, guide fees, food and accommodation, this is an expensive circus – and one packed with Chinese tourists to boot. In fact, if you choose to stay at the five-star-rated **Jiuzhai Paradise Holiday Resort**, you won't see much change from US$200 a day (standard rooms rates start at US$180 and escalate from there). No need to worry about bad weather: this place has several huge wings entirely enclosed with Plexiglas domes – including artificial hot springs and a whole Tibetan village (that's artificial, too). See the park website, www.jiuzhai.com, to check on current entry and transport fees.

Around Jiuzhaigou, horses can be arranged to ride up the two main valleys, which contain numerous vibrantly-coloured pools connected by small waterfalls on the valley bottom, while the forest extends to the snow peaks above. The scenery is stunning but, although it is a panda park, you are unlikely to see any black-and-white furries – or indeed any wildlife – most probably because the animal populations have been decimated by poachers.

Huanglong Park Huanglong Park is closer to Songpan, lying on the eastern side of Shar Dungri, a Bon holy mountain, and is cheaper and less visited than Jiuzhaigou. Huanglong is famed for its terraced travertine pools of many colours. On the downside, admission is a steep Y200. Many tourists, however, simply negotiate horses and guide for other treks in the mountains around. The most popular currently is a one- to three-day journey into the Niao Me (Nyenyul) Valley. In this valley lie several Bonpo monasteries, including the important Gyagar Mandi (which is built on an Indian model) and the Sakya monastery of Jara, as well as a famous waterfall called Zaga Pubu and a set of hot springs. It is also possible to reach this valley by road from a turn-off 30km to the south of Songpan. Be sure to check out the guide and precisely what services you are paying for before parting with any money. Most horse trekking is arranged from Songpan.

Songpan This has long been an important trading town for tea, musk, furs and gold. Songpan is an ancient Chinese garrison town with drum towers and walls. Qiang and Tibetan women visiting the market wear elaborate headdresses of amber and coral. It has become a major tourist destination due to the impressive nearby national parks. New guesthouses and budget hotels are built every year, so the best place to stay would usually be the newest as it has not had time to acquire a coat of filth from the spittle-happy Chinese. The best advice is to leave your luggage at one of the restaurants and wander down the single main street checking places out. Basic accommodation costs around US$5, but en-suite rooms with tiles and granite veneers will run US$20 a night or more.

There is an airport at Songpan, used by tourists who fly from Chengdu *en route* to Jiuzhaigou. The bus ride from Chengdu to Songpan takes at least a full day, and delays are frequent after summer rains due to landslides and heavy traffic.

The Min Valley is a well-forested gorge (where it hasn't been deforested) and many of the villages are set high above the road. The area is the home of the Qiang people, who are believed to be descendants of the ancient Ch'iang tribe that ranged widely across the north of the plateau before the period of the Tibetan kings. Nowadays they are principally agriculturalists, with wheat and maize as their main crops, although many keep a few domestic animals stabled in large courtyards or on the ground floor of their three-storey stone and timber houses.

From Songpan, you have about 330km to go south through the Min River Valley to Wenchuan and Dujiangyan, then out onto the Sichuan Basin to Chengdu. On this route, you witness severe destruction in the Min River Valley caused by the 2008 Sichuan earthquake. If you're taking one of the routes to Chengdu via Pingwu, you may wish to stop at the excellent **Sanxingdui Museum** of prehistoric bronze works located outside Guanghan, 40km north of Chengdu. Another 22km farther south, the **Buddhist Monastery of Divine Light** (Baoguang Si) near Xindu is also worth a stop. For information on the large yet appealing city of Chengdu, see *Gateway: Chengdu* in this chapter, page 268, and also the entry on Chengdu in the *Practical information* chapter, page 63.

THE TIBETAN WORLD
Tibetan Cultural Sphere

KEY
(inset only)
Tibetan enclave

Inset

Arunachal Pradesh

Thimphu
Lhasa
Shigatse
BHUTAN
Sikkim
Darjeeling
BANGLA-DESH

TIBET

Everest Region
Langtang
Manang
Kathmandu
Mustang
Dolpo
Humla
Kirnaur
Spiti
Lahaul
Zanskar
Leh
Ladakh
Aksai Chin
Mt Kailash

N E P A L

Gaya

DHARAMSALA
Delhi

I N D I A

RUSSIA

Sea of Japan

NORTH PACIFIC OCEAN

East China Sea

Yellow Sea

RUSSIA

MONGOLIA
Ulaanbaatar

KAZAKHSTAN

KYRGYZSTAN

TAJIKISTAN

UZBEKISTAN   AFGHANISTAN

PAKISTAN

C H I N A

BEIJING

N
Bradt

ETHNIC TIBET

Lhasa

Mt Everest
8848m

N E P A L

BHUTAN

INDIA

BANGLA-DESH

Kathmandu

Delhi

VARANASI

I N D I A

Mundgod

MYANMAR (BURMA)

LAOS

BAY OF BENGAL

See inset

0   800km
0   500 miles

9

The Tibetan World

A prophecy is attributed to the great sage Padmasambhava (8th century AD): 'When the iron bird flies and horses run on wheels, the Tibetan people will be scattered like ants across the face of the earth, and the Dharma will come to the land of the redskins.' Whether this is what he actually said, or whether somebody made it up later to suit the situation, the Tibetans are certainly widely scattered, but not across the face of the earth. They are mostly scattered across the Himalaya. In the old Tibetan flat-earth world view, however, they would be at the edges of the earth as the Tibetans knew it (which did not much extend beyond the Asian/Indian continent). Of the following destinations, the most rewarding trips are those to the high Himalayan regions inhabited by Tibetans. Journeys to these places can be stymied by formidable obstacles, both physical and bureaucratic, but if you make it you are rewarded with glimpses of the traditional way of life and festivals no longer seen in Tibet itself.

Probably the most surprising thing you learn as you visit different parts of the Tibetan world is that the Tibetans are not really unified, except in their common beliefs. Tibetans are a very tribal people. Historically, while different groups recognised the power of the Dalai Lama (centred in Lhasa), they were never obligated to the central Tibetan government, and were beyond its control. Centuries ago, rivalry between sects of Tibetan Buddhism openly took place, sometimes leading to battles. Tension between 'clans' and rival sects is ongoing, even in exile.

For a great overview of these diverse Tibetan regions, a remarkable guidebook is *Mapping the Tibetan World* (Kotan Publishing, 2000). This book is a very ambitious project, covering the entire Tibetosphere in 420 pages, with over 280 maps. Check out the website www.kotan.org for more details.

TIBET IN EXILE

Until the mid-20th century, there was little motivation for Tibetans to leave the sanctuary of Tibet: some Buddhist masters travelled back and forth to India, and certain groups like the Sherpas migrated southward over the Himalaya. The exodus of Tibetans from their homeland really began in earnest with the escape of the Dalai Lama in 1959, who was soon followed by some 60,000 of his people. Today, Tibetan refugees continue to escape, dodging Chinese bullets and biting snowstorms to negotiate high passes when crossing from Tibet into Nepal.

In exile, the Dalai Lama has established nearly 200 monasteries, with over 15,000 monks. There are estimated to be about 145,000 Tibetan refugees living in exile, mostly in India (101,000) and Nepal (perhaps 16,000), with 26,000 in the rest of the world. The West has been very reluctant to accept Tibetan refugees, although occasionally the doors have opened a crack, allowing 2,000 to settle in Switzerland,

3,500 in the US and 1,700 in Canada. In pockets of the Himalaya in India and Nepal, you can see Tibetan culture in a more pristine environment, without Chinese troops and police. Traditions disrupted in Tibet, or festivals that are no longer permitted in the TAR, can be seen in places like Dharamsala. The main Tibetan exile location is India. A rough breakdown of where they live is as follows: in northwest India, there are about 21,000 in Himachal Pradesh, 6,500 in Uttar Pradesh, and 5,000 in Ladakh; in central India, about 8,000; in south India, approximately 30,000; in northeast India, an estimated 8,000; while 14,300 live in West Bengal and Sikkim.

India's relations with China are cool, perhaps even cold – as in Cold War. Although India was quick to recognise the PRC when it came to power in 1949, tempers flared over border disputes, with a major showdown in 1962. China considers parts of Sikkim and Arunachal Pradesh to be its territory, as it has never recognised the India–China border drawn up by the colonial British in 1914. China lays claim to 90,000km^2 of territory in Arunachal Pradesh. In late 1962, the PLA invaded, humiliating the Indian defenders: their artillery and trucks failed to work in the high-altitude conditions and many Indian soldiers fled. Thousands of Indian soldiers were killed. The PLA were within a few days' march of Calcutta when the US airlifted military supplies to India, at which point the PLA abruptly turned around and left, withdrawing to the old border-line. A few months later, Pakistan ceded 25,000km^2 of disputed Kashmiri territory under its control to China, which enabled the Chinese to build a strategic mountain road connecting Xinjiang to Tibet through the zone of ceded territory (known as Aksai Chin).

In the late 1960s and 1970s China openly armed and trained separatist militants in northeastern India. Since the 1970s, China has given military support to Pakistan, and is believed to be the source of Pakistan's supply of Silkworm missiles – capable of striking Indian cities – and there are strong suspicions that China provided critical expertise and components to enable Pakistan's nuclear testing in 1998. China has given military support and training to three nations surrounding India: to Pakistan, Burma and Bangladesh.

India sees both Pakistan and China as border threats. In 1998, India's Defence Minister, George Fernandes, accused Beijing of stockpiling nuclear weapons and extending military airfields in Tibet. In May 1998, India went nuclear: it shocked the world by conducting a series of nuclear tests in Rajasthan. This resulted in economic sanctions by the US, which was hypocritical considering America's nuclear arsenal. Beijing got the message loud and clear: China is not the only nuclear power in the region. A few weeks later, Pakistan exploded a series of nuclear devices, raising the stakes of destabilisation dramatically. The spectre of three nuclear-capable nations facing off in the Himalaya is all too real, with India and Pakistan becoming very confrontational.

DHARAMSALA Arriving in India in 1959, exiled Tibetans did not fare well in the hot and humid conditions, and were susceptible to diseases and viruses not found on the Tibetan plateau. Where they could, Tibetans gravitated to mountain zones with cooler climates – to places like Manali, Mussoorie, Bir and Dehra Dun – which are all located in the mountain regions north of Delhi. There is a cluster of Tibetan settlements scattered throughout this area.

The base of the Tibetan government-in-exile is Dharamsala, a former British hill station in Himachal Pradesh, 520km north of Delhi. India tolerates this government-in-exile, but does not officially recognise it: India does not allow Tibetans to engage in political work, but as one exile put it, 'everything we do here is political'. Tibetans do not belong to India either. Most Tibetans are barred from taking out Indian citizenship, so they remain stateless – most just have Indian resident certificates. Even Tibetans born in India – who have never been to Tibet – may choose to remain stateless, although they have the option to take out Indian citizenship. This is due to their determination to one day see their homeland, independent as it once was.

Dharamsala is the lifeline for Tibetan culture. The Dalai Lama resides here, along with the ministers and cabinet of the government-in-exile, and the oracle of Tibet. At Gangchen Kyishong are the offices of the Central Tibetan Administration, with various ministries and information centres, as well as the Tibetan Computer Resource Centre and the Library of Tibetan Works and Archives (LTWA). The LTWA acts as a repository for ancient books and manuscripts from Tibet; a team of Tibetan scholars is engaged in translation, research and publication of books. Among other educational centres around Dharamsala is the Amnye Machen Institute, a small centre for advanced Tibetan studies; the institute also endeavours to expose Tibetans to Western literature and culture through translations. Among their publications is a fine map of Lhasa City.

Knowledge of Tibetan medicine is continued through the Tibetan Medical and Astro Institute, the only one of its kind in the world. It dispenses herbal medicines and trains students in Tibetan medical practices; research on new herbal medicines is also carried out here. The Tibetan arts have been revived through the Norbulingka Institute (for Tibetan artisans) and TIPA (Tibetan Institute of Performing Arts). The Tibetan Children's Village, mainly looking after orphans, is operated by the Dalai Lama's sister Jetsun Pema. In Dharamsala you can see festivals celebrated in full fashion, and Tibetan Buddhist ceremonies that carry real meaning (since they're not restricted, as they are in Tibet itself). Among the bigger celebrations are Losar (new year) and Monlam.

The Tibetan community-in-exile is not as cohesive as you might think. There are various points of view on Tibetan independence – some believe in full independence, others in limited autonomy. Some favour the use of force, by fighting a guerrilla war. When it comes to the government-in-exile, the Dalai Lama has tried to establish a quasi-democratic set-up, but this doesn't always work, as few would like to oppose him in public. This is where people get confused: opposing a point of view of the Dalai Lama is taken as a mark of disrespect.

Educated Tibetans say not enough steps have been taken for ushering the Tibetan community into the modern world – for example, translating modern literature into the Tibetan language. Nor is the faith of Tibetan Buddhism unified. Apart from the four main schools of Tibetan Buddhism, there are a number of offshoots or sub-sects. A major rift in the community developed in 1997 over a wrathful spirit with three bloodshot eyes, wreathed in the smoke of burning human flesh. Known as Dorje Shugden ('Powerful Thunderbolt'), this spirit seems to have originated in the 17th century: he is regarded by some as a protector deity, and by others as a murderous demon. The Dalai Lama, beginning in 1976, discouraged the propitiation of Shugden worship on the advice of the state oracle. In 1996, the Dalai Lama prohibited Shugden services in state offices and in government-in-exile-run monasteries, on the grounds that it is damaging to Buddhism. The subject is arcane and complex: several Dalai Lamas – the Fifth and 13th in particular – tried to stop the practice and teaching of Dorje Shugden worship. The controversy is ongoing: the Chinese, happy at any exile strife, have seized upon the rift to restore Shugden temples in occupied Tibet.

High points Dharamsala is divided into two very different parts: Kotwali Bazaar and lower Dharamsala, and McLeod Ganj in upper Dharamsala. The centre of activity for the Tibetan exile community is McLeod Ganj, set in forested mountain slopes. This laid-back town of perhaps 7,000 has lots of small restaurants and cafés where travellers hang out. There are numerous attractions related to Tibetan culture. As well as seeing the temples, you can visit the Tibet Museum – near the Dalai Lama's residence – offering two floors of displays. Apart from these attractions and the opportunity to take meditation classes, there is excellent trekking in the Dharamsala region, with camping trips of up to a week possible. Other activities include paragliding.

Low points During peak tourist seasons (June and November), the tiny town of McLeod Ganj gets so crowded that it's difficult to find a room in a hotel or guesthouse. People find the place so relaxing they just stay on: there's a very real danger of lingering over apple pie or chocolate cake in the cafés of McLeod Ganj and completely losing track of time.

Bizarre notes Nechung Monastery – the former Lhasa seat of the state oracle – was rebuilt in Dharamsala, with 70 monks studying the sacred rituals surrounding the oracle. The oracle is a man who acts as a medium to convey messages to the Dalai Lama from Dorje Drakten, a protector-deity. The messages are used in important decision-making. Ceremonies where the oracle goes into a trance are secret: the oracle is dressed in a traditional brocade costume and a heavy headdress of precious metals. The ceremonial headdress is thought to weigh 20kg: normally it is too heavy to be worn without support. However, when in a trance, the oracle's strength increases considerably, and attendants quickly strap on the headdress. During the trance, the oracle is said to dance around as if the headdress weighs nothing.

Best time to go March to June, plus October to November. Watch out for the monsoon (July to mid-September). Winters can be very cold in Dharamsala, but February is when Losar (new year) is usually celebrated.

Red tape Indian visas are valid for up to six months (and longer is possible); multiple-entry visas are also available.

Getting there You can reach McLeod Ganj by day or overnight **bus** from Delhi, taking about 12–15 hours for the 520km drive. The closest **railway** station is Pathankot. There's an airfield at Gaggal, connecting to Delhi, Kulu and Simla, but it does not appear to be much used, and **flight** schedules are erratic.

Following up A slew of mini-guides to Dharamsala appear on the site dharamsalanet.com (click on 'Holiday and Travel Guides').

BODHGAYA, SARNATH AND SOUTH INDIA Bodhgaya, in Bihar state (in north-central India, due south of Kathmandu, and 15km from the town of Gaya), is the place where the Buddha attained enlightenment under a Bodhi tree. The original Bodhi tree was destroyed, but a sapling taken from it was introduced back from Sri Lanka and this exercise was then repeated half-a-dozen times. The present tree is part of the grounds of Mahabodhi Temple. Bodhgaya is today a site of special significance because the Dalai Lama has conducted Kalachakra initiations there. These esoteric initiations were once highly secret and exclusive, and were only conducted in Tibet. In the ceremony, the initiator would harmonise inner elements of the body and mind to bring about harmony and peace in the outer world. In an attempt to counter humankind's destructive forces, the Dalai Lama has dispensed with exclusivity, conducting Kalachakra initiations around the world: up to 150,000 devotees have attended initiations in Bodhgaya.

Another Kalachakra empowerment site and Indian pilgrimage site visited by the Dalai Lama is Sarnath, 10km from Varanasi. Sarnath is the site of the Buddha's first sermon at Deer Park, 'Setting in Motion the Wheel of the Law'. Symbolising this sermon is the golden sculpture of the wheel with two deer that sits over the entrance of most temples in Tibet and is the national emblem of Tibet.

Like neighbouring countries, the Indians are not keen on large groups of Tibetans amassing, which explains scattered settlements in central India (8,000 Tibetans) and south India (30,000 Tibetans) where frontier-type settlements were hacked out of humid jungle. The temples of Sera, Ganden, Drepung and Tashilhunpo were built anew at Mundgod, Mysore and Bylakuppe.

TIBETAN KINGDOMS AND FIEFDOMS

Apart from the Tibetan realms already mentioned in this book (Tibet proper, Tibet outside the TAR, Tibet in exile), there is another realm: a fourth Tibet. It is largely composed of kingdoms and fiefdoms that broke away from Tibet centuries ago, when Tibet itself still had ruling kings. The people in these places speak and read Tibetan, and follow Tibetan cultural practices, but otherwise have developed their own worlds. They do not identify with Tibetan exiles, nor do they particularly want to attract them.

INDIA
Ladakh and Zanskar The kingdoms of Ladakh and Zanskar (northwest India) originally splintered from west Tibet. Tibetans settled in Ladakh between AD500 and 600. Upon the death of the King of Ngari (western Tibet) around AD930, his kingdom was split between his three sons, one taking Guge and Burang, another Ladakh, and the third Zanskar and Spiti. The kingdoms of Ladakh and Zanskar changed hands numerous times. The most famous king of Ladakh, Senge Namgyal (1616–42), overran the kingdom of Guge in west Tibet, and even threatened central Tibet. By the end of the 17th century, Ladakh's power was in decline, leaving it vulnerable to Muslim incursions.

Due to its strategic location, Leh (the capital of Ladakh) once hosted a busy trading bazaar, attracting caravans from Kashgar, Khotan, Yarkand, Lhasa and Rawalpindi. With India's independence in 1947, Ladakh was absorbed into the Indian state of Jammu and Kashmir. Pakistan contested the borders and seized Baltistan, plus a part of Ladakh and a part of Kashmir. In 1962, the Chinese attacked Ladakh and took over the region east of Nubra, effectively ending any trade. There's now a heavy Indian military presence in Ladakh, to counter potential threats from Pakistan and China.

High points Dominating Leh is a derelict palace, built in the same monumental style as the Potala. There are many monasteries within easy driving range of Leh; some, such as Hemis Gompa, host traditional festivals and monastic dances. Most imposing of the lamaseries is Tikse Gompa, a fantastic complex that occupies a whole hillside 17km upstream along the Indus River from Leh; the main hall houses a 15m-high seated gold image of Maitreya. Another real high point is Khardung La, a pass 40km north of Leh that sits at 5,606m and lays claim to being the world's highest motorable roadway. There are excellent trekking and mountaineering opportunities in Ladakh and Zanskar – you can put your own small group together and head out with a guide and donkey to carry gear.

Low points In snow-blocked months, the only way in is to fly to Leh from Delhi, and flights are often overbooked or cancelled, or both. Travellers have also experienced the opposite – they've made it into remote Zanskar but then have been unable to get out due to heavy snowfall. Faced with the prospect of being trapped in Shangri-La for six months till summer, there are two ways out: radio for an Indian helicopter airlift (expensive), or hike out along the ice on the frozen Zanskar River (slippery).

Bizarre notes Although royalty has largely disappeared from Ladakh, Zanskar still has two kings. The King of Zanskar lives in Padam, and the King of Zangla controls one castle and four villages.

Red tape No special permits are required to visit – an Indian visa suffices. However, certain areas are out of bounds to tourists.

Getting there Due to sporadic fighting between the Indian Army and Kashmiri militants, the Srinagar to Leh route is not recommended (although you can travel from Leh to Lamayuru and back to Leh). Travellers use the Manali to Leh route to enter or exit Ladakh and Zanskar (you should also be aware that foreigners have gone missing in the Kulu Valley near Manali under mysterious circumstances – *do not trek alone in this region*). Although **buses** have been known to wheeze over the high passes on the 475km Manali–Leh route, it is best negotiated by a **4x4** vehicle like a jeep. Along the route lies Tanglang La – at 5,330m, one of the highest road crossings in the world. The Manali–Leh road is generally open from July to October.

Following up Andrew Harvey's *A Journey in Ladakh* (1983) is the classic travelogue about the region, based on his 1981 trip.

Lahaul, Spiti and Kinnaur

The little-visited valleys of Lahaul and Spiti, accessed from Manali, are very Tibetan in character. No special permits are needed to enter Lahaul, but permits are required for parts of Spiti. Lahaul is reached over the 3,980m Rohtang pass, while access to Spiti is via the 4,550m Kunzum La pass. Long ago, both Lahaul and Spiti were ruled by the kingdom of Guge in far west Tibet. This is reflected in the now-rare Kashmiri style of artwork found at Tabo Gompa in Spiti, which is similar to that of Tsaparang (Guge Kingdom) in west Tibet. Tabo Gompa houses one of the Tibetan world's finest collections of Buddhist art, with seven chapels bearing frescoes and a number of Guge-style *chortens*. May to June is the best time to visit these areas. Getting around is possible by bus, hired taxi or trekking. You might consider hiring a Landcruiser for the journey, splitting the cost with several others. Inner Line Permits for Spiti are obtained in Rekong Peo, and will be scrutinised at the military checkpoint of Sumdo.

Southeast of Spiti is the Kinnaur region, where local people wear green felt hats. Like Lahaul and Spiti, Kinnaur was once part of the Guge Kingdom. The main focus of pilgrims to Kinnaur is the sacred mountain of Kinnaur Kailash (6,050m), which Hindus set out to circle clockwise. It is thought that Shiva comes from Mount Kailash in west Tibet to winter at Kinnaur Kailash – and to smoke hashish. Kinnaur can be accessed from Shimla; there is also a route leading from Kinnaur to Spiti.

Darjeeling, Kalimpong and Sikkim

Darjeeling and Kalimpong in northeast India were once controlled by Sikkim, but in the 18th century Kalimpong was lost to the Bhutanese while Darjeeling fell to the Nepalese. Eventually, the lands fell into the hands of the British East India Company, which developed the region as a tea-growing centre. Darjeeling is a former British hill station – a cool place at 2,100m, and the base for trekking in the area. From Darjeeling there are views of Kangchenjunga, at 8,595m the third-highest peak in the world. There are several Tibetan monasteries around Darjeeling; great places to visit are the zoo – featuring rare Himalayan animals like the red panda and the snow leopard – and the Himalayan Mountaineering Institute (HMA) which was run by Tenzing Norgay until his death in 1986, and now houses a climbing museum and climbers' training centre. Apart from being a resort, Darjeeling is a major educational centre, attracting the children of wealthy Sikkimese and Bhutanese.

From Darjeeling you can take a bus, jeep or taxi to Kalimpong. In the days of the British Raj, the main wool-trade route to Lhasa was via Kalimpong and Sikkim through Yadong to Gyantse. This trading route closed in 1962 as a result of border clashes between China and India, and was reopened in mid-2006. Kalimpong is a pleasant trading town – famed for its cheese – with several Tibetan monasteries. The town attracts Indian tourism.

Sikkim used to be a Tibetan kingdom – a kind of vassal state. Later, it was run by the Rajas of Sikkim; in 1975, it was annexed by India (China also claims the whole of Sikkim). The story of the demise of Sikkim has all the elements of a fairy tale – with a bad ending. In Darjeeling in 1959 the crown prince of Sikkim, Palden Thondup Namgyal, met Hope Cooke, an American on a study trip in India. He married her in 1963 at a ceremony at Gangtok Monastery; two years later he became king and she was given the title of queen. But the match did not sit well with the people of Sikkim. Hope Cooke remained distant: she never converted to Buddhism and she made frequent trips to Europe and America with the couple's two children. In 1973 there was a wave of unrest in Sikkim, and Indian troops took advantage of the situation to place the royal family under house arrest. Hope Cooke eventually left the king, returned to New York with her children, and filed for divorce. In 1975, the Sikkim National Congress voted to incorporate Sikkim into India. The monarchy was abolished, and Sikkim was annexed as the 22nd federal state of India. The deposed king died in 1982 in a New York cancer clinic.

Gangtok, elevation 1,500m, is the capital of Sikkim. Here you can find the former royal palace, the royal chapel and the Institute of Tibetology, with a fine collection of Buddhist literature. About 25km from Gangtok is Rumtek Monastery, built as a replica of Tsurphu Monastery (near Lhasa – see the *Exploring Central Tibet* chapter, page 171, for more about Tsurphu) by the exiled head of the Kagyu sect, who fled Tibet in 1959. There are excellent treks north of Gangtok, usually arranged in small groups with permits, porters and horses. The prize trek is up towards the base camp of mighty Kangchenjunga.

Most roads in Sikkim are in excellent shape. A few trekkers have managed to walk along the old British roads between monasteries. There's a small network of relatively unknown and unused old British service roads that can be used as alternatives to the main roads or steeper walking tracks. However, you will need your own maps as some roads are overgrown, and there are few (if any) guesthouses so you will need camping equipment, too.

Another highlight is the trip up to 4,350m Nathu La on the Sikkim–Tibet border, to wave Tibetan flags at PLA border guards. There are rumours that group tours may one day be allowed access to cross into Tibet here. By road from Gangtok to Lhasa is around 480km and the direct drive can be completed on the same day. Far preferable would be to break the journey at Gyantse and rest there a while.

When to go The best months are April–May (spring flowers in bloom) and October–November (post-monsoon). Winters are cold, with occasional snowfalls.

Red tape Darjeeling is open without permit. You can easily obtain a two-week permit for Sikkim in either Darjeeling or Siliguri, and an extension of two more weeks should be possible (longer permits for Sikkim may require booking a trek with an agency in advance).

Getting there Half of the thrill is getting there: the '**toy train**' – a narrow-gauge railway completed in 1881 – winds up from Siliguri for the 80km to Darjeeling, passing tea plantations and misty mountains. The closest **airport** to Darjeeling and Kalimpong is Bagdogra. You can **overland** from Darjeeling via the border town of Kakarbhitta to Kathmandu.

Following up A mixed photographic work and travel narrative is *Footsteps in the Clouds: Kangchenjunga a Century Later*, by Pat and Baiba Morrow (Raincoast, 2000).

NEPAL Nepal is a small country sitting on a border shared with an up-and-coming superpower. The Nepalese have no desire to confront the PLA, so the Nepalese government has worked closely with the Chinese since their invasion of Tibet, and fully supports the Chinese position in Tibet. In the late 1960s the Chinese requested help in snuffing out Khampa resistance operating from Nepalese territory, in the region of Mustang. After the Dalai Lama appealed to the Khampas to lay down their arms, the Nepalese Army surrounded the last guerrillas in Mustang and ambushed them. Most were killed; the rest were thrown in jail for lengthy periods.

Since the entire royal family was gunned down in mid-2001, Nepal has experienced great instability. Civil war erupted, with fierce battles between the Nepalese Army and Maoist insurgents. Thousands of civilians and military were killed, particularly in remote border regions. In November 2006, a peace accord was signed between the government and the rebels, with a new constitution and new national anthem. In 2008, Nepal became a republic. An air of uncertainty and unease prevails: it's best to keep updated on the situation in Nepal through news websites.

Nepal is the main conduit for refugees escaping Tibet, intent on reaching Tibetan settlements in India. They hike over high passes to the south of Tingri and Sakya to reach Nepal. Refugees run a gauntlet through Nepal – Nepalese police routinely rob Tibetans and there have been cases of them raping Tibetan women. Tibetan refugees entering Nepal used to be taken care of by the UNHCR, and allowed to travel on to the safe haven of India. However, this policy changed around 2004: some refugees have been handed back to Chinese authorities (in contravention of UN guidelines) and others have been jailed in Nepal.

About 20,000 Tibetan exiles live in Nepal, but no politicking is allowed – Nepalese officials have sworn to co-operate with the Chinese and swear they will not allow any demonstrations by Tibetans in Nepal. Nepalese police regularly crack down on 10 March gatherings, and have even broken up indoor gatherings of Tibetans when sensing a political undercurrent. The office of the representative of the Dalai Lama in Kathmandu was closed down in 2005, along with a Tibetan refugee organisation. That same year, after India suspended supplies of arms to the Nepalese Army, the Nepalese turned to the Chinese for help. The Chinese immediately pledged US$1 million in military aid and dispatched truckloads of weapons overland from Tibet into Nepal.

The Nepalese press is blatantly pro-Chinese, muzzling voices that support the Tibetan cause. Nepalese police and authorities will go to ridiculous lengths to silence Tibetans living in Nepal. In July 2011, Nepalese authorities even shut down gatherings by Tibetans celebrating the birthday of the Dalai Lama. Oddly, however, Kathmandu is the best place in Asia or the Indian subcontinent to buy materials on Tibet, such as Free Tibet stickers, Free Tibet T-shirts, Tibetan flags, HHDL pictures, books, magazines and tapes. It is this material that roadblock searches in Tibet are directed at if you head towards Lhasa by road from Kathmandu.

Two of Nepal's major foreign exchange earners centre around Tibetans: carpets and tourism. The flourishing Tibetan carpet industry – centred in Kathmandu – was initially set up by exiled Tibetans in the early 1960s as part of a Swiss aid project to benefit Tibetan refugees in Nepal. The venture became wildly successful. Tourism in Nepal is prominently connected with Tibetans: several of Kathmandu's popular temples are Tibetan, and the commonest trekking routes are through Sherpa or ethnic Tibetan regions.

Sherpas, a group that migrated from Tibet centuries ago, are directly involved in the tourist, trekking and mountaineering industries. They are often wealthy businesspeople who run lodges, guide groups and so on. Sherpas speak a language similar to Tibetan – they can converse with Tibetans, but have no written language. They are followers of Tibetan Buddhism. Sherpas have been sympathetic to the Tibetan cause, and have formed a kind of 'underground' to help refugees arriving in Nepal. There are probably around 20,000 Sherpas living in Nepal, with the strongest base around the Khumbu area. Sherpas are identified by their last name 'Sherpa' as in Jangbu Sherpa or Tashi Sherpa. Other Tibetan-related groups in Nepal are the Lhobas from Mustang and the Dolpopas from Dolpo.

High points In Kathmandu, Bodnath Stupa is the main Tibetan temple area, surrounded by Tibetan-run shops and businesses; further out from Kathmandu is the Monkey Temple in Swayambunath. Nepal is the most 'developed' of any of the trekking destinations in the Himalaya. Teahouse trekking is the easiest way to visit regions with Sherpa or Tibetan-related populations – places like Solo Khumbu, Langtang and Annapurna. A visit to the restricted Mustang, Dolpo or Limi regions requires self-sufficient camping trips, usually only in groups, with a liaison officer and special permits worth US$500–700 per trekker. Both Dolpo and Mustang used to lie on old salt-trading routes from Tibet: Tibetans took salt and wool south to exchange for grains from India.

Low points In peak seasons – October especially – popular trails can be jammed with trekkers, and lodges can be full. Near Namche Bazaar, Lukla airstrip waiting room can get pretty wild as trekkers and mountaineers duke it out to get on the overbooked light aircraft back to Kathmandu. Failure to make it onto a flight may mean a meaningless ten-day walk back.

Bizarre notes Mustang is a Himalayan kingdom governed by King Jigme Parbal Bista – who is the 25th monarch in a line stretching back to the 14th century. Actually, he is the former king: he lost his title when Nepal became a republic in 2008. His wife is originally from Shigatse in Tibet. Trekkers take a week to reach the town of Lo Manthang, where the king lives. This is one of the rare Tibetan-style citadels with walls still intact. If the former king is around, trekkers can most likely drop in for a quick audience over a cup of butter tea. Not having the time or the stamina to trek for a week, Nepalese dignitaries have been known to drop in for tea by helicopter, landing in a wheat field next door to the monarch's humble palace. The former king, if he goes out to Jomosom, relies on neither of these transport options. He rides one of his horses, escorted by a mounted bodyguard. He breeds the best horses in Mustang: one of his horses can fetch several thousand dollars.

Best time to go Go in the October–early December or March–April trekking seasons. Avoid the mid-June to late-September monsoon season, when trails are slippery, and roads can be washed out, with frequent landslides and mudslides.

Red tape One-month visas are available on arrival at Kathmandu Airport, or when coming in by road from Tibet. Longer visas are easy to get, and visas are easily extendable. If you go trekking, you need a permit for each region to be visited. These are obtained in Kathmandu.

Getting there Most trips have a start or end point (or both) in Kathmandu. Good trekking equipment can be bought in Kathmandu – a lot is left behind by expeditions.

Inspiration *The Snow Leopard* by Peter Matthiessen (Penguin, 1996 – reprint of 1978 edition) is a finely wrought account of a journey to Dolpo. Matthiessen also wrote the text for *East of Lo Monthang* (Shambhala Publications, 1995), a photobook featuring pictures of Mustang by Thomas Laird. In the fiction line, *Escape from Kathmandu* by Kim Stanley Robinson (St Martin's Press, 2000 – reprint of 1989 edition) takes the reader on a wild ride, with some hilarious excursions to the Tibetan side. A walk on the mystical side is *Surfing the Himalayas* by Frederick Lenz (St Martin's Press, 1997), claiming to discover mystical insights via snowboarding. Lenz created his own cult in the US, bilking his followers of large amounts of cash. On the net, a website with many links is run by Amaa Consultants at www.catmando.com. You should be aware that newspapers in Nepal are subject to heavy-handed censorship. A 'news' site from Kathmandu is www.nepalnews.com.

BHUTAN In the Himalaya, of the vast area that was once the spirited domain of the Tibetan religion and culture – stretching from Ladakh to Yunnan – only the tiny enclave of Bhutan survives as a self-governing entity, with Tibetan Buddhism as its state religion (Outer Mongolia, far to the north, is also independent and follows Tibetan Buddhism, but its people and language are Mongolian). With an area of 47,000km², Bhutan is roughly the size of Switzerland, and seeks to be as neutral. It allows India to control its foreign policy in exchange for military protection from China. To protect itself from a takeover by India, Bhutan has held a seat at the UN since 1971.

Although Bhutan was self-governing since the 17th century in a kind of theocracy, the Bhutanese monarchy is a hereditary dynasty begun in the early 20th century. Ugyen Wangchuck, previously the governor of Bhutan, was crowned hereditary monarch of Bhutan in 1907 with British support, after his role as intermediary between the British and the Tibetans during the Younghusband expedition of 1903.

King Jigme Singye Wangchuck, who came to power in 1972, fostered the entry of Bhutan into the international community, establishing diplomatic relations with many countries. King Jigme Wangchuck also fostered the traditional culture of Bhutan to the point of strong-arming other ethnic cultures. The predominant ethnic groups in Bhutan – the Drukpas and Monbas – migrated from Tibet centuries ago. Bhutan, however, is not a safe haven for refugee Tibetans, whom the Bhutanese fear will build up in greater numbers and power (there are several thousand currently living in Bhutan). Due to a falling-out over Tibetan refugees, Bhutan has few contacts with the Tibetan government-in-exile. Nor are the Bhutanese keen on a large Nepalese presence. The southern lowlands are mostly occupied by people of Nepalese origin. In November 2008, the king stepped down and handed the crown to his son, Jigme Khesar Namgyal Wangchuk, the fifth king in the lineage.

Figures on population in Bhutan vary wildly from 600,000 to 1.8 million. How you can lose over a million people on a census is hard to fathom, but it seems that in a 1988 census ethnic Nepalis may have actually outnumbered Drukpas in Bhutan, so the government could have rearranged the population figures to suit. The government banned the speaking of Nepalese, and has an ongoing programme to boot as many ethnic Nepalis as possible back to Nepal, citing their failure to assimilate to Bhutanese culture and learn the language as the reason for marching orders. Numbers of these people languish in refugee camps in southeast Nepal.

The official faith of Bhutan is Drukpa Kagyu, a tantric form of Tibetan Buddhism (and a sub-sect of the Kagyu order); also practised is Buddhism of the Nyingma school; in Nepalese areas, the faith is Indian- and Nepali-influenced Hinduism. Bhutan's national language, called Dzongkha, is related to Tibetan but is quite different from the Lhasa dialect. Dzongkha is a compulsory subject at school, although the medium of instruction is English.

High points Bhutan has a pristine environment, untouched by industrial development, or in fact any kind of development. Over 25% of Bhutan's land area is devoted to national parks and reserves. The best way to see this beautiful land is by trekking or jeep safari; more recently, white-water rafting and mountain biking have been introduced. Top treks include the one north towards Mount Chomolhari on the Tibetan border. Bhutan is famed for its traditional festivals – elaborate affairs with parades, Cham sacred dances and archery contests. And Bhutan is the best place in the Tibetan world to see traditional-style architecture – such as the parliament buildings of Thimphu and the numerous *dzongs* across the country.

Low points The crippling cost of getting into Bhutan may prove hazardous to your wallet, but it's also the factor that keeps the tourist masses at bay.

Bizarre notes Bhutan is so intent on preserving the traditional way of life that it is an offence not to wear the national robe (*kho* for men, and *kira* for women) – a fine can be levied. In addition to the national dress, men or women may wear a ceremonial scarf, and men often wear argyle socks.

Best time to go The best seasons are autumn (November) or spring (April/May). Avoid the June–October monsoon. However, if you are looking for flora, May and June are the months when glorious rhododendrons and blue poppies are in bloom.

Red tape Access is restricted – visitors are allowed only in a group tour or by personal invitation from a party in Bhutan. This policy keeps the numbers down to around 20,000 visitors a year. They fly into Paro (west of the capital of Thimphu) or come overland through Phuntsoling. There are three domestic airports under way at Tashigang and Bumthang (in the east) and Gelepgu (in the south). With advance clearance, visas are issued at the place of arrival. On group tours a set fee of US\$180–240 a day is levied on each visitor, depending on the kind of trip and the season. This may sound very high, but it includes all the bills (accommodation, food, trekking equipment and transport). The tariff must be paid upfront by wiring money to the Bhutan tourism authorities. Paperwork can take several months to complete if going through an agent outside Asia; in Kathmandu, the red tape can be completed in a week.

Following up Barbara Crossette's book *So Close to Heaven* (Vintage Books, 1996) explores the vanishing Buddhist kingdoms of the Himalaya. Jamie Zeppa's travel narrative, *Beyond the Sky and the Earth* (Riverhead Books, 1999) is an excellent personal take on the kingdom. For up-to-date information and news snippets on Bhutan, check these websites: www.kuenselonline.com (national daily English newspaper) and www.bootan.com (online outfit with a lot of information provided about Bhutan – the domain name bhutan.com is reserved by a cyber-squatter).

MONGOLIA Apart from a few monastic visitors, there is no Tibetan presence in the independent nation of (Outer) Mongolia. It is not a Tibetan kingdom or fiefdom, but the country is mentioned here because it preserves Tibetan Buddhist practices: the national faith of Mongolia is Tibetan Buddhism. Mongolia makes an interesting case study: it was a Tibetan Buddhist nation under communist (Russian) domination and then regained its independence soon after the collapse of the Soviet Union in 1991. In the 1996 election, the Mongolian Democratic Coalition garnered most of the seats, ending 75 years of communist rule. This is the scenario that intrigues Tibetans most – a similar fall of the Chinese Empire (with breakaway slabs being Tibet, Xinjiang and Inner Mongolia).

In the Stalin era, 700 larger and 1,000 smaller monasteries were destroyed in Mongolia, and thousands of monks were executed by the Russians in an attempt to wipe out Tibetan Buddhism, the predominant faith in Mongolia. A handful of larger monasteries survived (such as the one at Karakorum) and now, out on the grasslands, felt tents (*gers*) are converted for use as temples as Tibetan Buddhism enjoys a comeback. Also staging a comeback is Mongolian military hero Genghis Khan. After the last Russian troops left in 1992, Genghis rode back in, appearing larger than life, on the screen in a four-hour epic movie playing at cinemas in Ulaanbaatar. His fat bearded face also popped up on banknotes, and on the label of Chinggis Khan Vodka, a twist on the national Russian beverage.

All of which makes the Chinese very nervous – they're not keen on Genghis nationalism spilling over the border into their zone of Inner Mongolia (Genghis Khan's tomb is located in Inner Mongolia). Genghis brings back bad ancestral memories for the Chinese – in the early 13th century his hordes of horsemen surged with ease over the Great Wall, which was designed to keep them out. The Mongols weren't in any hurry to leave, either – the sons and grandsons of Genghis (particularly Kublai Khan) hung around China for the rest of the 13th century. Thus relations with Chinese-controlled Inner Mongolia are testy. There are hardly any Mongolians left in Inner Mongolia anyhow – out of a population of 20 million, perhaps only two million are reckoned to be Mongolians (the rest are Han Chinese settlers). This is what the Dalai Lama points his finger at: Inner Mongolia has been swamped by Han Chinese and has totally lost its identity.

Relations between Tibetans and (Outer) Mongolians, by contrast, are good. The Sakya sect established relations with the court of Godan Khan in the 1240s – an ongoing link. At the court of Kublai Khan in the 13th century, a great contest took place to see which philosophy had the greatest power – Islam, Nestorian Christianity, Confucianism, Taoism or Tibetan Buddhism. The last prevailed, but it was not until the 16th century, under Altan Khan, that Tibetan Buddhism really took hold in Mongolia. Altan Khan conferred the Mongolian title Dalai Lama (meaning 'Ocean of Wisdom') on Sonam Gyatso (the Third Dalai Lama). Despite Chinese protests, the current Dalai Lama has visited Mongolia a number of times since 1990, drawing huge crowds. He has established teachings there through his own monks. With the revival of Tibetan Buddhism in Mongolia, the Dalai Lama has a new ally. Buddhism is also rejuvenating in the Mongolian-populated areas of Russia – Buryatia and Tuva – on China's sensitive border zones.

High points Ulaanbaatar is a dump, with Soviet-style apartment blocks blotting the skyline, but it has an incredible fine arts museum, with intricate bronze statuary and stunning woven or painted *tankas*, some showing scenes of Lhasa and the Potala. The beautiful statuary in this museum is largely the work of 17th-century master sculptor Zanabazar, who studied in Tibet and returned to Mongolia to spread Tibetan Buddhism.

There are more animals in Mongolia than people – many more – with animal husbandry the mainstay of the economy. With a population of 2.3 million spread over an area of 1.56 million km², Mongolia is very sparsely inhabited and largely untouched. It's one big wildlife sanctuary in a sense, with herds of gazelles, wild camels, wild asses and bighorn sheep roaming the wilderness. That's what is most surprising about a visit to the Gobi Desert – the unexpected amount of wildlife. This is probably the way Tibet used to be. To see this kind of pure environment, go to the mountainous Lake Hovsgol region in the northwest, or to the Gobi in the southwest.

Low points Food in Mongolia – at least supplementary food, aside from the main course – is hard to find, and revolves around meat. Bring your own in the form of freeze-dried soups or meals to supplement the Mongolian meat-based staples.

Bizarre notes Large, whimsical postage stamps feature subjects like a Mongolian cosmonaut (sent into space on a Russian craft), Mickey Mouse, and Fred Flintstone riding a dinosaur past some *gers*. Also featured on stamps are Taras (Tara is the goddess of compassion), and tantric deities locked in *yabyum* (see *Glossary*, page 327) embraces. On the 1 tugrig banknote, the snow lion appears, as it used to on pre-1950 Tibetan money (the watermark on this bill is an image of Genghis Khan).

Best time to go Winter is severe with possible heavy snowfall and sub-zero temperatures, made even more sub-zero by howling winds. In other words, go in the summer, from June to September. The Nadam Fair – featuring horse racing, wrestling and archery – takes place in July.

Red tape Individual travel restrictions have eased up since the 1990s. The easiest way to get into Mongolia is to extend your stay off the TransMongolian Express. Some long-term visas are available direct from embassies from places like London or Vientiane (Laos). It's hit and miss: some embassies issue them, others don't. Monkey Business (aka Monkey Star), a Belgian travel agent with offices in Hong Kong and Beijing, seems adept at getting these visas on short notice – they run tours to (Outer) Mongolia. You can also get (Outer) Mongolian visas in Ulan Ude (on the TransMongolian, near Lake Baikal), and in Hohhot, the capital of Inner Mongolia. Ulaanbaatar is a very good place to pick up a long Chinese visa.

Getting there Journeys to Mongolia invariably start and end in Ulaanbaatar. A single passenger **rail** line traverses the country from north to south, linking

Moscow to Beijing via Ulaanbaatar. There are few roads in Mongolia, but a **jeep** can go almost anywhere on the grasslands in the summer, so no road is required. As an individual, you'll most likely have to get together with other travellers to rent a jeep. The trick is to find a jeep that has gasoline/petrol, as there's a severe shortage of the precious stuff. Mongolia is one of the few countries left where ancient Russian turboprop jets are still in use, on domestic runs. And you may even stray across an old AN-2 biplane parked at an airfield – it may be on display as a vintage **aircraft**, or it might actually still be in service.

Following up Tim Severin's book *In Search of Genghis Khan* (Atheneum, 1991). On the net, www.infomongolia.com and www.ub-mongolia.com carry snippets of news and other data.

Appendix 1

FAUNA EXTRAORDINARY

Adapting to the harsh high-altitude conditions of the Tibetan plateau is some remarkable wildlife. Some animals, like the wild yak, are so well adapted to the altitude that they cannot survive at lower elevations.

This is a brief introduction to some of the unusual mammals and birds of Tibet, and their links to mythology. Sadly, rather than a listing of fauna you might be able to spot, it is more a listing of endangered species – these species may soon end up being mythical. In the 1940s, American adventurer Leonard Clark reported about Tibet: 'Every few minutes we would spot a bear, a hunting wolf, herds of musk deer, kiang, gazelles, big horned sheep, or foxes. This must be one of the last unspoiled big game paradises.' Tibetans only took what wildlife they needed, so impact was minimal. The coming of the Chinese in the 1950s changed all that: Chinese soldiers machine-gunned wildlife not only for food but for export to China – and for sport. Tibet's once-plentiful wildlife now faces extinction: in the last 50 years, large mammals have gone the way of the bison in north America.

Due to poaching for its valuable undercoat, the Tibetan antelope's days are numbered. The fleet-footed Tibetan antelope can easily outrun any predator (except a wolf), but it cannot evade poachers equipped with 4x4 vehicles and high-powered guns. The Tibetan antelope's undercoat is the finest wool in the world, gossamer in weight and texture, soft yet incredibly warm. Poachers feed an underground network that supplies Kashmiri weavers, who spin shawls for wealthy buyers. The trade is outlawed, but poaching continues. The snow leopard is hunted for its pelt and for parts used in Chinese traditional medicine.

If you want to view Himalayan wildlife and birds, the best bet is Bhutan, which has a network of national parks and strong conservation policies in place. American biologist George Schaller has worked for the last two decades to get reserves established in parts of Tibet and Pakistan. He has been instrumental in the creation of a huge Changtang reserve in northern Tibet (see page 11).

The species at the start of the following list are 'flagship species' and have been given longer text. The names in parentheses are Latin (scientific name), followed by the Tibetan name(s).

MAMMALS

Tibetan antelope (*Pantholops hodgsoni*) Tibetan: *chiru, tso*. The Tibetan antelope inhabits high desert plateau. The females are hornless, but the males sport a pair of long slender upright horns, which could make them the source of unicorn myths in Tibet that date back several centuries (viewed in profile, the chiru would appear to have one long horn). The chiru's fine wool is a special adaptation that traps layers of warm air close to its body so it can survive snow blizzards where the thermometer plummets to –40°C. The chiru's underwool, known as *shahtoosh*, is the finest animal fibre in the world. The chiru has never been tamed or reared in captivity: the only way to get *shahtoosh* is through killing the animals and skinning them. Although the trade in *shahtoosh* is illegal, it has pushed the chiru to the brink of extinction, with fewer than 100,000 remaining. Their last hope is the creation of a Changtang nature reserve with adjoining ones in Xinjiang and Qinghai.

Snow leopard (*Panthera uncia*) Tibetan: *ganzig, saa.*

Unique in its camouflage – a greyish spotted coat, blending in with its terrain – the snow leopard is a nocturnal hunter, mostly active at dusk and dawn, and particularly fond of stalking blue sheep, ibex and marmots. By day it sleeps in caves or on rocky ledges. It inhabits remote high-altitude terrain from 3,000–5,500m, with the largest numbers left in northwest India – in Ladakh, Spiti and Lahaul. The snow leopard is about the size of a large dog. It has adapted ingeniously to life in extreme snowy terrain: its large paws act like snowshoes, and its enormous tail is used

to stabilise acrobatic leaps – and at night is wrapped around body and face like a scarf to withstand freezing temperatures. Because of its throat-bone structure, the snow leopard is a non-roaring cat, but is known to make strange howling cries during the January–March mating season. So elusive and stealthy is the snow leopard that the first movie film to capture it in action was not taken until the dawn of the 21st century. The snow leopard is highly endangered, with numbers remaining estimated at under 7,000; it may soon become as mythical as the snow lion. Seeing one: captive animals are held at the Darjeeling snow leopard breeding programme in northeast India.

Takin (*Budorcas taxicolor*) Tibetan: *bamen, dong gyemtsey.*

The takin is a hairy hoofed herbivore with a bulbous nose and backward-facing horns. It is a strange mix of moose, musk-ox and wildebeest, and can weight up to 400kg, with a body 2m long. The takin favours the forested slopes of the eastern Tibetan plateau, particularly in southeast Tibet and in Bhutan, where it inhabits dense forest. There are four subspecies: the Bhutan takin, Mishmi takin (Tibet), Shensi takin and Sichuan takin (China). There are probably fewer than 5,000 remaining. Seeing one: the takin is the national animal of Bhutan; a handful of captive takins are kept at a reserve overlooking Thimphu.

Wild yak (*Bos mutus*) Tibetan: *drong.*

An enormous creature: an adult male can weigh up to 1,000kg (equivalent to double the weight of a domestic yak), and can stand almost 2m high at the shoulder. *Bos mutus* is the Latin name given to distinguish the wild yak from the domestic one (designated as *Bos grunniens*, which means 'grunting ox' – a nod to the yaks' habit of grunting when agitated or when calling their young). Inter-breeding between the two species occurs when wild yak males enter domestic herds and abscond with females. Wild yaks graze mostly on grass and herbs. They are superbly adapted to altitude and are sure-footed over rough terrain. Herds travel on snow in single file, carefully stepping on footprints left by the lead yak. The wild yak's long shaggy coat enables it to withstand violent winds and snowstorms. A sighting of wild yaks is rare today, although possible in remote parts of Qinghai.

Tibetan wild ass (*Equus kiang*) Tibetan: *kyang.*

The largest of the Asiatic asses, this animal actually shares a lot in common genetically with the zebra, minus the stripes. But it follows a very different social system. The kyang is now mostly found in the Changtang in Tibet. The British Army attempted to domesticate them in 1904 for use as pack animals, but failed. Huge herds of kyang used to graze the highlands of Tibet, but today sightings are rarer. They may be spotted in groups of 20 to 200 in remote regions of Tibet.

Alpine musk deer (*Moschus sifanicus*) Tibetan: *lawa, larna*. The musk deer does not have antlers. Instead, both males and females have two large fang-like extruding upper canines for defence purposes. The musk deer has been hunted for centuries for the male's musk pod, located in front of the genitals. The musk obtained fetches a high price, used for its medicinal qualities and in the preparation of perfume, although most modern perfumiers use synthetic musk. Hunting has severely depleted numbers of the musk deer.

Blue sheep (*Pseudois nayaur*) Tibetan: *naya*. Blue sheep combine features of both goat and sheep. They have a slate-grey coat that appears more bluish in winter but turns brownish in summer, to blend in with its surroundings. Adult rams have large horns that curve up, outward and downward. The females have smaller horns. Blue sheep can congregate in herds of up to 200.

Marco Polo sheep

(*Ovis ammon hodgsoni*)
Tibetan: *nyen*. Huge males have massive curling horns, and thus are prized in hunting as trophy animals. The sheep is found in the Pamir region, at the intersection of China, Afghanistan, Tajikistan and Pakistan. The sheep is named after Marco Polo: in his day, nobody in Italy believed his story about the preposterous horns of this wild sheep. An estimated 11,000 remain. There is a close Tibetan cousin, the Tibetan argali sheep.

Tibetan brown bear (*Ursus arctos pruinosus*) Tibetan: *dremo, tremong*. The Tibetan brown bear can stand up to 1.8m, as tall as a man, which is probably why the species (and its footprint) are likely to be mistaken for a yeti. The highly endangered Tibetan brown bear ranges into higher altitude zones. Lower down in forests is the smaller Himalayan black bear (*Ursus thibetanus laniger*).

Red panda (*Ailurus fulgens*) Tibetan: *og dong kar*. This mammal has long been thought to be a distant relative of the giant panda because it shares the peculiar habit of feeding largely on bamboo, and because it has similar teeth and paws. But the red panda is actually more closely related to raccoons; this chestnut-coloured 'cat-bear' is small, with a ringed bushy tail half its length. It is a tree dweller, inhabiting dense bamboo forests to the eastern side of the Tibetan plateau, including parts of China, Nepal, India, Bhutan and Burma. The red panda is hunted for its pelt, used to make traditional hats in Yunnan. Seeing a live one: Darjeeling Zoo in northeast India holds several.

Tibetan sand fox (*Vulpes ferrilata*) Tibetan: *wa, wamo*. This species is endemic to the Tibetan plateau, and inhabits open steppe like the vast desert of the Changtang. Its sandy colouring allows it to blend in easily with the desert. The Tibetan sand fox has a peculiar chunky head and is bigger than the common fox, which is also present in Tibet (mostly found in forested zones). The Tibetan sand fox keeps the rodent population in check, especially pikas (mouse-hares). The sand fox is hunted for its pelt, which is made into hats.

Himalayan marmot (*Marmota himalayana*) Tibetan: *kunpo, sho, jibi*. Also known as the 'Tibetan snow pig', this species is commonly seen throughout the plateau on the plains and in grassy mountain valleys. This large rodent is related to the north American marmot. Himalayan marmots live in large colonies in networks consisting of deep burrows. Their shrill whistling call alerts all animals in the vicinity to danger from predators. The marmot is hunted for its thick golden-brown fur.

BIRDS There are over 500 species of birds recorded in Tibet, 660 recorded in Pakistan and 800 in Nepal. Bhutan is the best place for birdwatching in the Himalaya, with over 700 species, including magnificent pheasants like the satyr tragopan. For many years, it was believed that no birds flew over the high peaks of the Himalaya. Now, it appears that half-a-dozen species do fly over the world's highest peaks, the ultimate high-fliers of the avian world. Yellow-billed choughs have been sighted at altitudes of 7,000m by climbers attempting Everest, and snow pigeons have been spotted flying over peaks at 8,300m.

Himalayan griffon vulture (*Gyps himalayensis*) Tibetan: *mkha, khor*. The Himalayan griffon vulture has been sighted riding 'blue thermals' over Everest, at altitudes of 9,000m. As with other vultures, the bird feeds mainly from carcasses of animals, with one peculiar twist in Tibet: this bird gathers in clusters at sky burial ceremonies to consume human corpses. It is thus an iconic bird in Tibetan lore. In Tibetan, *jhator* (sky burial) means 'offering to the birds'. The bearded vulture also shows up at sky burial ceremonies.

Lammergeier (*Gypaetus barbatus*) Tibetan: *gobo*. Also known as the bearded vulture, this bird soars across the length of the Himalaya. It has a wingspan of up to 2.8m, making it Eurasia's largest raptor. The lammergeier has an unusual feeding routine: soaring to a great height, this vulture drops bones from its talons onto rocks far below, and then swoops down to feed on the exposed bone marrow.

Bar-headed goose (*Anser indicus*) Tibetan: *kalaha, gangpa*. Astronauts on the wing: bar-headed geese can fly at altitudes up to 9,000m, clearing the Himalaya twice each year to complete an epic migration. When winter is over, the geese leave their feeding grounds in the lowlands of Nepal and India, going from near sea level straight up to 8,000m, heading over Himalayan peaks to breeding grounds in Amdo (Qinghai Lake), Outer Mongolia and Kyrgyzstan. An inner layer of down feathers helps stop the bird from freezing to death, while an outer layer of tightly woven feathers apparently waterproofs the goose and prevents build-up of body ice that would cause the bird to plunge to its doom. The bar-headed goose has been clocked flying at 80 km/h, but with a tailwind it can rocket along at up to 160 km/h. The honking of the bar-headed goose in the mountains is a sure sign you are in Tibet. Seeing one: some have been sighted in parks in Lhasa, mixed in with other geese. Look for geese with several black bars visible at the back of the head – that's where the name comes from.

Black-necked crane (*Grus nigricollis*) Tibetan: *trung trung*. This is the tallest of the birds in Tibet, up to 1.5m high; much of its height is in the neck, which is black with a red cap. There are estimated to be fewer than 9,000 black-necked cranes remaining in the wild.

In mating rituals, pairs of cranes leap into the air and utter loud bugling sounds. Most cranes migrate every year from Tibet to Bhutan. Gangtey Gompa (central Bhutan) hosts an annual festival to welcome flocks of cranes that arrive in late October, and depart again for Tibet in mid-February. In Buddhist lore, black-necked cranes are regarded as highly auspicious, and are depicted in temple frescoes.

Appendix 1 FAUNA EXTRAORDINARY

A1

311

Appendix 2

LANGUAGE AND USEFUL GESTURES

TIBETAN LANGUAGE Any attempt you make at speaking Tibetan, however awkward, will be greatly appreciated in a place where the language has such a low profile compared with the use of Chinese. It's worthwhile carrying two phrasebooks to handle situations: one Tibetan, the other Mandarin Chinese. Many Tibetans – particularly in the towns – understand some Mandarin, but will most likely not appreciate attempts to communicate with them in Chinese. Phrasebooks become doubly useful if they have Tibetan script: you can point to phrases if the pronunciation is not getting through (this is limited by a literacy factor, however). Good non-verbal communication can be achieved through use of pictures. Examination of pictorial subjects can lead to long dialogue – carry a book with pictures of Tibet, or brochures about Tibet, and carry photos of your family and your city. You can derive a lot of dialogue from learning numbers in Tibetan, and not just for pricing. Numbers can be used in other creative ways: how many children do you have? How many yaks?

Tibetan is a difficult language to speak, with a number of different dialects. Lhasa dialect (the standard dialect) employs a series of rising and falling tones – up to eight of them. Tonal usage increases with talking in a polite manner. There are also letters that are retroflex, glottal, aspirated or non-aspirated. Unfortunately, there is no accurate way to render these complexities in English phonetics, so what follows is a rough attempt, and one that you should polish by reviewing with a Tibetan speaker.

Tibetan is an ancient language that borrows modern words like 'post office', 'fax machine' or 'airport' from the nearest language. Within Tibet, these terms may be taken from Chinese, while in India the word might come from English or Hindi, which all leads to a standardisation headache. But consider this: it's sometimes possible to use an English word (with a twisted accent) and be understood – the Tibetan for 'jeep' is *jip*, and the Tibetan for 'Landcruiser' is *landkrusa*. It's difficult to find Tibetans to practise with in the West. You can attune your ear by listening to Tibetan-language radio broadcasts (see *Internet resources* opposite).

Tibetan terms used in this book can be put to good use as speaking vocabulary. A yak is a yak, and *tsampa* is *tsampa* (nobody else in the world eats the stuff). Also usable are things like *dzong* (castle), *gompa* (monastery) and *tsangpo* (river). For more vocabulary, check the *Glossary* (see page 326; some terms are Sanskrit, not Tibetan).

Useful phrases Here are a few useful phrases for pidgin Tibetan speakers: *tashi delek!* is an all-purpose opener, meaning: greetings! how are you? congratulations! best wishes! *Yapodu* or *yabadoo* means 'good' (thumb up) while *yapo mindu!* means 'bad!' (little finger down). Vital to your survival is the phrase *kale kale*, which means 'slow down', when spoken to a maniacal driver. Etiquette when you reach the prayer-flags on the top of passes in Tibet requires you to shout, at the top of your lungs, *Sso-so-so-so-so! Lha Gyalo!*, which means 'Victory to the gods!'

Phrasebooks and recordings There are several Tibetan phrasebooks available for English speakers, but phrases are only as good as the sounds you can elicit from them. If you don't have an audio recording, go over the sounds with a Tibetan speaker, or have a native speaker help you record your own English–Tibetan version.

Giving access to a much wider range of spoken Tibetan are DVD packages which cost around US$50 each, like *Learning Tibetan* (EuroTalk Interactive) with innovative games and quizzes. The EuroTalk version can be purchased online as an app through iTunes, with several caveats. EuroTalk uses a stock list for all its language products. Questions like 'Where is the beach?' have limited currency in Tibet. And a lot of entries are vocabulary, not phrases. Watch out also for the cover art! More serious language learners should look into comprehensive Tibetan language packages from Snow Lion Publications (*www.snowlionpub.com*), such as *Fluent Tibetan*, with 26 hours of audio on CD or DVD.

Internet resources More advanced tuning of the ear can be achieved by listening to radio broadcasts in Tibetan on the web, at three sites: www.vot.org (with QuickTime MP3 downloads), www.rfa.org and www.voa.gov (video news). These sites are blocked in China: Radio Free Asia and Voice of America are both Washington-based, with part of the broadcast in Tibetan. Voice of Tibet, established in Norway in 1996, is the one of the oldest dedicated radio stations broadcasting in the Tibetan language. To try your writing skills in Tibetan script, go for a spin on a Mac. Most Mac computers come with a Tibetan keyboard installed. Go to the flags at the upper right of the screen (real Tibetan flag is not shown for some reason).

Openers

greetings (good fortune)	*tashi delek*	བཀྲ་ཤིས་བདེ་ལེགས།
goodbye (spoken to the person staying)	*kaleshu*	ག་ལེར་བཞུགས།
goodbye (spoken to the person leaving)	*kalepay*	ག་ལེར་ཕེབས།
pleased to meet you	*kerang tukpa gapo chung*	ཁྱེད་རང་ཐུག་པར་དགའ་པོ་བྱུང་།
how are you?	*kerang debo yinbe?*	ཁྱེད་རང་བདེ་པོ་ཡིན་པས།
I'm fine	*nga debo yoe*	ང་བདེ་པོ་ཡིན།
where are you going?	*kerang kawa droga?*	ཁྱེད་རང་ག་པར་འགྲོ་ག
what's your name?	*kerangi mingla karey re?*	ཁྱེད་རང་གི་མིང་ལ་ག་རེ་རེད།
my name is . . .	*nge mingla . . . yin*	ངའི་མིང་ . . . ཡིན།
I only speak a little Tibetan	*nga perkay teets teets shingi yur*	ངས་བོད་སྐད་ཏོག་ཙམ་ཏོག་ཙམ་ཤེས་ཀྱི་ཡོད།
I don't understand	*ngay hako masong*	ངས་ཧ་གོ་མ་སོང་།
Do you understand?	*kerang hakosong ngay?*	ཁྱེད་རང་གིས་ཧ་གོ་སོང་ངས།

Getting personal

where are you from?	*kerang lungpa kane yin?*	ཁྱེད་རང་ལུང་པ་ག་ནས་ཡིན།
I am from X	*nga X ne yin*	ང་ X ནས་ཡིན།
UK/Canada/Australia	*injilungpa /kanada / ostrelia*	ཨིན་ཇིའི་ལུང་པ / ཁ་ན་ཌ / ཨོ་སེ་ཊི་ལི་ཡ།

English	Transliteration	Tibetan
America/France	ahri/farenci	ཨ་རི་ / ཕ་རན་སི།
Tibetan/Chinese/Nepalese	perpa/gyami/pelpo	བོད་པ་ / རྒྱ་མི་ / བལ་པོ་
How old are you?	kerang lo katsay yin?	ཁྱེད་རང་ལོ་ག་ཚད་ཡིན།
nomad/farmer	drokpa/shingpa	འབྲོག་པ་ / ཞིང་པ།
monk/pilgrim	trapa/nekorpa	གྲྭ་པ་ / གནས་སྐོར་བ།
married/single	changsa/migyang	ཆང་ས་ / མི་རྒྱང་ (མི་བྱེད་)
husband/wife	kyoka/gyemen	ཁྱོ་ག་ / སྐྱེ་སྨན།
mother/father	ama/apa	ཨ་མ་ / ཨ་པ།
children/son/daughter	puku/pu/pumo	པུ་གུ་ (ཕྲུ་གུ་) / བུ་ / བུ་མོ།
younger brother	chungpo	གཅུང་པོ་
younger sister	chungmo	གཅུང་མོ།
older brother	jojo	ཇོ་ཇོ་ (ཅོ་ཅོག་)
older sister	aja	ཨ་ཅེ།

Flattery

English	Transliteration	Tibetan
good/very good	yapo du/yapo shedra re	ཡག་པོ་འདུག / ཡག་པོ་ཞེ་དྲགས་འདུག
The food is great!	kala shimpo du!	ཁ་ལག་ཞིམ་པོ་འདུག
I love this place!	nga sacha dila gapo yur!	ང་ས་ཆ་འདི་ལ་དགའ་པོ་ཡོད།
beautiful	nying jepo du	སྙིང་རྗེ་པོ་འདུག
very interesting	nangwa dropo shedra re	སྣང་བ་འགྲོ་པོ་ཞེ་དྲགས་རེད།
I feel happy	gyipo du	སྐྱིད་པོ་འདུག
we had a good time!	ngantso gyipo chung!	ང་ཚོ་སྐྱིད་པོ་བྱུང་།
good luck	lamdro yongbar shok	ལམ་འགྲོ་ཡོང་བར་ཤོག

Negatives, questions, requests

English	Transliteration	Tibetan
yes, that's it	re, de rang re	རེད། དེ་རང་རེད།
yes, okay	digi re	འགྲིག་གི་རེད།
no problem	kay chegi mare	གང་ཡང་(གལ) བྱེད་ཀྱི་མ་རེད།
no	mare (mindu)	མ་རེད་ (མིན་འདུག)
not okay, no good	yapo mindu	ཡག་པོ་མི་འདུག
thank you	tujeche	ཐུགས་རྗེ་ཆེ།
that's enough	dik song	འགྲིག་སོང་།
need	gerh	དགོས།
don't want (don't like)	mo gerh	མི་དགོས།
I don't know	nga shingi meh	ངས་ཤེས་ཀྱི་མེད།
sorry, excuse me	gohnda	དགོངས་དག
can I take a photo?	nga par gyapna digi rebay?	ངས་པར་བརྒྱབ་ན་འགྲིག་གི་རེད་པས།

what's this called in Tibetan?	perke nangla di kandres lab gire?	བོད་སྐད་ནང་ལ་འདི་ག་འདྲ་ས་ལབ་གྱི་རེད།
what does this mean?	di thondak karey re?	འདིའི་དོན་དག་ག་རེ་རེད།
where/where is?	kapa/kaba du?	ག་པར / ག་པར་འདུག
what?	karey?	ག་རེ།
when?	kadu?	ག་དུས།
who?/why?/how?	su?/karey jeni?/kandres?	སུ་ / ག་རེ་བྱས་ནས་ / གང་འདྲ་ས།
how much (how many)?	katsey?	ག་ཚད།
how far?	ta ringpo rebay?	ཐག་རིང་པོ་རེད་པས།

Red tape

passport	chikyur lakteb	ཕྱི་སྐྱོད་ལག་དེབ།
permit	chokchen	ཆོག་མཆན།
PSB office	gonganju (Chinese word)	གུང་འན་ཅུད," (རྒྱ་སྐད་)
	sangwe nyen tokbe lekung! (Tibetan)	གསང་བའི་ཉེན་རྟོགས་ལས་ཁུངས། (བོད་སྐད་)
tourist	takorwa	ལྟ་སྐོར་བ། (ཡུལ་སྐོར་བ་)
I need a translator	nga la gegyur cheken chik gerh	ང་ལ་སྐད་སྒྱུར་བྱེད་མཁན་གཅིག་དགོས།
what's the problem?	gang ngel karey tresong?	དཀའ་ལས་ག་རེ་འཕྲད་སོང་།

Medical

sick/very sick	nagi du/shedra nagi du	ན་གི་འདུག / ཞེ་དྲགས་ན་གི་འདུག
altitude sickness	zatuki natsa	རྫ་དུག་གི་ན་ཚ། (ལ་དུག)
headache/fever	gonagi du/tsawa pargi du	མགོ་ན་གི་འདུག/ ཚ་བ་འཕར་གྱི་འདུག
diarrhea/stomach ache	troko shegi du/troko nagi du	གྲོད་ཁོག་བཤལ་གྱི་འདུག/ གྲོད་ཁོག་ན་གི་འདུག
cold/cough	champa nagi du/lo gyabgi du	ཆམ་པ་ན་གི་འདུག / སྐོ་བརྒྱབ་གྱི་འདུག
feel dizzy	goyu korgi du	མགོ་ཡུ་འཁོར་གྱི་འདུག
I was bitten by a dog	khi chik gi sogyab song	ཁྱི་གཅིག་གི་སོ་བརྒྱབ་སོང་།
I need a doctor right away	nga la gyokpo amchi laten gerh	ང་ལ་མགྱོགས་པོ་ཨེམ་ཆི་ (སྨན་པ་) དགོས།
oxygen	sog lung	སྲོག་རླུང་། (འཚོ་རླུང་)
emergency	zatrak	ཟ་དྲག
hospital	menkhang	སྨན་ཁང་།
pharmacy	men tsongkhang	སྨན་ཚོང་ཁང་།
medicine	men	སྨན།

Transport

ticket	*pasey* (Indian-Tibetan word)	པ་སེ། (དཔྱིན་སྐད།)
	zinyik (Tibetan)	འཛིན་ཡིག (བོད་སྐད།)
plane	*namdru*	གནམ་གྲུ།
motor vehicle	*mota* (Indian-Tibetan)	མོ་ཊ།
	noomkor (Tibetan)	སྣུམ་འཁོར། (བོད་སྐད།)
bicycle	*gangkor*	རྐང་འཁོར།
horse	*ta*	རྟ།
I'd like to hire a jeep	*nga jip chik lander yur*	ང་འཇི་བ་ཅིག་གླ་བླ་འདོད་ཡོད།
I'd like to hire a Landcruiser	*nga landkrusa chik lander yur*	ང་ལ་ནྡྲི་ཀུ་རུ་ས།(སྐྱ་མ་འཁོར་ཏེ་ལོ་ཏ་) གཅིག་གླ་འདོད་ཡོད།
Do you rent bicycles?	*gangkor laya yurbe?*	རྐང་འཁོར་གཡར་ཡ་(རྒྱུ་)ཡོད་པས།
how much for an hour?	*chutsu chik la katsey re?*	ཆུ་ཚོད་གཅིག་ལ་ག་ཚད་རེད།
how much for a day?	*nyima chik la katsey re?*	ཉི་མ་གཅིག་ལ་ག་ཚད་རེད།
what time is the bus?	*jijger lun korte chutsu katserla drogi re?*	སྤྱི་སྤྱོད་རླངས་འཁོར་དེ་ཆུ་ཚོད་ག་ཚད་ལ་འགྲོ་གི་རེད
guide	*lamtriken*	ལམ་འཁྲིད་མཁན།
driver	*siji* (Chinese word)	སི་ཇི། (རྒྱ་སྐད།)
	kalowa (Tibetan)	ཁ་ལོ་བ། (བོད་སྐད།)
go slowly please	*kale kale drorok nang*	ག་ལེ་ག་ལེ་ར་འགྲོ་རོགས་གནང༌།
please stop here	*dila kag rok nang*	འདི་ལ་བཀག་རོགས་གནང༌།

Trekking

tent	*kur*	གུར།
sleeping bag	*nyeche*	ཉལ་ཆས།
stove	*tapga*	ཐབ། (ཐབ་ཀ)
I want to hire a yak	*nga yak chik ladoe yur*	ང་གཡག་ཅིག་གླ་འདོད་ཡོད།
porter	*jalak kyerken*	ཅ་ལག་འཁྱེར་མཁན།
is this the trail to X?	*di X la dro sai lamka rebay?*	འདི་ X ལ་འགྲོ་སའི་ལམ་ཁ་རེད་པས།
how many hours will it take to reach X?	*X pardu chutsu katsey gorgi re?*	X བར་དུ་ཆུ་ཚོད་ག་ཚད་འགོར་གྱི་རེད།

Places

I want to go to X	*X la drondoe yur*	X ལ་འགྲོ་འདོད་ཡོད།
airport	*namtang*	གནམ་ཐང༌།
post office	*drakhang*	སྦྲག་ཁང༌། (ཡིག་ཟམ)
bank	*ngukhang*	དངུལ་ཁང༌།

316

PSB office	gonganju	གྲུང་འན་ཅུ་ད།
temple	lakhang	སྐུ་ཁང་།
market	trom	ཁྲོམ།
photo shop	barkhang	པར་ཁང་།
bookshop	teb tsongkhang	དེབ་ཚོང་ཁང་།
museum	dem tonkhang	འགྲེམས་སྟོན་ཁང་།

Lodging

hotel	drukhang	འགྲུལ་ཁང་།
guesthouse	dronkhang	མགྲོན་ཁང་།
room	khangpa	ཁང་པ། (ཁང་མིག)
bed	nyetri	ཉལ་ཁྲི།
can I see the room?	khangpa la migtana digi rebay?	ཁང་པ་ལ་མིག་བལྟས་ན་འགྲིག་གི་རེད་པས།
do you have a room with private toilet?	khang panang lola sangcher yur rebay?	ཁང་པའི་ནང་ལ་གསང་སྤྱོད་ཡོད་རེད་པས།
where can I leave luggage?	nge jalak dintso kawar shakka?	ངའི་ཅ་ལག་འདི་ཚོ་ག་པར་བཞག་ག (འཇོག་གས)
telephone	kapa	ཁ་པར།
key	deymi	དེ་མིག
blanket	nyejay	ཉལ་ཆས། (གཉལ་པའི)
candle	yangla	ཡང་ལྭ།
toilet/paper	sangcher/sangcher shuku	གསང་སྤྱོད་ / གསང་སྤྱོད་ཤོག་གུ
shower/hot shower	trukhang/chu Tsapoe tru	ཁྲུས་ཁང་ / ཆུ་ཚ་པོའི་ཁྲུས།
towel	ajo	ཨ་ཙོར།
Thermos of hot water	chu tsapo chadam gan	ཆུ་ཚ་པོ་ཇ་དམ་གང་།

Food

hungry	trokok toki du	གྲོད་ཁོག་ལྟོགས་ཀྱི་འདུག
thirsty	kha komgi du	ཁ་སྐོམ་གྱི་འདུག
restaurant	sakhang	ཟ་ཁང་།
tearoom	jakhang	ཇ་ཁང་།
can you bring me . . . ?	. . . chig kyer yongrok nang?	· · · ཅིག་འཁྱེར་ཡོང་རོགས་གནང་།
bowl of noodles	tuk pa porpa chig	ཐུག་པ་ཕོར་པ་གཅིག
meat dumplings	sha momo	ཤ་མོག་མོག
stir-fried vegetables	tsoma ngowa	ཚོད་མ་རྔོས་པ།
meat	sha	ཤ
yoghurt	sho	ཞོ།
water	chu	ཆུ།

boiled water	chu kolma	ཆུ་འཁོལ་མ།
sweet Indian tea	cha ngarmo	ཇ་མངར་མོ།
yak butter tea	cha suma	ཇ་སྲུབ་མ། (པོད་ཇ)
homebrewed beer	chang	ཆང་།
salt	tsa	ཚྭ།
sugar	che makara	ཇེ་མ་ཀ་ར། (ཅི་ནི)

Bargaining

how much is this?	gong katsey re?	གོང་ག་ཚད་རེད།
do you have any ...?	kerang-la ... yurbe?	ཁྱེད་རང་ལ་ ... ཡོད་པས།
big/small	chenpo/chung chung	ཆེན་པོ་ / ཆུང་ཆུང་།
old/new	nyingpa/saba	རྙིང་པ། / གསར་པ།
too expensive	di gong chenpo shedra du !	འདི་གོང་ཆེན་པོ་ཞེ་དྲགས་འདུག
can you give me a better price?	gong jak tupki rebe?	གོང་གཅག་ཐུབ་ཀི་རེད་པས།
discount	gong jakya yurbe	གོང་གཅག་ཡས་ཡོད་པས།

Time

today	tering	དེ་རིང་།
now	tanda	ད་ལྟ།
tonight	togong	དོ་དགོང་།
yesterday/tomorrow	kesa/sangyin	ཁ་ས། / སང་ཉིན།
morning/afternoon/evening	shoke/chitro/gongtak	ཞོགས་ཀ། / ཕྱི་དྲོ། / དགོང་དག་(དགོང་དྲོ།)
year/month/week/ day/hour	lo/dawa/zankor/ nyima/chutsu	ལོ། / ཟླ་བ། / གཟའ་འཁོར། / ཉི་མ། / ཆུ་ཚོད།
Monday	sa dawa	གཟའ་ཟླ་བ།
Tuesday	sa migma	གཟའ་མིག་དམར།
Wednesday	sa lhakba	གཟའ་ལྷག་པ།
Thursday	sa pubu	གཟའ་ཕུར་བུ།
Friday	sa pasang	གཟའ་པ་སངས།
Saturday	sa pemba	གཟའ་སྤེན་པ།
Sunday	sa nyima	གཟའ་ཉི་མ།

Numbers

0	lekor	ཀླད་སྐོར།	1	chik	གཅིག
2	nyi	གཉིས།	3	sum	གསུམ།
4	shi	བཞི།	5	nga	ལྔ།
6	druk	དྲུག	7	dun	བདུན།
8	gye	བརྒྱད།	9	gu	དགུ།

10	*ju*	བཅུ།	11	*ju chik*	བཅུ་གཅིག
12	*ju nyi*	བཅུ་གཉིས།	13	*jok sum*	བཅུ་གསུམ།
14	*jub shi*	བཅུ་བཞི།	15	*jo nga*	བཅོ་ལྔ།
20	*nyi shu*	ཉི་ཤུ།	30	*sum ju*	སུམ་ཅུ།
40	*shib ju*	བཞི་བཅུ།	50	*ngab ju*	ལྔ་བཅུ།
60	*druk chu*	དྲུག་ཅུ།	70	*dun ju*	བདུན་ཅུ།
80	*gyeb ju*	བརྒྱད་ཅུ།	90	*gub ju*	དགུ་བཅུ།
100	*gya tamba*	བརྒྱ་ཐམ་པ།	500	*nyab gya*	ལྔ་བརྒྱ།
1,000	*chik tong*	གཅིག་སྟོང་།	2,000	*tong-trak nyi*	སྟོང་ཕྲག་གཉིས། (ཉིས་སྟོང་།)
1 million	*sayachik (or: bumju)*	ས་ཡ་གཅིག (ཡང་ན་ འབུམ་བཅུ།)			

Geographical terms, map features

river	*gyuk chu* (also: *tsangpo*)	རྒྱུག་ཆུ། (དེ་བཞིན་ གཙང་པོ)
spring	*chumi*	ཆུ་མིག
hot spring	*chutsen*	ཆུ་ཚན།
village	*trongsep*	གྲོང་གསེབ།
town	*trongte*	གྲོང་ཇེ།
fort	*dzong*	རྫོང་།
monastery	*gompa*	དགོན་པ།
ice/snow	*kyakpa/kang*	འཁྱགས་པ་ / གངས།
rain	*charpa*	ཆར་པ།
pass	*la*	ལ།
hill, mountain	*ri*	རི།
plain, plateau	*tang*	ཐང་།
lake	*tso* (also: *yumco, caka, nor*)	མཚོ།
map	*sabtra*	ས་ཁྲ།
compass points:	*chang* (N), *lho* (S), *shar* (E), *nub* (W)	བྱང་། ལྷོ། ཤར། ནུབ།

USEFUL GESTURES Tibetans respond to some gestures common in the West, but others can throw you for a loop. In old Tibet, a respectful form of humble greeting was to extrude the tongue (which had better be pink, because the tongue of an evil person was reckoned to be brown or black). The gesture is still used in remote parts of Tibet. Belgian cartoonist Hergé has some fun with this: when confronted by cheeky Tibetans poking out their tongues at him, Captain Haddock in the comic Tintin in Tibet responds with rude hand gestures. Once you get started on gestures, it's easy to build a repertoire for repeat situations: pointing vigorously to your watch or a camera, for instance, to get a certain message across.

Approval, or not

Good *yagodu!*
Fist with thumb up, indicating positive approval, also signals 'okay' *yapodu!*
gucci gucci! Two thumbs up (jiggled up and down) is a begging gesture, demanding money or otherwise

Bad *yapo mindu!*
Fist with little finger down – applied to things or people or concepts ('what you are doing is bad'). The little finger held to edge of eye indicates 'evil eye'.

Commands

Come here *del-phi*
Similar to Western gesture, but hand down (not up) and use whole hand, not finger

Go away *pa-phi*
Flick hand out, using whole palm, not finger

Slow down *kale kale*
Hand parallel to ground and move up and down, slowly, to tell your Landcruiser driver; also used as hitchhiking signal.

No thanks! Had enough!

Up to here *yasong!*
Bring open palm up under the chin.
Used to indicate enough food or drink.

Placing open palm on chest can convey similar idea – when you don't want something offered, like cigarettes.

Requests

Need a place to sleep *nyi nyayri*
Place palm to side of head and tilt head

Need a telephone *kaba*
Mimic phone with hand to ear

Signalling confusion

Don't know *nga hako masong*
Twist hand with fingers apart in a screw-in-the-lightbulb
gesture. Can also use head-shaking and head-scratching to
indicate doubt.

Crazy *nyon-pa*
Twist fingers at temple

Stupid *koog-ta-chen*
Slap forehead with open palm

Hello

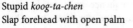

Greeting hello *tashi delek*
Bring single hand up to the forehead, with edge of palm
outward

High-level greeting
Palms together in prayer,
head slightly bowed – religious gesture of humility, used by
prostrators, and frequently used by the Dalai Lama.

Goodbye

Goodbye *kaleshu* (spoken to the
person staying)
kalepay (spoken to the person leaving)
Wave, like Western gesture

High-level goodbye
Palms up, facing inward, and bow slightly. Used
when saying goodbye to monk or important
person. Another gesture is touching foreheads.

CHINESE LANGUAGE Such is the dominance of Mandarin Chinese in Tibet that, in order to get hotel rooms, obtain food in restaurants, talk to truck drivers or deal with officialdom, you need some knowledge of Chinese. However, if you are talking to a Tibetan, it's far preferable to stay with Tibetan language.

Though there are eight major dialects in China, the standard version is Mandarin, or Beijing dialect. Mandarin is a tonal language – it takes a musical ear to get the hang of the tones. Without mastery of the tones, your efforts at Chinese will be unintelligible, reducing you to a gibbering curiosity. Written Mandarin Chinese is no easier: it draws on a fund of about 50,000 characters (originally pictographs), although literate Chinese need only knowledge of about 5,000 characters.

Pinyin is the romanisation system used for rendering Chinese sounds into approximate English. There are several quirks in Pinyin pronunciation. The vowels are rather tricky, and some consonants are pronounced differently: Pinyin 'c' is pronounced 'ts', Pinyin 'q' sounds like 'ch', Pinyin 'x' comes out as 'sh', and Pinyin 'zh' is pronounced 'j'. Thus on Chinese maps you may see the place names 'Xigaze' (Shigatse), 'Qamdo' (Chamdo) and 'Zhangmu' (Jangmu). Pinyin romanisation, in addition, uses accents over the letters to indicate tones (these are not employed in this book). The word *ma* for example, can have four different meanings depending on whether the tone is flat, rising, fall-rising or falling ('mother', 'hemp', 'horse' or 'swear'). Thus you could be trying to rent a horse and end up with a bag of hemp. For tones, accented Pinyin is of limited help: the best thing is to go over phrases with a Chinese native speaker to get the sounds right.

Useful phrases Good all-purpose words are *keyi* (OK, yes, agreed), *mei wenti* (no problem) and *hen hao* (thumbs up, very good). Another form of 'yes' in agreement is *dui*, which is often used in a rapid-fire sequence, as in *dui-dui-dui-dui-dui*. A catchy idiomatic phrase for 'so-so' is *mama-huhu*, which literally means 'horse-horse-tiger-tiger'.

Phrasebooks and recordings Phrasebooks become doubly useful if they have Chinese characters next to them: you can point to the characters if the pronunciation is not getting through. Another feature to look for is a mini-dictionary at the back of the phrasebook. There are a number of pocket-sized phrasebooks on the market, including those in the Rough Guides, Berlitz, BBC and Eyewitness series. Because Mandarin Chinese derives its meaning from tones, it's well worth chasing audio-enabled language-learning versions to get the sounds right. Rosetta Stone Language Group puts out DVDs with full audio. Easier to get at are apps under iTunes, where free Chinese phrases with script and audio can be accessed – or you can purchase more extensive versions which are self-driven once downloaded.

Internet resources Attune your ear to Mandarin by listening to radio and video broadcasts in Chinese at www.rfa.org (Radio Free Asia) and www.voa.gov (Voice of America).

Openers

hello	*ni hao*
goodbye	*zaijian*
pleased to meet you	*hen gaoxing renshi ni*
how are you?	*ni hao ma?*
very well, thank you	*wo hen hao, xiexie*
where are you going?	*ni dao nali?*
what's your name?	*ni jiao shenme?*
my name is ...	*wo jiao ...*
I only speak a little Chinese	*wo ju dongde idiendien hanyu*
I don't understand	*wo budong*
do you understand?	*dong ma?*

Getting personal

where are you from?	*ni cong nali lai?*
I am from Britain/Canada/Australia	*wo cong yingguo/jianada/oadaliya ... lai*
America/France	*meiguo/faguo*
Tibet/China/Nepal	*xizang/zhongguo/niboer*
how old are you?	*ni ji sui?*
my job is ...	*wode gong zhuo shi ...*
I'm married/single	*wo jiehunle/wo shi danshen*
husband/wife	*zhangfu/qizi*
mother/father	*mama/baba*
children/son/daughter	*haizi/erzi/nuer*
brother/sister	*xiongdi/jiemei*

Flattery

good/very good	*hao/hen hao*	beautiful	*piaoliang*
terrific food!	*hen hao chi!*	that's great!	*haojile!*
cheers! (toasting)	*ganbei!*	I had a great time!	*wo hen kaixin!*
I love this place!	*wo hen xihuan zhege difang!*	good luck!	*zhu ni hao yun!*

Negatives, questions, requests

yes	*shi*	I want to take a photo	*wo yao zhao ge xiang*
OK/no problem	*hao*	what's this called in	*zhege zhongwen jiao*
no	*bu*	Chinese?	*shenme?*
no (don't have)	*mei you*	please write it down	*qing ni bang wo*
not OK/no good	*bu hao*	for me	*xiexialai*
please/thank you	*qing/xiexie*	what does that mean?	*shenme yisi?*
enough, thank you	*goule, xiexie*	where/where is X?	*nali?/X zai nali?*
I want/need	*wo yao*	when?/who?/	*shenme shihou?/shui?/*
don't want/don't like	*bu yao*	why?/how?	*weishenme?/zenme?*
sorry, excuse me	*duibuqi*	how much/many?	*duoshao?*
I don't know	*wo bu zhidao*	how many kilometres?	*duoshao gongli?*

Red tape

passport	*huzhao*	tourist	*lu-ke*
visa	*qianzheng*	I need a translator	*wo xuyao fangyuan*
travel permit	*tong xing zheng*	what's the problem?	*yo shenme wenti?*
PSB office	*gonganju*		

Medical

sick/very sick	*sheng bingle/bingde hen zhong*	doctor	*yisheng*
altitude sickness	*gao shan bing*	need a doctor	*jao ge yisheng*
I feel dizzy	*wo touyun*	please help	*qing bang mang*
headache/fever	*touteng/fashao*	emergency	*jinji qingkuang*
diarrhoea	*laduzi*	hospital	*yiyuan*
stomach ache	*xiaohua bu liang*	oxygen	*yangqi*
cold/sore throat	*ganmao/hou-long teng*	pharmacy	*yaodian*
		medicine	*yao*

Transport

ticket	*piao*	let's go!	*zouba!*
plane	*feiji*	for a whole day?	*yitian duoshao qian?*
taxi	*chuzuche*	we want to hire a	*women yao yiliang jipu*
jeep	*jipu*	jeep	
truck	*kache*	where is the bus	*qichezhan zai nar?*
bus	*gonggong qiche*	station?	
bicycle	*zixingche*	what time is the bus	*dao X de gongche*
driver	*siji*	to X?	*shenme shihou kai?*
I want to hire a	*wo yao zu yiliang*	guide	*daoyou*
bicycle	*zixingche*	slow down please	*qing ni man idien*
how much for an	*yige xiao shi duoshao*	stop here!	*qing zai zheli ting!*
hour?	*qian?*		

Trekking

tent	*zhangpeng*	where can I hire	*wo sheme difang keyi*
sleeping bag	*shuidai*	yaks?	*gu yitou mao niu?*
how much a day?	*yitian duoshao qian?*		

Places

I want to go to X	*wo yao qu X*	PSB office/foreign	*gonganju/waishi ke*
airport	*feijichang*	affairs branch	
bus station	*qichezhan*	Buddhist temple	*fo si*
railway station	*huochezhan*	market	*shichang*
post office	*youju*	bookshop	*shudian*
cybercafé	*wang ka*	museum	*bowuguan*
Bank of China	*zhongguo yinhang*		
(foreign exchange)			

Lodging

main tourist hotel	*binguan*	dormitory	*duorenfang*
smaller hotel	*fandian*	single room	*danrenfang*
guesthouse	*zhaodaisuo*	double room	*shuangrenfang*
can I see the room?	*wo keyi kan fangjian a?*	room with bath	*dai yushi de fangjian*
where can I leave	*wo xingli fang narli?*	toilet/paper	*cesuo/shouzhi*
luggage?		shower/hot shower	*linyu/re linyu*
telephone	*dianhua*	towel	*maojin*
key	*yaoshi*	Thermos of hot	*yo re kaishui de*
room	*fangjian*	water	*shuiping*

Food

hungry	*duzi e*	meat	*rou*
thirsty	*kouke*	water	*shui*
restaurant/café	*fandian/kafeiguan*	boiled water	*kaishui*
let's eat!	*chi fanba!*	mineral water	*kuangquan shui*
do you have ...?	*ni you .... ma?*	tea	*cha*
noodles	*miantiao*	black tea	*hong cha*
rice	*mifan*	green tea	*lu cha*
biscuits	*binggan*	coffee	*kafei*
soup	*tang*	beer	*pijiu*
stir-fried vegetables	*chao shucai*		

Bargaining

how much is this?	*duoshao qian?*	too expensive	*taigui*
do you have ...?	*ni you ... ma?*	do you have	*yo pianyi yidian de*
big/small	*da/xiao*	anything cheaper?	*ma?*
old/new	*jiu/xin*		

Time

today	*jintian*	Monday	*xingqi-yi*
now	*xianzai*	Tuesday	*xingqi-er*
tonight	*jinwan*	Wednesday	*xingqi-san*
yesterday/tomorrow	*zuotian/mingtian*	Thursday	*xingqi-si*
morning/afternoon/	*zaoshang/xiawu/*	Friday	*xingqi-wu*
evening	*wanshang*	Saturday	*xingqi-liu*
year/month/day/hour	*nian/yue/zhi/xiaoshi*	Sunday	*xingqi-tian*

Numbers

0	*ling*	15	*shiwu*
1	*yi*	20	*ershi*
2	*er*	30	*sanshi*
3	*san*	40	*sishi*
4	*si*	50	*wushi*
5	*wu*	60	*liushi*
6	*liu*	70	*qishi*
7	*qi*	80	*bashi*
8	*ba*	90	*jiushi*
9	*jiu*	100	*yi-bai*
10	*shi*	500	*wu-bai*
11	*shiyi*	1,000	*yiqian*
12	*shier*	2,000	*liangqian*
13	*shisan*	1,000,000	*yi baiwan*
14	*shisi*		

Geographical terms, map features

river	*he* (also *jiang*)	province	*sheng*
lake	*hu*	snow	*xue*
mountain	*shan*	map	*ditu*
summit, peak	*feng*	compass points	*bei* (N), *nan* (S),
pass	*shankou*		*dong* (E), *xi* (W)
valley	*shangu*		

Appendix 3

GLOSSARY

For details of popular icons, refer to the *Jokhang* section of the *Lhasa* chapter, page 142.

ani	nun
Bon	pre-Buddhist religion of Tibet
chang	fermented barley beer, a potent milky liquid
chorten	inverted bell-shaped shrine containing relics, or the ashes or embalmed body of a high lama (*stupa* in Sanskrit)
dharma	the word of the Buddha and his teachings
dorje	'thunderbolt' – a sceptre-like ritual object, made of brass and used against the powers of darkness
dzong	castle or fort, usually grafted onto a high ridge
gompa	active monastery
gonkhang	protector chapel at a monastery
Kalachakra	the 'Wheel of Time', a complex supreme tantra associated with the mystical land of Shambhala
kata	white greeting scarf, made of cotton or silk, presented on ceremonial occasions or offered at monasteries
kora	clockwise circuit of a sacred temple, lake or mountain
lakhang	chapel or inner sanctuary
lama	master spiritual teacher or guru
Losar	Tibetan New Year, usually celebrated around February
mandala	mystical circle (often enclosing a square) representing the Buddhist cosmos and used as a meditational aid (*chilkor* in Tibetan)
mani stone	stone tablet inscribed with a mantra, often included as part of a *mani-wall*, composed of many such stones
mantra	sacred syllables repeated many times as part of spiritual practice, such as *Om Mani Padme Hum* ('hail to the jewel in the lotus heart,' a phrase addressed to the Buddha)
momo	Tibetan meat dumpling
Monlam	the Great Prayer Festival, around the time of Losar
nirvana	release from the cycle of mortal existence and rebirths
potrang	palace
prayer-flag	small flag printed with sacred prayers, activated by the power of the wind
prayer-wheel	large fixed wheel or small hand-held wheel containing mantras and activated by the spinning of the wheel
prostrator	pilgrim who measures the distance to a sacred destination with the length of his or her body, flung prone along the ground

rinpoche	'precious one'. A reincarnate lama, also known when young as a *tulku*
Saka Dawa	day of Buddha's enlightenment, celebrated around June
Shambhala	Buddhist 'Pure Land', a Tibetan utopia where disease and ageing are unknown, said to be located deep in the mountains to the north of the Himalaya
sutra	sacred text, the written or spoken teachings of the Buddha
tanka	painted portable scroll, usually depicting a deity, on fine cotton or silk; can be used as a teaching aid
tantra	the 'web of life', or *vajrayana*, is the form of Buddhism most often associated with Tibet. It employs radical steps to seek enlightenment within a single lifetime
torma	ritual 'cake' sculpted from *tsampa* and yak butter
tsampa	ground barley flour, a Tibetan staple food
tulku	reincarnate lama
yak	hairy high-altitude cattle, or 'cow with a skirt'
yabyum	tantric sexual pose of deity and consort, symbolising fusion of opposites, and often misconstrued by Westerners as sexual activity without any tantric significance.

CHINASPEAK Chinese rhetoric on Tibet is an odd mix of the irrational and the predictable. This quote is taken from the magazine *Beijing Review*, 1983, describing the Lhasa uprising of 1959:

> The imperialists and a small number of reactionary elements in Tibet's upper ruling clique could not reconcile themselves to the peaceful liberation of Tibet and its return to the embrace of the Motherland. The reactionary elements were intent upon launching an armed rebellion, negating the agreement and detaching Tibet from China. Abetted by the imperialists, they continued to sabotage and create disturbances. Despite the central government's consistent persuasion and education, they finally launched an armed rebellion on March 10, 1959. But, contrary to their desires, this rebellion accelerated the destruction of Tibet's reactionary forces and brought Tibet onto the bright, democratic, socialist road sooner than expected.

This puts forward the standard Beijing position on Tibet, unchanged for the last 60 years. For maximum effect, try and listen to this stuff spoken out loud, with a shrill Chinese accent and lots of static.

China's Tibet To reinforce the idea that Tibet is not a separate country, attach the word 'China' to it. Chinese-produced tourist brochures and maps all specify 'Tibet, China', or 'China–Tibet'. China branding is found all over: China Post, Chinapolice, China Mobile. There's even a book titled *Chinese Tibetan Opera*.

Counter-revolutionary Anyone who opposes official policy, an enemy of the state, or someone 'committed with the goal of overthrowing the political power of the dictatorship of the proletariat and the socialist system'. Despite an official Beijing repeal of this crime to placate international critics, those previously convicted of it still languish in prison. Now, prisoners continue to be convicted and are either held without charge or trial, or charged with being either a spy or a terrorist (the latter term more in vogue since 9/11: 11 September 2001). Another term is 'reactionary'.

The Dalai In June 1998, when President Clinton went on national Chinese television to say he thought the Dalai Lama was 'an honest man', this must have been news to a billion Chinese, who are more used to hearing him cursed as a treasonous demon. In rhetoric, the Chinese often employ the abbreviated form 'the Dalai', which is considered insulting by the Tibetans. Followers of the Dalai Lama are called 'the Dalai clique'. Chinese news sources call the exiled leader a 'splittist' and even 'a major hindrance to the development of Tibetan Buddhism'.

Democratic reform Chinaspeak for the period immediately after the 1959 Lhasa uprising and the flight of the Dalai Lama, when authorities set about dismantling the Tibetan culture in earnest – wading in there with machine guns where necessary. In 2005, when pressed by President Bush about greater freedom for the Chinese people, President Hu Jintao reassured him that China would pursue 'democratic politics with Chinese characteristics'.

Demonising the people This term surfaced during the 2008 Beijing Olympics, when protests staged by foreigners in support of human rights in Tibet were decried by the Chinese press as 'hurting the feelings of the Chinese people'.

Foreign imperialists General all-purpose scapegoats. It is never specified which country they're from, but the popular candidates are 'bad elements' from Taiwan, the USA, the UK and Germany. After the Dalai Lama received the Nobel Peace Prize, Norway was added to the blacklist.

Harmony and unity The cornerstones of Chinese national policy. And if it takes machine guns and mass arrests and torture to maintain the cornerstones, so be it. Unity means one party only.

Hot topic This denotes anything like taxes or price increases that dissidents (reactionaries) supposedly capitalise on to foment unrest and demonstrations. Tibetan independence is, of course, very hot. So is the Dalai Lama; when asked what they think of him, most Chinese squirm and try to drop the subject like a hot potato.

Internal affairs Chinese shorthand for 'back off, it's a domestic dispute, it's no concern of yours what we do behind closed doors, so don't meddle in our affairs'.

Minority nationality The minorities, or non-Hans, are viewed as being part of the big happy Han family, even if they don't speak the same language. A minority theme park outside Beijing presents them spending their time dancing and singing, rather like happy children. Within Tibet, however, the Tibetans are less politely referred to as 'barbarians'.

The motherland As well as referring to mainland China, this term embraces any parts of Asia that China wants to occupy. A number of China's neighbours have had trouble with this concept, including Russia, India, Taiwan, Vietnam and the Philippines. 'Love the Motherland' was the name of a campaign for Chinese schoolchildren in 1998. Splitting the motherland is an all-embracing, heinous crime in Chinese eyes.

Peaceful liberation A reference to the entry of the People's Liberation Army into Tibet in 1950. Some Chinese sources admit that the invasion was in fact not entirely peaceful – some Tibetans resisted, so the PLA was reluctantly forced to machine-gun the hapless Tibetans to clear them out of the way. Mostly, however, the people loved the PLA, according to official sources.

Princess Wencheng The tale of the Chinese bride of 7th-century King Songtsen Gampo is often trotted out by the Chinese propaganda machine in efforts to stake an early Chinese claim to Tibet, saying that she had great influence over the king. In fact, he had a Nepalese wife and three Tibetan queens as well.

Re-education Mainly for monks, teaching them to see that black is white, and white is black, to say the Dalai Lama is bad, and to say the Chinese-chosen Panchen Lama is good. Sometimes monasteries are closed to tourism while this is in progress. The authorities might as well hang out a sign: Closed For Revision.

Serfdom The pre-1950 state of the ordinary Tibetan, locked into exploitation by Tibetan nobility and monastic overseers. The Chinese broke down this class system by replacing the Tibetan masters with harsher Chinese ones.

Soul Boy The 11th Panchen Lama, a child into whose soul the Tenth Panchen was reincarnated. The boy is the most hotly disputed reincarnate in Tibetan history. 'Soul Boy' is a translation of the Chinese term applied to reincarnations, *Lingtong* (*ling* = soul, *tong* = boy/child). Tibetans find the translation annoying and misleading.

Spiritual pollution An odd term for an atheist nation to develop but this refers to interference from outside sources, such as Westerners, in the form of books, tapes, videos and so on. Some of these are 'black' (political pollution), others 'yellow' (pornographic pollution).

Splittists Favourite Chinese term for those advocating independence for Tibet, or separatists. The idea here is that the motherland must stay whole; anybody who splits off a piece will ruin the symmetry. Other chunks where splittists seem to be hard at work include Xinjiang, Mongolia and Taiwan.

State secrets Though there is no clear definition of what they are, revealing state secrets is an act punishable by years in jail. This charge has been applied to Tibetans who email abroad about demonstrations. The secrets are whatever the authorities deem to be sensitive matters at the time. People can also be jailed for 'spreading rumours'.

Appendix 4

FURTHER INFORMATION

BOOKS Some of the following books, multimedia materials and websites are frowned upon, restricted or simply outlawed in China. Do not attempt to bring in risqué material if travelling to Tibet. Books with straight printed material should not be a problem, but visual material is different – customs and soldiers will flip through a book looking for artwork like the Tibetan flag or pictures of the Dalai Lama.

Kathmandu is the best place in the subcontinent to find materials on Tibet, especially maps and books. Just about everything published on Tibet (in or out of print) can be found in Kathmandu. Mention of Tibetan or Taiwanese independence or criticism of Beijing's policies is in theory forbidden in Hong Kong SAR. In practice, however, books continue to circulate freely, and protests not possible in China itself (such as marking the anniversary of the Tiananmen Massacre) are tolerated in the colony.

For such a little-visited place, Tibet has generated an extraordinary amount of literature. What's listed here is just the tip of the iceberg. You can glean lots more information from the websites of specialist publishers. These include:

www.snowlionpub.com Snow Lion Publications, US
www.shambhala.com Shambhala Publications, US
www.wisdompubs.org Wisdom Publications, US and UK
www.tricycle.com Tricycle Books and quarterly magazine
www.paljorpublications.com Paljor Publications, India.

History, political intrigue

Avedon, Richard, *In Exile from the Land of Snows*, HarperCollins, 1998. A classic that first appeared in 1984.

Brown, Mick, *The Dance of 17 Lives*, Bloomsbury, 2005. About the intrigue and controversy surrounding the 17th Karmapa.

Hilton, Isabel, *The Search for the Panchen Lama*, Penguin, 2000.

Lustgarten, Abrahm, *Tibet's Great Train*, Times Books, 2008. Ace reporting, mixing political history and the building of the railway to Lhasa.

Shakya, Tsering, *The Dragon in the Land of Snows*, Columbia University Press, 1999. Definitive history of Tibet since 1947, from a Tibetan scholar.

Human rights, testimonials, activism

Amnesty International, *Persistent Human Rights Violations in Tibet*, London, 1996.

Choedrak, Tenzin, *The Rainbow Palace*, Bantam, 2000.

Gyatso, Palden, *Fire Under the Snow*, Harvill Press, 1997 (published in the US as *The Autobiography of a Tibetan Monk*).

Marshall, Steven, *Tibet Since 1950: Silence, Prison or Exile*, Aperture, 2000. This collaboration between Human Rights Watch and Aperture books draws on a wide range of sources and photographers.

Pistono, Matteo, *In the Shadow of the Buddha*, Dutton, 2011.

Buddhism

Batchelor, Stephen, *Confessions of a Buddhist Atheist*, Random House, 2010.

Thurman, Robert, *Inside Tibetan Buddhism*, Collins, 1995.

The Dalai Lama (as author)

My Land and My People, Warner Books, 1997. A reprint of the 1962 edition of the autobiography of the Dalai Lama.

Freedom in Exile, Harper, 1991. Part two of the Dalai Lama's autobiography.

Ethics for the New Millennium, Riverhead, 2001. The Dalai Lama delivers his timely message to a world sadly lacking in moral values.

The Dalai Lama (as co-author)

Chan, Victor, *The Wisdom of Forgiveness*, Hodder Mobius, 2005.

Cutler, Howard, *The Art of Happiness: A Handbook for Living*, Hodder & Stoughton, 1999.

Tibetan culture

Baker, Ian, and Shrestha, Romio *The Healing Arts of Tibet*, Thames & Hudson, 1997.

Goldstein, Melvyn, and Beall, Cynthia *Nomads of Western Tibet: The Survival of a Way of Life*, UC Press, 1990.

Larsen, Knud, and Sinding-Larsen, Amund *The Lhasa Atlas: Traditional Tibetan Architecture and Townscape*, Serindia, 2001.

Exploration, mountaineering, adventure

Anker, Conrad, and Roberts, David *The Lost Explorer: Finding Mallory on Mount Everest*, Simon & Schuster, 1999.

Berry, Scott, *A Stranger in Tibet*, Kodansha, 1989.

Buckley, Michael, *Eccentric Explorers*, Canada, 2009.

Hammleb, Jochen, et al, *Ghosts of Everest: The Search for Mallory and Irvine*, The Mountaineers, 1999.

Harrer, Heinrich, *Seven Years in Tibet*, Harper Perennial, 2005 (originally published in 1953).

Hopkirk, Peter, *Trespassers on the Roof of the World*, Oxford University Press, 1982.

Norgay, Jamling Tenzing, *Finding My Father's Soul*, Harper, 2001 (written by the son of Everest's premier summiteer).

Peissel, Michel, *Barbarians at the Gate*, Henry Holt, 1997.

Thubron, Colin, *To a Mountain in Tibet*, Chatto & Windus, 2010. At age 70, veteran British travel writer Colin Thubron heads off to tackle the Kailash *kora*.

Venables, Stephen, *Everest: Kangshung Face*, General Publishing, 1989.

Travel narratives

French, Patrick, *Tibet, Tibet: A Personal History of a Lost Land*, HarperCollins, 2003.

Kerr, Blake, *Sky Burial*, Snowlion Publications, 1997.

Le Sueur, Alec, *Running a Hotel on the Roof of the World*, Summersdale, 1998.

Guidebooks

Dorje, Gyurme, *Tibet*, Footprint, 2009.

McCue, Gary, *Trekking Tibet*, The Mountaineers, 2010.

Osada, Yukiyasu, and Kanamaru, Atsushi, *Mapping the Tibetan World*, Kotan Publishing, 2000. A very ambitious project, and highly recommended.

Photobooks

Borges, Phil, *Tibetan Portrait*, Rizzoli, 1996.

Harris, Brian, *Tibetan Voices*, Pomegranate, 1996.

Nomachi, Kazoyoshi, *Tibet*, Shambhala, 1997.

Rowell, Galen (photographer, with text by the Dalai Lama), *My Tibet*, University of California Press, 1990.

Young readers

Rose, Naomi, *Tibetan Tales for Little Buddhas*, Clear Light Publishing, 2004. Three traditional tales that exemplify Tibetan Buddhist beliefs are superbly illustrated by artist Naomi Rose.

Fiction

Davidson, Lionel, *The Rose of Tibet*, Gollancz, 1962. A terrific read.

Hilton, James, *Lost Horizon*, William Morrow, 1933 (reprinted many times since). The book that gave the world Shangri-La.

Mitchell, Ken, *Stones of the Dalai Lama*, Douglas & McIntyre, 1993.

Norbu, Jamyang, *Sherlock Holmes: The Missing Years*, Bloomsbury, 2001. Written by a Tibetan iconoclast and scholar.

Rampa, Lobsang T, *The Third Eye*, Corgi, 1956 (reprinted many times since). Masterful New Age hokum.

Tshe Ring Dbang Rgyal, *The Tale of the Incomparable Prince*, HarperCollins, 1996. An 18th-century classic revived in translation from the only novel in the Tibetan language.

OTHER MEDIA
CD

Freedom Chants, Gyuto Monks. Cerebral sacred music from India.

In a Distant Place: Quiet Mind. Two albums of the many performed by Nawang Kechog.

Tibet Tibet: Coming Home. Two albums by exiled female singer, Yungchen Lhamo.

CD-ROM

Tibet Outside the TAR. 2,700-page report crammed onto a single CD-ROM by Steven Marshall and Susette Cooke, 1997. Available through ICT, Washington (*www.savetibet.org*).

DVD, film and video

Tibetsites.com carries a listing of over 200 Tibet-related films and videos, with further links; the more recent films have been added upfront with poster art. Here are some major movies related to Tibet, in order of release date.

Lost Horizon, directed by Frank Capra, Columbia TriStar, 1937. The movie that spread the legend of James Hilton's Shangri-La far and wide.

Kundun, directed by Martin Scorsese, Touchstone Pictures, 1997. Superb biopic about the early years of the Dalai Lama.

Red Corner, directed by Jon Avnet, MGM, 1997. Set in Beijing, but concerned with the judicial system and human rights. Stars Richard Gere.

Seven Years in Tibet, directed by Jean-Jacques Annaud, Columbia TriStar, 1997. Stars Brad Pitt and David Thewlis, and introduces Tibetan actress Lhakpa Tsamchoe (later to star in *Himalaya*, see below). Based on the adventures of German POWs Heinrich Harrer and Peter Aufschnaiter in the early 1940s.

The Cup, directed by Khyentse Norbu, 1998. The first major movie directed by a Tibetan, a Rinpoche resident in Bhutan. It's about soccer-crazed monks at a monastery in northern India. In Tibetan and Hindi. Norbu followed this up with *Travellers & Magicians*, filmed in Bhutan.

Saltmen of Tibet, directed by Ulrike Koch, Switzerland, 1998. About the salt route caravans from Tibet to Nepal, a trade now mostly extinct. Filmed in Tibetan and in the secret salt language (with cryptic salt-language subtitles).

Windhorse, directed by Paul Wagner, Paul Wagner Productions, 1998. Based partly on a true story about a singer who must flee Tibet. At great risk, the director took video of actors on location in Lhasa. This 'docudrama' was filmed in Tibetan and Chinese and stars Dadon, a famous Tibetan singer who escaped into exile in 1992 and now lives in the US.

Himalaya, directed by Eric Valli, 1999. A stunning French–Nepalese co-production with an all-Tibetan cast, filmed in Dolpo, Nepal, in Tibetan. Stars Lhakpa Tsamchoe. The movie offers great insight into the nomadic way of life.

The Touch, directed by Hong Kong cinematographer Peter Pau, 2002. A family of acrobats are called upon by a Buddhist monk sect to retrieve a valuable artefact. Corny plot, but superb cinematography, some scenes shot on location in Lhasa and central Tibet. Stars Michelle Yeoh.

Tibet: Cry of the Snow Lion, directed by Tom Peosay, 2003. A vivid documentary about the situation in Tibet, with a wealth of interview material and unusual archival footage.

We're No Monks, directed by Tibetan cinematographer Pema Dhondup, 2004. Shot on a shoestring budget with unknown actors, this movie tells the fictional story of four disaffected young Tibetan exiles in Dharamsala who are catapulted into a violent mission of protest.

Dreaming Lhasa, directed by Tenzing Sonam and Ritu Sarin, 2005. A terrific dramatic feature involving unknown Tibetan actors, about an ex-monk who has escaped from Tibet into India to deliver a charm-box to a missing resistance fighter.

10 Questions for the Dalai Lama, directed by Rick Ray, 2007. An intimate look at the Dalai Lama – the man and the philosophy – through the lens of filmmaker Rick Ray, who tends to over-simplify key issues.

Murder in the Snow, directed by Mark Gould, 2009. A gripping documentary that recounts how Chinese troops opened fire on Tibetan escapees on a high pass in September 2006, in full view of Western climbers attempting a nearby peak – and the moral morass that resulted.

The Sun Behind The Clouds, directed by Tenzing Sonam and Ritu Sarin, 2010. Filmed mostly in 2008, this documentary focuses on the Tibetan struggle for freedom and where it is heading.

When the Dragon Swallowed the Sun, directed by Dirk Simon, 2010. This documentary examines the Free Tibet movement from different angles over a seven-year period, with a wealth of interview material.

USEFUL APPS In tandem with the website directory that follows, you might consider bringing a small mobile Wi-Fi device like Apple's iTouch. A device like this can store music, books and other material for passing time on the road, and can provide access to a huge range of information via apps. Useful apps for the road include a currency converter, maps, Tibetan phrases (with audio), Chinese phrases (with audio), and so on. There are several stumbling blocks, however. Apps are only reliable if self-driven (no net connection required), because Wi-Fi access within Tibet is found only at hotels for foreigners in large cities like Lhasa or Xining. The Wi-Fi strength can be weak, with slow connections. And you may run into another big hurdle: the site you are searching for could be blocked within China; YouTube, iTunes and Facebook are periodically blocked. Apple's iTouch and iPad use flash memory, which should not be affected by altitude. The lithium battery, however, will have a shorter duration under cold conditions.

WEBSITE DIRECTORY Accessing the 'wrong' sites has landed Chinese surfers in jail. That does not happen to foreign surfers, but it gives an idea of just how sensitive the internet is in the Middle Kingdom. Periodic purges of cybercafés in China have resulted in a number of them being shut down; those that stay in business are required to install monitoring software (called 'Internet Police 110') that shields banned sites and flags local authorities when such sites are being accessed. There are thought to be over 40,000 Internet Police at work in China – real people whose job is to entice and catch cyber-dissidents. Networks in China are required to use domestically produced software.

A number of the following sites are banned in China and are most likely firewalled. Some, like those listed in the section on human rights, are extremely sensitive. At the same time, it is surprising what is still accessible from within Tibet and China. Strangely enough, sites that were firewalled in Lhasa did not appear to be so in Chengdu (and vice versa for other sites). Maybe it's a case of different sensitivities in different places? To check if a website is blocked, go to this handy site and enter the URL: www.greatfirewallofchina.org.

A few tests here will show that YouTube is blocked all over China. Sometimes sites become unblocked. Other times, sites are blocked in some parts of China but not other parts. Go figure.

The net is your news lifeline in a place like Lhasa, where no foreign print news sources can be found. Staying up to date on current politics and travel conditions is very important. The following sites can assist with trip preparation, and give you the latest information.

In many cases, you can eliminate the www prefix, although some sites require exact transcription, even the use of capitals. If you can't get through to a site, play around with the syntax (especially use of hyphens or underscores), or run a search for it under metacrawler. com. If that doesn't work, you've hit the Great Firewall.

Regional information
Searching for it
www.google.com
www.metacrawler.com
www.amazon.co.uk or www.amazon.com To use Amazon, go to travel and browse by subject.

Currency conversion
xe.com/ucc Universal currency converter, one among many such sites.

Weather
www.cnn.com/weather Extended forecasts for Lhasa, Shiquanhe (Ali) and more.
weather.yahoo.com Go to 'Asia' for five-day forecasts for Lhasa and other Asian cities.

Travel warnings
www.fco.gov.uk/travel
travel.state.gov
www.smartraveller.gov.au
www.voyage.gc.ca UK, US, Australian and Canadian official travel warning bulletins.

General news
www.worldnews.com
www.iht.com

www.guardian.co.uk
www.bbc.co.uk
www.globeandmail.ca

Asia/India news
www.worldnewsasia.com
http://edition.cnn.com/ASIA/

Airport information
www.airportcitycodes.com Ever wondered where your bags are being routed to? This site can bring up many Chinese airport codings.

Banking
www.visa.com Use the ATM locator to find Agricultural Bank branches in Lhasa.
www.mastercard.com Use the ATM locator to find a machine in Kathmandu or Chengdu.

Health
high-altitude-medicine.com Delves into the high-altitude health strategy.
basecampmd.com/expguide/highalt.shtmlbasecampMD Delves into the high-altitude health strategy.
www.drwisetravel.com
www.cdc.gov/travel
travelhealth.co.uk

Surfing Tibet Some websites appear in other relevant parts of this book. For links on the Tibetan World (Bhutan, Nepal, northwest India, Outer Mongolia) see the *Tibetan World* chapter, page 293. For links on Tibetan Language, see *Appendix 2*, page 313.

www.himmies.com In support of the book you now hold is a special website with travellers' tales, dodgy advice, warped insights and provocative discussion related to travel in the Tibetan world. Log on to find out more.

Gateway sites
www.tibetsites.com Comprehensive listing of all Tibet-related websites, arranged in categories.
www.tibet.net Official site of the government-in-exile, offering loads of links.
www.kotan.org/tibet The website for the publishers of the book *Mapping the Tibetan World*. Click on 'Tibet Cultural Region Directory' for a host of links.

Current travel conditions in Tibet
landofsnows.com and kekexili.typepad.com Two good sites from an American who goes by the name of Losang and has been touring Tibet for some time.
cafespinn.com/en/ Café in Lhasa that dispenses some good travel advice on getting itineraries together.
www.atc.org.au There are pages on Tibet travel on a drop-down menu under 'Tibet'.
www.khamaid.org/travel Excellent on travel to the Kham region.

Virtual Lhasa
www.tibetgame.com Cool interactive travellers' game (and it's free). You have limited money and three Dalai Lama pictures: the object is to give acquisitions away, thereby increasing your

karma to attain bodhisattva-hood. This site, created by Sydney-based Peter Danford, gives you the feeling of being on the ground, exploring Lhasa via 24 linked panoramas with some audio. You need some plug-ins to run this game.

Everest homepage

everestnews.com Every 8,000m peak should have one: this site has everything you need to know about the Big E and all the climbing trivia. If you want to know what the view looks like from the summit of Everest, go to this site: www.panoramas.dk/fullscreen2/full22.html.

Tibet's environment

meltdownintibet.com Website by the author focusing on China's massive dam-building plans for Tibet.

sftuk.org/campaign/environmentcampaign Site hosted by SFT UK. From this link, you can download a PDF booklet covering the main issues at stake.

stopminingtibet.com Site hosted by SFT aimed at Western companies involved in mining joint-ventures in Tibet.

www.tew.org Click on 'Geography' for satellite maps and theme maps from Tibet Environmental Watch.

Tibet maps

http://www.google.com/earth/index.html Fantastic free web access that allows you to zoom over the Himalaya and fly low over Lhasa, though it's sketchy on Tibet and on Asia. These 'moving maps' offer a quasi-3D simulated view, similar to virtual maps that pilots use in the cockpits of modern jets.

Airlines

www.airchina.com.cn/en
www.cs-air.com/en Websites of Air China and China Southern Airlines, the main domestic carriers flying into Lhasa.

Chinese viewpoints

www.china-embassy.org From Washington: click on 'Topics' and go to 'Tibet' for Chinese rhetoric.

en.tibet.cn China–Tibet Information Centre: official source with some news and touring.

www.tibet-tour.com Slick site from Tibet Tourism Bureau, Shanghai branch (TTBS).

www.goldenbridge.net/offices.htm This travel agency is affiliated with the Chinese military, which explains how they get permits sewn up.

chinasite.com A gateway site with many links, many in the Chinese language and a number banned in China.

www.cnd.org China News Digest, compiled by a group of Chinese scholars in New York (another banned site).

Tibet news sources

www.thetibetpost.com Online newspaper from Dharamsala, available for viewing in three languages: Tibetan, Chinese and English.

www.phayul.com News source for the Tibetan community in exile, based in India.

www.tibet.net Government-in-exile site. Tibetan Bulletin, from Dharamsala, can be accessed from this site.

www.tibet.ca World Tibet Network News is archived here, via CTC, Canada. The archives go back two decades.

Tibetan bloggers Inside Tibet, brave bloggers have been shut down and are unable to reach an international audience. Or they have been jailed for trying to do so. An exception is Tibet's most famous blogger, Woeser, who lives in Beijing. The following sites and more are listed at www.tibetwrites.org.

www.highpeakspureearth.com Has English translations of Woeser's blog, Invisible Tibet.
www.jamyangnorbu.com Tibetan pundit and controversial essayist Jamyang Norbu runs his blog, Shadow Tibet, at this site.

Activism
www.tibetnetwork.org Acts for co-ordination of 180 Tibet support groups, and gives information on how to locate groups around the world.
www.tibet.org/Resources/TSG Worldwide listing of support groups. Site is case-sensitive, so needs capitals.
www.tibetsociety.com Website of the oldest Tibet support group, founded in the UK in 1959 by Hugh Richardson.
www.savetibet.org Site for ICT Washington and branches in Europe. Tibet Press Watch newsletter can be accessed from the website.
www.freetibet.org UK organisation, Free Tibet Campaign.
www.studentsforafreetibet.org Students for a Free Tibet.
www.tibetjustice.org Tibet Justice Centre, based in California.

Human rights
www.un.org/rights Gives the full text of the Universal Declaration of Human Rights.
www.dfn.org Digital Freedom Network, operating from New Jersey, gives lesser-known voices a chance to be heard.
www.hrw.org
www.hrichina.org Human rights in China are under scrutiny on these sites.
www.tchrd.org Dharamsala-based centre.
www.amnesty.org An organisation banned in China.

Tibetan Buddhist leaders
www.dalailama.com The Dalai Lama's homepage, which includes webcasts.
www.kagyuoffice.org
www.karmapa.org Homepages (of sorts) for rival Karmapa candidates.

Index

Page numbers in **bold** refer to main entries; those in *italics* refer to maps